Writing for Visual Media

Writing for Visual Media

Third Edition

Anthony Friedmann

Amsterdam • Boston• Heidelberg • London• New York
• Oxford • Paris • San Diego • San Francisco • Singapore
• Sydney • Tokyo
Focal Press is an imprint of Elsevier

Focal Press is an imprint of Elsevier
30 Corporate Drive, Suite 400, Burlington, MA 01803, USA
The Boulevard, Langford Lane, Kidlington, Oxford, OX5 1GB, UK

Notices
Knowledge and best practice in this field are constantly changing. As new research and experience broaden our understanding, changes in research methods, professional practices, or medical treatment may become necessary.

Practitioners and researchers must always rely on their own experience and knowledge in evaluating and using any information, methods, compounds, or experiments described herein. In using such information or methods they should be mindful of their own safety and the safety of others, including parties for whom they have a professional responsibility.

To the fullest extent of the law, neither the Publisher nor the authors, contributors, or editors, assume any liability for any injury and/or damage to persons or property as a matter of products liability, negligence or otherwise, or from any use or operation of any methods, products, instructions, or ideas contained in the material herein.

Library of Congress Cataloging-in-Publication Data
Friedmann, Anthony.
     Writing for visual media / Anthony Friedmann. — 3rd ed.
        p. cm.
     Includes bibliographical references and index.
     ISBN 978-0-240-81235-9 (alk. paper)
1. Mass media—Authorship. 2. Visual communication. I. Title.
     P96.A86F75 2010
     808'.066302—dc22

                2009046287

British Library Cataloguing-in-Publication Data
A catalogue record for this book is available from the British Library.

ISBN: 978-0-240-81235-9

For information on all Focal Press publications
visit our website at www.elsevierdirect.com

10 11 12 13 14   5 4 3 2 1

Printed in the United States of America

Working together to grow
libraries in developing countries

www.elsevier.com | www.bookaid.org | www.sabre.org

ELSEVIER   BOOK AID International   Sabre Foundation

Contents

PREFACE TO THE SECOND EDITION xv

PREFACE TO THE THIRD EDITION xvii

INTRODUCTION xxi

WHAT'S ON THE WEBSITE xxvii

PART 1   **Defining the Problem**

CHAPTER 1   Describing one medium through another 3

Writing not to be read but to be made 3

Writing, producing, and directing 4

Moving from being a viewer to being a creator 6

The producer cannot read your mind 6

Instructions to the production crew 7

What is the role of a scriptwriter? 7

The "Script" writer is a new kind of writer 8

What is visual writing? 9

Meta-writing 11

Where do we go from here? 12

Differences compared to stage plays 12

Writing with dialogue 12

Writing without dialogue 13

Conclusion 15

CHAPTER 2   A seven-step method for developing a creative concept 17

Step 1: Define the communication problem 18

Ivy college: An admissions video 19

American Express: American travel in Europe 20

PSA for battered women 20

Shell gas international 21

Step 2: Define the target audience...23

    Information overload 24

Demographics 25

    Age 25

    Gender...25

    Race and ethnic origin 26

    Education 26

    Income 26

Psychographics...27

    Emotion 28

    Attitude 29

Step 3: Define the objective..30

Step 4: Define the strategy 32

    Attention Span 32

Step 5: Define the content 33

Step 6: Define the appropriate medium..34

Step 7: Create the concept..35

A concept for an antismoking PSA..39

    The communication problem..40

    The target audience 40

    The objective 40

    The strategy..40

    The content 40

    The medium 40

    The concept...40

Conclusion...41

CHAPTER 3   The stages of script development 43

Background research and investigation...44

    Interviewing..46

    Location research 48

Brainstorming and freeing your imagination 49

Concept..49

    A concept for a PSA: Smoked to death..50

    Pitching 50

    Treatment..51

    A treatment for a PSA: Smoked to death 51

First draft script 52

A first draft script for a PSA: Smoked to death 52

Voice narration and dialogue...54

Revision 55

Final draft 56

Shooting script 56

Conclusion 57

CHAPTER 4 Describing sight and sound...59

Describing time and place 60

Describing action 61

Describing the camera frame or the shot 62

Describing camera movement 64

Describing graphics and effects 64

Describing transitions between shots 65

Describing sound...66

Writing for voice 67

Format for radio 67

Shot, scene, and sequence..69

Finding a format for the page 69

Master scene script 70

Dual-column format 71

Storyboard 73

TV studio multi-camera script 73

News anchor script format..75

Conclusion...76

PART 2 **Solving Communication Problems with Visual Media**

CHAPTER 5 Ads and PSAs: Copywriting for visual media...79

Copywriting versus scriptwriting 80

Client needs and priorities..81

The 20-, 30-, and 60-Second miniscripts 81

Visual writing...82

Devices to capture audience attention 83

Define the creative idea or concept...84

More on ADS and PSAs 89

Humor..90

Shock...91

Suspense 92

Drama 92

Kids 92

Testimonial..93

Special effects 94
    Sexuality 95
Recruiting the audience as a character 95
Writing for audio and radio 96
Infomercials 96
Video news releases 97
Billboards and transportation Ads 97
Advertising on the world wide web 100
Formats 102
Conclusion 102

CHAPTER 6 Corporate communications: Selling, telling, training, and promoting 105
Video versus print media or interactive media 106
Video as a corporate communications tool 106
Corporate television 107
Training, instruction, and education 108
    Formative evaluation 109
    Summative evaluation 109
Focus groups 110
Questionnaires 110
Typical corporate communication problems 110
Getting background and product knowledge 113
Using subject matter experts 114
Devices for video exposition 114
Show and tell 114
Job and task description 115
Educational/instructional use of video 116
How-to-do-it videos 116
Interactive applications 117
Other corporate uses of media 117
Meetings with a visual focus 118
Devices that teach and entertain 119
Devices that work for corporate messages 119
    Dramatization 120
    Humor 122
    Visual metaphor 123
    Narrators and anchors on camera 125
    Television formats 126
    Documentary 126
    Vox pops 127
    Logical argument in documentary narrative 128

Graphics 129

Visual seduction 129

Interview 130

Case histories 130

The story of a day 131

Writing the corporate treatment 131

Script formats for corporate videos 132

Length, pacing, and corporate style 132

Writing voice commentary..132

Developing the script with client input 133

Selling creative ideas...133

Working with budget limitations 134

Conclusion..134

CHAPTER 7 Documentary and nonfiction narrative...137

Documentary comes first 137

Truth or fiction 140

Scripted and unscripted approaches...142

Research and formulating a theme 143

What is the role of the writer?...143

The proposal 144

The treatment 144

Types of documentary technique...144

Reportage..144

Observation..144

Interviews 145

Investigative documentary...145

Narrative documentary 146

Dramatized documentary...146

Expository documentary...147

Propaganda 147

Other documentary applications..148

Expedition documentary...148

Travel documentary 148

Documentaries about the making of feature films...149

Wildlife documentary 149

Current affairs features..149

Writing commentaries..149

Narrative voice-over and postproduction..149

Wall-to-wall commentary 150

Commentary counterpoint and commentary anchors...150

Dual commentators 150
Commentary clichés..151
On-camera/Off-camera combinations..151
Conclusion..152

PART 3   Entertaining with Visual Media

CHAPTER 8   Dramatic structure and form 157
Origins of drama..157
Conflict 158
Three-act structures for film and television 160
Three-act story structure 165
Other narrative structures 165
The flashback...167
Genres 167
 Westerns 167
 Romantic comedies 168
 Horror movies..169
 Road movies...169
 Science fiction 170
 War movies 170
 Buddy movies 171
 Crime movies 171
 Private eye (film noir) 171
 Murder mysteries 171
 Gang movies...172
 Undercover cops 172
 Disaster movies 172
 Martial arts...172
 Epics 173
 Action-adventure..173
 Monster movies 173
 Biography..174
 Satire...174
 Cross genre 174
Script development...175
 Adapting the seven-step method 175
 Log lines...176
 The premise 177
 Tag lines...178
 Concept or synopsis 178
 Story engines 180

Writing a movie treatment...181
Screenplay 182
Scene outline 184
Master scene script format 184
Scripting software...185
Shooting script 185
Conclusion...185

CHAPTER 9 Writing techniques for long-form scripts 187
Characters and character 188
Dialogue and action...189
Plot or storyline 192
Comedy..193
     Comic devices 193
     The comic character as victim...194
     Verbal comedy 194
     Running gag...195
     The cover-up/impersonation 195
     Disguise and mistaken identity..196
     Dramatic irony..196
Drama...197
     Cover-up/mistaken identity 197
     Disguise..197
     Dramatic irony..198
     Ambition/pride 199
     Challenge and survival 199
     Greed 199
     Love gone wrong...200
     Desire/lust 200
Writing techniques for adaptation 202
The problem of adaptation...202
Length..205
Point of view..205
Narrative tense and screen time 206
Setting and period 206
Dialogue versus action 207
Descriptive detail and the camera frame...209
Implied action..209
It's a wonderful life..210
Bartleby 215
Conclusion...220

CHAPTER 10 Television series, sitcoms, and soaps 223

The premise for series, sitcoms, and soaps 224

Three-act structure and the TV time slot 226

Using commercial breaks 227

Visualizing for the small screen 227

TV dialogue 228

Realism/realistic dialogue 228

Breaking up dialogue 231

Pacing 231

The beat sheet 231

Team writing 233

Hook/teaser 233

The series bible 233

Condensing action and plot 233

Target audience 234

Script formats for television 234

TV comedy and its devices 235

   Running gags 236

   Visual gags 241

   Double takes 242

   One-liners and laugh lines 242

Sitcoms 243

New techniques and innovations 243

Spec scripts 244

Conclusion 245

PART 4 **Writing for Interactive and Mobile Media**

CHAPTER 11 Writing and interactive design 251

Defining interactive 251

Linear and nonlinear paradigms 252

Combining media for interactive use 254

Breakdown of script formats 257

   Branching 258

   Flowcharts 260

   Storyboards 260

Authoring tools and interactive concepts 260

Multimedia components 264

Finding a script format 264

Conclusion 266

CHAPTER 12   Writing for interactive communications...267

Different writing for websites 269

Multilayered writing 271

Conceptual writing versus content writing 272

Website concepts...273

Writing to be read on the web 274

Navigation: The third dimension 275

Writing issues 276

Concept 276

Design document...276

Flowchart 276

Breakdown for production 276

Text..277

Video, stills, and audio..277

Applying the seven-step method..277

Concept 278

Instructional and utilitarian programs...279

Interactive catalogues and brochures 279

Education and training 280

Kiosks 281

Conclusion...281

CHAPTER 13   Writing for interactive entertainment 283

Interactive reference works...283

E-Commerce and interactive books 284

Games, narrative, and entertainment...285

Video games 285

Graphics versus live action...290

The order of writing 291

Formats...292

Interactive television...294

Webisodes and television web content..296

Interactive movies 296

Conclusion...297

CHAPTER 14   Writing for mobile media 299

Antecedents...300

Technical antecedents 301

Video and cell phone use 304

Webisodes 308

The mobisode™ 310

Writing dos and don'ts..318

Conclusion..318

PART 5   **Anticipating Professional Issues**

CHAPTER 15   You can get paid to do this 323

Writing for the entertainment world 323

Writing contracts 324

Pitching 326

Ideology, morality, and content 328

Emotional honesty and sentimentality..330

Writing for the corporate world...333

Client relationships 334

Corporate contracts 334

Work for hire 335

Marketing yourself and your work 335

Copyright 336

Work-made-for-hire and freelance 337

Agents and submissions..338

Networking, conventions, and seminars...338

Surfing the web 339

Hybrid careers 339

Conclusion..339

APPENDIX: Script formats...341

BIBLIOGRAPHY 361

GLOSSARY 367

INDEX 389

Preface to the Second Edition

The first edition was printed twice and found support in many writing programs. I have used my own book as a textbook in a media writing course and learned a lot that has contributed to improvements in this second edition. I continue to believe that brevity and economy in the length of chapters is suitable to the contemporary college student's reluctance to read. Also in a writing course, reading about writing must be to the point and lead to the practice of writing.

In the interval between the writing of the first edition and the second, technological changes underline the importance of interactive media in the internet and the ubiquitous use of websites for corporate communications. The emergence of DVDs increases the importance of interactive design and the importance of video games as an industry whose size and dollar value rivals the traditional entertainment media. New chapters expand Part IV to look more closely at the emerging issues in writing for interactive media. The convergence of all media into one digital domain on the computer desktop impacts on writing courses and writing training. This convergence is increasingly reflected in the curricula of communications programs such that writing skills have to follow suit and diversify. An introductory course in media writing always faces the dilemma of what media to cover and how much time can be devoted to each.

The aim is to devise a textbook that addresses contemporary writing issues in an accessible way, that incorporates contemporary, interactive technology for the delivery of learning, and that takes account of contemporary script formatting software.

Creation of content for a medium proceeds from writing. Visual imagination lies at the heart of this writing. Visual writing is still the key. In the hunt to pin down the elusive quality of that visual writing, I have come to see that this is fundamentally conceptual writing, what I have come to call meta-writing in this edition. Meta-writing unfolds at several levels. It is visual thinking that precedes and underlies the end product of visual writing that is the script. Visual writing is behind or within the writing that is read as a script. It is embedded writing that underlies the writing we read. A concept dissolves into a treatment, which in turn dissolves into the instructions for a production in a document we call a script. I have come to see this as the key to understanding how visual media work and, therefore, how we can construct the content for those media. Thus visual writing, or meta-writing, is not the words of the final script but the imaging that makes the words of the final script possible.

Preface to the Third Edition

The success of previous editions, thanks to those readers, instructors and students who have expressed confidence in the content of this work by using it, drives the need for a third edition. While motivated to improve the book with each successive edition, I am concerned to preserve many chapters and retain the approach that I can only presume accounts for the relative success of previous editions. With each successive edition, embarrassing mistakes both small and large are printed and distributed. One gratification of a new edition is the opportunity to correct them.

Creating interactive media is fraught with hazard. Some interactive navigation that did not work on the DVD has been corrected. We also regret the failure of the Focal Press website to maintain certain links from the DVD to documents that are now going to be part of the larger website that replaces the DVD for this edition. This will mean on-going maintenance and updating together with added functionality such as a blog and a discussion page. This should expand the interactive component of the book and extend the ways in which readers and users can interact with the author and one another.

Reviewers invited by the publisher to comment on the book have obliged me to re-examine my approach sometimes leading to changes but sometimes confirming for me that I needed to stick to the convictions that underlie the book, that inspired me to write it in the first place and that found acceptance among instructors, students and general readers. When preparing the second edition, I had toyed with the idea of rearranging the first four chapters. The comments of reviewers confirmed some of my thinking that we can approach the problem of scriptwriting by a slightly different sequencing of key concepts. When several ideas are clustered together, they do not necessarily dictate a logical order of exposition. Nevertheless, a key principle behind this book is that the order in which you transmit key ideas matters to the success of your transmission and the consequent assimilation of those ideas. One way is better than another even though, in the end, you must assimilate them all and possess that integrated understanding. Hence, discussing the method of analysis, brainstorming, and thinking that precedes actual script writing now comes earlier than explaining the problem of describing sight and sound and the necessary stages of script development. Every instructor has an individual approach, and no doubt no order or exposition will suit everyone.

With the passing of time, the examples from many ads, television and movie content inevitably become dated. Some of these I need and want to retain because they are either classic or because I have the scripts and video clips for the website (formerly the DVD) and face restrictions of copyright for material that is desirable in an ideal world but unobtainable in a real one.

It made sense to merge the old chapter on educational and training video with the corporate chapter. Most chapters have been modestly expanded to elaborate the ideas they contain for the sake of greater clarity. We have introduced a list of key terms at the head of every chapter and printed those terms in bold in the body of the chapter to help readers assimilate ideas. These terms form part of the glossary but are set apart from other terminology by bold type so as to make them more readily identifiable and accessible. From chapter to chapter, these key terms are often repeated. I decided that key terms should be specific to a chapter as far as possible. This does not exclude repetition where useful and germane to the chapter but avoids ending up with a text block increasingly overwhelmed with bold type.

Although the premise of the book that is expressed in its title must control the content, the audio component of the visual medium now receives fuller treatment. Since we have to describe both sight and sound in visual media, writing for the voice is a component of visual writing even though audio is heard not seen. Nevertheless, it supports the visual. Writing for radio, which is sound only, receives treatment particularly in connection with writing PSA. Writing for radio is then a cognate discipline that we can explore to help us define more clearly what is meant by visual writing. The script format of writing for radio is now included in the appendix.

The argument of the premise that writing broadcast news is not visual writing equivalent to other forms of scriptwriting needs a more nuanced explanation. The production medium is visual, and the production script has a visual component. Certainly, investigative reporting demands visual input. News, however, does not need visual metaphor and is principally made up of and controlled by the concept of talking heads. That still sets apart this kind of writing, which must apply the disciplines of journalism to the task and leads in another direction. However, for the sake of comprehensiveness and contrast, we include the script format for broadcast studio production in Chapter 4, in the appendix and on the website.

Some curricula are organized in such a way that media writing is considered to be broadcast journalism and taught from a foundation in journalism that sets it apart from other forms of writing for media. The foundation course is broader and served by another kind of textbook with a different premise. Several good textbooks of this kind exist and take a different approach.

I have realized, partly in retrospect, that this is not just a book about how to write for visual media; it is also by turns, a reflection about the history, evolution and origins of this kind of writing. Media writers have to understand the forces that are changing the very media they write for. Nowhere is this more critical than for new mobile media platforms. This is not just a writing manual. It is also a book about the economic, production and social contexts in which writing for visual media occurs.

Since I regularly use *Writing for Visual Media* to teach an introductory course in scriptwriting, I learn a lot from students and their struggle to master script writing. They have sometimes shown me by their honest mistakes the shortcomings of certain passages that need either more or clearer explanation. I am indebted to Samantha Camacho, my student while I was teaching at Sam Houston State University, for her help in identifying out of date media examples and suggesting newer ones, based on her love of and knowledge of film.

The wholly new addition to the third edition is a chapter devoted to writing for mobile media platforms. To some extent, this is going out on a limb and more predictive than prescriptive. There seems to be enough evidence that new formats are emerging for small mobile platforms even though they are not strongly defined. I want to thank a number of people who gave their time and interest by talking to me about mobile media and by others who read the chapter in draft and offered comments, namely, Glenn Reitmeier Vice President, Technology, at NBCUniversal, Daniel Tibbets, Executive Vice President and Studio Chief at GoTVNetworks, and Mike Fry of Columbia University School of Film and Television. For telephone and email discussion that helped me prepare to write Chapter 14, I am indebted to John Hane of Pillsbury Winthrop Shaw Pittman LLP, Stephen Elfman President, Network Operations and Wholesale, at Sprint, Jana Venerka the scriptwriter and Joe Rassulo the director of the Fox mobisodes™ for informative conversations that helped me prepare to write Chapter 14. For any errors of commission or omission in all matters, the responsibility must be mine alone.

I am grateful for the support given me by Elinor Actipis, my editor, Associate Editor Michele Cronin, Assistant Editor Jane Dashevsky, and the Production Manager, Melinda Rankin at Focal Press for many creative and practical suggestions.

Introduction

THE PURPOSE

Although this textbook is intended mainly for students in colleges and universities who are taking an introductory course in writing scripts for media, it is also meant for all writers making the transition to writing for visual media. It assumes that the reader begins with minimal understanding of the nature of writing for visual media. Most beginners have had a large number of experiences viewing visual media: films, television, and video. They probably contemplate the originating creative act that lies behind such programs without much idea of how it's done. They may not understand visual thinking, or if they do, they don't know how to set it down. They don't know formats. In short, they don't quite know where or how to start. This book is designed to get the beginner started. It is not intended to make fully fledged professionals out of beginners nor to deal with every type of media writing, nor all the issues of scriptwriting, but it does cover all the material a beginner will need to write viable scripts in the main media formats.

Other books offer more exhaustive and more specialized information about how to work at a professional level writing for film, television, corporate video, or interactive media. Broadcast journalism for current affairs and sports is another discipline that is well covered in more specialized works. A selected bibliography at the end of the book lists many of these more advanced books that focus more narrowly on a special type of writing for a single medium together with more general works and the sources quoted or referenced in the chapters that follow.

THE PREMISE OF THIS BOOK

This book is based on the premise that the fundamental challenge of writing for visual media arises in learning to think and write visually, that a script is a plan for production, and that visual media are identifiably different from print media. Although broadcast journalism overlaps visual writing in some of its forms, journalists have concerns about sources, objectivity, and editorial issues that predominate. Shaping a news story delivered to a teleprompter does not really require visual writing. If anything it is writing for the ear. Even though a news script might make allowance for B-roll and story packages, those inserts are not written in. Therefore, this form of scripting is excluded except for a mention of the format for a production script.

Although writing for the audio track has been part of the job of scriptwriting since sound was added to motion pictures some 80 years ago, writing for the ear alone concerns only words that are to be heard rather than words to describe a visual experience on screen. Our focus is a body of technique that is concerned with writing for audiovisual media that are based on sequencing images. Writing for radio, with the exception of a show like *Prairie Home Companion* on National Public Radio, usually consists of writing radio ads, which are a form of copywriting and, therefore, guided by advertising concerns, or it is news and involves the journalistic issues already mentioned. Therefore, writing purely for radio is limited to radio public service announcements (PSAs) as an adjunct to visual PSAs. However, in context, writing dialogue, voice-over narration, and other audio concerns are given the importance they deserve.

OBJECTIVES

To become good at your craft, sooner or later you need to specialize. You need to hone and refine your writing skills for the way in which a particular medium is used. This does not mean you can never cross over from one form to another, but the chances are that if you are going to make a living writing for a visual medium, you will have to be good enough in at least one area to compete with the *pros* already practicing the craft. That is a few stages away.

To get there from here, you need to learn:

- How visual media communicate
- Visual thinking
- Visual writing
- Scriptwriting terminology
- The recognized script format for each visual medium
- A method to get from brain static to a coherent idea for any media script
- The role of the writer in media industries

SECONDARY OBJECTIVES

Even if you don't end up writing for a living, you may have a job that requires you to read, interpret, evaluate, buy, or review scripts. There are dozens of activities that require you to be able to evaluate the written plan that is the script. The script is cheap to produce compared to producing the script. You may need to be able to construe the final product from words and ideas on a page.

Some of the people who have to do this are producers, directors, casting directors, cinematographers, story editors, literary agents, studio and TV executives, film and video editors, and actors. Other positions in the visual communications industry might also require that you be able to read a script and deduce what it will cost to make a product that an audience will see. In addition to the people who have to evaluate and buy or reject scripts, these positions include art directors, set designers, talent agents, casting directors, lighting directors, and sound designers. Virtually anyone who has a role in bringing a script to the screen needs to be able to read the blueprint from which a program is made.

So even if you don't succeed specifically as a scriptwriter, you still need to understand scriptwriting and what makes a script work well. You must be able to follow the way a script translates into narrative images that communicate to an audience. You must be able to read the coded set of instructions that a script embodies.

THE BASIC IDEA OF A SCRIPT

When musicians want someone else to play their music, they must write it down as notes in a form that other musicians can read, decode, and then turn back into music. This problem has been solved in the music world by inventing the musical staff, treble and bass, with a clear set of rules for describing what pitch, what loudness, and what rhythm should be reproduced. Even composers who don't write music need arrangers to write it out for them because most music involves groups of musicians playing different instruments simultaneously. There is always a barrier between the page of music and the auditory experience of hearing the music. You can't hear the score unless you are a trained musician. Even then, you need to play the notes to understand what the composer intended and create a musical experience for a wide audience, most of whom cannot read music or play an instrument.

Likewise, you can't see the script for a film or a video. If you are a trained director or editor who knows how to read a script, you can visualize in your mind's eye what is intended, just as a musician can hear in his mind's ear what the music should sound like. You can translate a static page into a sequence of images flowing in a time line. Today's nonlinear video editors display programs in a graphic time line, which is a kind of storyboard metaphor for the content of a program. In the end, the production process is needed to make the script into images that are accessible to all viewers even though they cannot read a script, frame a shot, or edit a sequence to make narrative sense.

Like all analogies, this one breaks down. Musical scores are used over and over again for numberless performances, whereas a script is used only once. So another useful analogy is the blueprint, the drawings an architect makes for a builder or contractor to erect a building. After the building is finished, the blueprint has little interest except perhaps for maintenance or repair. The person who buys a house or who lives in it might not be able to read the architect's plans any more than the audience at a concert is able to read music or an audience for a film is able to read a script. The home dweller hardly thinks about the plans of the house, even though this person may have strong views about how successful the building is to inhabit. If you like living in the space, then that is a measure of the building's success even though you do not necessarily know how to design a house.

Likewise, if you watch a TV series, like a movie, or understand a corporate message, you don't think about the scripts on which they are based. You get an audiovisual, intellectual, and emotional experience. You laugh, cry, reflect, or go into a rewarding imaginative or mental space. So a script has little value except as a blueprint to make something. Think of it this way. You couldn't sell many scripts of *Star Wars* or *Jurassic Park* (name your favorite movie), but you can sell a lot of tickets to see the movie made from it—millions of tickets in fact.

META-WRITING

The term meta-writing, coined by the author, was introduced in the second edition to clarify and explain how visual writing works. The process of visual writing is elusive because it originates in the imagination before writing happens. Writing of any kind arises in the mind in some pre-verbal phase that seeks words to embody the idea. Languages are many, and the writing process is not confined to any particular language. Anyone who knows another language well can be faced with a dilemma of which language accommodates the idea. I am fluent in French and have written scripts, stories and letters in that language. Writing does not originate simply in words although words might enable the process. Writing for visual media involves yet another complexity, namely that the language used to describe the visual idea is not what the audience itself experiences. The language we use as visual writers is a referent for images or a construct of images that underlies the produced result and accounts for how and why it works. The term meta-writing refers to that *ur*-writing or pre-writing activity of the creative imagination. It is expressed as a concept, a premise, or some such pre-script document that then has to evolve through further elaboration in a treatment into a set of written instructions that become the script itself. That script is sustained by a vision that the audience grasps visually and not through words. So the audience is responding to what is in effect the meta-writing.

The website has a link to some CSX television commercials (www.csx.com/?fuseaction=about. tomorrow_moves). One of them consists of a montage of brief shots of all kinds of people breathing in. We then see another montage of the same people breathing out and swimmers racing. It incorporates the following text intercut with images: CSX trains move one ton of freight 436 miles on 1 gallon of fuel. Less fuel=less emissions. Good news for anyone who breathes. The tag line—"good news for anyone who breathes"—completes an idea that can only be assimilated visually. If you see this television ad, you understand it and know what it means. If you try to express your understanding in words, you might have difficulty. Expressed in words, something is lost. Let's try and then view the ad on line.

We live in a gaseous atmosphere just as fish live in water. That atmosphere is being altered by human activity burning fossil fuels and changing the gaseous makeup of that atmosphere. This same activity also emits pollutants which contaminate the environment and impact the health of the human organism that must breathe that gas polluted with carcinogens and other particulate matter detrimental to the respiratory system. Reducing that pollution benefits everyone who breathes, indeed every animal that breathes (a shot of a dog exhaling is included). So if we can get trucks off the road and do the same job of transporting goods by rail, which uses fossil fuel energy more efficiently, we all benefit. We are a railroad. We understand this. Every year, our train operations reduce the amount of $CO2$ being pumped into the air by over 6.5 million tons. It would take 152 million tree seedlings 10 years to absorb that much carbon. We want you to appreciate how important our older technology is for the survival of the planet and its life forms—you. Although railroads are old transportation technology, they are the solution for tomorrow.

Expressed in words, the idea is lengthy and somewhat clumsy; expressed visually; it is elegant and can be accomplished in 30 seconds. The tag line for the campaign is in words: How tomorrow moves™.

The transmission of a visual idea cannot take place without live action images that have to be produced. The audience then experiences the meta-writing. The audience gets the idea that started the whole process. This is why understanding how you do meta-writing is so important to visual writing. It happens before you write, but you have to find words to explain it to someone else so that it can be produced. Learning how to do this entails more than the traditional writing skills. It is less dependent on facility with language or fine expression than a capacity to think in images. This is meta-writing for visual media.

THE LEARNING TASK

Your job right now is to begin to understand how you put this plan, this score, or this blueprint for a movie together. Whether it is a public service announcement, a corporate communication, or a feature film, you have to figure out the process. You have to learn in what forms media industries communicate, buy, sell, and produce their ideas. You have to try it out before big bucks or your next month's rent are at stake.

The most difficult part of writing is the constant revision. We have to rewrite and revise until we get it right. Writers whose work you watch on TV and in the movie theater have spent a long time studying how it's done. One day, I was explaining this to a communications student who played on the college basketball team. I asked him what the coach had him do in basketball practice. His eyes lit up and he described some of the shooting drills. Then I asked him what he thought the equivalent drills would be for a writer. He wasn't so sure and did not understand that a similar degree of practice is the foundation for successful writing.

We need to think about how we can score some points in this writing game. If you have to shoot thousands of baskets so as to be confident about sinking a foul shot, let's think about what it takes to get to be good enough to score consistently in a competitive writing game. Some people will put in a lot of time practicing basketball because they love the game. Scriptwriters keep writing because they love the medium and they love to create. Isn't it the same idea? Practice, practice, practice! Don't give up! Don't get discouraged when your ideas don't work out right away, and, above all, enjoy the creative act, even if you don't make points every time!

CONCLUSION

This book is about learning the fundamentals of scriptwriting. It is designed to take you from nowhere to somewhere, from no experience and no knowledge to a basic level of competence and knowledge of what the issues of scriptwriting are. It gives you a chance to explore your visual imagination and try out your powers of invention. Later, you can confront the full range of writing issues particular to each genre in each medium by taking more advanced media writing courses dedicated to specific media formats, or by reading more advanced texts, or by further self-directed writing experience.

In the end, you learn, not by reading alone, not by thinking alone, and not by talking about doing it, but by doing it. "Just do it!" as the Nike ad says. Write!

What's on the Website

USING THE WEBSITE

This text is designed to work in tandem with a website. Interactive media technology provides us with a new opportunity, hitherto impossible to achieve in a textbook, to link script blueprint and resultant image in the visual medium itself. Although the printed book contains some examples of scripts, the website provides many more and also more complete scripts. On the website, script samples are frequently linked to finished video clips. It also provides a visual glossary of script vocabulary for camera shots and movements. An icon has been placed throughout the text whenever the website contains supplementary material. The interactive navigation is modeled on the chapter outline so that all the links for a given chapter are accessible under the heading for that chapter. There are also other options for interactive navigation that follow useful themes or topics. The text is linked to the website by an icon placed in the margin throughout the printed text whenever there is supplementary material on the website that enriches the matter under discussion. The website provides an interactive menu that corresponds to the chapters of the book. All supplementary materials referenced by the disk icon in the printed text can be accessed via this menu. In addition, other ways of navigating allow readers to consult:

- many corporate, and feature film scripts
- storyboards
- video clips of scenes produced from many script examples
- an interactive glossary of camera shots, movements and transitions
- links to relevant websites

Please note many URLs mentioned in the text become active links on the website. Some endnotes provide URLs for reference that are not permanent links. Over time, some URLs become invalid because the World Wide Web is a changing environment in which many websites are not permanent or undergo revision. The website will undergo revision from time to time to supplement material or remove links that are no longer active. New content and new links will be added to the website during the life of this edition so that the site can be consulted continuously for material that may not be flagged in the text. There will also be a forum for discussion and submission of syllabi, scripts, and documents of interest.

Readers should understand that the website contains a lot of material, especially video clips that can take several minutes to download depending on the speed of the Internet connection, the clock speed of the computer processor being used, and the available RAM.

Defining the Problem

Many people, and perhaps some readers of this book, will start out with confidence in their basic ability to write but be unsure of how they should apply it to writing a script. To know how to write for the visual media, it is important to understand how such writing differs from the writing most of us have learned to do until now. To change these habits and learn how to write a script, we need to see the specific problems that this different kind of writing solves. Above all, we need some kind of method to solve those problems. The first part of this book is devoted to a logical and pragmatic analysis of the reasons that scripts are written a certain way.If you understand the problem, you will understand the solution. This part also introduces you to a basic process of thinking, a method of devising content, and a method of writing in stages or steps. You need to know how to do it.

I had always thought of myself as a good writer, and I liked writing before I ever wrote a script. Many of you might feel the same way. I started writing scripts to have something to shoot in film school. After all, I could hardly hire a professional scriptwriter, and people around me were too busy doing their own projects to help out with mine. Besides, I wanted to write my own script. A lot of you are probably students in media production and will have to invent content for production projects. We all learn the hard way, by trial and error. The following chapters are intended to minimize those errors. Although there is a considerable body of craft to learn, this part of the book is about what a writer should understand before dealing with specific media and their formats. Let's begin.

Describing One Medium Through Another

The essential problem of writing for visual media comes from the difference between print as a medium, or words on a page, and the medium of moving images. You have to describe an audiovisual medium that plays in real time using a written medium that is abstract and frozen in time. So, a description in words on a page of what is to be seen on a screen has limited value until it is translated into that medium itself.

WRITING NOT TO BE READ BUT TO BE MADE

The fundamental premise of **scriptwriting** is that you are writing not to be read but to be made. This does not mean that a script is not read by producers, directors, and others who must decide whether to put resources into producing it. It means that the audience doesn't read the script. By contrast, a novelist or a poet or a journalist writes what the reader reads. I am now writing what my readers will experience directly as written language. Not so for a scriptwriter! Just as the musical score is a set of instructions to musicians and an architectural blueprint is a set of instructions to builders, a script is a set of instructions to a production crew to make a film, a video, or a television program. Only the ideas, scenes, and dialogue that are written down get made. This is the first principle to keep in mind.

Doi: 10.1016/B978-0-240-81235-9.00001-8

Whatever your vision, whatever your idea, whatever you want to see on the screen, you must describe it in language that a team of technicians and visual image workers can understand and translate into perceived moving images and sound.

A **script** is fundamental to the process of making a movie, video, or any type of visual program. It is the basis for production. From it flow a huge number of production decisions, consequences, and **actions**. The first of these is cost. Every stroke of the pen (or every keystroke) implies a production cost to bring it to reality on the screen. Although the techniques of filmmaking and special effects are seemingly without boundaries these days, extravagant ideas incur extravagant cost. A writer must keep in mind that a production budget is written with every word by virtue of the visual ideas contained in the script, whether that script is for a feature film or a training video. A script writer can reach an audience only by visualizing and writing potential scenes for directors and producers to shoot and edit. The finished work often reflects a multitude of creative choices and alterations unspecified by the writer.

WRITING, PRODUCING, AND DIRECTING

It is often said that a good script can be ruined by bad producing and bad directing, but good producing and good directing cannot save a bad script. Producers and directors have more recognizable roles in the process because production is visible and material. However, the writer's role is sometimes combined with that of either producer or director. Some writers can direct, and some directors can write. Writing and producing can also be combined. If you study program credits, you will see some of these dual roles and combined responsibilities. Some individuals attempt triple responsibilities. Among the Academy Award nominees for 1998, James Cameron had writer, director, and producer credits for *Titanic* (1998). He has combined these roles again for *Avatar* (2009). Atom Egoyan, a lesser known Canadian director, had a triple credit in *The Sweet Hereafter* (1997). The Coen brothers have written and directed many very successful films such as *Fargo* (1996), which won an Academy Award for best original screenplay, and *No Country for Old Men* (2007), which won for best adapted screenplay. They also directed these films.

As a rule, audiences pay little attention to the scriptwriter and often don't recognize the producer or director. Audiences identify with the actors they see on screen. However, they do so only because the writer has created the story that the audience wants to hear, the characters that it believes in, and the words that it accepts as those characters' words. A film or a television series gets made because a producer, a director, and sometimes key acting talent respond to the potential of the script idea. The script expresses the primary imaginative vision that can become a successful program or film.

The writer's work is somewhat isolated because the writer is the originator, with no one else to lean on. Others are waiting for the scriptwriter to deliver before they can do their work. However, strong collaboration can occur between the writer and the producers and directors and sometimes with other writers. The scriptwriter's work is less isolated than that of the traditional novelist, poet, or biographer because those writers write their words to be read directly by the audience. They do not need any intermediary, except perhaps a publisher, whereas a scriptwriter is never read directly by the audience and needs a team of skilled technicians as intermediaries and a risky investment of millions of dollars to create a result visible on screen.

In the entertainment world, the viewing audience is usually much larger than the reading audience for a book. It is a measure of the media age we now live in that visual media are so predominant in our imaginations. In fact, the very word *audience* is a carryover from another age when audiences listened. The word derives from the Latin *audio,* meaning *I hear.* Perhaps we should invent a new word, vidience, from the Latin video, meaning *I see.* Printed media no longer have the monopoly they have enjoyed for 500 years since the Gutenberg era and the invention of the printing press. With the invention of the motion picture camera/projector by **Louis Lumière** in 1895 and the movie projector by **Thomas A. Edison** in 1896,[1] a visual medium was born—one that, with its electronic derivatives, has probably displaced the print medium as a primary form of entertainment and now rivals it as a form of communication. Audiences today are primarily viewing audiences.

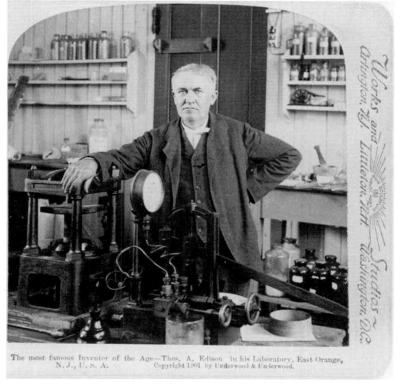

FIGURE 1.1
Edison in his laboratory.

---

[1] The Edison company demonstrated the Kinetoscope in the United States in 1891, which enabled one person at a time to view moving pictures. In 1896, Edison brought out the Vitascope projector.

Since the invention of the motion picture on film, these visual media have multiplied in type and nature so that a range of visual communication types now exists that require **scriptwriting** of many different kinds. After movies came television and a dozen different types of program requiring a variety of writing talents. From television came portable television or video, programs recorded on a single camera and edited to be distributed on videotape rather than broadcast. Other exhibition media based on microchip technology synchronizing slide projectors led to extravagant multi-image and multimedia projections for business meetings, museums, and exhibitions. This led to video walls that involve composing images across banks of 9 or 12 TV screens. New combinations of video and computer technology have led to the creation of interactive multimedia both for entertainment and instruction published on CD-ROMs, DVDs, and Websites.

Scriptwriters are indispensable to all these visual media. Their craft and art lie behind every program. Every time you watch a program on television or see a movie or watch a corporate communication, remind yourself that it began as a script—as words on a page. Don't walk out of the movies or switch the television channel when the credits roll—look for the **scriptwriting** credit! According to the Writers Guild agreement with the producers of movies, in both the United States and the United Kingdom, the script credit must come immediately before the director's, which is always the last credit.

MOVING FROM BEING A VIEWER TO BEING A CREATOR

This brings us to the next point in your transformation from a beginner into a competent scriptwriter. Most of us begin with the experience of being in the audience. We grow up going to the movies and watching television. A complete media experience written, produced, and edited is presented to us for our enjoyment. We are conditioned to be passive consumers of these images. We learn to interpret them. We do not think intensively about how they were created, although some viewers might have had a mild curiosity about this. We just enjoy them.

You begin to be a scriptwriter when you start to think about how the story got invented, who wrote the dialogue, who decided what the voiceover should say, whether they could have been better or different. It is a change of mindset. A member of the audience decides to get up and cross over to the other side and become a creator. The writer creates for an audience. A writer has to know what it is to be in the audience, but no-one in the audience has to know what it is to be a writer. This transition in awareness and in point of view must take place before you can function successfully as a scriptwriter. The following chapters are designed to engender that transition. It will take time. You are an apprentice to a craft. Where do you begin? Because you are **writing in one medium for another**, you have to change the way you have been used to writing, which was meant to be read by an audience, and instead write so that your writing works as a set of instructions for a production team.

THE PRODUCER CANNOT READ YOUR MIND

Everything begins in your mind, in your imagination. Unless you write down what you see and hear, no one else knows about it. Beginning writers sometimes forget this. Unless the script contains a clear description of your vision from beginning to end, with no gaps, your vision will not reach the screen. The production people who make the script into screen images cannot read your mind. Rule number one: Do not hand over your **scriptwriting** prerogative and responsibility to the director or actor, or anyone else whose job it is to translate your script into a program. Too often they will take it and do something other than what you intended. If you leave blanks, they will fill in those blanks from their own perspectives. They have to—it is their professional responsibility. There are no empty frames in movies or television.

INSTRUCTIONS TO THE PRODUCTION CREW

Consider the differences between the following sentences:

> A man is sitting in a car watching the entrance to a building ....

and

> A young man, unshaven, sits in a sports car, watching the entrance to a run-down apartment building through binoculars.

To shoot the first statement leaves a number of decisions to the director and art director: What type of car? What year? Is it period? What street? What else is in the shot? Crowd? Extras? Day? Night? What is the man doing in the car? Does he drive up? Time has to be allowed to set up the shot and rehearse. Permits are required to shoot in the street. These details may not be critical to your scene, but writers have to think all the time about what they should specify and what they can leave up to the good judgment of the production people, mainly the director. As a general rule, be specific. However, to provide answers to all these questions would result in an unusable script, encumbered with unnecessary and unacceptable production detail.

There is a prevailing sentiment that everyone wants to get the script right before proceeding with production. To change a script involves work and expense. However, until there is agreement about this crucial document, it is difficult to advance the project. So rewriting is almost unavoidable. The script becomes the common denominator of a production to which everybody refers. Production people use the script to make budgets, schedules, sets, select a cast, and choose locations.

WHAT IS THE ROLE OF A SCRIPTWRITER?

Because scripts are indispensable to production, writers are indispensable to the producers in the industry. This would seem to put writers in a powerful position. In practice, though, the scriptwriter seems to be the least valued contributor and the most abused.[2] Once a writer delivers a script and is paid, the power to shape the end result wanes rapidly or even ceases. The producer and the director

---

[2] "In terms of authority, screenwriters rank somewhere between the man who guards the studio gate and the man who runs the studio (this week)." William Goldman, *Adventures in the Screen Trade* (New York: Warner Books, 1983), p. xii.

take control of the process. That is why the script must express a convincing vision and be a clear plan. Successful collaboration between a writer and a director is the basis for good films and television programs. The producer's role is to bring about such collaboration and make it possible by finding financial backing.

The "Script" Writer Is a New Kind of Writer

The invention of the motion picture also brought about the need for a new kind of writer. In the early days of silent film, one- and two-reelers could be shot without scripts. The first writing job was to write the title cards and **dialogue cards** that were intercut with **action** scenes from time to time. More complex stories and longer films needed a **scenario** (the precursor of the **treatment** of today) that was written down by writers who could visualize and write **action** continuity.[3] **Scenario, photoplay, photo-drama**, now replaced by **screenplay** or **script**, were all new terms to describe this kind of writing. The new visual medium required a new kind of writing that described what was to be made visible on the screen. It had to describe the visual content of the frame or shot. It had to describe sequences of shots that would make narrative sense. It had to be a document that could be used as a plan for production. It required **visual writing.** It required screenwriting. Seeing how early scriptwriters invented techniques and ways of writing for the screen tells us a lot about the problem.

Many of the early writers for the new medium were women. Anita Loos (*Gentlemen Prefer Blondes*) wrote for D. W. Griffith and the Biograph Company. Margaret Turnbull, Beulah Marie Dix, and Marion Fairfax wrote for Famous Players-Lasky.[3] Literary writers of novels and plays were recruited by William de Mille to dignify the vulgar image of movies, with sometimes disastrous results because writers despised the medium and condescended to write mainly for the money.[4] It seems clear that nobody really knew how to do this kind of writing. By the 1920s, the idea of writing for the movies had taken hold, and many phony writing schools were advertising to the public: "No physical exertion required—invalids can succeed. Learn in five day's time. Start to write immediately."[5] Very quickly the need for **visual writing** that translated to the screen and for writing that anticipated practical production realities led to a new writing profession.[6] In the 1930s, after the advent of sound, the **Academy of Motion Picture Arts and Sciences** set about finding a standard form for the screenplay.

Everyone who tries to write for the moving picture medium and its derivatives goes through a personal evolution, somewhat as the industry did. You learn about the problem of composing for a visual medium and struggle with finding a form in which to express it. You do not have to reinvent the wheel, just understand why the wheel was invented. Your job is to learn the conventions of the form and layout of a script that the industry has worked out by trial and error. If you do not follow these conventions, you set up barriers to having your work accepted.

---

[3] Kevin Brownlow, *The Parade's Gone By* (New York: Alfred A. Knopf, 1969), p. 270.

[4] Ibid, p. 275.

[5] One literary writer, Edward Knoblock, wrote hopelessly: "Words fail to describe the scene that follows." Brownlow, p. 276.

[6] Brownlow, p. 278.

WHAT IS VISUAL WRITING?

Everybody has heard the old adage that a picture is worth a thousand words. **Visual writing** means making images stand for words. A clock face tells you that time is passing. In the classic Western *High Noon* (1952), the characters frequently look at the clock, and the audience sees a cutaway because the time left before the noon train is a powerful plot element. An outlaw recently released from prison and sworn to revenge is arriving on the noon train. The former marshal who put him in prison, just married and now in a dispute with his Quaker wife before they have even left on their honeymoon, desperately tries to recruit a posse but finally has to confront his enemy alone. Although **visual writing** for the screen involves description, it is not necessarily descriptive prose with a lot of adjectives. The clock in *High Noon* could be described in two words—CUTAWAY clock. The art director picks the clock to fit the period. We don't need to describe it and say whether it has roman numerals or a pendulum. The clock is a visual idea that communicates the importance of time in the plot. It is a functional visual idea. An image communicates both by logical deduction and emotional implication. A visual medium makes demands on both by using signs, symbols, and icons. You can tell the bad guys from the good guys in a Western without subtitles. Their hats, style of gun belt, clothes, and whether they are shaven or unshaven all let the audience know how to understand the character. **Visual writing** means writing and thinking with images that the audience will see rather than words they will read.[7]

How do you write with visual ideas as opposed to writing visually descriptive prose? We are all familiar with descriptive prose:

In the late summer of that year we lived in a village that looked across the river and the plain to the mountains. In the bed of the river there were pebbles and boulders, dry and white in the sun, and the water was clear and swiftly moving and blue in the channels. The troops went by the house and down the road and the dust they raised powdered the leaves of the trees. The trunks of the trees were too dusty and the leaves fell early that year and we saw the troops marching along the road and the dust rising and leaves, stirred by the breeze, falling and the soldiers marching and afterward the road bare and white except for the leaves.

The plain was rich with crops; there were many orchards of fruit trees and beyond the plain the mountains were brown and bare. There was fighting in the mountains and at night we could see the flashes from the artillery. In the dark it was like summer lightning, but the nights were cool and there was not the feeling of a storm coming.[8]

This visually descriptive opening to Ernest Hemingway's *A Farewell to Arms* is, no doubt, admirable prose fiction. However, it would not work for a film script. The freedom of the novelist to assemble impressions and condense impressions over time (written in the past tense) into a mood or atmosphere that is the setting for characters and **action** is hard to duplicate in film or television. It is barely

---

[7] "Writing for films was a new craft, having little to do with established literary forms. An elegant turn of phrase was of no use in a silent-movie script (unless it appeared as an intertitle). The plot and the visual ideas were what mattered." Eileen Bowser, "The Transformation of Cinema 1907–1915," in *History of the American Cinema*, vol. 2, ed. Charles Harpole (New York: Charles Scribner's Sons, 1990).

[8] Ernest Hemingway, *A Farewell to Arms* (New York: Charles Scribner's Sons, 1957), p. 3.

conceivable that a moviemaker would reproduce all of these visual images, even in a montage. A scriptwriter cannot assume the freedom that the novelist has. A lot of descriptive imagery is irrelevant to the visual medium. If the nights are cold, saying so in the script does not translate onto the screen; to do so with a line of dialogue would be heavy handed. You have to show someone shivering or putting on a sweater—all very costly in screen time unless critical to the story.

The **omniscient narrator** is a novelistic device that is hard to duplicate in a screenplay unless you create a voiceover narrator. In a novel, the narration is verbalized. In a screenplay, it must disappear. Whether you are adapting an existing work or writing an original script, the imaginative challenge is to select a key setting and a key image. Do we choose the flashes of artillery at night? That would be quite demanding to shoot. A script can't deal with the simile of comparing it to summer lightning. Do we choose the soldiers marching by raising dust with the crops, orchards, and mountains in the background? This is probably more concise cinematically and requires the right location. If we describe it too closely, the location search becomes impossible. Do we need to see the stream and the pebbles? Do we need to see the dust on the leaves? It is unrealistic for the writer to impose this kind of detail on the production. The director will resist when faced with the concrete task of choosing a location and a camera angle.

Essentially, the script writer has to introduce **action**. This is true not only for movies and television but also for corporate and instructional programs. The description that sets the scene is usually subordinate to character and **action**. The art is to combine them. Six pages on and some time later, Hemingway gets to a street scene with characters and interaction. On the seventh page, the first dialogue interchange between the narrator, a priest, Lieutenant Rinaldi, and a captain occurs in the mess hall. Two pages of dialogue in which the mood of war is introduced could easily take 5 or 10 minutes of screen time and a lot of money to create with lead actors, a crowd, sets, props, costumes, and locations. Yet by the end of Hemingway's Chapter 2, we barely have a title sequence for a movie. Good novel! Bad script!

A scriptwriter has to invent a visual sequence that will condense background and **action** in such a way as to advance a story. This could be achieved by a number of devices:

Solution 1: Create an observer. A character could be riding a bike down the road with the scene in the background and the column of soldiers in the foreground. He arrives in the village. The street scene is established. Cut to the mess hall.

Solution 2: Create a montage. We see quick cuts from artillery flashes in the night. Cut to a column of soldiers marching past. Quick cut to ambulance. Cut to civilians hiding from gunfire. Cut to ripe fruit in an orchard. Cut to Lieutenant Rinaldi in the mess hall.

Solution 3: Use audio to add value to the scene. Interior, night, mess hall, Lieutenant Rinaldi, a captain and a priest in terse conversation with an American. Between phrases, the sound effect of an artillery exchange rattles the glass faintly from the shock wave of an explosion. Flashes of nearby artillery illuminate the faces near the windows.

Some screenwriters invent scenes in their adaptations that are not in the original work, or even change the plot, often to our great annoyance. Is it laziness? Is it legitimate adaptation? Sometimes what works in a novel doesn't work on screen. A novel can be hundreds of pages long. A feature film is 120-odd pages of script for 100 minutes of screen time. As we saw earlier, there are plenty of ways to achieve the necessary economy of **action**. This linking and condensing of **actions** is **visual writing**. We might be better off calling it writing with visual ideas. It works by narrating through **a sequence of images**. The scriptwriter has to think in terms of physical **action** because everything in a screenplay is seen on the screen. The scriptwriter's job is to describe **action** as the camera sees it.

When screenwriter Ben Hecht adapted Hemingway's novel for the movie of 1957, he adopted a narrative voiceover technique (see Website).[9] Lieutenant Frederic Henry sets the background of the story of the war as we see him return from leave. He walks past a military column of pack mules and a company of Italian troops against a backdrop of the village of Orsino and evidence of war damage. He gets a wave from a girl from the window of a brothel over a local bar before he enters the ambulance pool adjoining the hospital. Now we meet characters, and dialogue between them moves the plot along.

In the final analysis, the solution to adapting Hemingway may be to cut out this opening and start deeper into the story. At this point, you might decide you'd rather be a novelist. On the assumption that you are still open to **scriptwriting** as an option, let's proceed.

META-WRITING

So the first understanding of **visual writing** means writing for the media result, providing a description of what the audience will experience. There is another aspect to **visual writing** that I call **meta-writing**. This writing, or perhaps this thinking (sometimes an unwritten concept), often determines the structure of media content. However, it is not necessarily the plot itself, nor the story; it is the visual idea that makes the content work for a given medium. It can be a dramatic conflict for a story, but it can also be the visual idea that makes a billboard work or a television commercial succeed. Often it requires a **visual metaphor** that carries the theme. It is usually embodied in the written **creative concept**.

To understand this concept better, let's illustrate **meta-writing**. *Titanic!* As soon as you say the word, you conjure up a major shipwreck, tragic loss of life, survivors, all things that you can see. The love story in the film is a storyline and plot that is superimposed on the **meta-writing**. *Jurassic Park!* The genetic reconstruction of dinosaurs in an island theme park is a visual idea. The characters and the storyline are superimposed on it.

Meta-writing has great importance in corporate communications, which often depend on finding a visual correlative for an abstract idea-change, for instance. Although change itself is an abstract idea, it can be understood through **visual metaphors** such as weather, a river, a speeded-up growth sequence of a plant, or speeded-up sequence of decay. The Website has a clip for an EMC Corporation video on management of information flows. It is made comprehensible emotionally and intellectually by images of water in motion, such as waves, rivers, and waterfalls. So, **meta-writing** is that writing or thinking that enables the writing of the key concept.

---

[9] Ben Hecht wrote a screenplay for the movie version of *A Farewell to Arms* (1957). There was also an earlier production in 1932 starring Gary Cooper and Helen Hayes.

WHERE DO WE GO FROM HERE?

We are ready to look at some of the specific problems of setting down the writer's vision—namely, describing images and sound for production. We will learn how to do so in incremental steps. One way is to reverse-engineer a scene from a movie or a television program. From your experience of seeing a scene, turn your role around and try to describe what a production crew would need to know to remake that scene. Even though you don't yet know how to write scripts, trying to do so introduces you to the essential problem. This will start you thinking about how you describe things and how you lay out this information on a page.

A good way to approach this task is to find a movie with a published script and study the way the visuals on screen relate to the script. A word to the wise, however: published scripts are usually postproduction scripts. They are made from the finished movie for distribution, dubbing foreign language versions, and publicity purposes. A postproduction script seldom corresponds word for word with the production script, and it is usually written by a person other than the scriptwriter.

DIFFERENCES COMPARED TO STAGE PLAYS

Another way to isolate the special nature of **scriptwriting** is to compare it to playwriting. Stage plays do not usually describe **action** in detail. Stage directors and designers have greater latitude to decide on the staging and the blocking. Stage plays assume a constant point of view based on the proscenium stage with a consistent sight line. In contrast, the scriptwriter has to be concerned with physical **action** and a specific point of view anywhere within a 360-degree compass. **Action** must be described as it is framed by a camera lens and by a camera movement. The words spoken by characters, the dramatic dialogue, although part of the script, do not present a **visual writing** problem except perhaps when dialogue stops the **action** (see a discussion of this issue in Chapter 9).

Plays are not always visual and depend heavily on dialogue. Novels describe emotions. Visual media have to show emotions. So a script is not a novel, though it may be adapted from a novel. It is not a play, though it is sometimes adapted from a play and becomes a screenplay. It is a unique form. A screenplay and many shorter scripts can be original, not based on a source work. A writer can also write or compose directly for the visual medium.[10] Although **visual writing** means thinking in terms of images rather than describing visual things, **visual writing** also means leaving out obvious and unnecessary scenes, no matter how visual. The scriptwriter has to construct visual meaning out of sequences of images, whether he is communicating a corporate message or adapting Hemingway. Original **visual writing** for a script means doing this in your head.

WRITING WITH DIALOGUE

Colin Welland wrote an original script, *Chariots of Fire*, produced by David Puttnam, about two British runners, Eric Liddell and Harold Abrahams, who competed in the Olympic Games of 1924. *Chariots of Fire* won the Academy Award for best picture in 1982. Here is the scene of a college race in which

---

[10] See Paul Schrader's screenplay for *Taxi Driver* (London: Faber and Faber, 1990) and his other writings.

we meet Abrahams, a main character. Welland introduces the theme of running and competition and establishes the social setting and the social class of the characters in this Cambridge University setting[11]:

```
EXT. TRINITY COURT MID-DAY

                         ROBIN
         Mr. Abrahams—your position please!

HAROLD MOVE FORWARD. A HUSH DESCENDS ON THE COURT. THE CROWD CRANE THEIR
NECKS AS HAROLD TOES THE LINE TO FIND THE BEST GRIP.

                         ROBIN
                  (addressing the throng)
         Owing to the absence of any other
         challenger, Mr. Abrahams will run
         alone.

A VOICE CUTS IN

                         VOICE
         Not so Mr. Starter!

ALL HEADS TURN—TO SEE, HURRYING THROUGH THE CROWD, HIS COAT THROWN OVER
HIS SHOULDER ANDY LINDSEY. CROOKED IN HIS ARM IS AN UNOPENED BOTTLE OF
CHAMPAGNE. HAROLD IS AS AMAZED AS THE REST. ANDY TOSSES HIS COAT TO THE
OPEN MOUTHED AUBREY AND THE BOTTLE TO HARRY. HE'S RESPLENDENT IN ETON
RUNNING STRIPE.

                         ROBIN
         Your name and college if you please
         sir.

                         ANDY
         Lindsey. I race beside my friend here.
         We challenge in the name of Repton,
         Eton and Caius.
CHEERS AGAIN.
```

The dialogue, although natural to the characters, advances the plot. The description is necessary to the **action**. It also sets up an **action** scene, which creates interest and anticipation for the audience.

WRITING WITHOUT DIALOGUE

Consider the opening of *Bartleby*,[12] a contemporary adaptation of the story *Bartleby, The Scrivener*, by Herman Melville. The images establish an urban setting, the anonymity, alienation, and isolation of the main character.

---

[11] Unpublished script of *Chariots of Fire* (1982), written by Colin Welland.
[12] *Bartleby*, unpublished screenplay, Pantheon Film Productions Ltd., distributed by Corinth Films, New York. See Website for complete version

INT. TUBE TRAIN -- DAY

BARTLEBY is sitting next to the window in silhouette. Light rain streaks
past the window as the train flashes past London suburbs. The train
plunges underground. Fade in Music.

                                                          CUT TO:

INT. TUBE STATION -- DAY

A train arrives in the station and stops. People pour out across the
platform. In the middle, we catch a glimpse of BARTLEBY.

                                                          CUT TO:

INT. TUBE ESCALATOR -- DAY

Side shot from parallel escalator descending of BARTLEBY riding up the
escalator. He is motionless. The background moves by.

                                                          CUT TO:

INT. TUBE ESCALATOR -- DAY

LS of BARTLEBY, one of a line of people riding up escalator. MS BARTLEBY.
He is motionless. Most of them are looking straight ahead. BARTLEBY looks
towards camera as it descends past him.

                                                          CUT TO:

INT. TUBE STATION -- DAY

CAMERA TRACKS and PANS past a long bank of 24 hour lockers coming upon
BARTLEBY putting a bag into a locker at chest height.

                                                     DISSOLVE TO:

This visual sequence without dialogue is the cinematic equivalent of novelistic description. Cinematic description is often implied by the setting, crowd, **action**, and movement of the camera. All good scriptwriters try to write with images and show **action**.

Some **scriptwriting** is down to earth. Here is a description of a shipping sequence from a corporate video:

MONTAGE OF 55-foot Truck and trailer backing up to a loading bay,
hand signals between driver and bay. Forklift loads the Truck.
Securing for the journey. Shutting the trailer door.

This is not inspired prose. It just describes essential **action**. What it looks like on screen will be decided by the director on location, by the placement of the camera, and by the chance availability of certain trucks and forklifts. **Scriptwriting** is primarily an art of organizing images and describing **action** to tell a story or communicate a message.

CONCLUSION

In this chapter, we have looked at how you adapt existing material and invent original dramatic writing. Starting with an examination of something familiar, such as a novel, reveals some of the ways that **scriptwriting** is different from writing prose. A later chapter deals with more of these issues. There are many other kinds of **scriptwriting**. Some have particular page formats governed by production methods such as multicamera live production. All **scriptwriting** involves clear description of **action**. A hundred years of development since the beginning of motion pictures have led to techniques of writing and a specific camera and audio vocabulary to help do the job. You need to learn these recognized conventions for describing certain recurring visual frames. This subject requires a chapter of its own.

Exercises

1. Write your description of a short scene from a TV series or a movie so that another production crew could recreate that same scene. Invent your own way of writing a one-page script.
2. Look at a video of a film with a published script and read the script while you study the video. Start by using a silent film, say, a Charlie Chaplin film such as *Gold Rush*. Here are a few movie titles for which you can find a postproduction script: *Citizen Kane*, *Casablanca*, *Taxi Driver*, and *The Piano Player*.
3. Select a scene from a Shakespeare play or any other play, by Bernard Shaw or Henrik Ibsen, for instance. Then identify what would not be clear in the scene for film production. What do you have to add to make a film or television sequence? Can you use all the dialogue? Do not write a script; instead write an analysis of what would have to change or be added to adapt the scene to film.
4. Write a present-time **action** description for the opening chapter of Hemingway's *A Farewell to Arms*. Decide how to condense the **action**. Make a list of shots describing visuals only. Set yourself an objective of no more than three minutes of screen time.
5. Write a present-time **action** description of the opening of a movie adaptation of J. D. Salinger's *The Catcher in the Rye*. Make a list of shots describing visuals only. Decide what screen time will work.
6. Compare a book you have read with the movie based on it. See if you can identify a key scene in the movie that wasn't in the book. Analyze why. Also look for a scene in the book that wasn't in the movie. Analyze why. Find a scene that is in both the book and the movie and examine how the adaptation has worked.
7. As an exercise in **visual writing**, try to create an image or a one-shot scene that communicates primary emotional situations: anger, fear, humor, curiosity, conflict, danger, deceit, hope, fatigue. The challenge is to show it without words and without literal-minded solutions, such as a close-up of an angry face representing anger.

CHAPTER 2

A Seven-Step Method for Developing a Creative Concept

KEY TERMS

analytic steps
axiom
behavioral objective
communication objective
communication problem
communication strategy
content
copy platform
creative concept
demographics

ethos or an appeal to ethical values
seven-step method
first-person plural
first-person singular
friedmann's first law of media communication
friedmann's second law of media communication
hopefully
informational objective

logos, an appeal to reason and argument
meta-writing
motivational objective
pathos, an appeal to emotion
present tense
psychographics
public policy problem
target audience
which medium

Knowing how to describe visuals, sound, and action so that a production team can understand your intentions is the essential task of a scriptwriter. However, knowing this does not help you come up with a program idea or construct a script. How scripts get started is often a mystery to the beginner. One thing is certain. You do not just start describing scenes and immediately write a first draft script. That is a recipe for failure. Scriptwriting is preceded by a great deal of thinking. It is probably true to say that writers in the media business are paid to think as much as to write. Once you have done the right thinking, the writing follows as night follows day. A strong **creative concept** is the foundation of successful scriptwriting. We now need to outline the steps needed to develop a **creative concept**.

Doi: 10.1016/B978-0-240-81235-9.00002-x

The visual media of the twenty-first century are sophisticated communications tools. From their roots in photography and film, they continue to evolve in electronic form with dazzling innovations. To succeed in writing for these media, we need to see how the choice of the medium and its application result from a thinking process. It is the quality of this thinking process that determines the quality of the writing and the effectiveness of the communication. This is the idea of **meta-writing** introduced in Chapter 1: writing that is not the finished document, but the thinking beneath, or behind, the actual writing that supports the visual idea. And let's be clear; this thinking is often written out for the benefit of the writer, the producer, or the client. If you watch a film or video, or even if you read a script, you do not see all of the analytic and conceptual thinking on which it is based. This is the part of the iceberg that is unseen below the surface.

Let's start with an **axiom**. An axiom is an undisputed given from which argument or investigation can proceed. Our **axiom** states that every program is a response to a **communication problem**. If there were no need to show, tell, or explain something to an audience, if there were no need to attract, entertain, seduce, delight, or distract an audience, there would be no reason to make a program and, therefore, no need to write a script. Common sense tells us that any program addresses and solves some kind of communication need. Before we can start any job, we have to identify and define this particular communications need. Going through this analysis is not only essential but highly creative. Moreover, it is a method that will always prepare you for any writing job. As you learn your scriptwriting craft, follow the seven-step process described in this chapter. When you are experienced and a proven producer of scripts, you can adopt your own way of defining a solution to a communications problem.

STEP 1: DEFINE THE COMMUNICATION PROBLEM

Most of this method is logic and common sense. The first shorthand question to answer is "What need?" Sometimes, you will come across the term "needs analysis," referring to the investigation that discovers a communication problem. Basic communication means that someone (a person or corporate entity) expresses a thought, idea, or message that is delivered via some kind of medium—speech, print, video, interactive multimedia—to a receiver. The message can be designed and sent but not necessarily received or, if received, not necessarily understood. We all experience unsuccessful communication both as senders and receivers. Talking or writing to your friends, parents, or strangers, although it could be important, is easy to do and doesn't cost you anything except, perhaps, a telephone call or a postage stamp. Creating, sending, and receiving a public service announcement, a corporate public relations video, or a training video is a very expensive exercise. Doing it haphazardly or improvising as you go is too risky. Professionals have developed ways of tipping the odds in favor of success by careful analysis and thought about the nature of the communication problem that is the reason for making a program.

Defining the communication need or problem is the first step. Collaboration is needed between the scriptwriter and the producer or between the writer and a client. Very often you write for others, not for personal expression or for artistic reasons, but to help them communicate successfully. Until you know what the communication problem is, you cannot begin. Until writer and client define it and both agree what it is, the enterprise is fraught with hazard. You risk misunderstanding, multiple revisions, wasted money, and, finally, an unsuccessful result. The seven-step method discussed here is particularly successful for scriptwriting commissioned by corporate clients.

Think of it this way! Unless you can identify an audience that needs to know, understand, or perceive something that you, the communicator, want them to grasp, there is no basis for a script or a program. Simply put, you do not know what to say, to whom, or why you should demand an audience's attention. Too often, corporate clients decide to make a video or create a website without thinking through what precise problem it will solve. It is important to grasp this basic point: you must think for your client because your client may not have thought through the problem. A client can ask an architect to design a bad building without realizing it. A client can ask a producer to produce a bad video without knowing. Architects can design buildings that do not solve the problem that led to the need for the building, and producers can make videos that do not solve the communication problem.

Let us illustrate this with some examples. First, we will go through the analysis of the communication problem so as to define the media need. Then we will see how to write it down in an acceptable and convincing way. Such a document is an intelligent form of insurance for the writer as well as being a service to the producer or client.

IVY COLLEGE: AN ADMISSIONS VIDEO

Most college students have seen a video made by a college or university to recruit students. There must be hundreds of them. Now there are CD-ROMs and websites that provide an interactive opportunity for the prospective students to get information. Because you can identify strongly with this particular audience, put yourselves in the recruitment video creator's shoes and think about the communications problem for the academic institution. What is it? The institution has to think about the needs of the student. What information will satisfy the high school senior's need for facts about courses, curricula, dorm life, the campus environment, sports, and recreational facilities? Is it just a need for information? Doesn't the institution want to project itself to a certain kind of student, to differentiate itself from other institutions? Does it want any student at any price? Is there something special about the institution and its traditions? What role should the video play in the whole process of recruitment that involves print media, applications, phone calls, campus visits, and counseling?

How can we define the communications problem? The students who might want to apply to Ivy College don't know enough about the institution to enable them to make a decision to apply or perhaps to make an inquiry about applying. They might not know where it is, what it looks like, what the courses are like, what the other students are like, whether it matches a special interest or requirement. They might not know that Ivy College has a strong program in, say, marine biology. They might not know things the college wants them to know, or they might want to know things that the college doesn't want them to know.

The question then arises, "What is the objective of the video?" After your audience has seen it, what do you want the result to be? Three questions quickly come into play that are closely interrelated: (1) What is the nature of the communication problem you want to solve? (2) Who is your audience? and (3) How can you define the successful outcome of that communication, namely, the objective?

Now that several issues are on the table, you have to be able to state clearly what each one is. This means being able to write them down for someone else to read and evaluate. The beginning script-writer is typically impatient and wants to get started on the actual writing, and thus may be tempted to brush off the questions that this chapter addresses. Whatever you do, resist the temptation to shortcut the analytic thinking that precedes writing. At the outset of a scriptwriting job, all is prom-ise, all is possible, and you have a great deal of freedom to invent. With each step, the script becomes more and more concrete, more and more specific, and has to deliver on the easy promises of the con-cept you put forward at the beginning. These **analytic steps** ensure that you stay brief and on target.

AMERICAN EXPRESS: AMERICAN TRAVEL IN EUROPE

American Express has an interest in the success of European hotels and restaurants that accept its card. American Express is sometimes perceived as an agent taking a percentage of revenue rather than as a contributor to the travel and tourism industry. Its market research indicates that the pattern of American tourism is changing and that the European tourist industry is in danger of losing its market share.

What is the communications problem? It is complex. First, there is a need to communicate informa-tion. The client knows something the audience doesn't know. If we tell that audience what we know, they will see a business problem in a different light. They will also change their perception of the client from a passive intermediary to a contributor and a partner. So the second communications problem is to shift perception or attitude. You will be able to measure the success or failure of the speech, publication, or video by the transfer of information and by the change of attitude.

Next you must ask: who is the audience and what is their current mentality? Unless you can answer these questions, you cannot ever design a successful communication. Even when you answer the question of who the audience is, you still don't know what the content should be nor how you will persuade the audience to see your point of view. If you define your communication problem clearly, at least you can start thinking about the other problems with some hope of success.

In this case, the target audience is European travel professionals such as hotel management staff, restaurateurs, and tourist authorities (but not the general public). Research shows that this audience is somewhat complacent. They think the tourists will keep coming because it is a law of nature, like the migration of elk across the tundra. They are ignorant of American trends and tastes and unaware of competitive destinations. (See the complete script on the website.)

Let's look at another communications problem.

PSA FOR BATTERED WOMEN

A shelter, also an advisory service for battered women, wants to make a PSA to reach women who need a refuge from abuse. This is a real challenge to think through. You may think it is obvious. Your target audience is battered women. You just tell them about the safe house and where it is. However, there are a dozen different messages that serve different communication needs. Some are purely informational, such as where is it and what is the phone number? There are women victims who don't know about it. Your PSA tells them. Communication problem solved! Job done!

But there are also women who are abused who don't think of their treatment as abuse. They are in denial, as the current psychological language describes it. Some are in real physical danger. Others may be sliding into a pattern that will lead to abuse. Some have children; some don't. Some are educated; some aren't. Some are afraid and confused; some are aware of the abuse but powerless to overcome their problems.

Suddenly, we realize that a good PSA for one type of battered woman would be unsuccessful for another. A meaningful message for one would be of limited interest to another. The communication problem has to be defined very closely to accomplish a meaningful objective. One problem might be informational; another might be motivational. You have to get your audience to think and go on thinking. Another problem you might want to solve could be defined by behavior—you want your audience to pick up the phone and call the number you publicize in the PSA. In fact, all media communication can be summed up as a combination of informational, motivational, or behavioral objectives. The mix or proportion of one to the other is infinitely variable. Sometimes one is dominant, sometimes another.

You have almost certainly seen PSAs that address the issues of drugs, smoking, or drinking and driving. All of them involve complex decisions about what communication problem is in play. What is certain is that the problem varies with the **target audience**. Hence, the objective varies with both. It is like an equation in algebra. If you change the value of one unknown, you get a different answer.

SHELL GAS INTERNATIONAL

An oil company has invented a process that can turn natural gas into lubrication oils at an economical cost. Huge reserves of natural gas exist in both developed and undeveloped countries that are practically worthless because there is no nearby market for the gas. However, there is a market for lubrication products because they have higher value and can be delivered to market at less cost. The decision to buy the process, make the investment, and enter into a joint venture would be made by a handful of people in the world—oil ministers and senior geologists or advisors. The countries involved number about a dozen.

The target audience for this video is going to be about 25 people, 50 at most in the entire world. Contrast that with the audience for a college recruitment video, or an exercise video that shows you how to get six-pack abs. How different are the communication problems? How different are the target audiences? How different are the objectives of each video? Until you define the answers to the key questions, you don't stand a chance of writing a successful script. Your interest may be in writing for entertainment media. Although the problems are slightly different, you still need to be able to answer a variant of the same questions. For instance, you need to know who your primary audience is—children, thirty-somethings, women, or youth. Your objective could be to make them laugh or cry. You might intend to write drama, comedy, or documentary. For television you might be writing a game show or a children's adventure or an animated cartoon. All of these have different premises and, therefore, demand different thinking.

In summary, defining a communication problem is a "needs" analysis of a communication deficiency of some kind. Somebody or some group needs to know something that they don't know. Having established what it is, you follow the steps to find a media solution that will tell them what they need to know. Ask yourself why the program should be made. It must solve a communication problem that you must identify clearly. Sometimes people confuse the communication problem with another larger problem that lies behind the immediate reason for making the program. This could be a social problem or a marketing problem, which is the reason for the need for communication. However, the communication problem is not the social problem or the **public policy problem**. For example, smoking is a public health problem. The objective of public policy is to stop people, especially young people, from getting addicted to nicotine. The communication problem, however, is not to stop people smoking. It is to increase awareness, change attitude or motivate a change of behavior. It is an incremental step deploying media in a public policy objective. The communication problem is not the same as the **public policy problem**.

An antismoking PSA might address a specific communication problem, which is that teenage smokers are unaware or dismissive of the health hazard of smoking. They've heard it all before. They dismiss the warnings and believe they are immortal. Getting through this specific problem of denial is the communication problem. Behind it lies a larger social, and public health, problem: persuading teenagers to stop smoking, or not to start in the first place. Beginners often and easily confuse the marketing problem or the social problem with the communication problem. Someone who says the communication problem is the need to show that drinking and driving do not go together is stating an objective, not a problem—not stating the problem but the solution.

Take another topic! What is the communication problem that lies behind a college recruitment video? Someone who says, "The communication problem is to show high school students, mostly seniors, how to apply to college through a video" has not found the problem. The problem is better stated by asking, "What do those who are unsure about the application process to college need to know in order to apply successfully?" Or "Many high school students are insecure about the college application process and do not know how to go about applying." That states a problem for which there is a media solution.

You can see that several different PSAs could be made from the same generalized premise in each case. So, to get off on the right foot, it is really important to nail this question accurately. Smoking is a social problem or a health problem; domestic abuse is a social problem; college recruitment is a marketing problem. But within these, there are communication problems that will be specific to the programs, that will define your PSA and lead to clear ideas about the target audience and the objective.

Understanding what communication problem lies behind a media project is so critical to getting the script right that you should not proceed until you have achieved clarity about exactly what problem you are trying to solve. Once again, let us emphasize that many people confuse the public policy problem or the marketing problem with the media communication problem. We must remember that the role of a media piece whether PSA or TV ad or even a corporate video is particular and subordinate to the larger communication problem. We can illustrate this by referring to the 50-year-long campaign against smoking. Beginners frequently make the mistake of stating that the communication of the antismoking PSA is to get people to stop smoking. It almost never is. The public policy objective of the whole campaign surely is, but that can involve multiple media strategies, lobbying, changing legislation, and so on. The television PSA is going to have to be focused on some subset of the problem. For instance, where adolescents are the target audience, the communication problem could be more accurately and precisely stated—that they are not aware how addictive cigarettes are and that adopting smoking as a way to claim maturity and independence conceals a huge danger. Now switch the target to veteran smokers. The communication problem of the PSA, not the public policy campaign, is that these addicted smokers do not realize that even though they may have been smoking for years and damaged their health, there is a huge health benefit from quitting that can prolong life and the quality of life.

In almost every case of scripting an ad or a PSA, there is a subtle and critical distinction between the campaign and marketing objective and the objective of the particular piece of media. Even when you are selling a good or a service, the communication problem is almost never to sell the product but to change an awareness that creates the context for selling. If a product solves a problem of daily living or satisfies a need, then the change of understanding, perception or awareness creates the condition for a sale to take place. All media solutions solve problems that are a subset of a global campaign objective. Get this right and your thinking or **meta-writing** will fall into place.

STEP 2: DEFINE THE TARGET AUDIENCE

The shorthand question to answer is, "To whom?" From the previous examples, you can see it is impossible to talk about any communication problem without bumping into the question, who is the **target audience**? If you change the audience, you change the kind of problem, and hence, the objective. If you want to warn smokers of the dangers of smoking, you will write a completely different script if you are addressing adolescents or high school students compared to adults or veteran smokers. Getting someone to stop a 20-year-old habit is a different communication task than discouraging a young person from starting. Selling a process to turn natural gas into lubrication oils will never have the customer of those oils as its audience. Its audience is decision makers who will give a green light to the investment of hundreds of millions of dollars. If you do not accurately profile your audience, you will endanger your communication.

To illustrate how much the target audience changes the communication problem and the objective, let's play with the variables. It is Valentine's Day. The message is "I love you." You have had an argument with your boyfriend or girlfriend. You want to make up. Suddenly, the message takes on a different weight. How you will communicate suddenly becomes very important. Sincerity is crucial. But some kinds of sincerity are better than others. How the message is delivered is critical.

Try another variation. The target audience for your "I love you" message is your mother on Mother's Day, or your grandmother on her 90th birthday. Does that color the problem differently and suggest a completely different objective? Or your audience is someone to whom you are expressing this feeling for the first time. You have never uttered these words to this person before. Does that feel different? You get the point. Every time you vary the target audience, you change the communication problem and the kind of strategy that is going to make it succeed.

Information Overload

In our day and age, the amount of information presented to us through print media, radio, TV, and now the Internet is overwhelming—and that is before you consider deeper levels of information that you can search out in books, libraries, or archives, or on the Internet. We all have to limit our intake in order to process it. Thinking about the rate at which an audience can absorb information is important.

You will hear the terms **target audience** and *primary* **target audience**, secondary, even tertiary target audience. What do they mean? Target is a metaphor. You shoot at a target. The idea is to aim at and hit the bull's-eye. Concentric rings on the target near the bull's-eye are less desirable but useful nevertheless and score points. Even with the exhaustive research that advertisers do to market products, a certain averaging of audience characteristics is necessary. Dominant factors have to govern your approach. We all quote Lincoln's phrase about not being able to fool all of the people, all of the time. You can, however, fool some of the people some of the time.[1] How many can be included is the writer's challenge. You make your judgment and hope that you bracket the largest and most important part of your audience. The others are called the *secondary* **target audience**. You want them, but you are not going to jeopardize gaining the larger audience to get them. You know that you might lose some of the secondary audience, but the success of your communication does not depend on them.

Take the Ivy College recruitment video discussed earlier. What if your **target audience** is nontraditional or returning students? What if your video is for a graduate program? Consider an extreme case. What if your audience is openly hostile? A company takes over another company and intends to rationalize the operation leading to layoffs, relocation, and changes in job titles. You are not going to construct the same video as if you were addressing company personnel about pensions or safety issues in the workplace. You have to address the deep distrust the audience will bring to the company's message. In general, awareness of what the audience thinks, feels, knows, understands, does for a living, does for recreation, and so on could change everything. Their educational level, income, gender, age, married status, political views, or consumer preferences could flip your approach one way or the other.

---

[1] You can fool some of the people all of the time, and all of the people some of the time, but you cannot fool all of the people all of the time. Abraham Lincoln, *16th president of the United States* (attributed)

Most beginners tend to be too vague about their target audience. Here's an example of a student attempt at defining the audience for a college admissions video:

> My target audience consists of males and females who are interested in attending a small, diverse college in a town on the outskirts of Boston that offers a wide variety of majors.

This is too vague and mixes the statement up with objectives about "majors." In fact, some of the audience might not know they are interested in a small college or in the geographical location. The point is that we want to define who they are. Male and female is clear. They must be high school seniors or graduates. Are they all American, or are there also international students? Income might be a factor for private college tuition. Location is part of the content or the strategy of persuasion rather than a definition of the identity of the audience.

There are two words you need to know about that refer to techniques of measuring and identifying the characteristics of audiences. They are **demographics** and **psychographics**. For most scriptwriting, you need to think about both.

DEMOGRAPHICS

Trying to identify the common characteristics of a group of people so that you can define them as a target audience is a professional preoccupation of advertisers, public relations practitioners, pollsters, marketers, television ratings researchers, and more. Millions of dollars are spent on audience research and market research to identify the profile of a buyer or a viewer. Just because you don't have a large budget to commission such research does not mean you can ignore demographics when you try to define who your audience is. You can, and should, do some amateur demographics. A lot of it is common sense.

Let's put down the major characteristics that delimit the nature of a person and categorize him or her as part of one grouping or another.

Age

Age will affect the vocabulary you can use and the sort of devices that will work. You would not use a stuffed animal or a dinosaur character to explain company pensions, but you might use them to warn young children about the dangers of crossing the road. The college admissions video has a fairly well-defined target age. Many other projects do not have well-defined age targets.

Gender

If you could identify a majority female audience, you might opt for a different approach than if it were a majority male audience. You can see this in TV advertising for products with a gender bias such as shampoos, hygiene products, or perfume. A PSA targeting battered women is easier to write because the gender of the target audience is more likely to be women. However, you could write a PSA targeted at male abusers also, trying to increase awareness of destructive behavior. The approach would have to be entirely different. Yet again, women also abuse men although it is less well known. This would entail a complete rethink of the way to approach the PSA message.

Race and Ethnic Origin

The sociology of race and ethnic origins tells us that groups have identities. There are common cultural assumptions and values that might aid or hinder communicating with these groups. The United States is home to numerous subcultures that might respond differently to certain nuances in language, music, or style. A good example is the campaign by the Milk Marketing Board with the well-known tag line "Got milk?" Translate this into Spanish and you get "Are you lactating?" If your audience is international, the possibilities for cross-cultural misunderstanding are considerable. The most obvious way this could affect your message design is in casting. You might want the actors in your production to be representative of a minority group. A recent TV recruitment commercial for the U.S. Army showed a young African-American youth with his mother. He says that it is time for him to be the man now. Interestingly, this ad implies that we are seeing a stereotyped single parent family presumed to be prevalent in this demographic. Moreover, the ad is clearly pitched at a disadvantaged racial and economic demographic. The target is race.

When Wal-Mart started doing business in Germany, the greeters who approach shoppers at the entrance to Wal-Mart (the smiley face) offended Germans, who complained to management about being approached and harassed by strangers. In the United States, people are more familiar and personal with strangers than in Europe. American sales personnel and telephone marketers call you by your first name, which Europeans consider a breach of etiquette that is offensive. There are regional differences in the United States. This is often exploited in advertising food that is regional, for instance. A southern accent might sell the barbecued spare ribs or the sauce better than a Boston accent, which might give the New England clam chowder an identity.

Education

The educational level of an audience governs the vocabulary you can use, the general knowledge you can assume, and the kind of argument that will be readily understood. When writing a corporate video for Shell that is aimed at decision makers in petroleum-producing countries, you can assume a certain level of language and concept, but you have to know the difference between an audience of geologists and an audience of ministers or high-level civil servants who are not scientists. The larger the audience, the lower the educational denominator is likely to be until you reach a national average.

A pharmaceutical company making a video about a new cholesterol-lowering drug aimed at cardiologists has a very high educational demographic. If the video is aimed, however, at the eventual users of that same cholesterol-lowering drug, the demographics change. The patients, who are likely to use the drug, cut across the educational demographic and would be less educated and knowledgeable than the doctors who prescribe to them.

Income

Advertisers have studied socioeconomic classes intensively so that they can define their characteristics. You may have heard of the letter classifications that designate income, with "A" being those people with the highest disposable income. Income is usually associated with professional occupations.

Wealth might correlate with a political bias toward conservative views. You want to advertise expensive cars, perfume, and cognac to the group of people who have the disposable income to afford the product.

In the final analysis, most audiences are defined by complex variables. Whatever you can do to narrow down the classification of your audience's cultural preferences, disposable income, or cultural attitudes will help. Advertising and public relations practitioners maintain large departments devoted to audience research and demographics.

PSYCHOGRAPHICS

A concern with **psychographics** means worrying about what is going through the mind of your **target audience**. So just as you can classify the social and cultural characteristics of a person, you can also identify attitudes and mental outlook or state of mind. A person's attitude might overwhelm the demographics for certain messages. Most people are driven by emotions to a greater or lesser degree. How they feel governs how they act and how they respond. Visual media such as film, video, and television communicate emotionally. For one reason, they show the human face and figure with all the body language and nonverbal communication that people intuitively understand. They tell stories that invite emotional responses. They use visual images that signify emotions or engender strong emotional responses. An image of an explosion or a plane crash provokes awe, fear, and fascination. Think of an archive shot of a hydrogen bomb going off with its signature mushroom cloud, or the dark vortex of a tornado touching down. These images compel attention.

Think about the ways that audiences can be "turned off." The very phrase is a metaphor. A knob or a button on a radio or television set or remote control gives the user the power to interrupt the transmission or switch to another channel. Even if you were strapped to a chair and left in front of a television with your eyelids taped open, your attention could wander or even switch off entirely. We all have a "turn off" function in the brain, and we have filters that screen out what we don't want to hear.

Corporate television and video often play to captive audiences. Unless the program designers give thought to the **psychographics**, they will lose the audience because of the "turn-off" switch in their brains. A client once argued to me that his internal corporate audience of middle managers was paid to watch the program we were making, and he therefore rejected my imaginative ideas to motivate them. This person did not understand **psychographics**. Audience response involves passive assent at a minimum. A stronger posture would be neutral consent. Even more positive would be getting the audience to actively seek and participate in the experience of the program in a way that involves a level of enjoyment.

Students sometimes tell me that a certain subject is boring to write about. My reply is always that there are no boring subjects, only boring writers. As a scriptwriter, I believe, and you must believe, that there is always a way to reach an audience. This is especially true for corporate communications.

Safety is a huge problem that costs corporate America millions of dollars. Companies are strongly motivated to reduce insurance premiums and lost workdays by communicating safe work practices. This subject probably sounds boring to you, but if you are good, you can find a way to make the topic watchable. The point is not whether you would choose to view a safety video on how to use ladders at home on a Saturday night and invite your friends. Nevertheless, in the right context, at the right moment, many outwardly uninteresting subjects become relevant to what you need to know in your job or in your life.

Video Arts is a company that has made millions out of videos on management training often written around a comic character played by John Cleese, the Monty Python actor. The videos are often funny and clever. The audience swallows the message with the comedy and remembers it. Delivered as a straight message, the audience might reject that which it willingly accepts when presented with humor. This is applied **psychographics**.

Emotions are complex, volatile, and difficult to categorize. For these reasons, **psychographics** is an art rather than a science. You don't have to be a psychologist or psychic to make use of **psychographics** in your writing. Once again, a great deal is commonsense deduction. You can analyze your audience's **psychographics** by putting yourself in its shoes. You can investigate your own feelings and attitudes to extrapolate what is likely to be shared by another. You have to be self-aware and self-analytical. Your own strong preferences might not represent the masses. Your taste in music, whether it's Mozart or Motley Crüe, Handel or heavy metal, seems right to your ear, but it may turn off a large segment of your audience.

This, incidentally, makes it difficult to choose music for a sound track. Surprising successes can result from daring choices. For example, *2001: A Space Odyssey*, Stanley Kubrik's classic film, made a huge audience listen to and appreciate a modern classical composer, Ricard Strauss. This mass audience probably didn't know the name of the composer or the name of the composition, *Thus Spake Zarathustra*, or that it was played by the Berlin Philharmonic conducted by Herbert Von Karajan, but they responded to the music. Now most people instantly recognize the theme. The theme was imitated and copied and jazzed up and played on different instruments. Millions hummed it. Another example was the huge jump in sales of a Mozart piano concerto (No. 21, C major, K. 467), whose slow movement was used in the sound track of a Swedish film, *Elvira Madigan* (1967). People who would normally never listen to or buy a recording of Mozart were sending this record off the charts because the director made them experience the lyrical and romantic feeling of the music. All this is to remind you that you have to use intuition. Sometimes you have to go beyond the obvious, the conventional, and the predictable to tap into the receptivity of an audience.

What are the main psychological issues that make up a person's mind? They are things you know about already.

Emotion

We all have moods and sensations that are colored by emotions that range from down or depressed, sad and anxious, to happy, elated, playful, or wild. Individuals have emotions; groups have emotions; and crowds react with emotions. Most rock concerts are exercises in crowd mood creation. Emotions are tricky and volatile, especially when crowds are involved. An audience is sometimes a crowd and sometimes a large number of individuals in a serial response to a program. Think of a book that has sold a million copies. The audience is large, but each one of that million encountered the book individually. They do not all gather in a stadium for a mass reading, whereas the audience for a movie made from the book is a different entity. Groups of hundreds of people sit together and experience the same moments together, perhaps laugh together or cry together. Even a television audience is a simultaneous mass audience of single viewers or small groups of viewers.

As a scriptwriter, you have to deal with emotions, with the anticipated emotional response of your audience. It is almost always important to communicate emotionally to an audience in the visual media as well as by reason and logic. The mixture varies with the nature of the communication. Dramatic narrative tends to work through emotional communication, whereas documentary or training videos lean on logical argument. Getting battered women to use a shelter probably requires reaching the audience through emotion rather than reason. The selling of Shell's natural gas conversion process, in contrast, should be based primarily on logic and rational exposition.

Attitude

An audience frequently has an attitude, not in the slang sense of the word, which corrupts the original meaning, but in the sense that their disposition can be characterized by it. Think of these different audiences.

After the Rodney King beating by four Los Angeles police officers, you have to write a police PR video about police and community relations in the inner city. Simply put, your audience is going to be hostile. You cannot make a move without dealing with the open distrust and skepticism that will block their hearing what you want to convey.

We mentioned previously the problem of a merger and the internal PR problem of explaining the benefits of the merger to the employees. People are fearful of losing their jobs, their seniority, or their pensions. You cannot proceed without taking into account the attitude of this audience.

The opposite condition can arise. Audiences can be receptive as well as hostile. You are writing a recruiting video for an elite volunteer military unit such as the Marine Corps or the Green Berets. You are probably preaching to the converted. If they are watching, it's because they are already thinking about joining up. You don't have to break down mistrust, skepticism, or hostility. You do not design the message to turn pacifists into warriors.

Yet other audiences are neutral or indifferent. They do not bring strong negative or strong positive predisposition to the table. You have to wake them up or arouse interest or curiosity by your images and your creative ideas. It seems constructive for a scriptwriter to think carefully about whether his audience falls into one or other of these categories—receptive, hostile, or indifferent.

The importance of **psychographics** cannot be emphasized enough. The attitude and outlook and mental receptivity of your audience are critical. I have read too often the dismissive statement that this PSA or this program includes all ages, all genders. The broader the message, the less effective it will be. Let me introduce **Friedmann's first law of media communication**. It states that the effectiveness of a message varies in inverse proportion to the size and breadth of its audience. That means that as an audience increases in size, the chances of including all of them in your communication falls off or decreases proportionately. It is easy to grasp the **psychographic** and **demographic** of an audience of one. If the audience doubles, the effectiveness is going to be half. If multiplied a hundred times, it is going to be 1/100 as effective. The relationship is not mathematically precise because as the size of the number increases the changes are barely noticeable.

Friedmann's second law of media communication is that the simplicity of the message must be in inverse proportion to the size of the audience: the larger the audience, the greater the need to simplify the content to reach the lowest common denominator of any given audience. An extreme example is a Stop sign. Exit is another. The only audiences excluded from this message are children who cannot read. Even they might get the meaning from the color red. That's why a message for an audience of one is the most effective. It is addressed to you and you alone. Every increase in the size of the audience reduces to some degree the effectiveness of the message. We all practice this principle every day. If we are talking to one person, we think and speak differently to when we have to talk to a group. Teaching an individual is easier than teaching 20, 40, or 100. The congruence of an audience of one with its message must generally break down. That is why all junk mail tries to personalize a letter by using your name in the text. It creates the illusion of an audience of one. Clearly, the way to overcome the decay in effectiveness of the message or communication to a mass audience is to find the common denominator so that you reduce the fraction to get as near to one as possible. Attention to the **demographics** and **psychographics** moves you in that direction. Clearly some messages can be more effective when matched to an audience **demographic** and **psychographic** than when watered down for all. Take drinking and driving. A teenage or college audience has a completely different **psychographic** than a general audience. The first audience basically considers itself bullet proof, immune to death, disease, and misfortune.

The best way to test yourself is to ask whether you can describe that audience profile. Can you say who is not part of that audience? Can you carry your defined audience through the program? Can you connect it to the communication problem? You are now answering the question "to whom?" So now you've got a shorthand guide—what for, and to whom? Next we need to answer the question "why?" Answering "why?" means you can define the objective for the video or program.

STEP 3: DEFINE THE OBJECTIVE

The **communication objective** is closely associated with the communication problem. One states the problem, the other states the outcome. So if teenagers do not appreciate or understand the health hazards of smoking, which is the problem, the objective is to change their perception of smoking. The shorthand questions to answer are "why?" and "what for?" In military terms, an objective would be to capture a position or to win the battle. The larger objective is always to win the war. The objective is usually easy to see. The hard part is knowing how to obtain it. The same is true of scriptwriting. In business terms, an objective would be to achieve a 10 percent increase in sales or a 5 percent decrease in costs. These objectives are clear. The hard part is how to achieve them. Likewise with scriptwriting!

A TV program, film, or video must have an objective that is clear. It is the net result that you are working to achieve at the end of the viewing—the message. It is what the audience is left with as a general effect. A lot of programs are meant to entertain. That is too general. Entertainment can mean many things. Comedy is designed to make the audience laugh; drama, to make the audience worry; romance, to make the audience fantasize; horror, to make the audience fearful, and so on.

Many programs do not have an entertainment objective. The primary objective could be to impart information. That is not to say they are not watchable or entertaining. Lots of programs try to give you facts and figures about a product, about a country, about a health issue, about the history of the country, about the environment, or about the life of an animal species. You assimilate information from the program that you did not possess before watching the program. You may have had other experiences during the program, but taken as a whole, your main acquisition is that you know something or understand something you didn't know or understand before. The objective was to convey information. What is the primary objective of your script concept? An **informational objective** appeals to the mind and to the reasoning side of the brain.

Another common way to design a visual communication is to think about shifting the audience's attitude or point of view. Information might also be part of the package, but the primary net result you desire is to get the audience to see things differently. For example, you can communicate a mountain of facts about the dangers of smoking—how many people die of smoking-related diseases, a list of the negative consequences of smoking. A thinking person might draw conclusions. Almost anyone can draw the conclusion that smoking involves a serious risk to health. Nevertheless, many such people will dismiss the communication and not change their thinking, let alone their behavior.

So facts and information alone won't work. We have to get the audience to acknowledge the facts and infer consequences for the individual's health. A nicotine addict has already been bombarded with facts. So try another approach! Turn facts and figures into graphic images that will disturb the audience. Make use of drama and imagination to get the audience watching! Let the audience draw its own conclusion.

How would you respond? Not with your head! Images bring your emotions into play. You are forced to see something commonplace in a smoker's daily life in a different context. If you are a smoker, you might be disturbed. You might start seeing your habit differently. Your attitude could shift. If the shift is strong enough, it could be described as motivating. Remember! The word "motivate" comes from the Latin root meaning "to move," and so does the word "emotion." If emotions are affected in a coherent and sequenced fashion, the result is motivation—a **motivational objective**. Most advertising depends on visual stimulation of the emotions to shift attitudes. This is sometimes known as the soft sell. The challenge is to create a sequence of images that compel the viewers to lead themselves to a position from which they cannot go back.

Apply this to more complex problems. You have to make a 15-minute video that communicates safe handling of materials in an industry or explains how to drive defensively. Or you have to make a 10-minute video that persuades the audience to recycle. In this communication problem, your objective is slightly different. The difference is that you not only want to motivate the audience, you also want to activate them. You want them to do something—to put their bottles and cans and plastics into receptacles for collection. This is the most demanding objective because you want to change their behavior. A lot of marketing videos (not TV commercials, as you will see in a later chapter) try to do just that. We have now defined an action objective, commonly called a **behavioral objective**.

Let's revisit our examples. The objective is to make high school teenagers think twice about getting addicted to nicotine. The objective is to make battered women seek counseling before they end up in a hospital with broken bones. The objective is to get European travel professionals to think about their tourist product for American tourists and whether it corresponds to what those customers are looking for. The objective is to get a high school graduate or senior to call admissions and ask for an application. And when you revisit the objective of a personal communication (the "I love you" message), the objective is to get your estranged girlfriend to let bygones be bygones and come back to you.

In every case, you can make a definite and specific statement about the successful outcome of the communication. Until you can do that, you will never write a successful script to solve the communication problem because you haven't thought about what you are trying to achieve.

One way of defining an objective is a change of knowledge, perception, or awareness. Once you have learned that Santa Claus doesn't exist, you cannot go back to a state of consciousness in which you believed in Santa Claus. Your childhood is in some sense over. Similarly, once you know something about smoking or using drugs, you cannot restore your mind to a previous state when you did not have that knowledge or awareness like we can restore a computer to a state before a virus infection or before some undesirable alteration of its operating system. If you can achieve that change of consciousness in an audience, you have succeeded in putting in place the foundation for all subsequent thinking and eventually action. So the motivational awareness induced by an antismoking PSA is the prerequisite for the action of a change of behavior—quitting. So your **behavioral objective** is engendered by the motivational even though it is not directly targeted.

We now have three clear steps down on paper. One defines the problem, another defines the audience, and the third defines the desired result or objective we are working toward. Answering these three questions does not finish the job because we haven't answered the question "how?" How are we going to solve the communications problem, reach the audience, and achieve the objective?

STEP 4: DEFINE THE STRATEGY

The shorthand question to answer is, "how?" To write a successful script that solves the communication problem, we need to figure out how to achieve the objective, reach the target audience, and suggest the content that leads to effective communication. This is a moment of creative challenge. If you want an audience to think, feel, or act in a certain way, you have to have a **communication strategy**. A military commander plans to pound the enemy position with artillery, then divide his forces into two groups who will attack from different directions. A marketing executive has a plan to increase sales by offering an incentive such as a 2-for-1 sale or a free baseball glove with every full tank of gas. This is the "how." How are you going to achieve your objective?

Attention Span

How long does it take you to change the TV channel if something doesn't catch your interest? You've been pampered all your life by a multitude of choices. You are merciless. If you don't like something, you change it. You switch to another channel, or you switch off the TV. Now you are on the other side of the game. You have to hold your audience by the pacing, content, and imagination of your script. They have the remote control. Andy Warhol, the controversial American artist, made an 8-hour film of one of his favorite stars sleeping. Needless to say, it did not have a large box office. It was a rebellious stunt by an outrageous artist.

Think about how network news programs try to keep you interested with little previews and announcements about what's up next. They use good-looking anchors who smile at you through the lens and seduce you into staying with them. How many times do you hear the line "Don't go away?" You can't give frequent-flyer miles to your audience for watching. So how can scriptwriters get the job done? They think up strategic ways to hold the attention of the audience while they deliver the message. For example, they use humor, a story, suspense, shock, intrigue, unique footage, a testimonial, or a case history. Everyone will listen to a joke. If the joke has a clever point, your audience will get the message while they laugh or chuckle.

Many ads use humor. A recent ad shows a dog and a man sitting in front of one another. The dog is training the man to balance a piece of cheese on his nose and on command flip it in the air and eat it. Reversing the roles of dog and man and having the dog talk captures people's attention with a smile. You will remember that brand of dog food.

Communication strategy involves getting attention by humor or shock or audience involvement so that you can deliver a packet of information or an idea. We can draw on an understanding that was articulated by Aristotle in his *Rhetoric* over 2,400 years ago. You can sum up strategy by noting that it almost always relies on **pathos**, an appeal to emotion, or on **logos**, an appeal to reason and argument, or on **ethos**, an appeal to ethical principles.

STEP 5: DEFINE THE CONTENT

The shorthand version of defining the content is to ask the question, "what?" What are we going to see and hear on the screen? What is the program going to be about? What happens in the story or narrative of the program? Clearly, the content cannot be defined first. You may well argue that you can define the **communications problem**, the **target audience**, and the **objective** in almost any order. However, they must all be defined before you can designate content. In fact, you really need to have some kind of strategy or creative device to make it all work before you fill in content.

Content is what you see. Content is what your program is about. It is the objective matter or substance of the piece. When a program is shot, the camera has to be placed in front of something to capture its image. The script has to describe what is going to be in front of the camera. How it serves the **communication objective** may not be apparent from shot to shot.

We can illustrate this by revisiting the several script ideas we have discussed throughout this chapter. In the college recruitment video, the content could be described by a list of the things we are going to shoot: classrooms and teachers, dorm life with students, sports and extracurricular activities. From this list, you can quickly see that content does not often define what is unique about a program. This list could cover hundreds of recruitment videos, if not all of them. What makes one different from another is the **strategy** and the **creative concept**. In the natural gas video, we have to show the process. In this case, we could shoot a pilot plant and show the process working. In the American Express video, the content is testimonials and shots of the type of tourist setting that market research shows appeals to American tourists.

STEP 6: DEFINE THE APPROPRIATE MEDIUM

The shorthand question to answer is, **"which medium**?" All media have particular qualities and peculiarities that give them strengths and weaknesses. What works for film on a large screen projected in a darkened room might not work on a 21-inch TV screen. The intimacy of the television image would not work on a 40-foot movie screen. Dense information that should be presented in the form of graphs works in a slide show but not on video. In short, the concept we devise has to work for the medium, or we have to pick the medium that will work for the concept. We have to write so as to exploit the special advantages and qualities of the medium.

Interviews work well on television and video. Action and long shots work better in film. Corporate clients frequently ask for communication objectives to be put into a video that clash with the medium. For instance, a detailed instruction about how to install a piece of equipment is better done in print. An audience is not able to take in written instructions on a TV screen. They won't remember them. In print, you can look at the page as long as you need to and refer back to it. If the communication has a long shelf life, an interactive CD-ROM would work better than linear video programming and possibly better than print. A small TV screen won't work at an exhibition or a trade show. You need something that commands attention visually. A video wall of 9 or 12 programmable TV screens does the job.

What makes a PSA for television different from a PSA for radio, for instance? A student wrote a PSA on domestic abuse that, although conceived for video, works successfully as a pure audio script. It is only secondarily a visual script. The creative idea is a sequence of spoken statements that compels an audience to think. The message is carried in the spoken voice-over more than in the images. Although it also works with visuals, the test is to take the images away and see if it works. A visual concept and visual writing relies on a sequence of visual images: Although the images have been visualized, you can hear this script. It relies heavily on the spoken commentary. You can easily imagine this as a successful radio commercial. Visual ideas work best in a visual medium-.

INT. BEDROOM - DAY	
CAMERA PANS ACROSS A SMALL BEDROOM, PAUSING BRIEFLY TO SHOW THE BROKEN GLASS AND SHATTERED TABLE STREWN ACROSS THE HARDWOOD FLOOR. BROKEN PICTURE FRAME HOLDING A PHOTO OF A MAN AND WOMAN KISSING.	MALE V.O.
CUT TO WINDOW WITH RAIN FALLING AGAINST THE GLASS.	A woman is beaten every fifteen seconds

PAN DOWN TO WOMAN SITTING ON THE FLOOR HOLDING HER KNEES TO HER CHEST, SHAKING.	FEMALE V.O.
SUPER TEXT: HOTLINE 800 NUMBER.	Which means ... every minute, four women are beaten ... every hour 240 women are beaten ... and every day 960 women are beaten ... every week, 6,720 women are beaten. MALE V.O. What did you do last week?

You need to ask yourself whether your idea is visual? But print, billboards, and posters can be visual. The question to answer is why this idea will succeed and come alive uniquely in the video/television medium as opposed to putting it on a billboard, in a print ad, or creating a website. So if it is going to be for television, ask what are the values that make that medium work. First, there's color. Do you use color? Then there's motion. Do you exploit the moving picture medium, or are you running a slide show on television? Do you use emotion? Do you have stunning graphics or animation or special effects? The fewer of these element present in your concept, the less likely it is to be an effective television commercial or PSA! At this point you could ask whether you should be working in another medium. Some campaigns use several media and vary the concept to suit the medium. Although the Milk Marketing Board *Got Milk?* campaign has been seen on television, it probably works best as a billboard because you can convey the essence of its visual idea in a still—the milk moustache on a celebrity—that can be read in a matter of seconds as you drive by. The visual idea is so strong that you could take away the text even though they reinforce one another.

STEP 7: CREATE THE CONCEPT

This is the seventh step. You are thinking: "That's enough. Let's get started. I've done my homework." Not yet! Before you take the seventh and final step, you should answer these questions in writing so that they are crystal clear. You may get impatient with this method and resist going through this analytic prewriting process. Rest assured that any problem that shows up in your script concept will be traceable to these issues. The most important realization that you can have at this point is that addressing these six issues will enable you to generate creative ideas. Now the hidden process of writing comes out into the light. This arc of ideas that lie behind the creative concept, we are going to call **meta-writing**. This writing is the creative thinking that will be embodied in the final production document.

Before we go to the final step, let's review the sequence of analytic thinking. The order of analysis is ideally as follows:

1. Define the communications problem (What need?)
2. Define the target audience (Who?)
3. Define the objective (Why?)
4. Define the strategy (How?)
5. Define the content (What?)
6. Define the medium (Which medium?)

The seventh step is the seed of your script. Let's call it the **creative concept** or, if you want, just the concept. This is the first visible step of the scriptwriting process. In a professional assignment, you may not write out all of the thinking you did to answer the six questions although it is common practice to write out some response to a client's communication problem. I like to set down my thinking for all scriptwriting assignments that are not entertainment so that my client will buy into the thinking that lies behind my creative idea. So now you are going to explain in writing to your client, producer, or director what the key idea is, what the approach is, and how you will use the specific medium to make the communication work. This creative idea or **creative concept** will solve the **communication problem**, reach the **target audience**, achieve the **communication objective**, embody the **communication strategy**, provide the **content** of the program, and show how it will work in the chosen medium.

To some extent, almost anyone can go through the six steps and get to reasonable definitions of each. In the advertising world, this is commonly referred to as a **copy platform**. It is slightly different because it will involve a product and a summary of its benefit or selling points. The rationale is the same—think through the communication before writing copy. And so finally we come to the creative embodiment of all this preparatory work. The seventh step—devising a **creative concept** or device that will translate all those needs into a working script—is different. It is a creative task, not an analytic task. It is the work of a scriptwriter's imagination. This is the source of freshness, originality, clarity, and visual intelligence that makes a program compelling to watch or a pleasure to watch. It is hard to explain and perhaps harder still to teach. This is the imaginative talent that you get paid for.

From this concept your script will grow or die. Until you have a convincing concept or proposal that addresses all of the issues expounded in this chapter, you shouldn't continue. No professional would. You might pull it off for one assignment because the topic is congenial to you. Don't let yourself do this. You will be digging the grave of your scriptwriting career. Succeeding in this business is about consistent results, producing again and again whether you are inspired or not. It is about becoming a pro. Confidence comes with practice and experience.

We have kept up a running discussion of several communication problems. Now we can float some creative concepts for them. Just in case you are unsure of what creative concept means, let's clarify.

SEVEN-STEP QUESTIONNAIRE

Many people do not honestly and effectively answer the **seven questions**. They mix up issues belonging to each area and end up with a less than clear reasoning for a strong **creative concept**. So here are some of the questions you can ask to double-check whether you are genuinely answering the primary questions of the **seven steps**:

Step 1: What Need?

1. Have you stated a problem for the potential **target audience** in terms of something they do not understand, don't know, don't want to know, or could not know until you tell them with your video or other communication?
2. Have you made the common mistake of substituting for a communication problem a social problem or a public policy problem?

Step 2: Who?

1. Have you stated all the **demographic** characteristics of your audience? Have you evaded the question by making a lazy, general statement?
2. Have you addressed the all-important issue off **psychographics**?
3. Have you asked yourself what the mental and emotional state of your audience is?

Step 3: Why?

1. Have you stated an **communication objective** that is informational, motivational, and behavioral or some combination of those?
2. Can you see that the objective is the reverse side of the coin of the **communication problem**?
3. Could you have put the objective down as the problem and ended up repeating the objective in the third step?

Step 4: How?

1. Does your idea achieve the objective?
2. Does your idea get the attention of the target audience defined in step 2?
3. Does your idea get past the defenses of the target audience defined in step 2?
4. Is your idea visual, a visual metaphor, and one that completes itself in the audience's imagination?

Step 5: What?

1. Is the content about the objective?
2. Is the content, action, or activity something that uses the visual medium?
3. Does this description of the content preempt and take away from the creative concept?

Step 6: Which Medium?

1. Is the idea dependent on visual qualities that are unique to the moving picture medium?
2. Have you relied on talking heads or voice commentary to a degree that misuses the medium?
3. What is visually unique about this idea that means that this cannot be produced in print, on radio, or for a billboard, poster, or any other medium?

Step 7: What Is the Creative Concept?

1. Does your **creative concept** test out against all the questions for the six prior steps?
2. Are you writing down the driving creative idea?
3. Are you summarizing the content and in effect writing a treatment before time?
4. Are you pestering the client/producer with camera directions that don't belong?

Everything we've discussed so far—the "need," the "who," the "why," the "how," and the "what content" issues—still doesn't give us images or actions to describe from scene to scene or a way of approaching the topic. The trick is to come up with some creative ideas that will encapsulate all of the definitions for a particular medium. One of these ideas will translate into a living, breathing visual idea that will make a script.

Some ideas sound great but don't work out in practice; so you have to test them. If you are writing a college recruitment video, how are you going to avoid the predictable shots of campus buildings with voice-over superlatives extolling the praises of the place? You're creative. You wake up one morning with a brainstorm. You'll do the college recruitment as a Broadway musical. You can see it now— a chorus of coeds singing and dancing instead of a boring voice-over. It's entertainment. The audience will keep watching. It's creative, but somehow it's not right. The idiom doesn't suit the target audience. Ignore the fact that it will quadruple the production costs. The problem is that the **creative concept** runs away with the **communication objective**. It doesn't serve it. You lie in bed wondering how you're going to crack this one. Suddenly, you jump up, hit the word processor, and type out your idea. Use your own experience to show the audience what a typical day is like, perhaps with a bit of embellishment to work in all the points you want to make. So this will be—a day in the life of an Ivy College student. That gives you a concept that provides the content, the structure, and the objective. It will give the target audience a character to identify with. Any leftover points could be carried by a commentary voice-over.

Most beginners make the mistake of thinking their first idea is the only idea and the one to work with. You should put down at least three different creative concepts for the job, test them out, and then pick the best. So we still have one to go. What would be another way to get at this objective? How about a student who comes on campus and, through a series of interviews, which we carefully craft to reveal the information we know to be necessary, finds out everything about Ivy College?

How do you choose between them? One way is by pitching them to a client, or the class, or your instructor. Another is by your feel for how well the concept will play out through the detail of the content. There are usually trade-offs. Interviews may be good, but scripting them makes them sound stilted and false. On the other hand, how do you know that you'll get what you want if you film unscripted interviews? There's a risk. If you define the six questions with integrity and try out creative concepts, you will isolate a creative concept that works.

The **communication problem** for American Express was to convey the fruits of its market research to its **target audience** so that audience would shift its erroneous perception of American tourists in Europe. The research defined categories of travelers such as Grey Panthers, Business Travelers, and Adventurers. They all had different ideas about what they wanted to find in Europe. It was apparent to the writer that the audience of European tourist professionals was complacent and needed to be persuaded by undeniable evidence to change their point of view. In this case, interviewing dozens of each category in unscripted video recordings at an airport yielded enough evidence to corroborate the published market research. It was expensive and risky, but it paid off. That's the nature of a creative business. It involves risk. That's part of what makes it exciting to be a scriptwriter—to have an idea and see it working in a finished program.

We also mentioned the oil company with the process to convert natural gas to lubrication oils. A hundred million dollars (more in today's money) had been spent over 10 years in research. A pilot plant had been built to prove it worked. Here the problem was to get scientific and technical information into a form that would be comprehensible and convincing to the small audience of decision makers. The **creative concept** that worked was governed by the fact that there was a lot of archive footage that had to be used. The solution was to tell a story—a news story. So the script was built around a current affairs format with an actor playing an investigative reporter talking to the camera and taking the audience through the story. It enabled the stock footage to be bracketed with an explanation. It made the patented process sound like a suspense story. It gave a structure and a variety to difficult material.

How about a **creative concept** for a Valentine's Day message? This is to get your imagination going. Don't send a card. It's predictable and conventional. You telephone your girlfriend. You say, "Look out the window up at the sky!" A Microlite is flying around trailing a banner that reads, "I love you, Mary Jane. Will you marry me?" Outside your budget? Go to the exercises and try out some of your ideas.

To finish, let us bring it all together and write a document that sets all these issues down. Sometimes, you need to do this for a client as a first step. Sometimes you need to do this for yourself to prepare for your concept. There is no fixed format or industry-wide convention for doing this. A simple solution is to use the headings we have used in this chapter.

A word of warning before we write it out! Write in the **present tense**! Never use the future tense in media writing! If you use the future or the conditional, you put off the prospect of the PSA, ad, or corporate video being real. By using these tenses, you introduce into the mind of your reader that (the future always being uncertain) this may not happen. You appear to the reader to have less conviction about what you are proposing than if you write as if it is happening now. You can see it, and you want your reader to see it as if it already exists. Another verbal give away in writing and verbal pitching in meetings is to use the word "*hopefully*." That instantly communicates to your immediate audience, client or producer, that you do not really believe in your idea and that you are not sure that it works. Until you can arrive at that state of conviction and convey it in your writing and presentation, you should not begin.

Another fatal error is to use the **first-person singular**. As soon as you write *my* PSA, or *my* idea, or *my* video, you instantly create a tension. First of all, it is not yours. You are being paid to create something for someone else. You are putting your creative talent at the service of your client. It is theirs. They are paying for it. By attaching your person to the communication, you create a psychological problem. If someone wants to criticize your work, your ideas, or your thinking, it becomes personal. That critic has to confront you or attack and criticize you by implication because you have identified yourself with the product. Consider now what happens if you employ the **first-person plural**. As soon as you write or say "we," you include your client. You put both of you on the same side, on the same team. Thus, any criticism, modification, or difference of opinion becomes the group thinking through a problem to find a collective and collaborative solution.

A CONCEPT FOR AN ANTISMOKING PSA

All antismoking PSAs face the problem of having to convince addicts to quit. We need to get past their defenses and their denial. All the facts about health hazards are already out there. We have to make them real and emotionally affecting. In Massachusetts, there were a number of effective antismoking campaigns. One had a billboard the exact size of a room with the dimensions shown and a punch line: "Second-hand smoke spreads like cancer." The image and the punch line conspire to make you think. The smoke that fills a room when anyone smokes in it obliges everyone else to smoke. So the spreading smoke is also spreading cancer. Another referred to the number of toxic substances in a cigarette with a tag line saying that it would be illegal to dispose of them in a garbage dump. Another has a simple statistic: "Last year smoking killed 470,000 people." A recent television campaign against smoking breaks down this number into how many people die each day. The creative visual shows crews piling that number of body bags in a city street. By making the audience see the number as a heap of body bags in a street, the creators turn a dull statistic into a graphic image and make the audience think. You get the idea.

7-STEP ANALYSIS FOR AN ANTI-SMOKING PSA

The Communication Problem

Young adults and teenagers do not know or understand how vicious the addiction of nicotine is and do not realize how serious the health hazards are. They may have some information, but it is probably not organized and arranged into a conclusion. Even though packaging carries warning signs, they do not heed the warning or take it seriously.

The Target Audience

Our target audience is primarily young adults and teenagers with a secondary audience of older smokers.

Demographics: Our focus is an age group between 14 and 21, sometimes not well educated, and often from lower socio-economic groups. We may have to consider targeting the younger or older end of this audience as the primary target.

Psychographics: The young think they are immune to the health hazards and to the difficulties of addiction. They dismiss the legal warnings. They might think that smoking is cool or a way to demonstrate maturity. The audience will not accept a lecture and is not really impressed by statistics. They are responsive to images of their own lives. We have to show them in a scene that matches a plausible lifestyle for them.

The Objective

The objective is in part informational, to convey further information about the hazards of smoking. It is also strongly motivational, to shift the attitude of the target audience and make them start thinking and start worrying. It is to haunt them with troubling images that won't go away. It is only through the motivational shift that the possibility of an indirect behavioral outcome can occur.

The Strategy

The strategy is to create a little sexy vignette with romance and style that does not reveal itself as an antismoking PSA until it is too late for the audience to disengage. They respond to it piecemeal until they are stuck with the conclusion. The logic must be visual, not verbal. We use powerful special effects derived from contemporary fantasy horror films (such as morphing) to reveal a sequence of aging, sickness, and death from smoking-related disease. The reality is like a bad trip or a hallucination.

The Content

An attractive young man and young woman are in the kitchen after a date sharing a beer and a cigarette.

The Medium

Our message is primarily visual. The message needs close-ups and depends on special effects that are easy to do with video. It could not be conveyed by audio only for radio, nor for a static medium such as a billboard. The medium necessary to convey this message is television. This idea exploits the visual potential of video and television.

The Concept

We are going to involve the audience in a familiar scenario of a date but with a difference. The character is going to hallucinate and see the inside of a kitchen refrigerator turn into a morgue draw showing a corpse. He acquires x-ray vision and is able to see the damaged lungs of his date and the transformation of skin damage happen before his eyes. The abstract medical consequences of smoking are made graphic and physical to our audience.

From the concept you can pitch the solution to the communication problem to the client. Once it is agreed, you can elaborate the concept as a *treatment* that narrates in chronological order what happens on screen.

CONCLUSION

At this point, you understand the essential scriptwriting problems. You have seen how important it is to think before you write. Thinking through the **communication problem** with this **seven-step method** will enable you to generate **content**. You can ask and answer **seven questions** to analyze the problem. However, they must be answered honestly and rigorously. This capacity to break down a communication problem and come up with creative solutions is part of the job of scriptwriter, especially in the world of corporate communications that includes advertising, public relations, sales, training, and corporate image videos. If you can become proficient at doing this, you will bring an invaluable skill to any media enterprise.

Exercises

1. You are going to send a Valentine's Day message. You will not use the words "I love you." Using the **seven-step method**, come up with five creative concepts for five different audiences. Let the changing **target audience** modify your **communication objective** and your **strategy**. The message does not have to be sent as a video. The question of **which medium** to use is important. For example, a dozen red roses with a card could be your **creative concept**. Unchain your imagination.
2. Your job is to devise a **creative concept** for an antismoking PSA using the **seven-step method**. Come up with five **creative concepts** for these different **target audiences**: pregnant women, preteens, college students, and adult addicts.
3. Your assignment is to devise a **creative concept** for a safety video about (a) carbon monoxide hazards in the home, (b) how to use a ladder, or (c) pedestrian rules for children under age 7.
4. Your assignment is to devise a **creative concept** to launch a new product to a company sales force: a new car, a new can opener, or a holiday package. Could this be a website?
5. Your assignment is to write a **creative concept** for a video to get people to recycle. How do you define the **target audience**?

CHAPTER 3

The Stages of Script Development

KEY TERMS

background research and investigation	follow-up questions	revision
beat sheet	format	scene outline
brainstorming	funnel technique	script
camera plot	hypothetical questions	scripting software
closed questions	index cards	self-assessment questions
concept	inverted funnel	shooting script
content	leading questions	subject matter experts (SMEs)
creative concept	location research	
decorum	log line	treatment
dialogue	open questions	tunnel
double-barreled questions	outline	visual metaphor
final draft	picture researchers	voice narration
first draft script	pitching	voice-over commentary
	process	

Scriptwriting is a **process**. It begins with gathering information, thinking, analyzing, and questioning, and it ends with devising a **creative concept**. This visual idea then needs to be developed through some kind of outline or **treatment** and then be scripted in a **format** appropriate to the medium concerned. This **script** format lays out a set of descriptive instructions in a special language about what is to be seen on the screen and heard on the sound track. We can break the scriptwriting process down into well-recognized stages. In fact, they are so well recognized that the stages have names that are also reflected in the contractual agreements that usually govern professional writing of this kind. Let us outline this process by stages. Some of these stages may change places in the sequence depending on the nature of the writing job:

- Background research and investigation
- Developing a creative concept

Doi:10.1016/B978-0-240-81235-9.00003-1

- Pitching or verbal presentation
- Concept outline
- Treatment
- First draft
- Revision
- Final draft

BACKGROUND RESEARCH AND INVESTIGATION

Part of the process of scriptwriting often involves **background research and investigation** of the subject matter before you define the objective or outline the content. Experience tells you when you need to get information. Sometimes it is at the beginning of the creative thinking process. Sometimes it is in the middle. Research could be necessary to define the target audience. Consider a public service announcement (PSA) on smoking. Although you have general ideas about the effects of smoking on health, you do not have facts and figures. Research enables you to say with conviction how many Americans die annually from smoking-related diseases. If you are devising a PSA about battered women, you need statistical facts and possibly psychological background before you can think about what is relevant, let alone make an assertion about the topic. Before you can say it, you need to know it. So research is gathering information that enables you to be authoritative and specific about the subject.

Even entertainment concepts require research. An imaginary story is often set in a time period or has a background. To make a story more believable, you need authentic detail embedded in the scenes. If your story concerns airline pilots, you need to know how they talk and what their world is like. To write a scene that involves cockpit talk, dialogue has to be credible and realistic. To write an episode of *ER* or any other hospital drama, you have to describe medical procedures and use meaningful dialogue between characters who are doctors. If you want to appreciate the research that might precede writing a screenplay, read about William Goldman's research before writing his original screenplay *Butch Cassidy and the Sundance Kid*.[1]

Research can be undertaken in any of several well-proven ways. You can consult encyclopedias, visit a library, or search the Internet. You have probably used a library catalog for a research paper. Research for scriptwriting is not much different. Everyone finds a particular style or method that works for him or her. Index cards are effective because they enable you to shuffle and reorder the material, and they help you to find the right sequence for ideas. Some **scripting software**, such as Movie Magic Screenwriter (see the website link), has an electronic index card system that allows you to do it all on computer.

If you are working on a documentary project, background information about your topic is necessary to construct a meaningful narrative and to write a voice-over commentary. Researching a project for visual media is different from term paper research because you not only need a factual background, you also need images—old photos, engravings, artifacts, and locations. Every scene in the **script** must be represented by an image. Suppose your **script** is historical. A good example would be the Civil War documentary by Ken Burns.[2] You cannot interview Civil War veterans, but you can interview historians who

---

[1] William Goldman, *Adventures in the Screen Trade* (New York: Warner Books, 1984).
[2] See http://us.imdb.com/Title?0098769.

are knowledgeable about the Civil War. You can film locations of some Civil War battlefields. Location research is critical to this kind of project. You can shoot existing images such as photos, engravings, and paintings. All of these images have to be found. A number of **picture libraries** sell the use of pictures from their collections, including the Library of Congress, which has a huge collection of Civil War photos that are in the public domain. Finding the right picture is a specialized task. There are people called **picture researchers** who make a living doing this particular kind of research.

Beginners will often propose short projects and pick documentaries about big topics such as AIDS or drug addiction. Most people find that their knowledge is very general and that the archive of available images is limited. Choosing such a project means doing research. A student of mine wanted to make a video about stress and how to combat it in college life. To do so, you need definitions of stress, statistics, and reliable information. One of the issues was healthy diet and exercise. You need to make statements about diet in the voice-over commentary that are true and authoritative. All of these requirements lead to research. Obviously, research takes time and sometimes money (if you have to travel to research a location or visit a library).

Before you can order a copy of an image or the text of particular statistics, you have to find them. The emergence of the World Wide Web has made research easier both for getting information and finding images. Clearly, picture libraries and photo agencies will become prime users of the web because they can show their product online, sell it online, and even deliver it online in one of the picture file formats such as GIF or JPEG. The cost of digitizing a photo library is high, but it is the way of the future because commercial users of pictures are now able to buy pictures as digitized files ready to download onto their computers and manipulate in a program like Adobe Photoshop. It also simplifies the task of searching a collection for the image you want.[3] This will be particularly relevant to production of websites, CD-ROMs, and DVD programs for which most writers should be preparing themselves. Technology changes the way we have to think about media.

Another example of research is collecting background information about a product or a process for a corporate program. To write about the client's product, you may need to read manuals and brochures and interview people in the company who are knowledgeable about the product. These people are sometimes known as **subject matter experts (SMEs)**. This is particularly true if the content is technical. You have to learn enough about the subject to be able to make decisions about what is relevant or interesting to the designated target audience. If you are writing about a medical product, pacemakers, for example, you have to pick the brains of a cardiologist. This means you have to know how to get to the right people and how to formulate the right questions. In a corporate context, your client usually guides you to many of the contacts you need. You need to arrive with a plan of investigation and a list of questions thought out beforehand.

At what stage do you do your research? Some kind of research and investigation is usually necessary to get going and to stimulate your thinking; so it logically precedes everything else. Research could also come later in response to your need to know about specific things in order to make accurate statements. At a later stage, you may need to do audience research. If your production has a commercial purpose, it is quite possible that questionnaires, surveys, or focus groups would be called for.

---

[3] Look up a photo archive such Getty Images at http://gettyimages.com.

Then when you have defined your objective, communication problem, and target audience, you might have to research background information in order to devise your content. You might see a specific need for expert knowledge at this point.

For the PSA on smoking, you know you want to make a dramatic statement about how many people die each year from smoking-related diseases in America. You might want to compare it to another figure such as how many people die in automobile accidents or how many Americans died in the war in Vietnam. Making a statement like that is effective because it puts the statistics in perspective for the audience. A statement that makes the audience realize that smoking kills more people every year than all those who died in Vietnam can have lasting impact. It makes the audience think. The populace would not accept American war casualties of that order every year without huge political consequences. Yet for some reason, the lingering deaths of hundreds of thousands of people from all sorts of smoking-related diseases are acceptable. Our attitudes shift based on our knowledge and awareness.

To get information about smoking-related deaths or drunk driving deaths, you might look at government statistics. These are published annually in reference works that are available in public libraries.[4] The Vietnam War statistic is a fixed historical fact that you would need to find. It would be extremely effective to say, "Four hundred twenty thousand Americans died last year from smoking-related diseases. That is more than eight times the number of American casualties in the whole Vietnam War.[5] Do you want to be one of them?" Being able to say, "Roughly 48 percent of all traffic deaths in the United States are caused by alcohol" is a stronger statement than some generality about the dangers of drunk driving. You need a fact to reinforce a good punch line, such as "If you drink and drive, death could be the chaser."

Investigation and research overlaps with journalism. The difference is that research for visual writing is not just about verifying facts; it is about finding pictures and getting visual information from which you can construct a **script**. Knowing facts or background information does not tell you how to construct a **script**, or persuade or entertain an audience. The same kind of information could be the basis for an article by a journalist or a book by an author.

Interviewing

People are another source of information. Some people are experts in their field. If they speak with authority, you might want to use them directly on camera as part of your program. Sometimes you need the point of view of the man in the street or you need to interview someone who represents a certain class of people. For documentaries and corporate programs, you need to find **subject matter experts**, people who have extraordinary knowledge based on a lifetime of research or direct personal experience. Because these interviews are often once-only opportunities, you need to prepare intelligent questions and have **follow-up questions**. There are a number of classic concepts for structuring an interview. There are a number of types of questions, each with a different purpose and usefulness in the interview process:

---

[4] Statistical Abstract of the United States, published annually by the U.S. Department of Commerce, Economics and Statistics Administration, Bureau of the Census. Figures for 1990 are documented in *Substance Abuse: The Nation's Number One Health Problem*, prepared by the Institute for Health Policy, Brandeis University for the Robert Wood Johnson Foundation, Princeton, NJ, October 1993. Alcohol-related deaths are also documented.

[5] A total of 47,072 U.S. servicemen were killed in combat in Vietnam. This and other facts about the conflict can be found on the PBS website, www.pbs.org/wgbh/pages/frontline/shows.

1. **Open questions** allow the interviewee to volunteer information, to express opinions, and to warm up: What is the most exciting aspect of your job? How did you get interested in the reproductive life of sub-Saharan scarab beetles? Or, what do you like to do in your spare time? Questions that ask who, what, when, where, why, or how typically lead to open questions.

2. **Closed questions** generally have a limited choice of answers. Do you like caviar? The answer can only be yes or no. Logically, it could also be, I don't know, if, for example, you haven't tasted it. In legal cross-examination and police interviewing, closed questions play an important part in pinning down the facts. Did you see the victim on the night of . . .? Closed questions can be hostile or threatening. In documentary investigation, the result might be refusal to answer or to go into detail on controversial matters.

3. **Double-barreled questions** ask two or more questions in combination: Why have you asked for political asylum, and what will you do if you get it, and if not, how will that change your view of this country? The subject will tend to answer the questions he wants to answer and ignore those that might be awkward or revealing. Being interviewed puts people under pressure. Sometimes they forget one of the questions. Experienced interviewers avoid overloading the subject with multiple questions.

4. **Leading questions** imply an intent and can involve logical entrapment: When did you stop beating your wife? The answer involves an implicit confession. They can be positive: Is the fact that your brother was imprisoned by the regime the only reason you decided to work for Amnesty International? The interviewer prefaces the question with information based on research. These questions lead the interviewee to reveal more information or motivation.

5. **Hypothetical questions** ask someone to imagine a situation or choice that has not yet occurred or may never occur and to describe how they would respond. The answer reveals the character and mentality of the subject. The interviewer describes a situation to the subject and then asks what he or she would do. Such questions often involve ethical issues: If you knew a terrorist had information that could save hundreds of lives, would you use torture to get that information? If your brother or sister needed a kidney to survive, would you donate one of yours?

6. **Self-assessment questions** ask people to offer judgments or evaluations of themselves and their conduct. Political candidates get asked this kind of question all the time: Why should you be elected president of the United Sates? Or it could be in retrospect: When you chose medical research as a career, did you ever think you might regret not becoming a professional actor? These difficult questions hand the interviewee an opportunity that can be exploited—by a glib politician, for instance. They may bring a disadvantage to interviewing someone who is shy or inarticulate.

Capturing the opinion of people on camera is a universal documentary technique. News reports often do vox pops to reflect the views of the man on the street. An unrehearsed interview cannot be scripted although the questions can and should be written down ahead of time. To interview successfully, you should follow one or other of the well-established methods for constructing an interview. An interview needs to have an objective and a purpose. Why are you doing the interview, and what do you want to achieve through the interview?

Then the structure of the interview matters. Do you start with a general question that is open so that the respondent can choose the scope of the answer? Sometimes, interviewers use this approach to put the subject at ease. This is called the **funnel** approach. You start wide and narrow down the questioning to finish with close questioning of a focused kind. Sometimes an aggressive interviewer will start deceptively with open questions and work the subject down to difficult, embarrassing, closed questions that go for the jugular.

Let's imagine you are doing a documentary on terrorism. You have obtained a blindfold interview with a high-level, practicing terrorist. At the broad end of the **funnel**, you might ask, what made you become a terrorist? At the narrow end you can ask specific closed questions or detailed questions: Were you involved in the planning of the 9/11 attacks? If you were to invert the process, you would start with a specific closed question that might establish the point of departure: Are you holding the three journalists hostage? This could lead to broader questions that create a free-ranging discussion about terrorism, world politics, and values. This is known as the **inverted funnel**.

Lastly, there is the **tunnel** approach, which avoids the narrowing or broadening strategy but combines both and simply pursues a logical, consistent line of questioning. For instance, you are interviewing a cardiologist about pacemakers for a pharmaceutical-sponsored documentary about heart disease. For this you need instruction and explanation. You need to structure the interview to get the information you need. So if you ask what is the most important advance in treating heart disease, you present an expert with probably too wide a choice. There are so many types of heart disease. If you ask what is the most important development in pacemakers, you will get an informed answer. This is why you must do your research and inform yourself ahead of time.

Follow-up questions can make a difference to what you get from a subject when someone unpredictably opens up a topic or reveals a fact or interest that the interviewer did not think of. Improvised follow-up questions extend the responses of unanticipated answers. If you have not done your pre-interview research, you will have difficulty asking good follow-up questions. Regardless of whether an interview is with a **subject matter expert** or a celebrity personality, preparation makes the difference. Although the answers can only be paraphrased in anticipation, the questions can be carefully written to provide a good structure from which it is easy to depart when the interview demands it.

An interview can be conducted by telephone and by email, as well as in person. Whatever the method, it is also critical to record the interview accurately with an audio or video recording device. Sometimes, you discover that the interviewee is interesting enough to write an interview into the program and use what you have recorded.

Location Research

For film and video production, **location research** is very important. Unless you have the budget to create artificial interiors in a studio set, you have to find a setting in which to shoot. For exteriors, you have no choice. You are obliged to find a location. If you want a seashore with a sandy beach, you or your producer must go and find it. If you want historical buildings, you have to find a town or a street that fits the period. Rather than write and create locations searches, it often makes sense to research the locations first because they give you ideas for visuals. This is particularly true for corporate programs. Because the story or message usually has little visual information, you have to make it visual.

Abstract ideas become concrete when you stand in a place or see the surroundings. **Location research** can make the difference for a writer. Visual writers need visual ideas. You get visual ideas by being in the environment of your topic. This is important to remember when negotiating a writing fee. Including an allowance for travel time, research time, and related travel expenses is important.

Writers of scripts still have to make the transition to the visual medium concerned. This is why the seven-step method discussed in Chapter 2 is so useful. To write a **script**, you have to think in the medium itself. This process starts with the loose, wide-ranging activity of creative sketching and digging for ideas. It is popularly called **brainstorming**.

BRAINSTORMING AND FREEING YOUR IMAGINATION

You can't write a **script** with just facts or information. You have to write with visual ideas. These ideas may allude to facts or information, or they may even embody that information. Getting a **script** going depends on your imagination and, more specifically, on your visual imagination. There isn't a surefire method for stimulating this process that works for everyone. By trial and error, you learn what helps you think visually and creatively about the medium. Nevertheless, we can enumerate several techniques.

Brainstorming usually means just writing down all your ideas as they come to you without constraint or formality. It means stirring up your imagination by free association and by doodling. Making lists, drawing diagrams, and sketching images in storyboard sequences usually does the trick. The most important element of this process is to feel free to think or visualize whatever comes to mind. Very little should be rejected at this stage. By its very nature, this kind of writing produces more material than you will finally need or use. Therefore, it leads to a necessary selection or editing process.

Sooner or later you need to make some kind of **outline**. One good way to work on your program is to outline it by listing key sequences or key images. You can use **index cards**. This allows you to shuffle the order to experiment with finding the most logical or the most meaningful order. Logic is not the only way to communicate, though. Sometimes, visual communication works best by being an emotional communication, such as showing a shocking image that disturbs the viewer. Visual exposition is not the same as writing essays in English composition. For example, there is no good verbal equivalent for a kaleidoscopic montage. And above all, you need **visual metaphors** both for individual scenes and structural organization. On the website there is a video about managing information flows that uses water, in all its forms and movement, to explain the abstract problem of capturing, finding, using, and managing digital information.

CONCEPT

The first formal document you create in the scriptwriting process is called a **concept** or a **creative concept**. Whatever you call it, its function is the same: namely, to set down in writing the key ideas and basic vision of the script **content**. This document is written in conventional prose. There is no special format for it. It does not provide any details of plot or content, nor does it include dialogue or voice narration. It is primarily an idea in a nutshell from which the **script** in all its detail will grow. A **concept** is written to persuade a key decision maker, such as a producer, director, or client, that the project idea is on track and should go forward to the next stage. Very often the **concept** is presented verbally at meetings, which has come to be known as **pitching**. The metaphor taken from baseball implies that you are going to get an idea across the plate in the strike zone. The metaphor has to break down because the producer or developer who is receiving the pitch is not trying to hit it with a bat and score. In the entertainment world, the **concept** has a short form known as the log line. A **log line** is a written phrase or sentence that encapsulates the very essence of the premise. It is part of the **script** development process of the entertainment world and will be discussed in greater detail in chapters devoted to that kind of scriptwriting.

The importance of a **concept** for the writer is that the vision of the **script** is clearly expressed and clearly understood. Like a sketch that precedes a painting or a model that precedes a sculpture or a drawing that precedes a building, a **concept** shows others the scope and potential of what the final result will be. The writer needs to know that whoever pays for the work gets what he wants. A script-writer is ultimately writing something that is validated by someone else wanting to collaborate to realize that expressed vision. That collaboration may take the form of money invested by a backer or a producer; it may take the form of creative consent invested by a director or an actor; it may take the form of client consent to proceed with the vision.

It is difficult to characterize a **concept** because it has no fixed length and no fixed form. It just has to convince, persuade, and embody the seed of the **script** to come. Generally, the **concept** can be stated in a paragraph or a page at the most, depending on the length of the program. It is important for the writer to get reactions and for the producer to give reactions before significant effort goes into the next stage, the **treatment**. A **concept** for our antismoking PSA might look like this.

A Concept for a PSA: Smoked to Death

A young, attractive couple, at the end of a date, sit in a kitchen. As they light up, he offers her a beer from the fridge. The young man seems to hallucinate so that the fridge from which he gets a beer opens into a morgue with corpses and as he snaps back he can see the effects of smoking on her. By means of stunning special effects and clever cutting, we show the unsuspecting youth audience the consequences of smoking. We see the young man's hallucination of seeing the inside of his date's lungs and a vision of her morphing into a sick older woman ravaged by the effects of smoking-related disease.

Pitching

Most beginning writers don't know much about pitching. **Pitching** is talking, not writing. It is part of the communicating and selling of ideas in both the entertainment and the corporate communication industries. You have to be able to talk your ideas as well as write them down. To make a living as a writer, you often have to sell your ideas in meetings. It is a notorious part of the entertainment business that decisions to develop projects are often based on short pitches. The art of pitching is difficult to master. There are commercial pitching workshops that veterans and coaches from the industry run for the benefit of writers wanting to break into the industry. The Robert Altman movie *The Player* (1992) contains a number of scenes of pitching story ideas to producers and studio executives. It gives viewers a good idea of how pitching works in the entertainment business.

Pitching is not restricted to entertainment writing. When you write for a corporate client or a producer of corporate programs, you spend a lot of time in meetings and briefings in which you have to present your ideas succinctly and clearly to win the job. Even though the concept has been written down, you usually have to present it verbally in a meeting with the client. A good pitch should capture the essential idea in a nutshell and tease the listeners so that they are motivated to read what you have written. You should never read your **concept** to clients. If you do, then when they read it, they experience an anticlimax. This is because there is nothing new. Thinking on your feet and communicating ideas orally is part of the writing business whether in entertainment or corporate communications.

Treatment

After the **concept** comes the **treatment**. Both of these terms are universally used and understood. A writer must know what they are and how to write them. Writing the **treatment** involves expanding the **concept** to reveal the complete structure of the program with the basic content or storyline arranged in the order that will prevail in the final **script**. A **treatment** is about structure and the arrangement of scenes. The narrative order must be clear. All the principal characters should be introduced. All the principal themes and points of exposition in a factual or corporate program should be laid out. Although this document is still written in normal prose, it can introduces key moments of voice narration or dramatic dialogue. Some writers base the **treatment** on a **scene outline**. In television series, the **scene outline** is known as a **beat sheet** and can substitute for a **treatment**. A **treatment** is always written in the present tense—always. It is a prose description of the action and not yet a **script**. It is not appropriate to describe camera angles in abundance or shot concepts. Do not "ZOOM," because it is a difficult shot to shoot and an awkward shot to edit. An occasional CLOSE UP or CUT TO might contribute to clarity. However, the treatment is not a production document and therefore not filled with technical instructions. It must communicate clearly to nonproduction people.

A Treatment for a PSA: Smoked to Death

Interior kitchen, a good-looking young man has lit up a cigarette with his girlfriend. He offers her a beer. He goes to the fridge and opens the door. Suddenly, it is as if he is opening the door of body refrigerator in the interior of a morgue. A white-coated assistant pulls out a drawer from the freezer. Back to the kitchen. He is visibly shaken, dismisses it, opens the beer for himself and her, hands his attractive date the beer.

Putting on a grin, he starts to make seductive small talk. We see her inhale and, as the camera pulls back, a special effect reveals the inside of her lungs like an X-ray. We see his worried look. We see the same woman morphing into a much older woman with wrinkles brought on by smoking. His face registers alarm. The next vision is of the girl morphed into an older woman with emphysema in a hospital bed, on oxygen. The couple in the kitchen clink beer bottles. His line: "Your health."

In a cemetery we track past a headstone. The inscription reads, "Died from Smoking-Related Disease." We see another headstone showing the same inscription: "Died from Smoking-Related Disease." And another and another in more rapid succession. In the kitchen, she puts out her cigarette and coughs once. Superimpose text: "Smoking kills 450,000 Americans every year!"

FIRST DRAFT SCRIPT

The name of this document is fairly self-explanatory. The **first draft script** is the initial attempt to transpose the content of the **treatment** into a screenplay or script format appropriate to the medium. This is the crossover from prose writing to scriptwriting in which all the special conventions of camera and scene description are used. The layout of the page serves the special job of communicating action, camera angles, and audio to a production team. It is the idea of the program formulated as a blueprint for production. The producer, the client, and the director get their first chance to read a total account for every scene from beginning to end. Until now the program idea has existed incompletely as a promise of things to come. Now it has to work in every scene with little or nothing left to chance for actors, directors, and anyone involved with production. Only now do we write a **script**, which has to communicate to production personnel.

A FIRST DRAFT SCRIPT FOR A PSA: SMOKED TO DEATH

1. INT. KITCHEN - NIGHT	
Establishing shot of a young, attractive couple in a sitcom sort of kitchen. The style is contemporary. They light up. She nods to accept the beer. The man turns to open the fridge door.	MAN: Beer?
CUT TO	
2. INT. MORGUE - NIGHT	
The young man finds himself opening the door to a body refrigerator. A white-coated assistant pulls out a corpse.	FADE UP ATMOSPHERIC MUSIC
	FADE OUT MUSIC
CUT TO	

3. INT. KITCHEN – NIGHT

The man turns back with the
beers. He is visibly shaken.
Cut to the girl who raises
an eyebrow. He recovers and
smiles and hands her the beer.
He is about to launch into
some suave small talk when he
reacts again to something we
haven't seen.

                    CUT TO

4. SPECIAL EFFECT

We see the girl inhale, but as
if by X-ray vision, so that the
inside of her tobacco-polluted
lungs are seen inside out. CUT
TO a BCU of her smiling mouth
blowing smoke.

5. INT. KITCHEN – NIGHT	FADE IN MUSIC UP AND UNDER
He is disturbed once again at this horrific hallucination. The girl is back to normal. She is chattering away.	
6. SPECIAL EFFECT	MUSIC UNDER
As we watch her, her face starts to wrinkle showing the aging effects of smoking.	
7. INT. HOSPITAL – DAY	FADE UP MUSIC
We see an older woman recognizable as the pretty young girl. She is older. She is suffering from emphysema and on oxygen and breathing with difficulty.	MUSIC UNDER
8. INT. KITCHEN – DAY The couple clink beer bottles.	BOTH TOGETHER: Your health!

9. EXT. CEMETERY – DAY	FADE UP MUSIC
Quick track to a headstone. CU of inscription: DIED FROM SMOKING-RELATED DISEASE. CUT TO another headstone with the same inscription. And another and another in rapid succession. PULL BACK to see a whole cemetery full of headstones like a military graveyard.	
10. INT. KITCHEN – DAY	FADE UP MUSIC
The girl puts out her cigarette in an ashtray and coughs once and smiles. FREEZE.	
11. CG	FADE UP MUSIC
Text SUPERS over the freeze frame: "Smoking kills 450,000 Americans every year! Do you want to become a statistic?"	
Sponsoring Organization Name	MUSIC FADES OUT

VOICE NARRATION AND DIALOGUE

One of the particular skills that a writer needs to bring to the writing of a script is the ability to write **dialogue** and **voice narration**. The obvious point is that language written to be read on the printed page has a subtly different ring to it than language meant to be spoken sound on an audio track. Whereas spoken language in a **voice**-over commentary works better in short sentences that are readily understood, in printed media, longer and more complex sentences can have value. Printed sentences can be reread, but spoken language on the sound track of a program must communicate effectively right away because the viewer usually has no opportunity for a second hearing.

Spoken language is often more colloquial than written language, which is usually more formal. Spoken language allows contractions, shortcuts, and even sentence fragments that are inappropriate in print. This is particularly true of dialogue. If you are creating a character, the lines that a character speaks must be credible and plausible. A rap artist does not talk like a senator. A construction worker doesn't talk like a college professor. Whatever kind of character is on screen, his or her dialogue should come across as natural and believable.

One of the principles of oratory that goes back to classical treatises on rhetoric by the Greek philosopher Aristotle and the Roman senator Cicero is **decorum**. The language must be appropriate to the occasion, the person, and the subject matter. Not all spoken language is casual and colloquial. Great moments in history have been marked by spoken language. Every American student has been referred to Abraham Lincoln's Gettysburg Address as an example of a clear, eloquent, and succinct statement. It was written to be spoken. Yet it is formal, stylized, and not at all colloquial. It has **decorum**. It uses language appropriate to the time, place, and occasion of a public ceremony of memorial. In a sense, the writing of commentary and dialogue simply observes the rules of classical rhetoric. In our time, we have lost this knowledge and judgement about how to use language appropriately and effectively.

Whatever you write for the sound track, whether dialogue or commentary, you should always test it out by reading it aloud, or better still by asking someone else to read it back to you. Wildlife documentaries are particularly prone to bad commentaries. They are frequently intrusive, cute, or, worse still, monotonous.

Language destined for the sound track should do the following:

- Be clear
- Complement the image
- Match the character or subject matter
- Be pronounceable or speakable
- Be suitable for the target audience.

Voice-over commentary must fit the picture in two particular ways. First, the duration of the words spoken should not extend the picture beyond its intrinsic visual value. Then the visual becomes wallpaper. Put it this way! Are we watching the picture just so that more words can be spoken? Too much of this turns the video or program into an illustrated lecture, a kind of moving picture slide show. If the visual narrative expressed through images is strong, however, those images can communicate meaning with less propping up by words. A strong way to use commentary is to set up an expectation of visual exposition by providing key themes illustrated by images. We could introduce a series of related images of suspension bridges by making a statement about the engineering: "All suspension bridges are held up by cables, which translate the weight to the load-bearing tower." Then you can stop talking and show a montage of bridges in long shot and close-up that illustrate your point. Commentary should cue the audience, not bludgeon it with verbal information.

REVISION

Every stage of the scriptwriting process involves readers and critics. Most writers are paid to write by a producer or corporate client who is entitled to ask for changes at each stage of the process. This is normal and proper. The writer's skill in conceiving visual sequences is a valued skill. It requires a lot of work and a special talent. Although writers write their own scripts on *spec* (without being commissioned), eventually any **script** has to be read and understood by an enabler such as a producer, a director, or an actor. Anyone who is going to lend energy or resources to bring a **script** into production has views and will want to modify the script in some way. This means revision.

Revision is the hardest part of a writer's job because it means being self-critical. It means throwing out ideas or changing them after you have invested time and energy to make them work. Sometimes you have to give up ideas you believe in. You have to trust that the process will work out in the long run. If you cannot prevail in vigorous debate at a meeting and get all your ideas accepted, you have to accommodate alternatives. Willingness to revise and the capacity to make revisions mark the most successful and professional writers. You have to learn to see revision as an opportunity to make your work better. You have to develop a thick skin. If you are oversensitive to criticism, you will have a hard time. You must learn to see writing as collaboration and to see your writing as a creative service rather than personal expression.

There are different levels of **revision**. **Revision** does not mean correcting spelling or grammar. This should be corrected before submission. It means throwing out unneeded material. It means adding new scenes. It means changing the order of scenes. In an extreme case, it could mean abandoning a concept and starting again. However, the custom and practice in this industry, which is reflected in contracts, allows you to demand more money for rewriting something that had been accepted at an earlier stage. You can see the need for these stages of the process that have developed over the years. People change their minds. By submitting work in stages, you gain acceptance for your work before you invest time and energy in the next stage, knowing that each stage is more laborious. If your client or producer demands something that overturns a previously accepted stage of the **process**, you should be paid to do the work again. This is unusual, but it does happen. In the entertainment industry, this often means paying off one writer and bringing in another. The stages of the **process** are important to the success of the scriptwriting enterprise because they support the creative development of ideas in a methodical way, and they provide a comprehensible system for the business arrangement that accompanies writing work.

FINAL DRAFT

The **final draft** is another self-explanatory term. It is the final document that incorporates all the revisions and input of the client or producer and all the improvements and finishing touches that a scriptwriter gives to the writing job even when not explicitly asked for. Scriptwriters, like all writers, look at their work with a critical eye and seek constant improvement. This document should mark the end of the writer's task and the completion of any contractual arrangement.

SHOOTING SCRIPT

You have probably heard the term **shooting script**. What is the difference between a **script** and a **shooting script**? The simplest way to distinguish them is to say that the scriptwriter writes the **script** and the director writes the **shooting script**. The difference is that the **shooting script** translates the **script** into a production document concerned with detailed camera angles usually based on location surveys and a **camera plot**. It breaks down the **script** into shots and camera setups. It represents the director's technical conception of how to shoot the program. A scriptwriter cannot write a **shooting script** unless that writer is also the director. It is inappropriate and irritating to a director when a scriptwriter tries to direct from the **script** by peppering it with camera angles and camera directions. The director

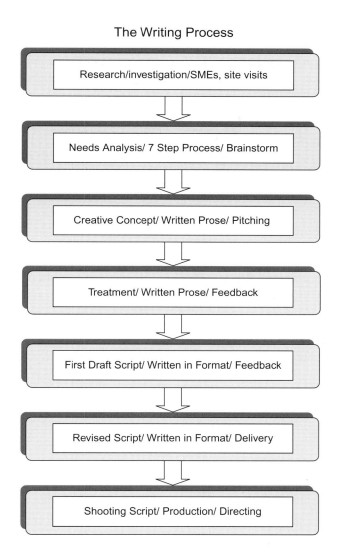

The Writing Process

- Research/investigation/SMEs, site visits
- Needs Analysis/ 7 Step Process/ Brainstorm
- Creative Concept/ Written Prose/ Pitching
- Treatment/ Written Prose/ Feedback
- First Draft Script/ Written in Format/ Feedback
- Revised Script/ Written in Format/ Delivery
- Shooting Script/ Production/ Directing

FIGURE 3.1

The writing process.

is responsible for the execution of the vision set down in the **script**. That means choosing locations, production resources, and camera angles. It also means editing.

CONCLUSION

What we have learned up to now is that scriptwriting is a **process**. It has stages. Scripts have special formats and use technical shorthand for many descriptive tasks. This kind of writing is unique to the new media that evolved throughout the twentieth century. It requires **visual writing**.

We now know what a **script** looks like. We know the professional terminology of sight and sound. We know most of the theory. We have alluded to many different types of visual media. We have defined the problem of describing a moving picture medium in words on a page and shown how a scriptwriting convention has evolved to solve many of those problems. We now need to apply this knowledge to some of the more common media formats that we encounter in the world of writing for visual media. To do this, we should look at specific communication problems that require scripted solutions. We need to learn the language that the industry has adopted through years of trial and error and apply it to the creation of a **script**.

Exercises

1. Record or listen to a conversation in a cafeteria or a bus and transcribe it. Rewrite it to remove all the chaff and incoherence.
2. Take a piece of written prose and edit it for commentary.
3. Listen to a documentary sound track without looking at the picture. Watch a documentary without the sound track. Write an evaluation of the program structure based on each.
4. Conduct an interview of people you know to collect information for a piece on a controversy such as stem cell research, abortion, or gay marriage. Use an audio recorder or a camera.
5. Ask another writer to critique your work and write down that writer's comments. See if you can revise your script to take the criticisms into consideration.
6. Write a critique of a **treatment** or a **script** written by someone else.
7. Write a **concept, treatment**, and first draft **script** for a PSA on smoking, drinking, or domestic violence.

CHAPTER 4

Describing Sight and Sound

KEY TERMS

act
angle of acceptance
audio writing
camera angles
camera directions
camera movement
character generator
character names
cinematography
computer graphic imaging
   (CGI)
commentary
DAY/NIGHT
depth of field
dialogue
dual-column format

EXT.(exterior)
graphics
INT.(interior)
master scene script
marked-up script
montage
multimedia time continuum
music
music bed
music bridge
music cues
music sting
rack focus
scene
scene heading
script format

scripting software
sequences
shot
slug line
shooting script
sound cues
sound effect
specialized kind of writing
storyboard
sync
transitions
videography
voice narration
visual writing
writing for audio

Writing a script, simply put, involves describing what the eye sees through the camera lens and what the ear hears on the audio track. This is where we should start. It sounds easy enough. The problem is, as we found out in the first chapter, knowing what to leave out. When you try to write a script for the first time, you usually end up describing too much or not thinking concretely about what is visible within the frame. You must describe the essential visual event that happens in front of the camera,

Doi: 10.1016/B978-0-240-81235-9.00004-3

but without preempting the basic production responsibilities of the director. Describing what the camera sees means understanding the basic technique of shooting and what separates one shot from another. To communicate your intentions (and a script is nothing but a set of intentions that others must realize), you must let go of some habits that have been drilled into you for writing expository prose. Other habits must take their place.

DESCRIBING TIME AND PLACE

Consider this example. Look out of the window and describe what you see. First write it as prose. It might go something like this:

> It was a drizzly fall day. Leaves had collected in the gutters and created wet skid traps on the asphalt. The wind was stripping the last few leaves clinging to the branches. A car went past with a screaming fan belt. A jogger slapped through the soggy leaves exhaling rhythmic puffs of vapor and disappeared around the corner. The phone rang. Alessandra turned to answer it. Tears made rivulets of mascara down her cheeks.

This is descriptive prose for an essay or a novel, not Hemingway, but the problem is similar. The events are brought together as an assembly of impressions without reference to order in time or place. To describe a scene is not the same as visualizing the sequence of images on a screen and then describing it so that a production crew can shoot it. The camera is like a robot. It sees only what it is in front of it. Anything not in front of it cannot be admitted to the description of the scene. What the camera sees is always in the present. **Cinematography** and **videography** record in the present—now. Therefore, the description of what the camera sees is always in the present tense—always.

Human vision scans a scene. The eyes move; the head moves; and the **angle of acceptance** of the human eye is very wide. Most important of all, the eye is connected to a brain that selects and interprets the visual information delivered by the optical nerve. The brain can assemble and arrange impressions in any number of ways. A camera interposes an artificial eye between the scene and the eye of the audience. That is what makes the medium an art. The audience only gets to see what the camera lens frames, which issues from the scripted scene. The artificial image on an emulsion (film) or an electronic scan (lines, pixels) are visual experiences separate from reality, just like an artist's canvas is a visual experience apart from the reality that inspires it.

So let's take the same scene and explore how it would work to write it as a script. Always ask the question, what does the camera see? This means thinking about where the camera will be set up physically and in which specific direction it will point. The camera always expresses a point of view. Therefore, you must use it. The director has the final decision about these matters. You describe the possibilities.

Your first decision as a scriptwriter is to imagine whether we see the scene from the interior looking out or whether we play the scene as an exterior. You express this with an abbreviation: **INT.(interior)** or **EXT.(exterior)**. The director, the camera crew, and anyone working on the shoot know the practical implications of this abbreviation. The next piece of essential information is to describe where the action is taking place. This can be a word or two, such as STREET or LIVING ROOM. Next you have to decide what time it is, day or night. Again this has implications for lighting and production. You write **DAY/NIGHT**. Occasionally, you can specify a particular time such as dawn or sunset. We now have three critical pieces of information necessary to every scene in a script that tell a production crew a great deal about what they have to do and what they have to plan for. These three pieces of information are arranged in a well-recognized sequence called a **scene heading** or a **slug line**, for example:

INT. LIVING ROOM - DAY

DESCRIBING ACTION

So far so good! Your next job is to describe some action or object or person that you want to be seen within the camera frame. Now you need to think about how large or how small this frame is and about what is in the **foreground** and **background**.

The description could go like this:

INT. LIVING ROOM -- DAY

We see a figure in silhouette against a window. Through the window, we see a suburban street lined with trees. Leaves are falling. It is windy and raining. A car drives past. with a screaming fan belt. A jogger runs past. His breath is visible. A telephone rings. The figure turns toward camera, and we see tears on her face.

This could be enough. What has changed from the written prose we looked at earlier? The description is in the present tense. Descriptions of action in scripts are always in the present tense, as if we are seeing everything in front of us right now playing on a movie or TV screen. Another difference is that most descriptive adjectives and poetic embellishments are removed. We reduce the description to simple, short statements of action. Sometimes it is permissible to write in incomplete sentence fragments that would usually get red ink corrections in composition classes. Try this:

INT. LIVING ROOM -- DAY

LS with figure in silhouette in foreground against a window. In background through the window a suburban street with trees. Leaves are falling. It is windy and raining. A car up and past. SFX a screaming fan belt. A jogger runs past. His breath is visible. SFX telephone ring. The figure turns. We see ALESSANDRA's face in CU, tears running down her face.

This is probably enough. It could be shot as one shot by **racking focus** (see definition below) or it could be broken down into two different shots, one interior and one exterior. Also, specifying a CU (see the definition that follows) or deciding what size of shot should frame the figure is optional and must not be overdone.

Try another version with an exterior:

```
EXT. STREET — DAY

LOW ANGLE of a woman at a window. REVERSE ANGLE of the street -- leaves
are falling. It is windy and raining. A car up and past. SFX a screaming
fan belt. A jogger runs past. We see the steam of his breath. The figure
turns away from the window.
```

Now we have to visualize a different shot, which involves a different camera setup. So the scene has to be written as two separate shots that have to be produced separately. Even a script written the first way might inspire a director to cover the scene with an exterior and an interior. In fact, a director might shoot close-ups of the runner, or cutaways of the leaves, or a long shot of the window, none of which are specifically written into the script.

```
INT. LIVING ROOM -- DAY

The street scene of the previous shot in the background. The phone rings.
ALESSANDRA, in silhouette against a window, turns to the camera and reveals
a tear-stained face. She answers the phone.
```

Deciding which way to play the scene is a writer's prerogative. The scriptwriter is all powerful for the moment. In reality, once the script is turned over to production, the writer's power wanes, as we learned in the previous chapter, and the director assumes control. The interior version is cheaper to produce because it involves only one setup. The interior/exterior combination is visually more interesting and introduces more dramatic complexity. It takes more time to do two setups, one interior and one exterior under different lighting conditions and, therefore, more money.

DESCRIBING THE CAMERA FRAME OR THE SHOT

You may have picked up other features of scriptwriting style in these examples. **CHARACTER NAMES** and **CAMERA ANGLES** are usually typed in uppercase. Most important of all is the specialized language that describes the way a lens produces an image, often written as an abbreviation such as CU. This is not a book about production. Therefore, we do not want to go into camera work in an exhaustive way. However, the following commonly used terms and abbreviations—and their meanings—must become part of your working vocabulary. The website provides an interactive glossary of live-action video or stills to illustrate every type of shot.

Although you should know these terms and although they will be needed from time to time to convey what your vision is, you should be careful not to pepper your script with minute **camera directions**. Too much directing of the script by trying to choose camera frames clutters up the script and encumbers the director. The director has to make a decision based on the real scene in front of the camera on the day of shooting. I have shot many of my own scripts and had to abandon visions of

Standard Camera Angles	
VLS	VERY LONG SHOT: A very long shot has no precise definition other than that it should include the whole human figure from head to foot, all of the action, and a good view of the background.
LS	LONG SHOT: A long shot should include the whole human figure from head to foot so that this figure (or figures if more than one) is featured rather than the background.
MS	MEDIUM SHOT: A medium shot, like all of these shots, is defined with reference to the inclusion or exclusion of parts of the human body. So a medium shot is usually just below the waist. Keeping the hands in is one way to visualize the shot. It is definitely well above the knees.
CU	CLOSE UP: A close-up frames the head and shoulders leaving headroom above the head. A close-up captures facial expression or the detailed characteristics of an inanimate object.
2 SHOT	TWO SHOT: Although this is not an abbreviation, it is a common term that describes two people in close-up or medium shot. The wide-screen format (2.75:1 ratio) of the movie screen and the new high-definition television (HDTV) format (16:9 ratio) make good use of this frame.
BCU or ECU	BIG CLOSE UP/ EXTREME CLOSE UP: A Big Close-Up or Extreme Close-Up frames the head so that the top of frame clips the forehead or hairline and the bottom of the frame clips the neck with chinroom.
WIDE ANGLE	This term is somewhat loose. It generally means a long shot or an establishing shot that shows the whole scene. It refers to a shorter focal length lens.
OTS	OVER-THE-SHOULDER: This shot, as the name implies, frames two figures so that one is partially in the frame in a quarter back view to one side while the other is featured in a three-quarter front view.
	This shot is usually matched to a reverse angle of the same figures so that the values are reversed.
REVERSE ANGLE	A Reverse Angle is one of a typical pairing of two matched shots with converging eye lines. They can be Medium Shots, Close-Ups, or over-the-shoulder shots and are shot from two separate camera setups.
LOW ANGLE	A Low Angle means pointing the camera lens up at the subject, whether an object or a person.
HIGH ANGLE	A High Angle means pointing the camera lens down at the subject, whether an object or a person.
RACK FOCUS	Racking Focus, also known as pulling focus, refers to a deliberate change of focus executed by twisting the focus ring on the barrel of a lens during the shot. This technique is typically used to shift attention from one character to another when they are speaking and the depth-of-field is insufficient to hold both in focus at the same time. It is commonly used in television drama and movies.

how it was supposed to be because the lens would not accommodate the idea. The performance of lenses is governed by the laws of optics, which limit what they can do. The principal limitation is in the way foreground and background can be contained in focus in what is called the **depth of field**. This could be a weakness of the interior version discussed earlier. The figure and the exterior scene will not both be in focus. As the figure turns, the camera crew will have to **rack focus** to feature the face. All of these problems of execution are the province of the director and his crew. A rule of thumb might be to give a **camera direction** only when it is indispensable to the visual idea on which your scene rests. Otherwise, leave it to the common sense of the director.

Describing Camera Movement

You need to learn the terms that describe camera movements. **Camera movements** change the size or perspective of a frame, the angle of view, or a combination of these. (See the website for live-action video of each camera movement.)

Standard Camera Movements	
PAN	Pan stands for panorama. It is the most common movement of the camera. A pan can move from left to right or vice versa, sweeping across a scene to give a panoramic view. The most common use of this camera movement is to follow a moving figure or object while the camera platform remains stationary.
TILT	A tilt is a movement of the camera platform to angle up or angle down in a continuous movement along a vertical axis. It is useful for following movement. Panning and tilting are often combined in one movement to follow motion in two dimensions.
TRACK	A track refers to the continuous movement of the camera platform in one direction, usually alongside a moving figure. This is accomplished by putting the camera on a dolly that runs on tracks or by handholding the camera while walking alongside the action. Professionals often use a gyroscopic Steadycam mount. This enables the camera operator to maintain a constant frame around a moving object or person and to track movement without camera shake. A camera platform can also be mounted on a vehicle or any other moving object. Tracking was an early innovation in camera movement in silent movie days.
DOLLY	A dolly shot is similar to a tracking shot in that the camera platform moves, but it moves toward or away from the subject so that the frame size gets larger or smaller. A similar but different effect is obtained with a zoom lens.
ZOOM	A zoom is an optical effect created by changing the focal length during a shot with a specially designed lens that has a variable focal length. The effect makes the frame larger or smaller like a dolly shot. The important difference is that a dolly shot maintains the focal length and depth of field throughout as the camera moves nearer or farther away. The zoom uses an optical effect without moving the camera to change from a wide-angle lens to a telephoto lens so that it appears to the viewer that the subject is closer or farther away. The depth of field changes as the focal length changes.
CRANE	A crane shot is made by raising or lowering a camera platform, usually with a crane or boom. It can also be achieved with a helicopter-mounted camera at great expense. In a low-budget production, a smaller-scale crane effect can be done by bending and straightening the knees while handholding the camera.

DESCRIBING GRAPHICS AND EFFECTS

In contemporary television and video, a significant proportion of program content, especially commercials, is generated by computer imaging software output to video. This includes titles, 2-D and 3-D animation and computer-generated optical effects that produce layers of video. **Graphics** and live action can be combined to create almost anything imaginable, including images that defy logic and natural laws. Metallic insects, hybrid creatures, science fiction worlds, a face metamorphosing into a different face or object (known as morphing)—all of these images are created without using a lens or light-sensitive medium to record a real-world scene. Therefore, the **scene heading** has no meaning when describing a computer-generated graphic. A useful convention to adopt in place of the **slug line** is a heading: GRAPHICS or **CGI**. This graphics **slug line** announces to all production people that this scene does not have to be shot but must be scheduled for postproduction by the editor or by a graphic artist.

If you need a graphic image or graphic animation in your script, you need to describe it as you see it. If it is a 3-D animation, you can resort to the conventional frame descriptions to visualize the scene. For example:

```
CU spaceship, seen from a low angle, filling the screen.
```

A title is created either in a **character generator** or as part of **computer graphic imaging (CGI)**. It is created in **postproduction** and needs to be identified by another **slug line** separate from a **shot** or a **scene**. You can indicate this by a simple slug: TITLE or CG.

DESCRIBING TRANSITIONS BETWEEN SHOTS

Transitions between shots are predominantly decided by the director and the editor. Although all scripts begin with FADE IN FROM BLACK and often designate a DISSOLVE or a MIX in place of a CUT, it would be inappropriate for a writer to try to pin down the director or editor at every transition between scenes. As with other camera directions, sparing use for specific cinematic reasons will command attention, whereas constant use will irritate postproduction people who will probably ignore them. Let's take a look at the terminology used to describe **transitions** between scenes (see the website):

Standard Transitions	
CUT	The most basic and indispensable transition on which modern visual editing relies is the cut. In the early days of film, movies were short, sometimes consisting of one shot that lasted for a few minutes. Modern motion picture editing was born when directors shot more than one angle so that the rhythm and pace of a scene could be controlled in the way shots were edited. Some scriptwriters write in a transition in uppercase at the end of every scene: CUT TO. Some scripts are written with the understanding that any transition is automatically a cut unless some other transition is specified. D. W. Griffith, the silent film director, is usually credited with the invention of editing innovations based on cutting shots together that are still in use today—cutting to a close-up for emphasis and cutting away to a detail of a scene, which is out of continuity.
CUTAWAY	A cutaway is a shot of some detail within the scene, something like a clock or a telephone that is not part of the continuity of action, or a cutaway of, say, the feet of a runner. An editor can cut away to it without concern for its match to the previous or the following shot. Experienced directors always shoot plenty of cutaways to solve continuity problems in the editing phase. For the writer, the use of the cutaway would be to emphasize the dramatic or narrative importance of an object. As mentioned in Chapter 1, the classic western *High Noon*, scripted by Carl Foreman, cuts away to the clock as a dramatic device to increase tension for the audience because the bad guy released from the state penitentiary is arriving on the noon train to take revenge on the marshal who put him away. This cutaway could be written in by the scriptwriter. Some cutaways, however, are created by directors and editors.
DISSOLVE/ MIX TO	In film production, anything other than a cut has to be created in the optical printer from A- and B-roll offsets. The editor marks up the film so that the lab technician can move the printer from the outgoing shot on the A roll to the incoming shot on the B roll. In video, the mix is made with a fader bar that diminishes input from one video source as a second is added. In video, the term MIX TO is preferred.
SUPER	In the middle of a dissolve when 50 percent of the printer light or video source comes from each picture, a temporary effect called a superimposition is produced. This effect is now created digitally within nonlinear editors. A superimposition is simply the mix or dissolve mixed into the midprinter light or midfader position and then out. Beginners often go to unnecessary lengths to describe the way titles superimpose on picture or a background. A sentence can be reduced to "SUPER TITLES over black," "SUPER TITLES over LS of street" or "SUPER flashback action over CU of face."

FADE IN FROM BLACK	All programs begin with this effect, which is simply a mix or dissolve from black to picture. Sometimes you might write in this effect to mark a break in time or sections of a program.
FADE OUT TO BLACK	All programs end with this effect, which is a mix or dissolve from picture to black, the opposite of the fade in from black. Logically, these two fade effects go in pairs.
WIPE	A wipe is the effect of an incoming image pushing off the outgoing image. A wipe is more commonly a video effect. Every switcher has a number of standard wipe patterns. The most obvious are a horizontal and a vertical wipe in which the two are images are separated by a moving line that bisects the screen. The other basic patterns are circle wipes and rectangle wipes in which the incoming image grows from a point in the middle of the outgoing picture as an expanding shape. The corner wipe is a variation. The incoming picture starts as a rectangle entering from any corner of the screen. Once again, a scriptwriter should think very carefully before writing in such detailed transitions. It is better to leave it to the director and editor in postproduction.
DVE	Transitions between shots have become so numerous, because of the advent of digital video effects (DVEs) in computer-based editors and mixers, that it would be impossible to list the dozens of different patterns and effects. Once again, this is the province of postproduction unless you have a strong reason to incorporate a specific visual effect into your script.

DESCRIBING SOUND

The sound track is an enormously vital part of any program. There are basically three ways that sound works to intensify the visual image. The most obvious element is voice. The human voice is our most important means of communication. Speech or **dialogue** is commonly recorded in **sync** with the image of people when they talk. So the words we write for sound track, the manner of delivery, and even the gender of the voice all contribute to the final result. If you listen to any sound track carefully, you will hear more than just the synchronized sound that was part of the scene when it was shot. Most dramas involve two other elements that are not part of the camera recording.

The second kind of sound that we use is the **sound effect**, either in **sync** with something on screen, or as a pure effect, natural or artificial. If we see an explosion, we expect to hear the **sound effect**. If we see a dog barking, we expect to hear it. Then there are ambient sounds that complete a picture or an impression of time and place without **sync**. An example would be a **scene** in the country reinforced by the sound of birdsong or a city scene given greater realism by the distant sound of sirens and traffic.

Lastly, the makers of theatrical films, documentaries and corporate and advertising programs well understand the emotional impact of **music** on a scene. The right **music** can lift a **scene** that, in visual terms, is quite ordinary. Cutting footage to **music** allows the musical beat to reinforce a visual expectation and tie them together.

So **visual writing** has to include **audio writing**. You have to think about sound sometimes when you are writing visuals. The three elements of a sound track have to be mixed together in postproduction in what has become an elaborate and demanding multitrack mix. Both **music** and **sound effects** (often created by Foley artists in a special studio) are usually added later in postproduction. Scriptwriters do not normally describe every aspect of this multitrack mix. Audio recordists and directors and mixers make production decisions as to how to produce the sound track of your **scene**. The exceptions are when you want to emphasize the specific dramatic, comic, or informational use of **sound effects**. So we mention specific **sound effects** or **music cues** only when the production team might otherwise leave them out or because they have special significance. A character hears footsteps approaching or hears a door opening off screen. That has dramatic significance.

If you are an editor or have been involved in editing film or video, you likely have discovered how ordinary shots can be transformed by **music** or **sound effects** or how cutting a **montage** to a beat can transform ordinary and mundane shots into something visually interesting. So aesthetically and technically, we have to acknowledge that sound alters the value of images for a viewer. **Sound cues** are part of the scripting language that we need to learn.

We are discovering that writers need to know as much about production as possible, but they also need to know when not to intrude on the work of production and postproduction personnel. Only a limited number of detailed decisions in making and finishing a program can be incorporated at a given moment in the production. It is unnecessary and silly to give instructions that cannot be used.

Writing for Voice

Since sound was added to picture in the 1930s, **dialogue** and **voice narration** has assumed a significant role in moving picture media. We need to write for the voice. What better way than to examine radio and consider writing for voice only or audio only. There is a fuller discussion of writing for **commentary** and voice over in Chapter 7.

Format for Radio

Although this book is concerned with writing for visual media, **writing for audio** is inevitably part of the writing task for an audiovisual medium. As a footnote to these issues, it seems useful to look at what a **script** that is dedicated to radio would look like. Whereas radio used to produce drama, soap operas, and series, it now consists of music, news, and talk with a few exceptions like Garrison Keillor's *Prairie Home Companion* on National Public Radio. In effect, the only real audio scripting that is left to do on radio is for the advertisements on commercial stations. Both ads and public service announcements (PSAs) for radio have to be written. To communicate to production sound engineers and voice artists, there has to be a workable convention for these instructions and a page format to accommodate them. Because radio is a linear medium that unfolds in time and is strictly timed, the script needs to show clearly both the sequence of audio events and the relation of simultaneous events. **Sound effects** have to be described so that they can be recorded or taken from a sound library of prerecorded effects. Likewise the use of music must be clear in the script. Clearly, **music, sound effects**, and speech cannot all be recorded or rather mixed together at the same level or amplitude. The audio/radio script has to show the approximate relation in loudness of one element to another.

Music cues have a language of their own that indicates the function of the music and therefore is a guide to the type of music sought as well as how it should fade in and out.

A **music bed** is a longer piece of music that usually goes under dialogue and sound effects or segues to that dialogue or effect. Music can be part of an imagined scene such as the background of a car radio or a band in a parade that is not featured.

A **music bridge,** as the term suggests, is played or laid in a multitrack mix to link scenes or a change of place, time, or action.

A **music sting** is a short prominent musical phrase or note that is used to underline a line of dialogue or a dramatic moment. We see this use in film and television, especially in suspense and horror films.

Let's imagine an audio **script** for a radio PSA about drinking and driving. Note that character names and **music** and **sound effects cues** are in uppercase. **Dialogue** and speech is in lowercase. Audio events are generally numbered. **Transitions** and **cues** are important.

```
 1. SOUND FX:        INTERIOR CAR SOUND OF MOTOR AND
                     EXTERIOR TRAFFIC
 2. MUSIC BED CAR RADIO—HEAVY METAL FADE UNDER.
 3. COLLEGE STUDENT 1 What a great party!
 4. COLLEGE STUDENT 2 I'm wasted.
 5. COLLEGE STUDENT 1 Are you all right to drive?
 6. COLLEGE STUDENT 2 Hell yes.
 7. COLLEGE STUDENT 1 (PANICKED) Look out!
 8. MUSIC BED         SEGUE TO
 9. SOUND FX:         SCREECH OF BRAKES THEN CAR CRASH
10. SOUND FX:         AMBULANCE SIREN
11. ANNCR:            If you drink and drive, death
                      could be the chaser.
12. MUSIC STING       ORGAN CHORD
```

Here are the abbreviations you should learn when working with sound directions:

Sound Directions	
SFX	This is a convenient abbreviation for SOUND EFFECTS. Instead of describing a thunderstorm and the sound of thunder at length, it is sufficient to write SFX thunder. In postproduction, whoever assumes responsibility for the audio tracks will pull a stock effect from a bank of effects on a DVD or from an audiotape. A sound effect is anything other than speech or music.
MUSIC	A music track is created independently of camera production. Music videos begin with a defined sound track. Other programs have music added in postproduction to fit the dialogue, sound effects, and mood. The writer does not usually pick music or decide where music is necessary. The exception is when the music is integral to the idea or in a short script such as a public service announcement (PSA) in which detailed conception might include ideas for music. If you do write in music cues, there is a correct way to do it, by using the following terms.
FADE IN	Almost all audio events are faded in and faded out to avoid a click as the playback head picks up a snap cut to music or effects at full level. This also permits us to use music cues that do not necessarily correspond to the beginning and end of a piece.
FADE OUT	This is the audio cue that most people forget to use. They fade in music or effect and then forget to indicate where the audio event ends. Mixing multitrack sound depends on fading in and out of different tracks. The fade-out diminishes the loudness of the sound down to zero over an interval, short or long, according to taste so that it avoids an abrupt cutoff and does not shock the ear or draw attention to itself. Many commercial recordings of popular music are faded out at the end, whereas classical music has a specific ending to the composition, the loudness of

	which is controlled by the performer. Library music that is sold by needle time for specific synchronization rights for designated territories is generally recorded without fades so that the audio mixer of a program can make the decisions about the length of fades. This music is recorded in convenient lengths of 30 and 60 seconds. Some pieces are longer with variations on the same basic theme so that the piece can be reprised at different moments on the sound track. Also, small music bridges, riffs, and teasers are available off the shelf for editors and audio mixers to use.
FADE UP	A fade-up is a change of level in an audio event that needs to be featured again after being faded under. Music tracks need constant fading under and up to clear dialogue. A writer seldom needs this kind of cue.
FADE UNDER	Fading under an audio event such as music is necessary when you want the event to continue but not compete with a new event that will mix from another track, typically dialogue or commentary. You should understand that audio mixers and editors largely make these types of decisions. Nevertheless, you should know these terms for the rare occasion when you need to lock in a specific audio idea in your script.
SEGUE TO	This term means to cross-fade two audio events. It is the audio equivalent of the video mix. You do not need to write this into the audio side of a script every time you use a MIX TO (see above) transition. All involved understand that one goes with the other.

SHOT, SCENE, AND SEQUENCE

Now that we know the nuts and bolts of describing sight and sound in an individual **shot**, we need to think about how those shots go together to make **scenes** and how **scenes** go together to make **sequences**. In dramatic writing, there is a larger structural unit carried over from theatrical writing called an **act**. This is used in television scripts (see the templates on the website) and is usually implicit in screenplays. Chapter 8 discusses large-scale story structure that gives a script shape, rhythm, pace, and meaning.

A **shot** is the minimal element of the moving picture medium. It has a beginning when the camera is switched on and an ending when the camera is switched off. The beginning and ending can be adjusted in length in an edit suite, but that is all. Theoretically a **shot** could be one frame long, but it would not then have movement. It could only work as part of a **montage**.

FINDING A FORMAT FOR THE PAGE

The last problem to solve for the beginning scriptwriter is to determine the accepted way of laying out a script on the page. You must respect well-established conventions. They evolved by trial and error for specific reasons. In a professional setting, using the right **script format** is crucial. Not to do so proclaims your ignorance of the business you are trying to break into. Your script will probably also be harder to read if you don't follow the accepted conventions. Fortunately, computer software makes this part of the job easy. Most word processing applications can be formatted with macros to create any script layout. Dedicated **scriptwriting software** is also available. Some of the specialized software such as Movie Magic Screenwriter also plugs into budgeting and scheduling software that saves time and money for producers. In the professional world, you must get to know some of these systems.[1] (See the companion website.)

---

[1] Visit www.writersstore.com to see the range of formatting and story development software. This is also useful source for book, seminars, and courses on writing.

MASTER SCENE SCRIPT

Two broad types of script formats or page layouts are in common use. The first, called a **master scene script**, reads down the page and is close to a theatrical script in that way (see sample script format in the appendix). It is written according to a plan that includes a **slug line** or **scene heading** for every **scene**. In fact, if any information in your **slug line** no longer applies to the action you are describing—that is, if the time and place have changed—you must start another **scene** with a new **slug line**. The scenes are not numbered. Character names are typed in uppercase, as are **camera directions**. **Dialogue** is centered, indented, and separated from the description of action, which is margin to margin. This format it used for feature film and TV film and usually anything that involves characters and lines of **dialogue**. TV series and serials are written in variants of this **script format**. Some adopt the convention of putting **dialogue** in uppercase. Some series have idiosyncrasies in their **script formats** that spec writers should learn.

```
FADE IN:

INT. SEMINAR ROOM - DAY

A group of people eager to learn the secrets of the Master Scene Script
format are sitting around a seminar table.
A projector shows the text being created.

                         INSTRUCTOR
                    (smiling)
               The film industry has a standard
               format for screenplays that everyone
               follows.

                         EAGER LEARNER
               What are the margins?

                         INSTRUCTOR
               Good question! Left, 1.5 inches.Right,
               1.0 inches. Top, 1.0 inches to the body,
               0.5 inches to the number. Bottom, 0.5 to
               1.5 inches, depending on the position
               of the page break.

The instructor shows an example on the projector.

                         SECOND EAGER LEARNER
               I get it. Scene headers stay attached
               to action description, and a line of
               dialogue would be pushed to the
               next page.

                                                  CUT TO:
```

```
EXT. CAMPUS - DAY

The sun is shining. Everyone is sitting on the grass having a picnic
lunch.

                                                      DISSOLVE TO:


INT. SEMINAR ROOM - AFTERNOON

The eager learners are taking notes while the instructor explains more
format issues.

                            INSTRUCTOR
                  Let's talk fonts. Always Courier,
                  12 point, 10 pitch. That is the
                  industry standard.

                                                       FADE OUT:
```

DUAL-COLUMN FORMAT

A **dual-column format** is the other main type of **script format**. It has to be read from left to right because audio and visual elements are separated into two columns (see a sample script in the appendix). The description of everything that is seen on screen is placed in the left-hand column. The description of everything that is heard on the sound track is placed in the right-hand column. Each scene therefore consists of a pair of descriptions. For anyone involved in production, this is an ideal arrangement because it accommodates production techniques. For a reader, it is awkward to integrate what you read in left and right columns and then move down to the next pair.

What we are discovering is the difficulty of describing visual media in a print medium. That is the nature of the problem. Remember the analogy of the blueprint. An architect or designer has to represent a three-dimensional object in two dimensions on the page. Likewise, we, as scriptwriters, have to represent a **multimedia time continuum** in writing. Writing is a 4000-year-old technology that is still indispensable for many forms of communication, and the printed page is a 500-year-old technology that is still an immensely successful medium. You are using it right now. However, writing and printing do not do justice to audiovisual media. Writers have written prose for as long as language and alphabets have existed. Playwrights have written for theatre since the fourth century BC in Athens. Scriptwriting is new and arose in response to the invention of a historically new medium of moving pictures. A script is, in effect, a **specialized kind of writing**, just as a blueprint is a specialized kind of drawing. To solve the problem, a script would need to be a kind of musical score, a visual representation, and a verbal description combined. There is a suggestion of this in the documents that describe interactive media, as we shall see in a later chapter in Part 4.

In the end, each format—that is, each way of organizing the page—has its advantages and disadvantages. A **master scene script** has to combine visual and audio descriptions. In production, these have to be disentangled. Because such scripts are usually driven by **dialogue**, the main audio event is read in alternation with the description of action, so the reader has to assimilate them and integrate in alternation going down the page. In the **dual column script**, the problem is presented in a different way to favor production and requires the reader to assimilate pairs of audio and visual elements while parsing down the page.

```
FADE IN:

INT. SEMINAR ROOM - DAY

A GROUP OF PEOPLE EAGER TO        INSTRUCTOR:(smiling) The
LEARN THE SECRETS OF THE DUAL     industry has a standard
COLUMN FORMAT ARE SITTING         layout for dual column
AROUND A SEMINAR TABLE. A         scripts using for corporate,
PROJECTOR SHOWS THE TEXT          documentary and public
BEING CREATED.                    service announcements.

                                  EAGER LEARNER: Why is the
                                  action in caps?

THE COMPUTER PAGE IS              INSTRUCTOR: It doesn't have
PROJECTED ONTO A SCREEN.          to be. I have seen the
                                  reverse where spoken dialogue
THE GROUP TAKES NOTES             is in c72aps and action is in
                                  lower case.

                                  SECOND EAGER LEARNER: Can we
                                  choose?

                                  INSTRUCTOR: I advise putting
                                  speech into upper and lower
                                  case because it is easier to
                                  read. Action description can
                       CUT TO:    also be in lower case.

EXT. CAMPUS - DAY                 EAGER LEARNER: What font do
                                  we use?

THE GROUP IS SITTING ON THE       INSTRUCTOR: I use Courier New
GRASS HAVING A PICNIC LUNCH.      12 point, but outside the
                                  entertainment industry, the
                                  rules are less rigid.

                                  FADE MUSIC UP AND UNDER
```

```
                              INSTRUCTOR: The most
                              important point about the
                              dual column format is that
                              the columns should be equal
                              in width and action and
                              speech should be related by
                              horizontal position opposite
                              one another. Audio cues
                              should be in caps.
                  CUT TO:     FADE MUSIC UP AND OUT
```

STORYBOARD

Meanwhile, the best answer that the industry has devised to represent the moving picture media is known as a **storyboard** (see the companion website). It was developed by art departments in advertising agencies to get over the problem of clients reading and interpreting scripts visually by supplying them with sequential drawings of key frames. It is similar to the problem of understanding blueprints. Architects visualize the result for nontechnical clients with models and sketches. TV ads and PSAs are almost always rendered as storyboards before going into production. Some directors storyboard dramatic scripts, especially sequences involving special effects. A scriptwriter might not be a good artist and, although capable of writing excellent scripts, might not be capable of drawing. An artist who can sketch the key frames probably has no scriptwriting skills. So creation of a **storyboard** generally requires collaboration. It is a good idea to sketch a **storyboard** for certain sequences even if your drawing consists of crude stick figures. It helps you to visualize what you are trying to describe in scripting language.

New computer software has transformed traditional roles by creating libraries of characters and backgrounds with powerful routines that can vary camera angles, size objects, and change perspectives. Text can be imported into caption areas. This allows almost anyone to create a **storyboard**. The more film and television rely on sophisticated computer-generated effects, the more important storyboarding will become. There is already a trend to create program content directly with images in an imaging medium that sequences frames. StoryBoard Artist, a program developed by PowerProduction Software, will even let you add sound files to the frame. The **storyboard** as produced by such computer software is halfway to an animated movie.

TV Studio Multi-Camera Script

Television scripts, whether for news or for other programs that are intended to be shot in a television studio with a multicamera method and switched live in the control room, require a slightly different formatting of the script. Because news emphasizes the news anchor reading from a teleprompter, it only makes sense to adopt a two- or three-column format with the right hand column for the audio.

The visuals are either medium shots or closeups of the presenters. This can be indicated in the next column to the left and can identify which camera will take it. Most television news is put together from standard setups with very little camera movement. The cameras are increasingly robotic with one operator. The other elements are B roll from tape VTR, or CG, still store, or live feed. These are produced separately and can be incorporated into the left-hand visual column for cueing. They would have to be produced independently beforehand. For more elaborate productions involving sets and movement of talent, a rehearsal would enable the floor and the control room to anticipate the camera moves from a rundown sheet and a shot list separated out for each camera to follow. Prerecorded video and music cues would be marked.

A television script really takes shape as a production script. Switching live means you must have precise cues for picture and sound. Whereas editing footage shot on a single camera in postproduction allows edit decisions to be made on the basis of a marked-up post-production script. This **marked-up script** is produced by the script supervisor to show the relationship of multiple takes and angles shot out of script order that cover a **scene** identified by their unique slate numbers and logged and digitized in bins. Here another level of information is superimposed on the **master scene script** to show what is covered and what is not for any given take. The **marked-up script** is strictly production and post-production and no part of a writer's work.

A television drama might be written as a **master scene script** and then turned into a **two-column script** for production if it were going to be shot live in a studio. A **script** for live multi-camera production is best written as a **dual column script** to enable ample **camera directions** in the left hand column. The **master scene script** layout would fight with the conceptual thinking about assigning cameras to action because it reads down the page. The dual column shows the relationship of camera and **shot** to **dialogue** or to-camera speech. For this type of production, more **camera direction** is required. Later, a director can mark up the **script** with actual camera assignments during a camera rehearsal and produce a shot list for each camera. The production must be rehearsed from such a script and is closer to a **shooting script** for single camera production. Directors write their own shooting scripts (see *American Travel in Europe* on the website); they are not the province of scriptwriters. Once again, we are straying into the realm of shooting and production scripts that involve directorial talent.

```
FADE IN:
CG title                              MUSIC INTRO FADE UP AND UNDER

SEMINAR SET
WIDE SHOT of instructor and
learners

Instructor to camera                  INSTRUCTOR:(smiling) The
                                      industry has a standard
                                      layout for dual column
                                      scripts using for corporate,
                                      documentary and public
                                      service announcements.
```

	EAGER LEARNER: Why is the action in caps?
WIDE ANGLE of seminar table	INSTRUCTOR VO: It doesn't have to be. I have seen the reverse where spoken dialogue is in caps and action is in lower case.
STILL STORE script page	SECOND EAGER LEARNER: Can we choose?
CU Eager Learner taking notes.	
WIDE ANGLE of the group	INSTRUCTOR: I advise putting speech into upper and lower case because it is easier to read. Action description can also be in lower case.
MS of Instructor CU Eager Learner	EAGER LEARNER: What font do we use?
LS Instructor	INSTRUCTOR: I use Courier New 12 point, but outside the entertainment industry, the rules are less rigid. The most important point about the dual column format is that the columns should be equal in width and action and speech should be related by horizontal position opposite one another.

NEWS ANCHOR SCRIPT FORMAT

News scripts primarily show text to be entered into a teleprompter and then read by one or more anchors from the teleprompter. The only **visual writing** involves designating which anchor reads what portion of the text and which camera takes the **shot**. It is a production document and part of the writing necessary for one aspect of television production. In fact, it is more like a production **script**. Nevertheless, it has to be written prior to production.

```
        ON CAMERA: SHERRY              DRIVERS BETTER KEEP THEIR
                                       EYES PEELED.
                                       NEW 55-MILE-AN-HOUR SPEED-
                                       LIMIT SIGNS ARE GOING UP... TO
                                       KEEP OUR POLLUTION DOWN.
                                       W-B 39'S KATIE McCALL TELLS
                                       US ABOUT THE CHANGES.

        TAKE VTR
        :17 SUPER: JANELLE GBUR        SOT 1:38
        DEPT. OF TRANSPORTATION
        :32 SUPER: KATIE MC CALL
        REPORTING
        :40 SUPER: MIKE STAFFORD
        HARRIS COUNTY ATTORNEY
        1:38 TAPE OUT

                                       1:38 STD OUT CUE
```

CONCLUSION

After reading this chapter, you should have a useful repertoire of scriptwriting terms and conventions that enable you to deal with the detailed problems of describing sight, sound, and **transitions**. You now have the building blocks of scriptwriting. You need to try them out in small-scale exercises. Then the larger issues of devising script concepts and content and of writing scripts for specific program formats can be brought into perspective. The chapters that follow show you how to solve communication problems through **script** development and this newly acquired visual language so that a production team can carry the work to completion resulting in a finished, viewable product.

Exercises

1. Write a camera description of yourself getting up and having breakfast. Use the camera vocabulary you have learned from this chapter. Think about what you would describe and what you would leave out.
2. Watch a simple real-life scene, such as people having an argument, a cop giving a driver a ticket, or action in the street, on a bus, or in a restaurant. Now describe what a camera would see. What would appear on a screen if it were a movie? Describe it as you want to see it on the screen.
3. Listen to an auditory event or experience that involves more than one type of sound, namely, voice, sound effects, and, if possible, **music**—a restaurant **scene**, for example, or a **scene** in nature. Write an audio-only **script** using the terminology you learned in this chapter. You can add your own music to your scene.
4. Write a **scene** that comes from your imagination, describing both visual and audio elements. Don't be concerned about format. Just confront the problem of describing what you want to be shot.
5. Take a short **scene** from a short story or novel and adapt it for the screen. How do you want to lay it out on the page? Choose a **master scene script** format or a **dual-column format**. (See the appendix and website.)
6. Choose a short **scene** from a short story or novel and make a **storyboard** for it.

Solving Communication Problems with Visual Media

In the beginning, television was simultaneously a production medium and a live distribution medium. Its production technique was matched to the necessity to broadcast live over the airwaves. After the invention of videotape recording and the evolution of postproduction video editing, television could be produced with single cameras by nonbroadcast companies as well as by the broadcast behemoths. The television signal can be produced outside the studio, recorded, and edited on videotape. We can call this video. Television is now a distribution medium as well as a production medium. Let's not confuse the distribution medium with the production medium. Television programs can be delivered to the end user by broadcast radio signal, by satellite, and by cable. To this now add podcasting via Internet web pages and mobile platforms. Other methods of program distribution are theatrical exhibition in movie theaters, videocassette sales and rentals, and optical disks such as CD-ROMs and DVDs.

A program delivered via a given medium might not be produced in that medium. For example, a feature film, shot on film, even a series shot of film produced mainly for television can also be exhibited in a movie theater and broadcast, or cable-cast, or delivered by satellite transmission or on all of the media mentioned. A television quiz show or a news program would probably be restricted to over-the-air broadcast, cable, and streaming to the web. A documentary could be delivered to you on many of the media mentioned. Multiple-camera studio production, the traditional and original television production technique, is different from single-camera video production, even if the final product is shown on television. The script is a production document, not a distribution document. Therefore, the writer must think in terms of the producing medium, not the distributing medium. Knowing that you can see documentaries on television does not help you write them. Knowing that you can see a feature film on television does not help you write one. Writing for television is different to writing for the big screen. And writing for mobile platforms and websites, we will find out, requires yet another approach.

The logical progression of our learning process is to apply what we know to specific media formats. Many of them have special requirements. Many of them have preferred formats that the industry has adopted. Each type of program has a definable characteristic that we need to learn about and practice writing. Although these formats are all visual media, the writer has to think about them in different ways.

In this section, we will pay close attention to the use of visual media to solve communication problems that are principally informational, promotional, instructional, and persuasive. This includes solutions to both corporate communications needs and commercial messages, as well as factual documentary and educational content.

CHAPTER 5

Ads and PSAs: Copywriting for Visual Media

KEY TERMS

algorithm	hyperlink	shock
Aristotle	infomercial	special effects
audience as a character	minidramas	storyboard
banner ads	miniscripts	strategies
billboards	meta-writing	suspense
click mapping	metonymy	testimonials
copywriting	popups	video news release
digital signage	PSAs	visual metaphor
dual-column format	reason (logos)	visual writing
emotion (pathos)	scriptwriting	voice commentary
ethical values (ethos)	search engines	
humor	sexual innuendo	

Before television, there was radio advertising and film advertising in movie houses. You still see local ads in some movie theaters before the program starts. So the principle of selling time between programming for commercial messages grew up with the visual media. A format that is probably unique to television was developed to deliver short visual commercial messages very efficiently and effectively in breaks between programs. The airtime was sold to advertisers to generate the operating revenue and profit for the television companies. This is now the principal business model for mainstream media that are free to the viewer.

Television provides access to the majority of homes and, therefore, to the largest audience. Before television, few people had dealt with the pressure to communicate product or commercial information in a rapid, attention-getting way that television needs. It was, and still is, very expensive to buy airtime. Because television is the most expensive advertising medium, it has driven the writers and

Doi: 10.1016/B978-0-240-81235-9.00005-5

producers of commercials to refine their techniques so as to deliver a complete message in a short amount of time. The cost of this time far exceeds the production cost of making the message itself.

The short ad has become a kind of twentieth-century art form with a constantly evolving style. It has attracted much writing and directing talent from around the world, drawn partly by the money and partly by the opportunity to graduate to longer forms. Ads are special because they are so short—usually well under a minute. Everyone has seen them, which is not so true for some other formats.

Almost all television viewers have seen public service announcements (**PSAs**), which are messages that are broadcast for the public good. Sponsoring organizations sometimes pay for **PSAs**, but they are usually furnished to broadcasters to fill any unsold time in the commercial breaks. This is one way in which television stations help the community to which they broadcast and fulfill a public service obligation of their Federal Communications Commission (FCC) license to broadcast over public airwaves. Of course, **PSAs** usually run late at night or in other less commercially desirable time slots. Not everyone can write a feature film script, but anyone can write a 30- or 60-second PSA; so it is a good place to start.

COPYWRITING VERSUS SCRIPTWRITING

Let us distinguish between **copywriting** and **scriptwriting**. **Copywriting** includes print and media writing. National advertising campaigns on television are devised and produced by advertising agencies retained by the client company. Learning about this kind of writing and the business of advertising and public relations usually takes place in a specific track and specialized courses in communication studies. Although **visual writing** is involved in some kinds of **copywriting**, there are so many other issues involved in **copywriting** that it is better to leave those dedicated issues aside and deal with **visual writing** that happens to be part of **copywriting**.

However, small markets in the broadcasting world serve local clients who cannot afford an advertising agency. Somebody has to write these ads for the station's clients. It could be a staff member, part of a unit that sells the station's time, or it could be a freelance writer or a local ad agency paid to do this writing work when needed. We need to keep in mind that these kinds of local ads are made on small budgets, sometimes at cost, by the station selling the airtime because their profit comes from selling that airtime. They often have spare production capacity—a studio, cameras, a camera crew, and an editing facility. This means that the ad must be written for that budget range without slick effects or expensive graphics, without travel to expensive locations, and without expensive talent. It brings us back to the perennial challenge that every scriptwriter faces: to write creatively and invent original visuals within a tight budget framework. The same holds true for local **PSAs**, sponsored by organizations with a limited budget to spend on production.

PSAs offer an excellent training ground for student scriptwriters. They are short and complete **mini scripts**. They require all the disciplines of **scriptwriting**. You can easily settle on a public service issue such as smoking, domestic violence, education, drugs, or drinking and driving. You know the issues. You can test-drive your creative imagination. If you are enrolled in a related production course, you might be able to make your PSA into video. You can also take a familiar product and try to devise a TV spot for it. However, a lot of ads rely on specialized production companies to get pack shots or create computer-generated effects that might be difficult to duplicate in a college production setup. Another good exercise is to write and produce an anti-ad. You satirize and expose the false logic of many ads exposing the shallow strategy of communication. A good one running at the moment takes the message of the coal industry that it has enough energy to power America for years to come, generating well-paying jobs and alluding to a new clean coal technology. The anti-ad exposes the complete absence of fact and logic in the ad. A presenter invites you to look at the new clean coal technology. You go through a door to an empty landscape. There is no clean coal technology (www.thisisreality.org). Another one has a family using a can of clean coal *clean* to create a cleaner atmosphere in the home. The black dust coming from the spray can of *clean* has them coughing. The presenter exposes the patent deception in the idea of clean coal—an oxymoron. What we are learning here as writers also enhances our media literacy.

CLIENT NEEDS AND PRIORITIES

The PSA and the TV ad are works commissioned by a client. The client needs a solution to a communication problem that the writer must provide. We alluded to this discipline of the professional writer in Chapters 2 and 3. You write for someone who represents the interests of an organization or a corporation. Later we will look more closely at another kind of **script writing** for a producer of entertainment films or programs. The entertainment script is different from commissioned works because neither the producer nor the writer can know for sure what a good script is until it is produced, shown to an audience, and validated by box office or audience ratings. Commissioned programming doesn't have an audience measurement expressed in terms of box office revenue. Successful communication can only be measured by quantifying audience responses as changes in sales or behavior.

Advertisers expect to measure the effect of an ad in increased sales. Otherwise, there is no business sense in spending money on it. A PSA often aims to change people's behavior. It is much more difficult to garner information that positively proves the effectiveness of the PSA. A good example would be the Ad Council's campaign launched in 1983 against drinking and driving and the slogan "Friends Don't Let Friends Drive Drunk," sponsored by the U.S. Department of Transportation/National Highway Traffic Safety Administration. Changes in behavior are much more difficult to achieve than changes in the buying choices of the public. However, by 1998—15 years later—alcohol-related fatalities had declined to a historic low.

Writing for clients is often challenging and exciting precisely because you are given a problem, know the desired result, and have to devise a solution. The seven-step method explained in Chapter 2 is an excellent way to approach this challenge. The process of analysis is really important for writing PSAs. Although you do not now have a client, you must practice **script writing** as if you had a client to satisfy. Your creative ideas must work for a client. One of the constraints of this kind of writing is that the client fixes the length. Because the resulting product is transmitted in commercial breaks, its length must be exact to the second, as that is how airtime is bought and sold.

THE 20-, 30-, AND 60-SECOND MINISCRIPTS

Ads in the form of 20- or 30-second **miniscripts** are almost a new art form. They are a popular art form born of the television age and the need to compress visual messages into very short, very expensive time slots. The style and tempo of these ads continues to evolve at a furious rate. The style of camera work, directing, and editing is quite specialized. Some companies produce nothing but TV commercials, just as some directors spend their whole careers making these minimovies. From their ranks have come a number of feature film directors such as Ridley Scott, Hugh Hudson, and Alan Parker.

Some TV commercials for national campaigns of major brands, based on millions of dollars worth of airtime, have very high budgets. With bigger budgets than half-hour documentaries and budgets as big as a half-hour television episode, these productions are made on 35-mm film with production crews that sometimes rival those for a small feature film. The local market spot for a car dealer or furniture store, however, is often low budget. Clearly the national campaigns are developed by advertising agencies whose copywriters develop the ads in collaboration with creative directors, art directors, and account executives. The copywriter is not a full range scriptwriter and also usually has to write print media ads. Although this book primarily serves the interests of scriptwriters, the visual thinking that underlies billboards and transport ads relates to both **copywriting** and **scriptwriting**.

VISUAL WRITING

We think of writing as words forming an exposition, but media writing, particularly television advertising, needs a visual idea. This is another layer of writing. The visual idea is what we refer to as **meta-writing** in earlier chapters. There is a difference between visual **meta-writing** and the writing found on a page of script for a visual medium, whether in the minidrama of an ad or a full-length feature film. The scene descriptions contribute to a visual idea that transcends the screen moment and rests on many of those moments, hence **meta-writing**. It is an idea that informs and governs the written detail of the script. The dialogue, which is an integral part of the writing and exposition, is not itself **visual writing** but a necessary component of it. Radio ads need dialogue writing but not a visual idea. So visual writing is the idea as well as the description of specific images or shots. It needs what we will call a **visual metaphor**. Let's look at an example.

A few years ago, an ad by AOL tried to explain spam by comparing two sandwiches, one protected from spam and the other one ruined by ketchup, mayonnaise, and relish smothering it. That kind of organizing **visual metaphor** is often the key to successful visual communication.

A current ad that is an even purer form of **visual metaphor** underlies a series of ads for Red Bull. We see a propeller-driven aircraft flying an air rodeo obstacle course in Monument Valley in the Arizona desert and performing outrageous maneuvers ending with a vertical stall, allowing the plane to fall out of the sky into a dive. We get a closeup of the pilot happy and high. His line is "Welcome to my world." There is no voice-over, no computer graphics or text on screen, and no identification of the product as a drink. Red Bull sponsors air races and rodeos all over the world. So what is the visual communication here? As with many other Red Bull ads featuring extreme sports, there is a **visual metaphor** at work—the images of extreme sports represent skill, daring, and exceptional performance. The audience sees this, perceives this, and without the benefit of words makes the connection between the high achievers and the qualities and benefits of this energy drink—the world of Red Bull. The stunt flyer is the product or the implied effect of the product. The audience extrapolates the meaning by a mental interpretation through the visual not the auditory cortex. So **visual metaphor** can make an image meaningful in the moment, but **visual metaphor** is also the organizing metaphor underlying narrative structures. This metaphorical thinking in images is **meta-writing**. Together they constitute **visual writing**.

In an ad for Doritos, a young woman hails a taxi and while munching Doritos looks at another car. The scene inside lights up and changes color; everywhere she looks there is a Doritos transformation. It ends with her stepping out of the taxi and striding past the bouncer into a chic club. Again, there are no words, and there is no text except for the name of the product. The **script writer** is trying to find a **visual metaphor** for taste. What we are seeing is an objective correlative—what used to be a part of a literary critical theory advanced by T. S. Eliot. An objective correlative meant that an image in all its complexity stands for a meaning that is understood visually whether in poetry or a TV commercial. The transfer of meaning is hard to achieve, but when it works it is stunning and engages the audience. Apple's billboard campaign for Mac discussed later in the chapter also illustrates **visual metaphor**.

DEVICES TO CAPTURE AUDIENCE ATTENTION

Most of you have engaged in the subtle war between the viewer and the television advertiser. Hands up everyone who has hit the mute button during the ads, or gone to the bathroom, or gone to the fridge, or made a telephone call during the commercial break! This nullifies the advertiser's effort and expense. Sometimes, either by accident or by choice, we find TV commercials entertaining or fun to watch. The challenge is clear. The advertiser has a lot of resistance to overcome and must **capture audience attention**. Now you are on the other side of the box. You have to be creative and capture the audience's attention in spite of itself so that it pays attention to your message. Your device has to work for others. Measured by your own viewing behavior, no audience will give you any quarter. You live or die in seconds.

What are some of the ways you have noticed **script writers** of these **miniscripts** hooking the audience so that it will pay attention to the message? You can recognize definite **strategies** such as **humor, shock, suspense, minidramas, testimonials**, special graphic effects, music, and, of course, **sexual innuendo**. These **strategies** are more elaborately developed in commercial advertising because for-profit companies have the dollars to spend on high-end production values. **PSAs** cannot command the same resources. They are made on lower budgets or created through the pro bono work of advertising agencies and production personnel. Working with a low budget is a creative challenge. Production dollars don't automatically buy creative and effective communication. Some of the most ingenious ads and PSAs are both cheap and effective.

Consider how a PSA about a public issue such as gambling works. In this case, the Massachusetts Council on Compulsive Gambling needs to communicate to a population that suffers the destructive consequences of this kind of addictive behavior. How do you solve the communication problem? Let's apply the` seven-step method we learned in Chapter 2. This is the equivalent of a **copy platform** in the advertising world. From account executive to creative director to copywriter and art department—each party involved in creating the PSA needs to have a common understanding written down that defines the communication problem. Agencies develop their own ways of essentially defining the communication problem by identifying the product, the medium, the product's benefits and selling points, and the creative strategy. Our approach is more thorough and more universal in its potential application because not limited to advertising.

CASE HISTORY: GAMBLING PSA

Define the Communication Problem

The population of compulsive gamblers includes gamblers who are isolated by their problem and do not see that they are not alone. They do not fully comprehend the consequences of their addiction or are unable to do anything about it. The Massachusetts Council on Compulsive Gambling does not have a handy database of compulsive gamblers and cannot easily reach isolated individuals who need help to tell them about a confidential help line. The council wants to reach out to a hidden population.

Define the Objective

The gambling PSA alerts compulsive gamblers and those who know them to the existence of their addictive behavior and communicates an 800 number to call for help. An informational goal includes letting gamblers know that gambling is a common social problem. A motivational objective is to get gamblers to think about their problem and move them closer to changing their behavior. The highest goal is a behavioral objective: Gamblers will stop gambling, or they will at least call the 800 number.

Define the Target Audience

The *target audience* demographic is difficult because it cuts across age, gender, and social class. The audience has to be identified by a behavior pattern. Many gamblers, like alcoholics, don't want to acknowledge their problem. The psychographic of the audience is probably resistant. Many in this audience will have ways of dismissing the message, believing they have everything under control.

Define the Strategy

The audience has to recognize its problem in the powerful images shown in the PSA. The PSA must get their attention and get to their hidden thoughts and awaken a secret wish that all those losses due to gambling could be reversed, undone, or at least stopped. We use a strongly visual device that is emotional rather than logical in effect because compulsive gambling is an emotional weakness, not a logical choice. We show acts of gambling as if time were running backwards by running the video backwards.

Define the Content

Recognizable scenes of gambling dominate the 30-second PSA (Figure 5.1). A montage is shown of close-up shots of rolling dice, cards being shuffled and dealt, scratch card numbers being revealed but in reverse. This is accompanied by a voice-over (Figure 5.2).

Define the Medium

This PSA is uniquely conceived for a visual medium because its essential visual idea is impossible in any other medium. Time runs backwards when video plays in reverse, suggesting that the addiction can be undone. This is an effect unique to the moving picture medium and video in particular. Television lends itself to emotional appeal and motivational messages.

DEFINE THE CREATIVE IDEA OR CONCEPT

The effective creative concept is to use a strongly visual device to make the emotional connection to the audience by turning back the clock. Footage of gambling action is run backwards while a voice-over articulates the wish that time could be turned back and losses undone. The visual effect of seeing the fantasy realized compels attention. Again, this device of reversing time and showing action undoing itself is a visual effect unique to the medium. The voice-over drives home the message of how these images relate to the buried wish to escape compulsive gambling. The message is, you are not alone; more than 2 million Americans are in the same boat. There is an 800 number help line to call. We finish with an invitation to call and talk.

You see that the seven-step approach breaks down the problem and identifies the solution. You can read the script and see the PSA as it was produced on the accompanying website.

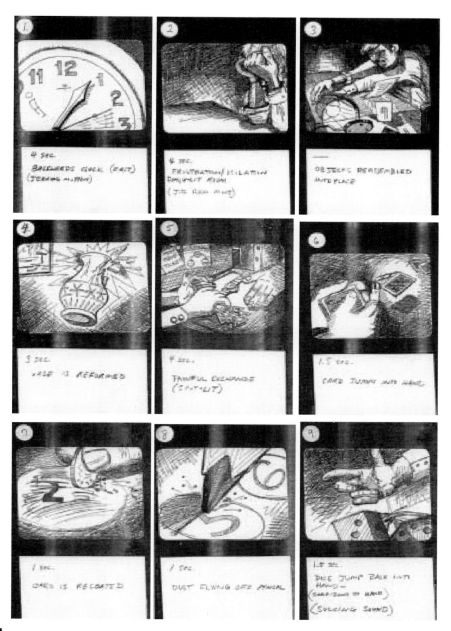

FIGURE 5.1

Storyboard for "Turning Back the Clock," a PSA on gambling sponsored by the Massachusetts Council on Compulsive Gambling.
(Storyboard by permission of Pontes/Buckley Advertising.)

MASSACHUSETTS COUNCIL ON COMPULSIVE GAMBLING

Turning Back the Clock (30 second TV Spot)
Written by Jerold Gelfand

Note: All action takes place in reverse. In addition voice-overs alternation male and female voice (possibly overlapping) with the final words "my life" simultaneously spoken (staggered) by several of the characters.

VIDEO	AUDIO
CUTAWAY A clock going backwards in fast motion with an optical jerking effect	VO: I want to go back to a time when life had promise . . .
INT. HOME OFFICE-NIGHT Tight shot of man at home office desk full of papers, envelopes, bills, booklets as well as a light and a drink. With pen in hand, he slams both hands down and sweeps the contents of desk onto the floor then clutches his hands to his forehead cradling his head in pain. 4 seconds	VO: . . . to a time when giving up wasn't an option to a time before running away seemed to be the only answer
INT. PAWNSHOP-DAY Tight shot at pawnshop counter where customer is giving up a watch (with clasp) for cash. 4 seconds	VO: . . . and before family heirlooms were sold for cash.
MONTAGE Gambling situations shown backwards (i.e., tights shots of cards being undealt, dice jumping back into person's hand, person unfilling-in lottery ticket numbers, person unscratching scratch ticket. FADE TO BLACK 5 seconds	VO: . . . back to a time when gambling didn't control my life. SFX crowd noises then "sucking" sound on fade to black.
FADE IN TEXT Over two million Americans suffer with problem gambling. 3 seconds	VO: Do you need help turning your life around?
FADE IN TEXT You're not alone! 2 seconds	VO: Call us and let's talk about it.
FADE IN TEXT Massachusetts Council on Compulsive Gambling 1 800 426-1234 We're in the Yellow Pages	

FIGURE 5.2

Script for "Turning Back the Clock." (Reproduced by permission Pontes Buckley Advertising.)

Client: The New England Home for Little Wanderers
Agency: Boston ITVA PSA Committee
Title : Family Portrait
Medium: 30 second television spot

VIDEO	AUDIO
The visual look is cold, monochromatic blue.	(MUSIC-increasing tension.) (SFX-The pulse of a racing heart.)
FADE UP ON . . . EXT. ALLEY. DAY. (4 seconds)An urban alley in a poor part of town. Garbage and debris litter the ground.	(Over this sound, we hear a series of DESPERATE VOICES.)
From a low angle, we look up at a tough,angry thirteen-year-old BOY. A CIGARETTE is jammed into the corner of his mouth. He walks through the alley with anger and attitude, kicking at the trash and smashing his book bag against the wall.	WOMAN'S VOICE (VO) (angry, frustrated, desperate, rising in pitch, losing control) (slight echo) "The school called again. What am I going to do with you?!"
The image in the alley is interrupted by a FLASH CUT (1 second)(Full color.) A happy family PORTRAIT. A single mother and the thirteen-year-old boy. He's dressed neatly in a tie. A jagged CRACK slices across the glass.	(SFX-Glass cracking.) (1 second)
CUT TO . . . INT. ROOM. NIGHT. (4 seconds) A young BOY, six or seven, huddles against a wall, terror and pain in his eyes. Behind him, we see the SILHOUETTES of a man hitting a woman.	(SFX-Woman crying. Struggling. Bottle breaking.) FATHER'S VOICE (VO)(angry, drunk, slurred speech)(SFX-SLAP.) "Don't you ever turn away (SLAP) from me when I'm talking!" (SLAP)
FLASH CUT (1 second) The family PORTRAIT. Father, mother, sister, and the young boy. A jagged CRACK slices across the glass.	(SFX-Glass cracking.)

FIGURE 5.3

Script for "Family Portrait," a PSA for the New England Home for Little Wanderers.

CUT TO . . .
EXT. ALLEY. NIGHT.
(4 seconds) A young GIRL,
eight or nine.Tight on her
face. She cringes at her
disturbing memories. We
move in closer and closer
until all we see are her
haunted, tear-stained
eyes.

YOUNG GIRL'S VOICE(VO)
(pleading) (slight echo)
"Please don't. Please
don't touch me there.
Daddy, I'm scared."

FAMILY PORTRAIT
The young girl in happier
times with her mother and
father. As if struck from
behind, the family
portrait SHATTERS into a
million pieces.

(MUSIC stops and is
replaced by the sound of
shattering glass.)

Jagged pieces of the
portrait explode toward
the camera in slow motion.

NARRATOR (VO)
For some children-and some
families-life is a
shatteringexperience.
(MUSIC-brighter, hopeful)

(FULL COLOR)
As the shattered pieces of
the family portrait float
toward us, we DISSOLVE to
the LOGO-
    **The New England Home
for Little Wanderers**

NARRATOR (VO)
We help put the pieces
together again.

DISSOLVE to the phone
number-
1-888-The Home over a soft
focus background of rich,
spring time, green grass
and deep blue sky.

NARRATOR (VO)
To find out how you can
help, call 1-888-The Home.

In the background behind
the phone number, we see a
tiny CHILD'S HAND reach up
into the frame. A large
MAN'S HAND reaches down
and holds it tenderly.
Fade up the tag line-
    **Children Families
    Futures**

For people who really need
a helping hand.

FADE TO BLACK

FADE OUT MUSIC

FIGURE 5.3
(Continued) (Reproduced courtesy of Peter Cutler.)

MORE ON ADS AND PSAs

In the short form of the television commercial, visual communication is critical. It enables a great many ideas to be compressed into seconds. Doing this requires visual thinking and **visual writing**. A PSA produced for the New England Home for Little Wanderers (Figure 5.3) puts a 30-second story together that has to convey a dysfunctional home and domestic abuse. The **visual metaphor**, which also works for the sound track, is breaking glass. The shattering of a child's life, his family, and his future is captured by a single image.

Another excellent example is the corporate TV spot for First Union, subsequently taken over by another bank (see the website). Let's look at the context. Banking is regulated by state and federal laws and agencies. Formerly, banks were not allowed to have interstate branches, could not sell insurance, could not be stockbrokers, could not be merchant bankers, could not run mutual funds, and so on. Now banks can combine financial services in these different areas and compete with other financial institutions. This deregulation has led to mergers and fundamental changes in the banking industry. The communication problem is that most people don't know how to tell one bank from another and don't understand the changes that are taking place in the financial world. Explaining financial matters to the consumer is difficult because most people are confused by financial products and intimidated by financial institutions. Companies large and small, using different institutions for different financial services, find themselves having to rethink their relationships and having to use new financial products such as derivatives to manage risk or so-called junk bonds to raise capital.

The objective of the First Union commercial is to get consumers and potential customers to grasp the change and see First Union as an island of security in a dangerous world and the solution to their problems—one-stop shopping for all of their financial needs. The strategy is to show the financial world as a surrealistic nightmare, then to confront the problem, and then to have First Union provide the solution. The metaphor chosen is that First Union is a mountain. This visual image is backed up by the voice-over, which in a series of ads ends with a variation on the statement "… come to the mountain called First Union. Or if you prefer, the mountain will come to you."

It is axiomatic that the impact of the message here must be visual, not verbal, in essence. To do this requires images at the cutting edge, compositing cinematography, alpha channel effects, and computer-generated images that capture the audience's attention and set up and condense the message. In each of the ads, there is a visual narrative that makes sense on its own but is complemented by the verbal narrative, which functions on another level. The visual narrative is broadly emotional in impact. The verbal narrative is broadly rational in impact. Scripts of this kind almost always have to be storyboarded. Look at **storyboards** and view the video results for two First Union ads on the website.

For example, the **visual metaphor** of survival in shark-infested waters compels attention. The dorsal fin cuts through water with the financial wreckage of dollar bills and financial paper floating on it. The water is the runoff from a storm—a storm sewer that floods corporate boardrooms. The **storyboard** is 19 pages long for a 30-second commercial. With two or three key frames per page, the pace of visual flow is pushed to the limit. In contrast, the voice-over is measured and minimalist: "In the financial world … the one requirement … for long-term survival … is to keep on the move. It is not a world for the hesitant or the timid."

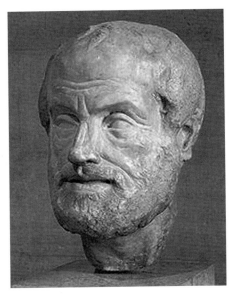

FIGURE 5.4
Head of Aristotle, Louvre.

What more effective way to suggest corporate merger than to show two skyscrapers crashing together or whole buildings being moved on huge caterpillar tracks? Such a **visual metaphor** exploits cutting-edge **computer imaging** techniques. A scriptwriter could not put the image down on the page without some understanding of the techniques that are available. As recently as the 1990s, the technology probably did not exist to make this TV commercial. It is extremely difficult to tell how these state-of-the-art TV commercials were made. **Visual writing** creates content that flows from contemporary production techniques. Hence, visual writers must understand the repertoire of techniques available to the producer. Compositing 3-D animation, graphics, and live action take the writer to the limits of verbal description—hence, the reliance on **storyboards**!

We should step back and reflect on the underlying principles. **Aristotle** (Figure 5.4) mapped out the basic techniques of persuasion in his theory of rhetoric. They involve an appeal to **reason (logos)**, an appeal to **emotion (pathos)**, or an appeal to **ethical values (ethos)**. Although there is a connection between what you learn in basic writing courses about argument and the techniques of visual persuasion, the persuasion is not accomplished by words alone. Images have a vocabulary and a grammar. Many devices and **strategies** are available for hooking audiences and planting the message. It is like the **strategy** of the flower in nature. Show bright colors, give off powerful perfume, and produce sweet nectar. Bees and other insects will be attracted by the color and aromas and feed on the nectar while coating themselves with pollen, which they will carry to the next flower so as to fertilize the plant. The clever message maker creates nectar or seductive qualities that attract the viewer who carries away the message whether he likes it or not, just as the bee carries the pollen away.

What are some of these devices? What follows is an informal **survey of strategies** of exposition that a scriptwriter can use to communicate in the television medium.

Humor

Most people are attracted by **humor**. If you watch an evening's ads on television, you will find about half of them use some kind of comic device. Either the characters in the ad are funny in their behavior (a man behaves like a dog and his dog like a man, tossing the man treats for clever behavior), or the spoken lines have an amusing or clever turn. Comic conception can be expressed in visual graphics. Cats, dogs, and babies can be made to talk. E-trade has a baby in a high chair talking about stock strategies in an adult voice. It shocks and is funny at the same time and perhaps suggests that trading stocks with E-Trade is child's play. Animation can create cute M&M characters or the Pillsbury chef. Morphing can change the expression of people's faces or distort them for effect. Arms can be lengthened to score amazing slam-dunks. Much of the humor we see is a form of exaggeration. Slapstick from silent film days continues to work in ads, such as dogs running away with toilet paper or physical struggles with equipment or materials. Dogs may behave like human beings or speak their thoughts, such as the dog requesting "bacon—want bacon" for Begging Strips. A pampered dog rides in a chauffeured Rolls Royce for Cottonelle toilet paper. An ad for Enzyte, a male enhancement product, shows an always grinning dufus, Bob, who is the envy of other men for the attention that he gets from women, his prowess at golf, and you name it. In the Santa Claus scene, he has women lining up to sit on his lap to ask for their Christmas present—the gift that keeps on giving. This approach contrasts with the self-conscious Viagra, Cialis, and other ads. Cialis is particularly confusing because it shows a pair of matching his and hers bathtubs on a rock overlooking the ocean. They are holding hands. As a **visual metaphor**, it is very confusing. Is this pill to get you to have baths in separate tubs? You would have thought getting in the same tub would be the beginning of successful sex. So much mocking comment grew up around this ad on the internet including satirical take-offs on YouTube that Cialis now tries to address this misleading image by a rationalization in more recent ads about the couple being able to choose when to get out of the twin tubs.

Using **humor** in an ad carries a risk. The risk is not being funny enough for your audience. Bad jokes can be a turn-off. Many corporate clients are nervous about **humor** as a device because they worry that their company or their product might not be taken seriously. Nevertheless, **humor** is an effective way to disarm hostility and skepticism in a target audience. It appeals to both **emotion** and **logic**. Capital One has a campaign built around the punch line, "What's in your wallet?" Improbable situations involve a gang of Vikings acting like gangbusters in department stores and gas stations, smashing things and behaving like, well, marauding Vikings who can't get to you because you have the Capital One credit card in your wallet. Sprint has a crowd of network users, all available on your Sprint network, that follows you around. The abstract idea of a network is made concrete and funny by seeing all the people on it. The come-on to look and listen is the **humor**. Fun relieves tedium. Jokes or gags often work on a logical principle by challenging that same **logic**. If you can get the audience to smile, they will probably listen to your message.

Mac and PC face off as two competing operating systems represented by two styles of nerd, cool and uncool. Geico has adopted a tiny green lizard as a presenter for its auto insurance products. The voice of the lizard is a London cockney who even uses English colloquialisms such as "free pie and chips," obscure to most Americans who do not know what this means (a greasy meat pie with French fries) or understand the accent or the other quirky phrases. There are even obscure references to the English television naturalist Sir David Attenborough, who plays cat and mouse trying to observe the gecko. The Geico gecko has become viral. In effect, the talking lizard is also a kind of **shock** device. You don't expect lizards to talk, and you particularly don't expect them to talk cockney.

Shock

Shocking an audience is a way of getting its attention. **Shock** can take many forms. It can be violent, such as explosions. It can be funny like talking geckos, or talking dogs, or the E-trade baby in the high chair who talks finance with the voice and knowledge of an adult dubbed over baby body language. Whatever you do to **shock**, you have to follow your own act. You have to use the attention you get to good effect. Many people are good at getting attention but not so good at holding it. Consider streakers at games. Taking your clothes off and running out into the middle of the field pursued by police officers and officials will get the attention of the whole stadium, but then what? You can be outrageous, surprise the audience, or do something unexpected, but if all the audience remembers is the device and not the message, you have failed. It is easy to **shock** but hard to fold it into an effective message.

Suspense

Suspense offers a different way of getting an audience's attention. Shocking images often lead into **suspense**. What's going to happen to the truck attached to the bungee cord falling off a bridge? Comic **suspense** works as well as a balancing act, juggling or a character in a predicament. **Suspense** means that the device makes the audience hold its breath until it knows the outcome. **Suspense**, like **shock**, is easy to start and hard to finish. The revelation at the end must justify the wait. We all experience feeling cheated by this plot device in certain movies of suspense that short-change the audience in the outcome. AT&T has a pair of lovers exchanging pictures on a cell phone. His final picture is of him in the same place she is, and he has found her on a park bench. There is a bit of **suspense** about where we are going with these characters; there is also some **humor** or witty exploitation of the picture-capturing and messaging capability of cell phones. **Suspense** often involves drama.

Drama

Can you tell a story in 20 seconds? Television commercials have got it down to an art. Quick cuts minimize the visual information and allow **minidramas**, mini–love stories, and miniplots to unfold. Ads for Brink's Home Security show a woman at home alone who gets off the phone as we see two burglars peeping through the window. She puts on her ear phones to listen to music while working out on the treadmill. The burglars break in; the alarm goes off; the woman is frightened; the phone rings because Brink's is monitoring the alarm. She picks up the phone and gets the reassurance that a Brink's agent is radioed to go to her aid even though the burglars fled, scared off by the alarm. So this is a story told in the form of a **minidrama** that illustrates the role and value of the product. These dramas can become little miniseries so that audiences become intrigued about the next episode. The Geico commercials, both of the lizard and the cavemen, create serial dimensions that the audience understands. Meanwhile, their message gets exposure. A credit card gets a character out of a scrape, like in an Indiana Jones adventure. Someone has a splitting headache or a migraine. An important life event, such as a key assignment at work, or a wedding, or a date is barely manageable. A friend urges the person to take the brand name painkiller. The crisis is averted, and it's smiles all round. The **strategy** is to mime little dramas typical of life and organize a happy ending dependent on use of the product.

Kids

Children, babies, and animals are always good for **pathos**. People respond to cute kids and cute animals. Temporarily, they stop using their brains and respond emotionally. Children aren't only used for breakfast cereal. As discussed earlier, E-Trade gets your attention with a child in a highchair who discusses investing in an adult voice dubbed over the child's mouth movements. Michelin achieved one of the cleverest and most effective uses of a baby ever in a television commercial. On screen are four tread marks from Michelin tires on a flat color background. The commentary makes the point that the main safety features of any car are the four points of contact with the road: "There's a lot riding on your tires." There is a match dissolve to a baby sitting on the ground in the middle. Viewers are forced to use visual logic to put together two ideas. You want to protect the most vulnerable passenger any of us will carry—a helpless baby. This is the advertising equivalent of the car sticker–Baby on board. The tire tread of your four wheels is your only contact with the road in all emergency situations. Your choice of tires is a factor in that safety. The sell is just the brand name on screen. The visual logic goes something like this: (vulnerable baby, standing for our indisputable wish for safety) + (choice of tire is your choice of tread contact with the road) = (brand name Michelin). It is elegant, simple, and brilliant as a piece of visual communication. A variation was to put a baby inside a Michelin tire smiling and gurgling happily. Again, the economy of the visual imagery forces the audience to understand the message through visual **logic**. This is a picture truly worth a thousand words. Effective visual imagery works through nonverbal communication. Michelin's ad is **meta-writing** at its best resulting in stunning **visual metaphor**. Simplicity is also a virtue in Michelin's highly creative and inexpensive ad. Such visual writing is not limited to advertising. It is essential to powerful dramatic writing for the screen.

Testimonial

There are two types of **testimonials: real and fake**. Another way to categorize them would be to contrast a celebrity **testimonial** with a simulated **testimonial**. If you can find a well-known personality to endorse your product, you get the attention of your audience. The public will give you the time of day because of the famous name. AT&T has a series running for its wireless Internet service that uses star, champion athletes to play a competitive challenge with the AT&T guy; he has wireless Internet, whereas they do not. The celebrities, whether the tennis player Andrew Roddick or the Olympic gold medalist swimmer Michael Phelps, say nothing but look on in dismay as they are put at a huge disadvantage because they do not have the AT&T service. Cosmetics, perfumes, and beauty products often use an actress as a poster girl for their products. Gillette uses Tiger Woods. Sleep Number Bed uses Lindsey Wagner.

Simulated **testimonial** is broadcast on television every day in ads for painkillers and cold remedies. We have become inured to them, but they must work well enough because advertisers keep using them. A white-coated actor playing a doctor, speaking earnestly into camera, affirms the effectiveness of the drug. An anonymous but professional-looking man or woman, usually walking along in a tracking shot and speaking into the camera, tells you sincerely how one painkiller is prescribed by more doctors than any other. The presenter mimics the role of a news reporter, expert, or anchor. Many ads for feminine hygiene products rely on simulated and acted testimonials by a suitably cast representative woman talking about relief from menstrual cramps or migraine headaches.

Real testimonials also have a place in this repertoire of **strategies**. Despite years of feminist revolt, housewives testify that a given laundry detergent washes whiter than another or that a household cleaner cleans "cleaner" or an old mop is rejected by a woman who makes love to her new and better mop. Or submitted to a double-blind test, they just happen to pick the load of laundry that was washed with the advertised product. Some years ago, AT&T ran a series of ads that were based on the real, spontaneous testimonials of people on the street saying that they preferred AT&T long-distance service. As the production company was filming, the lawyers were vetting the content and ruling whether or not the statements could be used. People in the shots used were paid and had to sign a waiver permitting use of the **testimonial**. This last example is an unscripted documentary technique. Most of the others are scripted ideas. Most of these devices can be used in longer corporate videos, as we shall see in the next chapter.

SPECIAL EFFECTS

Today, many of the images we see on screen are computer generated. The 1999 prequel of the *Star Wars* trilogy, *The Phantom Menace*, is rumored to contain at least 80 percent computer-animated images despite the presence of live actors. Industrial Light and Magic, the company founded by George Lucas, has been responsible for many of the extraordinary computer-generated special effects in theatrical films such as *Jurassic Park*. Now there are so many software toolkits on PCs and Macs that can create stunning graphics and animation that contemporary scriptwriters can fantasize scenes almost without inhibition.

A good example is the First Union ads that make skyscrapers merge and collapse, creating a visual metaphor for corporate merger (see the video on the website). The camera wanders in a surrealistic, computer-generated fantasy world, a futuristic urban landscape reminiscent of *Blade Runner* (1982), suggesting the predicament of the consumer trying to deal with the world of financial services. It is a visual statement about the alarming uncertainty of the financial world.

FIGURE 5.5
Schwab: posterizing.

Car ads often need visual metaphors to vaunt the qualities of the car beyond simple transportation. Acura sells the aspiration of the engine. We see a competitive swimmer gulping air cresting through the water and the image morphs into a car and then the engine. A voice-over talks about the breathing engine. Infiniti aerodynamic design is expressed through the image of a competitive diver flying through the air and then entering the water with minimum splash in slow motion. He then morphs into the car breasting the air. Modern computer-generated imagery (CGI) has increased the range of **visual metaphor** because its ideas are purely visual and haves no verbal equivalent. Movies like *Sin City* (2005), *300* (2006), *A Scanner Darkly* (2006), *Watchmen* (2009), and the 3-D *Beowulf* (2007) have changed the style and range of live-action visuals. Schwab has developed a line of ads in which live-action shots are treated with video special effects tools like rotoscoping and posterizing to make them look like animated artwork. In ads, there are also interesting ways of using animated artwork to elaborate an idea, such as the dynamically unfolding line drawings of T. Rowe Price ads explaining world markets. As a rule, these **special effects** are ways of getting attention by challenging visual norms and defying reality. Once again, the device has to serve the message or the audience will remember the effect and not the message.

Sexuality

Sexual innuendo is probably the oldest technique of all. Every new medium has exploited erotic interest, whether it be the early moving image peep shows (Edison's Kinetoscope, then the rival Mutograph), interactive CD-ROMs (*Virtual Valerie*), or the Internet, where so many websites purvey pornography. In the advertising world, sex sells. Is there an ad for perfume or aftershave that doesn't imply that the product will attract the opposite sex like flies? The same goes for most fashion advertising. Beer, alcohol, and soft drinks usually rely on the hoary proposition that consuming them makes you look so cool that members of the opposite sex will fall into your arms. A strong seductive technique of persuasion is the look straight into the lens. Another technique you recognize is the big close-up of lips or the framing of some part of the female body such as looks, smiles, or batting eyelashes. Somebody has to write this stuff into a script. What we see, however, is the finished ad, which has been produced and directed. The director has interpreted the script and talent has interpreted the role, but the intention is clear: to get audience attention by appealing to their sexual interest.

As I'm writing this paragraph, the television is on. An ad comes on for an herbal shampoo. A woman whose car has broken down is stopped at a gas station. She asks the mechanic under the hood where she can freshen up. He throws her a key. In the washroom, she washes her hair (fat chance!). Pack shot! As she washes, she starts to cry, "Yes, yes, yes." Dissolve to brushing out her dry, bouncing hair as she emerges from the restroom. "Yes, yes" becomes louder. The mechanic looks up and bangs his head on the hood. The radiator spurts steam. Get the allusion? She asks if the car is ready. He says it will be a little while longer. Pack shot with a title: Herbal Essence—A totally organic experience. Get the pun? Notice the rip-off of the film *When Harry Met Sally* (1989), in which Meg Ryan simulates an orgasm in a restaurant? A woman in the next booth tells the waitress she wants "to have what she's having." Somebody wrote this ad with the sexual **strategy** in mind. The shampoo confers sexual power on the woman who uses it. Many other ads have followed in the same vein. This tradition has continued for years and traveled around the world. In the French version, a woman leaves a trail of clothes on the floor. We find her in the shower. She applies Herbal Essence and has the climax. A middle-aged couple watches the ad on television. The grandma says she wants the same shampoo as the woman in the ad. The original allusion is still going strong.

A recent ad with Kate Walsh riding in her Cadillac argues that the real question is, when you turn your car on, does it return the favor? Or we find a young man who sprays Axe deodorant or body spray on himself, which brings a thousand young women in red bikinis pounding out of the surf to get him and another few hundred in yellow bikinis rappelling down the cliff above the beach. They converge on him, but we never see the ending, which is left to our imagination. This is relatively tame compared to some of the European scripts for the same product. You can find them on YouTube.

RECRUITING THE AUDIENCE AS A CHARACTER

One common and effective way to use the television medium is recruit the **audience as a character** in the spot. Television and video work well in close-up. When talent looks straight into the lens and addresses the audience, a direct connection to the viewer is made. The artifice of the camera creates a psychological effect that approximates someone speaking to you personally. Many spots are written so that a character speaks confidentially to the audience. It is the exact opposite of the fictional film technique, which depends on the actors never looking into the lens. In fact, the illusion of the film story would be instantly destroyed. Exceptions are certain comedies that deliberately use the technique of an aside to the audience, which derived from the theatrical device of a character speaking to the audience used frequently in Shakespearean and Restoration comedy. Ads frequently use asides and often rely on a to-the-lens address.

WRITING FOR AUDIO AND RADIO

Although the scope of this book signaled by its title identifies **visual writing** as a different and special kind of writing, the visual media are also audio media. The sound track, whether voice, music, or sound effects, is an integral part of the audience's experience. Whereas in dramatic writing, the dialogue of characters recorded as sync sound is taken for granted, in ads and PSAs, voice and words often have a specific value both apart from and complementary to the visuals. Many ads and PSAs have a punch line or a tag line that can stitch the message together such as "Friends don't let friends drive drunk."

Voice commentary that lives on the sound track and is written and recorded separately from any filming demands a consciously different kind of writing. First and foremost, the language and sentence structure must be speakable out loud. The succinct expression of short sentences makes it easier for the audience to follow and condenses the ideas so that the commentary takes less screen time. Because the words have no sync with images, if the words outlive the available images or extend beyond the time value of the images on screen, a commentary-driven piece results, which is driven by relentless and ultimately tedious spoken narrative. The visual narrative gets smothered and suppressed. Voice has to be subordinate to the image; it is complementary, supportive, and highlights and underlines meaning.

We understand more about the role of voice when we contemplate how voice works in the pure audio medium of radio. Radio spots often cram words in a limited time slot by accelerated delivery. Voice in video or film should not compete with picture or substitute for picture. In radio, the sound effects often conjure up visuals or work to draw in the visual imagination. If you hear the sound of a car crash followed by police and ambulance sirens, you have a generic image of a scene. The sound effects have visual correlatives that the audience understands, even if listeners do not visualize concretely. The sound effects are connected to a visual reality. Their value is visual in an audio medium.

INFOMERCIALS

The **infomercial** is a relatively new television format that has grown up with the emergence of cable television channels. It offers another way for a channel to make money. Companies or enterprises pay for the time at a cheaper rate than that which make money for the Cable channels selling spots in programming. You've all seen them. They masquerade as interview or talk shows, in which a guest or guests are talking to a presenter about a product or service. There are real estate schemes, get-rich-quick seminars

("I guarantee you will make money out of my scheme"), exercise devices, cosmetics, diet plans, you name it. They are periodically interrupted with buying breaks in which the 800 number comes on screen with images of the credit cards that can be used to purchase the service or product. Although some of this dialogue can be improvised as in a talk or interview show, the format itself has to be scripted.

VIDEO NEWS RELEASES

The **video news release** is another result of the proliferation of television channels. It is the video equivalent of a press release in print. Companies create a news story related to a product that is professionally produced and distributed free to TV stations in the hope that they will insert it into the news. Many smaller markets are short on material and find that a professionally produced story about a new pharmaceutical drug embedded in a story about scientific research into cancer fits nicely into a science-reporting category. The fact that this particular manufacturer's new drug is featured as part of the story is acceptable if it is not too blatantly promoted. It is not advertising. It is a new form of publicity planted in newslike stories. A lot of this type of writing is given to journalists because it resembles journalistic writing. It mimics the objectivity of the news story and utilizes the same techniques of to-camera presenters and documentary footage.

BILLBOARDS AND TRANSPORTATION ADS

Billboards are a form of visual communication for commercial purposes that has evolved with the increase in consumer ownership of automobiles. Of course, people riding on surface public transportation also see city billboards, as do pedestrians. Large surfaces such as the sides of buildings become canvases for outdoor ads that have developed a style and technique appropriate to the medium. The primary determinant of how a billboard works is its method of delivery. Delivery of the message depends on drive-by duration. You do not see crowds gathering around billboards, as the dominant audience of billboards is the motorist or passenger of a motor vehicle. The sight line from the billboard to the viewer exists for a matter of seconds as the vehicle drives by.

This fundamental context for reading billboards and posters leads to several logical axioms about billboard copywriting:

- The message has to be comprehensible within seconds.
- There has to be a strong visual idea behind the billboard.
- Text takes too long to read and has to be limited to large phrases.
- The visual idea can work independently of text.
- Messages use strategies of **humor** and **shock**, just like TV ads.
- Successful campaigns become series (Got Milk?).

The billboard illustrates very well the difference between informational, motivational, and behavioral objectives. Clearly, information that is mainly text dependent has a limited place. Although behavioral objectives can work and billboards can deliver 800 numbers to act on, the primary objective is going to be motivational. Billboards are interesting examples of visual communication because of the severe constraints imposed on their content, which must be read in an instant. Their message has to achieve an extreme economy in audience capture and communication.

In 1999, the Outdoor Advertising Association of America commissioned a study to measure motorists' response to outdoor advertising using special "ShopperVision" eyeglasses that document the actual seeing experience from a passenger's perspective.[1] The study showed that the following elements are important and register with an audience as follows, in descending order of importance:

- Bright/cheerful colors: 30 percent
- Uniqueness (movement/extensions): 26 percent
- The color yellow: 18 percent
- Catchy/clever/cute/humorous: 14 percent
- Personal relevance: 14 percent
- Familiarity/repeat exposure: 12 percent
- Product illustration: 12 percent

If a campaign deploys more than one medium, like the "Got Milk?" campaign, it allows billboard design to trade on the print ads and exploit the familiarity and repetition. A print ad can use more text because readers can study the page. In the billboard, the image predominates. The milk moustache becomes the main visual idea, coupled with celebrity. So two **strategies** are combined. First, there is repeat exposure across media, which helps. The **humor** is important. All kinds of celebrities are, in a sense, brought down to the level of you and me. The visual makes a great common denominator. The image of the milk moustache makes a wordless statement.

Again, Apple's "Think Different" campaign uses a celebrity value in its print ads and billboards. However, they are not like the "Got Milk?" celebrities because they are, more often than not, historical celebrities. They are creative geniuses, usually unconventional, not necessarily beautiful. Because they did not follow convention or the crowd, they were innovators, inventors, thinkers, scientists, and artists. The visual statement is, "Here is a genius who changed human history." They are not using Macs; indeed, most could not have. The association implies that people like these tend to choose Macs; this is communicated visually. They thought differently. The ad invites you to do the same. Buying a Mac and using a Mac by association links you to genius and originality. This kind of visual elision between thoughts that compresses a syllogism into a single glance has to rank high as visual communication. It is more than just a picture; it is a train of thought. Of course, the text, "Think different," is itself a verbal and grammatical embodiment of the picture. So they are apposite. One is a clue to the other. "Think" is a verb in the imperative mood. Adjectives ("different") do not modify verbs despite the vernacular misuse of the language in phrases such as "I did good." The correct expression would be, "Think differently!" So the deliberate grammatical mistake underlines the message, which expresses the unconventional mind.

Although **visual writing** is generally narrative, this narrative needs key moments and key images that compress the meaning into a single glance. Most good films have such moments. Even corporate communications, as we have seen, depend on this visual poetic device, which is the equivalent of a figure

---

[1] See www.oaaa.org/images/upload/research/200324847362083611150.pdf.

of speech. It is called **metonymy**. Apple's Mac stands for originality, for creators, for those who think differently than the crowd. The **viewer is a character** or a player in the ad. A key component of the ad is the viewer's recognition or the viewer supplying a missing link. It is the visual compression of a statement: if you know who Maria Callas (a famous opera singer and artist) is, you are part of a certain elite. If you recognize Einstein or Bob Dylan, you are part of that elite that thinks "different." That elite uses Macs. It is part of the same world. You could argue that it is the opposite of "Got Milk?" "Think Different" is exclusive; "Got Milk" is inclusive. The one is for the few; the other is for the many.

FIGURE 5.6
(left) *An advertisement from the "Got Milk?" campaign.* (right) *Muhammad Ali in Apple's "Think Different" ad campaign.*

As you drive into or out of Boston on the Mass Pike, you see a number of billboards. The one that most merits our attention was dedicated to gun control. It was not a normal billboard, but the side of a long building. The ad consisted of a statement in large letters, "Bullets Leave Holes." At the end of this phrase, we saw a series of frontal shots of kids. One of them was an outlined blank hole where a child was. The verbal cleverness in the double entendre on "holes" matches the visual image and gives it value. The billboard messages contract and compress verbal and visual meaning once again in apposite ways.

Another example of ingenious visual communication found in downtown Boston concerned an anti-smoking campaign. The billboard was the approximate size of a room with the dimensions marked on the billboard. The text message was "Secondhand smoke spreads like cancer." The double meaning of "spreads" anchors the visual idea that is instantaneously understood—the way cigarette smoke diffuses throughout a room is a potential cause of cancer for nonsmokers in the room. The image is the smoke, which is the cancer spreading. The power of this idea is that the audience fills in the blank billboard with the visual—a room with furniture and a smoke haze. The audience has been co-opted

FIGURE 5.7
Billboard on the Massachusetts Turnpike.

to create its own visual. This is a very effective **strategy** because each viewer has an individual personal image, which is more powerful than a generic image that the advertiser might try to create.

The billboard and signage industry is the domain of the copywriter rather than the **scriptwriter**. The **copywriter** is going to have to work closely with a creative director or a graphic designer so that the very few words allowed on the billboard achieve concision because they complement the visual. The text stripped out would probably mean very little unless it were a company slogan or motto with an independent existence. However, there is little writing that precedes the design in the form of concept or needs analysis because agencies probably use an artist or graphic designer to draw roughs and then pitch the concept verbally at a creative meeting. Once again we see that **meta-writing** or visual thinking underlies the creative idea.

So we see that **visual writing** is critical to an advertising copywriter's arsenal. It applies to transportation posters and to full-page print ads, which often work like posters with a key phrase that unlocks an image. The visual has to be strong to attract the reader flipping through pages of ads to get to the articles in a magazine. This way of constructing messages as a kind of informational and motivational sandwich is very effective and is essentially the same mode of imagination that informs the work of the **scriptwriter**. The kind of writing we are trying to develop—compressed, elided, visual—is common to **copywriters** in an advertising world or **scriptwriters** in a corporate or entertainment world.

ADVERTISING ON THE WORLD WIDE WEB

In 1996, there was little or no **advertising on the Internet**. In 2010, advertising is a problem. There now exists a battery of new ways to reach audiences by inserting messages into web interaction, from animation to **popups**, to **click mapping** that tracks the browser. There is a new form of **digital signage** that puts contextual messages on the desktop of web users, via the Internet Service Provider or their Internet portal, that relate to their browsing choices. Writing web copy has to reflect a new medium and how it functions.

Advertising on the web has many advantages. It is cheap to produce and can be updated quickly and easily compared to print and television. We see **banner ads**, sometimes animated. The online edition of *The Boston Globe* frequently interposes a full-screen ad in front of the reader's chosen **hyperlink**. All web-based ads can get the viewer to respond by providing interactive cues to click on something that is fun, instructive, or logical and that will produce a result, answer a question, or show a product. The links allow the ad to occupy very little real estate on the desktop, but it connects to client web pages where an unlimited amount of detail can satisfy any level of consumer curiosity. The traffic can be measured by clicks and hits on websites, a much more precise measure than ratings on television or circulation of print media. In the latter media you, do not have any measure of how many viewers see or read your ad other than the ratings and audience share. This is a guess, whereas web hits can be counted.

Banner ads condense even further the visual language of ads and **PSAs**. They resemble billboards on line but with the addition of animation. Once they advance beyond plain text and graphics, they begin to call on metaphor which appeals to that faculty of the audience that can engage in visual reasoning. Metaphor is a kind of reasoning. If we say something is a two-edged sword, we mean that it can cut in two ways, one of which may be disadvantageous. CSX has an extensive multimedia campaign to advocate rail freight as an efficient and environmentally friendly mode of transport. The banner shows a landscape with a line of trees in the background. Superimposed on it is the signature outline of the CSX freight car. Inside the freight car graphics is a succession of phrases: 2,000 pounds of freight; 1 gallon of fuel; 423 miles. Then the graphics freight car moves across the banner. The visual argument conveys in seconds that this mode of transportation is green and good for the environment (see website). It has a feature unique to **digital signage**—a **hyperlink** to a website that invites a response with the text button Learn More. Web portals are businesses that need to build significant value for customers. Their objective is to get people in front of their content. To do this, they have to personalize sites, browsers, and portals to flatter the user. **Search engines**, formerly simple utilitarian tools, are evolving so that searching becomes embedded in other activities such as downloading music, viewing pictures, reading articles, and collecting information. The new generation of search engines learns your interests and habits.[2] Association of products and services with personalized **search engines** will provide more efficient advertising. You can see this **strategy** working by using the Google **search engine**. Product placement increasingly provides a click-through link that takes you to a website where you can buy the product. Paid-for click advertising becomes a major source of revenue.

Copywriting for the web has changed so that the advertising is structural and contextual. More important than the text or design of the message is the **algorithm** that tracks the browsing and presents an ad in the context of the web page content. The function of advertising, which is to deliver a message about a product or service to an audience that potentially needs or wants it, is served by delivering the surfer to the relevant site. The message is enacted based on embedded intelligence

---

[2] This is the vision of Jerry Yang, cofounder of Yahoo!, expressed in a television interview with Charlie Rose on PBS television in March 2005.

in the browser gathered from the way you use your browser rather than offered to an audience for response. You don't need to respond to a particular message because your responses, at least your range of responses, are already known. You see ads that correspond to your interests.

As advertising on the Internet increases in quantity and interactive complexity, **copywriters** and creative directors have to comprehend interactivity and conceptualize campaigns that integrate with Internet services and interactive content on websites and interactive entertainment media. **Interactive television** will allow the future viewer to click on items in the picture, which may be put there by product placement, and take the viewer to an online boutique where a purchase can be made. We discuss these methods in Part 4.

FORMATS

Applying **visual writing** techniques to commercial messages involves the whole gamut of devices and **strategies** that are available to the medium of moving pictures, whether video or film. Advertising and promotional budgets often allow writers and producers to exploit all the special effects and technology of the medium. The most adaptable format for the writer is the **dual-column format**. It is much easier to communicate precise, split-second timing of shots, effects, and voice-overs by lining up numbered shots in parallel so that the producer knows exactly what to shoot and the editor knows exactly what to edit. To communicate to clients who may not be able to read the **dual-column format** easily, **storyboards** serve the important function of visualizing the key frames for the client so that the image can be related to voice and effects. The **storyboard**, however, does not describe all of the detail of the shot as well as the **dual-column script** can. Camera movement has to be described, as do transitions and effects. The **dual-column script** is sort of like the architect's blueprint, whereas the **storyboard** is somewhat like the architect's sketch of what a building will look like. The client needs the sketch; the builder needs the blueprint.

CONCLUSION

Ads and PSAs are highly concentrated **miniscripts** that embody many of the techniques of longer form entertainment scripts. They rely on visual communication and require strong **visual writing**. They are an excellent training ground for beginning writers. Many of the techniques discussed in this chapter apply to longer forms of video communication that corporations and organizations need in order to promote, sell, or market products and services. They are also used for training, education, and self-help. The chapters that follow will look at these applications.

It is not difficult to see that many ads and PSAs combine more than one of these **strategies**. You can be sexy and funny. **Special effects** can be a means of creating **humor**. Mix and match! It works. Television is a powerful medium, and it is not surprising that commercial organizations quickly worked out ways, helped by public relations practitioners, of establishing a presence and making use of the power of the medium in ways other than paid television advertising.

Exercises

1. Watch **PSAs** on television and analyze how they work by writing down the seven-step thinking behind them. In other words, reverse engineer the ad.
2. Call up a local advertising agency or a local public service organization and ask what public service announcements the agency is working on and offer to write one.
3. Pick out an advertisement or **PSA** that really holds your attention. Analyze how it works. What is the creative **strategy** that keeps you watching and therefore being exposed to the message?
4. Write a **storyboard** of an existing commercial or **PSA**. Try out the software program Storyboard Artist.
5. Pick one of the strategies or devices described in this chapter and use it to write a TV spot or a **PSA**. For example, use a **shock** effect in a **PSA** on drug or alcohol abuse, use **sexuality** to sell a healthy diet, or use **humor** to promote racial tolerance and diversity tolerance.
6. Write an **infomercial** for the business idea of an on-campus laundry service.
7. Write a **video news** release for a new birth control drug in the context of research into human reproduction.

CHAPTER 6

Corporate Communications: Selling, Telling, Training, and Promoting

KEY TERMS

asynchronous	humor	synchronous
authoring software	interactive multimedia	summative evaluation
business theater	instructional designer	task
case history	interviewing	testimonials
cost benefit	jobs	the story of a day
dramatization	linear	treatment
dual-column format	nonlinear	visual metaphor
educational documentary	narrative argument	visual seduction
focus group	on-camera anchor	voice-overs/voice
formative evaluation	questionnaires	commentary
graphics	show-and-tell	vox pops
how-to-do-it videos	subject matter experts (SMEs)	

Corporations, nonprofit organizations, government departments, and businesses large and small often use a visual medium like video to communicate important information and ideas to both internal and external audiences. Before video, they used film. Corporate use of visual media started early, although infrequently, in the days of silent film. Armour & Company, the Chicago meatpackers, used the Polyscope Company to make a promotional film about their stockyards to counter the negative publicity brought about by Upton Sinclair's novel *The Jungle* (1906), which exposed the less-than-desirable practices of the meatpacking industry.[1]

---

[1] Charles Masser, "The Emergence of Cinema: The American Screen to 1907," in *History of the American Cinema*, vol. 1, ed. Charles Harpole (New York: Charles Scribner's Sons, 1990), p. 476.

Today, making video and television for corporate clients, often called the nonbroadcast industry, is a huge business, larger even than the more visible broadcast television industry. It is hard to see that because of the way television and cable dominate most people's lives. The general public sees very little of the output of the nonbroadcast producers for the simple reason that the target audience for these videos is rarely the general public, and the videos are seldom seen on cable or broadcast networks. You may get to see an industrial or commercial video as a customer of a service or a purchaser of a product. Most people do not know about the vast number of writers, producers, and directors who make their livings creating these videos for corporate clients. Many of these creative talents migrated from the broadcasting and entertainment worlds. Some of them work in both.

The "modern age" of mass communication began in 1924, when sound was linked to pictures for the first "talkie." Though it's not widely known, the first time sound was synchronized with film was for a classic public relations use—a 1924 informational tour of Western Electric's Hawthorn plant, hosted by the company's vice president.[2]

VIDEO VERSUS PRINT MEDIA OR INTERACTIVE MEDIA

The world of corporate communications is dynamic and in a state of constant evolution. Once, 16-mm film was the only production medium for visual communication. In the 1970s, Sony's industrial U-matic videocassette format (1966) was joined by the domestic half-inch formats, of which only JVC's VHS format survives. Video recording and portable video liberated television from the exclusive province of broadcasters and studio production. Location and production costs came within the budget of corporate departments. Then the convergence of video and computers in a digital domain led to a form of production that allowed multiple media to coexist in digital form on a computer hard drive. Then programs could be made that were menu driven and **nonlinear**. **Linear** program content runs from beginning to end in a predetermined order and period of time that the viewer must follow, whereas **nonlinear** media allow random access determined by the user. Video was then subordinated to an **interactive multimedia** world. This **interactive multimedia** experience could be stored on a CD-ROM or DVD and could also exist as a complex cluster of web pages at a site on the World Wide Web.

Finally, we must remember that traditional print media are still valid and unbeatable for certain kinds of communication. A great deal of information is most easily accessed and absorbed by using the old Gutenberg technology. What we have now is a repertoire of communication media and communication methods, each of which has advantages and disadvantages. The choice of medium has to be matched to the communication problem.

VIDEO AS A CORPORATE COMMUNICATIONS TOOL

Although film and video are both **linear** media, there are differences between them. Film is exposed to light and processed in a laboratory and then printed to positive. Its postproduction time is longer

---

[2] See the website of the Media Communication Association International at www.mca-i.org/articles/mediapro.shtml, an organization of media professionals who work in this area.

and less versatile in terms of effects and transitions. Film produces a better quality image, but it needs a special darkened room with a projection booth, a projector, and a projectionist to give an audience the full experience. Modern digital high definition video can match 16-mm quality, and film is no longer in use as a corporate medium. Video production is quicker to produce and thus more responsive to urgent business needs. The final product can be distributed on a familiar VHS cassette, DVD, or streamed over the web. It can be played by anyone on equipment that is found everywhere. The screen size, and, hence, the audience size, is limited, but that has not inhibited its growth and popularity as a medium for corporate communicators. For large audiences, more than one projection screen or more than one monitor can be provided.

Another reason for the success of video is its use of the familiar idiom of television, an idiom that every member of the population understands. Everybody is educated in the language of the television screen from an early age. Therefore, corporate producers can exploit the devices and styles of television programming to get their messages across.

The television screen on which the messages are delivered is an intimate and personal medium because only small groups can view it, sometimes a single individual at a time. Video and television make good use of close-ups and communicate the body language of human expression, particularly the face, very effectively. Hence, video communicates emotion effectively. Emotional themes and concepts work well. Another advantage of video is that you can get instant playback, both when you shoot it and when you view a finished program, merely by rewinding the tape. Now video has incorporated most of the stunning special effects that can be created with graphics tools developed for computers. Both computer-generated graphics and live-action video images can be manipulated electronically in extraordinary ways by postproduction tools that digitize the video image. This contemporary style is well illustrated by the TV spots for the former First Union Bank (see the website).

Corporate video has often innovated beyond broadcast television because corporate producers were free to use new formats and tools initially not admitted to the realm of the broadcast signal by the guardian engineers who ruled NTSC broadcast standards. Corporate producers have always experimented with new devices and formats that would make their work easier, cheaper, or more effective regardless of whether it met broadcast standards. Video can embody film, television, photography, computer graphics, and music. It is a **linear** experience starting at a specific frame and ending after a specific duration of time. This has advantages. We are used to it. So video is versatile and offers a range of narrative techniques and styles that we need to study, master, and learn to write. Its disadvantage today is that it is not interactive and does not allow for user input. Interactive communication and how to write for it is discussed in full in Part 4.

CORPORATE TELEVISION

Many large corporations set up their own closed-circuit television channels. They acquire studios, equipment, crews, and creative staff to produce daily programming, which is distributed by cable or satellite to its branches and offices around the country or around the world. The television medium, originally the exclusive province of public broadcasters with FCC licenses, has escaped and been reinvented in private networks to serve business communication needs. This nonbroadcast world, largely invisible to the general public, constitutes a large industry with a turnover in billions of dollars that employs a large number of professionals, probably more than the broadcast world. Corporate television, although not held to the same technical standards as the public broadcasters, uses much of the same equipment and for the most part is produced to the same standards.

The only reason a company would spend all that money on television or video programming is because it gets value for it. The efficient functioning of a business depends on successful communication, a great deal of which is visual and more effective on television. Television brings the internal corporate audience together. It therefore has an internal public relations potential that is incalculable. Think of the difference between seeing a CEO explaining a takeover crisis compared to reading a memo about it! Think of the advantage of being able to communicate to employees in a visual medium that is understood by all! Product launches, training, company news, and company benefits can all be narrowcast on the corporate TV network. Some international corporations have a business turnover as large as small countries. Many large geographically dispersed corporations, like Fedex, maintain private television networks to communicate with their workforce or sales force. Others have their own production studios and post-production facilities. They are largely self-sufficient producers of their own video needs. As such, they are like a production company within the corporation that employs writers, producers, directors, graphic artists, editors, and the supporting personnel to produce a large number of videos or programs each year. The management decision to invest in the equipment and overhead to produce in-house would only be triggered by a large and ongoing need for visual communication within the company.

Even so, some companies contract outside vendors or video production companies, of which there are many in each major commercial center, to make their videos for them. Some companies do both. They make some productions in-house and contract out others. Many buy services from freelance creative talent such as directors and, in particular, writers. It is probably true to say that most scriptwriters are freelance although there are staff positions within these corporate studios. One way to see the size of the industry that services corporate video production needs is to look at the Yellow Pages for your city under "video producer." You will see that most companies listed, other than the producers of wedding videos, produce commissioned audiovisual work for clients.

TRAINING, INSTRUCTION, AND EDUCATION

Business, government, and the military all have vast training needs. Ever since television escaped from the broadcast television studio when Sony introduced a portable format in the form of (3/4)-inch U-matic cassettes, organizations have seized on video to create standardized training modules. A visual medium lends itself to showing how to do things and to explaining procedures and behavior. In fact, many products are now sold with video manuals as well as printed manuals. Video is an instructional tool for educational and industrial training. Broadcast and cable television abound in how-to-do-it shows about home maintenance, auto maintenance, cooking, gardening, and so on. With the dissemination of the VHS format and the consumer VCR, now superseded by DVD players, either stand alone or as a read/write drive in a computer, many different types of training and how-to-do-it videos are sold or rented to the general public, ranging from aerobic exercise tapes to do-it-yourself videos. Here again is a vast market that needs writers, producers, and directors.

In the 1980s, attempts were made to make videotape **interactive**. The **linear** tape medium did not lend itself easily to this function because the time required to spool backwards and forwards to different sections of the tape took too long. With the advent of laser disks—first the 12-inch format, then the CD-ROM, and now the DVD—a real marriage between computers and audiovisual media became possible. Programs can be designed to be **interactive** so that the user input is made part of the program concept. This **nonlinear interactive** structure lends itself perfectly to training needs. Self-paced learning can accommodate all learners. It allows tracking of performance and effective testing. That same interactivity is now accessible on websites over the Internet. What used to be exclusively **linear** video now becomes a component of multimedia that demands a different kind of conceptualizing and writing. Further discussion of writing for **interactive media** can be found in Part 4.

Finding out whether a writer's idea for a corporate video is right or wrong can be an expensive business. Training and instructional programs are different because the desired end result can be closely defined and then tested or measured. Therefore, the content can be evaluated in a controlled way. Evaluation becomes a crucial part of the writing process. Evaluation comes in two kinds: formative and summative.

Formative Evaluation

Formative evaluation is a process that takes place before committing resources and time to a project. The word "formative" suggests that it is part of the forming or shaping process. There are a number of techniques, both formal and informal, that you can apply to your writing. The most accessible one is to make up a questionnaire and use its answers to guide you to the content of the program. If you want to make a video about parallel parking, you would ask people to reveal what they find difficult about it, what their fears are, how they learned to do it, and what they think would be useful to see in a video.

Summative Evaluation

"Summative" is a word, like "formative," that derives from a Latin root. The word "sum," or "total," is related. The "summation" of arguments at the end of a trial is similarly derived. So we understand that this **summative evaluation** takes place at the end of the process of communication to see whether the message worked as planned. The process tries to verify whether the objectives defined at the outset were met and whether the target audience is effectively receiving the intended message.

Formative and **summative evaluations** work in tandem. What you find out in the first evaluation becomes the basis for the second. Sometimes, they can be used independently and serve a purpose. Normally, though, one leads to the other. If you ask formative questions about parallel parking to define what you would show in your video, you would then want to ask the audience whether they understood how to parallel park after viewing the video. The message sent is not always the message received, hence the elaborate exercise to test whether your intention is working as planned. For a production company and its client, success or failure has commercial consequences. **Formative** and **summative evaluation** is a sort of insurance policy. You might think of a carpentry analogy. You measure your wood before cutting it. You check the result afterwards to see if it is right before assembly. Media communication is an inexact science. Any way of stacking the odds in your favor to achieve a successful result is highly desirable. Numerous techniques have been developed in the advertising and public relations industries to ensure the success of campaigns for specific publics. **Formative** and **summative evaluations** rest on many techniques that work equally well to assess training needs.

FOCUS GROUPS

A **focus group** is a handpicked group of people who represent a cross section of your target audience and who have agreed to participate in the evaluation process. This might involve questionnaires, meetings, and discussions with a view to collecting detailed responses about a product, a service, or the effectiveness of the message. Most **formative** and **summative evaluation** works best with **focus groups**. It is advantageous to measure hypothetical responses and actual responses with the same group of people. It would not be hard to do an evaluation exercise with a **focus group** in a college environment.

QUESTIONNAIRES

Questionnaires can be used on their own without a **focus group** to conduct **formative** or **summative evaluations**. A good questionnaire provides an efficient way to collect information about the audience and its attitudes. In an informal way, every writer asks and answers questions about the target audience. A formal **questionnaire**, however, needs to be designed to elicit specific results and eliminate faulty assumptions. At the high end, this requires training. The use of polls and research into public attitudes on given issues is a specialized field

TYPICAL CORPORATE COMMUNICATION PROBLEMS

To understand the business of corporate media, you need to look at some of the communication problems that corporations and organizations face for which media can become a solution. For example, when I bought an early model cellular phone, Bell Atlantic, then Nynex, now Verizon supplied a video to explain how to use a cellular phone and how their cellular system worked. A professional anchor or presenter talked to camera. Cutaways to close-ups showed how the phone worked. The video answered a number of the questions that come up for a person using such a product for the first time. Most videos of this kind have a **cost benefit**. That is to say, the cost of making the video is compensated by a saving to the company in customer service calls and the employee time and overheads needed to deal with basic questions. In other words, this company anticipated a problem and found a solution by making a video. There are other factors and other benefits. Forestalling customer problems and making the product or service more successful is a strong benefit that is hard to value in dollars and cents. It is worth a lot and justifies the video dollars that a management decides to spend on the communication exercise.

This example shows that there is a rationale behind any video that is commissioned by an organization or corporation. Now corporate marketing and public relations employs **nonlinear** as well as

linear media. Brochures and catalogs are produced on CD-ROMs and DVDs. Product catalogs are searchable databases on a website. So the need to match a solution to a corporate communications problem extends beyond plain "vanilla" video.

Production companies have to be more versatile than they used to be. The range of media solutions has increased, and video has become a component of fixed **interactive media** and websites. Corporations and organizations have multiple types of communication problems that need solutions. Solving those problems is a creative service that production companies provide. They also offer production and postproduction services. They deliver a finished product ready for distribution. Small business-card size CDs can hold a promotional brochure for products and services. Video is primarily motivational rather than informational, often a component of fixed interactive and online media. The range of media solutions has expanded so that step 6 of the seven-step method that queries what medium is appropriate and why becomes more urgent and a key part of developing a creative concept.

In this process, the scriptwriter has an important role. You need to understand that role, and you need to see how to develop your thinking and writing skills to make a career in that field. Breaking into that market is easier than breaking into the entertainment market, which is smaller and highly competitive. It is easier to sell your talent to write a $1500 script for which the client or corporate producer is taking a small risk than to persuade a TV producer that you can write a series or even an episode of a series, let alone a feature film for which budgets run into tens of millions of dollars. Let it be said, though, that you should not limit yourself or your ambitions, and that you can migrate from one market to another and back again.

To understand the kind of problem that writers are given in the corporate market and for which they have to devise solutions, you have to start thinking from the clients' point of view. You have to see their needs, their predicaments, and, sometimes, their shortsightedness about their own communication problems. Corporate video is not about self-expression, or saying what you want to say. It is about expressing what others want to say. Sometimes they don't know what to say or how to say it. Selling your visual writing talent to help them find a solution can be creatively demanding and personally satisfying, as well as financially rewarding. It does mean, however, that you won't necessarily deal with themes or topics that you would freely choose to write about.

Because the client determines the subject matter and the message, the writer often has to learn about fields of activity, manufacturing processes, or technical information that are totally new. This makes the field intellectually exciting and challenging. You never know what is going to be thrown at you. You learn about all sorts of things that you would otherwise never come across. That is why a good general education, an understanding of science and history together with strong verbal and analytical skills, is important. Every company's business has unique products or special preoccupations that you have to assimilate and communicate to an audience. You have to read and digest manuals and brochures and do background research, not to mention absorb verbal input from managers, **subject matter experts (SMEs)**, and employees on site visits. You are often entrusted with confidential or sensitive commercial information. You need to get up to speed quickly and be able to discriminate between essential information and background noise. Corporate scriptwriting demands a creative imagination combined with a realistic understanding of business environments.

Corporate communication problems are never ending. A pharmaceutical company wants to get the attention of cardiologists, so it makes a video about pacemakers and the latest technology instead of trying to hard sell a particular drug. In this way, it can get the attention of its target audience, create an event, and promote the drug indirectly. Shell invents a bitumen compound that won't wear out but is more expensive than traditional road asphalt. It also results in a porous road surface that allows rainwater to drain away, thereby putting a stop to hazardous plumes of spray behind trucks and other vehicles. How can a petroleum company persuade municipal and highway authorities to use the new product when it is more expensive than traditional asphalt surfaces? One effective communication tool is to show how the product works. When trucks pass from a conventional road surface to the patented porous surface, the camera shows how the plume of spray drops instantly. Then there is a story to tell—how the product was invented, case histories, **testimonials**, and benefits. The scriptwriter is the one who has to learn the story and interpret it to the chosen audience.

A department of education wants to ensure safety in school laboratories where Bunsen burners and chemicals pose a hazard. How do you do it? How about getting a known television comedian to dress up as a school kid and pretend to be going through all of the mistakes that schoolchildren go through? It is funny and serious at the same time. You have found a way to reach a young audience and get them to pay attention to a message and absorb safety information. Designing a successful script and seeing it made into a working video is exciting. Getting paid to do it makes it an even greater pleasure. Are you getting interested?

A telecommunications manufacturer supplies state-of-the-art light-wave multiplexers (get your mind around that one) and has to respond to an enhanced delivery and installation timetable imposed by its main customer, who is losing a million dollars a week in revenue because of lack of capacity to handle traffic. You have to communicate a new schedule and plan for a way to deliver and install exchanges and motivate the people involved to achieve the objective. You get a 2-inch-thick manual for technicians to read and have to figure out what it all means, what will make meaningful video, and what information is best left in print form. Maybe this is not much fun, but you are a professional. You can read the manual and filter the information so that you concentrate on the relevant passages. You can think through the communications problem and come up with a solution. The corporate world is willing to pay big bucks for these solutions. Consider these examples:

- An oil company faces perennial safety issues because hydrocarbons are volatile and flammable in both liquid and gaseous form. Every maintenance procedure involves serious hazards because teams with different skills are involved and may not know what the others are doing. A lockout safety procedure is in place that protects the life of each worker, not to mention the physical plant of the refinery or tank farm. When it has been ignored, it has led to loss of life in accidents. How do you get the lifesaving message across? The audience must watch, listen, and learn. Perhaps more important, the audience must change its behavior or put into practice what it learns from your video. You are the ringmaster, the impresario.

- A laboratory department in an oil company needs to show the executive board that its research facility saves its cost many times over because of specific improvements to drilling mud and a process that saves the loss of expensive chemicals in the refining process.

- A national chain of record stores wants to train its personnel in procedures that reduce shoplifting and to make sure that they know how to deal with a shoplifting situation correctly if it occurs.

- A construction company that has built cooling towers for a nuclear power station wants to show its engineering innovations in managing the job with precast concrete sections and coordinating teamwork in erecting the tower. Construction takes longer than 2 years. What makes their engineering different or better than anyone else's? You have to find a **visual metaphor** or way of telling the story that makes the difference.

- The regional government of Midi-Pyrénées in France wants to promote itself as a dynamic region for investment to aerospace and biotechnology companies that can benefit from the existing national research laboratories and research university of Toulouse. You have to find a way to blend history and modernity and weave together a bundle of separate stories.[3]

- A company wants to educate new hires in the corporate jargon that is full of acronyms and abbreviations that are like a foreign language and must be learned by all new hires to understand written and spoken communications.

GETTING BACKGROUND AND PRODUCT KNOWLEDGE

The most important job a writer has to do is to think, not just write. If the right thinking takes place, the right writing will follow. When you write for clients, you have to get inside their business, inside their mentality, and adopt their communication problem. Of course, you bring an outside point of view to their problem, which is one of your strongest points. You see with fresh eyes some salient feature that to them is habituated and sometimes no longer visible.

There are several ways to get background: by reading, visiting places, and talking to people. Reading could start with an encyclopedia and end with a memo. Most clients dump all the literature, manuals, and brochures they can find on you. Usually, there is more than you need. You have to apply a selective filter to it all. You have to formulate in your mind an inclusion/exclusion mechanism, learning to discard the material that is beyond the scope of your communication brief. You also have to measure the depth of knowledge you need about a given detail. You cannot become a cardiologist overnight, or a petroleum chemist, or a telecommunications engineer. You can, on the other hand, think through the audience's need and read intelligently on their behalf.

Another way you can collect information is by visiting the client's place of business, production sites, and sales outlets. This visual input is crucial for most writers. It shows you the most likely locations for action settings. It provides you with visual background and images that help you to write for the camera. Sometimes, it also enables you to see and understand industrial and manufacturing processes or technical problems that remain abstract if all you do is read about them.

[3] *Midi-Pyrénées: Nouveaux Espaces* is represented by video clips on the website.

The last way of collecting information, talking to people, is also indispensable. This could mean talking to your client's managers, employees, or customers. You frequently have meetings with small groups of people called together by your client because they all have expertise, experience, or interest in the subject matter. You have to listen carefully, think quickly, and ask relevant questions. Take names and contact numbers so that you can consult particular people when you are on your own and baffled by a question which one of these people will surely be able to answer. One or more of these people will be **subject matter experts**, often referred to as **SMEs**.

USING SUBJECT MATTER EXPERTS

A **subject matter expert** is someone designated by the client as an authority on a particular topic or subject matter. If a video project involves technical or scientific subject matter, an **SME** is a necessity. If an **SME** is not assigned to the job, you should ask for one or more. Talking to this person is often the breakthrough that you need. A good tactic is to ask the **SME** to explain things to you in response to specific questions that you prepare beforehand so as not to waste time. Most **SMEs** love to explain things. Most videos are targeted to an audience that is much less knowledgeable than subject matter experts. Therefore, your interrogation of an **SME** makes you an ambassador or a representative for that audience. It is an exciting and responsible job entrusted to you as a writer researching the topic or theme.

DEVICES FOR VIDEO EXPOSITION

In Chapter 5, we saw how ads and public service announcements (PSAs) are organized around a number of structural devices that help to organize content and keep the audience's interest. Humor, shock, suspense, and other strategies are useful for corporate video. Dramatization and case histories are also good ways to organize and communicate training content. There are a few formats that are perhaps more typical of training videos.

SHOW AND TELL

The older training videos tend to be very basic and of a certain type known as **show-and-tell**, which usually involves some kind of task description. It is a tried-and-true technique because that is exactly what it does. Most writers have been pushed into doing one of these. The military and government agencies traditionally relied on this approach to reach a broad common denominator. If you want to teach hundreds or even thousands of recruits how to, say, change the caterpillar tracks on a tank, you need to simplify the job into a number of separate, clear tasks. As the phrase "**show-and-tell**" suggests, the technique is to show on screen how to do something and then explain what you are seeing in a voice-over on the sound track. Many training tapes go on for 30 or 40 minutes and are unwatchable for anyone but the trainee who needs the instruction to pass a qualification. The **show-and-tell** technique is usually a standardized demonstration captured on video. A talking head introduction and a conclusion are typical of this kind of program, which is particularly useful and cost effective for training tasks that have to be repeated and are subject to variations in quality and style at each session depending on the instructor. A video training tape standardizes the content and the quality of delivery. This is important whenever a large number of trainees is involved. **Interactive** modules created for a computer and stored on a drive or a disk now provide an alternative to video and have more versatile applications.

The learning of a task can often be packaged in a **show-and-tell** videotape. Maintenance—operating radar, servicing a motor, or testing electrical circuits, for instance—is a good example. Learning how to drive a car or a forklift, or how to back a truck into a loading bay, or how to sell a product are other examples. **How-to-do-it videos** are really training videos that the general public buys or rents from video stores. They include cooking, exercise routines, or gardening topics. They use the visual medium to show by means of a moving picture what would have to be described at length and be difficult to follow in print. Many television shows are based on the **show-and-tell** technique. The difference is that there is an anchor or presenter who is generally a personality of some kind, whether it is a celebrity chef showing us how to make a soufflé or some other personality showing us how to install storm windows or remodel a kitchen.

In all of these programs, the common thread is that the subject matter, the content, is primary. An audience is going to be watching because it is interested in the subject matter per se, either because they want to be or, in the case of corporate training, because they have to be for their jobs. This kind of video does not always demand highly creative or imaginative use of the medium. How many ways can you show someone changing a spark plug? It does, however, require clear thinking and good organization of the material.

On a number of occasions, this writer has dealt with clients who wanted basic training videos and resisted all creative innovation. Once a client representative said to me that because the members of his audience were paid to watch the video, they didn't need anything creative or fancy. This thinking is mistaken because, even though an audience may be obliged to watch the video as part of a job responsibility, there is always a motivation factor. You can oblige someone to sit in a room and be present for a screening, but you cannot control his mental attention. The person's mind can wander. You cannot stop someone from dozing off in a darkened room after lunch. You cannot control message retention by force-feeding someone a video. There is always a virtue in creative, thoughtful scripting that works to hold the audience's attention and improve message retention by imaginative use of the medium.

JOB AND TASK DESCRIPTION

Most training concerns learning how to perform jobs. **Jobs** are broken down into tasks. The distinction is important. **A task** is specific, identifiable, and short. If you were dealing with driving a car, starting the car would be a task. Parallel parking would be another task. Several **tasks** in a sequence add up to a **job**. A **job** is then an undertaking that leads to a terminal action that completes the defined end objective. Many training videos are broken down into **tasks** and organized around task description.

EDUCATIONAL/INSTRUCTIONAL USE OF VIDEO

Education is a universal preoccupation. Overhead projectors are still a popular presentation tool for educators. Now computer presentation software such as PowerPoint allows bulleted points and headings to be spiced up with graphic objects, audio, and video. The computer has basically subsumed the role of a slide projector when coupled to an LED projector. Slides can be stored as picture files and called up as needed. A training program can be stored as a computer file and called up for live presentations. There is a role for writers in serious slide presentations for training. We can approach this from the opposite direction and suggest that managers and employees with communication roles in their work should learn to think and write visually to make more effective presentations.

All companies have training needs. In every field, technology and the constant evolution of ideas means that employees need to be retrained and their knowledge and skills upgraded. Companies also need to train new hires who may have an inadequate education or who need knowledge about the company's products, history, policies, and benefits. Such training needs are ongoing.

In educational institutions from grade school through college, there is a constant need to acquire information, learn methods, and supplement classes or lectures. The advent of video in cheap portable formats opened up a vast educational video market. Live lectures can be recorded and replayed, which is the simplest application. Video can be produced on specialized topics, such as the study of an artist, an historical figure, or a social issue. Videos containing extraordinary images, archival material, or interviews, which are scripted and shot with an organized structure, offer valuable extensions to the classroom lecture technique and standard textbooks traditionally used for teaching. Most students have seen this kind of **educational documentary** during their careers.

Most college libraries now have a significant video collection almost as diverse as their book collection. The only difference between a television documentary and an educational documentary is probably length (because there is no scheduled slot to fit into) and subject matter. Television documentaries have to appeal to a general viewing audience. Educational documentaries can presume some background knowledge and can be more specialized.

HOW-TO-DO-IT VIDEOS

If a picture is worth a thousand words, then showing an audience how to do something is the best example of it because explaining in words is nearly always long and often ambiguous. Everybody has had the experience of trying to follow written directions to assemble a piece of furniture or the operating instructions of an appliance, not to mention the instructions for a piece of computer software. For many retail items needing instruction, it is neither practical nor economical to provide a video manual. However, more expensive goods or services do sometimes come with a video manual. There is a commercial market for videos that show you how to do things: cooking, gardening, house repairs, exercise routines, and even how to make love. Although many are offshoots of television shows, plenty of videos are made specifically for this market. Video rental stores have a small section devoted to **how-to-do-it videos**. You see them advertised in magazines, sold by mail order, and promoted through infomercial programs on cable television.

INTERACTIVE APPLICATIONS

Interactive training came into its own with the invention of the laser disk. A computer interface with instant access to 50,000 frames of information made **nonlinear** instructional design a practical reality. The CD-ROM, successor to the 12-inch laser disk, has now largely been replaced by the DVD. **Authoring software** has been created that enables sophisticated **interactive multimedia** design. The ultimate medium for training is now **interactive**. Individuals absorb knowledge at different rates. Interactive media now allow self-paced learning. Computer-based training enables testing and scoring of individual performance. **Authoring software** allows the **instructional designer** to create feedback loops that not only foster self-paced learning but oblige the user to complete a test or learning module before proceeding.

Nevertheless, there is still room for the **linear** training video. One reason is that it costs much more to design and program a complex **interactive** training program than to produce a videotape. This cost is not justified unless the training program will have long life and a large audience will need numerous copies of it. If training content changes rapidly or has a small audience, **linear** videotape can do a useful job of instruction at low cost in conjunction with print manuals. Lucent Technologies (since merged with the French company Alcatel in 2006) adopted this solution to facilitate installation of light wave multiplexers for which I wrote a couple of scripts of this very kind. The main objective of the videos was to improve the speed and efficiency of installation and the target audience was the installers. They had a 3-inch ring binder of printed instructions. It was impossible to use the medium effectively because **linear** video does not allow the audience to retain detailed information, which is what they had to do. So clearly they would be reading the manual. Video works best to motivate and communicate emotionally. To communicate abstractions, you need **visual metaphors**.

The fastest growing application for training is online, using real-time synchronous and **asynchronous** sharing of information to an unlimited audience who can log on to a website. Microsoft is promoting its meeting software, NetMeeting. More interesting is a tool like Adobe Acrobat Connect Pro, which allows video, audio, and white board **synchronous communication** and as well as **asynchronous** stored media such as stills and video for later access. So, increasingly, video will become an asset to be produced for uploading to a more versatile, **interactive** environment, either on fixed media or on websites. The traditional instructional video may well dwindle in value.

OTHER CORPORATE USES OF MEDIA

Corporate communications is a fast-moving and dynamic world. Producers are quick to innovate and propose media solutions that exploit the latest technology. So corporate video has changed over the years. It has become shorter, more motivational, and targeted at specific opportunities. There is no better way to capture a CEO's message to shareholders or to employees, now more likely to be streamed to the corporate website rather than distributed on videotape. Think of video as a component in increasingly **interactive** solutions on the web. This makes sense, especially when content needs to be updated regularly.

Fixed media are ideal for cheap distribution of catalogs, interactive brochures, and service manuals when the content will have a reasonable life expectancy. Corporate marketing can choose between a product launch in a meeting with a video component or a website with its potential for viral marketing as well as traditional video, increasingly likely to be on DVD, and therefore offer interactive options. So annual general meetings, product launches, product promotion, sales training, technical installations, service manuals, and product updates can all be delivered via **interactive** solutions on a website or on fixed media. There are public relations stories, annual reports to shareholders, and prestige corporate image videos. There are internal public relations explaining policy changes, product changes, and health and pension benefits. There are endless training needs including safety training, personnel training, and management training. Training is a big part of corporate communication. A later chapter in Part 4 dedicated to writing for **interactive media** has more on **interactive** corporate communications.

MEETINGS WITH A VISUAL FOCUS

Management means meetings. Management constantly needs to communicate new policies, information, and strategies to submanagers and employees; so they have meetings. Small meetings might be built around a computer-produced slide presentation. These sorts of PowerPoint presentations with graphic presentation of facts and figures and bulleted points can be projected on larger screens for larger meetings. Big companies also hold big meetings because they have hundreds of managers or sales representatives. They want to motivate these people to do a better job or to put a new policy into practice. They want to bring all their dealers together to launch a new product or a new model. Good marketing starts by getting the dealers to believe that the new product or new model is competitive and that they can make money selling it. The manufacturer might spend what to us is a small fortune on a meeting with visual focus. This might include slides, video, music, live demonstrations, and the "reveal," which is a dramatic unveiling of the new model or product that inspires the audience of dealers. Without the visual focus, the meeting would boil down to speeches by sales executives and CEOs. Talk is talk. You can only take so much. High-level executives need meeting openers and focused videos that encapsulate a corporate story.

Meetings are also about rewards. IBM used to mount an annual awards event for its best salespeople called the Golden Globe Awards. They were often held in an exotic location, such as Honolulu, Cannes, or Las Vegas, with presentations and keynote addresses by senior executives in the company. It was a reward but also an opportunity for internal public relations and promotion.[4] If a company brings together 1000 or more of its salespeople or its dealers, it has an unparalleled opportunity to communicate corporate vision and motivate its people. Such meetings can be elaborate, big-budget extravaganzas with highly original concepts accompanied by elaborately produced multimedia presentations designed to motivate the sales force. Motivation, as we have said before, derives from the same root as emotion. Motivation with words alone is possible but difficult. Historically, great orators have changed public consciousness with memorable language, whether Cicero in the Roman Senate, the representatives of the first Continental Congress of the States, Abraham Lincoln at Gettysburg, F.D.R. telling

---

[4]See the website for a speculative proposal for such a conference.

the American people that the only thing they had to fear was fear itself, or Winston Churchill in his address to the British House of Commons after Dunkirk confronted with the possible invasion by Nazi Germany.[5] However, great orators are not common in corporate management. Video commentary can be voiced by experienced actors. Visual media can call on powerful visual images and multitrack stereo sound that impacts the senses so that messages are experienced as well as heard or read. Guess who is needed to think up these visual experiences and develop the management themes? Yes, scriptwriters! More work for scriptwriters who know how to deal with corporate communication! This is big business. It is also exciting to do. It is a kind of **business theater**.

Mars, a candy manufacturer, is having an internal meeting of salespeople to launch a marketing and sales program. To dramatize the meeting and its rivalry with other candy bar manufacturers, the conference is built around a giant chessboard on which key pieces of the sales strategy correspond to chess pieces. A real chess game is worked out that ends in checkmate for the competition. Key executives speak to the themes, which are dramatized by moving a life-size chess piece on the floor. Writing the speeches and writing the scenario for the marketing chess game is work for a writer.

DEVICES THAT TEACH AND ENTERTAIN

The challenge with a corporate video is to hold the audience while a great deal of information is delivered in such a way that the audience retains it. Sometimes the way companies use training video sinks the medium like an overloaded vessel. Because the medium is **linear**, it is hard to retain information beyond a certain amount. The writer's skill is to create a device that gets the information across while keeping the audience's attention. A number of devices can do this. Most of them involve pretending that the training task is, for example, a game, a television show, or a story. Above all, we need some kind of structural device that holds the material together and which the audience can follow. This can take many forms. Once again we need **visual metaphors**. We need images that impart emotion and meaning straight to the perceptive mind through the visual cortex in a way that language often cannot.

DEVICES THAT WORK FOR CORPORATE MESSAGES

The beginner looks at a corporate communication problem and probably thinks that the message is so factual or so specific to a product that it can only be tedious. However, some of the most creative and exciting opportunities for writing and program making come out of corporate communication problems. It is precisely because the message content is presented in the raw that the writer and production

---

[5]"We shall not flag nor fail. We shall go on to the end. We shall fight in France and on the seas and oceans; we shall fight with growing confidence and growing strength in the air. We shall defend our island whatever the cost may be; we shall fight on beaches, landing grounds, in fields, in streets and on the hills. We shall never surrender and even if, which I do not for the moment believe, this island or a large part of it were subjugated and starving, then our empire beyond the seas, armed and guarded by the British Fleet, will carry on the struggle until in God's good time the New World with all its power and might, sets forth to the liberation and rescue of the Old."

team have wonderful opportunities to innovate strategies to reach the audience and invent devices that make the program watchable.

Writing a script, whether fiction, documentary, or corporate, involves finding a structure. A writer's fundamental problem is to find a structure that will organize the material in such a way as to take the audience along. Therefore, it has to be an idea that the audience grasps. This idea can be either explicit or implicit. It can be announced as a key for the audience to the organization of content. Or it can be a sort of rack on which points hang. Most stories have implicit structures whether novels, plays, or films. An exposition such as a lecture or a business presentation is usually laid out as a plan with headings and subheadings so that the audience knows where it is going. The structure that enables the scriptwriter to bring together all the details and communicate a comprehensible message usually rests on one of a number of devices. We need to know what they are and see how they can be used. In corporate video, it has become commonplace to borrow from television and imitate other types of program.

Dramatization

A common device is **dramatization**. Even though corporate drama or comedy productions might not equal entertainment vehicles in production value or talent, dramatizing a message is an effective way to engage an audience because it tells a story and creates characters with whom the audience can identify. It is particularly effective for training videos. In *The Right Direction*, a training video for financial advisors, the scriptwriter wants to make a point about communicating financial information to customers who are not familiar with financial matters. One effective way to make the point is to invent a dramatic situation with characters. First get the audience involved in the story. A driver, lost in the country, asks for directions from a local. The audience readily understands that the road and the map of where we are going is a good metaphor for the client's journey down a financial road. Road signs are adapted to warn of regulatory and other problems, Getting lost is the metaphor. Once the audience gets into the story, the moral of the situation can be made clear. In fact, this piece uses several devices in combination—**dramatization, voice-over narration**, and **graphics**.

AT&T produced a video for a wide public called *Connections*. Its target was a nontechnical audience. Its objective was to imagine the future of telecommunications and how it might impact our lives. To bundle together all the diverse points, it needed a device like a story in which the audience would encounter the future telecommunications technologies in the context of work and leisure activities. A young woman who has been working in Asia has become engaged to a Belgian doctor. When her mother and father meet her at the airport, she uses a future AT&T phone with voice recognition and simultaneous translation of foreign languages. The father is rather taken back. He faces his own struggles as an architect and city planner when one of their rebuilding projects meets resistance from a community teacher who needs classroom space. We are introduced to a universal terminal that functions as a video telephone and computer, networked to huge databases that enable efficiencies we are just beginning to see since the film was first conceived in the early 1990s. We learn how the mother, who is a doctor, can practice telemedicine and prescribe a prosthesis for a hockey player consulting a physician in China. The *Connections* video is an excellent example of corporate production values being used to communicate a complex message about where technology is leading (see the website).

Dramatization means creating characters and situations that embody the training points. A safety training video might use serious drama to make a point about the consequences of ignoring safety procedures in a factory or a warehouse. Many other kinds of training programs make use of comic drama. John Cleese, of *Monty Python* fame, cofounded Video Arts to exploit the situation comedy format to make management training films that are entertaining and instructive. The company has been very successful. Learning how to close a sale or interview a job applicant by watching John Cleese caricature how not to do it is an unforgettable experience. An omniscient **voice-over** watching this tells him what he is doing wrong and he replays the scene the correct way. Comedy captures the audience's interest. The errors and mistakes are hilarious to watch. The audience laughs at them and, of course, at their own errors. They are softened up to receive the training point about how to carry out some management function the right way. Job done!

The same approach is adopted in *Charley Wheeler's Big Week*, which teaches securities sales personnel the rules and regulations of the Securities and Exchange Commission (SEC). The wrong behavior and key infractions of regulations are dramatized in a character named Charley Wheeler. A training video is an invaluable aid that pays for itself many times over. John Hancock has a legal obligation to train the people who sell its financial products. *Charley Wheeler's Big Week* employs humor from time to time as well as dramatizing the message. We get a smile out of Charley's obvious lies and subterfuges. He also breaks every rule.

It is more memorable to show a fictional character who does everything wrong than to explain what is right. A fictional character provides the writer with a great deal of license. It also means that the audience can laugh at a scapegoat or see faults that might be harder to acknowledge in a factual recitation. *Charley Wheeler's Big Week* tells a moralizing tale of malpractice by creating a fictional securities salesman who is careless about SEC rules and regulations. It would be awkward, if not impossible, to use real case histories as examples of how not to sell, or how not to follow Securities and Exchange Commission rules of conduct, to drive home the importance of regulation in the mutual fund industry.

When you have a lot of information to convey, you can deliver it as factual documentary narrative: "You must do this, you mustn't do that." In other words, you could create a video lecture. The scriptwriter of *Charley Wheeler's Big Week* instead chose to organize the points within a moral tale of what not to do as a mutual fund salesman. The fact that we meet Charlie in the lower grade job of short-order cook after he has been barred from the securities industry for violating its professional codes makes sure that we, the audience, see the story from the correct ethical perspective. Clearly, the audience is trainees and salespeople in the mutual fund industry. They are given a fall guy to explore all the dos and don'ts from a safe emotional position. This is a common and useful technique. The character is recognizable. He may even have a bit of us in him. However, we can laugh at him, despise him, look down on him as a loser while at the same time realizing that there's a Charley lurking in all of us somewhere if we let him have space. It is usually more effective to **dramatize** a situation that allows your message to be sent via emotional attitudes or through character conflict than deliver a straight exposition. An audience is more inclined to give its attention to dramatic treatments and to remember the points more easily than from a recitation of dos and don'ts. (Read the script and see video clips from *Charley Wheeler's Big Week* on the website.)

Humor

Another helpful device to capture audiences is humor. A lot of clients are nervous about jokes and **humor**. This is not comedy hour. The humor has to serve a purpose that delivers the message. **Humor** can help make a point that if, put in the form of explanation, would not be nearly as effective. So you enliven the situation with **humor**. The predicament of people lost in the country is amusing to most of us who have had a similar experience. This scene from *The Right Direction* helps the target audience to understand the predicament of the client, getting multiple directions from differentsources.

POINT OF VIEW—DRIVER (8 SECONDS)

The car pulls up to another younger country farmer walking along the road. This fellow is the opposite of his older cousin. Where the older farmer was slow and thoughtful, this fellow seems to have overindulged in his morning caffeine. The younger farmer looks in the window and addresses the driver. (Also shoot alternate straight delivery.)

YOUNG FARMER
(extremely fast delivery)

You can't miss it. Just take forty-three three miles to two-twenty-two then go north five minutes on twenty-five or twenty-five minutes on five. Got that?

POINT OF VIEW—FARMER (2 SECONDS)

Stunned look on the driver's face. His mouth hangs open. He blinks his eyes in disbelief.

POINT OF VIEW—DRIVER (9 SECONDS)

YOUNG FARMER
(not waiting for an answer
or taking a breath)

Good. Turn right on seven for one point seven miles then take a left on one-seventeen 'til you hit the seven-eleven. At the seven-eleven you'll see a sign for seventeen cross seventeen then back over seven to one-eleven. You with me?

POINT OF VIEW—FARMER (2 SECONDS)

The driver twitches his head, nodding, trying to follow the torrent of numbers raining down on him.

The audience understands the way a salesperson can confuse a customer by delivering reams of facts and figures familiar to the seller but unfamiliar to the customer. The other point made is that the customer needs to know these things just like the lost motorist needs to get directions. The situation is recognizable, humorous, and drives home the point.

Visual Metaphor

The same example uses a technique of **visual metaphor**. A metaphor is a figure of speech that shows one thing to be like another in a different context. In prose or poetry, it is commonplace. To speak of the sword of justice or the scales of justice is to use a metaphor. In a visual medium that strings images and actions together, it is extremely difficult to make up good metaphors and even more difficult to elaborate them without disrupting the narrative continuity of the piece. *The Right Direction* uses a visual and dramatic metaphor to make a point. In long hand, the argument goes something like this: If you are lost in the country and you ask a local to give you directions, the local is often so familiar with the area that the directions—although perfectly clear to him–are confusing to you. Such directions are usually given too fast and in too much detail. You end up being confused by the person helping you even though he feels he is trying his best. Most people have experienced this dilemma and get the point of the scene. They get lost. Can you give good directions?

As a scriptwriter, you have a voice-over say something like, "Listening to a financial advisor talk about money and investment involves unfamiliar vocabulary." You convey to your audience of financial advisors that even though potential customers want to go in that direction and learn the necessary background to make good decisions about their investment, they are confused and lost. If you, the financial advisor, speak to them as if they know what you know, they won't get it. You will not be providing the necessary service and, worse yet, you could lose the customer. You could put all this in a voice-over and show a meeting going on with occasional cuts to staged dialogue between advisor and customer. This is the lazy way, and too often the weak way, of presenting a message that gets into corporate videos. The writer of *The Right Direction*, Peter Cutler, has found the kind of device that will carry the point in a way that the audience will grasp without realizing that they thought about it.

The **visual metaphor** of the driver lost in the country asking a local farmer for directions is a situation with which the audience can identify. The extrapolation to financial advising can also be made in the **voice-over** once the audience is emotionally and imaginatively prepared. That is how this script works. Moreover, *The Right Direction* does something else worth noting as we learn the craft of corporate communication. It builds a **visual metaphor** into the structure of a script. Hence, the title! This allows the writer to use road signs and warnings signs about detours and dead end to continue the metaphor and its financial correlative. This is meta-writing—finding a **visual metaphor** that can organize the narrative for the viewer.

EMC Corporation's original business was data storage but has now become information management. Storage is measured by digital capacity, but the value of the information stored is determined by accessibility and functionality. Managing information flows makes storage work. So how do you express this abstract idea visually? What flows and changes shape and speed and has multiple applications in personal, industrial, and natural spheres? Water! Images of surf, streams, mighty rivers, dams, waterfalls, and raindrops all illustrate information flow in all its variety and allow voice-over commentary to carry greater weight. An elegant video results that makes the abstract ideas concrete, visual, and highly watchable (see the video clip on the website). *Sea Change* is composed almost entirely of stock shots edited together with music and commentary to make a provocative short video sequence that does not once mention the product. If you can identify the problem and imagine a solution for which your client corporation's product is the solution, you get your audience's attention and make it receptive to a sale at some later point. **Visual metaphors** are the key to visual writing and effective scripts.

I once had a large construction company as a client. The company was building the cooling towers for a nuclear power station. The project managers wanted me to define their efficient methods and their uniquely innovative solutions to the engineering problems of the job. They had to work to a deadline to synchronize with the rest of the project. There was a lot of visually exciting action with a huge crane at the center of the tower. The complexity of the project and the orchestration of the different interlocking phases of the project, which unfolded over 2 years, explained the construction company's prowess. The last sentence contained a metaphor—orchestration. It became the breakthrough idea to bring the story together and explain the nature of the achievement. The plans were like the score. Getting 70 or 80 musicians to play together to the same beat and create great music is difficult. Not all orchestras are the same or as good as one another. Getting seven or eight teams of specialized craftsmen to work together efficiently is more than just a hiring job. The different teams of ironworkers, riveters, cementers, and scaffolders were like sections of an orchestra. They had to play in turn, in sequence, to produce the desired result. At the center was a conductor—the chief engineer. We wanted to differentiate this construction company from several others in the same business. The Boston Symphony Orchestra might play the same music as the Podunk Symphony Orchestra, but the end result, although similar, is not the same.

After obtaining footage of a regional symphony orchestra playing Beethoven's Fifth Symphony, I had the basis for a script. I also had the music for the sound track—heroic, dramatic, well known. I didn't have to buy the performance of the orchestra because I could buy a music library version of Beethoven and sync it to the images of the players that we had permission to use. Once the metaphor was set up, it could run throughout the video and be turned on and off at will, ending with a great finale as the dramatic shots of the two towers from a distance were cut to the *tutti* of the Beethoven finale. At the end I got a shot of all the worker teams with tools in hand standing in and around a huge cooling duct 10 feet in diameter taking a sort of a bow as the sound track played the applause of the concert audience.

The video I wrote and directed for the Conseil Régional de Midi-Pyrénées in France uses **visual metaphors**. How do you explain that a region that is as old as Cro-Magnon man (whose drawings can be found in local caves), that has been inhabited by ancient Celtic peoples who raised stone monuments (dolmens) in ways that are beyond our understanding, that was conquered by Julius Caesar, and that is a traditional wine-growing region, is also a white-hot technological center of research and innovation in the aerospace and biotechnology fields? In the video, there is a shot of a traditional peasant in a beret tending his vineyard with a medieval village in the background. He looks up as a modern jet flies overhead leaving a trail. We cut to the Airbus assembly line in Toulouse (see the website). A visual language that can condense thought and make a point in pictures that is more succinct than words is what scriptwriters try to achieve.

Another device used to organize the multiple sections of the same video was to open the video with a computer screen on which titles appear as someone types on the keyboard. After each section, you return to the same device and introduce the next section.

Once you get a good metaphor going, it makes for strong structure and provides visual ways of communicating that use the medium with flair and imagination. The also-rans just do wall-to-wall voice-overs, which say "crane" on the sound track then show a shot of a crane. Every major word has an image to go with it that is controlled by the audio track. The whole video becomes predictable. It also becomes a struggle to find images that go with the commentary once you start. It becomes like a slide show with commentary. It results from writing the right-hand side of the script first—the classic mistake of the amateur. Never write the structure into the sound track when the medium is visual! The rare exceptions are documentaries in which the voice is important, such as the voice of a historical character in a biography. The point is that you need a visual concept and a visual lead in a visual medium. Otherwise, you are not using the potential of medium.

A number of devices for video have basically been borrowed from program concepts evolved for television. Because the visual language of television has become a universal idiom of popular culture, writers and producers of corporate video know that their clients and their clients' audiences will understand programs cast in that format. Some of these formats are broadcast news, the use of an anchor or presenter, documentary features, **interviews**, **vox pops**, quiz shows, and, from television advertising, **testimonials**.

Narrators and Anchors on Camera

Most factual or informational programs, whether news features or corporate videos, need some kind of narration. Although the use of **voice-overs** works some of the time, television producers have learned that audiences identify with people on screen. It is often more effective to have an **on-camera anchor**, presenter, or narrator take the audience through the story, whether it is about global warming, a political situation in a foreign country, or a product launch. Broadcast news relies on anchors to present the news. A great deal of experience has been accumulated about how to work with the camera so as to relate to an audience. These techniques differentiate the professional from the man on the street talking to a camera. Professionals know how to deliver lines to a camera and carry an audience. Sometimes, a simulated investigative documentary style can work well in corporate videos.

Shell Gas International is a company in the giant Shell group. As mentioned in an earlier chapter, their research side had developed a new catalyst that would allow natural gas to be turned into high-value lubrication oils and kerosene, which is jet fuel. There are huge reserves of natural gas in the world, much of it in underdeveloped countries where it has no value. Natural gas is only valuable when it is near a large population that would justify the huge investment in infrastructure of pipelines required to deliver it to the consumer. Investment in the research had reached $100 million in yesterday's money, including a working pilot plant in Amsterdam. The CEO of the operation wanted a video to explain the breakthrough and sell the technology to a key decision-making audience of oil ministers and petroleum engineers in developing countries where the natural gas reserves could be found. There is a lot of archive footage in the Shell film and video library about everything the company has done. More to the point, the story to be told was complex and had to persuade the target audience to entertain a joint venture involving a multimillion-dollar investment. This all amounts to a big communication challenge. How do you construct a video that will carry the story, integrate all of the available material, and be persuasive?

One of the main psychographic problems for the audience would be believing Shell advocating and promoting its own patented process. The success of the video depended on convincing the high-level audience that the process was cost-effective. The device that seemed to solve the communication problems and suggest a watchable video of tolerable length was to have an **on-camera narrator** reporting and explaining the story. In this way, an intermediary between the audience and Shell moderated the commercial propaganda. The audience would have a guide and a friend to take them through the story and make it into an exciting discovery like an investigative documentary. It would work because there was a story and because it was an interesting development in the history of petroleum chemistry. For decades numerous enterprises (including the Nazi regime during World War II) had tried to find a way to convert coal and natural gas into gasoline without commercial success.

To create this script, the writer borrowed a device from broadcast television. The story opens with the anchor looking at video footage of natural gas being flared off in huge flames in a Middle Eastern oil field. Turning to the camera, he asks, "Why would anyone burn off natural gas and waste colossal amounts of energy?" He launches the program by asking, "What if there were a way to convert natural gas to liquid fuels and save this energy?" Roll title: *Natural Gas: The Liquid Alternative*. On-camera presenters are used in science documentaries, investigative news reports, historical documentary, and cultural series. The device is well understood and quite versatile because the narrator's voice can be run as audio only behind cutaways to location footage, archive material, and interviews.

Creating a Loyal Client [6] relies on a **to-camera narrator** as its fundamental strategy. The host in the script is sometimes on camera and sometimes off. The narrator's role is to persuade, cajole, and instruct the audience so that the corporate message is secure. This is a common strategy in corporate video. The host becomes a kind of interpreter for the audience and an insurance policy for the corporate client. It is a way of borrowing from the format of television shows whose audiences are accustomed to being led by the hand and carried through the show.

Television Formats

All of the television formats get used now and then as models for corporate video. The basic strategy is to use a small screen idiom that we know the audience will understand. It is a given that every audience knows television and has been culturally trained to accept its formats and conventions. Variety shows, quiz shows, interviews, documentary narrative, television news, sitcoms, how-to-do-it demonstration shows, and more have been used in corporate videos.

How do you present retirement benefits to young employees who would be turned off by cold facts and figures? You present it as a television show with audience participation anchored by a young host who can make it sound acceptable to the target audience. This is what happens in *Check It Out* for Fidelity Investments. This program about the outwardly boring subject of benefits combines the TV show format with humor, and employee **testimonials** cunningly embedded in the variety format keep the message entertaining. Employees learn that benefits can make a significant difference in their lives later on.

Documentary

Another style of television documentary is the compilation documentary with an unseen narrative voice-over. This is common in wildlife, historical, and reportage documentaries. Again, this device

---

[6]Creating a Loyal Client, written by Peter Cutler for John Hancock.

can be adapted to corporate narrative in all kinds of sales, public relations, and corporate image videos. Corporate histories and product histories are often quite involved and complex, especially when applied science is involved. Corporate messages can also involve economics and public policy. Businesses and nonprofits alike have a constant need to narrate, explain, and communicate factual information.

As you will remember from discussion in earlier chapters, American Express in Europe had spent a large sum on market research into American tourist destinations, preferences, and spending habits. The research revealed that Europe's market share was declining as Americans discovered Caribbean, Far Eastern, and domestic destinations. The demographic of the American tourist was changing. European tourist organizations and businesses were complacent about their market share. American Express, like other cards, charges the establishment accepting the card a percentage of the charge. Sometimes restaurants and hotels resent having to pay this fee. A public relations opportunity existed for American Express to educate the member establishments and European tourist professionals and show the relationship as a partnership. American Express had valuable marketing know-how, historical perspective, and worldwide experience. With frequent opportunities to interact with travel professionals at conventions and meetings, high-level management needed a vehicle to present this valuable marketing information for mutual benefit. After all, if American travel to Europe declines, so does the card business of American Express.

You could give the target audience printed brochures of the market research. That approach is passive and would not profile the company. A good video, on the other hand, is an invaluable opener for meetings and also a useful internal communication that could reeducate European employees of American Express.

So what approach would carry off this communication? You are talking to professionals. You have complex marketing data to interpret. You have a public relations function to perform. You have to achieve an informational and a motivational result. During my research visits, I found the attitudes of Europeans about American tourists to be not only complacent but patronizing, ignorant of the nature and breadth of American tastes and interests. There was a real need to shift the attitude of the audience and start them thinking. I came to the decision that one device was essential to the mix: to prove that the costly market research carried out by an outside contractor was accurate, we would need to match its categories to **testimonials** from real American tourists.

Vox Pops

Vox pops stands for *vox populi*, or "voice of the people" in Latin. This technique consists of sampling opinions on the street or some other location using unscheduled, random interviews. News reports often capture the unrehearsed opinion of the man on the street. That is relatively easy to do. For the most part, a television audience sees edited excerpts. A lot of footage gets shot, but only a short sound bite is rolled into the broadcast. For a corporate video, and for American Express in particular, the interviews had to be authentic, unpaid, and unrehearsed in order to be convincing. It was a gamble—a creative gamble and a production gamble. I could not guarantee the availability of the mix of demographic types that governed the market research. These types were defined as Business Travelers, Big Spenders, Gray Panthers, and Adventurers.

Choosing to use **vox pops** would result in production problems and costs. The obvious place to capture interviews of American tourists was at the Heathrow Airport check-in lounge in late August or early September. At least a dozen flights a day departed Heathrow for U.S. destinations. Most of the passengers were likely to be returning summer tourists. Shooting in an airport, however, is costly. Airports demand facilities fees and also require you to insure yourself for several million dollars worth of public liability. The point to keep in mind as a writer is that although you can write the questions, you can only write in a paraphrase of what you hope the interviewees will say. The questions have to be well researched and well thought out. Whoever does the interviewing off camera has to have follow-up questions and be able to get the subject to talk. Anyone appearing on camera has to sign a waiver that has been approved by the corporate legal department. Waivers are commonplace.

Basically, the technique is a strategic fishing expedition. You know something is out there. You try to use the right bait to catch it. Of course, anything that is not suitable can be edited out. However, you cannot make up material that is not genuine. In Chapter 5 we alluded to the use of this technique by AT&T. The company ran a series of long-distance carrier ads based on the **vox pops** technique.

The fishing expedition in Heathrow Airport was successful. We had American Express personnel with clipboards canvassing the passengers to find out if they were American, if they would agree to be recorded, and if they had the time to be interviewed before their flights. Most people are pleased to express opinions on camera if given the right opportunity. This filter provided a steady trickle of American travelers to be interviewed on video. Afterwards, the interviewees were offered refreshment and a small goodwill gift of an American Express calculator.

Logical Argument in Documentary Narrative

The American Express video combined a number of techniques: **voice-over** narrative, **vox pops**, and documentary narrative. Another commonplace technique that works well for corporate videos is an adaptation of documentary technique that could be called **narrative argument**. This technique requires voice narration to support it. It is based on editing images that have relevant content but are not usually shot in continuity or covered from different angles. Therefore, editing can only mean arranging the sequence of shots and deciding on their length. It is a basic form of visual exposition found in news features, documentaries, and corporate videos.

In the American Express video, we wanted to put forward an argument based on the extensive market research and economic statistics about trends in travel destinations and the impact on American tourism in Europe. This involved drawing conclusions about projected growth in long-haul destinations and the statistics about tourist spending to make the point that Europe could lose market share if the trend continued. To retain market share, action could be taken to satisfy the preferences of the principal types of American tourists as analyzed in the market research.

Documentary argument often works by using a metaphor of some kind. Earlier in the chapter, we explained how visual metaphor works. Corporate videos are often called on to make wide-ranging philosophical arguments about adapting to change, about understanding change, or about ecological vision or social policy. In *Sea Change*, produced for EMC Corporation, the message is about the impact of information technology in the business world as a way of introducing a company that makes storage disks and storage systems. The documentary metaphor about change becomes a platform for introducing the relevance of the product without a hard sell.

Graphics

A strong way to represent statistical information visually is by means of graphs and charts. Effective **graphics** that are clear and colorful are a powerful means of communication for corporate videos. Today, computer graphics tools and animation software provide us with virtually unlimited capabilities at a reasonable cost. In the early days, computer graphic animation was a high-cost item in the budget because of the cost of hardware and software. Although costs have come down as computer processing power has become cheaper, animation can still be expensive. For instance, Industrial Light and Magic creates effects for feature films like *Titanic, Jurassic Park*, and *Star Wars* that are off the scale for corporate production. Adobe Photoshop, Illustrator, and Infini-D enable low-cost desktop solutions that will get you a long way toward exciting graphics produced by high-end animations tools like Soft Image.

Corporate communications such as annual general reports and financial statements deal in facts and figures all the time. **Graphics** help get across statistics as in the familiar bar charts or pie charts. This is fine for Power Point presentations or print, but in a moving picture medium, you should animate the **graphics**. Even simple step frame animation will help, but we are still talking 2-D graphics. Now low-and high-end tools are available for all budgets to create 2-D and 3-D animation. This is particularly helpful for explaining a process. For example, the Shell video about natural gas had to explain the chemical process of catalysis to explain the innovation that Shell used to achieve the change in molecular structure. Good 3-D graphic animation can show how the complex long chain hydrocarbon molecule changes when it comes into contact with the catalyst.

Visual Seduction

The television screen, or computer screen for that matter, is everywhere. It is a visual space on which all kinds of images, text, and scenes are projected. Some of it is ordinary, even banal. Some of it is visually stunning. Photographically powerful images captured on film by a skilled cinematographer compel attention and lift the medium to another level. Shots of nature or people can make the difference between something that passes before your eyes and something you watch with awe. **Visual seduction** is a technique that is only minimally available to the writer and depends on the videographer and director to bring to the screen.

A writer can describe the intent and suggest the visual power of images. For example, exotic or dramatic locations often furnish the kind of breathtaking images that hold attention. These can be industrial images, such as a stunning crane shot, suspended from the cable of a crane turning around so that the camera pans the outside of the cooling tower of a nuclear power station under construction. The height and the point of view make it a compelling shot. Strong location visuals can be written in. *Natural Gas: The Liquid Alternative* required stunning shots of natural gas flaring off in the desert to make the point about wasting energy. The roar of this flame, like a jet engine, makes the point on the audio track. This type of footage already existed as archive material in the Shell library, so it could be written in as a predetermined image in the final video. In *American Travel in Europe*, I chose to shoot in Ghent, Belgium, for the quaint period architecture and the canals. When the writer is also the director—frequently the case in corporate video production—location research is sometimes more efficient and more effective.

Interview

Of all the documentary and corporate techniques, **interviewing** is the oldest and most basic way of capturing expert opinion. You film a person answering questions that will illuminate the points you are trying to make. Usually we are accustomed to seeing the person speak to an off-camera interviewer so that the eyeline is to the left or right of camera. This distinguishes it from the **to-camera presentation of an anchor**. The news style delivery or confidential and personal delivery of someone speaking into the lens implies consciousness of the audience. It is by nature manipulative. When the camera observes someone speaking to an off-camera interlocutor, the statements come across as more authoritative and more objective. In *Natural Gas: The Liquid Alternative*, we interviewed the head of Shell Research to explain the breakthrough in catalysis. We interviewed the chief executive because of his vigorous, dynamic conviction about the future potential of the process. Although the point we wanted them to make was planned, it looks authoritative and objective, especially when it is seen in counterpoint to the to-camera anchor who takes us through the story.

Case Histories

A more specific technique that may be made up of several interviews is the **case history**. As the name implies, this technique involves in-depth documentation of a personal story to illustrate an idea or a point. The **case history** can become the governing structural idea of a program. *Charley Wheeler's Big Week* for John Hancock is a fictional case history built around a dramatic character invented by the scriptwriter to illustrate all the points about how not to conduct yourself as a securities salesperson. The **case history** is an effective way to structure a corporate program when you want to bring together a number of points whose order is not as important as the context in which they are understood. **Case histories** work well because they are basically stories. The story structure takes precedence over the points you want to make. If you were to make the points in some kind of order, the audience would experience it as a glorified bullet list. Ideas that are abstract and hard to remember out of context become concrete and easy to remember in the context of a story. *Charley Wheeler's Big Week* has it both ways by creating a supplementary review video in which the points are recalled as the key points John Hancock wants to get across to its audience.

Consider the difference between explaining the way cholesterol-lowering medication works and introducing the audience to a number of particular patients of different ages and types of lifestyle who have high cholesterol. You meet people. You get their story. In fact, even better, you do both. You provide case histories, and you have an animated graphic that explains how the blood chemistry works when arteries become clogged, how this produces angina or more critical heart attacks, and you use the same animation to show the intervention of the cholesterol-lowering medication in reducing bad cholesterol. This makes another point, namely, that adopting one device or technique does not exclude another. In this case, you set up the problem with case histories. Then you educate the audience about heart disease. You sell the particular drug product indirectly by association. The same company might make a 30-second television spot that would sell the brand. The two uses of video are completely different.

The Story of a Day

Sometimes a writer's material or the content that the client wants to see included is so disparate that none of the structures we have so far examined seems to work. Also we might be dealing with a process or a sequence of events that is time sensitive. A useful device is the slice through time, a unit of time, during which most of what you need to look at occurs. A company story can sometimes be nicely told in a day's activity—**the story of a day**. I used this technique in a script I wrote for the Saudi Aramco's Aviation Department. Finding, lifting, and refining petroleum is a 24-hour operation for an oil company. Aviation is vital to company operations. To explain how the aviation department affected every aspect of the operational day was part of the story. To summarize the structure and organization of the aviation department would have resulted in a deadly dull recitation of images and explanations that would soon pall. The diversity of information and activities—including the repair and maintenance of aircraft, pilot training, and transport—had no natural order. The answer to the scriptwriting problem was to show a 24-hour cycle in the operation. The idea was to cross-cut between multiple stories of flights in preparation. The preflight check runs on the sound track as you cut away to simultaneous activities in other areas. Meanwhile, on an oil platform, a helicopter delivers a relief crew. Shots of cargo being loaded, from mail to drill bits and spare parts, take you into other stories. The clock becomes your narrative structure. At night, an executive Gulfstream flies an emergency mission to bring a pregnant woman with a breach baby from a remote site to a Dhahran hospital. Through this device, all of the different types of aircraft and missions can be covered in different locations.

In the final analysis, the corporate video has to tell a story. Whether the story is factual or fictionalized, it has to make a number of points. It has to convince an audience to respond to the informational, motivational, or behavioral objectives that we discussed in Chapters 2 and 5. In other words, the corporate video has to do a job, although it might entertain as a means toward that end.

WRITING THE CORPORATE TREATMENT

These organizing devices must now be expressed in a **treatment**. We discussed treatments in developing PSAs, but for a 30- or 60-second message, the **treatment** stage is less critical. In reality, it is sometimes possible to go from your creative concept to a first draft script. This is not true for corporate videos of 5 to 10 minutes in length. You have to go through the stage of outlining the narrative in chronological order in a prose **treatment** that describes action and suggests the role of commentary. You do not and should not write out the **voice-over** commentary at this stage or the dialogue you wish the talent on camera to speak. You can paraphrase the gist of what they are going to say. You can even paraphrase the content of interviews by suggesting what might be said in interview or what you hope will be said in response to interview questions. The final document that you want your client to read should give a complete account of action and activity that is to be filmed. You cannot generalize content by saying. We have interviews of managers or sales reps or tourists. You need to characterize the expected content of those interviews. You cannot say we see the manufacture of the company's products. You have to say what products and at what location and what physical action, perhaps because you have researched it. If you do not, your client cannot evaluate what is likely to be in the script. Moreover, when you get to writing the script, you will have to do it anyway. A script is a con-crete document that describes what happens in front of camera for every scene. So you are only put-ting off the evil day. More importantly, for both client and writer/producer, you can see and evaluate the structure and scope of the video. A good **treatment** simplifies the job of scriptwriting. Writing a script is really translating the content outlined in the **treatment** into video production language. (An example of a corporate treatment that is too long for the printed page can be found on the website.)

SCRIPT FORMATS FOR CORPORATE VIDEOS

It is probably fair to say that the most common format for corporate video is a dual-column format (see the appendix). Remember that in the **dual-column format**, the visual description of what appears on screen is written down in the left-hand column. The audio description of what is heard on the sound track is written down on the right-hand column. These two columns are read together so the producer can assimilate all of the information needed to produce the scene. It is the easiest way to write for video once you get over the beginner's tendency to mix up the two categories of audio and visual. In practice, corporate video uses any and all types of production concepts including drama, news, and documen-tary. Instead of using the **dual-column format**, scriptwriters may adopt formats that are typical of those other types of productions, such as a master scene script for a dramatic concept (see *Charley Wheeler's Big Week* by Peter Cutler on the website).

LENGTH, PACING, AND CORPORATE STYLE

What is the length of a corporate video? Answer: It is as long as it takes to do the communications job at hand. Some corporate videos can be a few minutes; others are as long as 30 minutes. Over the years, since video has become a commonplace corporate communication tool, practitioners have studied the success or failure of videos with audiences. When an audience is watching a television screen for reasons other than entertainment, the attention span is short. You will happily watch a 2-hour program with characters, plot, story, conflict, and action. When the content concerns ideas, information, products, management policies, or other informational subject matter, your capacity to concentrate and retain information falls off exponentially after 15 minutes. If a program can stay under 10 minutes, it might be more effective. The 15-minute limit has always seemed a good one. In recent years, the ideal length has come down to 10 minutes. There are exceptions. In every case, the length must be justified by the inter-est of the content and the effectiveness of the program making. Narrative styles that wrap a message in a **dramatized** story always play longer than factual recitations or talking heads.

WRITING VOICE COMMENTARY

Commentary takes up program time. Running time for a program can sometimes be critical, whether it is a PSA or commercial, a corporate promotion or a documentary. It takes a long time in screen time to say things. Long-winded or overly detailed explanations can burden a program. Continuous commentary from beginning to end is tedious for the audience. It is always better to have pauses and rests in spoken sound track to allow music or natural sound to carry the program. A voice artist has to be well cast and well directed.

Most important of all, we must constantly remind ourselves that in visual media, visual communication through images is more effective than the spoken word. Any corporate or documentary program should work at some level without a sound track. It is a good test to view a program without commentary and to make it as effective as possible in purely visual terms. **Voice commentary** should complement the visuals and support them, but the structure of a program must derive from visual sequences, not from spoken commentary. Innumerable documentaries and corporate programs violate this principle. Writers, particularly those who are not professional scriptwriters, often write the commentary first and then add visuals to cover the commentary. The visuals become a kind of fill-in wallpaper. Do not write what we might call wall-to-wall commentary! If you catch yourself writing the right-hand column of a **dual-column script** first, the quality of your work will suffer. The best programs are always conceived as visual statements first and are driven by visual ideas. A **voice commentary** should be subordinate to the visual story. **Voice commentary** is best written in two stages. First write a draft commentary to help cut the visuals and pace the editing. Do you need to edit picture or edit voice-over to fit the picture? So the second stage is a final draft ready for voice recording. If you record the commentary first, then picture editing is driven by the commentary. A director or producer has to choose which is dominant. Some prefer to record a voice artist to video playback. So a writer might be given a rough cut to polish the final version—much easier when the writer is also the director.

DEVELOPING THE SCRIPT WITH CLIENT INPUT

Corporate scripts are not written for the writer; they are always written for the client. Before writing anything, you need to consult with the client and research the communication problem as explained in Chapters 2 and 3. At each stage of development, presentation of the concept, **treatment**, and first draft script involves informal feedback and finally formal acceptance of the work. Each stage needs client approval before you continue. This process is critical to the success of the project. Every writer has had the experience of working with a client who barely reacts, or reacts after the script is written. There are clients who do not understand their role in advising and collaborating to achieve a successful corporate communication. Books devoted solely to corporate writing provide greater insight into this problem, which is part of the writer's job but not part of the writing.[7] The writer of corporate work has to be able to manage relationships and gently orchestrate the necessary responses if they are not forthcoming. Writers who work in the corporate field learn that clients sometimes waste their time and waste their own resources.

SELLING CREATIVE IDEAS

When you write, you sell. All writing for corporate communications involves selling the creative ideas on which your communication is based. This means that not only must your ideas work for

---

[7] See Ray DiZazzo, *Corporate Scriptwriting, A Professional's Guide* (Burlington: Focal Press, 1992); see also William J. Van Nostran, *The Scriptwriter's Handbook: Corporate and Educational Media Writing* (Burlington: Focal Press, 1996).

the medium, but they must also persuade the client who is myopic about the message and cannot see the wood for the trees. Many clients, indoctrinated with "corporate speak," have difficulty hearing any other voice or mode of communication. They are nervous about creative ideas that may dilute the pure message. They have difficulty seeing that their audience, even a captive employee audience, is not necessarily going to absorb and retain the message in its pure corporate form without some strategy of communication that gains audience assent. The creative strategies outlined in the previous section are what the writer works with to exploit the medium and reach the audience effectively.

Although our principal concern here is with writing, we should alert the beginner that most corporate writing involves presenting ideas in meetings—a form of pitching. Writers in this field need to be able to talk their ideas. They need to encapsulate them for the corporate client in such a way as to get this client to read the **treatment** or the script with understanding and assent. They want the client to "buy" the script.

WORKING WITH BUDGET LIMITATIONS

Every project has a budget. Even the grandest feature film has a budget. Cost is relative to length, location, and production values. Cost is paramount in corporate work. All corporate departments work with budgets. Audiovisual communications have to be designed and written within some kind of cost guidelines. Although in the learning stage one need not be hampered by cost, in professional work, creative ideas come with a price. If a creative solution is too ambitious and too costly, it will be rejected. Many corporate clients do not have discretion to spend more than a fixed figure. Often that figure is unrealistic for what they want. Every corporate producer has been in a meeting in which after finding out what the client wants, learns that the money available to do the job is totally unrealistic. Compromises have to be worked out. Writers have to learn how to compromise and modify creative ideas and concepts based on the amount of money available.

CONCLUSION

The corporate world makes liberal use of visual media to solve a wide range of communication problems, from marketing to external and internal public relations, promotion, brochures, service manuals, and training. Providing these solutions is big business for a large and diversified industry of media producers who employ writers to think through corporate communications problems and come up with creative solutions. Corporate scriptwriting involves designing media messages on behalf of a client. All of the creative devices of the medium are potentially useful to this end. Working in the corporate field involves a contractual and consultative relationship that is unique

In this chapter, we learned that writing training programs involves specific goals that can be more closely measured and defined through techniques of **formative** and **summative evaluation**. Training and educational needs usually involve explaining or demonstrating an operation or a process. Media solutions deliver standardized content that meets agreed objectives. The scripts are usually written in a **dual-column format** like their corporate cousins. Imaginative devices are still a valuable part of the writer's repertoire to communicate how to perform a task or improve performance. The corporate need for training is virtually inexhaustible. Its needs are increasingly met by interactive instructional media, which are the subject of Chapters 12 and 13.

Corporate scripts typically adopt a **dual-column format** unless other formats work better, for instance, a dramatized work. The nonbroadcast industry is probably larger and more innovative than the broadcast industry. It is a highly creative and dynamic industry that is responsive to new technology and communications media. It offers more opportunities for employment than the entertainment industry.

Exercises

1. Write a short training video for a simple task such as tying a tie, parallel parking a car, or cooking an omelet. This should include a short **formative and summative evaluation**.
2. Write a plan for a **formative evaluation** for a college recruitment video. Use an existing video to do a **summative evaluation**. Optional: Put a focus group together to do the evaluations.
3. Write a task description of a familiar activity, say, brushing your teeth.
4. Go to the training department or human resources department of a local company and find out if the department has any training needs. Try to get information so that you can write a script for the human resources personnel.
5. Go to the training department or human resources department of a local company and find out if the department has any training videos. Ask to see them and find out as much background as you can about their development.
6. Make a list of **visual metaphors** to explain situations or problems, for example, driving, rules of the road, conflict resolution, or using a piece of machinery.
7. Visit the admissions office of your college or university. Find out what the communication problems are with recruiting. Write a concept and **treatment** for an admissions video that would address those problems.
8. Contact the public relations or advertising department of a local company and find out if the department has any corporate video needs. Submit a proposal to write a script for them.
9. Contact the public relations or advertising department of a local company and find out if the department has made any corporate videos. Ask to see them and the script and see if you can get some background on the development of the project.
10. Find an organization on campus that you imagine needs a video. Interview the staff and design a video concept for them.

CHAPTER 7

Documentary and Nonfiction Narrative

KEY TERMS

3-D	historical documentary	reality
actuality	interviews	reportage
archives	inverted funnel	research
biographical documentary	investigative documentary	science documentaries
commentary	location research	scratch commentary
concept	narrative documentary	travel documentary
documentary	objective documentary	treatment
dramatized documentary	photography	truth
expedition documentary	picture research	voice-over
expository documentary	point of view documentary	wall-to-wall commentary
fiction	propaganda	wildlife documentary
funnel	proposal	

DOCUMENTARY COMES FIRST

Everybody has seen a documentary. The documentary is an important program format that has roots in **photography** and painting. If you think about it, the most fundamental urge we have is to record reality. Some 25,000 years ago in the south of France, Cro-Magnon man struggled to document the fauna of his world on the walls of caves. There are no portraits of the painters of those exquisite rock drawings. At the site of Pêch Merle in France, there is, however, a prehistoric signature in the form of an outline of a human hand. The need to record ourselves in the form of an image is central to all cultures, whether on Greek pottery or temple friezes, Roman coins or Egyptian obelisks. The portrait is our most intimate documentary. For centuries, painters have been commissioned to create likenesses

Doi: 10.1016/B978-0-240-81235-9.00007-9

of people for public display, for family, or for posterity. Much of this function has been assumed by **photography** since the latter half of the nineteenth century. We have a photograph of Abraham Lincoln. We only have paintings of George Washington. We take our own photographs of friends and family. In this respect, we are all documentarians. What is our objective? We want to record reality so that someone else can experience that moment either with us or without us at a later time.

The first moving picture **documentary** was inspired by a $25,000 bet—a tidy sum in its day. The challenge was to prove that a horse either does or doesn't lift all four legs off the ground at a full gallop. In the 1870s, Eadweard Muybridge rigged up a system of trip wires so that a galloping horse would release the shutter on a line of still cameras as it passed.[1] In this way, he could prove that a horse lifts all four legs off the ground and does not keep one hoof in touch with the ground as his adversary maintained (Figure 7.1). What could be more essentially **documentary** than that?

Others,[2] including Louis Lumiere and Thomas Edison, worked on capturing motion. What excited the first movie audiences was seeing realistic shots of motion—such as a train rushing toward camera, which gave a feeling of such realism that the audience ducked in fear of being hit. The same

TRANSVERSE-GALLOP.

FIGURE 7.1
"The Horse in Motion," photographed by Eadweard Muybridge in 1875.

---

[1] The "zoopraxiscope" was patented in 1867 by William Lincoln. Moving drawings or photographs were watched through a slit in the zoopraxiscope.
[2] Leland Stanford, who was his patron, published a book in 1882, *The Horse in Motion*. The two quarreled over the credits, and Muybridge went on to publish further works: *Animal Locomotion* (1887) and *Animals in Motion* (1899). See the video at http://photo.ucr.edu/photographers/muybridge/contents.html.

phenomenon was repeated in **3-D** movie experiments in the 1950s and 1960s. I remember going to a Cinerama film and seeing a shot of a lion jumping at the camera, which gave the audiences of that day a thrill such that we all screamed and ducked. If you have ever been to an *IMAX* theater, you will find the same psychology applies. The huge wraparound screen on which a 70-mm film image is projected creates a realistic experience of "being there." I remember feeling dizzy watching a shot from an ultralight plane flying over the Grand Canyon or Niagara Falls or some other spectacular landscape. Not many dramatic fiction films are made in this format because of the cost. However, **3-D** production is becoming more popular for feature film production. In 2009 **3-D** television sets became available for domestic use.

The first attempts to make moving pictures were **documentary**. Dramatic storytelling uses of the medium came later. In reality, however, the **documentary** format in film, video, or television also narrates stories, but of a factual kind. Early **documentary** filmmakers, such as John Grierson and Robert Flaherty, were, in a sense, reporters. Film quickly became a news medium, and television continued the use of the moving image to convey reports of people, places, and events.

Recently, as happens from time to time, some **documentary** films have been distributed as theatrical feature films competing with fictional dramas and comedies. The Academy of Motion Picture Arts and Sciences awards Oscars for both short and long **documentary** films; *Bowling for Columbine* won in 2003 in the feature length category. *Spellbound* (2002) documents the agonies of children competing for the prize in the Scripps Howard National Spelling Bee. Then there is an extraordinary wildlife film, *Winged Migration* (2001) that allows us to fly along with migrating geese and cranes and know the life of birds that fly thousands of miles to seasonal feeding and nesting grounds. Others like *Touching the Void* (2004), a reenacted **documentary** of surviving a climbing accident, and *The Endurance: Shackleton's Legendary Antarctic Expedition* (2000) can command theatrical audiences because they are extraordinary tales of human endurance. Other personal **documentary** essays by Michael Moore, *Fahrenheit 9/11* (2004), *Sicko* (2007) and *Capitalism: A Love Story* (2009), generated political controversy and also a record-breaking box office for the genre.

Even though some **documentaries** may be shot on film, it is risky and expensive to distribute them on film. However, recent history suggests people will buy tickets to see these **documentaries** projected as films in a theatre. We conclude that the desire to know reality or be told about reality is an abiding need of film and television audiences. With time, DVDs and the World Wide Web will probably become more important to the dissemination of **documentaries**.

Despite these successes, television remains the main distributor of **documentary** programs. Most **documentary** filmmakers look to television to commission or buy the broadcast rights of their work. With its inexhaustible appetite for **documentary** material that communicates information, explains ideas, or records history, television and cable have kept the tradition alive. Now we have television news features and whole channels more or less devoted to **documentary** programming. The Discovery Channel, A&E, and the History Channel come to mind. PBS, especially WGBH in Boston, is a consistent producer of **documentary** series, carrying on a great tradition that originated with early producers of 16-mm film **documentaries**. They produce some of the best **documentaries** on television. *American Experience* tries to capture uniquely American people, places, and events. *Nova* documents new discoveries and new thinking in science. *Frontline* is a current affairs program that addresses contemporary social, political, and ethical issues.

You could also argue that the sports channels are, in a sense, **documentary** channels because they show you real games. Perhaps the most basic **documentary** function of television is performed by C-SPAN, which records senate hearings and public events, debates, and so on. However, real-time, live broadcasts are different. They are not scripted. Could you script the progress of the World Series or the Super Bowl? They record an event as it happens. Even sports commentators or announcers ad-lib their broadcasts. No writers are needed. This is an important distinction because we are now proposing to examine the role of the scriptwriter in the **documentary** form and learn how it is done. How does the writer approach **documentary**? What is the role of the script? How is writing for a **documentary** different from writing sitcoms, movies, or broadcast news?

TRUTH OR FICTION

Let us think about the word itself: *documentary*. Obviously we recognize the word "document" in it. Its root is the Latin word **documentum**. According to the Oxford English Dictionary (OED), its first appearance in English is close to the Latin, meaning a teaching, an instruction, or a warning. Later, in the seventeenth century, the meaning shifted and the word came to refer to something that is written or inscribed that furnishes evidence, such as a deed or a contract. The growth of trade made documents important. A ship's manifest would show who owned the cargo. Hence, a document is a record of something that establishes a fact. Then it becomes a verb, to document, meaning to establish the truth, furnish the evidence. In 1802, the OED records the use of **documentary** as an adjective, meaning that something consists of **documentary** evidence. Only with the invention of the **documentary** film does the adjective then become a noun again that is shorthand for this type of film.

So **documentary** contains the idea or intention that it is evidence establishing a fact, that it is telling the truth. This raises all sorts of interesting problems. For instance, the video footage on the news is supposed to be truthful reportage. That is our expectation, but it is not always so. Shots can be staged and sometimes are. Shots are framed for effect. We do not see what is behind the camera or outside the field of view of the lens. The footage is also edited. A point of view is both contained in it and imposed on it. Nevertheless, we expect the truth. If a **documentary** is about an expedition to climb Mount Everest or reveals the life of a pride of lions in the Serengeti, we expect it to be a truthful account. **Documentary** scholars and theorists argue about the relationship between truth and reality. For instance, to be controversial, ask whether a pornographic website that shows live sexual activity is truthful. Is it reality? Perhaps it is real but not truthful because it is performed, even though it may involve real sexual acts. It is easy to confuse **actuality** with **reality**, and **actuality** in behavioral **documentary** is not necessarily reality because of the presence of the camera or because of the cultural differences between the observer and the observed.[3]

The name of the genre suggests an action of documenting a factual story in moving and still pictures. It can be a story of a person, a historical period, a historical event, an animal species, a work of art, or any other topic of investigation. The essence of the **documentary** form is that it attempts to tell or show the truth in its totality. This commitment to recording reality can result in shocking or disturbing

---

[3] See Barry Hampe, *Making Documentaries and Reality Videos*, Henry Holt and Company, New York, 1997, p. 87.

material. Georges Franju, in *Le Sang des Bêtes* (1949), makes us look at the hidden horror of slaughter-houses. Alain Resnais, a French director, made a famous **documentary** called *Nuit et Brouillard* ("Night and Fog," 1955), which was probably the first attempt to reflect on the horror of Nazi concentration camps. The allied armies that liberated the camps had documentary film units that recorded the first images of that horror. The power of images to show the truth makes visual media compelling and per-suasive. On the other hand, the same power can be devoted to fabricating falsehood and propaganda. Leni Riefenstahl's Nazi propaganda film, *Triumph of the Will* (1934), commissioned to commemorate Hitler's Nüremberg rally, is a masterful use of the medium.

That is why we should consider whether all nonfiction narrative is **documentary**, even though all **docu-mentary** is nonfiction narrative. We have to distinguish between telling a true story and telling a story about historical events, which is based on the truth. A dramatized documentary tells a story of real peo-ple and real events, but it does so by inventing scenes and employing actors to portray what the writer imagines could have happened. The line between truth and fiction becomes blurred. If we cross the line completely, we end up with a biopic, as it is called in *Variety*-speak. **Truth** takes a back seat to entertain-ment. **Documentary** is still narrative, but narrative that is dedicated to telling the story of history.

Remember that the word "story" comes from the Latin word for "history." "Story" and "history" often overlap. The Old Testament and the New Testament tell stories, but some consider them to be history. Cultures tend to convert history into stories that become more compelling than the real thing. For exam-ple, the Boston tea party is both a story and an historical event, as is the ride of Paul Revere. Sometimes, the story becomes more important than the history, as is the case with the ride of Paul Revere. In history, he rode to Lexington; in legend, according to the poem of Longfellow, he rode to Concord.

How do you construct a **documentary** idea? How do you tell the **truth** in a visual narrative? True representation of something rests on knowledge. Knowledge rests on **research**. **Research** takes many forms. It can be picture **research**, location **research**, factual **research**, background **research**, **interviews** with people, or historical **research**. Until you have done that work, you cannot meaningfully write down a **treatment** or outline for a **documentary** production.

Of course, you get an idea for a **documentary** based on an insight, a supposition, or a hunch that there is a **truth** to reveal about something. It could be commonplace, such as what happens to a letter once you post it, or something unusual or exotic, such as the story of an expedition. We still call this a **concept**. It is an idea that guides your thinking, your **research**, and your discussion with producers and editors of program formats. Once you have a **concept**, you have to **research** it.

We say that seeing is believing. The scriptwriter should understand that film and television are media that are made by editing footage in postproduction. They are assembled shot by shot according to a script or a vision of the maker. Because editing involves choice—choice of what to leave in and what to cut out—the editorial point of view can be biased. So **documentary** is not necessarily objective truth. It can be an argument against war or for the environment. Its point of view may be partisan and consciously adopted by the maker. Wherever the camera is pointed, some things are excluded while others are included. Camera placement on location and editing choices in the cutting room determine the final result.

Documentaries fall broadly into two types according to their point of view. There is **objective docu-mentary** and **point of view documentary**. The first strives to be a record of true observation, showing things as they are. It is the most difficult because the production method so often alters the reality in front of the lens. The latter is an examination of factual matter but from a point of view that is declared. An example of the latter would be Michael Moore's documentaries.

Usually, the director imparts the point of view. This is why **documentary** is primarily a director's medium. The writer, if independent of the director, is not going to have as strong an influence on the final shape of the program, for the obvious reason that the shooter chooses the images and frames the shot. Because the writer is subordinate to the director, documentaries are often made by writer/directors who can carry through their intentions from script to shooting and, finally, in the cutting room. The general public is not really aware of how the medium of film and video can be manipulated in postproduction or how the person looking through the viewfinder chooses the frame, which once again includes and excludes objects or people in front of the camera. Both of these actions constitute a form of continuous visual editing that imposes a point of view. It can easily be abused—and often is—in news reporting to create more dramatic footage.

For this reason, true **documentary** is a noble form because it seeks to reveal the **truth** about a subject. Being truthful can be compatible with expressing a point of view, just as, in print journalism, editorial opinion can be stated in conjunction with factual reporting. The important point is to make a clear distinction between fact and opinion, or between the camera as an observation device and the camera as an editorial device manipulating what the audience is allowed to see.

SCRIPTED AND UNSCRIPTED APPROACHES

Most directors shoot unscripted documentaries. Such productions can be undertaken on the basis of a **treatment** expressing the idea or intention of the **documentary**. Wildlife documentary is particularly unlikely to be scripted before shooting because you don't know what you are going to get until you shoot it. You cannot script moves for a pride of lions or plan what a gorilla will do. You just keep shooting and, very often, acquire footage of opportunity that could never have been planned. You can and must script a reconstruction of the assassination of President Lincoln.

Documentaries can be divided into two broad categories: those that are highly researched and structured and those that are observational or a filmed record of things as they happen. **Historical and biographical documentary** tends to need scripting to establish a structure and a narrative order. Like any production, a **documentary** script has to be broken down into sequences and shot lists and then budgeted. If you need a certain shot or an archive picture, that location or that photo has to be researched, found, and rights or permission obtained. This all adds up to cost. Therefore, the greater the detail of your script, the better you can plan the shoot and control the budget. All scripts, for every format, are an exercise in efficiency. If you know what you are going to shoot, you can organize better and limit shooting things on the spur of the moment that may ultimately have no use. On the other hand, shots of opportunity often occur on location, and a good director knows when to improvise or grab an unforeseen opportunity. It comes down to simple pragmatism. It is worth paying a writer or spending the time writing a script or plan for what you are going to shoot in order to save money. If we recall the blueprint analogy, we can remind ourselves that construction is the expensive part. So scripts save production costs, just as drawing up accurate building plans saves construction costs.

RESEARCH AND FORMULATING A THEME

Factual background, **location research**, and **picture research** are also necessary when creating a documentary. They are specialized services that are often independent of the writer. **Research** is based on reading background, on **interviews** with experts, on site visits, and on **archives** of both still and moving pictures. From the **research**, a writer can establish what material exists, find a theme, and choose a way of organizing the narrative exposition. To undertake **research** without some kind of formulated project that is acceptable to an eventual buyer involves risk. The expense of time and money might not lead to production. Initial **research** might be enough to establish the topic or theme. Serious **research** enabling a script to go forward would then be part of any budget.

Research means, above all, picture **research**. It is no good writing in a shot of Sigmund Freud analyzing a patient on his couch if either the picture doesn't exist or the rights to the picture cannot be acquired or are too expensive. Picture rights are a huge part of **documentary** budgets. Therefore, a writer must write around the images that are available. If an **archive** image is not available, then a location shot of, say, a historical place such as a Civil War battlefield could be substituted. That means a location shoot with all the attendant expenses. Another alternative is to write in a dramatized reenactment. This means spending production money on actors, costumes, and sets. Every solution costs money. A writer has to write a visual narrative that is based on known resources as far as possible. At the same time, the story has to be credible and substantial. It is always tempting to carry the story in words rather than visuals. Ultimately, the program will fail if it becomes commentary heavy. **Research** empowers the writer to write intelligently, exploiting the resources in a judicious way while keeping the program alive.

Sometimes, a **documentary** is made because of the discovery of new material. After the dissolution of Soviet Russia, a whole new film archive about World War II was discovered in Russia shot from the Russian point of view. The archival material itself warrants a **documentary**, even though other **documentary** series about World War II already exist. This type of **documentary**, based on the compilation of existing footage linked by narration, is common. Obviously, writing this kind of script depends on viewing the **archive** footage and arranging it in some kind of order with a narrative **voice-over** and some selected **interviews**. It makes the writer into an editor. Indeed, an editor is like a writer who writes directly on the screen with the available images that have made it to the cutting room.

WHAT IS THE ROLE OF THE WRITER?

At this point, we can understand that the role of the writer can be different for different types of documentaries. Writing is largely restricted to the development phase for other types of media writing but is coexistent with production and postproduction for documentary. Writing is critical for two preproduction documents. The first is a **proposal**. The second is the **treatment**. Then in postproduction the writer returns to write **voice-over** narration. Only **dramatized documentary**, in which real events are reconstructed or historical characters are portrayed, is fully scripted because you need settings, action, and dialogue.

The Proposal

The **proposal** is the dealmaker. Like all media content, documentaries cost money. Typically, they are financed by presales to channels for certain rights. The **proposal** or **concept** sets out the idea of the **documentary**, the potential, and the promise. Essentially, a distributor such as a television network, here or abroad, buys the idea with a promise to make payment on delivery for a specific number of broadcasts in a specific territory over a specified time. All documentaries have an element of unpredictability. Therefore, the **proposal** and the proposer are all that the network or cable channel has to go on. The **proposal** matters because it will lead to the **treatment**.

The Treatment

We know what a **treatment** is from previous chapters, and for a **documentary** it is not really different except that it is probably the final document before production. Unless there is reenactment or dramatized narrative, there is no way to script a scene you don't know you are going to get. The importance of the **treatment** is to organize the structure and the argument of the **documentary** and the intended sequence of visuals. It should also establish its point of view. The **treatment** could also be a scene outline that would identify locations and interview subjects.

TYPES OF DOCUMENTARY TECHNIQUE

There are a number of recognizable **documentary** techniques in use today. Sometimes they are combined, just as techniques of corporate video are. However, on the whole they tend to work better when a consistent style is maintained throughout. What follows are simply commonsense definitions meant to help us discriminate between different types of writing. They have no formal standing.

Reportage

Reportage is a French word meaning, literally, "to bring back." The journalist, writer, or filmmaker brings back information that gives an account of an event. Because **reportage** involves telling the story as you find it, it is really a contradiction to write down shots you plan to shoot or things you plan to see. There is an implicit understanding that you will record what you see as you see it. Of course, putting yourself and your crew in a place and time that will enable you to get the footage depends on choice and implementation of opportunity. Writing is primarily going to take place in postproduction in the form of commentary.

Observation

The camera can be used as an observing eye from within the environment in order to introduce the audience to an unfamiliar world. As a general rule, the camera and its crew intrude in the world that is being recorded. People react to the camera. The crew, even a crew of one, is a presence that is not part of the environment. The camera disturbs the environment it is trying to record. Therefore, it cannot observe the natural behavior of subjects. If you put a camera into a classroom, it will be difficult for the students not to be aware of the camera and, as a result, they will probably change their behavior. The same would be true for, say, a prison, a street gang, or a family. It is a challenge to a certain kind of documentary filmmaker to approach human environments somewhat like a wildlife photographer. The technique is to introduce the camera and wait until people are used to it and forget about it. They can then render the camera neutral. Flaherty's documentary about Eskimos, *Nanook of the North* (1922), has attracted controversy because he can be accused of staging actions and behavior for the camera. This kind of documentary is basically constructed in the cutting room. In this silent film, there is no commentary. Other documentaries of this kind have to be postscripted after the footage has been recorded.

Interviews

Whether an **interview** serves as research before actual production or whether it is going to be filmed as footage for inclusion in the edited **documentary**, successful interviewing underpins every **documentary**. The questions may not appear in the final edit. Audio only of the answers can also be used for commentary **voice-over**. **Interviews** are based on questions and answers to those questions, which might be recorded on camera or off. The techniques of interviewing were discussed at length in Chapter 3. Let us recall that there is a range of rhetorical techniques in different types of questions and a number of ways of structuring **interviews**. The **funnel technique** begins with broad and general open questions and narrows down to specific closed questions. The **inverted funnel** does the reverse. (Refer to the discussion in the previous chapter). Strong interviewing is central to so many documentaries. Thinking about the purpose and method of any **interview** in advance is necessary to its success.

Investigative Documentary

Investigative documentary uses the medium of film or television to record an inquiry into the **truth** or falsehood of a certain question. Numerous controversies exist in a pluralistic society. Conflicts of interest occur between corporations and public interest, between new advances in science and technology and public conservatism, between political policies and the public good. Global warming is of enormous consequence for the human race. Yet scientific evidence has to be sifted and presented before we can know the **truth**. Establishing that a disproportionate percentage of the prison population in America is black then demands an investigative analysis. Or revealing that prisons have become the dumping ground for the mentally ill as states cut budgets, the subject of an *American Experience* **documentary**, requires that the producers obtain extraordinary entry into a restricted environment to get footage and interviews of inmates, prison administrators, and psychiatrists. The class-action lawsuit against Corning Glass by women who had silicone breast implants led to another documentary—*Breast Implants on Trial*—produced by *Frontline* at WGBH.

Investigative documentary depends on in-depth research. It is important to marshal all the facts and separate them from rumor, popular opinion, and corporate **propaganda**. You generally need to have a few good case histories on which to draw. This means getting the cooperation of individuals and paying experts for testimonial. Many well-prepared **interviews** with a good cross section of opinion are desirable.

Investigative documentaries always face a problem of balance. It is easy to create a bias by omitting, as well as by including, certain evidence. We expect impartiality. The question is, do we expect a conclusion? A trial in court of law must reach a verdict or a mistrial is declared. Does an **investigative documentary** have to reach a conclusion? It seems unsatisfactory to leave things up in the air after arduously leading us through the evidence. A successful **investigative documentary** should point to a conclusion and make clear an editorial view set beside the arguments and the evidence. The audience can form its own opinion, but with the knowledge that those who dug up the evidence would not make a program unless they could resolve the issues themselves.

Narrative Documentary

One of the most appealing forms of nonfiction is **biography**. Every life has some mystery. Famous and infamous lives invite all the emotions of curiosity, admiration, and amazement. Documenting a life in pictures through the recollections of friends and relatives, through the evidence of the public record, or through private papers can get closer to the **truth**. A human life has a natural narrative structure—a beginning, a middle, and an end. We all recognize it. We all empathize. Putting the facts in order, balancing the differing views, or debunking a myth is absolutely a **documentary** endeavor. Who doesn't wonder about the personal life of Marilyn Monroe and question the manner of her death? Who is not curious about the life of a genius like Albert Einstein? Figures of wealth and power in history forever fascinate us. The Discovery Channel and A&E program a lot of biographies, particularly of celebrities. The story of a life may also be a window into the historical period in which the person lived. *TR: The Story of Theodore Roosevelt* puts a mythical figure in perspective. **Narrative documentary** can tell us the history of a town, a work of art, a war, a political movement, or a revolution. The story, leaning on the Latin root of the word, becomes history.

Dramatized Documentary

The **dramatized documentary** has become a popular form on television. Instead of hopping between **archive** images, narrators, **interviews**, and location shots, you abandon those techniques and give yourself license to recreate or reenact a factual story with actors in costume. The purist might object to the invention of dialogue or scenes that may or may not have happened but whose exact content is not known. A case in point would be the life of Shakespeare, perhaps the world's most famous playwright. Very little is known about his life beyond official records and some comments by his contemporaries. One treatment would be to construct a narrative with a presenter showing us where documents about his life exist and linking present-day sites to historical engravings; another approach might be staged reenactment of probable or plausible scenes.

Where is the borderline between a Hollywood biopic and a **documentary**? A biopic has acts and structure. A story of a life has shape, but not necessarily three acts and a dénouement. So there are different dynamics. What is the difference between a movie like *Little Big Man* (1970, directed by Arthur Penn), about the defeat of General Custer at Little Big Horn, and a **documentary** about the same subject?[4] Arthur Penn is also a **documentary** filmmaker. It is interesting that the movie is structured around a simulated **documentary interview** of a 111-year-old man who witnessed the event. The movie tells a story that concentrates on the trials and misfortunes of a particular character who lives in both the white and Indian cultures. There are also **documentary** accounts of these events that try to establish the facts from sources. *Legends of the West* (1993) is a **documentary** film that goes over the same ground. The result of a fictionalized movie is different from that of a **documentary** and creates a different experience for the viewer.

---

[4] Some documentary background can be found at www.garryowen.com, www.curtis-collection.com/tribe%20data/custer.html, and www.mwac.nps.gov/libi.

In practice, **dramatized** and **narrative documentaries** can be, and often are, combined. Sometimes the gaps in **archive** material or location can be filled with an actor playing the character of the biographical subject. An actor's voice can be used to read letters and create emotional impressions that would not come across in the stricter form of exposition by **voice-over**, **archive**, and **interview**. This is how the life of Albert Einstein is treated in a WGBH *Nova* production. An actor playing Einstein on screen narrates parts of his life story; these scenes alternate with the broader story of Einstein's life and science narrated by a **voice-over**.

Expository Documentary

The term **expository documentary** is meant to describe the kind of documentary that explains something. It is typical of **science documentaries** that explain a hypothesis or a theory and the way the experimental evidence supports it. These are often constructed as narratives that unfold in a kind of suspense story. Exposition is a nondramatic function of film and video. It shows us a place, or an artist's work, or how a life form grows, or how a product is manufactured. *The Triumph of Evil* documents the failure to prevent genocide in Rwanda. *Inside the Tobacco Deal* tells the "inside story of how two small-town Mississippi lawyers declared war on Big Tobacco and skillfully pursued a daring new litigation strategy that ultimately brought the industry to the negotiating table. (WGBH website)"

Now compare this last **documentary** story with the dramatized, feature film version, *The Insider* (2000), starring Al Pacino and Russell Crowe. By doing this, you will see clearly how drama embellishes a true story. They are both powerful narratives. The question to ask is whether the **truth** is revealed more accurately in factual **documentary** narrative or in emotionally convincing dramatic narrative portrayed by actors.

Propaganda

In democratic societies, we do not like to think that we produce **propaganda**—politically or socially targeted messages that are dictated by a government, political party, or commercial organization—but such documentaries have been made since the beginning of the moving picture medium and will continue to be made. All governments in time of war make them. The Nazis made use of film to advance their political and racial philosophy. Leni Riefenstahl made a classic political **documentary** for the Third Reich, *The Triumph of the Will* (1934). It is brilliant filmmaking but for an unpalatable cause. Britain and the United States also produced plenty of biased **propaganda** films during World War II.

More disturbing are the social **propaganda** films produced in post-war America. An example of public policy **propaganda** is the film made in the United States to show the population how to survive a nuclear attack—pretty much a pack of lies. Then there were FBI films, such as *Reefer Madness*, that were made to show the effect of smoking marijuana and how it leads to uncontrolled sexuality and madness. Marijuana undoubtedly modifies behavior in certain ways, but the film's hysterical bent is grotesque social **propaganda**.[5]

We live in an economy in which advertising is rife. You could argue that advertising is a form of commercial **propaganda**, which is, after all, hardly concerned with **truth** but with persuasion. It is

---

[5] See the *Frontline* documentary titled *Busted: America's War on Marijuana* (www.pbs.org/wgbh/pages/frontline/shows/dope).

not difficult to turn those talents to making nonfiction programs to persuade audiences about social or political issues. Political parties do it. Presidential candidates do it. Public relations firms and advertising practitioners sell their expertise to all comers, even foreign governments. The government of South Africa retained public relations firms to counteract the negative publicity of apartheid. **Propaganda**—whether social, political, or commercial—usually masquerades as **documentary**. That is why a strong, true **documentary** tradition is a priceless cultural asset that contributes to the free speech and cultural health of a nation.

In the United States, the government, particularly the White House, tries to influence the media and the public perception of policy. Why else is the press secretary such an important appointment of any president? The Pentagon and other interests manipulate foreign policy and actions abroad, especially military action, to inculcate a favorable public perception.[6] If you want to understand the difference between managed media coverage and the truth, a fruitful study is the American invasion of Panama in 1989, ostensibly conducted to deal with the corrupt government of General Manuel Noriega. To understand what really happened, view the Academy Award–winning documentary *The Panama Deception* (1992), directed by Barbara Trent and written by David Kaspar. It can be seen as an **antipropaganda documentary**. It is an excellent example of an **investigative documentary** that goes beyond what any news special or news feature would dare to air. Nevertheless, controversy surrounds it because it makes harsh and damaging claims about the way the United Sates conducts its foreign policy.[7] It reveals a **propaganda** model that is strikingly similar to the one used in the run-up to the invasion of Iraq in 2003.

OTHER DOCUMENTARY APPLICATIONS

Expedition Documentary

Archeological, mountain-climbing, and other types of expeditions often include a documentary film project, which is a record of the voyage and a possible source of revenue through television and video sales. Common sense tells us that it is going to be difficult to script an **expedition documentary** in advance. So writing becomes a postproduction exercise, especially **voice-over** commentary.

Travel Documentary

Everyone has seen one. In the days when travel was more difficult and more expensive, film and video could provide a vicarious visit to an exotic country or region. Of course, **travel documentary** has a marketing or promotional function and was often sponsored rather than motivated by an investigation. Now there is a wider television audience for **documentaries** of exotic places. In the days when movie houses had shorts and supporting features, **travel documentaries** were common. Travel and exotic places are often the subject of documentaries shot in super-widescreen format for IMAX theaters. A lot of people would watch a **documentary** about Antarctica who wouldn't spend their

---

[6]A powerful study of this evidence can be found in the video *Manufacturing Consent—Noam Chomsky and the Media* (1994; http://uk.imdb.com/Title?0104810).

[7]A bonus of the World Wide Web is the opportunity to read reviews on amazon.com, where the video is for sale, by individuals who served in the military in Panama during the Bush intervention, Operation Just Cause (http://uk.imdb.com/Title?0105089).

vacation dollars on a trip to the South Pole. These now tend to be television programs with a host appearing on camera while on location and taking you on a tour.

Documentaries About the Making of Feature Films

This is becoming increasingly important for DVD releases, which are interactive and offer the viewer a menu of outtakes and background on the film's story, actors, and the shooting itself. Documentaries such as these have to be shot on the basis of an outline and are largely written in postproduction. They have to include shots of the movie's final cut, intercut with interviews of the actors and production personnel. Of course, they have to be planned before the production of a film and require permission from the producers.

Wildlife Documentary

This almost needs no comment. This genre is omnipresent in the television schedule. Such programs are the mainstay of Animal Planet, NGEO and the PBS stations. **Wildlife documentary** programs have endless appeal to a wide audience demographic. Seeing the secret life of a rare species, being taken into the life of a pride of lions, or seeing the life of an ant colony is an experience that would not be possible without the help of the wildlife filmmaker. Because wildlife shooting is unpredictable, the program is constructed in the editing phase when the writer becomes an important contributor in constructing the commentary.

Current Affairs Features

Documentary works best when there is a topic of investigation. Too many current affairs features are weak, in my view, because they simply collect sensational material, juxtapose conflicting points of view, and end with a question or a kind of shoulder shrug, leaving the viewer to weigh the evidence. Although it is all done in the name of objectivity, it is a cheap and easy out. The mystery documentaries always use this technique. After showing evidence that there might be extraterrestrial visitors and UFOs, they leave the mystery unsolved and their point of view uncommitted. The question they started out with remains unanswered at the end. *Frontline* produced by WGBH in Boston probably represents the highest achievement of current affairs investigative documentary.

WRITING COMMENTARIES

Narrative Voice-Over and Postproduction

Probably the most noticeable writing in the documentary form is the writing of the **commentary**. This requires a special kind of writing that must function in conjunction with the images on screen. Therefore, all **voice-over** narratives or **commentary** are finalized in postproduction based on the running order and the running time of the sequence. The salient fact is that every word written must be spoken. Every word spoken takes time. Beginners always underestimate how long it takes to speak a **commentary**. The **commentary** cannot extend beyond the relevant images that the audience sees while listening to the **commentary**. Typically, a "scratch" **commentary** is written and recorded and laid against the rough cut. When the two are finalized, then the true recording with the **voice-over** artist is recorded, often against a projected picture. Alternatively, some directors will record the **commentary** and cut the picture to fit. The problem with this approach is that if your picture and **commentary** don't match either in length or emphasis, you have to pay for the recording process all over again.

Wall-to-Wall Commentary

You must let the **commentary** breathe, that is, give the audience a break from a droning voice. After all, film and video are visual media. Their success lies in the power of the images on screen that have intrinsic meaning without need of **commentary**. Some documentaries and corporate videos have what I call **wall-to-wall commentary**. The **voice-over** starts at the beginning and continues with scarcely a break until the end. The result is monotonous and exhausting. It is made worse when there is a continuous music track running underneath it. **Commentary** should support the picture when it augments the visual or supplies indispensable information about the image. Even great documentaries fall down in this respect. Alain Resnais's great essay on the holocaust, *Nuit et Brouillard*, suffers from an interminable verbal assault on the ear, which deprives the images of their power to evoke a self-made **commentary** in the mind of the viewer.

Commentary Counterpoint and Commentary Anchors

One way to combat the **wall-to-wall commentary** effect is to set up topic sentences of **commentary** that are then completed by the visual sequences that follow. Skillful use of **commentary** sometimes results in an effect similar to musical counterpoint. You create a deliberate tension between the spoken **commentary** and the visual content. The **commentary** can give a clue to the deeper meaning of the images. It resembles the way music can be used both as an ironic comment on the visuals and as an emotional intensifier. The NBC miniseries *500 Nation* exhibits some examples of this. The devastation of European invasion and settlement of the Americas is explained but played out in a visual sequence that makes a statement independently of the **commentary**. It is advisable to use this technique as a change of pace. It sometimes works as a commentary anchor for a sequence. **Commentary** often has to bridge and combine disparate and diverse images in a montage. It is impossible to comment on every image; this is not the purpose of **commentary**. **Commentary** can set up a sequence that then runs better without **commentary** because the audience is cued and sees what it is supposed to see. The writer must search for a generic phrase or a collective idea that anchors the sequence so that it can float free visually.

Dual Commentators

Most programs have a single voice narrating the **commentary**. There is no reason why you cannot have more than one. Two voices could break the potential monotony of one voice in a long program. It also offers the advantage of having both a male and a female voice. Although it is really a director's or a producer's decision, the writer might write the dual narrator concept into the script. Female voices do not necessarily go with so-called female subjects. As a corporate producer, I sometimes used female voice-overs for male target audiences as a form of counterpoint to expectations so as to get attention. The female voice is attractive to the male ear and messages that might make little impression in male tones can sound intriguing. There is nearly always an element of seduction. The female voice can also be maternal and persuasive. It can be a teacher's voice and, therefore, authoritarian, or shrill, nagging, and possibly off-putting.

The psychology of voices is complex. Some voices are pleasant to listen to, and others are not. Some voice artists make small fortunes each day running all over town from studio to studio providing voice-overs for ads and corporate videos. Others cannot make a living. If you listen to voice-overs on TV spots, you can recognize certain recurring voices.

Commentary Clichés

The most obvious abuse in writing **commentary** is the predictable and obvious linking of image and **commentary** such that the **commentary** either follows literally what is shown on the screen or telegraphs exactly what we are going to see just before we see it. This kind of literal linking reduces **documentary** to a kind of slide show. Unfortunately, programs continue to be made in this way. Sometimes it is better to say nothing and let the pictures tell the story. **Commentary** can destroy the visual life of a film. Another chronic problem of **documentary commentary** is the use of predictable phrases and clichés that lazy writers use, such as "age-old," "Nature's fury," "a land of hope," and so on. You know when you hear them. You've heard them before in a dozen other commentaries.

Writing **commentary** for **wildlife documentaries** seems to present a great challenge that is rarely met successfully. Although this is a personal view, it is fair to say that the **commentary** of a large number of **wildlife documentaries** is obvious, predictable, or too sentimental. It has become commonplace to personify places and animals leading to flowery language and sentimentality: *The Serengeti breathes a sigh of relief as the rainy season brings life back to the parched earth.* Or we get a warthog personified as Leonard: *Leonard is playful and wants his brothers and sisters to play with him. Leonard's dad is an unsociable male whose only role is to fertilize the female.* We may have a need to explain animal behavior in terms of human behaviors, but to do so is scientifically misleading. It is easy to parody this kind of **commentary**.

On-Camera/Off-Camera Combinations

The classic **voice-over commentary** is spoken by a talent, sometimes a well-known actor, who never appears on screen. The audience accepts this voice narrator without needing to see the person. This script has to be written carefully for the spoken voice and in short phrases that flow naturally and fit the visual sequences. The **commentary** has to be apposite to the picture. Above all, where no **commentary** is needed because the meaning of the picture is self-evident, it is a writing skill to say nothing.

A **scratch commentary** is written in postproduction against a rough cut, if not a fine cut, of the program. It has to be timed to fit the running time not only of the overall program but of individual sequences. It is no good writing brilliant **commentary** that runs beyond the visual sequence. If you are still explaining the dry season on the Serengeti and there are no more dry season shots and thunderclouds and rain is sheeting down on the screen, you are forced to curtail your dry season remarks. It is easier to rewrite the **commentary** than to recut the film. Moreover, you want to avoid a rewrite in the recording session when you are paying big bucks for the studio, the engineer, and the voice talent. So you need a breakdown of the film with timed sections in order to write. You have to test out what you write by reading it aloud against the picture.

There are two ways of fitting **commentary** to film or video. You record a roughly timed **commentary** and then lay it over the picture as a separate audio track. Where it doesn't fit exactly, you edit out pauses in the audio track or edit images so that you get the picture and **voice-over** to line up for the emphasis and effect that you want. Once it is set, you lay the music and then mix the tracks so that the levels fade up and down or in and out to achieve the final result.

The second technique is to record the **commentary** to play back. You loop sections of the final cut and cue the voice artist to deliver the **commentary** while watching the sequence. This sometimes has the advantage of getting a more nuanced and effective delivery compared to reading a text in a recording booth without the benefit of picture. Voicing lines to picture, or ADR (automatic dialogue replacement) for lip sync is indispensable to the postproduction of dialogue films or for dubbing a foreign language, but for ordinary documentary it is usually too expensive.

Narration can also be delivered to camera by a talent that appears on screen. Sometimes this can be a celebrity or a well-known actor who lends interest to the topic. Obviously, if the narrator stays on screen all the time, you end up with a continuous talking head. This type of **commentary** always involves running the voice track of the narrator while cutting away to shots of something else, usually what the **commentary** is talking about. In that way, you can alternate between an on-screen narrator who looks into the lens and engages the audience emotionally and a **voice-over** whose identity you know while liberating the screen for images that support the story. This technique requires writing prior to production and commits the director to shooting the narrator in certain locations and backgrounds. It is usually reserved for programs that advocate a point of view rather than try to be objective.

One of the earliest of these documentary series was *Civilization*, produced by the BBC in the 1960s with Kenneth (Lord) Clarke, the distinguished art historian, as on-screen narrator. Alistair Cooke, the well-known columnist and radio commentator, narrated a **documentary** series titled *America* (1972) in a similar way. More recently, Kevin Costner made and narrated a **documentary** series, *500 Nations* (1995), about the North American native peoples, their rich civilization, and its destruction by European invasion. The reasons for using this technique are numerous. It works when you have an on-screen authority or personality whose presence enhances the audience experience. Sometimes, it can get in the way of showing the audience the pictures you want them to see instead of this intrusive character. It works in conjunction with interviewing techniques. Your narrator can interview experts, characters, or passersby and seamlessly integrate **interviews**, on-screen narration, and **voice-over**. This versatility is attractive to makers of factual programming. This choice has to be made before production and commits both writer and director to that decision.

CONCLUSION

Documentary and nonfiction narrative have an honorable place in the history of the medium and will continue to do so. Now most Internet content falls into the category of nonfiction narrative of some kind. Immense numbers of websites are now dedicated to documenting and **documentary** objectives. Informing a public, as well as entertaining a public, remains a significant goal of all media formats. **Documentary** investigation is essential to news analysis, although it is largely excluded from regular news because of the airtime required for in-depth exploration of a topic. The cable channels continue to buy and commission **documentary** work. Stories about people, historical figures, and historical events make for compelling nonfiction narratives.

Although **documentary** is probably a writer/director's medium more than a writer's medium, the background research and the writing of a treatment are a crucial contribution to the form. In post-production, writing good **voice-over** can make or break a **documentary**. Whether the director/writer or an independent writer composes this text, it remains a key writing job in factual narrative film and corporate video.

Exercises

1. Record a **documentary** from television. Then, with the sound turned all the way down on playback, write your own **commentary** or **voice-over** narrative for the visual content.
2. Find an example of a good **documentary**. Play the audio track without looking at the screen, or dub off the audio track. Time the phrases and time the pauses.
3. Write an outline or **treatment** for a **biographical documentary** on a celebrity or historical figure. Make a list of **research** needs for pictures, locations, and **interviews**.
4. Write a set of **interview** questions for the subject of a biography of someone you know or of someone whose life you would like to document.
5. Write an outline for a **documentary** on events at the Little Big Horn. Make a shot list of key images.
6. View *Manufacturing Consent—Noam Chomsky and the Media* (1994); *The Panama Deception* (1992); the WGBH–Boston documentary *War and Peace in Panama* (1991); and *Missing* (1982) a feature film written by Donald Stewart II and directed by Costa-Gavras about American involvement in a Chilean right-wing coup d'état. Make a list of those features that make a film a **documentary** and those qualities that make it dramatized entertainment with a message.

7. Compare the investigative **documentary** *Smoke in the Eyes*, produced by *Frontline*, with the feature film *The Insider* (1999), in which Al Pacino portrays Lowell Bergman, the CBS *60 Minutes* newsman who later became a Frontline producer when he resigned over CBS's refusal to air the story about Dr. Jeffrey Wigand blowing the whistle on Big Tobacco. It was suppressed by the CBS parent company, Westinghouse.

Entertaining with Visual Media

In *Get Shorty* (1995), John Travolta plays Chili Palmer, an enforcer for loan sharks who want to collect from a movie producer. As he gets caught up in the movie world, he comes out with the perfect line with which to launch this part of the book: "I've got a great idea for a movie." Let's face it. Everybody has an idea for a movie. We've all seen more films and television movies than we can count. We can all imagine a story, a character, or an imaginary world that would be just as good as some of the movies we have seen. Now is the time to look more closely at what it means to conceive and write a feature film or a long-form television script. Many dream of a concept, but not many have the perseverance to write a 2-hour screenplay. Even if you can complete a screenplay, the fact is that many are written, but few are chosen. Hollywood is reputed to spend $500 million on development of stories and screenplays and buy at least 10 times more scripts than are ever produced. Most professionals would agree that there is always room for good writing and original ideas. The lure is the lucrative fees that are paid for good scripts and even for some not-so-good scripts.

The market changes constantly. Unknown writers and directors sometimes strike a chord that resonates with the public imagination and see their creation soar into the spotlight. Some low-budget movies such as *The Blair Witch Project* (1999) have grossed millions. In 1969, Dennis Hopper and Peter Fonda made a low-budget movie, *Easy Rider*, that spoke to a new generation of moviegoers and threw Hollywood into confusion in an era when it was making big-budget musicals and spectaculars that lost money. The studios at that time did not understand the youth market that made up a large portion of moviegoers. Studios usually try to back known quantities and spend the bulk of their development money on projects written by writers with demonstrable talent.

Let's backtrack a little and look at how it all started. The companies that were making films for the arcades and nickelodeons competed fiercely. There was no talk of art. The objective was to sell the novelty of the moving picture sensation and visual amusement for profit. This meant finding ways to appeal to the general public. Within a short time after the invention of the moving picture medium, early filmmakers experimented with short fictional narratives. With the first attempt to tell a story on film, a need for scriptwriting arose. To set a camera in front of an onrushing train doesn't require a script, but to tell the stories of the *Perils of Pauline* (1914) in which we see her tied to the track by a villain and wonder what will happen in next week's episode requires storytelling. It requires a sequence of shots to be set up. Although directors might keep simple stories in their heads, the economy of the medium dictates that production be planned and produced for a known cost. In order to plan and budget, there has to be a written script. The American inventor of the motion picture projector[1] created the Edison Company to make films for the new and growing entertainment industry. The archives are part of the film collection of the Museum of Modern Art in New York. You can examine the scripts and the distribution scripts for foreign versions and quickly realize that production was highly organized, even in the first decade of silent movies.

Of all the forms of film and television, the most captivating is the feature film. The power of the medium to hold audiences the world over has endured for a century. The public has embraced this experience of escapism, laughter, tears, fantasy, and **drama.** Talented writers and directors, in spite of the studio film factories, have made out of the medium a seventh art.[2] Visual storytelling was firmly embedded in the popular culture of the twentieth century and promises to be a significant part of twentieth-first-century media. Therefore, the writer who conceives the story or adapts the story and writes the dialogue must continue to be indispensable to program creation.

---

[1] The Edison company demonstrated the Kinetoscope in the United States in 1891, which enabled one person at a time to view moving pictures. In 1896, Edison brought out the Vitascope projector.
[2] Andre Bazin, in *Le Septième Art* (New York: Penguin Books). The other six arts are music, drama, painting, sculpture, literature, and dance.

CHAPTER 8

Dramatic Structure and Form

KEY TERMS

action	key moment	screenplay
acts	log line	sequence
adversary	low-concept film	setbacks
antagonist	master scene script	seven-step method
archetype	photoplays	shooting script
character	pitch	shot
comedy	pity	story engines
concept	play-within-a-play	subplot
conflict	plot	tag line
dénouement	premise	tension
deus ex machina	problem	three-act structure
dialogue	protagonist	three-stage process
drama	resolution	through line
fear	revenge	tragedy
flashback	reversals	treatment
genre	scene	Writers Guild of America
hero	scene heading	(East and West)
high-concept film	scene outline	

ORIGINS OF DRAMA

The origin of drama in Western culture is rooted in the Greek theater. The playwrights of ancient Athens created dramatic structure. Its philosophers and rhetoricians, principally Aristotle in the *Poetics*, defined the theories of **tragedy** and **comedy**, concepts that hold true to the present day. Its architects created amphitheaters. The Romans continued the theatrical tradition by writing and performing plays. The remains of their amphitheaters as well as their viaducts survive to this day in places far from Rome in what were then their colonial outposts in Europe.

Although performance, singing, juggling, reciting poetry, and storytelling never ceased over the centuries, there is little evidence of theatrical culture after the Romans until Medieval morality plays and the Elizabethan theatre in sixteenth-century England. In this extraordinary ferment of poetry, of rediscovery of the classical literature of Greece and Rome, and of reinvention of the theatrical stage, the genius of Shakespeare flowered and endowed us with 37 plays consisting of comedies, histories, and tragedies. Ever since, English-speaking culture has continued to produce playwrights, plays, and players.

If you were alive at the beginning of the twentieth century and somehow became involved with the new medium of movies and wanted to create dramatic films, you would have naturally drawn on the theatrical tradition that you knew. Plays and **photoplays**, as they were initially called, had certain things in common that made them work. To have drama you have to have **conflict**.

CONFLICT

Conflict is the basis for all dramatic plots. Conflict creates **tension**. **Tension** demands change and resolution of that **tension** through **action**, choice, and **dialogue**. This is the energy that drives a plot forward. You can identify the **conflict** engine in any film or television drama. The **conflict** can be between characters, between a character and his or her own nature, or between a character and natural forces. **Conflict** produces a situation that is by definition unstable. Something has to change. In the first few scenes of *Hamlet*, we know that his uncle murdered Prince Hamlet's father, his right to the throne of Denmark was usurped, and his mother has married this same villainous uncle. He is in love with the daughter of a high-ranking courtier who is currying favor with the new king and sees this relationship as a way to advance his career. Hamlet is alone, and his life in danger in a treacherous political situation. What is he going to do? He must choose **action** or speech that impacts on the other characters and moves the play forward. Watching this tragedy unfold until all of its complications are resolved in a magnificent duel scene grips audiences in every new generation and will do so until the end of time.

Aristotle summed it up pretty well 2400 years ago. He explained **tragedy** as an **action** that is serious, complete, and of a certain magnitude. This action evokes the emotions of **pity** and **fear** in the audience, which are then purged through their witnessing the spectacle. **Pity** is aroused when we see someone suffer the consequences of mistakes or human frailty, and **fear** by the recognition that the tragic character is like ourselves. We identify with the tragic hero—*there but for the grace of God go I.* Aristotle also defined a key characteristic of good drama, namely, that "the unraveling of the plot … must arise out of the plot itself … not be brought about by the **deus ex machina** as in *The Medea*, or in the return of the Greeks in *The Iliad*." A lot of Hollywood producers ought to be made to memorize this. Of course, maybe they have, and, in the absence of box office figures from Athens, don't consider those ancient Greeks to be A-list writers.

So we see deliberate violations of this principle that ruin the play or the movie by having some external force, like the gods in Greek mythology looking down, interfering in the destiny of characters and resolving the tension of the plot. **Deus ex machina** means, literally, "a god outside of the mechanism"— that is, a force or event outside the **premise** of the plot invented by the writer that fixes the problem of the plot. Somebody wins the lottery. The cavalry rides over the hill and rescues the hero. Such contrived intervention short-circuits the completion of the purge of the emotions of **pity** and **fear** that are engendered in the **conflict**. Tragedies don't, or shouldn't, have sequels.

What about **comedy**? **Comedy** has the same **premise**—a **conflict** of interests, a **conflict** of expectation and reality, a predicament that cannot stay the same. It must be resolved. The need to resolve it drives the characters and the plot forward to increasingly hilarious dilemmas until the problem is resolved and we can all go home contented. Aristotle said that **comedy** aims at representing men as worse, **tragedy** as better, than in actual life. Try this! A brother and a sister are shipwrecked in a foreign country. The young woman disguises herself as a man and seeks favor at the court of the local count. This count is courting a beautiful lady and uses the cross-dressing woman as a go-between. The lady falls in love with the messenger who (herself) is in love with the count on whose behalf she must woo. Her good fortune depends on pretending to be a man. If her true gender is discovered, the game is up. The harder she works at being the messenger of love to the lady, the worse the situation becomes. What a delicious spectacle for the audience! For the Elizabethan audience, there was the added irony that female parts were played by young male actors.[1] Between this situation and its resolution, there's going to be lots of hilarious confusion. And we haven't even brought in the subplots.

Do you recognize Shakespeare's *Twelfth Night*? Shakespeare is the master. The Elizabethan English of 400 years ago does not obscure the sheer theatricality of his plays and the plain fact that his theater was commercial entertainment for a paying audience of all classes.[2] The parallel to the birth of the movies as a new form of commercial entertainment is interesting. Some of the problems are the same. There is a great literary tradition, technical innovation, and a bottom line. The difference is that the cinema was, from the outset, an industrial enterprise based on mass production rather than individual artistic talent. Nevertheless, artistic talent was necessary both in front of, and behind, the camera.

Lots of people—studio heads, producers, and agents—have ideas for movies or buy rights to novels, plays, and musicals to turn into movies. Rarely can they write the scripts. Even if they have the talent, they don't have the time because they are making more money running the business. Therefore, movies and television series cannot be made without scriptwriters. The people in control of the process of production cannot function without writers. From the beginning, they have sought to control this creative person whose work is difficult to measure. The friction between creative artists and industrial moviemakers continues to this day. Hollywood is a town dedicated to deals and to making money. It is no wonder that writers are organized into a trade union, the **Writers Guild of America (East and West)**.[3]

To some extent, the **screenplay** is a form created by Hollywood. It is true that playwrights have, since the theater of ancient Athens, found structures that, when analyzed, help us to create our own plays. If the aim of Hollywood film production is to mass produce entertainment or, more recently, to find

---

[1] This type of mix-up was part of the fun in the Academy Award–winning movie *Shakespeare in Love* (1998).
[2] For those who want to bypass serious background reading, the film *Shakespeare in Love* (1998) paints a picture of the trials of the new medium, although its tale of Shakespeare is wholly fictional and improbable.
[3] Consult their website: www.writersguild.org.

the formula for product that will quickly produce cash flow avalanches from box office hits, then it becomes important to be able to pick the right scripts. It is probably more important to be able to define the script (or script elements) that will form the basis for box office success. Industrializing the script is a consequence of industrializing movie production and distribution. It became the practice to employ more than one writer on script development in order to keep creative control. The practice continues to this day.

THREE-ACT STRUCTURES FOR FILM AND TELEVISION

When we go to the theater, we experience scene changes, a division of the play into **acts**, and an intermission. When we watch television, we get commercial breaks that usually happen at a significant point. So television appears to have **acts**. When we go to the movies, however, we have a seamless narrative experience from beginning to end. In reality, most movies have an intrinsic **three-act structure**. The popular audience does not think about **acts** or structures. Nevertheless, this structure is what makes the form work, even if the audience is not conscious of it. There is a parallel to music. Music has structures that the composer uses: counterpoint, refrain, repetitions, key changes that follow conventions and rules based on chords and harmonies. People may not be aware of the rules of musical composition, but they unknowingly respond to them. Music without structural form is noise, and movies and television without a dramatic structure leave audiences confused or dissatisfied, even if they can't explain why.

Many stories, legends, myths, and folktales exhibit a natural form of storytelling from an oral tradition. It seems to correspond to how the human psyche responds emotionally to stories. Perhaps it is akin to forms in nature like the golden ratio in the shell of the nautilus, or the spiral of nebulae, or like the mathematical ratios of musical notes. This cultural story fabric shows patterns that are probably universal or **archetypal**. If you can find that pattern and embed it in your film story, you will probably find a wide audience. That is what Hollywood writers and directors have learned.

What are the characteristics of good stories? They have a **main character** or hero. That hero has a **problem** that is life altering or life threatening. The hero has an **adversary**, either animal, such as a monster or dragon, or human, such as a rival, a wicked uncle (as in *Hamlet*), or a stepmother, which leads to significant **conflict**. The story unfolds with a rising action that includes heart-stopping **reversals**, **setbacks**, and turning points. The hero learns something about the world or about himself and delivers his family, village, city, or tribe from harm. This **archetype** of the hero was identified by Joseph Campbell in *The Hero with a Thousand Faces* and was discovered by Hollywood decades later as a kind of talisman for storytelling.[4] Hollywood storytellers have identified it as a structure having three acts. Many movies exploit and enhance a natural **three-act** storyline and **archetypal** heroes that are recognizable in myth and legend. The folktale *Little Red Riding Hood* has a basic structure that is easy to follow and has worked for generations of children. What is important is that it works even if you know the story. Stories that work, work forever. Children know the story but still respond with the same emotion each time they hear it or read it. In fact, the repetition of the story enhances

---

[4] *The Hero with a Thousand Faces* was first published in 1949, was revised in 1968, and has been reprinted many times since. The archetype is an idea he borrowed from Jungian theory to find universal meaning in primal stories. George Lucas acknowledged the influence of Campbell in *Star Wars*.

its value. When you read to your children, you discover the unschooled responses of humankind to narrative. Homer's *Odyssey* or *Iliad* do not wear out. Shakespeare's great tragedies are revisited in every generation, whether it is *Hamlet* (1990) played by Mel Gibson, a modernized *Romeo and Juliet* (1996) with Leonardo DiCaprio playing Romeo, or *The Merchant of Venice* (2004) with Al Pacino playing Shylock. Filmmakers can't stay away from them. Let us now examine the structure of the story through the intuitive responses of children to discover what makes it work.

Little Red Riding Hood is given a task by her mother. She has to take a basket of food to her Grandma, who is not well. To get there, she has to walk through the forest. It is a journey. She is instructed not to wander off the path or talk to strangers. So the young girl is the **protagonist**, the lead character. The audience identifies with her. She has a **problem**. She has to find the way to her Grandma's house. This is a test of character and resolve and an adventure that is seemingly innocent but is fraught with serious moral and character issues. You might argue that Little Red Riding Hood's mother should be had up for child abuse and neglect exposing to her to such risk, but clearly we have become soft and weak. Life was tougher then.

The sun is shining. The sky is blue. The birds are singing. What could happen? Little Red Riding Hood sees banks of wildflowers, starts to gather them and chase butterflies, and ends up wandering off the path. Many movies start in the same way. Then Little Red Riding Hood loses her way. Soon the audience learns that there is a Wolf in the forest, who spies the little girl, sees high-quality protein and an easy meal, and intends to eat her. This character is the **antagonist**, or the villain. Now we know something she doesn't know. This creates suspense. It also creates sympathy, **fear**, and **pity** for her and concern about her destiny. She is alone and lost in the woods with a hungry, cunning Wolf slinking around who wants to eat her alive. What will happen to her? Being lost in urban society is an inconvenience; being lost in nature—a desert, a forest, a jungle, at sea—is a life-threatening trial. You can run out of food or water, be overcome by the weather, and be attacked by wild animals. Now we have MapQuest and GPS. Now we have signposts, and animal predators are threatened with extinction and are protected—like wolves for instance. We have forgotten what children know. The fear of being lost is primordial.

This is Act I. Act I has to establish several fundamentals for the audience:

- Introduce the main character.
- Introduce supporting characters.
- Establish a task, an intention, a desired outcome.
- Establish an obstacle, a **problem**, an adversary.
- Create **conflict, suspense, tension**.
- End with a **reversal** or a **setback**.

If the story stopped now, the audience would be frustrated. By the end of Act I, we want to know what is going to happen. When the audience reaches this state—understanding the **problem**, knowing the main character, and wanting to know the outcome—Act I is complete. This does not mean you have to mark this point. On television, this is where you would place a station break because you give the audience a reason to stick around to see what is going to happen. Act I is simply the completion of a response pattern.

Now Little Red Riding Hood is lost in the forest and a little worried. Although the sun is still shining and the birds are still singing, the hours of the day are numbered. In our movie version, we could have dark clouds blot out the sun or a storm build up on the horizon. This would signal the audience that danger threatens (in literary rhetoric, when nature seems to mirror human emotions, it is called a pathetic fallacy). In many versions, the Wolf goes up to her, smooth-talks his way into her confidence, and finds out where she is going. We hear the sound of an ax chopping wood. We come upon a Woodcutter. Little Red Riding Hood is so glad to see him because she can ask him the way. This is the seeding of a **subplot**, not fully developed, but indicative of movie structures. The Woodcutter gives her directions and sends her on the way. There is temporary emotional relief. Little Red Riding Hood is going to make it. Then cut to the Wolf who has overheard the conversation and now knows where she is going. So he runs ahead and gets to Grandma's cottage first.

This is the R-rated version, by the way. If you are under 17, you need your mother's written permission to continue reading. We now have a terrifying scene in which the snarling Wolf eats the helpless Grandma alive. The horror of this is amplified in intensity because it now sets up a fearful apprehension about what will happen to our heroine. Turn the screw a little tighter. The Wolf now dresses in Grandma's clothes and with an evil chuckle goes to her bedroom and gets into bed. We show the Wolf rehearsing imitating Grandma's voice (the Wolf is played by Jack Nicholson). Now the audience is really worried. Whatever problems Little Red Riding Hood had in Act I are now intensified and complicated. Sometimes the main character knows and sees the problem. Sometimes only the audience knows. After rushing along through the forest, Little Red Riding Hood suddenly comes into a beautiful clearing and sees Grandma's cottage. She rushes up to the front door and knocks. This is the end of Act II.

Now the audience is really invested in the fate of Little Red Riding Hood. What is going to happen? If the story stopped now, the audience would go out of its mind. The situation has become worse. The predicament of the main character is as serious as it can get. It has to be resolved. There has to be a conclusion, a **resolution**, or a **dénouement** as it is called. That's when you know Act II has finished and it is time for Act III to begin. Once again, it is not announced. It is a point in the emotional response pattern of the audience to the story.

Act II must accomplish the following:

- Complicate the predicament of the **main character**, raise the stakes.
- Introduce a **subplot**.
- Introduce subordinate characters.
- Create an overwhelming need for final **resolution**.
- End with a **setback** and a new level of crisis.

Now the Wolf (pretending to be Grandma) calls her to come in, or maybe the door is left open by the earlier arrival of the Wolf. Little Red Riding Hood wonders where her Grandma is. We could write in shots that show evidence of a struggle and a fleeting reaction of puzzlement on her face mixed with joyful anticipation of seeing her Grandma. "I'm in the bedroom," calls the Wolf in his granny voice. We cut to the surprise on Little Red Riding Hood's face as she sees the false Granny. The Wolf encourages her to come nearer. She goes through the classic dialogue: "Oh Grand Mama, what big eyes you have!" "All the better to see you with," replies the Wolf. "What big ears you have!" All the better to hear you with, my dear," replies the Wolf. And then the climactic line, "Oh Grand Mama, what big teeth you have!" Children hold their breath and squeal with anticipation—"All the better to eat you with," cries the Wolf and rips off his disguise with a snarl.

The **sequence** ends with the terrifying revelation of the true identity of the Wolf. Little Red Riding Hood screams in total, absolute terror. This is the ultimate horror story and the paradigm for many horror movies. The audience is in agony at the prospect of her downfall. The jaws open wide. She screams as the Wolf devours her. She is gone. This is the ultimate **setback**.

At this point, the audience is in a state of shock. Could this be the end? Surely not! While the Wolf rips off the Grandma's clothes, we cut to the Woodcutter with his ax coming into the clearing. Just as he is about to go up to the door, he stops as he catches sight of a Wolf through the window. He sneaks up and notices the signs of struggle and the blood of the victims and then sees the Wolf triumphant. Audience morale rebuilds. There is hope again. The Woodcutter catches the Wolf off guard and with a roar splits his skull with his ax. Audience emotion soars with elation. The Wolf dies in agony. The audience rejoices in the violent and painful end of the Wolf. This is the fundamental emotional mechanism through which movies introduce violence and slake the audience's thirst for **revenge**.

Although **revenge** is satisfied we've lost Grandma and Little Red Riding Hood. For some narratives this is the trade-off, the only satisfaction, and we must accept the loss.

In many children's books, this doesn't happen. This is the R-rated version, the European version. The earliest known version was collected and set down by Charles Perrault in 1697.[5] In the nineteenth century, the brothers Grimm introduced or set down a version that brought in a Huntsman who kills the Wolf and rescues Little Red Riding Hood and her Grandmother.

FIGURE 8.1
Engraving by Gustav Doré.

Now we hear the strange sound of cries from inside the Wolf. The Woodcutter takes his knife and slits the Wolf open and pulls out Little Red Riding Hood and Grandma. They are slimy, bloody, and exhausted but whole. Sobbing, she falls into the Woodcutter's arms. It could end here, or we could see them cleaned up and recovered saying goodbye to the Woodcutter as he goes off into the woods. Of course, one variation of the Woodcutter **subplot** is that because he saves the heroine, he gets the girl and they get married and live happily ever after. You recognize that scene in a many movies.

---

[5] *Histoires et contes du temps passé, avec des moralités. Contes de ma mère l'Oye*. In this version, the Wolf triumphs and there is no rescue and no happy ending. The author draws a moral about how young girls should not talk to strangers. It has clear sexual or seductive implications about predatory males.

FIGURE 8.2
Woodcut by Walter Crane.

Act III must accomplish the following:

- Intensify the **problem**.
- Close the **subplot** by resolving it into the main plot.
- Create an ultimate **reversal** or a **setback** in the predicament of the **main character**.
- Bring about a **dénouement** or **resolution** of the final **setback** and the whole story.
- Create the triumph of the hero, **protagonist**, or main character and the downfall of the **antagonist** or villain.

Little Red Riding Hood is the **archetype** of the majority of horror films in which there is always a female victim and always some menacing man/beast/alien/mutant/ creature who threatens her. This ending could be happy or tragic, funny or serious. Every turn of the story can be nuanced by writing, by directing, or by casting to express horror, drama, or comedy. Ever since Perrault introduced the sexual nuance to the plot in the seventeenth century to warn girls and young women about smooth-talking, deceptive strangers, there has always been an implicit sexual threat in the story that is made specific in many horror and suspense films. *Red Riding Hood* (2004, released in 2006), a recent film version intended for children, bears out the Perrault interpretation of the story with clear sexual innuendo that is ostensibly inappropriate for its target audience. Notice the "Little" is left out of the title. The *Little Red Riding Hood* plot was loosely adapted into a contemporary suspense thriller in *Freeway* (1996) with the tag line, "Her life is no fairy tale." A similar storyline of a woman menaced by male (wolf) aggressors showed up in a low-budget thriller *While She Was Out* (2008). Indeed, the cultural assumption is that the wolf is male, even though a female wolf could be equally dangerous just as a female lion or tiger is as deadly as the male. We also have the cultural marker in the term "wolf whistle" and the idea that single males are potentially sexual predators despite the millions of devoted husbands, grandfathers, brothers, and sons—among them a few woodcutters too.

To summarize, Act I usually must accomplish three main tasks: introduce the **main characters**, establish a **problem** or **conflict** that will drive the movie forward, and establish the setting. How do you know when Act I has ended? It usually ends with a major crisis for the **main character** or **protagonist** (we are still using the language of Greek theater) and a temporary triumph for the **antagonist**.

Act II brings complications and a **subplot**. It usually ends with a **reversal** in which the **main character** is in even greater difficulty.

Act III must bring a **resolution** of the original **conflict**, sometimes through the agency of a character from the **subplot**.

THREE-ACT STORY STRUCTURE

The three-act movie has evolved into a Hollywood convention for plot-dominated stories. It accommodates a variety of movie genres. Although there are a thousand variations, broadly speaking, most film stories fit themselves around a skeletal structure. This structure is not just the plot; it is more a map of the emotional response pattern of an audience. It is the difference between life and art, fact and fiction, reality and fantasy. You can't watch life, your own or anyone else's, like a movie. Life is what we are living and experiencing every day. It has no beginning and no ending for us because we are always in the middle, in the present. Time does not exist before our birth, even our first memory, nor can it exist for us after death. In some sense, life has no apparent plot, no dramatic structure. In fact, we are constantly trying to give it shape and structure by ceremonies, by time divisions, or by self-invented narration. In a movie, we have to give the experience of story a beginning, a middle, and an end. That is why the **three-act structure** works. It also works for television. Television episodes sometimes have four **acts** so that commercial breaks can be inserted with the least disruption. Indeed, the breaks are used cleverly to heighten the audience's anticipation by leaving them at key unresolved moments in the natural rhythm of the drama.

Why three **acts**? Shakespeare had five. Modern stage plays seem to have two separated by an intermission. Movies run for approximately 2 hours without any break. So why three **acts**? The reason is, it works. Nobody has legislated that screenplays have to have three **acts**. It is just the case that most of them do. They are not marked down as **acts** in the **screenplay** and most certainly not indicated in the screen image that the audience sees. It is a virtual structure that seems to accommodate the way stories can be told in moving pictures. However, not all movies use the **three-act structure**. There are **alternative story structures**.

Some stories are developed around characters. Eric Roehmer, a French director, has made a series of films over thirty years that examine dilemmas of human character that do not depend on the **three-act structure**. There does not have to a single dominant **protagonist**. These are often referred to as **low–concept films**. Of course, big Hollywood (revolving around movie stars and box office megabucks) holds this kind of film in contempt as low-budget, no-account art film. Hollywood favors the **high–concept film** that turns on plot and has clear leading roles. Woody Allen is another unconventional storyteller whose films often evolve around characters and situations. So at the risk of confusion, we should learn the classic three-act form while at the same time keeping in mind that there may be other narrative techniques for film and television.[6]

OTHER NARRATIVE STRUCTURES

Other narrative forms have an ancient pedigree that probably conforms to another human emotional template. Since ancient times, minstrels have sung and recited epic poems and mythical stories for communal audiences. These stories have exerted a powerful influence on poets and storytellers for centuries: the story of the war of Troy, told by the Greek poet Homer in *The Iliad* and continued by the

---

[6]A valuable critique of the traditional three-act structure and an examination of other narrative strategies for film can be found in *Alternative Scriptwriting*, 2nd ed., by Ken Dancyger and Jeff Rush (Burlington, MA: Focal Press, 1995).

Roman poet Virgil in *The Aeneid*. These epics and their subject matter have dominated Western civilization for two millennia. The structure of epics is episodic, multilayered, and populated by numerous heroes and figures, often including divinities. The wanderings of Odysseus returning from the war of Troy told by Homer in *The Odyssey* is, in a sense, a subplot of *The Iliad*. In the epic, there are often stories within stories. This multilayered form of storytelling reappears in Boccaccio's *Decameron* and Chaucer's *Canterbury Tales*, in which characters in the story tell one another (and the reader) stories while they are part of a larger story.

Multiple interweaving story structure is replicated in the television series and soap operas, like *The Bold and the Beautiful* or *The Young and the Restless*—narratives that are a kind of modern minstrel tale for the community, telling multicharacter, multiplot tales of greed, love, revenge, and justice. Soap operas, crass as many of them are, thrive on parallel storylines that do not follow a **three-act structure**. Now that many television series like *The West Wing* and *The Sopranos* are available on DVD, audiences can see them as television novels or epics with complex storylines.

Another device with origins in the complex weaving of epic narratives is the **play–within–a–play**. Shakespeare uses it more than once. In *Hamlet*, it reveals the truth that underlies all of the deceptions of the various characters. It is no accident that the players that Hamlet asks to perform his play ("wherein to catch the conscience of the King") are asked by him to recite a speech about the murder of Priam, the king of Troy, from a play based on *The Aeneid* (which connects the story of Troy to the origin of Rome through a survivor of the sacking of Troy). Those lines, often cut from modern productions, set in epic context the meaning of the murder of the king, Hamlet's father, for the Elizabethan audience. The **play–within–a–play** technique, beloved by Shakespeare, has a parallel in the film-within-a-film technique. The appeal of the movie within the movie device has been exploited by Francois Truffault in *La Nuit Americaine* (1973) and by Robert Altman in *The Player* (1992), which has a kind of allusion to Hamlet in its plot. We've mentioned *Get Shorty* (1995), which is a film about how the film we are watching gets to be made. There is an offensive movie called *8 mm* (1999) about an illicit market in snuff films, which is essentially a film within a film. *The Blair Witch Project* (1999) is a film about making a documentary about a supernatural phenomenon, which effectively disguises the low budget production techniques of handheld 16 mm in the device and recruits the audience as a partner in the plot of investigation. It is an eternally appealing way to conceal and reveal meaning at the same time.

Mark Twain's *The Adventures of Huckleberry Finn* is an episodic and peripatetic (meaning "wandering") story. The peripatetic form of the novel is a distant cousin of *The Odyssey*. Henry Fielding's eighteenth-century novel *Tom Jones* was turned into a hugely successful movie.[7] Even a mainstream film like *Forrest Gump* (1994) has a story structure that is peripatetic and almost helical and spiral in its structure. The road movie is a modern American equivalent in which the hero, or often a pair of lovers (*Bonnie and Clyde*, 1967) or a pair of friends, cross the country or trace out a career. The buddy movie was probably established with *Easy Rider* (1969). It is about two hippie bikers who travel through American culture and landscape, trying to get to the Mardi Gras in New Orleans. *The Defiant Ones* (1958) is about two convicts—one white, one black—bound together, escaping from a chain gang. One of the most successful of this genre is *Butch Cassidy and the Sundance Kid* (1969).

---

[7]The script adaptation was written by an important modern British playwright, John Osborne, and directed by Tony Richardson. It won the Oscar for Best Picture, a nomination for Best Screenplay, and a host of other awards in 1963. See http://uk.imdb.com/Title?0057590.

THE FLASHBACK

Citizen Kane (1941), the Orson Welles masterpiece, is considered to be one of the greatest films of all time for its storytelling power, its cinematography, and its direction, and it is also probably the greatest example of the **flashback** structure. It begins with the death of Kane, a ruthless and egomaniacal newspaper baron whom everyone understood to be a portrait of the real-life William Randolph Hearst. The story unfolds as a newspaper reporter interviews a number of key characters who knew Kane and who recount their differing recollections. We flash back to the dramatized scenes of Kane's life in long sequences and flash forward to scenes of the reporter, who is a kind of narrator, interviewing Kane's drunk ex-wife or his senile former colleague and employee of many years. The script by Herman J. Mankiewicz and Orson Welles is brilliant movie writing.

Quite a few filmmakers have experimented with alternatives to the linear narrative line by making **flashback** part of the plot, as in *Memento* (2000) in which a character has no short-term memory and has to reconstruct events to find out who raped and killed his wife. The linear narrative is in black and white, whereas the contemporary events are in color. **Flashback** is a psychological phenomenon usually recalling trauma of some kind. Writers and directors are interested in the relation of time to consciousness. We live in the present moment but also in memories that are part of our present. The television series *Lost* makes use of **flashback** in almost every episode as characters try to figure out how they got to the island on which they are lost.

GENRES

Genre is a French word that means "type" or "class" of things. Another way to look at movie structure is to see repetitive characteristics in movies that have similar stories and plots. These recognizable conventions of plot and setting are useful shorthand descriptions that most of us use to describe something we saw. We say that it was a western, a horror film, a suspense thriller, or a romantic comedy in order to convey a certain type of entertainment experience—one that we have had before and recognize. We cannot describe all of the patterns, and anyway, **genres** can be mixed. We would risk sounding like Polonius describing to Hamlet the acting range of the players coming to Elsinore: "pastoral-comical, historical-pastoral (tragical-historical, tragical-comical-historical-pastoral)."[8]

Westerns

This **genre** began with published stories of the outlaws and other colorful characters of the frontier and the American West. It is the American version of the pirate and outlaw tale of European fiction. In many ways the western recapitulates the story of Robin Hood. Robin Hood could be the **archetypal** story of the good guy wronged, who has to live beyond the law, whereas the bad guy, the Sheriff of Nottingham, is the law. Maid Marian is the love interest. The good king Richard Coeur-de-Lion is away at the crusades while his bad brother John usurps the throne. Robin, a dispossessed nobleman, robs from the rich and gives to the poor. You could be forgiven for thinking that this piece of English history was invented by a Hollywood scriptwriter. No wonder this story has

---

[8] Act II, scene ii.

been made into a film a dozen times, most recently by Kevin Costner in 1991.[9] Its storyline serves the western.

No sooner had motion picture been invented than the theme of the western furnished rich material, starting with *The Great Train Robbery* (1903) and retelling the story of characters such as Jesse James, Billy the Kid, and Wyatt Earp. Wyatt Earp, his two brothers, and Doc Holiday confront the Clinton gang in the famous gunfight at the OK Corral, which has been made into film several times.[10] The classic *My Darling Clementine* (1946), directed by John Ford, stands out among them. But the best Doc Holiday is played by Val Kilmer in *Tombstone* (1993). Some of my favorites are *Winchester 73* (1950), *The Gunfighter* (1950), and *High Noon* (1953). The Clint Eastwood series of westerns beginning with the spaghetti westerns of Sergio Leone is a newer reworking of the **genre**, but without the realism. A television masterpiece in this **genre** is the miniseries *Lonesome Dove* (1989), adapted from Larry McMurtry's western novel. The western has declined in importance over the years. Clint Eastwood has a consistent record of acting in and directing westerns from the days of his role in the television series *Rawhide* through spaghetti westerns, *The Outlaw Josey Wales* (1976), and his award-winning *Unforgiven* (1992).

Romantic Comedies

Romantic **comedy** often deals with social issues about love, money, class, and society. The essential element is an attraction usually between a man and a woman who either start out by detesting one another or by loving one another and then have to overcome amusing obstacles.

A classic romantic **comedy**, which required strong male and female leads, is *The Philadelphia Story* (1940). The hostile banter between the male and female leads is in inverse proportion to the warmth of the union with which it will finish. *Sleepless in Seattle* (1993) is a popular romantic **comedy** that errs on the sentimental side. *Liar, Liar* (1997) has a great comic premise. What if a little boy's wish as he blows out his birthday candles, that his divorced father would stop lying, were to come true? It leads to endless complications and hilarious scenes in which Jim Carrey says exactly what he thinks to everyone he meets. His son's wish eventually brings the father and mother back together in a second chance at repairing the American marriage.

Another brilliant **comic premise** lies behind *The Bachelor* (1999). A man is going to inherit $100 million on the condition that he is married by his 30th birthday. Guess what! Tomorrow is his 30th birthday and his girlfriend has just turned him down on a botched marriage proposal. In desperation, he now frantically starts contacting all his ex-girlfriends with a proposal. They all turn him down. Each refusal heightens the tension and incites the audience's interest to a fever pitch. We won't reveal how it ends, but you can recognize a brilliant **comic premise** in this plot. *High Fidelity* (2000) is a quirky, music-oriented romance about breaking up and reuniting; the main character talks to the camera, using a cinematic version of the theatrical aside. *My Big Fat Greek Wedding* (2002) was a

---

[9] See http://uk.imdb.com/Title?0102798.
[10] Please consult the very complete online database (http://uk.imdb.com) of movies for credits and plot summaries of all the movies mentioned.

low-budget sleeper that became a box office success because of the ethnic conflict that the heroine has to break out of the confines of expected gender role and then get her non-Greek fiancé to be accepted by her extended Greek family. *Something's Gotta Give* (2003) takes the **genre** into senior territory and the taming of the womanizing confirmed bachelor. The TV series *Sex and the City* (1998), a serial romance without the comedy and an homage to the chick flick, became a movie 10 years later.

There is also a kind of ironic antiromantic comedy that has more social realism or more character realism in which love and marriage are not the be-all and end-all. *Lost in Translation* (2003) explores emptiness and alienation. Woody Allen's script *Vicky Christina Barcelona* (2008) explores cultural contrasts between the European and American idea of love and marriage. Two recent European films about love and loss illustrate the adult alternative to Hollywood romantic comedy. *The Edge of Love* (2008) explores the destructive marriage of a brilliant womanizing drunkard who happens to be one of England's great modern poets—Dylan Thomas. *Il y'a Longtemps Que Je T'aime* (I've Loved You So Long, 2008) explores the rehabilitation of a woman after coming out of prison on parole for murder as she remakes the relationships with her sister and her family.

Horror Movies

This **genre** has origins in folk literature and fairy tales that children learn. It has a literary pedigree in the classic gothic novel *Frankenstein* (1818) by Mary Shelley. Then there is the vampire legend, which was fixed in its literary form by John Polidori in *The Vampyre* while holed up in a Swiss castle with Lord Byron and Percy and Mary Shelley in 1816, and in Bram Stoker's *Dracula* (1897). *Nosferatu* (1922) began the long career of Dracula and vampire stories in the movies (see the website). Seventy years later, Frances Ford Coppola's vampire movie title reflects the original, *Bram Stoker's Dracula* (1992). *Interview with the Vampire* (1994) adapted from the Anne Rice novel created a mainstream hit with the tag line "Drink from me and live forever." Vampires have populated the movies in endless variations and broke into television in *Buffy, the Vampire Slayer. The Lost Boys* (1987) was a teenage variant, which reappeared recently in the high school setting elaborated in *Twilight* (2008) and its sequels.

In the American tradition, we have the macabre tales of Edgar Allan Poe. It is now very much a movie **genre** that has its own traditions that are almost stronger than any literary tradition. Many of its effects used to depend on lighting, but nowadays depend on computer-generated special effects. Whether it is psychological horror like Hitchcock's *Psycho* (1960) or supernatural horror films such as *Dracula* (many versions) or *The Exorcist* (1973), there is always a strong element of suspense and shock created by playing on the audience's fear of the supernatural and violent threats to normal existence.

Road Movies

The road movie involves a journey that is both literal and figurative at the same time. It could be a journey of search or a journey of escape. These have ancient pedigree. The original road movie archetype is probably Homer's *Odyssey* or *Jason and the Argonauts*, which was remade in May 2000 as a television miniseries. In these cases, the **three-act** structure is not always necessary. The structure becomes episodic. A seminal road movie is *Easy Rider* (1969), which is a journey across American culture and counterculture of the late 1960s accompanied by a chorus of rock-and-roll anthems. It is also a buddy movie. *Thelma and Louise* (1991) is road movie with girls as buddies. *Mad Max* (1979) mutates the genre into a futuristic fantasy world. An original family road movie, *Little Miss Sunshine* (2006) reminds us how often this genre, as with *Easy Rider*, becomes a lens for examining American culture (the child beauty contest) and American landscapes. The screenplay by Michael Arndt won the Oscar for Best Original Screenplay in 2007.

Science Fiction

H. G. Wells wrote a science fiction novel called *War of the Worlds*, which was produced as a radio play in a documentary fashion by Orson Welles so convincingly that people began to flee New York and New Jersey believing that a Martian invasion was actually taking place. Then it was made into a movie in 1953, and it still stands up well for its special effects. Steven Spielberg remade the movie in 2005. The **genre** of science fiction was relegated to B movies until Stanley Kubrick's *2001: A Space Odyssey* (1970) broke out into the big time box office. *Star Trek* established the genre on television and spawned 11 movie offshoots with the most recent in 2009. The six-part epic *Star Wars* has since firmly claimed top box office status for science fiction, together with classics such as Spielberg's *Close Encounters of the Third Kind* (1977) and *E.T.* (1982).

There are many subgenre variations, but the basic plot is recognizable. Aliens invade the earth either as a single threat, as in *The Thing* (1956), or as a race, as in *Invasion of the Body Snatchers* (1956). We usually cannot tell who is human and who is alien. By the time we get to *Men in Black* (1997), we have combined the science fiction movie with the buddy movie and comedy. *The Day the Earth Stood Still* (2008) is a remake of a 1951 classic of science fiction that explores the hypothesis that we are not alone in this universe and that superior beings or more powerful beings with greater knowledge than we have exist, which provokes an examination of what is human. The most recent exploration of that theme can be found in *District 9* (2009), in which aliens stranded on earth with a broken-down spacecraft are herded into ghettos. A film like *Alien* (1979) combines science fiction, horror, and suspense. Almost a generation later this subgenre is still going strong in a movie like *Species* (1995). In 2009, James Cameron extended the range and story matter of the **genre** with 3-D and special effects in *Avatar*.

War Movies

This **genre** hardly needs definition. These movies describe on a huge canvas the sweep and confusion of war and the way it impacts the lives of individuals and civilian populations. Most war movies are ambivalent about war. The **conflict** between realism and myth animates the **genre**. They can be divided between those that celebrate heroism, nationalism, and victory, and those that show suffering and futility. *D-Day: The Sixth of June* (1956), *The Guns of Navarone* (1961), *The Longest Day* (1962), *Tora, Tora, Tora* (1970), and *Midway* (1976) try for the historical sweep. The First World War movie classic, *All Quiet on the Western Front* (1930), is an antiwar movie as much as a war movie. *The Deer Hunter* (1978), stemming out of the Vietnam War, is a modern antiwar movie, as is *Apocalypse Now* (1979). *M*A*S*H* (1970), later turned into a television series, is an ironic view of the Korean war from a behind-the-lines medical unit. *Saving Private Ryan* (1998) tries to have it both ways by combining extreme realism with a sentimental, patriotic storyline. Now the enemy is terrorism and terrorists, intensified after the terrorist attack on the World Trade Center, which turns the genre into a type of mission film, such as *Black Hawk Down* (2001). Elite units of the military are pitted against an anonymous but racially and culturally identified enemy. *Behind Enemy Lines* (2001) is set in the Balkans theater; *Rescue Dawn* (2006) revisits the Vietnam era. A counter trend critical film, *Rendition* (2007), challenges the extremes of antiterrorist illegal policies. The British-made reenacted documentary *Battle for Haditha* (2007) dispassionately reveals the how war crimes happen in Iraq. Recent films examine the personal consequences on individuals serving in Iraq, *The Hurt Locker* (2009), and in Afghanistan, *Brothers* (2009). Nevertheless, World War II is continuously revisited and reexamined. The true story of Nazi officers who tried to assassinate Hitler is chronicled in *Valkyrie* (2008). *Defiance* (2008) tells the true story of Jews who escaped roundup by Russian collaborators with the Nazis, became partisans in the forests of Belorussia, and survived the war.

Buddy Movies

The beginning of the buddy movie was *The Defiant Ones* (1958), in which Tony Curtis and Sidney Poitier escape from a chain gang while still shackled together. The buddy theme is very much a part of *Butch Cassidy and the Sundance Kid* (1969), although it is also a western. The relationship between the two lead characters is in one way what the movie is about. *The Odd Couple* (1968), originally a Broadway play by Neil Simon, with the classic pairing of Jack Lemmon and Walter Matthau, became a movie and then a TV series. Buddy movies, because they are about character and relationship, lend themselves to low-budget originals like *Swingers* (1996), a portrait of the American male mating quest. Although the buddy movie is about male bonding and is a classic "guy thing," a female variant is *Thelma and Louise* (1991). *Wild Hogs* (2007) is a comedy variant of the biker and buddy movie.

Crime Movies

This is broad category that has several subgenres that have identifiable themes. From the early days of movies, crime has been a major subject matter of motion pictures. The chronicling of prohibition, Chicago mobsters, and legendary figures of crime like Al Capone and Dillinger and led to films such as *Little Caesar* (1930), *The Public Enemy* (1931), and *Scarface* (1932 and remade in 1983) and introduced what has become a recognizable genre. Its latest version is *Public Enemies* (2009).

Private Eye (Film Noir)

Humphrey Bogart as Sam Spade in *The Maltese Falcon* (1941) and Philip Marlowe in *The Big Sleep* (1946) is everybody's idea of the private eye. Bogart established the style of the private eye as a tough loner and outsider. Again, a popular literary tradition of detective fiction is the source. Dashiell Hammett and Raymond Chandler were detective fiction writers who also wrote Hollywood scripts, later followed by Mickey Spillane. A hallmark of the **genre** is the voice-over narration in the first person by the main character and the wise guy dialogue. *Chinatown* (1974) is a darker variant. A spoof version of the genre is *Dead Men Don't Wear Plaid* (1982), which incorporates footage from all the classics of the genre.

Murder Mysteries

Body Heat (1981), written as an original screenplay and directed by Lawrence Kasdan, is a small masterpiece with a cunning plot and excellent performances. In the literary tradition, Sir Arthur Conan Doyle's *Sherlock Holmes* and Agatha Christie's *Hercule Poirot* laid the foundations of the genre, which also blends into the detective story or private eye movie. Typically, the plot is very involved and the audience cannot guess who the culprit is until all is revealed at the very end. Detective series have proliferated on television. An elegant variation on the theme, which involves a scathing exposé of the hypocrisy of British class values at the time of World War I, is the understated, brilliant *Gosford Park* (2001), directed by one of the world's great directors, Robert Altman. *Basic Instinct* (1992) is a murder mystery that is almost a film noir but the protagonist is a police detective.

Gang Movies

Movies about criminal organizations and gangs are numerous. The one movie that rises to the level of art is *The Godfather* (1972) trilogy made by Francis Ford Coppola. The mafia has become so much a part of American culture that we almost accept them as an alternate route to success in America. The TV series *The Sopranos* normalizes the life of crime as the family next door with the mafia boss getting psychotherapy to adjust to his lifestyle. *The Outsiders* (1983), *Heat* (1995), *Snatch* (2000), *Carlito's Way* (1993), and *Pulp Fiction* (1994) provide various takes on the struggle of characters to survive and escape a life of crime. The summer of 2009 saw the release of *Public Enemies* in which the Feds go after the notorious gangsters John Dillinger, Baby Face Nelson, and Pretty Boy Floyd, remaking and updating the subject matter of the 1930s and 1940s.

Undercover Cops

An early example of the genre based on a true story is *Serpico* (1973), which deals with corruption in the police force and the ostracizing of the honest cop. *LA Confidential* (1997) explores corruption in the LAPD. Ethical conflicts and dangerous undercover work give us *The Untouchables* (1987), *Donnie Brasco* (1997), and *The Departed* (2006).

Disaster Movies

Airport (1970), *Towering Inferno* (1974), *Virus* (1995), *Volcano* (1997), *Armageddon* (1998)—disaster movies favor one-word titles. The city, the country, the world (choose one) is threatened by a natural force that transforms someone into a hero as he orchestrates the struggle to save the world in clipped and tense dialogue and reminds us of the place of man in the scheme of things. It is interesting to compare *The Day After Tomorrow* (2004) with the real tsunami of December in that year, which killed hundreds of thousands of people in the Indian Ocean basin. *Outbreak* (1995) is about another type of environmental disaster—deadly viruses. Disaster movies really explore those forces that human beings cannot control. Invisible infections become enemies that for millennia have terrified all civilizations. The Black Death of medieval Europe, the plague, AIDS, and the Ebola virus all strike fear into the hearts of us all. A futuristic elaboration of the same premise gave rise to *28 Days Later* (2002).

Martial Arts

The martial arts movie is really about a theme. The theme crops up in other genre and probably began with the Samurai movies of the great Japanese director Akira Kurosawa. A great example is his movie about a young man learning judo in *Sugata Sanshiro* (1943) and *The Seven Samurai* (1954), which was adapted into a western in the United States, *The Magnificent Seven* (1960), produced by and starring Yul Brynner. The Hong Kong movie industry developed the kung-fu genre, which focused on the set piece dueling of good and bad guys. It has come to depend on a single actor/martial arts practitioner, the model being Bruce Lee. Other actor/martial artists have movies built around them, including Jackie Chan, Chuck Norris, and Steven Segal. The television series *Kung Fu* (1972-1975) introduced David Carradine and the martial arts to a wider public. The fighting style has now invaded many other types of movies; James Bond movies, police stories, and action-adventure movies incorporate it, not to mention television series such as *Walker, Texas Ranger,* and *Martial Law.* We find more serious exploration of martial arts in *The Rebel* (2006) and *The Last Samurai* (2003), which explores the end of the samurai tradition in nineteenth-century Japan's transition to the modern era. *Kill Bill* volumes 1 and 2 (2003, 2004) brought David Carradine back in a major martial arts story of revenge among a gang of assassins.

Epics

Ben Hur (1959), *Spartacus* (1960), *Cleopatra* (1963), and *Gladiator* (2000) have led to more sword and sandal renditions of ancient history such as *Troy* (2004), based on the mother of all epics, Homer's *Iliad,* and *Alexander* (2004). These films usually involve historical settings and historical characters whose lives affected millions or who are affected by great historical events. The plot usually involves battles, armies, and national destinies. They are therefore always big-budget entertainment spectaculars with costumes, large casts, and remote outdoor locations. They are difficult to write and difficult to produce. Nevertheless, new epics have come to the screen in recent years. The film *300* (2006) tells the story of the Spartan resistance to the Persian invasion of Greece at Thermopylae. *Beowulf* (2007), innovating because of its use of the 3D process, visualized the singular Anglo-Saxon epic poem again (another film of the same story was produced in 2005) about a hero who overcomes the monster Grendel and his mother. So it could be classified as a monster story as well.

Action-Adventure

Raiders of the Lost Ark (1981), *Indiana Jones and the Temple of Doom* (1984), *Romancing the Stone* (1984), *Indiana Jones and the Last Crusade* (1989), and *Indiana Jones and the Kingdom of the Crystal Skull* (2008), with a final appearance of Harrison Ford, are some of the recent examples of a genre that probably originates from literary works like H. Rider Haggard's *King Solomon's Mines,* which was made into a movie in 1937 and 1950 with excellent results each time. Then there is Tarzan from the novels of Edgar Rice Burroughs, which spawned an endless number of Hollywood movies and was remade lovingly by Hugh Hudson as *Greystoke: The Legend of Tarzan, Lord of the Apes* (1984). These are all stories of fantasy and fiction tenuously connected to reality. Recent examples are *National Treasure* (2004) and *The Mummy* (1999), itself a remake, that are now turning into multiple sequel franchises.

Monster Movies

Mary Shelley's novel *Frankenstein* (1818) is the great ancestor of all monster movies. Monster movies always involve some creature, either man-made or a mutant human. There is *Dr. Jekyll and Mr. Hyde,* which involves again the theme of the mad scientist whose knowledge leads to unpredictable and frightening results. It becomes a kind of parable about the fear of knowledge as power, leading to unintended consequences when man interfere with nature. The genre reached network television in *Beauty and the Beast* (1987) with a story about a cultivated lion-man, who lives in a subterranean society of outcasts, and his love relationship with a beautiful New York district attorney. It presents interesting parables about sexuality and innocence.

Herman Melville's classic American novel *Moby Dick* chronicles Captain Ahab's vengeful pursuit of the White Whale. *Jaws* (1975) really borrows this **premise** and turns the whale into a great white shark. Following its success, the **premise** was reworked with alligators, piranhas, squids, and many more; the list includes films such as *Piranha* (1978), *Alligator* (1980), and *Lake Placid* (1999). The monster always has to have a personality and a motive to save its young or get back at its antagonist, the character in the title role. *King Kong* (1933) was remade twice, in 1975 and again in 2005. *Cloverfield* (2008) introduces a huge unknown monster who, instead of climbing the Empire State Building like King Kong, proceeds to wreck Manhattan. You wonder why this fascination with mythical and fantastical monsters endures. It has to be the survival of primal fear in some limbic part of our brains that has always been aroused by monsters in fairy tales and folk legend.

Biography

The Hollywood rag *Variety* refers to them as *biopics*. The genre hardly needs explanation. Certain lives of real people have either historical importance or a story in them of triumph over adversity or achievement in sports or the arts. The story has to involve something out of the ordinary. We can usually identify with the character who will be played by a major actor. In the old days, we had something as straightforward as James Stewart in *The Glenn Miller Story* (1953) about the great jazz clarinetist. Most recently, Jamie Foxx playing Ray Charles in *Ray* (2004) is little more complex. George C. Scott played General Patton in *Patton* (1970). An award-winning French film, *La Vie en Rose* (2007), told the story of the famous French singer, Edith Piaf, with a stunning Academy Award–winning performance by Marion Cotillard.

Satire

American Psycho (2000), adapted from a novel by Brett Easton Ellis, although crossed with the horror movie theme of a psychotic serial killer, is really a social satire and an attack on male culture and attitudes. *Cannibal Women in the Avocado Jungle of Death* (1988), one of my favorite bad movies, is a camped-up satire on contemporary gender issues starring Bill Maher, later the star of *Politically Incorrect* (abandoned by ABC in 2001 after Maher's politically incorrect remarks about the terrorist attack on the World Trade Center) and the late night television show *Real Time* on HBO. A satire of the private eye film noir movie is *Dead Men Don't Wear Plaid* (1987), in which Humphrey Bogart appears by virtue of clever intercutting of classic film footage.

Cross Genre

Many excellent movies cannot be classified in a single **genre** but are hybrids that combine more than one type of **genre**. For instance, *The Mummy* (1999) is a combination of action-adventure, monster, and horror. Some writers and directors manage to create their own genres. Ironic observation and even comic moments can be introduced into the midst of serious and brutal crime. The Coen brothers film *Fargo* (1996) is a good example; it is a story of state troopers who are trying to solve a crime of kidnapping and murder that is combined with wry social observation of both the main and peripheral characters. It is almost the cinematic equivalent of the omniscient narration of the novel. The more recent Coen brothers film *Burn After Reading* (2008) combines comedy, satire, and suspense. *The Cooler* (2003), a beautifully made and acted film, initially appears to be about the mob and Las Vegas but turns out to be a moving love story as well as an antiheroic exposure of all the characters' behaviors. It defies classification. There are many more. The Woody Allen film *Manhattan* (1979) presents a certain type of character, references to movies and relationships, therapists, and so on. His type of movie is almost a **genre** in itself. Charlie Chaplin was perhaps the first to create a unique character and a **genre** of his own.

SCRIPT DEVELOPMENT

Adapting the Seven-Step Method

It is probably true to say that the **seven-step method** is most useful when applied to corporate communications. The communication problem of entertainment is more elusive. The basic communication problem is that potentially huge audiences want to be entranced, made to laugh, cry, or transported out of their daily reality. They don't know how, and they don't know exactly what they want. They just want entertainment that is going to work for them, an end result that is satisfying. Because we cannot interview individuals, and because most people don't know what they want to see until the day of their choice, it is difficult to answer question number one about the communication problem except in the most general terms. If Hollywood could find the answer, it would be able to avoid the risk entailed in every film production.

Question number two, which asks us to define the target audience, helps a great deal more because we need to think about our audience. Some choices are obvious. If children are the target, or teenagers, or a general audience, we know how to write differently for them. **Audience demographics** are very important. It is easier to measure at the front end than at the back end of the process. As a writer you must be a million people who all want to see your movie.

What is the objective? It is, in Hollywood terms, always, to entertain. If you are writing **comedy**, the objective is to make people laugh. If you are writing suspense, the objective is to make people sit on the edge of their seats. As you write or revise, you can evaluate what you have written by reference to this objective.

The strategy that is the answer to the "how" question is about how you are going to entertain them, how you are going to make them laugh or cry. In effect, the answer becomes **comedy, tragedy,** suspense, or some other mode of engaging the audience. These are essentially story structures and **character**. So in some sense, the strategy becomes the **premise** that we discuss below.

The content is the storyline, the narrative, or what will become the **treatment**. What will happen in the movie? The medium is going to be film or television, but there is a difference between theatrical film and television film, between multicamera live-to-tape sitcom and single-camera recording whether on film or video. This is important for scripting.

The seventh step, which is the creative concept, is the **premise**. Getting to the **premise** is a lot of work. Getting it clear, getting it right is half the battle. Setting it down in such as way as to attract development money is to embody all six of the previous steps in one compelling outline. It could be what is called a **log line** in the industry.

Log Lines

The **log line** is a term you will often hear mentioned in the movie business. It is an even more concentrated form of the **premise**. It is a short statement that sums up the movie, a kind of teaser to make someone think about the script and ultimately want to read it. It is often the means by which an agent, a producer, or a studio decision maker will be introduced to your script and, according to many, the basis for any decision to read further. From your point of view, your script is unique. From the industry point of view, your script is one of hundreds that someone has to sort through and make decisions about whether to recommend it to others for consideration. Given a problem of choice, human psychology typically approaches the problem by eliminating the also-rans, whether it is choosing clothes, vacation destinations, or job applicants. So most people agree that the **log line** has a primary function of ensuring that your script gets read and considered.

A **log line** is also really the foundation for a **pitch**—the verbal presentation of the project in a meeting. You may **pitch** your own **script**, but it also highly likely to be pitched by someone else on your behalf, such as an agent, a producer trying to raise finance for the project, or a studio executive who believes in the **script** and needs to persuade others. So the **log line** actually continues to work for you and your **script** by supplying others with a readymade handle for your **script**. In recent years, a few websites have emerged that serve as market places and bazaars for independent producers to search for interesting new talent and new scripts. Once again, the **log line** does duty as the pocket version of the **script** that allows an interested party to make a preliminary decision. Sometimes this has to do with **genre**. If you are a producer looking for a kung-fu action story, you do not want to be bothered with romantic comedies. You cannot always tell from the title alone.

The **log line** has become a minor art form almost. Many professional writers and others concerned with creating entertainment content for the media argue that if you cannot sum up your script or movie idea in, say, three sentences, you don't truly know what your **screenplay** is about. Can it be two or could it be four sentences? That's not really the point. It has to be short, pithy, express the essence of the story, and make someone want to read further.

A **log line** must have the following characteristics:

- It has to be in the present tense, as always. It is as if you are seeing it now before your eyes on a screen.
- It has to identify implicitly or explicitly the **genre** for the reason given earlier.
- It has to establish a **main character** and that character's **problem** or challenge.
- It has to show a **conflict** or a situation that will drive the story.
- It should suggest a climax and a **resolution** or **dénouement**.
- It doesn't have to do the preceding in any particular order.

Screenplays are developed through a **three-stage process** similar to the one we examined for the shorter film and video formats. The **concept** and **premise** is the first job of writing. Although storylines and premises are sometimes invented by actors, producers, directors, and studio executives, a writing skill is needed to set one down in a convincing form that everyone can study and discuss. Most projects begin as a **concept** in the writer's imagination. Either the project gets written on spec, as they say, or it gets financed, in which case it has to be sold by pitching it to a decision maker who will finance the development. The **concept** and the **pitch** are really about the **premise**.

The Premise

A **premise**—a shorthand way of referring to the essence of the story idea—can be summed up in a phrase or a few sentences. The **premise** has to be in the **log line**, but it could also be expressed as a slighter longer plot outline. A great deal of business is done on the basis of pitching a **premise**. You can think of it this way: if a friend who had not seen a movie that you had seen asked you what a movie was about, what would be your answer? At the moment, you probably don't make a supreme effort to capture the essential driving idea. You just say something like, *I liked it. It's about this guy who …* Now imagine that instead of telling a friend, you have to tell someone about a movie that hasn't yet been made and needs a million dollars to develop the script and another $30 or $40 million to produce. These days that is a low budget. The **premise** has to be the idea that defines a movie, the reason for writing it, and the reason for making it. Ultimately, the reason for writing it and the reason for making it have to be congruent.

Sometimes the **premise** can almost be the title itself. Some argued that Paul Schrader's movie *American Gigolo* (1980),[11] based on his **screenplay**, contains the **premise** in the title. The idea of a male prostitute sets up a tension with the idea of the American maleness. It also explores an interesting gender issue of male sex for hire. His lover, a senator's wife, has to provide an alibi for him when he is suspected of murdering one of his clients. It is a nice irony that Richard Gere plays opposite Julia Roberts in *Pretty Woman* (1990) a decade later in the moral mirror image of this sentimental sex fantasy. In any case, the title and the **premise** should connect with one another. *Titanic* (1997) is another title containing a premise as are many disaster movies.

Later we will discuss *It's a Wonderful Life* (1946) and *Bartleby* (1970). The **premise** for the first might go like this: A decent man, pushed to suicide by bad luck, is saved by an angel who grants him the wish that he had never been born. Seeing how altered the lives of people he cared about would be in that alternative reality, he begs to reverse the wish and is reconciled with his wonderful life. The **premise** for the second might be: A social drop-out takes passive resistance to the ultimate conclusion in a battle of wits with his employer who, trying to save him, then rejecting him, cannot get rid of him and ends by feeling guilt and responsibility for his death.

The **premise** is really the cinematic idea that forms itself in the writer's imagination. When it won't go away and cannot be ignored, it should be written. This is the seed idea. This seed of a **screenplay** has to be grown through stages into a finished production-ready script.

---

[11] You can see a trailer of the movie through a hyperlink in the CD-ROM or by pointing your browser to http://us.imdb.com/Trailers?0080365&546&56.

We can take a movie title that we know and construct a **log line** for it: The **premise** of the movie is as follows:

> *The Bachelor* (1999)
> After his marriage proposal is rejected by his girlfriend, who then leaves on a trip, a man finds out that he has 24 hours before his 30th birthday the next day to find a woman to marry him, which is his grandfather's condition for inheriting $100 million. After he exhausts his list of old girlfriends, his friends and relatives try to fix him up to save the company and their jobs by putting an ad in the paper. A thousand would-be brides show up to be married, chasing the hero until he is reunited with his girlfriend who returns from a trip oblivious of what has happened.

From this would come a shorter, pithy and concentrated essence of the movie, we call a **log line**:

> One thousand brides. One hundred million dollars. Jimmie Shannon is about to discover the true value of love.

This was the **tag line**. In some cases, this **log line** can also be the **tag line**. The difference is that the former is selling the producer or studio or distributor prior to production, whereas the latter is selling the audience after the film is in distribution on the prospect of becoming immersed in a story and carried away for a couple of hours.

Tag Lines

A **tag line** is really the postproduction cousin of the **log line**. It is created after production in the distribution phase to market the movie. It is usually shorter than a **log line** so that it can appear in advertising copy. It is a provocative phrase that sums up the audience interest or the way the audience might respond to the **premise**. So it often has an oblique relation to the **premise**. It is designed to make you curious and to want to see the movie: "In space nobody can hear you scream" (*Alien*, 1979). It is the kind of writing that goes with creating the trailer for a movie. It's the line you will find on the poster or on the DVD cover. *Shattered Glass* (2003) has the **tag line** "Read between the lies." Earlier, we mentioned *Freeway* (1996) as a contemporary *Little Red Riding Hood* premise and its **tag line** "Her life was no fairy tale." This, like the *Alien* tag line, is a pure **tag line** and could not be a **log line**.

Concept or Synopsis

In Hollywood, movies are often referred to as "**high concept**" and by opposition "**low concept**." A **high-concept** film generally depends on strong **plot** and storyline within a **genre** and often furnishes a vehicle for star actors. A **low-concept** film, by contrast, depends to a greater degree on **character** and **dialogue**. They are often low-budget vehicles for first-rate actors who are not necessarily box office titans who create compelling performances and break new ground. A good example would be *The Visitor* (2008), which explores the life-changing encounter that occurs when a widowed professor returns to his New York apartment to find illegal immigrant squatters living there. The man happens to be a musician who plays the drums and who teaches the professor how to play. Priorities in the professor's life change as he is transformed by the discovery of new worlds and different types of people than those found in the academic world of which he has become tired. So-called **low-concept** films are often more realistic and more truthful about human experience and human emotions than are **high-concept** films, even when they are really well written and produced like the latest Batman film, *The Dark Knight* (2008).

So what is a **concept**, high, low, or neither? The **concept** is a statement of the **premise** of the movie stated in a few paragraphs or, at most, a page. From this essential idea, the **drama** or **comedy** must unfold. The idea can be simple, but it must somehow be unassailable. It compels us to want to follow the idea to some necessary conclusion. Sometimes, the same or a similar premise can lead to different movies with different outcomes. Many argue that there are only a limited number of **plots**. All movies are just variations of this finite pool of storylines. This has led to the development of **story engine** software such as Dramatica Pro, which tests out story **concepts** and develops a storyline and characters out of the premise.

A good example of a **concept** might be this: A guy makes a bet with a friend that the friend cannot seduce a certain woman. Although the romance starts out as a bet, it turns serious when the guy really falls in love with the woman he has to seduce. She finds out about the bet by accident and is heartbroken. How does it end? In fact, several movies have been built on this same **premise**. Although they share the same **premise**, the movies are quite different in time, place, and character. One is the classic, worldly French film *Les Grands Manoeuvres* (1955), directed by René Clair with Gérard Philipe and Michèle Morgan. Another is the commercial Hollywood comedy *Worth Winning* (1989), starring Mark Harmon and Leslie Anne Warren.

In the French film, the setting is nineteenth-century provincial France. The guy is a French cavalry officer and a lady's man. In the officer's mess, while drinking and fooling around, he accepts a bet from a fellow officer that he cannot seduce a certain lady of the town before the regiment leaves on maneuvers. He woos the lady. She falls in love with him and he with her. One day she comes to the officers' quarters to seek him and overhears the teasing about the bet. She is heartbroken. He doesn't realize she knows. His wooing has become serious. He is no longer interested in the bet. He has fallen in love with her. As the regiment rides out to the cheers of the townsfolk, he looks up anxiously at her window. She is inside in tears. It is tragic, bittersweet, and ironic. The maneuvers of love have parallels to the maneuvers of war, hence the irony of the title. The bet has become a trap.

In the American film, a handsome weatherman who is a bachelor and has enviable success with women is challenged by his married buddy to seduce three women of his choice and get them to accept a marriage proposal and prove it by a certain date. The married buddy's wife happens to own a Picasso, and the wager becomes the painting, unknown to the man's wife. His proof of seduction has to be a videotape of the successful proposal. He really falls in love with the third woman and wants to marry her. The bet catches up with him because the videotape of a previous seduction is seen accidentally, after it is left in the VCR, by his (now) fiancée when she visits the wife of the buddy who made the bet. The women get together to teach him a lesson. At the marriage ceremony, his bride confronts him, refuses him, and exposes his two-timing. He is made to repent. To get her back, he has to bid for his would-be bride at a charity auction, donating not only to charity but publicly making promises to her. They are reconciled. You can see the how differently the same premise can be developed and how each movie expresses the varied European and the Hollywood approaches. The same **premise** lies behind comedy and tragedy. One is nuanced, textured, and ironic. The other is staged, sentimental, and ideological. The European film is an observation about the fickle nature of love and sexual attraction in which there is understanding with a realistic ending and without a moralizing text. The American film reveals a hidden cultural code and a cultural agenda. It is a **comedy** about the taming of the male fantasy by the female in which there is a moralizing subtext and a sentimental happy ending that saves face. It embodies the subtext of so many American films and television series in which the male is ultimately subject to the female. The American male bachelor is tamed and conscripted into marriage. There are recent variants on this classic plot such as *Made of Honor* (2008). *She's All That* (1999) and *Mean Girls* (2004) are both crossed with another genre, the teen comedy.

Story Engines

Most of the stories in the world can be broken down into a finite number of basic **plots** with different variations. An American distributor is reported to have said, "Listen, in television and film, there's only one goddamn plot. There's a guy in Zanzibar with a cork up his ass. There's only one guy in the world who can get it out, and he lives in Newark, New Jersey. We spend the next fifty minutes seeing the second guy fighting overwhelming odds to reach the first guy before he dies of toxic poisoning. Okay?"[12]

Ideas about story structure are certainly strong in Hollywood. The pressure to find the magic formula for a successful movie is great. Some might worry that **story engines** reduce all movies to a limited number of **archetypal plots** and their variations. If you now see movie storylines and **plots** starting to resemble one another, it could be because of the search for formulaic stories reduced to **archetypes** by **story engines**. Whether it is the use of **story engines** or the copycat mentality of studios trying to make money by doing their disaster movie or their science fiction adventure of the season, it is hard to know. We all know that there are stereotypes and fads for certain kinds of subject matter. Of course, **genres** lead to certain predictable storylines whether it is a western or a road movie. We know what we are in for. Even though **genre** movies have conventions that are understood, there is always room for originality and innovation.

Traditionalists might argue that most of the world's literature and **drama** has been composed without the benefit of **story engines**. By the same token, most of the world depended on the horse and buggy rather than the internal combustion engine and the quill pen rather than word processors. It probably boils down to deciding that whatever helps you is a good thing. We owe it to ourselves to examine **story engines**.

In previous chapters, we have emphasized the importance of the thinking that precedes the writing. Getting to the creative premise, concept, or outline and getting it right are fundamental to success. This is what **story engines** help the writer to do. **Story engines** analyze **plot** structures and story elements so that writers can generate **plot** possibilities from the **premise**. **Story engines** use computing power to examine a huge number of choices that represent permutations and combinations of a similar **premise**. **Story engines** rest on certain assumptions about **plot** and story.[13] Dramatica Pro, which is one of the programs in Screenplay Systems' stable of scripting software, rests on a theory of story structure. The software asks questions that lead to a definition of the story type, **plot**, and **characters**.

---

[12] Reported by Eric Paice in *The Way to Write for Television* (London: Hamish Hamilton, 1981), p. 8.
[13] Melanie Anne Phillips and Chris Huntley are the authors of the Dramatica theory of story.

Dramatica Pro could be described as a writer's tool for creating a **treatment**. Dramatica Pro certainly teaches the user a great deal about how stories work. In it, the StoryGuide is an elaborate process that asks questions about **character**, story, and issues to establish the fundamentals of your story. "Storyforming" deals with "the underlying dramatic skeleton of a story"—the structure, theme, and **through line**, which can result in 32,768 possible "storyforms," presumably the number of permutations and combinations of the **archetypal** variables. All stories begin with a **problem** that must be **resolved**. The theory posits that all stories have four **through lines**:

- The overall story **through line** (the big picture)
- The main character **through line** (the protagonist)
- The main versus impact **through line** (passionate and subjective perspective)
- The impact character's **through line** (perspective forces change)

The overall story **through line** is what the story is about. It involves all the **characters**. In *Star Wars*, this **through line** is about a war between the Empire and the Rebellion. It takes place in several locations, but there is always a struggle between the two forces, in some sense a struggle between good and evil. The main **character through line** is about the **problem** of the main **character** and how it drives the story and leads to some **resolution**. The impact **character** is not necessarily the **antagonist** in the classic theory of **drama**, but a **character** who makes the main **character** question his or her basic assumptions, and therefore choose, **act** and change. In the Dramatica Pro demo analysis of *Star Wars*, Luke Skywalker is a main **character** and Obi Wan Kenobe is the impact **character**. The main versus impact **through line** charts the **conflict**—the interaction between these two key **characters** that determines the outcome for each of them.

Storytelling describes **characters**, their **problems**, problem-solving style, **actions**, concerns, situation, and environment; how things are changing; and the time and option locks that limit the story and create the **drama**. By question and answer, the **characters** and **plot** are defined and refined. However, the questions have to be very much in the vein of the structural theory that the authors set up behind the software. The software is a patented way of getting someone to think through all the issues of a story.

"Storyweaving" involves creating scenes of specific **action** from the storyforming and storytelling bank of raw material. The "end result is a complete narrative **treatment** of your story, a rough first draft if you will (Dramatica Pro)." This document can then be exported to Movie Magic Screenwriter as a formatted **screenplay** or as a novel, or even as a text document for a word processor.

WRITING A MOVIE TREATMENT

Once the **concept** has been accepted, the next stage is to expand the idea into a **treatment**. We have already defined what a **treatment** is in the context of writing other types of script. In terms of a film, a **treatment** is a contractual stage in the writing process that is recognized in the standard contract negotiated by the screenwriters' union, the **Writers Guild of America**. A **treatment** for a feature film or a television movie is a substantial document running 25 pages or more. The producer who pays for the **screenplay** usually makes suggestions and requests changes to the story and character development before the first draft **screenplay** is commissioned. Of course, **treatments**, like **screenplays**, are also written on "spec," that is, without payment.

A **treatment** for a **screenplay** is a prose narrative of the main storyline (in chronological order) with **characters** described and occasional samples of **dialogue**. A movie **treatment** should be a complete account of what happens, a complete storyline, and a readable narrative that looks forward to the **screenplay**. A **treatment** is written in conventional narrative prose without any special formatting but always in the present tense.

The purpose of the **treatment** is to allow producers, directors, studio executives, or whoever is going to pay for the script to evaluate the story and its entertainment potential. It serves the purpose of getting writers to show their hand and tell the story. It also allows all of the aforementioned people who have a say in the creation of the final product to react to an early version and respond with comments, concerns, and encouragement. The **treatment** is less expensive to create than the **screenplay**. It is, if you like, a prototype for the **screenplay** that enables everyone to test out how it will play. It is a lot easier to revise a **treatment** than a **screenplay**, just as it is a lot easier to revise a **concept** than a **treatment**.

Another way of understanding what a **treatment** is would be to ask what is missing from it that will eventually be delivered in the **screenplay** or script based on it. The foremost missing element is **dialogue**. The exact words to be spoken by all the **characters** are essential to the **screenplay**, but not to the **treatment**. Every **scene** to be shot must be described in the **screenplay**, but not necessarily in the **treatment**. Major **scenes** and major **actions** are going to form part of the **treatment**. The supporting **scenes** and the detail of many **scenes** only come to the fore in the **screenplay**. Because a screenplay describes every **scene** and every word spoken, it decides the pacing and flow of the movie. This cannot be delineated precisely in the **treatment**.

If we go back to the blueprint analogy of Chapter 1, then the **treatment** could be roughly compared to the sketches of the finished building. The **screenplay** is the equivalent of detailed drawings in plan, elevation, and section that provide exact dimensions. The sketch allows you to see what the building will look like and appreciate many of its features. The plans allow you to know how large the living room is and how many bedrooms there are. Above all, it allows the builder to build it just as the **screenplay** allows the director to shoot the movie.

SCREENPLAY

A **screenplay** or script is the translation of the **treatment** into a visual blueprint for production, laying end to end the particular **scenes** employing the specific terminology of the medium to describe what is to be seen on the screen and heard on the sound track. This means the **action** and its background and each new **character** in the **scene** must be delineated. Every word of **dialogue** must be written down. Every **scene** must be described. The **scene** is the basic unit of visual narrative for the **screenplay** and the writer who writes it, whereas the **shot** is the basic unit of narrative for the camera and the director who shoots the movie. Why do we say, "Shoot a movie?" The verb "shoot" corresponds to the noun "shot." A movie is made out of **shots**. The standard margins and layout of the page for a screenplay are as follows:

This transition from **scene** to **shot** is the last barrier between the writing and the making of the movie. The director has to compose the **scene** out of **shots**. This means a director has to create a **shooting script** out of a **screenplay**.

[top margin--approximately 1.0"]

[dialogue margins   DAISY   [character name centered:
approximately 3.0-6.2"   (fluttering eyelashes)   ALL CAPS]
            I'm late. I'm sure you didn't mind waiting.

                            WINTERBOURNE   [character name centered:
                    Not at all.   ALL CAPS]
                                DAISY
[dialogue   I just didn't want to go to Chillon by
single space]   carriage. I have such a passion for those
                        lake steamers. They're so sweet.

    They walk out the front door of the hotel.
                                                        CUT TO
                                    [transition: ALL CAPS]

    EXT. LAKE FRONT -- DAY   [slug line: ALL CAPS]
[single space break]   [description--single space]

    There is a lot of commotion as passengers board a steamer moored
    along side. DAISY and WINTERBOURNE in LONG SHOT. She is quite sudden
    in her movements as she moves up the gangway. The steamer blows its
    whistle and prepares to cast off. There is a summer breeze rippling
    the lake.
                                    [description margins
    EXT. LAKE STEAMER DECK -- DAY   approximately 1.7"-7.5"]

    WINTERBOURNE feels they are on an adventure as they stroll the deck.
    DAISY is animated and charming. She is not flustered when she is
    aware that people are staring at her. People look at her because she
    is pretty and because of her unconventional manners and apparent
    liberty with her escort. They find a seat on the deck and
    WINTERBOURNE looks at her enchanted while she chatters on.
                                DAISY
                    I wish we had steamers like this in America.
                            WINTERBOURNE
                    Well what about on the Mississippi?
                                DAISY
                    I don't live near the Mississippi.

                            WINTERBOURNE
                    Well, we've got the trip back to look
                    forward to.
                                DAISY
                    What's your first name, again?
                            WINTERBOURNE
                    Frederick!
        [bottom margins--between 1.5"-.05" depending on description or
                        dialogue break]
                                [always number pages]25

FIGURE 8.3

Although writers may indicate the importance of certain camera shots (always capitalized) and certain transitions from **scene** to **scene** (CUT TO, DISSOLVE TO), the director has both the right and the responsibility to break down the **scene** into camera setups or shots that will cover the **action** of the **scene**. A director must shoot the same **scene** from several angles so that **action** and **dialogue** are repeated in different camera angles in order for the editor to create continuity. Without this "**cover**," a **scene** cannot be edited. This thinking about setups is not really part of the writer's thought process. The **screenplay** is the writer's construction of the sequence of **scenes** in the order and length that will make the story come alive. Although the writer may dip into detailing a **shot** for particular emphasis—for instance, to describe a CUTAWAY that carries dramatic and visual significance—as a rule, the writer leaves **shots** to the director. You cannot and should not try to direct a movie from the **screenplay**.

To pursue the blueprint analogy to the bitter end, it would make sense to say that the shooting script is the plan for the builder. It gets down to a list of **shots**. This list of **shots** makes up the shooting schedule and leads to each individual camera setup that defines the method of working. This is why the director is so important to a movie production, or indeed any production, because it is the director who makes that final translation of words describing visuals on paper to images in a moving picture medium by means of camera setups in shooting and scenes edited together in postproduction.

SCENE OUTLINE

Another step that can be very useful in constructing both a **treatment** and a **screenplay** is the **scene outline**. In essence, film and television narrate by **scenes**. **Scenes** are defined by the SLUG LINE or **scene heading** (see Chapter 2). Every time there is a change of time or place, the scene changes. It is the sequence of **scenes** that tell the story. The audience only experiences what is enacted in the given **scenes**. If you can put a skeleton narrative together by means of brief **scene** summaries, you have a solid structure for a **screenplay**. Each **scene** should have a **key moment**. The **key moment** is really the distilled moment or **action** that advances the narrative. Lots of **scenes** are possible, even probable, but not necessarily essential to the hundred-minute story.

One way to think of this narrative skill is to ask what you see rather than what you hear. On the whole, narrative unfolds through the **action** and choices of the principal **characters** rather than what they say. It is probably preferable to see it first and hear it second. In other words, narrate through **action**; or put another way, try to show the story rather than tell the story. Nevertheless, most **scenes** need **dialogue**. The point here is not to talk the **plot**.

MASTER SCENE SCRIPT FORMAT

The **master scene script** is the accepted script format that is now well understood and accepted in the industry. It has very clear conventions. It is best understood by looking at the sample page above. The description of **action** and **character** behavior runs from margin to margin. **Character** names are always capitalized and centered. **Dialogue** is separated from **action** under the name of the **character** speaking. **Dialogue** margins are set within the margins for **action**. It is a way of organizing visual narrative on the page to show **scenes**. Every **scene** begins with a slug line. Each slug line announces a new **scene** because of change of place or time. The slug line abbreviates the information summarizing whether the shoot is inside or outside, where it is, and whether it is day or night. The slug line is always in caps. The **action** is described in lowercase and is single spaced. If the **scene** contains **dialogue**, the **character**'s name is centered in the middle of the page and typed in caps. **Dialogue** is written in lowercase and is single spaced. The breaks between slug lines and **action** or between **action** and **character** name are double spaced. The breaks between **scenes** are twice that. Doing all this on a typewriter involves considerable typing skills with tab settings and spacing. Current scriptwriting software systems make this job easy.

SCRIPTING SOFTWARE

With the advent of computers and word processing, formatting a script has become nearly effortless. Not only does dedicated scriptwriting software take the chore out of formatting the page by providing macro keystrokes to create slug lines or keeping lists of **characters** in memory, it has become an industry requirement. Script formatting software provides an easily manageable computer file that can be imported into scheduling and budgeting software that simplifies a difficult and costly preproduction task. A writer must adopt one of the accepted **screenplay** formatting software systems.

SHOOTING SCRIPT

Before we conclude this chapter, we must draw a clear distinction for the new screenwriter between the **master scene script** and the **shooting script**. The difference is not always apparent. As the name suggests, a **master scene script** is constructed out of **scenes** that describe a setting and the action that takes place in that **scene** together with all the **dialogue** spoken by the **characters**. It translates the narrative of the **treatment** into **scenes**. Because most of us know that a director will **cover** the action in the **scene** from more than one angle and cut between **shots** and because many beginning scriptwriters are also shooters and editors, many make the mistake of trying to direct the movie from the script. Writing in camera angles and camera directions is a distraction from the essential function of the **master scene script**, which is to tell the story visually and establish a strong clear **storyline**. Writing anything other than NIGHT or DAY in the slug line or **scene** heading, such as 3PM or AFTERNOON, must be justified by a clear need for this description to make the **action** and the story clear. Finally, writing elaborate transitions other than CUT TO or trying to edit the movie from the script is again unprofessional. Directors and editors will be irritated by all this intrusion into their domain; they won't be ruled by it; and it will make it harder for other readers to follow the story during the decision-making process.

When a **master scene script** goes into production, the director will translate **scenes** into **shots**, setups, and camera angles and number them so that production personnel on the shoot know what the specific technical problems are. Do not try to do this before time. Limit your camera directions and **scene transitions** strictly to what is indispensable to understanding the visual **concept** of the **scene**. Once again, tell the story, don't try to direct and edit the movie!

CONCLUSION

We now see that the **stages of development** of a **screenplay** are similar for most uses of the linear visual media we have discussed so far, whether public service announcements, corporate videos, or feature films. In fact, we need to bring forward everything we have learned from Chapters 2, 3, 4, and 5. We need to describe one medium through another. We need to be able to define the **problem** in terms of entertainment.

In writing for entertainment media, the **problem** is a **plot** problem or **character problem** in the form of a **premise** that will intrigue and hold an audience. So the objective is now entertainment for its own sake. It is a loose term. Fictional narrative in visual media has to be believable, or if not believable in the realistic sense, then it has to be seductive. A fantasy world, whether animation or science fiction or even a mixture of live action and animation (for example, *The Mask*, 1994), has to work for the audience.

Knowing who the audience is for entertainment subjects is an art, not a science. Many studio executives have been humbled and unknowns vindicated in the unpredictable judgment of the box office. Legion are the stories of scripts turned down by one studio or producer only to be made into gigantic successes by another. Small independent, low-budget films that nobody expects to do well end up capturing huge audiences. The British film *The Full Monty* (1997) defied the usual Hollywood formula for a big box office success. This film has now become adapted as a musical set in Buffalo. *Billy Elliot* (2000) is yet another—about a young boy in a coal-mining town who wants to become a ballet dancer. It is safe to say that these films would never have been made at all by standard Hollywood practice. They are full of local British accents and have no American stars. For some reason, the two stories and situations struck a chord with a huge American audience.

We now have an overview of the forms and structures and a broad understanding of the stages of the process of developing a **story** and a **screenplay**: **premise, log line, concept, treatment**, first draft script, or **screenplay**, followed by a second draft. This process has well recognized contractual stages in the industry. In the next chapters, we need to examine some of the specific problems and creative techniques of the scriptwriting process.

Exercises

1. Watch a movie and summarize the **conflict** that lies at the root of the **plot**.
2. Everybody in your class is to think up an idea for a movie and then **pitch** those ideas to the rest of the class. Take a straw vote to get an instant reaction to the ideas. If class members were in control of a production budget, would they commit development money for the script based on the **pitch**?
3. Write a list of five **conflicts**—physical, moral, or historical—that could be the source of a dramatic movie.
4. Write a list of **conflicts** that could be the source of a comedic movie.
5. Consider three movies that you know and write a paragraph about the **premise** of each.
6. Develop one of your ideas of **conflict** into a **premise** for a movie.
7. Write a **scene** for your **premise** that is **action** only, without **dialogue**.
8. Write a **scene** for your **premise** with **dialogue**.
9. Write a **treatment** for a feature-length movie based on your **premise**.
10. List three of your favorite movies and then write a new **log line** for each.
11. Take a movie you know well and outline its **three-act structure**.
12. Take the **plot** of *Little Red Riding Hood* and rework it as horror movie with different characters but the same **plot**.

CHAPTER 9

Writing Techniques for Long-Form Scripts

KEY TERMS

action
adaptation
audience
character
character as victim
comedy
cover-up
cross-cutting
deus ex *machina*
dialogue
disguise

dramatic irony
gag
hubris
key moment
mistaken identity
narrative tense
omniscient or third-person
   narrator
plot
point of view
public domain

realism
realistic
running gag
scene
slapstick
storyline
title cards
tragedy
verbal comedy
visual narrative

So far we have outlined the broad process of developing and writing without going into the craft of how you do it. Many good books are dedicated to writing for the movies and for television that expound on techniques and share the tricks of the trade. This chapter is an introduction to basics on which the student must build. In other words, if you have never written a screenplay or tried to conceptualize a narrative in a visual medium that lasts for an hour and a half or two hours, here are some of the issues you need to think about.

Previously, we said that a writer is paid for thinking as much as for writing. We mean by this that the quality of the meta-writing or thinking that underlies the writing determines the quality of the final product. Writing screenplays is not about putting words on paper so much as thinking out storylines, visualizing **scenes**, and imagining **characters**. Although we can identify elements of the screenplay form, singly, none of them will make a screenplay. Put together, they pretty much cover those issues

Doi: 10.1016/B978-0-240-81235-9.00008-0

that scriptwriters have to think about and for which they have to execute technically the finished working documents that will manifest in actors' performances and directors' shots. We are talking about creating a complex structure that you can travel through or examine from a number of points of view. Let's start with **character**.

CHARACTERS AND CHARACTER

Every story must have at least one **character** whose identity is clear and whose destiny is engaging. Otherwise, we, the **audience**, have nothing to relate to and identify with. Hemingway's *The Old Man and the Sea* pits one man against the sea, the elements, and the great fish that he struggles to bring in. We identify with his struggle, his hunger, and his fatigue. Herman Melville's *Moby Dick* is a more complex story of Captain Ahab against the white whale. The genre probably goes back to heroic, mythical stories such as the Anglo-Saxon *Beowulf* and St. George against the dragon. A more recent version of this archetype is *Jaws* (1975), in which the animal adversary is replaced by a Great White shark. This has spawned a host of similar beast and monster movies based on the premise of a confrontation with an outsize animal opponent discussed in the previous chapter under genre.

Normally, we assume **characters** to be human, but in this genre the animal is a **character** in the story with personified characteristics of will, motive, and intelligence. Don't tell me animals are not **characters**! A whole franchise, as they call it nowadays, was built around a sheepdog, Lassie. Dozens of *Lassie* movies were made, and a television series of the same name ran for many seasons. Don't tell me characters have to have lines! Lassie barks—no lines. Think of Frankenstein's creature! There's another **character** without lines and also a variation on the theme.

Most stories need more than one human **character**. They need a protagonist and an antagonist, or a hero and a villain. The struggle between them is typical of archetypal stories. Think of Achilles and Hector in Homer's *Iliad*, Julius Caesar and Brutus, or Octavius Caesar and Cleopatra, or Grant and Lee in the American Civil War. The entire Batman series is about a struggle between a protagonist, Batman, and his adversary, the Joker. There are usually two points of view or two sets of values that define each **character**. In its most commonplace and generic version, we have the cop and the criminal. Then there are the hero's friends, lover, parents, children, and all those possible relationships that fill out the plot. The list of characters makes up the cast.

What makes characters interesting to an **audience**? A **character** has to be someone the **audience** can identify or with whom the **audience** can identify. What's the difference? Who identifies with Hannibal Lector in *Silence of the Lambs* (1991)? You recognize him as a fascinating psychotic personality, but you identify with the vulnerable young FBI agent, Clarice, who must navigate the mind games of the imprisoned cannibal for clues to capture a serial killer. This identification has nothing to do with gender. Her problem—to pluck knowledge out of danger—involves the **audience** and makes them feel concern for her predicament and want her to succeed.

The more subtle idea of **character** has to do with characteristics—the inner and outer nature of a person that defines who they are. Writers have to give **character** to their characters. They have to differentiate their characters and give them identities that make sense for the story and the world in which the characters live. The **audience** has to believe in the characters. A writer has to create that believable reality in act and speech. To do that, a writer has to think about the name of the **character**, the **character's** background and life story, so that he or she comes to life on the page and on the screen. That means hearing how the characters speak (what voice do they have?), seeing how they walk (what is their physical appearance?), and imagining their hopes and fears.

DIALOGUE AND ACTION

The two engines of story are **dialogue** and **action**. **Dialogue** must not drive the story; rather, the story must drive the **dialogue**. When **characters** speak, they define who they are. Their words can also give forward momentum to the story. **Dialogue** spoken by **characters** must be essential to the **plot** and essential to their **character**. So when George Bailey makes his impassioned speech at the board meeting in *It's a Wonderful Life*,[1] he expresses himself as a right-thinking, ethical **character** and sets in motion his own appointment to the manager's position of the savings and loan of Bedford Falls and the second frustration of his lifelong dream to travel, this time on his honeymoon.

The unit of composition in a screenplay is the **scene**. It has unity of time and place. Each **scene** must contribute to the necessary structure of the story. In the economy of the screenplay, a **scene** has to be a **key moment**. If it is not, it is not necessary and should not be there. If a **scene** can be defined as a **key moment** in the story, then the **dialogue** should be only what is necessary to carry the **scene**. It is no trouble to put words into the mouths of characters. Before you know it, your **character** is talking the screenplay and what is worse, talking the **plot**. As a rule, avoid having characters explain the plot; rather, let them speak from within the fiction. This goes back to Aristotle's criticism of the *deus ex machina* as a device. If characters talk about the **plot**, it destroys conviction. This is a common fault in suspense and mystery dramas, which can only be resolved by someone explaining the ambiguities that result from tying the story in knots.

Characters interact with their environments or with other characters by making choices and doing things that have consequences. In fact, *It's a Wonderful Life* turns on the choice to live or not to live (Hamlet's "to be or not to be"). This moves the story forward. Events in nature or in history act on characters such that they must change or perhaps die. The **action** that takes place is not dependent on **dialogue**. In the best writing, **dialogue** complements **action**. **Dialogue** creates the understanding of **action**. **Action** creates the context for **dialogue**. **Dialogue** must advance the **action** or **plot**. They work together. Sometimes **dialogue** is more important, sometimes **action**. In film, the narrative must be told by visual events as much as by the words characters speak.

When a **character** does speak, the **dialogue** must define something about the **character**, or at least be consistent with the **character** and appropriate to the moment. This brings us to a question of *realism*. Most people can write down words and phrases that are a plausible representation of the way people speak. The trouble is, the way people speak is usually long-winded, rambling, disjointed, repetitious, and boring. To check this out, take a recorder into the cafeteria. Listen to people conversing on a bus or subway. Listening in on a telephone conversation (cell phones sometimes give us no choice)

---

[1] This film is discussed in greater detail in the section on Adaptation. The complete script is on the website.

reveals speech that is the opposite of film **dialogue**. It goes nowhere. So strict **realism** is going to kill the screenplay.

Dialogue in films and television has to be **realistic**, not real. That means characters have to speak in **character**, have to be believable, and have to sound as if they are real. In actual fact, such lines are carefully crafted and edited to carry the **plot** and to convince the **audience** from moment to moment that the illusion is reality. We expect a doctor in *ER* to talk like a doctor or a nurse to talk like a nurse. We do not, for the sake of a moment, want to spend a day in a hospital hearing all the inconsequential utterances of an intern or ward physician. You can hang around a hospital emergency room for days and not experience anything that would be exciting enough for a television show. Perhaps you have had the misfortune to have to go to a hospital emergency room either for yourself or with someone else. It is really dull. To make an interesting television show about a hospital, you have to graft many separate moments together. You have to create an interaction of **characters** that will bridge imagination and reality. You exaggerate; you heighten; you intensify. If **characters** still get to say ordinary things, they do so while racing down the corridor with a gurney or answering the phone while looking at a lab workup on the patient.

What does movie **dialogue** do for the **plot** and the **character**? Compared to novels and even stage plays, movie **dialogue** is sparse. The reason should be apparent from the experience of going to the movies. The most successful way to tell a story on screen is by showing **characters** in situations or doing things that explain implicitly what is going on in the story, rather than showing **characters** jawboning with one another. When they do speak, the exchange has to be necessary to the moment, to the **plot**, and to the revelation of that **character**. So **dialogue** explains **character**, advances the **plot**, and informs the **audience**. **Visual narrative** is key to writing for the moving picture medium.

In the *Godfather* (1972), there is a great moment of American cinema that illustrates **visual narrative** without **dialogue** and narrative condensation by means of the quintessentially cinematic technique of **cross-cutting** parallel, simultaneous storylines. It also illustrates one way **visual narration** condenses **action**. The master **scene** is the christening of Michael Corleone's sister's baby in a large church. Michael Corleone is going to stand as Godfather to the baby, but during the ceremony will become godfather in the mafia sense as all the rival gang leaders are assassinated and his family's honor revenged. The sequence intercuts the intricate ritual of baptism with its unguents and intoning of the sacrament in Latin with the ritual preparation for the several assassinations. Priestly actions in the baptism correspond to preparations by the various hit men; applying holy oil to mark the baby's forehead cuts to a barber applying shaving cream to the face of one of the assassins; or a gesture of the priest corresponds to assembling a weapon. The only **dialogue** is the Latin ceremonial and the ritual questions put to the godfather. The pace quickens when we cut from the question "do you renounce Satan?" and the answer "I do renounce him" to the targeted victims being gunned down. It is a masterpiece of American cinema because of the writing that organizes the narrative to make Michael Corleone at once godfather in both senses, underlines the meaning of family in both senses, and creates the moral and ethical context in which we see the story as a world of hypocrisy, duplicity, and internecine murder, which leads to Michael alienating his wife and killing his brother.

One mistake beginners often make is to have **characters** make set speeches. Another is to gum up the forward motion of the movie with tedious small talk. It may be **realistic** and just the way people talk, but movies are not **realistic**. They condense life into **key moments**. Total **realism** would be unbearable. People have to sleep, eat, and go to the bathroom. They have to ride the subway, take a bus, or drive for half an hour to get somewhere. No one is going to pay money to see a truly **realistic** movie. Remember that Andy Warhol made an 8-hour movie of someone sleeping. That's **realism**. You could not survive without sleep, but sleep is not entertainment. In fact, it is the opposite. We all use the expression "puts me to sleep" to register that something is the opposite of entertaining.

What we feel to be **realistic** is a true representation of a moment of human experience. We accept the moment of fear, the moment of doubt, the moment of emotional expression, or the embarrassment of a comic predicament as convincing. So from moment to moment, the prevailing style of movies is to craft **dialogue** to sound natural and to show **characters**—whether in offices, crime scenes or homes—that are plausible. If you analyze the moment, it is a **key moment** stripped of excess **action** and **dialogue** so that we understand in that moment what went before and what consequences are likely to follow. Most of what we are saying applies to television as well, with the exception of sitcoms.

On the other hand, the drive to condense **plot** and make **dialogue** as dramatically efficient as possible leads to a number of recognizable clichés. For example, detectives stride purposely through a building issue serious-sounding orders, while another **character** enters and delivers a **realistic** comment about what forensics found out about the murder weapon, all shot with a sweeping, fast-moving Steadicam track showing background **action** that tells us we are in a police precinct. We end up in an office. The character grabs some coffee. The phone rings. A psychotic serial killer calls in a taunt. Trace that phone call! Or a new piece of information is delivered to set up the next stage of the plot. You could sit for days in a police station and be bored out of your wits. Rewrite the same cliché, and we are in a hospital corridor going into emergency, going up the steps of a courtroom, striding through an office at the Pentagon, tracking into an airport disaster room, at a fire—you name it. That is not how it really happens. It is a movie and TV convention for condensing the **action** and the **dialogue**.

Think how movie **dialogue** writing evolved. It began as **title cards** for silent movies interspersed between **scenes**. The words to be read by the **audience** had to capture **key moments**, key sentiments that would support the **scene** of intense looks and silently moving lips. From the beginning, movies had to reduce **dialogue** to the essential. If you compare older movies with today's product, you generally find that they are verbose. With the invention of synchronized sound, the "talkies" seemed to lean on the theatrical tradition again. Actors who looked good but couldn't deliver a line were replaced by actors capable of delivering **dialogue**, often trained in the theatre. Writers could go to town on the **dialogue** because hearing actors speak in lip sync while seeing them on screen was a novelty that exploited the new technology. Writing **dialogue** is an art. The words a character speaks can be ambiguous, nuanced, and mask who he or she really is. Such is the dialogue of Hannibal Lector, for instance, as is the dialogue of Hamlet simulating madness to fool his uncle and Polonius.

The danger of **dialogue** is that you talk the **plot**. This frequently happens in suspense thrillers and murder mysteries in which the audience is kept guessing. There is frequently a key scene at the end in which the hero confronts the culprit and then talks through the explanation of how he figured out the truth. The old television series *Columbo* consistently resolves the crime story in that way, as does Agatha Christie's Hercule Poirot in the TV series and movies based on the famous detective novels. You could argue that it was successful and that Peter Falk became a popular television character.

Styles change. Now you get it in *CSI*. Robert Altman brought about one of the great innovations in movie **dialogue** writing and delivery in his movie $M^*A^*S^*H$ (1970).[2]

Later that movie was spun off into a television sitcom. Until $M^*A^*S^*H$, characters spoke in turn. In real life, people hesitate, interrupt one another, talk at the same time, and overlap one another. Altman broke the old convention, and movies have never been the same since. We now hear more **realistic** speech with interruptions, half-finished thoughts, and speech fragments. We also get uninhibited vernacular speech that includes four-letter words that were formerly anathema.

Filmmakers soon learned that it was more interesting to tell a story through **action** and images rather than theatrical speech. Early scriptwriters got the point.[3] By contrast, in television soaps, most of the narrative is conveyed by duologues between two characters in medium shots and close-ups. They never stop talking. Talk is cheap; it just needs a few basic sets and a team of writers compared to movie locations and special effects, stunts, car wrecks, and exploding buildings. In the contemporary Hollywood movie, **dialogue** must carry its weight in describing **character** and advancing the story for the **audience**. This is particularly true of action films. Classic novels by writers such as Jane Austen and Henry James that are adapted for the screen usually allow lengthier **dialogue**. One reason is that green berets and kung-fu masters are not prone to extensive verbal communication, whereas a nineteenth-century lady or gentleman with an education is more expressive. It fits the **character**. There are other exceptions like Woody Allen films, which thrive on verbal interaction between characters. The Woody Allen talk is part of the **character**.

It's easy to write **dialogue**. It's hard to write good **dialogue**. Almost anybody can string together an exchange between **characters**. The difficult part is to develop an ear for the way words will play so that a **character** speaks consistently, so that an **audience** will believe in the **character**, and so that the lines don't slow down the movie. Remember that words take up time. Lots of words take up lots of time. What is your **character** doing while speaking? The **dialogue** has to fit the **action** and the circumstance. It has to fit the **character** so that a college professor doesn't talk like a car salesman, a teenager doesn't talk like an adult, and a Boston banker doesn't talk like a Southern farmer. Not everybody can find the words that sound right. You have to be observant of people and develop an ear for speech. Because most stories involve conflict, struggle, love, revenge, mistakes, or comic embarrassment, **dialogue** often expresses emotions. Writers have to find the words that fit the emotion.

PLOT OR STORYLINE

The **plot** seems to be the mechanism that most of us see as the embedded structure of the screenplay and movie. It is somewhat like a skeleton. By itself it can't stand up. It needs muscles and ligaments and a life force to animate the total organism. So the plot or **storyline** is one way of understanding a screenplay. What happens in what order? The way you arrange the sequence of **scenes** determines the way the story unfolds. That is important.

---

[2] Check out the screenplay by novelist Ring Lardner Jr. (www.geocities.com/Hollywood/8200/Mash.txt).

[3] Willar King Bradley, *Inside Secrets of Photoplay Writing* (New York: Funk & Wagnalls, 1926): "I once asked David Ward Griffith what he considered the best course for one to pursue in writing for the screen, and he answered, 'Think in Pictures!' He had just completed *The Birth of a Nation*" (p. 33). See also J. Berg Esenwein and Arthur Leeds, *Writing the Photoplay* (Springfield, MA: The Home Correspondence School, 1913): "it is action that is of primary importance. It is what your characters do that counts" (p. 112).

A **plot** is really the sequence of **actions** that traces out a progression of events. This constructed sequence distills the essence of life and shows us something about the way life works. When Polonius hides behind the arras or curtain to eavesdrop on Queen Gertrude's meeting with Hamlet, he creates a circumstance that leads to Hamlet reacting defensively to stab him through the curtain, thinking or perhaps hoping that it is his uncle Claudius, murderer of his father. Because it is Polonius, the **plot** intensifies and complicates things for other characters. Laertes now has to avenge his father's death. Hamlet has killed the father of the woman he probably loves but cannot acknowledge, Ophelia. Hamlet himself is now in greater danger because of his risky **action**. Claudius is very much alive and now fearful of Hamlet and therefore much more dangerous. So one **action** sends stress lines into every corner of the play. The tension is heightened. More **action** must follow. Choices and **actions** in life are usually less dramatic, but the choices of yesterday lead us to where we are today. Even if **characters** are not tomb raiding, saving the world form asteroids, or trying to defuse a bomb, they are always making choices. The choices they make spring from their values and their nature as **characters**, which then lead to consequences, another **scene**, and so the story moves forward.

COMEDY

As Sam Goldwyn once said, "Our comedies are not to be laughed at." Writing funny lines as you devise comic situations presents another kind of challenge. **Comedy** depends on **action** as well. Even if it is not **slapstick action**, it requires physical situations in which **characters** have to confront embarrassing situations and act in outrageous ways. **Comedy** requires **conflict** as much as **tragedy**. Whereas the tension that arises from **conflict** in **tragedy** is released in violence and suffering, the tension that arises from **comedy** is released in laughter. Silent film developed a visual vocabulary for comedy. Obviously, the slapstick traditions of vaudeville translated to film. The difference is that film had to develop stories not stage acts. The master of this new form, Charlie Chaplin, was writer, director, and star. In *The Gold Rush* (1925), the tramp is trapped inside a cabin in a snowstorm in Alaska with a huge, ugly fat man. They have no food. You could just as well imagine this **premise** as a survival drama. You have seen dozens of them on film and television. The big man starts seeing Chaplin as a meal, hallucinating that he is a large chicken. Chaplin sets about his own survival. He boils his boots for dinner and makes us laugh while he treats the shoelaces as spaghetti and sucks the nails like chicken bones.

Situations of physical danger lend themselves equally well to suspense that is dramatic and suspense that is hilarious. Later in *The Gold Rush*, the cabin is teetering on the edge of a cliff where it has been blown by the storm. The movement of the occupants threatens doom at every moment, obliging them to cooperate in order to escape. Some of you may have seen the Harold Lloyd silent **comedy** in which he is clinging to the hands of a clock on a clock tower. As the hands move, he is in constant danger of falling, but he miraculously avoids it. The line between **comedy** and drama is sometimes thin.

Comic Devices

Almost any comic device can also be a tragic device. Aristotle contrasted **tragedy** and **comedy** by saying that one makes **characters** look greater or better than they are in real life and the other makes them look worse. Almost all of them can be found in Shakespeare's plays. Even the hoary cliché of the comic spectacle of drunkenness is there. See Sir Toby Belch in *Twelfth Night* and the Watchman in *Macbeth*. We have **comedy** inside **tragedy**—the fool in *King Lear*. And we have **tragedy** and cruelty inside **comedy**—Malvolio in *Twelfth Night* or Shylock in the *Merchant of Venice*. By studying **comedy** and how it works, we hope we improve our comic writing. It must help to identify certain devices that underlie the comic experience.

The Comic Character as Victim

The comic **character** can be a physical victim or a victim of circumstance; we can call this the **character as victim**. Silent film relied on physical **comedy**, and physical **comedy** works. In *Modern Times* (1936) (see the website), Chaplin is selected from the production line to test the new feeding machine that a vendor is trying to sell to the factory owner that will allow workers to eat on the job and put an end to lunch breaks. Chaplin is strapped in and eager to eat, but the machine starts to malfunction and the corncob holder spins out of control until Chaplin stops it with his nose. The soup is thrown in his face. The spectacle of Chaplin desperate to get a bite of this food, which is mechanically delivered too fast or out of range, makes you weak with laughter. The audience empathizes with the hunger, the enjoyment of food and the frustration. Then there is the spaghetti fight in the official dinner in the *Great Dictator* (1940). In *Lost in Translation* (2003), Bill Murray is forced to run faster and faster on an out-of-control stepping machine. In the hospital scene in *Something's Gotta Give* (2003), Jack Nicholson gets out of his hospital bed and wanders around in a hospital gown that shows his bare butt just as his women friends are arriving to visit. He is oblivious, but we are not.

Verbal Comedy

In *Lost in Translation* the Japanese director of the whiskey commercial Bill Murray's character is making yells cut and then gives a long speech of direction. The American actor played by Bill Murray and we, the **audience**, wait with baited breath to find out what this is all about. The Japanese production assistant then translates it in a single sentence: "He wants you to turn to the camera." Then there is another minute of Japanese direction and discussion with the production assistant. And she then turns to him and conveys the direction: "with intensity." Bill Murray's character says, "Is that all? He must have said more than that." The anticipation of what the Japanese means is given a comic anticlimax in the short simple direction. We laugh at the contrast. The **dialogue gag** enriches the situation, and the **dialogue gag** works because of the situation. For the most part this bittersweet film depends on the visual irony of putting **characters** in background and letting us see how alienated they are. The **comedy** is situational. The alienation and culture shock is a fundamental driver of the **plot**. So miscommunication because of language, whether it is foreign language or emotional language (between Scarlett Johansson's character and her husband and between Bill Murray's character and his wife on the other end of the phone and fax), makes the **comedy**. The screenplay by Sofia Coppola won the Oscar for Best Original Screenplay in 2003.

In *The Devil Wears Prada* (2006), the tyrannical magazine editor treats her assistants like dirt and the new girl played by Anne Hathaway disappoints her. So she says petulantly something like, I thought I would take a chance on the "smart fat girl." The deadpan amazement on Anne Hathaway's face, seen in close-up, is masterful comic acting. The expression validates the line, which is itself hilarious because Anne Hathaway is not fat but amazingly beautiful. Meryl Streep understates the **comedy** and allows the **audience** in. It is a good example of a well-scripted line validated by great acting, authoritative directing, and perfectly timed editing.

Running Gag

A **running gag** is comic setup that because it has been introduced to the audience as a premise for humor keeps working over and over again. The repetition enhances and enriches the comedy. *Some Like it Hot* (1959), written by I. A. L. Diamond and Billy Wilder, is one of the great movie comedies of all time. You could argue that the premise of the movie is a **running gag**. Two musicians who unwittingly witnessed the St, Valentine's Day Massacre in Chicago are pursued by hit men from the mob who wants to eliminate all witnesses. The musicians disguise themselves as women and join an all-girl band going to a gig in Miami. Cross-dressing is a kind of **running gag** itself and also a mistaken identity device. Every encounter between Sugar, played by Marilyn Monroe, and the musicians, played by Tony Curtis and Jack Lemmon, reinvigorates the **running gag**. They are sleeping in the midst of a railroad car full of women in nightgowns. They want to make out but have to preserve their disguise in the sleeping car. Then in Miami, when a millionaire falls for Jack Lemmon and Tony Curtis assumes the identity of the same millionaire to woo Sugar, the **gag** gets richer and funnier because it is building on what we, the **audience**, already know. When Jack Lemmon steps into the elevator with Joe E. Brown as the millionaire, we cut to the floor indicator. The door opens again and Jack Lemmon slaps him for getting fresh. The comedic moment depends on this **running gag**.

The Cover-up/Impersonation

Miss Pettigrew Lives for a Day (2008) follows the misfortunes of Guinevere Pettigrew in what is called screwball comedy. A vicar's daughter, governess, and nanny, who has been fired from several jobs and dropped by her agency, sneaks a job file from the office and meets her new employer, a flighty ambitious American singer masquerading as a star. This **character** played by Amy Adams immediately recruits her into an elaborate and frantic scheme to juggle her simultaneous relationships with three men. The **comedy** of the cover-up into which Guinevere is thrust also involves her covering up her real identity as a nanny and pretending to be a social secretary. The excitement of the **comedy** for the **audience** is the unpredictable and precarious nature of each **scene** and its unknown outcome. In this **comedy** as in most **cover-up plots**, the truth must out to resolve the **premise**. Set in period before the outbreak of World War II in London, each **character** finds a truth and an identity that lifts the coverup. **Cover-ups** can be **plot** based or transitory comic devices that drive a **scene**.

Two cross-dressing impersonation movies—*Tootsie* (1982) and *Mrs. Doubtfire* (1993)—deserve mention because the **plot** of each depends on the **audience** understanding that the main **character** is a man pretending to be a woman. In the case of Mrs. Doubtfire, the **comedy** is also poignant because the **character** has adopted this disguise so that he can be with his children who are in the custody of the divorced mother.

The Marx Brothers made some great comic films that almost always turn on some kind of **cover-up**. In *A Day at the Races* (1937), Groucho plays Hugo Z. Hackenbush, a horse veterinarian who pretends to be the doctor of a sanatorium that is going bankrupt. Groucho doing medical exams is so funny it hurts. *A Night at the Opera* (1935) was scripted by a major American comic writer, George S. Kaufman.

The **plot** is too complicated to summarize but involves Groucho masquerading as a business manager Otis P. Driftwood with his accomplices who are friends of two opera singers who they want to help, now enabled by a rich social-climbing benefactress that Groucho has seduced. It starts in Milan and unfolds aboard ship where the accomplices and the aspiring operas singers are stowaways. When the stowaways hide in Groucho's cabin to evade ship's officers, it is another laugh-till-you-cry **scene**. This kind of zany whacky **comedy** seems to be nothing more than a romp, but all **comedy** conceals a meaning that is, for want of a better word, serious. Very few people are genuine. We all put on faces, behaviors to conform to what we think employers, friends, and lovers want to gain approval, success, or fulfill ambitions. We all masquerade, pretend, and **cover-up** who we really are.

Disguise and Mistaken Identity

Disguise is a variant of the cover-up. **Mistaken identity** is when cover-up happens in spite of the characters, and the **character** doesn't know. We can call on *Some Like it Hot* again to illustrate disguise. The cross-dressing is essentially a form of disguise. It has a wholly different meaning in *The Crying Game* (1992), in which an IRA defector fleeing to London looks up the girlfriend of the British soldier he had to guard, becomes attracted to her, and finds out that she is in fact a transvestite. In a previous chapter, we mentioned *Twelfth Night*, which turns on the transvestite disguise of Viola, which then leads to many comic complications. She falls in love with the duke for whom she is the love messenger but cannot reveal her true gender. She is mistaken for her brother Sebastian, which gets her into a sword fight with Sir Andrew Aiguecheek that they both desperately try to avoid. The entire plot of Shakespeare's early *Comedy of Errors* is based on an old **premise** from Latin comedy of twins being taken for one another and confusing those around them and the twins themselves. It is hard to top Shakespeare.

Burn After Reading (2008) involves a hilarious misunderstanding that the manuscript of a memoir of an ex-CIA agent is a secret document that can be used to get reward money. Every **character** in this movie misunderstands and mistakes every other **character** for someone else until finally the CIA agrees to finance Linda Litzke's plastic surgery makeover if she promises to keep quiet about a train of events and murders that they do not understand. Consider *Never Been Kissed* (1999), in which Drew Barrymore plays a reporter pretending to be a high school student to do an undercover story, or *Miss Congeniality* (2000), in which Sandra Bullock trying to be a tough guy FBI agent has to go undercover as a beauty queen to prevent a terrorist plot against the Miss America beauty pageant, or the original screenplay of *Dave* (1993), in which a character who looks like the president of the United States (who is seriously ill) is persuaded to fill in for him and govern the country. *The Master of Disguise* (2002) is comedy thriller whose title incorporates the comic **premise** itself. We'll finish with a remake of a Humphrey Bogart movie *We're No Angels* (1989) in which two escaped convicts disguise themselves as priests to get to the Canadian border and freedom.

Dramatic Irony

A simple kind of **dramatic irony** occurs when the **audience** knows more than the **character** or characters in the novel, play, or movie. So their **actions** or words have a meaning to us that is more complex than it is to them. Again, *Some Like It Hot* provides a comic example. Because we know that Tony Curtis and Jack Lemmon are men disguising themselves as women, we know something none of the girl band knows, but particularly Sugar and the Florida Millionaire. Without this knowledge, the **comedy** wouldn't work.

Burn After Reading (2008) also involves dramatic irony in that each character does not know what we know. So we see them working at cross-purposes. Chad, played by Brad Pitt, is shot by the treasury agent played by George Clooney when he discovers him in his closet and assumes he is a spy because he has no identification. So Chad, the innocent gym instructor who thinks he and Linda have found secret documents, ends up being caught up in a CIA drama even though it is all a complete and total misunderstanding on the part of all players. In fact, most comedies depend on **dramatic irony** that requires the **character** to know less than the **audience** about his or her own situation.

DRAMA

Almost any dramatic device can be turned to **comedy**, and almost any comic device can be turned to drama. How many times have you seen a nail-biting scene in which the hero or heroine is hanging by one hand from a building or stuck in a wreck about to fall over a bridge or cliff? Then they slip and fall to the next ledge, or the rescuer seems like he cannot hold on. The **scene** is milked for suspense, but you don't laugh like you do at Harold Lloyd hanging from the hands of a clock. Why? There's the difference between **comedy** and drama. In drama, such a scene is written and played for tension and suspense. The **premise** is identical to the **premise** for comic disaster. Drama means conflict, high emotion, and usually **action**. Suspense drama turns heavily on **plot**. The consequences of **action** are critical for life and death, success or failure, so that we worry about what will happen. In **comedy**, the consequences of **action** are also critical, but we are allowed to laugh at the victim who represents all of us faced with the indignities of life. Although the **premise** of **comedy** and drama may be similar, the outcome is always different—happy as opposed to serious. How is the writing different? **Dialogue** and **character** weigh heavily in pushing the concept one way or the other. **Comedy** requires **gags**, tension, and overreaction. Drama requires tension, conflict, and understatement.

Cover-up/Mistaken Identity

Cover-up and mistaken identity are usually essential to much detective fiction and many crime thrillers. Someone innocent is taken to be guilty. There is even film whose **premise**, our topic, is its title—*Mistaken Identity* (1999), also called *Switched at Birth*, a title that was used three times in the silent era. Two mothers find out that their babies were accidentally switched in the maternity ward. The same **premise** allowed Mark Twain in *Pudd'nhead Wilson* to explore the thesis that **character** and social status derive from conditioning in a story that revolves around the new science of fingerprinting. A light-skinned slave and his master's son are again accidentally switched in the cradle so that the scion of the plantation grows up as a slave and the Negro slave grows up to be a cruel plantation owner. In Mark Twain's hands, this **premise** is a devastating condemnation of slavery and racial prejudice.

Disguise

The Wolf disguises himself as Grandma in *Little Red Riding Hood*. Almost all the comic book superheroes–Batman, Superman, and Spiderman—go in disguise. Superman disguises himself as reporter Clark Kent, but Batman is a disguise for Bruce Wayne. *V* (2003) is about a masked avenger. Then there is the old Saturday movie serial hero Zorro, subsequently made into feature films. *The Man in the Iron Mask*, a novel by Alexander Dumas, which brings the **premise** into the title, has been made into a movie several times, most recently in 1998. *The Mask* (1994) again brings the **premise** into the title with Jim Carrey playing a timid character who finds a mask that transforms him into a daring and powerful character opposite to his reality. Horror films that play with the Halloween theme often use the mask and disguise as a suspense and frightener device: *Scream* (1996), *Halloween: Resurrection* (2002) and its predecessors, *2008* (2009) and its predecessors. All vampire movies basically turn on disguise. The vampire looks human and has human form but has another identity that is in conflict with human nature. *Interview with the Vampire* (1994) and recently *Twilight* (2008) discovers the disguise for the **audience**.

Dramatic Irony

Dramatic irony occurs when words or **actions** mean something different to the **audience** and the **character**. **Dramatic irony** that is not comic in effect but an intensifier of drama, suspense, and tension is central to *Little Red Riding Hood*. We know that the Wolf knows where she is going. We know that the Wolf has eaten Grandma and is waiting for Little Red Riding Hood. She doesn't. Every horror film and suspense thriller depends on **dramatic irony**. We watch knowingly as a **character** walks into a trap, a situation of danger or sometimes the opposite, a situation of triumph. The most powerful **dramatic irony** in **tragedy** is Oedipus. A man unknowingly kills his father and marries his mother.

We were just discussing horror movies. Almost every horror movie you have ever seen involves a key moment of **dramatic irony** when a **character**, usually a female victim, walks into a trap or into danger that we, the **audience**, know is there because of a prior shot of the lurking monster/rapist/slasher. The device is often used in suspense thrillers and caper movies.

The Bank Job (2008), a brilliant script that tells the story of true events, is about a 1971 bank robbery in London that was never prosecuted because the government wanted to **cover-up** scandalous photos of a member of the royal family that were in the bank vaults that were looted. It is monitored by MI5, the British secret service, who convinces a woman that she won't be charged if she helps them to recover the pictures. She gets an old flame, a shady car dealer, to put together a gang to tunnel into the bank vault. The irony is not only that they don't know that they have been put up to the job, but it is heightened when they get off scot-free when caught in the act because the scandal would threaten VIPs in government and the royal family.

In Bruges (2008) involves two hit men who are sent to Bruges in Belgium to wait for orders. Meanwhile they become out-of-place tourists interacting with a range of characters from a dwarf actor shooting a film, to a woman selling drugs, to the people on the set, to a hotel manager. The film ends in a bloody climax in which one of them, in carrying out a hit, kills an innocent boy. The **characters** are in a world that they do not understand, and they do not even know why they are there. The dark **comedy** turns into strong suspense because we learn with the **characters** why they are there and who their controller is.

Doubt (2008) is a title with a double meaning. It refers to the doubt that the Meryl Streep character has after destroying the career of the priest she accuses of pederasty, and it refers to the doubt that we, the **audience**, experience because we are momentarily receptive to her conviction but finally we are uncertain and left in doubt.

Ambition/Pride

Hubris is the Greek word for that delusion of invincibility or being in control that is pride, which goeth before a fall. The spectacle of human beings convinced that they are in control of their own destiny or of an ego that cannot give way has an implicit dramatic premise. Tragic characters are deluded into thinking that they are masters of their own destiny. Spiritual teaching, both East and West, tells us that "thine is the kingdom, the power and the glory." Many use the expression "What goes around, comes around." This is *karma*, the Vedic understanding that there is a law of cause and effect in the actions of human beings that plays out over more than one lifetime. Drama requires action and consequence to play out in a single lifetime, such as when Macbeth murders his liege lord out of ambition, showing a fundamentally good man who makes a bad choice. *Frost/Nixon* (2008) explores the downfall of a president who was impeached. *There Will Be Blood* (2008) explores the ambition of a man who wants to annihilate his competitors and be the king of oil.

Challenge and Survival

Treasure of the Sierra Madre (1948) is a classic story of greed about a down-and-out American in Mexico who teams up with a prospector who has a gold claim that needs to be worked. Once they mine enough gold to be rich for life, they then have to get it back to town to sell it. They have both inner and outer challenges. But this is also a story of greed for a category we discuss later. *La Vie en Rose* (2007) is the real-life story of Edith Piaf who basically survived an orphaned existence on the streets of Paris and became a beloved music hall singer. *The Wrestler* (2008) tells the story of a down-and-out wrestler who has lost his family, his daughter, and his friends and struggles to survive in ignominious jobs until he decides to make a final comeback against all medical advice. He dies in the attempt to claim his only identity. *Gladiator* (2000) shows us a character who, despite a terrible loss of status, wife, and children, learns to survive and confront his tormentor. *Jurassic Park* (1993) turns into a drama of challenge and survival as soon as the park structure fails and the visitors are at the mercy of the genetically engineered dinosaurs that inhabit the island. *Slumdog Millionaire* (2009), which won the Oscar for Best Picture, tells the story of a slum orphan who wins a "Who Wants to Be a Millionaire" million by turning his fantastic life experiences into knowledge and insight that enables him to answer the questions. Some survival stories lead to loss and suffering; others lead to triumph. In *Dances with Wolves* (1990) there is a temporary triumph in the flight and escape of the Sioux and Lieutenant John Dunbar before the U.S. Cavalry, but we know the ultimate fate of Native Americans; so it is a temporary survival.

Greed

Greed is one of the seven deadly sins. The pursuit of money and material things and the craving for wealth is a common denominator that any **audience** understands. In fact, the other six sins are a pretty good source of drama too: lust, gluttony, sloth, wrath, envy, and pride.

Treasure of the Sierra Madre (1948) begins with a down-and-out American losing a lottery with his last peso. Later, after becoming rich beyond his wildest dreams with two others up in the mountains, they fall into a paranoid state of suspicion about each other. Each fears that the others will kill him and take his share of the gold. It is based on a classic morality tale in Chaucer's *Canterbury Tales* told by the Pardoner. *There Will Be Blood* (2007), based on Upton Sinclair's novel *Oil*, is about a ruthless dominating **character** who cheats people out of their oil rights as he build an oil empire and great wealth. He loses his only son and gains nothing but emptiness and loneliness.

Wall Street (1987) is a classic story of greed. There is the famous line by Gecko, the film's corporate raider: "Greed is good." So this film focuses on greed as a phenomenon that motivates ambitious financial operators whom many want to emulate. It is suddenly relevant to the present day in which essentially greed and speculative fever brought down the American and world banking systems and brought about the worst recession since the Great Depression.

Love Gone Wrong

We all know *Romeo and Juliet* as the classic story of love gone tragically wrong. In this case, the world around the two lovers conspires to frustrate their union. *Sylvia* (2003) is the true story of the love and marriage of the American poet Sylvia Plath to the English poet Ted Hughes, the disintegration of their relationship, and her eventual suicide. *The Lover* (1992) adapts a novel by the French novelist Marguérite Duras, which is a recollection of a tragic love between her as a teenage girl and an older, wealthy Chinese man. They are divided by culture, race, and class. It is a powerful story of loss that haunts two lives. The lyrics of an old French song express it: the pleasure of love lasts but a moment; the pain of love lasts a lifetime.

Although *Doubt* (2008) is not about carnal love but spiritual love, it is nevertheless relevant because the caring of the priest accused by the head of the convent school of perverting a young black boy is probably a true expression of love, *agape* not *eros*. The Greeks had a distinction between erotic love and love that does not have a sexual dimension that is precious to human beings: the love of parents for children, of siblings for one another, of children for grandparents, and of friends for one another.

The Duchess (2008) is a biographical portrait of a woman who finds herself in a loveless marriage to the richest and most powerful duke of eighteenth-century England. She must find the strength to bring up children, endure his mistress, and renounce her love of a future Prime Minister of England for the sake of her children.

Desire/Lust

Everyone understands desire. We mentioned lust as one of the seven deadly sins. Whether desire is a sin is a religious question, but it is certainly an inevitable component of human lives and a cause of endless pain and drama as well as a certain amount of happiness. In **comedy**, we imagine the happy outcome of this force of attraction. In drama, we confront the ways in which this hormonally driven emotion enters our lives and unleashes possessiveness, jealousy, pain, and even hate when love is spurned or rejected. *The Lover* (1992) expresses truthfully the strength of desire as a driver in human relationships. It is different because the **characters** know they are doomed. The girl deliberately destroys their potential for love until at the end she realizes that she really loved and was loved. Not many Hollywood films can go the distance with this kind of story. Great works of literature such as Flaubert's *Madame Bovary* or Tolstoy's *Anna Karenina* deal with destructive adulterous love. *Anna Karenina* has been filmed for movies and television at least a dozen times. Adulterous love induces an instant situation of **conflict**, which can only resolve with unhappiness of one kind or another because it can involve up to four people and any number of children. Nevertheless, it happens over and over again in real life and in the movies.

Body Heat (1981), an original screenplay written by Laurence Kasdan, shows how a man can be set up by seduction into killing a woman's husband so that she can inherit his wealth, even though there is no intention on her part to continue the relationship.

Controversy surrounded *9½ Weeks* (1986), which explores eroticism and desire as a force of attraction and seduction without romance. The film involves a wealthy businessman who captivates a young, recently divorced woman. It tests extremes of trust and goes where most American films don't go. The most radical exploration of desire as an all-consuming force of almost any film ever made is Japanese director Oshima's *In the Realm of the Senses* (1976). Initially banned in North America, it chronicles the true story of obsessive love and desire that leads to sexual mutilation and death by strangulation because the character seeks greater extremes of sexual pleasure. A weaker version of this theme would be Madonna's role as a woman charged with knowingly murdering a man by causing him to have a heart attack during extreme sex in *Body of Evidence* (1993). She later seduces her defense lawyer, who then is forced to question the innocence he is defending. *Two Lovers* (2008) shows us a young man who misses the loving woman right under his nose and whom his family wants him to marry pursuing a more complex, mixed-up woman who is in a destructive affair with a married man. In *Elegy* (2008), an older man who is a professor makes advances to an attractive female student but does not have the courage to follow through when she responds. *Lolita*, the novel by Nabokov, was made into a movie twice—in 1962 with James Mason and in 1997 with Jeremy Irons. It tells the tragic attraction that a professor of French has for the daughter of the woman at whose house he boards because she recapitulates his teenage love who died. It becomes an increasingly destructive relationship, initiated by the 15-year-old Lolita. *The Reader* (2008) explores the initiation into sexual love of a young teenager by an older woman who has him read to her. We find out that she is illiterate. Iin her trial for being a prison guard under the Nazi regime and party to a massacre, she refuses to save herself by revealing her illiteracy. The young man doesn't speak up to save her. While she is in prison, she learns to read from the audio books he sends her.

Although most movies discussed here are adapted from another source work, the glory of the medium is the original screenplay. Writing directly for the screen is a great craft and difficult to do well. *Citizen Kane* (1941), written by Herman J. Mankiewicz and Orson Welles, is one of the greatest original screenplays ever written. Lawrence Kasdan is an accomplished writer/director. His *Body Heat* (1981) is a flawless murder-mystery thriller. Jane Campion wrote and directed *The Piano* (1993) to international acclaim. One of the true talents of movie writing in America is Paul Schrader. His writing and directing credits are numerous and include the original screenplay for Martin Scorsese's classic *Taxi Driver* (1976).[4] My favorite is *Mishima* (1985), about love and honor in a cross-cultural love affair in Japan involving an ex-GI. Don't forget to read William Goldman's original screenplay of *Butch Cassidy and the Sundance Kid* (1969), published in *Adventures in the Screen Trade*,[5] which tells you a lot about working realities for writers in Hollywood.

---

[4] Paul Schrader, *Taxi Driver* (London: Faber & Faber, 1990). See also *Schrader on Schrader & Other Writings*, "Directors on Directors Series," by Paul Schrader, Kevin Jackson (ed.) (London: Faber & Faber, 1992) and *Transcendental Style in Film: Ozu, Bresson, Dreyer* by Paul Schrader (London: Faber & Faber, 1988).
[5] William Goldman, *Adventures in the Screen Trade* (New York: Warner Books, 1983).

When you go to the movies, you should watch the screen credits and see who the writer is. See whether it is an original screenplay. Pay attention to the writer and to the writing talent that makes movies possible. Don't be one of those vulgarians who walk out as soon as the credits come on. Although the **audience** remembers the actors, whose lines we write, maybe the director, whose story we create, they rarely remember the writer. The basis of every movie is a screenplay. Every screenplay is the work of a writer.

WRITING TECHNIQUES FOR ADAPTATION

Let us reprise a point we made in Chapter 1 while working up an understanding of visual writing, the kind of writing that is special to the screen. We used Hemingway's novel *A Farewell to Arms* to show the difference between prose fiction and screen writing by asking how we would translate the opening descriptive paragraph into a screenplay. We were showing the difference between two types of writing, two types of storytelling. We now need to look at a much bigger issue, which grows out of that initial problem of what you represent in a **scene** when you adapt a source work for filming. We need to deal with techniques of **adaptation**.

In the entertainment world, writers are frequently called on to adapt their own or someone else's work, but **adaptation** also happens to be a really instructive exercise for the beginner; it can help the beginner learn how to write for the screen and discover the art of **visual writing**. Adapting can be one of the best ways to appreciate what screen writing is and, by the same token, what prose fiction is. If the storyline and the characters already exist, then the writer can concentrate on the problem of key moments and the 2-hour continuum of the movie.

THE PROBLEM OF ADAPTATION

Adaptation presents a special problem of translating one medium to another. Shakespeare, the master dramatist, was also a master adapter. Most of his plays drew from existing literary works. The parallel between the new medium of Elizabethan theater and the new medium of film is revealing. Although many great screenplays have been written originally for the screen, it is probably safe to say that most movies that we see are adapted from source works. They can be novels, short stories, stage plays, musicals, epics, fairy tales, and folk tales. You might think that a play is easy to adapt to film because it is made up of **dialogue** and **action**, but in a play, **action** takes place on a stage. A movie cannot just film a stage, although that is how many early silent movies were shot. People thought in terms of watching performance on a proscenium stage. It didn't take long for someone to figure out that you could move the camera and liberate the actors from painted scenery. Then camera angles were invented, which necessarily led to the art of cutting shots.

Although the original screenplay is, in a way, the glory of the medium, producers and movie studios look to properties that have succeeded with **audiences** in other media as a form of insurance. Producing and distributing movies is a high-risk business. Producers will look for any way to reduce the odds and increase the likelihood of recovering their investment. A best-selling novel has a ready-made **audience**. A Broadway hit has a prior reputation that helps to sell the movie. Successful new works in the theater or in print come with a price. Getting the rights to a John Grisham novel involves competitive bidding against other producers. So the insurance of buying a pre-sold **audience** and a ready-made story increases production costs and obliges the producers to share profits with the original writer. Increased production costs then demand the security of box office stars and known directors, what is known in Hollywood as "A list talent," which increases the production cost yet again.

For these reasons and because the rights are in the **public domain**, producers also look to classic works from Homer, through Shakespeare, to Dickens, and other classic writers. Not only are their stories in the **public domain** and therefore free, but they have withstood the test of time and held **audiences'** attention for generation after generation. The ready-made **audience** is proven. The trade-off is that it may be a smaller **audience** that is educated and literate, rather than the worldwide popular **audience** that does not read or does not know the great works of literature. The other element that sometimes dampens enthusiasm for these stories is that they are set in the historical past. This does not always appeal to **audiences** who have an appetite for seeing contemporary life reflected in the movies.

Period movies involve costumes, locations, and props that considerably increase the cost of production. In 1995, Jonathon Swift's satirical work *Gulliver's Travels* was turned into a television miniseries. The producers took advantage of modern computer-generated special effects. However, they introduced a shell story not in the original, in which Gulliver has a son and a wife who want him back. When he returns and is condemned as a madman, the son saves him by finding some of the miniature animals from Lilliput in their luggage. It tampers with the author's intention and sentimentalizes the final satire that has Gulliver preferring the company of horses (Houyhnhnms) to humans and going to live in a stable.

In the 1990s, producers discovered the works of Jane Austen and Henry James, two authors whose novels are not mass **audience** fare. Yet both authors have subtlety and texture that is surprisingly modern and cinematic. Hidden emotional forces in the lives of their characters can be portrayed in the visual language of cinema. Implied sexuality can be more readily understood in looks and gestures. Consider the film adaptations of *The Wings of the Dove* (1997) and *The Portrait of a Lady* (1996). Filmmakers can find contemporary values in old stories. Jane Austen's struggling and independent female characters can make contemporary interest in the changing role of women all the more poignant because of the social strictures of early nineteenth-century England or the conventions of social behavior in Golden Age America. Films such as *Pride and Prejudice* (1940 and again in 2005), *Sense and Sensibility* (1995), and *Emma* (1996) have won Oscars and have been remade several times since the invention of film and television.

Here is the author's adaptation of a **scene** from Henry James' *Daisy Miller*. Let us look at two versions to see how and why **dialogue** works and doesn't work in **adaptation**.

```
INT. MRS. WALKER'S APARTMENT - DAY

A SERVANT ushers WINTERBOURNE into the crimson drawing room of a Rome
apartment filled with sunshine. MRS. WALKER greets him and WINTERBOURNE
kisses her hand.

                              MRS. WALKER

             My dear Winterbourne! How nice to
             see you! How are you? How is Geneva?
```

                    WINTERBOURNE

         Geneva is less delightful now that
         you no longer winter there. I am
         very well and happy to be in Rome
         again. How are your children?

                    MRS. WALKER

         We have an Italian tutor for them,
         but he is not as good as the Swiss
         school and their teachers.

         THE SERVANT ENTERS AND ANNOUNCES
         DAISY MILLER AND HER FAMILY.

                    SERVANT
               (with italian accent)

         Signora e signorina Meellair!

The fault in the writing is that Mrs. Walker asks two questions. Winterbourne then answers them in series. It would be better to revise it as follows to facilitate the flow of dialogue:

                    MRS. WALKER

         My dear Winterbourne! How nice to
         see you! How is Geneva?

                    WINTERBOURNE

         Geneva is less delightful now that
         you no longer winter there.

                    MRS. WALKER

         How are you?

                    WINTERBOURNE

         I am very well and happy to be in
         Rome again. How are your children?

                    MRS. WALKER

         We have an Italian tutor for them,
         but he is not as good as the Swiss
         school and their teachers.

On the other hand, when Mrs. Miller speaks, her voluble aimless recitation is not a conversation. She has no social sense. While she rants on about her health, the camera shows Winterbourne trying to contain his boredom, his furtive glances at Daisy talking to someone else, and the leaping about of the restless Randolph, her 12-year-old brother.

LENGTH

Movies and television play in real time. A minute is a minute on screen. The movie narrative has a time limit. A paragraph or a page has no fixed time value. A novel can condense time and expand time. It can pack into descriptive prose numerous locations and casts of characters that would cripple a movie budget. Also, the novelist can describe characters and express their thoughts by means of the **omniscient narrator**. So the first problem of adaptation is to find a visual and action **storyline** that is not dependent on the **omniscient narrator**. In general, source works are longer than the movie can be because prose narrative is, in certain ways, more efficient than narration in visual media, which depends on **action**. Short stories and novellas generally make a better transition to the screen. A case in point is the classic western *High Noon* (1952). The screenplay was written by Carl Foreman, adapted from a *Collier's* magazine story "The Tin Star" (by John W. Cunningham), published in December 1947. The film is better than the original story.

POINT OF VIEW

Some readers might have tried their hand at prose fiction, either short story or novel. It is quickly apparent that the writer of fiction has options that the screen writer does not. The most important of these is the narrative **point of view**. Prose narrative must have a **point of view**. Although Melville's *Bartleby*, for example, is narrated in the first person from the **point of view** of a single character and the way he perceives events, the most common style of narration for the novel is usually referred to as the **omniscient or third-person narrator**. The writer can see everything and know the thoughts of all the **characters**. The writer can write objective description that sets time, mood, and place without reference to a character's point of view. Or the writer can describe what a **character** sees and thinks as well as put lines of **dialogue** in the **character's** mouth. This flexibility is part of the richness of fiction as a form. In some ways it is easier to write fiction because of the versatility of its narrative devices. Writing for the screen means, similar to the theater, confining the narrative to a certain duration. The story must be told within a time frame defined by the medium. We have all seen movies of a book we have read and felt the disappointment that the movie is not as good as the book. A movie can never be like the book because it is a different medium. Parts of the novel have to be left out. A novel can luxuriate in passages of description and describe the inner thoughts of characters in **omniscient third-person narrative**. For the film **adaptation**, however, the **plot** usually has to be tightened up. Sometimes the setting has to be changed. And a novel that one can read in 10 or 20 hours has to play in 2 hours.

The question of point of view is important for movies because the camera must point one way or another for every shot. As an optical recording instrument, it necessarily creates a literal point of view. The viewer cannot see anything other than that which is included in the frame. In some ways, this makes the medium powerful because it is concrete and because it creates emphasis. On the other hand, it also limits what the **audience** can see and experience by placing a specific image in the viewer's consciousness and excluding all others.

NARRATIVE TENSE AND SCREEN TIME

After point of view, the second great variable is the **narrative tense**. A novel can weave in and out of present time, but a movie camera narrates in the present tense because what we see is necessarily present time.[6] So screenwriters have to think in terms of seeing and hearing what characters do and say in front of us. We cannot represent their thoughts in the same way that a novelist does. We can only show them by **action** and reaction in situations. We have to narrate by means of **key moments**. A novelist can write in the past tense (which is the most common), can write in the present tense, or, to a degree, and with care, can even change tenses, depending on the point of view. This cannot happen in film unless you admit the flashback to be a tense change. Even in a flashback, the camera films in the present tense, as it were, and the viewer experiences the past now.

In some films, the manipulation of tenses of time relative to the main time of the story can become confusing. Viewers know when the story is in the past and when it is in the present. Some films create confusion when playing with chronological order. This is not the case with prose fiction. The signposts are usually unambiguous. This is probably because some of the time shifts in film are created by editing in postproduction. *Memento* (2000) comes to mind, even though the **premise** of the film posits a **character** with short-term memory loss.

SETTING AND PERIOD

The first issue that comes up concerns setting. Do you do the piece in period? Or do you transpose the story to another time? Is the story attached to its time? These questions came very much to the fore in adapting *Bartleby*. The question was whether an audience in the 1970s would respond to this story if it were set in a legal office in the New York of a century before. Could the timeless element of the story be transposed to the modern day and thereby reveal a meaning that many would not recognize in a setting of frock coats and quill pens? The passive resistance, the portrait of a loner who would not cooperate with an employer or with social norms, seemed intensely relevant to a post-Vietnam world of political protest and a generation of youth who did not buy into the social contract. The story seemed to be a commentary on the contemporary social phenomenon of the dropout. There were hundreds of Bartlebys. In fact, many people have said to me that they have met or known a person just like Bartleby. So the **character** seems to be timeless.

There are tremendous risks to transposing the story. A lot of elements change. For instance, a modern law office does not use scribes to make copies of legal documents. Legal secretaries, and now word processing, take care of that chore. So what is a modern equivalent? From my observation of dealing with lawyers and accountants, the answer seemed to be that an accountant's office, where bookkeepers' work with figures and balance sheets demands meticulous drudgery, would be the modern-day equivalent. Of course, with a contemporary setting, other details would have to change. However, setting it in London, England, in a kind of stuffy, retrograde British professional, gentlemanly environment seemed to be a perfect equivalent to the mannered stiffness of the New York lawyer of a hundred years earlier. Once you go in this direction, everything changes.

---

[6] See Kenneth Portnoy, *Screen Adaptation: A Scriptwriting Handbook* (Boston: Focal Press, 1998), p. 7: "In the novel, there are three time periods—past, present, and future. The screenwriter must deal in the present and devise ways to reveal the past."

A comparison might be that of changing the setting of a Shakespeare play. It is frequently done in the theater and in movie adaptations. *West Side Story*, the famous musical by Leonard Bernstein, reworks Shakespeare's theme of "star-crossed lovers" by placing them in modern New York among Puerto Rican gangs. Think of the recent film of *Romeo and Juliet* (1996), in which gangs with .45-caliber automatics in a Latin setting substitute for the houses of Montague and Capulet in Renaissance Verona. The emotional truth of the story is largely intact, but the text has to be severely edited for anachronisms. In many ways, that movie idea derives from Bernstein's musical crossed with *Miami Vice*. An English movie made in 1995 set *Richard III* in a ruthless fascist world that recalled Nazi Germany as a way of making the unprincipled villainy of Richard's political plotting more plausible. A new *Hamlet* came out in 2000 that set the play in contemporary New York. In it, Denmark is a corporation and the king a CEO.

DIALOGUE VERSUS ACTION

In novels, there is often more **dialogue** than can be used in a film **adaptation**. The question is whether the **character dialogue** that works in the novel will also work in the film. As we know from earlier discussion, it usually doesn't work to talk the **plot**. Bartleby's classic line ("I prefer not to") can be supplemented with looks and gestures. However, the opposite is true for Frank Capra's classic movie *It's a Wonderful Life* (1946). The short story on which it is based is thin on **dialogue**. The film script adds a great deal of **dialogue** that is not in the original story to good effect, **dialogue** that makes the **characters** come alive and **dialogue** that gives the audience information. For example, the angel in the original simply turns up and engages George in talk. In the movie, we get a shot of the sky with voice-over **dialogue** from some kind of heavenly administration that is assigning duties to angels until we get to Clarence, who hasn't yet got his wings. The movie opens with an original scene of people praying for George Bailey, which seems to activate the prayer-answering department of heaven:

CAMERA PULLS UP from the Bailey Home and travels up through the sky until it is above the falling snow and moving slowly toward a firmament full of stars. As the camera stops, we hear the following heavenly voices talking, and as each voice is heard, one of the stars twinkles brightly.

FRANKLIN'S VOICE

Hello, Joseph, trouble?

JOSEPH'S VOICE

Looks like we'll have to send someone down.

A lot of people are asking for help for a man named George Bailey.

FRANKLIN'S VOICE

George Bailey. Yes, tonight's his crucial night.

You're right. We'll have to send
someone down immediately.

Whose turn is it?

                    JOSEPH'S VOICE

That's why I came to see you,
sir. It's that clock-maker's
turn again.

                    FRANKLIN'S VOICE

Oh! Clarence. Hasn't got his wings
yet, has he?

We've passed him right along.

                    JOSEPH'S VOICE

Because, you know, er, he's got the
I.Q. of a rabbit.

                    FRANKLIN'S VOICE

Yes, but he's got the faith of a
child. Joseph, send for Clarence.

A small star flies in from left of
screen and stops. It twinkles as
Clarence speaks.

                    CLARENCE'S VOICE

You sent for me sir?

                    FRANKLIN'S VOICE

Yes, Clarence. A man down on earth
needs our help.

                    CLARENCE'S VOICE

Splendid! Is he sick?

                    FRANKLIN'S VOICE

No, worse. He's discouraged. At
exactly ten forty-five PM tonight,
Earth time, that man will be
thinking seriously of throwing away
God's greatest gift.

```
            CLARENCE'S VOICE

   Oh dear, dear! His life! Then I've
   only got an hour to dress. What are
   they wearing now?

            FRANKLIN'S VOICE

   You will spend that hour getting
   acquainted with George Bailey.
```

(See the video clip on the website.)

At this point, we get back to the earthly level of the movie and we get the angel's flashback of the life of George Bailey as a young boy when he saves his brother's life. So apart from the **comedy** of George getting a second-class angel who gets us on his side, we have inserted into the original story a cinematic device that enables the movie to tell us the story of George's life free of chronological sequence and to introduce the characters of Bedford Falls. None of this is in the original story. It is the decisive device that makes the movie different from the short story and makes the movie work.

DESCRIPTIVE DETAIL AND THE CAMERA FRAME

In Chapter 1, we discussed the opening of Hemingway's *A Farewell to Arms* and how the descriptive prose of the novel, if literally turned into film images, would extend the movie to unworkable length and impractical cost. The freedom of the novelist to describe detail presents the scriptwriter with a problem of choice—what to turn into a **scene** and what to ignore. What contributes to the story? What contributes to the atmosphere that is necessary to bringing that world alive?

Although novels frequently describe appearances or surroundings in detail, there is also a great deal that is left out. Everything that is in front of a camera lens has to be specific and concrete. Although some of these issues extend into production rather than scriptwriting, the screenplay might need to specify things that the novel does not—props or decor that need to be imagined to create a screen image. The novel can afford to develop a **character** at length by describing the past and by representing the character's inner thoughts. A movie has to reveal the **character** in the present and through **action** or interaction with other **characters**.

IMPLIED ACTION

Novels also imply **action** that a film version might not want to use. For instance, when Melville's narrator tells us that he finally moved offices to get rid of Bartleby, he doesn't describe moving. A powerful image suggests itself of movers taking away the furniture and leaving Bartleby standing in a bare office. When the lawyer drops into his office one Sunday to discover that Bartleby is living in his office, what should we see on screen? A novelist can leave it to the reader's imagination. A scriptwriter cannot. To convey that Bartleby is living in the office, a few **shots** can show him washing in the bathroom or getting dressed. Melville describes how the lawyer discovers evidence that Bartleby is living in his office. In the novella, there is a paragraph. In the screenplay, three short **scenes** expand on the prose. We need to see the lawyer arriving, his suspicion, his surprise, and his reactions. It is an opportunity to reveal a discovery in purely visual terms without **dialogue**. This is what makes movies work. Interestingly, in this case the script expands on the novella: whereas novels have to be cut down in length, short stories usually are expanded.

For instance, the adaptation of Melville's Bartleby presented a problem in that the novella is narrated in the first person from the **point of view** of the lawyer who employs Bartleby. He shares his thoughts with the reader. In a movie, you have the choice of rendering this as a voice-over narration or you have to create a situation in which some of his thoughts are revealed by interaction. It therefore seemed reasonable to create a lunch scene with a colleague in which the lawyer tries to rationalize his behavior toward Bartleby. The responses of the colleague spoken from convention and common sense set in relief the obsessional rationalizing state of this Wall Street lawyer. (Read the scene and see the video on the website.) This approach entails risk. You alter the original. Earlier in this chapter, I criticized the TV script of *Gulliver's Travels* because it creates a false shell story with a wife and a child. These are extra characters. The difference is that they fundamentally alter the meaning of Jonathon Swift's satire.

IT'S A WONDERFUL LIFE

It's a Wonderful Life is a well-written, well-made, and well-acted film. The story **premise** (see the website for the script) almost forms a genre—a movie story with recognizable or predictable elements. In this case, it is an angel movie. An angel or two intervene in the earthly drama of a human life with complex plot consequences about time, cause, and effect, and free will. It becomes a device that allows us to look at causality in existence. Everyone is fascinated by the problem of free will. You don't have to be a philosopher or a theologian. You just have to wonder if your life is fate or your own doing. Everyone, from time to time, has a notion that some greater force controls life's events, not individual choice. Most people wonder what would have happened if they had married or not married someone, made a different choice of major, job, or profession, or chosen to live somewhere else. There is also envy—some people seem to be getting a better deal in life than others. So the **premise** of the film, despite the unrealistic, supernatural elements, finds fertile soil in the imagination of any **audience** in which the **plot** can grow.

The basic **premise** of *It's a Wonderful Life* is that an angel trying to earn his wings intervenes in the life of George Bailey to save him from committing suicide when his life hits a crisis. The angel fulfills George's wish that he had never been born. George then visits the alternate world that results and discovers that his life has made a difference in the world. The moral is that each individual life counts and affects the lives of others. In other words, the universe is affected by our individual existence. Individual destiny is universal destiny. It is dramatically intriguing because it makes the **audience** into an omniscient observer. It's a film that has stood the test of time. This is why a number of contemporary television series and movies derive from it or make use of the same basic premise.

Quantum Leap (1989)[7] built a series on a science fiction premise, that a researcher time travels and finds himself in a different body each week. His only guide is a hologram angel or alter ego

---

[7] See http://uk.imdb.com/Title?0098151 for production details and plot summary.

who furnishes him with critical, omniscient information about his time and situation. Our hero is desperately trying to get back to his own body and own time. You can see how the premise lends itself to a series.

Groundhog Day (1993) is another variation on this same plot. The main **character** is a television weatherman who by some fluke is able to replay and relive the same day over and over again. When he catches on that time is repeating like a scratched record (or a dirty CD, for those who don't remember vinyl records), he takes advantage of his prescience to experiment with alternate choices. In other words, he is able to stand outside of time and see the causality of events and make different choices to have different outcomes for himself and those around him.

Touched by an Angel (1994)[8] is a popular TV series that explores the premise of angels intervening to teach people in crisis, who are about to make bad or destructive decisions, how to act positively. Poor mortals get the benefit of angelic counsel in the midst of sin and suffering, proving that the universe is benevolent and good can triumph over evil.

Michael (1996) is a feature film that looks at a *National Enquirer* story in which an angel with wings has come into the world of the owner of the Milk Bottle Motel somewhere in the Midwest. The reporters that investigate have their life problems untangled, and the angel works small miracles to bring lovers together and a dog back to life. The comedy of an angel behaving contrary to expectations is milked for all it's worth. Again, the **plot** turns around free will and intervention in destiny.

The television series *Now and Again* (1999)[9] explores the fiction that a man who dies in an accident is brought back to life by a secret government agency in a genetically engineered body. His brain, memory, and self-identity remain intact. He is not allowed to make contact with his wife or daughter on pain of termination. He is a fat-slob insurance salesman reborn as a superman. The premise produces numerous comic episodes in which he encounters his wife and daughter but cannot reveal his identity.

The satirical movie *Dogma* (1999)[10] is based on the plot idea of an alternative destiny that depends on intervention in the lives or actions of **characters** by supernatural beings. In this case, God is trapped by the devil in a human body, and the whole reality of the universe is at risk unless the good angels somehow manage to avert the contradiction that God's will is not absolute because two fallen angels are trying to get back into heaven.

Run Lola Run (*Lola Rennt*, 1998)[11] is a film about three different versions of the same scenario that explore alternate outcomes when slight variations in action alter the coincidences and events that follow. We see Lola run to save her lover in three plot outcomes. This makes the audience into the omniscient observer.

A classic exploration of this theme of knowing what is true or what is real lies behind the breakout Japanese film by Kurosawa, *Rashomon* (1950), which shows us three different views of a rape and murder from the **point of view** of three different characters. A newer variant is *Vantage Point* (2008),

---

[8] See http://uk.imdb.com/Title?0108968.
[9] See http://uk.imdb.com/Title?0212395.
[10] See http://uk.imdb.com/Title?0120655.
[11] See http://uk.imdb.com/Title?013082.

which narrates the attempted assignation of a fictional American president seen from the point of view of eight characters. We all know that reality can be complex and certain events not what they seem. To put it simply, we cannot know for sure what is real.

All of these variants of the angel/intervention plot illustrate different ways you can construct a movie plot from the same basic premise in original ways. You may be able to add to the list. In *Family Man* (2000), Nicolas Cage plays the central character in yet another destiny plot in which a rich capitalist bachelor gets switched into an alternative life in which he's married to an old girlfriend and has numerous children. This genre will continue to thrive on television and movies. Meanwhile, let us return to the granddaddy of them all and, in the process, learn more about the challenge of screen **adaptation**.

The story *The Greatest Gift*, on which *It's a Wonderful Life* (1946)[12] is based, is shorter and simpler than the movie. George and the angel are the only two main **characters**. Even George's wife is a minor character. In the movie, we see George's life from the time he was a boy to his falling in love with Mary, and we meet a huge cast of supporting characters including his brother and various townspeople, not to mention the savings and loan customers. Of particular importance is his alcoholic uncle who precipitates the ultimate reversal that makes George contemplate suicide. None of these are to be found in the original story. They were invented by the scriptwriters who needed to flesh out the detail of the essential **plot** idea and make it emotionally convincing in all the detail that brings Bedford Falls to life.

The story kicks off with voice-overs of people praying for a certain George Bailey. Who is George Bailey? This is, of course, a hook for the **audience**. We want to know who George Bailey is. Then we hear the voices (off-screen) of angels discussing the case and who will be assigned to it. When Clarence, angel second class, who still has not attained his wings, is summoned (this piece of droll invention has no basis in the original story), we are given a potted history of George Bailey by way of a briefing for the angel's mission. George Bailey is about to take his own life. This briefing takes the form of a flashback story (another device of the screenplay not in the original story) of George's life that takes us from his boyhood to early manhood. We are introduced to his father, the manager of the savings and loan association that finances the houses of low-income people in the small New York town of Bedford Falls. Mr. Potter, a kind of Scrooge character, dominates these townspeople's financial lives. George is all set to fulfill his boyhood dream of leaving Bedford Falls on a great trip abroad before going to college.

On the eve of his departure, we are introduced to Mary, the kid sister of his friend, at the high school dance where a relationship is seeded. Their night's romance is cut short when George's father, Peter Bailey, has a heart attack. Three months after his father's death, George, having postponed his trip to keep the savings and loan going, is present at the board meeting where Mr. Potter, the money-grubbing villain, moves to disband the savings and loan. George's passionate speech in defense of his father's work and of the importance of the institution for the ordinary people convinces the board to reject the motion and to appoint George to replace his father. Although George insists he is going to leave town to go to college, he stays and sends his kid brother to college with his savings, with the plan that they will trade places in four years.

---

[12] Directed by Frank Capra and written by Philip Van Doren Stern and Frances Goodrich, based on the novella *The Greatest Gift* (www.failuremag.com/arch_arts_ its_a_wonderful_life.html), and starring James Stewart, Donna Reed, and Lionel Barrymore. See http://sfy.ru/sfy.html?script=its_a_wonderful_life.

This is about the ending of Act I. We have met all the characters. George has made a choice to postpone his life. So it becomes a story about small town America and about a community.

In Act II, George's brother comes home from college married to a woman whose father has offered him a job in his company. The more George tries to break out of Bedford Falls, the more it seems to entangle him. He visits his old flame, Mary, who is being wooed by a rival, pushed by the mother. The mutual attraction between George and Mary results in their marrying.

As they are about to leave on their honeymoon, there is a panic run on the banks and the savings and loan during the Depression. Mr. Potter tries to buy the members' shares at a discount. George uses his savings to pay the depositors, who want all or some of their money, and manages to stave off the collapse of the bank, much to the disgust of Potter. After refusing an offer to work for Mr. Potter, George, always the man of principle, opts to defend the people and their savings institution. He and Mary have four children. World War II turns his younger brother into a fighter pilot and a war hero who wins the Congressional Medal of Honor. His uncle, who is a drinker and has an absentminded character, is taking the savings and loan association deposits to the bank when he runs into Mr. Potter. Showing him the headline about his war hero nephew, the uncle accidentally gives his envelope of cash deposits to Mr. Potter when he hands him back his newspaper. Potter, who now owns the bank, discovers the envelope and is about to return it when he sees his chance to realize a lifelong ambition to destroy or take over the savings and loan. The uncle now frantically retraces his steps looking for the money. At the savings and loan, George learns of the predicament on Christmas Eve. Meanwhile, a bank auditor has to go over the books. Evil is about to triumph over our Everyman hero who faces impossible odds. This is the end of Act II.

Now George must go to Potter and beg for a loan at any price. He offers his life insurance as a surety to cover the missing money. Potter not only refuses but acts to have George arrested for embezzlement and fraud. When George returns home, in despair of finding a solution, his erratic, impatient, and uncharacteristic behavior with his children alerts his wife Mary. After venting his frustration on his family, he goes out to the local bar to drown his sorrows. The children and his wife start to pray.

We have now completed the flashback. Snow is falling. George, now drunk, smashes up his car as he drives to the bridge. When George gets to the bridge over the falls and prepares to kill himself so that his life insurance will redeem the provident society, the angel, Clarence, finally intervenes to stop him. Instead Clarence jumps off himself and appeals to George's better instinct to save someone else. As they dry off in the tollhouse, Clarence reveals his identity. When George expresses the wish that he had never been born, Clarence seizes upon the wish as the way to teach him. He grants George's wish.

George goes back into town to find an alternate world in which he does not exist. All the people he knows, including his wife, have lived other destinies, much worse for the absence of George Bailey who has affected so many. This reversal seems disastrous, so George asks Clarence to give him his life back. At this point he returns with joy to his wife and children. The many people whose lives he has affected now turn up with baskets full of money as the word has spread. The crisis has been averted and George reconciled to his wonderful life as the people, affected by his life, sing a Christmas hymn and then "Auld Lang Syne."

Most of the movie is about George's growing up and falling in love and his defense of the townspeople from the rapacious banker and landlord, Potter, through the savings and loan created by his father. George never gets to go away and fulfill his youthful dreams. One circumstance after another conspires to keep him in small town America, hopping from decision to decision, which seems the right choice at the time. It leads to the ordinary life of a good man whose heroism is modest and whose deeds consist of doing the right thing. It is a paean to the life of the average American man, who is, of course, sitting in the **audience**.

Now let us go back to the source work—*The Greatest Gift*.[13] The original source turns out to be a short story of great simplicity that turns on the essential **plot** idea of a man called George in a nameless town who is standing on a bridge on Christmas Eve feeling suicidal. A nameless stranger appears to save him by granting his wish that he had never been born. Skeptical, he then returns to his hometown to find out that it is physically different and that the people in his life have lived different destinies because he, George, had never been born. After seeing this alternate reality (which poses a few problems in quantum mechanics and entropy), George rushes back to the bridge to find the stranger and have his wish undone. Rushing back into town he is overjoyed to discover his old life restored. It is a basic, simple moral fable about the value of the life of each individual. The big difference between the story and the movie is that the story provides little motivation, at least very general motivation that would not intrigue the audience, when an angel intervenes:

> I'm stuck here in this mudhole for life, doing the same dull work day after day. Other men are leading exciting lives, but I—well, I'm just a small-town bank clerk that even the Army didn't want. I never did anything really useful or interesting, and it looks as if I never will. I might just as well be dead. I might better be dead. Sometimes, I wish I were. In fact, I wish I'd never been born!

Taken by itself, this is just a bunch of petulant whining. The film script, based on this short story of a dozen pages, has invented and elaborated on huge amounts of detail and fleshed out the main character. The screenplay adds **characters** and alters the sequence of the story to construct the film as a long flashback.[14] This is why we believe in George's suicidal urge. When we get to the bridge **scene**, we have seen George's whole life; we know him, identify with him, and agonize over his final humiliation and final setback of losing the savings and loan deposit, playing into the hands of his lifelong adversary, the villainous Mr. Potter, who sees the opportunity to destroy George and take over the savings and loan. (See the scene at the bridge on the website.)

Are we worrying about what's going to happen? You bet! For the entire movie, George has thrown off every setback and disappointment. This ultimate reversal sets up the dénouement. Remember, the Woodcutter, a minor character in the second act of *Little Red Riding Hood*? In *It's a Wonderful Life*, George's woodcutter turns out to be one of his friends. George Wainright, now wealthy, who offered him a chance to get rich in his youth, hears of the problem and wires funds. All the townspeople contribute their dollars and cents. The dénouement is not just a happy ending, it ties up all the loose ends of the **plot**, which explain and motivate the **actions** of all the **characters**. In this case, the movie is far superior to the source work.

---

[13] Originally published privately by Philip Van Doren Stern in 1943. See *Afterword* by Marguerite Stern Robinson in the new Penguin Studio edition (New York, 1996).

[14] Note that no fewer than five scriptwriters contributed in varying degrees to this screenplay. See http://uk.imdb.com/Title?0038650.

BARTLEBY

The opposite is, in a way, true about *Bartleby* because it derives from a small masterpiece of American literature. The film becomes a commentary and a reinterpretation of it. Melville's story is short enough to read as an assignment. It also presents a number of challenging problems of **adaptation**.

In 1853, Herman Melville published a novella called *Bartleby, The Scrivener (a story of Wall Street)* in Putnam's *Monthly Magazine*.[15] The story is written in the first person. A lawyer, who remains nameless, hires a new scribe (or "scrivener") to work in his law office. He describes his law chambers and his employees and recounts the extraordinary relationship with the mysterious and impenetrable character called Bartleby. Bartleby, little by little, refuses to carry out the tasks that are asked of him. The lawyer does not know how to deal with this unpredictable character, his passive resistance to the work contract, and, finally, his refusal to obey instructions. Bartleby gets under his skin. He does not want to get angry. It becomes a psychological battle of wits.

In the end, Bartleby becomes a liability to the business. When Bartleby is fired, he won't leave the building. Eventually, the lawyer moves his office, leaving Bartleby behind. Then the next tenant comes to his new office to complain about the ghostly presence of Bartleby, who sleeps in the building. Finally, Bartleby is arrested and thrown into prison where the employer feels compelled to visit him and where Bartleby finally dies. The lawyer has gradually assumed a kind of responsibility and even a kind of guilt, early on, for the circumstance of this solitary and obstinate character. One Sunday, he visits his Wall Street office to find evidence that Bartleby is sleeping, eating, and living in his office:

> For the first time in my life a feeling of overpowering stinging melancholy seized me. Before, I had never experienced aught but a not unpleasing sadness. The bond of a common humanity now drew me irresistibly to gloom. A fraternal melancholy! For both I and Bartleby were sons of Adam.[16]

In the shooting script of the film, the scene is without dialogue. (See the website.)

EXT. STREET - DAY

During the weekend, the Accountant drives over to his office. His car pulls up at the curb. He gets out and walks into the building. He is dressed casually.

                                                    CUT TO

INT. CORRIDOR OUTSIDE OFFICE - DAY

The Accountant approaches down the corridor and opens the door to his office and goes in.

                                                    CUT TO

---

[15] See a scan of the original publication on the website.
[16] Herman Melville, "Bartleby: The Scrivener," in *Selected Writings of Herman Melville*, The Modern Library (New York: Random House, 1952), p. 23.

INT. OFFICE - DAY

The Accountant stops noticing something unusual as he passes through
reception. He sees a blanket on the sofa and then looks into Bartleby's
cubicle where he sees a piece of soap, a razor, and a towel on the desk.

CUT TO

INT BARTLEBY'S CUBICLE - DAY

He walks into Bartleby's cubicle half expecting to find Bartleby there.
Then he becomes curious about further clues. On Bartleby's desk are the
remains of some food, a cup, and a knife. The Accountant is agitated and
scandalized by this unheard of arrangement but also moved and depressed
by the implied solitude and poverty of Bartleby's existence. He goes to
Bartleby's desk and looks through to discover more personal belongings: a
change of underwear, money saved and wrapped in a handkerchief. He puts
everything back.

CUT TO

INT. OFFICE - DAY

When the Accountant has finished, he stands up and turns to confront
Bartleby who is standing behind him at the door looking mildly
reproachful. Without a word he turns and exits. The Accountant follows
him. FADE IN MUSIC.

The lawyer rather likes Bartleby: "there was something about Bartleby that not only strangely disarmed me, but in a wonderful manner, touched and disconcerted me." Later, he comments, "Nothing so aggravates an earnest person as a passive resistance." Then he rationalizes, "He is useful to me. I can get along with him."[17] When Bartleby continues to greet every request with the line "I prefer not to," the lawyer gets frustrated because he thought he could handle Bartleby. He suppresses his anger. This reflective narrative is difficult to turn into film. The solution for this writer was to invent a scene in which the lawyer, now an accountant, has lunch with a colleague. Psychologically, it works to have him try to rationalize his Bartleby problem and to hear an outsider with a commonsense point of view reveal to us how obsessed and isolated the character is becoming.

INT. RESTAURANT - DAY

THE ACCOUNTANT and a COLLEAGUE are sitting at a table eating lunch. THE
ACCOUNTANT is talking about BARTLEBY with animation, trying to justify
himself to his COLLEAGUE. The COLLEAGUE is mainly interested in his
lunch. For him it is a simple matter--fire Bartleby. We hear the general
background of a restaurant.

---

[17] Ibid, pp. 16–17.

COLLEAGUE

Why don't you just sack him? Could
I have the salt, please?

ACCOUNTANT

Sack him? I know it seems the obvious
solution, but I can't quite bring
myself to. He's so utterly civil, so
dignified . . .

> (THE COLLEAGUE shrugs and
> goes on eating)

He's actually a very efficient worker
except that he refuses to do certain
things from time to time. It's sort
of... passive resistance.

COLLEAGUE

Oh yes, what's he against?

ACCOUNTANT

Nothing, nothing! It's a mood; it's
his manner. If I humor him a bit,
I feel he'll come round. He could be
a first-class clerk. He needs someone
to take him in hand. In another firm,
he wouldn't have a chance.

The COLLEAGUE looks up and smiles
sourly.

COLLEAGUE

No, he'd be sacked immediately.

FULL SHOT

The meal progresses. A waiter's
hands are seen to clear the table of
plates and utensils. The ACCOUNTANT
is half thinking to himself, half
talking to his companion as he becomes
caught up with reflections about
BARTLEBY's rebellion against him.

ACCOUNTANT

Funny, I always end up giving him a
chance even though he irritates me.
I'm damned if I'm going to let him
get away with it. But then I just
wonder how far he'll go. I wonder
how far he would go.

COLLEAGUE

You ought to listen to yourself.
You're obsessed with this character.
Do yourself a favor. Get rid of him.
People in the profession are beginning
to talk about it. Your Bartleby will
queer your reputation and put off
clients.

> (THE ACCOUNTANT begins to
> perceive that his judgment
> is confused. His prudence
> and his business sense are
> stirred)

ACCOUNTANT

Really? Well there's a limit. But
you know he's there first thing in
the morning and last thing at night.
In his way, he works hard. I'll
bring him round yet. If not he'll
have to go.

The **scenes** extracts the essential conflict the lawyer narrates at length, but which has no filmable content. This is the kind of leap of imagination that a scriptwriter must have to adapt a work of literature. At the same time, it violates the sanctity of a literary classic. This is the dilemma. The adapter has to both add and subtract from the original, or find the equivalent. In the jail scene in the book, there is another **character** called the Grub Man. The film changes the prison to a mental hospital and the Grub Man to an anorexic inmate who is able to speak most of the lines in the original. You will have to judge by reading the 47-page novella, reading the script, and seeing the film. Others have wrestled with the problem and made changes to the characters when **adapting** the story for the screen in other productions.[18]

---

[18] See the account by George Bluestone, *Bartleby: The Tale, the Film, in Bartleby, The Scrivener: The Melville Annual*, Howard P. Vincent (ed.) (Kent, OH: The Kent State University Press, 1966), pp. 45–54.

Some adapters take a novelist's narration and read it as a voice-over to accommodate the thoughts and comments expressed. This seems to be an evasion most of the time to writing a film equivalent. Two films, however, come to mind in which this technique works. The first is a remake of Nabokov's *Lolita* (1997) with Jeremy Irons. The second is a superb adaptation of an autobiographical novel of Marguerite Duras, the French novelist. The voice-over narration for *The Lovers* (1991) is delivered by the throaty, world-weary voice of Jeanne Moreau. The other tactic of the filmmaker is to make the camera narrate visually and to frame close-up detail that reveals the emotional intention of the narration. When the two lovers meet, we see their shoes. He is an elegant dandy. She is a teenager, learning to walk in heels, unsure of herself but wanting to explore her emerging womanly allure. There is a wonderful moment as they board the river ferry and we see their mutual looks, the detail of their clothes and gestures. Their attraction now leads on to a tragic love affair.

A lot of Melville's characters are outsiders and social misfits. As a writer he explored the intersection of normal and abnormal behavior and the experiences of people at the edge of conventional society but engaged in real-world activities. He shows us how a slight shift in circumstance, character, or point of view alters everything. *Moby Dick* and *Billy Budd, Foretopman* have attracted filmmakers.[19] Adapting a literary masterpiece is a dangerous undertaking. The source work has a huge **audience** and lives as an independent work. *The Greatest Gift*, however, was bought as a story and was not even published until after the film had established itself as a classic.

Bartleby fascinated me because it was a psychological story and because, before its time, it seemed to explore the anonymity of modern urban life. It seemed to document a forgotten population whose lives are dominated by economic and social conditions that marginalize them. I had met people of my generation who had dropped out. They lived in the same environment I did, but they had no Social Security number, no health insurance, and squatted in abandoned houses. Some of them were just disoriented, but others were politically articulate and consciously rejected the social economic roles that are forced on us. *Bartleby* seemed to speak to the post-Vietnam world. It probably still does. The idea was to reveal the character in our own day. As soon as you decide to change period and setting, multiple problems arise.

One of the reasons why the story has cinematic potential is that it leaves a lot to the imagination. It also has a narrative **point of view**. Could you adopt that first-person **point of view** for the film? Possibly! One could imagine a film that explores the lawyer's perception of the character. It would make a very claustrophobic **visual narrative**. It seemed to me that if you were going to do it, you should explore both **characters** with the camera and invent **scenes** that visually define the psychological space in which the **character** moves.

So I wanted to reveal Bartleby as a loner in a crowd, in the world but somehow not of it. The urban landscape behind him of impersonal buildings and concrete spaces helped to make his **character** plausible without necessarily getting behind his impenetrable mask. His words are few. We see him as the anonymous commuter in the tube train. He rises on the escalator like a damned soul coming back from the underworld to redeem himself and to allow others to redeem themselves. When he sees the massed starlings in the square on one of his walks, we see that these birds live in spite of the urban landscape

---

[19] John Huston made *Moby Dick* (1956) and Peter Ustinov made *Billy Budd* (1962). See www.imdb.com for credits.

just like he does. The sights that he sees and the camera records for us legitimize his character. Instead of having him put in prison, implausible in our own day, he is committed to a mental institution. The through line of the **character** is the same, but the universe through which he travels changes color and texture compared to the original.

All literary classics have a rightful place in our cultural imagination. Adapting them for the screen risks alienating those who know and love the original. Then the **audience** that sees the film without knowing the original might get an experience of a great story but may not ever know the truth of the original. It is an interesting phenomenon that movies sell books, even literature, just as they sell the music of the film. Most entertainment conglomerates have a book publisher somewhere in their empire. When the movie is an original screenplay, media companies often commission a novel of the movie to garner the sales in their publishing market. When the source is a classic in the **public domain**, they also reissue the classic and sell the source story on the back of the movie release. One powerful reason to adapt a literary classic has to do with copyright. Many great works that have great cinematic potential, such as the works of Melville, Jane Austen, and Henry James, are in the **public domain**. That means no one owns the copyright. Any book or story that is copyrighted remains in copyright for the author's lifetime plus 70 years.

Henry James wrote a brilliant novella, a story of manners called *Daisy Miller*. It tells the story of a *nouveau riche* American family on the grand tour of Europe. The beautiful and wealthy young Daisy, her mother, and her small brother have no idea of manners and society. They are seen through the eyes of Winterbourne, a cultivated American who is attracted to Daisy but too cowardly to declare his love because of his social snobbery about this wealthy but gauche American family. When the family arrives in Rome, Daisy scandalizes the ex-patriot American community by socializing with an Italian who is married. The story is full of comic situations and colorful visual locations. It would make an excellent exercise for **adaptation** even though it has already been made into a film by Peter Bogdanovich in 1974.

CONCLUSION

Film writing seeks to exploit the large screen and the impact of surround sound and to narrate through **action** rather than **dialogue**. Writing visually is essential to good film writing. You compose narration out of images. Your story, its **characters**, and its world live for 2 hours through the collaboration of vast numbers of talented people in front of and behind the camera who bring the script to life. Film scripts are composed of **scenes**. Whether films are viewed on the big screen, television, video, or DVD, the experience is not exactly the same. Although films are shown on television all the time, other types of entertainment programming are produced for television only. Writing for television has its own issues and requires its own chapter. Before considering television writing issues, we should look at the problem of **adaptation**. It is an important way to understand scriptwriting and an important way to learn how to write for the screen.

Adaptation involves the translation of narrative from one medium (novel, play, or true story) into another, the motion picture. Writing a screenplay that adapts a source work usually involves compromises to make the story work in the new medium. The most basic problem is length. Films usually have to shorten the story and dispense with descriptive and reflective prose. Film narration depends on visual action in key scenes and sparse dialogue. A film must work on its own terms that can alter the proportions of the original. Some films, such as *It's a Wonderful Life* and *High Noon*, improve on the original story. The chances are that lesser-known, short works make better films than long, complex novels.

Exercises

1. Write a 2- to 3-minute **scene** without **dialogue** that tells the **audience** that one **character** is in love with another. You can explore variations, such as one **character** being in love but the other rejecting that love.
2. Write a 2- to 3-minute **scene** that builds suspense and anticipation.
3. Write a 2- to 3-minute **scene** in which no **character** is allowed more than one line of **dialogue**.
4. Record a real conversation in the cafeteria or some other public space. Transcribe 5 minutes of it on paper in screenplay format. See what **realism** is. Now try to edit the **dialogue** down to 1 minute.
5. Edit and rewrite the **dialogue** you recorded in Exercise 4 to create **comedy**.
6. Edit and rewrite the **dialogue** you recorded in Exercise 4 to create **drama**.
7. Find a novel that has been made into a film and write an analysis of how it has changed for better or worse in the film medium.
8. Take a children's story like *Little Red Riding Hood* or *The Three Little Pigs* and write a movie **adaptation** in the form of a **scene** outline. Change the names and the settings if need be.
9. Find a short story out of an anthology, a freshman English text for example, and **adapt** it for the screen.
10. Write an analysis of a movie **adapted** from a book you know or have read, and evaluate whether it works or doesn't work and figure out why.
11. Take a standard fairy tale or folk tale such as *Cinderella, Sleeping Beauty*, or *Beauty and the Beats*, and turn it into a film story with your own **characters** in a modern setting.
12. Read Bram Stoker's *Dracula* and write your own screenplay of the Dracula story. Compare the original with some of the screen **adaptations** of this story.
13. Read *The Greatest Gift* and compare it with the screenplay and the film of *It's a Wonderful Life*.

CHAPTER 10

Television Series, Sitcoms, and Soaps

KEY TERMS

4:3 academy ratio	one-liners	setup
beat sheet	pace	sitcom
double take	putdown	slug line
FCC language codes	running gag	soaps
HDTV 16:9	scene heading	"spec" script
hook	scene outline	teaser
laugh line	serials	trailers
master scene script	series bible	visual gags
miniseries	series editor	wide screen 2.85 to 1

Television is a huge maw that devours programming. Think of the number of channels! Think of the need for new ideas! Think of the need for writers to write episodes of long-running **series** that reappear season after season! Although the total program lineup for the medium includes news, documentary, sports, games shows, and so on, we are going to discuss only the program content that is acted entertainment, such as **series, sitcoms**, and **soaps**.[1] We need to understand the special requirements of television writing and learn the basic techniques of thinking and writing for television. Then we need to look at the premise and techniques for writing comedy and drama. Because television is changing all the time, we need to think about what's new. Then there is the question of script format—how you lay out the page. Many television series have developed their own idiosyncratic variations of script formats, which its scriptwriters follow and which have been reproduced in this chapter. Lastly, keep in mind that there are many books devoted exclusively to writing for television that will take you deeper than we can ever go in one chapter. Your job right now is to make a first effort at writing for this medium.

---

[1] We covered writing for documentaries in Chapter 7. News writing is journalism, and a different type of writing outside the scope of this book.

Doi: 10.1016/B978-0-240-81235-9.00010-9

In the first half-century of motion pictures, serial programming had evolved as a way of appealing to audiences. A weekly news report from Movietone News or Pathé was part of the program, as was a cartoon. People would go to the movies on a weekly basis. Kids would go to Saturday matinees. Each week brought a new episode of Charlie Chaplin, or Abbot and Costello, or the Lone Ranger, or Hopalong Cassidy. The idea of producing a new weekly segment of a continuing program formula was part of the movie distribution model. So the television formula was, in a way, anticipated by the movies. The television medium just makes it much easier to distribute program content and much easier for the audience to access that content on a regular basis.

The other source of television genres was its broadcast antecedent, radio. Radio had coped with the problem of devising formats to fill the day's schedule: news, variety, comedy, drama, sports, game shows, and children's programming. Radio **serials** such as *Superman* have been reborn as television **serials**. Comedy that had to be verbal could now be visual. Tuning in to the radio on a daily or a weekly basis transferred to television just as easily. Television was a convergence of radio and film in both technology (radio pictures) and programming. The idea of watching a program in **serial** segments was familiar to TV viewers because of their experience with radio and, to some extent, with movies and therefore was a natural fit for television, which developed it and refined it into the **series** for the new medium. The movie short and documentary, once a regular part of movie programming, vanished or migrated to factual programming on television. The emergence of television had a marked effect on the way movie programs were composed and marketed. It also altered the kind of movies that were made. To compete, movies were made so as to offer a unique experience in screen size and production scale and, of course, in those days, color when television was black and white.

THE PREMISE FOR SERIES, SITCOMS, AND SOAPS

The premise for a television **series** is slightly different than the premise for a movie. The television premise has to keep generating new episodes and new scripts each week, whereas a movie is conceived as a single story even though producers exploit some box office successes by making sequels and prequels. *ER* ran for a decade. An emergency room is at once a setting and a premise because it provides an endless stream of incidents and episodes. You have the constant throughput of patients during each episode with a drama that can reach out into a wider social world. You have the ongoing professional and personal relationships between interns, physicians, nurses, and technicians, interspersed with drive-by patients with interesting and quirky stories. Every medical series—*House, Bones, Grey's Anatomy*—shares a broadly similar premise.

There is the law premise. Think of the older series *L.A. Law*—a law firm with a cast of characters ranging from partners to legal secretaries. In its day, it was original. Now we have a new series, *Boston Law*. Another reworking of this series premise is *The Practice*, in which the district attorney and a defense lawyer are roommates and two of the defense attorneys have a love relationship. So we see more intense exploration of the working of the courts, and we see another city background, Boston. *Family Practice* is yet another way to vary this premise. Endless stories about social issues, childcare issues, and marital issues that intersect with the law can be spun out of this premise.

Each case is a new drama that provides a plot for a week or even two or three weeks. Each case introduces new characters. Some episodes present more than one case, each with a different lawyer or partner as the focus. Each episode can explore a new legal and social issue or an anomaly of human behavior. It's a natural. The **series** also gives its audience insight into the workings of the law business—the commercial pressures, the competition, and the internal politics of the firm. In all of these series, the courtroom creates dramas of confrontation because of its adversary system of prosecution and defense together with a citizen jury (really representing the audience), whose decisions will always provide a moment of climax and suspense. Cross this with the military and you get *J.A.G.*, which stands for Judge Advocate General (for the U.S. Navy). Now you have a way to spin stories about moral conflict between human nature and military discipline, not to mention social issues to do with race, gender, and cultural diversity. You also have superb opportunities to open up interiors to the occasional exterior of military theaters of action involving ships, aircraft carriers, and foreign locations. Can you do the next one? How about *Patent Law*? We see how new inventions, scientific discovery, and corporate skullduggery intersect. The little guys fight the big corporate interests. We learn about new economy startups, business law, IPOs (initial public offering of shares), biotechnology, information technology, and e-commerce.

The hospital series, such as *ER*, or the police series, such as *NYPD Blue*, are all virtually inexhaustible formulas for television **series** that are as old as television itself. The oldest **series** programming, **soaps**, derives from radio drama series sponsored by the soap and detergent manufacturers that wanted to reach the daytime audience of housewives who would buy their products. The tradition continued into television. Long-running chronicles of passion, ambition, jealousy, and revenge, such as *The Young and the Restless* and *The Bold and the Beautiful*, have loyal followings. The way they are written and produced follows a pattern that we need to understand to avoid writing clichés. Then there are the single-name shows like *Frasier*, *Harvey*, and *Seinfeld*, which are built around a star's character and particular brand of comedy.

There are two types of **series**. The first has a constant style and cast of characters, but each new episode tells a new and independent story. The plot of one program has no connection with the plot of another. Each week, we see another variation on the kind of theme that makes the series work.

The other model is a **serial**, more typical of the soaps in which the story continues from one episode to another. If you do not watch *The Young and the Restless* on a regular basis, you may not grasp the full significance of some storylines or relationships. You do not know the back story of the characters. This is true for an old **series** like *Star Trek* and newer series such as *The Wire*, *Nip/Tuck*, *The Sopranos*, and *Sex and the City*. The continuing **series** allows lengthier and more complex storylines that become almost epic in their proportions. This model leads to different writing problems. In the one-off episode, the storyline is brief, the formula for resolution known, and the audience given completion at one viewing. The continuing **series** leaves the story incomplete at the end of the episode and needs an audience that is willing to come back again and again. It is an interesting form because unlike the one-off episode and unlike a movie, the writers and producers do not know the eventual evolution of the story at the outset. Although both models are typical of television, the longer, multiple-episode story is rather unique to the medium. It allows a canvas that is more akin to the novel—full of texture and detail that would not be possible even in a feature film—although sometimes the writing is so simplistic that the opportunity is lost. Producers and writers have to deal with killing off or retiring characters and introducing new ones because actors do not renew their contracts or because the story needs new life

Miniseries

There is also the formula of the **miniseries**. This entails two, three, or more episodes that might be scheduled on consecutive nights or spaced out over weeks. *Roots* (1977) was one of the most successful of these extended **miniseries**. A dramatized adaptation of Alex Haley's documentary investigation of his African roots and family history through slavery to the present day, it was a complex and epic story about African-American history that worked far better on television than it would have as a movie. It was also very successful in terms of audience share, achieving one of the largest TV audiences ever. One of the best **miniseries**, and certainly one of the greatest works of the western genre, was *Lonesome Dove* (1989), which was adapted from the western novel of Larry McMurtry. Both the writing and the acting, particularly by Robert Duvall and Tommy Lee Jones, were outstanding. Now many of these works can be enjoyed on DVD.

The television **miniseries** is a long-form narrative that has a predetermined end as opposed to an open-ended, long-running **series**. It is an effective way to adapt major novels and classic works such as the novels of Charles Dickens. The great allegorical and satirical work by Jonathan Swift, *Gulliver's Travels* (1995), was adapted as a **miniseries** with a great deal of fiddling with the integrity of the original work. *The Thorn Birds* (1983) was one of the most successful **serial** stories on this model, followed by the sequel, *Thorn Birds: The Missing Years* (1996). The canvas for these two **series** was huge, covering 60 years in the lives of the Cleary family in Australia. A great **miniseries** that really took advantage of the scope of this long form of television program was *Shogun* (1980), adapted from the long novel by James Clavell and starring Richard Chamberlain. While keeping in mind the variety and scope of television writing, it is clear that the place to start is with the half-hour and hour episode because it allows writing to a basic three-act structure.

THREE-ACT STRUCTURE AND THE TV TIME SLOT

After appreciating the dramatic structure of long-form movies, you might wonder how that structure works for the television half-hour and hour episodes, which are interrupted by commercial breaks. In the series model in which each episode is a self-contained unit with the same main characters (e.g., *Buffy, The Vampire Slayer*), a problem is introduced, usually a challenge to the main character. This sets up an antagonist who delivers a number of reversals that rise in severity until some kind of dénouement occurs in which the hero triumphs and order and equilibrium are restored. Because the episodes are reborn each week, a recognizable structure is helpful to the audience. The basic formula of the three-act structure still works.

However, the **serial** structure, multiple storylines that extend beyond a single episode, works better for some **soaps, sitcoms**, and **series** that have complex stories. The **soaps** offer the clearest example. Each episode involves several story strands running simultaneously. None of the stories follows a strict three-act development structure, but rather they alternate as foils for one another. Just as one storyline reaches a crisis, we end with a close-up on the character doing "the look." An actor or actress holds a blank ambiguous look that conveys worry, thought, or some intense interior emotion, after having learned that their wife or husband has been unfaithful, that they have been disinherited, or that they are not the father of their child. Then, we cut to another parallel story strand involving another set of characters that develops to its temporary climax, and then we cut to a third or cut back to the second. Intercutting storylines adopts a sophisticated editing technique but for spurious reasons. It is not a clever writing technique. It is simply a crude way to keep several storylines in play at once and to disguise the lack of dramatic structure. Whenever you run out of ideas or get into trouble, cut to a commercial or another storyline. It is probably a way of keeping several audiences happy at once. This episodic structure has no real beginning and no real end. It is just a way of spinning out episodes for the cast of established characters. The series of indeterminate length, written as original work for television, illustrates both the most interesting and most bathetic potential of the medium.

USING COMMERCIAL BREAKS

Because most television programming is broken up by commercials, the writer has to take them into account and write scenes or acts with so that the audience's interest is held, if not heightened, by the break after a climactic moment. The commercial break has turned every episode into a four act structure because the hiatus of the break has to be incorporated into the dramatic rhythm and narrative structure of the story. Apart from the fact that we use breaks to go to the bathroom, or get a snack or a drink, or make a phone call, we also sometimes switch to other channels. It makes you think that the modern audience is capable of running multiple storylines in its head and taking in emotional and factual information at several levels. Sometimes, the television screen performs the function of a social, informational heads up display that modern urbanites consult almost like a pilot reads multiple inputs of information from the flight deck instrumentation. The modern audience interacts with the medium through the remote control, surfing multiple channels, sampling multiple programs, and watching more than one program simultaneously, whether by switching at commercial breaks or watching via picture-in-picture enabled TV sets, or time shifting with TIVO. To some extent, television writing has developed so as to work in short episodic bursts so that its comedy, dialogue, and characters are instantly recognizable, enabling the audience to pick up the program at random and figure out what's happening. The audience watches behaviors, styles, and mannerisms that it learns to model in speech and emotions. The social impact of television makes it difficult to know sometimes whether life is imitating art or art is imitating life.

VISUALIZING FOR THE SMALL SCREEN

Sometimes writers need to think carefully about the difference in size between movie and television screens. This difference can affect the way you write and the way you think about writing. Size of image counts. A large projected image has great impact and allows a different kind of cinematography and camera work. You may argue movies are shown on television all the time and movies are rented on video. This is true. Nevertheless, the experience is not the same. When I fly transatlantic,

I watch movies on a little LCD screen on the back of the seat in front of me. This does not give me the same experience I get in a movie theatre. The visual value of the images changes. The same may be said of the size of the viewing image on mobile phones. Panoramic shots or big actions shots are less exciting. A lot of detail gets lost. The same is true for television. Also, the shape of the screen changes from a **wide screen 2.85 to 1** ratio to a **4:3 academy ratio**. Parts of the picture are cut off on old TV sets. Now high-definition television is the standard, and the aspect ratio of the screen has changed to **HDTV 16:9 ratio**, which will fit Panavision wide-screen ratios for the most part. The resolution and the definition (crispness of detail) of the image together with the color reproduction have improved. Nevertheless, it is still a different experience than watching a movie at a large-screen movie theatre, sitting in the dark with an audience of strangers.

Television is a close-up medium. News anchors, interviewers, and their subjects come across better in medium shot or closeup. So this is how camera operators and directors tend to compose the shot for so much television material. They are thinking about what it will look like when the audience experiences the program. That is what counts. Think about the content of television **sitcoms** and **soaps**! Most of the scenes play in medium shots or two-shots. They deliver intimacy so that you can see the subtle emotional body language of the face of the character. This is what **soaps** are all about— showing feelings, looks, and concealing the same—up close and personal as the saying goes. The audience wants this intimate contact with the character. You have to think and write in terms of the screen size of the image and how it will communicate with the audience.

TV DIALOGUE

The characteristics of the screen image have an impact on dialogue. If you want the audience to feel the characters, you have to put them in proximity to one another so that they talk and relate. It is a talking medium as well as a close-up medium. You will notice that television writing tends to make characters talk more than in movies. Dialogue carries more of the weight of a television storyline. The dialogue may refer to action or events, but we experience characters through their interchange. *The West Wing* is a good example of drama and complex relationships carried in tightly scripted dialogue.

Television is more likely to be produced in studio sets, whereas movies tend to exploit action, locations, special effects, and stunts. Television shows are shot on smaller budgets and tighter schedules than movies. The **soaps** always come to mind as the primary example. Most scenes consist of two people meeting in an office, an apartment, or a restaurant or talking over the phone to play out some relationship drama in verbal exchange—consider *Seinfeld*, for example. The primary technique, which is also the most economical way to shoot, is two-shot and matching singles, or a two-shot and over-the-shoulder reverses. The content of the shots is talk and emotional body language. So the writer writes the storyline and the dialogue to carry it.

REALISM/REALISTIC DIALOGUE

When characters open their mouths, we always expect their language to correspond to their world and their personality. In cop shows, medical shows, and legal shows, characters have to speak like those professionals do. They have to use the professional jargon. This is a writing responsibility. Think of another kind of dialogue writing problem in a series such as *Star Trek*. Apart from the fact that the Klingons have their own language (can you write Klingon?), the setting is not just fictional but hypothetical. All sorts of vocabulary are invented to refer to futuristic technology. It is easy to parody. We see serious-looking people in colored lycra body suits leaning over winking panels of controls and turning to say things like, "The particle shield is down; there's no response," "Activate the thrust inhibitors," "Fire the gravity phaser," or some such nonsense. I just made those up. Technical background on weapons and other functions of starship *Enterprise* gadgetry are part of the plot and part of the **series bible**. You have to know what certain weapons are or what certain terms mean, such as the holodeck, where holograms can simulate alternative realities in other time periods. Science fiction establishes conventions of credibility. The idea of accelerating to warp speed or beaming someone down to a planet surface becomes accepted as concepts, which, in the case of *Star Trek*, have entered the general culture. So although it is invented language, it has its own realism in context.

In *The West Wing*, you expect senior staffers, whose world revolves around political and governmental issues, to use language that most people read in the papers; likewise for the journalists, advisors, and lawyers who live in the White House basement. At the same time if you study the script of a *West Wing* episode, you will not find realism but something that is realistic, a distinction we made in a previous chapter. Real staffers probably spend hours working on keyboards, reading memos and briefs without talking. When they do talk, they are probably more long-winded than their fictional counterparts in *The West Wing*, whose dialogue is taught, witty, and full of repartee. Just as real doctors and nurses probably don't behave like the fictional ones we see on *ER*, White House staffers probably do not trade witticisms in tight dialogue exchanges. As we have said before, simulating reality means making it believable, not necessarily realistic. Realism is too long winded, too messy, too complicated. So we can get an exchange that is good television. The high drama that erupts in every episode probably doesn't occur with the same frequency in the life of real staffers. The point is the events and the dialogue are believable. People are people as well as staffers.

```
INT. WEST WING/MAIN LOBBY/CORRIDOR/BULLPEN JOSH'S OFFICE -
SAME TIME
CONTINUED:

JOSH knows what this means and stops walking, holding onto DONNA's arm to
get her to stop walking as well. They speak in hushed tones.

                         JOSH
               What did I do?

                         DONNA
               How would I know?

                         JOSH
               Because you know everything.

                         DONNA
               I do know everything.

                         JOSH
               Donna . . .
```

                    DONNA
I'm saying you say that now, but
anytime I want to make a substantive
contribution . . .

                    JOSH
You make plenty of substantive
contributions.

                    DONNA
Like what?

                    JOSH
This. This could be a substantive
contribution.

                    DONNA
I need a raise.

                    JOSH
So do I.

                    DONNA
You're my boss.

                    JOSH
I'm not the one who pays you.

                    DONNA
Yes, but you could recommend that I
got a raise.

                    JOSH
Donna, she's looking for me. Do you
think this is a really good time to
talk about a raise?

                    DONNA
Mmm. I think it's the best time to
talk about a raise.

                    JOSH
Donna, you're not a very nice person.

                    DONNA
You gotta get to know me.[2]

---

[2] Aaron Sorkin, *The West Wing Script Book; Six Teleplays*, Newmarket Press, New York (2002), pp. 80–81.

BREAKING UP DIALOGUE

Dialogue has a certain rhythm that works and is different from real speech. As we have noted, real speech is rambling, disjointed, and static. One of the mistakes of a beginner is not to break up dialogue so that the characters ping-pong the lines back and forth as they do in *The West Wing*. There is a tendency to crowd too many thoughts into one speech rather than letting one character start an idea and then get a response, which leads to the next development of the thought. Long speeches slow down the show and lead to predictable responses. Beginning scriptwriters make characters say too much and deprive the other characters sharing the scene the opportunity to respond.

PACING

Another tendency of novice writers is to put too much of the story in the first scenes. Beginning writers typically are big in the first act and then find that their treatments underestimate how to **pace** the material. This fault is easily concealed in the treatment and always revealed in the script. One of the best ways to combat it is to make a step outline or a **scene outline**, also called a **beat sheet**. This prevents self-deception about the amount of material you really have to work with. It also shows you the storyline and structure in a way that the treatment does not. The beginner tends to peak too early and not to use subplots.

THE BEAT SHEET

The **beat sheet** is basically a numbered **scene outline** that lays out the narrative structure of the episode in a similar way to a treatment. It identifies the scene setting and summarizes the action or plot development with paraphrases of dialogue. It is an instrument of television writing rather than movie writing. It helps to navigate the fragmented intervals of television playtime. Let us consider a beat sheet for an episode of *ER*. It is broken down into a teaser and four acts to fit around the commercial breaks. Here is a beat from Episode #3 of an *ER* episode:

> ADMIT - Where Weaver is introducing TEAM ER—her latest brainchild to unify and motivate her troops. Romano is down in the ER. He makes a disparaging remark about Carter, still none-too-happy to have him working here. Weaver assures him that Carter's only working half shifts and no traumas. Before he leaves, Romano spots Chen. Asks who's the daddy? Nobody knows. Fine don't tell me—as long it's not me. Huh? Malucci figures somebody must know who the father is. Everybody has their own ideas. Bets are made. So begins the "Who's the Daddy?" pool. Abby overhears Kovac taking a phone call in Italian. It's brief but amorous, and Abby can't help but eavesdrop, even if she doesn't know what he's saying.[3]

This is fleshed out into three pages of production script. Some ideas are still left by the wayside. For instance, the betting pool about Chen's pregnancy didn't get into the final because it was probably

---

[3]

too much of a diversion from the forward momentum of the story. Also, the **beat sheet** does not hint at the dialogue exchange between Carter, Romano, and Weaver. Carter is a resident who has come back from drug rehab, which extends our understanding of the characters. Romano is a mocking, sarcastic, nasty guy, and Weaver is the quick-witted head of ER.

> ROMANO
> Doctor Carter, when did they let you
> out?

> CARTER
> A few weeks ago.

Romano stares into Carter's soul. Carter could try to do the same to Romano, but since the man has no soul, it's pretty pointless.

> CARTER
> I've got a patient.

> ROMANO
> Go forth and heal.

Romano gestures for Carter to go, but then while he's still within earshot—

> So who's watching the Drugstore
> Cowboy?

> WEAVER
> ER is my department. That makes Carter
> my responsibility.

> ROMANO
> Correct me if I'm wrong, Kerry, but
> didn't he develop his drug addiction
> under your watchful eye?

> WEAVER
> Did you need something, Robert?

> ROMANO
> Do I need a reason to stop by and
> say hello?[4]

The dialogue and the character development are all part of the writing of the script beyond the story structure work of the beat sheet.

---

[4] (c) Warner Bros. Television. All rights reserved.

TEAM WRITING

Most television scripts are rewritten by teams of writers who keep the production line going with scene and dialogue rewrites right up to the time of shooting. Play time is fairly critical in the television world because time slots with commercial breaks are exact. You cannot run over. Some writers specialize in dialogue and are assigned particular scenes to write. The team is managed by a **series editor**. So what appears to be the uniform work of a single writer is often a team effort of multiple writers rewriting a half dozen times.

HOOK/TEASER

A **hook** is a device that gets the attention of an audience, involves them, and makes them want to keep watching. A **teaser** is a short scene that precedes the commercial break before the episode starts that contains a **hook**. It may also be the premise of the episode, although that is not always possible and not necessary. Most television **series** and episodes have to provide something to whet an audience's appetite quickly because there are a dozen other channels, a dozen other choices. In the movies, this is less critical. Not that the movie does not need a **hook**, but if you have paid for a ticket and you are sitting down with your popcorn, you are going to accept a more complex development of story and plot. It takes an enormous failure to make you walk out of a movie; it takes a minor lapse for you to hit the remote and check out what's on another channel. Major **series** often build interest with quick **trailers** inserted into earlier programming on the same channel. These **trailers** are often the **hook**. They also play at the end of the episode to entice the audience back for the next episode.

THE SERIES BIBLE

All **series** have a "series bible" that describes each character, including backstory, personality, past life and details of props, settings, and other information that enables new writers on the **series** to stay faithful to the spirit of the **series** and true to character. For this reason, a head writer or editor will oversee the development of episodes. All writers eventually get worn out in **series** writing. Even the original writer who might have developed the idea for the series and written the first episodes becomes weary and runs out of ideas. So there is a regular rotation of guest writers. This is why writing a "spec" script of a long-running **series** can be a good way to show your stuff and help an agent to get you some freelance work.

CONDENSING ACTION AND PLOT

We have already commented on the difference between reality and realism. Life is mostly banal—eating, doing the laundry, flossing your teeth, sleeping. Even work involves paperwork, long meetings, and totally undramatic data-entry at a computer keyboard. You can't make riveting television programming out of such things unless you select key moments, condense activity and action, and shorten the screen time in a plausible way. So you need characters to walk and talk at the same time. You need to combine action and dialogue.

The scene from *ER* quoted above condenses action and plot in a walk/talk moment. In a *Nash Bridges* episode, Nash, Joe, and Katie are on the case of a psychotic serial killer who is murdering people who use cell phones. This dates it. They have called him on the cell phone he took from a victim. He hangs up. As they stride purposefully through crowds to the car, Nash says, "Get the triangular on the phone and check all patients released from mental hospitals in say the last six months." This scene condenses action and plot so that the viewers know some background detective work is going on. The writers get these points across by having the characters move from one scene to the next. This kind of efficient use of time, motion, and dialogue is typical of police and detective series, which always have to deal with a lot of off-screen detail that could never be filmed because of time constraints. In this same series, there is a lot of movement from one location to another. Nash's trademark is his souped-up yellow convertible in which he and Joe roar from one part of town to another. This type of motion scene is useful to get through a lot of dialogue that fills in the plot or fills us in on background and provides personal interchange between characters.

TARGET AUDIENCE

Although the seven-step method we developed in Part 1 does not apply in exactly the same way when dealing with a television entertainment objective, it is important, nevertheless, to give some thought to the demographic of a target audience. Shows that go on late at night are allowed to present more sexual themes and scenes than family shows. Broadcasters are bound by Federal Communications Commission (*FCC*) **language codes** that exclude the kind of realistic dialogue that movies allow and that some cable channels allow. So realism for underworld settings or gang worlds must find the style without the four-letter words. There seem to be fewer qualms, however, about showing explicit violence than showing explicit sexuality or including bad language. Cable television is less restricted. The brilliant show *Deadwood*, which came out in 2004 on HBO, portrays a lawless frontier town in South Dakota in the 1870s with a degree of realism about the western probably never before seen in movies or on television. The foul language is relentless and persistent among uneducated greedy people competing for gold, space, food, pleasure, and life itself. Wild Bill Hickok and Calamity Jane are passing through, and she is as foul mouthed as any. The story is convincing, the writing brilliant, and the acting first rate. The target audience is clearly adult and worldly wise. Another ground-breaking, realistic and uninhibited series is *The Wire*, which began in 2002. It has a documentary style that examines facets of ghetto life in Baltimore, Maryland.

SCRIPT FORMATS FOR TELEVISION

As with writing for other visual media, the project should also begin as a concept, an outline, from which you write a treatment. The treatment is then made into a script. For the most part, two formats with some variations cover most television script layouts. The format most resembles the **master scene script**. Each scene is announced by a **slug line** or **scene heading**. This is followed by action description in uppercase, which differentiates it from the screenplay. The character name appears above the dialogue and is centered; the dialogue follows and is also centered. (See formats on the website and examples in the appendix.)

```
INT. HELMER'S STUDY-NIGHT

HELMER AND NORA STAND IN THE CENTER OF THE STUDY.

                         NORA
          Oh, Torvald, it hurts me terribly to
          have to say it, because you've always
          been so kind to me. But I can't help
          it. I don't love you any longer.

                         HELMER
          And you feel quite sure about this too?
```

In a variation of this format, the script is aligned to the left margin and introduces act and scene numbers. The last variation is that stage and action directions are contained in parentheses. The **Writers Guild of America** has published a *Professional Writer's Teleplay/Screenplay Format Guide*, which it sells by mail order.[5]

TV COMEDY AND ITS DEVICES

Comedy has a great range on television, from crude put-down humor to witty and clever portraits of human behavior. Contrast *Married with Children* with *Seinfeld*! *Murphy Brown* was a very successful comic vehicle for Candice Bergen and was the pioneer series that uses the medium of television itself as a setting. Murphy Brown is a star television anchor and journalist, known for her acerbic wit, sarcasm, and vaulting ego. The comedy turns frequently on bringing her down to size with clever put-down lines. It parodies television production behind the scenes.

Most television dialogue involves some kind of subtle or not so subtle insult or putdown. Low-grade insulting humor continues a vaudeville tradition. Comedians like Jimmy Durante, Sid Caesar, Eddie Cantor, and Abbott and Costello were all familiar with playing visually to an audience. Radio comedy necessarily had to do without the visual comedy. Then the radio broadcasters also became the television license holders. The radio comedians like George Burns, Jack Benny, Fred Allen, and Ozzie and Harriet were co-opted into television. The writers were radio writers. Skit writing with clever one-liners migrated into television from radio comedy, which in turn had grown out of vaudeville. Some of this writing style of the **double take**, the **setup**, and the **putdown** still thrives in **sitcoms**. This writing developed in other ways when the shows moved to the West Coast television production facilities from their original production base in New York.[6]

---

[5] The price including postage is $4.55 from Writers Guild of America, East, 555 West 57th Street, New York, NY 10019.

[6] I am indebted to Nancy Meyer for this background information and research presented in her paper, "The Situation Comedy Script Format: Its Evolution from Radio Comedy and the Traditional Screenplay," delivered at the Broadcast Education Association Convention in Las Vegas in April 2000 at a panel I chaired, "Who Invented the Screenplay?"

Running Gags

We discussed **running gags** in the chapter on writing long-form movies citing *Some Like It Hot*. A **running gag**, as the name suggests, depends on repetition. It keeps running. The audience knows the premise of the gag so that each new exploitation of the gag gets a rise from the previous one. You keep going back to the same premise to work it from another angle. This device enriches a lot of comedy. *Just Marcy* is a student-written and student-produced pilot for a television series. The complete script and some video are reproduced on the website. It is about a college-age girl who needs to find a roommate. She has money problems, and her landlord is threatening to evict her unless she pays the arrears. This creates the pressure to find a roommate.

We can illustrate the comic device of the running gag with the following situation. Marcy has the landlord at the door. She is showing a new roommate around. The audience knows something that the roommate character doesn't. So her responses are doubly funny. The scene is built around the physical action of going back to the door where the landlord is waiting. Each time Marcy appears, the comedy ratchets up a notch. Marcy is showing the prospective roommate around when . . .

THE DOORBELL RINGS

                    MARCY
          Can you hold on for a minute

SHE ANSWERS THE DOOR, IT'S HER LANDLORD.

                    MARCY (CONT'D)
          Oh my god, Mr. Jacobs, hi.

                    MR. JACOBS
               (he says in a monotone voice)
          I want the rent.

                    MARCY
          Can you hold on for just a minute?

SHE CLOSES THE DOOR AND GOES LOOKING FOR SANDRA.

                    SCENE THREE

INT. MARCY'S ROOM—MOMENTS LATER (MARCY, SANDRA)

                    MARCY
          Sandra?

                    SANDRA
          Oh I just love this room.

                    MARCY
          This is my room. Let me show you the
          room for rent.

SCENE FOUR

INT. SANDRA'S ROOM—MOMENTS LATER

(MARCY)

THEY WALK INTO THE OTHER ROOM AND THEN THE DOORBELL RINGS AGAIN. MARCY GOES TO THE DOOR.

SCENE FIVE

INT. MARCY'S FRONT DOOR—MOMENTS LATER (MARCY, MR. JACOBS, SANDRA)

MR. JACOBS
$500 dollars for last month . . .

MARCY SHUTS THE DOOR AND RETURNS TO SANDRA.

SCENE SIX

INT. MARCY'S KITCHEN—MOMENTS LATER (MARCY, SANDRA)

SANDRA
WOW! I really like this place.

MARCY
About the rent . . .

SANDRA
You know I'm really desperate. My roommate just kicked me out and . . .

MARCY
$500 for last month's rent

SANDRA EXPRESSES CONFUSION.

MARCY (CONT'D)
. . . I mean this month's . . .

THE DOORBELL RINGS AGAIN.

MARCY (CONT'D)
I'll be right back

SHE HOLDS UP HER FINGER AND RUSHES TO THE DOOR.

SCENE SEVEN

INT. MARCY'S FRONT DOOR—MOMENTS LATER (MARCY, MR. JACOBS, SANDRA)

MR. JACOBS
(he has his arms
folded on his chest
and is glaring at
Marcy)
... and $500 for this month.

MARCY SLAMS THE DOOR AND GOES BACK TO SANDRA.

SCENE EIGHT

INT. MARCY'S KITCHEN—MOMENTS LATER

(MARCY, SANDRA)

SANDRA IS STANDING BY THE TABLE.

MARCY
Sorry to keep you waiting . . .
(she is slightly
out of breath as
she speaks and
smiles)
. . . and $500 for this month . . .
I mean next month . . . no, I mean,
you know, a deposit.

SANDRA TAKES OUT HER CHECKBOOK. MARCY'S EYES GO WIDE.

MARCY (CONT'D)
'Er . . . you wouldn't have cash by
any chance?

SANDRA
A thousand dollars in cash?

(Marcy shrugs)
How do you spell your name?

MARCY
Mr. Jacobs . . .

SANDRA DOUBLE-TAKES

MARCY (CONT'D)
. . . I mean, just leave it blank, ok.

SANDRA
Whatever you say, roomie.

SANDRA HANDS HER THE CHECK. MARCY GOES STRAIGHT TO THE DOOR AND OPENS IT.

SCENE NINE

INT. MARCY'S FRONT DOOR—MOMENTS LATER (MARCY, MR. JACOBS, SANDRA)

MARCY OPENS THE DOOR.

                    MR. JACOBS
          Now, or you're outta here.

MARCY HANDS HIM THE CHECK. MR. JACOB'S JAW DROPS. SHE SHUTS THE DOOR AND
GOES BACK TO SANDRA.

(Read the complete script and see how the scene plays on the website.) Each time Marcy answers the
doorbell, the gag builds and the scene intensifies the comedy at the door with the prospective roommate.

A good example of the **running gag** happens in the opening of the pilot episode of *Murphy Brown*.
The characters are sitting around in the production office discussing the lead character who is about
to make an entrance after a month's rehab at the Betty Ford Center. First, we see Corky, the ex–Miss
America beauty queen who has been hired to stand in for Murphy during her absence.

                    CORKY
          You know, when I was asked to fill in
          for Murphy, I couldn't believe it.
          It was kind of like the time I became
          Miss America. Did I ever tell you
          about it?

                    FRANK/JIM
          (NOT AGAIN) Oh, yes, uh-huh. You
          definitely did. I'm crazy about that
          story.

Frank now formulates a bet that Murphy will come back a changed woman.
Corky keeps plugging her ego-centric story.

                    CORKY
          It was so incredible when they
          announced my name . . . first
          runner-up, Corky.

                    JIM
          Murphy'll never change. Once a pain
          in the butt, always a pain in the butt.

                    FRANK
          Jim, we're talking a month at the
          Betty Ford Center. Remember the
          segment I did on that place? They
          knock the stuffing out of you. Come
          on. Ten bucks. (TAKES MONEY FROM
          POCKET)

Now the **running gag** about Corky and her self-adulation comes back while Jim and Frank continue to ignore her. The second **running gag** and the big one is the bet. It drives the opening scene and heightens the **hook** that keeps the audience watching because it also builds up anticipation of who this person is that they are all waiting for. Will she be like their description? The **running gag** serves a dual function of being funny and building the action. Now Jim on the other side of the bet argues:

> She'll insult at least three people,
> grab a cup of black coffee and bum a
> cigarette. Then she'll lock herself
> in her office until she has the perfect
> piece for next week's show. As usual.
>
>   (TAKES OUT MONEY)
> You're on.

THE ENTIRE OFFICE BEGINS THROWING TEN-DOLLAR BILLS ON DESKS AS MAJOR BETTING GETS UNDER WAY.

Now we get the grand entrance of Candice Bergen as Murphy Brown. She is nice to everybody, and Jim loses the bet and hands over money. Then we hear Murphy Brown:

>   MURPHY
>
>   (REALLY PISSED)
> Okay! Which one of you turkeys put
> their greasy fingerprints all over
> my Emmy?
>
>   FRANK
> All right! She's back!

MONEY ONCE AGAIN CHANGES HANDS. FRANK GIVES MONEY BACK TO JIM. JIM WALKS AWAY AS MURPHY COMES OUT OF HER OFFICE.[7]

The **running gag** of the bet gives momentum and structure to the comedy. The **running gag** of Corky's Miss America hangup will continue to work in this and other episodes. It is attached to the character. Each of the characters will have a trait that the writer and the actors will continually milk for effect. Most of them have to do with self-image. Murphy's self-conceit and bluntness or Jim's uptight personality are the fuel that makes the comedy run. Other series work in similar ways.

A character often has a foible that generates endless comedy. Take the character of George in *Seinfeld*. He is slightly pompous and always trying to get even for an insult or involved in a convoluted scheme to get one up on some adversary. We know his character and can't resist the pleasure of his downfall or of his being exposed and brought down to size. Part of the reason is that we see an aspect of ourselves in this character.

Visual Gags

Visual gags help comedy in a visual medium. If every joke is spoken, every piece of humor is verbal, the visual potential of the medium is wasted. In an office comedy, someone hiding under a desk, or in a domestic comedy, someone trying to dress up in disguise, or someone trying to hide evidence of a mistake, all make the camera an ally and engage the visual part of the audience's brain. The tradition goes back to vaudeville stage gags if not further. Shakespeare used visual gags. Think of Malvolio in *Twelfth Night* dressing in yellow stockings and cross garters to please Lady Olivia because he thinks she has suggested it in a letter forged by the Fool, Sir Toby Belch, and Sir Andrew Aiguecheek to trap his vanity. Chaplin articulated the visual gag for the camera together with Harold Lloyd and Buster Keaton in silent film. Without a sound track, the comedy depended on visual gags. The Marx Brothers evolved comedy for the screen by combining visual gags with verbal wit. Early television gave *The Three Stooges* a lot of scope for fairly crude visual comedy. Someone being hit with a ladder when his friend turns around has its limits. Comic violence shades off into a kind of sadism that is evident in huge numbers of animated cartoons in which Tom gets endlessly flattened or blown up by Jerry.

A student of mine developed a great visual gag. The story is about two Jamaicans coming to visit their cousin in New York. Immigration thinks that they are illegal immigrants, although we learn later that this is a case of mistaken identity. Meanwhile, they have to do something. So when the immigration officer comes to the apartment, he finds them dressed up as women. The dialogue is hilarious and the scene all together succeeds very well. It also complicates their other ambition, which is to find American girlfriends whom they can marry so as to stay in the country. Cross-dressing, which we discussed in the previous chapter, works as a kind of visual gag.

Visual gags carry over to animation comedy such as *King of the Hill* and *South Park*. As this edition goes to press, *The Simpsons* has become the longest running show on television. Here is a little visual gag combined with verbal a verbal one liner by Lisa.

`INT. SIMPSON HOUSE - BASEMENT - NIGHT`

Homer is at the pool table, carefully lining up a shot. Lisa is resting her head on the table, facing Homer.

> HOMER
> Steady, steady...

Homer **TAPS** the cue stick lightly and it neatly **KNOCKS OUT** one of Lisa's baby teeth.

> LISA
> Thanks, Dad. That loose tooth was
> driving me crazy. (Looking at tooth)
> Hey, I wonder if I could use this for
> my science fair project.

She exits.[8]

---

[8](c) Twentieth Centurary Fox Television

Double Takes

Like many comic devices, the **double take** is a compact with the audience. The character takes an extra long time to react to a putdown or before delivering a reply. Although it can be an acting technique, it is also very much a comic effect that can be written into a script. It needs the right line or situation with an indication in the script. You do this by writing PAUSE, BEAT, or even DOUBLE TAKE.

Here's an example of a a comedy beat from **Nanny**:

FADE IN:

INT. LIVING ROOM - NEXT DAY

(Fran, Niles, C.C., Grace, Yetta, Nettie)

FRAN SITS ON THE COUCH, CRYING. NILES SITS NEXT TO HER WITH HIS ARM AROUND HER, TRYING TO COMFORT HER.

>   FRAN
>   (Sobbing) Niles, my parents are
>   splitting up. What if Ma starts going
>   out with other men and meets one she
>   likes and gets married...(BEAT)
>   before me!

                                                   FADE OUT

One-Liners and Laugh Lines

One-liners are the staple of situation comedy. Characters say lines that stand alone and get a laugh track because they are snide, funny, sarcastic, self-evident comments about another character or a situation. Most **sitcom** characters, especially those that head up a **series**, are given one-liners as a regular feature of their episodes. The previous example of a beat from *Nanny* also illustrates the **one-liner**.

Consider this example from *Frasier*. It's Frasier's birthday. His father wants to make a fuss by making him a special breakfast. He announces, "I got you a newspaper from the day you were born." Frasier replies with a typical television comedy would-be clever one-liner, "I told you to clean out that closet." It's the kind of line that does not require a response. It is just comic embellishment for the audience's gratification.

South Park is full of one liner put downs and one liner exclamations that belong to the character's mode of talking.

INT. SCHOOL CAFETERIA - DAY

The kids are all in line for lunch. Cartman farts a huge fireball.

>   CARTMAN
>   OOOOWWWW!!! Ooh, I sure am hungry.

>   STAN
>   How can you eat when you're farting fire?

```
                    CARTMAN
          Shut up, dude. You're being totally
          immature.
```

SITCOMS

Laugh lines and **one-liners** are typical of **sitcom** writing. Although the line should fit the character who delivers the line, such lines rarely depend on the plot or advance the plot. They are opportunities that almost stand alone or are added on to the situation. In one sitcom, *The Nanny*, Fran Drescher is in the hospital about to have an operation or biopsy. One of the characters talks about notifying her parents:

> "They're on their annual pilgrimage to the Holy Land."
> "Jerusalem?"
> "Miami!"

It's cute; it's funny; it's in keeping with the Fran Drescher character. Then we move on with the story.

NEW TECHNIQUES AND INNOVATIONS

Once and Again, a new ABC series in 1999, was an exciting departure in television writing that took creative risks. It avoided the formulas of **soaps** and most of the clichés of potted plots and canned emotions. It was and is the polar opposite of the **soap**. It is the story of two families whose parents are separated or divorced and whose children, of teen, adolescent, and preadolescent ages, are trying to cope with growing up in a splintered household. The love relationship between the divorced father of one and the separated mother of the other family magnifies the problems of each family. The mature television writing manages to capture some of the texture of middle-class American family life. The portrait of angst adolescents feel about their parents and the parents about their children rings true. More than any other **series**, this one tries to document the scale and amplitude of people's emotions and reactions to the everyday events and crises of American middle-class life. It has comedy, tragedy, and ordinary and extraordinary moments. The writing is clearly at the foundation of this series, even though the acting is flawless, especially that of the young actors. At every moment, the depiction of a certain kind of contemporary living experience is seamlessly convincing.

```
                    JESSIE SAMMLER
          This isn't how I am.

                    KATIE SINGER
          What do you mean?

                    JESSIE SAMMLER
          Sarah's really giving the impression
          that… she's acting like this is just
          some big contest. Like you have to
```

```
                    choose. Like, if you're friends with
                    me then you can't be friends with her
                    and… that is SO not how I am, and
                    it's so stupid, and I just think that
                    we should…
                              KATIE SINGER
                    I choose you.
                              JESSIE SAMMLER
                    What?
                              KATIE SINGER
                    I choose you over her.
                              JESSIE SAMMLER
                    But I don't want anybody to choose
                    anybody.
                              KATIE SINGER
                    I know you don't, but… I can't help
                    it.
```

The writing also experiments with an innovative technique of cutting away at key emotional moments to a black-and-white interview of the character talking to the audience about his or her innermost thoughts. It is a television equivalent of the theatrical aside. It allows us to learn more about the character's point of view and to see the interweaving of past and present into a complex tapestry of emotions and gestures. This could have been artificial and disturbing to the emotional experience of the viewer. Quite the opposite occurs, however. The black-and-white shot differentiates the interior monologue from the external drama. We recognize a level of emotional truth in the characters that has rarely been seen on network television. This kind of complex narrative developing over many episodes is more difficult to write and produce.[9] The advantage can be that once an audience is hooked, it will follow the story week after week. However, *Once and Again* was above the low common denominator of television **series** and did not survive its third season.

Some of the innovation that we see in television **series** may be the result of direction or editing. There is a tendency to borrow flashy camera moves and jump cuts from car commercials (see *Nash Bridges*). Effects such as posterization of exteriors, or taking the chroma out of a scene, or the use of slow motion creep into drama and action-oriented series. Cutting techniques and camera movements are borrowed from the world of commercials where the need to condense messages and get the viewer's attention constantly pushes the envelope.

SPEC SCRIPTS

One of the best ways to train as a writer is to write a **"spec"** script for a television **series** you are familiar with. You know the main characters. You know the format. You can invent within the premise of

---

[9] The series, created by Marshall Herskovitz and Edward Zwick, won many awards. These two producers have been involved with numerous quality television and feature film productions, which you can explore on imdb.com.

the **series** or **sitcom**. This is also one of the ways to demonstrate writing ability to producers and **series** editors who are looking for new talent, and it also makes a good assignment in a writing course. It is a manageable assignment for all. Even if you don't succeed right away, it provides a valuable learning experience that will give you new respect for what you are used to consuming as a television viewer.

CONCLUSION

Television is a big marketplace for writers. The range of programs is enormous from daytime **soaps** to primetime **series** and **sitcoms**. Although it is commercial and dominated by ratings, good writing does get into production—*Once and Again*, for example—as well as run-of-the-mill half-hour comedies stuffed with **laugh lines**. There is a demand for writers and an opportunity, albeit highly competitive, for writers to break into established **series** with **spec scripts**. Almost all writing in the entertainment industry is freelance work, but television series hire staff writers on longer term contracts. Staff writers can become **head writers** who determine the content. Writers can also become producers and directors. The audience is large, and the demand for good new material never satiated. However, there is a disturbing trend in recent years for networks to reduce the amount of scripted programming and opt for talk shows, reality shows and other less scripted formats because the production cost is lower and the risk lessened, in spite of the fact that independent producers take the largest part of the risk of developing a new show. They have to recoup some of the production cost from syndication, foreign sales, and DVD boxed sets of a season.

Exercises

1. Pitch a new episode of *NYPD Blue*, *The Practice*, or *J.A.G.* to the class.
2. Write scene **outline** for an episode of *NYPD Blue*, *The Practice*, or *J.A.G.*
3. Write a scene for a hospital drama such as *ER*. Check the technical and professional vocabulary that each character would be likely to use.
4. Devise a short scene with a **running gag**. First write one with no dialogue. Then write a different one with dialogue.
5. Write a scene that gives the audience visual cues about character without using dialogue or a voice-over. For example, a young college-age couple in love, or a senior couple in love. Then write a scene showing an engaged couple in which one of them believes the engagement is now a mistake.
6. Write a scene in which one character is trying to hide the truth from someone he or she loves.
7. Write a comedy scene with plenty of **one-liners**.

Writing for Interactive and Mobile Media

In the 1980s, before interactive video became a reality, I was involved as a scriptwriter in a project to create a mail-order multimedia course to teach accounting to managers. A prominent business college in the U.K. saw a market for distance learning. It wanted to create a learning package that would enable working professionals to acquire the knowledge of the course without physically attending the classes. We built in some primitive interactivity by using three independent media: print, audiocassette, and videocassette. The videocassette was produced with planned pauses indicated by a subtitle on screen instructing the user to stop the tape and refer to a page in the manual to read in-depth background. Similar cues were recorded on the audiocassettes. The video dramatized a business situation; the text provided facts and figures and exercises; and the audiotape had testimonials from managers.

Today, we would create hyperlinks to audio files or video clips, or hyperlinks from picture to text. This kind of continuing education could now be run through a website and a listserve or packaged on a CD. So you can see that interactive multimedia is actually a technical response shaped by the long-standing need to interrelate media and build in user input. Current computer technology enables that need to be filled. Interactivity is now a fundamental component of new media and an increasingly common feature of traditional media. The term "new media" is often used to describe interactive media. The Writers Guild of America considers this kind of writing to include "not only video games, but also content developed for other digital technologies, including the Internet, CD-ROMs, DVDs, interactive TV, wireless devices, and virtual reality."[1]

In the early 1990s, the multimedia computer was a novelty. Now multimedia functions are standard. The idea of interactive multimedia developed in fixed media because all the media components (video card, graphics card, audio card) could be incorporated into the desktop. Code could be written so that by mouse click and key stroke, the user could navigate around the content. The first exploitation of interactivity on the multimedia computer was informational. Fixed interactive media preceded websites because the CD-ROM was in circulation before the web had become established. The importance of fixed interactive media was really signaled by the breakout Multimedia Convention that set up separately from the main convention floor of the National Association of Broadcasters in 1994. It occupied a ballroom in the Las Vegas Hilton. By 2001, it had grown so large that it occupied another entire convention center at the Sands. With the expansion of the Las Vegas Convention Center, the multimedia trade show moved back under the same roof as the broadcasters, which mimics the convergence of media on the desktop. At that time the World Wide Web, although in development, did not yet exist.[2] A year or two later it began to transform mass communication as we know it.

While this book was being conceived and written at the end of the 90s, the world of interactive media was in ferment. It continues to evolve and change. This phenomenon of change is something we have to learn to live with as Alvin Toffler pointed out in his seminal and prophetic work *Future Shock*.[3] It is a truism that media technology is evolving at an exponential rate. It is not just the increase in speed and memory and the decrease in the size of computers. It is the new applications and their impact on the skills we need to function in the workplace. Knowledge workers need tools to manage and process information. The speed, memory, storage capacity, and shrinking size of these systems drive the new economy of information technology.[4] The convergence of video in digital format and digital computer processing brings about the possibility of universal networked interactive multimedia. Broadcasting becomes netcasting and now mobile digital television or DTV (see Chapter 14). A screen becomes the display for any and all possible communications media. Since the first edition, we have seen the burgeoning of handheld computers, personal digital assistants, multifunction cell phones, and wireless networking. The recent emergence of the iPhone with an operating system and downloadable apps together with its smart phone competitors and competing operating systems by Google and Palm now suggest another metamorphosis of the media world. In our homes, we switched from analogue to digital video and TV. Producers will have to create program content in the new high-definition standard. Professional cameras are now all digital and switchable between the two aspect ratios of standard TV and high-definition TV (HDTV). DVDs offer 9 gigabytes of storage, which is sufficient to encode a full-length feature film plus outtakes, background story information, and eight channels of audio. Distributors can put multiple language versions of a movie on one DVD. Blu-Ray now supersedes DVD with more than five times the storage capacity of traditional DVDs.[5]

---

[1] www.writersguildeast.com.

[2] Tim Berners-Lee founded the World Wide Web Consortium in October of 1994, which was the foundation of the Web as we now know it.

[3] Alvin Toffler, *Future Shock*. New York: Bantam Books, 1991. See also *The Third Wave* (New York: Bantam Books, 1990), by the same author.

[4] Bill Gates, author of *Business @ the Speed of Thought* (New York: Penguin Books, 1999), makes the case that the success of any enterprise now really depends on the speed and efficiency of its digital nervous system, meaning its total internal and external communications.

[5] See the Writer's Guild of America West's website at www.wga.org.

This extra capacity combined with the use of advanced video and audio codecs will offer consumers an unprecedented HD experience. Movies are being distributed in interactive versions with outtakes and alternate angles included such that the viewer can alter the edit by remote control. Information about the production, the actors, and the making of the movie are also commonly included.

All this alters the way producers, writers, and directors have to think about media. It is hard to predict how this might impact television dramas and sitcoms, let alone feature films. Cable providers offer retrievable digital content and embed program and other information in all channels accessible through the remote control. Television programs are linked to websites, which extend the program. WGBH in Boston produces the documentary program *Frontline*, which puts up subtitles of the universal resource locator (URL) where further information about the program can be found and where online discussion about the program can continue. Since television and the Internet are delivered over the same network and on the same screen for certain models, television can become increasingly interactive so that viewers can shop for products that are "placed" in the program. One can imagine that objects will be clickable to take viewers to a website where they can make a purchase online.

Even before digital video, video boards in computers allowed us to bring live-action video into the computer and thereby combine live action, graphics, animation, still pictures, sound, and text. Computer games and other types of interactive software that take advantage of this multimedia environment are familiar to most of us. The Internet has given birth to the World Wide Web and a form of interactive communication that exploits the multimedia capabilities of computers. Every computer is now built with integrated video, sound, graphics, and Ethernet or modem network connections that make it a multimedia computer. We are now used to user input that modifies the playback or viewing experience by means of hypertext and hyperlinks.

The general conclusion we have to draw is that whatever we know and accept now as visual entertainment will change. Nor is it difficult to foresee ever-increasing instructional and educational use of this kind of interactivity combined with multiple media on CD-ROMs, DVDs, BDs, and websites. Corporations and universities use websites for interactive learning. Production companies whose business was creating videos now have to be able to design and produce DVDs and websites, or go out of business.

The interactive combination of the computer and the World Wide Web with its open architecture reveals new opportunities every day for learning, training, entertainment, and commerce. Think content! Wherever there is content, there is writing. More writers are needed. New media require changes in the conceptualizing and the writing that precedes production. Scriptwriters have to acquire new skills and learn new kinds of visual and structural writing techniques. However, these new writers have to be able to think differently (for Mac users, read "think different") and write for media that are no longer linear. They are nonlinear.

CHAPTER 11

Writing and Interactive Design

KEY TERMS

artificial intelligence
assets
authoring tool
branching
cross-platform
design document
flowchart
functionality
hierarchical
HTML

hub with satellites
hypertext
interactive design
linear
meta-writing
multipoint-to-multipoint
 communication
navigation
nodes
nonlinear

parallel paths
random access
scripting language
sticky
storyboard
visual metaphor
virtual space
wheel

DEFINING INTERACTIVE

First of all, we need to define more closely what we mean by the term "interactive." Although interactive media were enabled by the convergence of computer, video, and audio technology in the same digital environment at the end of the twentieth century, there are previous examples of interactive structures in our culture. Although the term "interactive" is new, the phenomenon is not. We can even see this before the Gutenberg era of print media, which is only now being displaced by digital information technology. Although we associate books with print technology, a book is a piece of technology that preceded the printing press. Medieval monks wrote books with numbered leaves of paper or vellum bound together in a sequence so that the reader could keep the printed matter in a compact space and access any part of it very readily. Consider some of the alternatives—clay tablets, parchment scrolls, or palm leaves sewn together—all difficult to handle and absolutely **linear**. Those more primitive technologies use the writing medium in a sequence that is analogous to a straight

Doi: 10.1016/B978-0-240-81235-9.00011-0

line. You have to move along it in one direction, forward or backward, starting at the beginning or at one particular point. If you are in the middle of a scroll and you want to consult the beginning, you have to roll the scroll backwards, just as you have to rewind a videotape.

In the fifteenth century, the printed book was a stunning piece of cutting-edge technology that changed European civilization and had a revolutionary impact on social and political culture somewhat like the computer and the Internet do today. Books and magazines will not disappear soon because this technology is still very effective. Consider this book you are reading now! In a flash you can look at the table of contents, the index, or the glossary and go back to the chapter you are reading. In addition, of course, you can open a book at any chapter. Surely, this is the beginning of user input—namely, interactivity. Early on in the 500-year history of printing, this structural design was exploited to make dictionaries and, later, encyclopedias. This type of book is **nonlinear** in design. You open it at any point of alphabetical reference and you move between pages that are cross-referenced. This is also the logical model for **hypertext** that is now integral to the World Wide Web. Dozens of reference books, including the commonplace telephone directory, were never designed to be read in a linear fashion but consulted in an interactive fashion. Did you ever meet anyone who reads the telephone directory, the dictionary, or even an encyclopedia from end to end? Can you imagine a telephone directory or an encyclopedia as a scroll? Most of the knowledge in the ancient world was recorded on these primitive handwritten media.

Interactive means that the reader or user can make choices about the order in which information is taken from the program. You cannot get information from the Yellow Pages without making choices. You cannot progress through a website experience or a game or a training program without making menu choices or activating a link that starts a new chain of choices. Whereas the information in a reference work is pretty much on one predictable level, the experience of a game or a website is an open-ended discovery. It is not only about a number of choices but about permutations and combinations of choices. So the number of choices becomes mathematically very great. This is becoming problematic for some giant websites. Users get lost. Sites have to incorporate search engines. The paramount issue of the day is how to design choice for the user that is efficient and clear so that hits on a website lead to burrowing and deep exploration.

LINEAR AND NONLINEAR PARADIGMS

Narrative works, whether in poetry or prose, appear to be **linear** in construction. Drama is **linear** because, like music, it plays out in time for a specific duration. We saw that one problem of writing screenplays is the **linear** play time that drives how you think and write. However, epic poetry from ancient time has usually been based, as with *The Iliad* and *The Odyssey* of Homer or the Sanskrit *Mahabharata*, on a huge mythological background web of stories that is not strictly a **linear** narrative but a cluster of interlinked narratives. Even European works such as Boccaccio's *Decameron*, Chaucer's *Canterbury Tales*, or the peripatetic novels of the eighteenth century, such as Fielding's *Tom Jones* or Laurence Sterne's *Tristram Shandy*, explore structures that are not end-to-end **linear** but layered or multidimensional and not necessarily chronological.

The Bible is an interesting example of both types of structure. Although the Old Testament is a broadly chronological sequence recording the history of the people of Israel, starting with Genesis, the New Testament is principally four parallel narratives. The Torah is still written out as a scroll and read sequentially throughout the year in a **linear** fashion. The scroll is housed in the Ark of the Covenant and worshiped as the word of God in synagogues. The Christian Gospels were recorded in a **nonlinear** format—parallel stories about the same events in the life and death of Jesus. The structure suggests the difference in the spiritual teaching. The former is based on 613 commandments elaborated in centuries of commentary to prescribe every detail of life in a tribal existence. The latter is based on a single commandment that is universal. The Gutenberg Bible, the vernacular book that launched the era of print media and changed the religious and political structure of Europe, embodies the two narrative paradigms.

Interactive narrative paradigms have evolved rapidly with the advent of video games. This new dimension to storytelling makes the audience part of the story. In the most sophisticated examples of the genre, the player of a video game interacts with an imaginary world, determines actions for characters, and influences the outcome. In multiplayer games, the player interacts with other players in a **virtual space** that all players can to some extent modify within rules and conventions. The development of **artificial intelligence** opens rich new opportunities for interactive illusion.[1] At the start of the twenty-first century, we are experiencing the burgeoning of information technology that alters and develops preexisting forms of narrative and exposition. Social websites such as Facbook, Myspace, and Twitter have becomes real-time interactive universes that depend on **multipoint-to-multipoint communication** and are now critical components of traditional broadcast channels and corporate communications.

It seems reasonable to argue that the human brain does not function in a **linear** fashion. It is more akin to a computer processor that multitasks and uses different types of memory. Physiologically, the human brain processes different sense impressions with different cells in different areas. Visual sensation is processed in the visual cortex and auditory sensation in the auditory cortex in the temporal lobe. Touch, which enables interaction through the mouse and keyboard, is processed in yet another sensory area of the cortex. We all know how we can hop between mental tasks and suspend one operation while we process another. Indeed, our lives seem to depend on being able to do this more and more now that we have the tools to exploit this potential of the human brain. All our memories, all our knowledge, and all our consciousness coexist with **random access**. We use them somewhat like a relational database but without the same efficiency or speed. We can even think and do two things simultaneously. Not only do we have to chew gum and walk at the same time, we have to multitask all day long. We drive a car, listen to the radio, drink coffee from a mug, plan the events of the day, and talk on a cell phone. The latter seriously endangers the driver and others on the road because of the limits of human multitasking. The way the human brain manages this reality stream and programs the actions that follow provides a **nonlinear** model. **Linear** media increasingly make use of multiple information streams. Television puts text titles on screen, or the stock market ticker under the news at the same time as the anchor is talking and the picture moving. It uses picture in picture so that the eye and brain must sort multiple streams of information simultaneously. Many channels have preview popups of the next program in the corner of the screen so that the viewer is engaged in program planning while engrossed in current viewing, even of dramatic material that calls on the

---

[1] See the discussion on the International Game Developers Association website: www.igda.org/writing/InteractiveStorytelling.htm.

audience's "willing suspension of disbelief" (Samuel Taylor Coleridge), something that would never occur in the viewing experience of film in a movie theater.

COMBINING MEDIA FOR INTERACTIVE USE

Although we have probably always had **nonlinear** imaginations, we have not always had **nonlinear** media nor the tools to make them interactive. Our entire linguistic education encourages us to think, read, and write in a **linear** fashion going from left to right and from top to bottom. For traditional script formats for television, film, and video, we had to write for two media that can exist independently—sound and vision. Now we have additional media—graphics, animation, still photos, and text. So just as it is a bit of an adjustment to write a script with two or three columns, writing for interactive media will require a new layout to accommodate not only more elements of media production but also the **nonlinear** form and the interactive possibilities of the program. This is true for both interactive instructional programs and for games and interactive narrative. Because a script is always a blueprint or a set of instructions for a production team, we have to figure out how to express the interactive idea for the makers to build in that structural possibility.

What comes first, the chicken or the egg? Do you design the interactivity first, or do you write the content? This is the key question for understanding the problem of interactive writing and design. This differentiates the challenge of writing content for **linear** media and writing content for **nonlinear** and interactive media. In the first, the presentation of content is predictable in flow and direction. Sequencing is critical to all the writing we have discussed so far. Suddenly, sequencing doesn't mean a thing because the user or player is going to choose the order of multiple possible content sequences by mouse click or button press. We are creating menus of choice. To continue the metaphor, we are used to starting with appetizer, soup, starter, going on to the main course, and finishing with dessert. We can serve wonderful sit-down meals in this way, whereas an interactive experience resembles a buffet. You eat what you want in any order at any time. Some people may want to eat dessert first, or stay with starters. Like all analogies, this one is limited.

The point is that the relationship of one scene to another, one page of script to another organizes the structure of the resulting film or video. For interactive media, there is no such relationship. The order in which you write down something does not reveal the final order of the program or even the order in which the user can access it. You can write words to be recorded as audio, pieces of text for display on screen, or images to be created by graphics tools or shot on video, but this has no necessary relationship to the way all these elements will be arranged in an interactive program. Nor would these individual pieces of writing express the interactive relationship between them. That interactive potential has to be conceived, designed, written down, or represented so that it can be made or rather programmed.

You have to know that an **interactive design** will work. Interactive content cannot meaningfully exist without **interactive design**, at least only to a degree. How do you prove that the interactivity will work whether it is on a website or a DVD? You have to write that interactivity into computer code that will make it happen. You have to use an **authoring tool**. The content, or **assets** as they are called—text, graphics, video, audio, or animation—cannot be created first before design. It may not always be clear at the outset what media you need. These bits of content that might be greater or smaller or added on later are written as descriptions of what is going to come. The final result, what you are purveying, is an interactive click stream or a potentiality of interaction. You have to model a kind of prototype. The plan for this is difficult to describe in prose. A diagram would seem to explain it better. This diagram is known as a **flowchart**. A **flowchart** can map the interactive idea more efficiently than lengthy prose descriptions of multiple opportunities for user choice.

However, the **flowchart** does not describe the content—the text, the dialogue, the pictures, or the video clips. Out of each node on the **flowchart** comes a piece of writing that describes a graphic, a photo, an audio element, a piece of video, or text. So you have to think in two dimensions. One relates to the content of a particular piece of media. The other relates to your overall interactive purpose across the whole. Let's illustrate all this by some communication problems for which an interactive multimedia design would be a solution. We need to recall the seven-step method:

1. Define the communications problem. (What need?)
2. Define the target audience. (Who?)
3. Define the objective. (Why?)
4. Define the strategy. (How?)
5. Define the content. (What?)
6. Define the medium. (Which medium?)
7. Write the creative concept.

Until you answer these questions, you cannot intelligently decide whether an interactive medium is the solution. Defining the objective is going to weigh heavily in making this decision. Many producers despair of corporate clients who come in and say we want a website or we want a DVD without knowing the communication problem and the objective. They see that rivals and competitors have these products, so they want one. It is essential to start by looking at the communication problem, rather than starting with the communication medium and then finding the solution that will use the medium.

A video game is an exception to this analysis because it is interactive by definition and by its very nature. If you are designing a video game, you do not wonder whether it will be interactive; you know it has to be interactive. You spend your energy defining the target audience closely and thinking about a strategy to make it different, new, or appealing to that audience. The objective might be to excel in graphic realism or to innovate in streaming video or to create a totally engrossing imaginary world.

Let's start with the website that accompanies this book. What communication problem does it solve? Beginning scriptwriters have difficulty seeing the relationship between words on a page and the finished product. They also have difficulty translating a visual concept such as a shot or an image into a descriptive **scripting language**. Descriptions and illustrations interrupt the flow of reading. Wouldn't it be an advantage to be able to show a script and have a video clip to illustrate the scene? Wouldn't it improve understanding of scriptwriting terminology describing camera shots and transitions if you could read the definition and see or hear an example? An interactive multimedia lexicon is a solution to a need to understand new concepts. The objective is to make scriptwriting terminology more accessible to a target audience of college students who are not always good readers and who might not retain the concept by reading a definition. The strategy is to make it easy to use, which could be enhanced by presenting it as a game or quiz.

Consider the following initial proposal document that is the formal beginning of the project:

Design Objective:

The main objective is to provide an interactive tutorial for scriptwriting terminology and its use. The idea is to provide a lexicon that combines text, image, and sound to explain each term. An efficient interface and clear **navigation** are important so that the module is easy to use. The user can select terms in any of the three main areas—camera, audio, and graphics—to increase familiarity with scriptwriting terminology and have a better understanding of the industry-wide conventions for this type of writing. The strategy is to create an easy interface with interactive links that make all definitions two or three clicks away from any place in the glossary.

Navigation:

The flow is **hierarchical** with links so that the user has an opportunity to connect traditional text definitions via hyperlinks to illustrations in the medium itself—video, graphics, and audio. Each page has a button link to the other branches so that the user can move at will between topics. Each page is designed to offer a choice to a deeper level with button or hyperlink options that move the user through branching to a graphic illustration. The hierarchy has three levels and then a return back to the top or a link to another branch. There is a link to a complete alphabetical lexicon that itself links to every definition (e.g., MEDIUM SHOT).

Creative Treatment:

Although the content is educational, the graphic style establishes a bright and user-friendly environment with clear navigational choices to click through the bank of information. Each link has a visual change such as a new color or a rollover effect together with a sound cue to support the navigational choices. Apart from the text that defines the term selected, we see a choice of visual icons for each type of illustration that embody links to that illustration. For example, the camera movements are represented by a camera icon, the camera shots by a TV frame icon, the audio by a speaker icon. When an illustration is a QuickTime movie, we set it in a quarter frame with relevant text. The usual player controls enable us to play, rewind, and stop. Likewise, audio illustrations have player controls including volume.

Text definitions travel with the **navigation** from level to level. Choosing camera leads to a choice of three subtopics: shots, movements, and transitions. So "movement" is added to the camera identity of the frame. Then at the next level, the specific movement is added: "movement—PAN." A short definition is fitted into the layout with a movie frame and controls so that the movement can be seen as live-action video. In this way the information is cumulative. Links to websites about scriptwriting and productions could add another dimension but would also distract from the central purpose, which is instructional.

The written proposal is a necessary start. It does not solve the many problems of design but rather states what they are. It does not enable you to experience the **navigation**, which is the key to the nature of interactive experience. In fact, between proposal and production, many things changed as the reader can verify by using the Website. The provisional flowchart included an interactive game that had to be abandoned because it would not really work in practice.

One of my students proposed an interactive project on national parks, something like a kiosk, DVD, or website. The idea appeals immediately. The Department of the Interior (specifically the National Parks Service) would be the theoretical client. The project provides a solution for dealing efficiently with public inquiries, but it goes even further and anticipates a need to promote tourism. Much of this type of information has no **linear** logic. Geographical location, wildlife, and recreational facilities need to be accessed through some kind of interface. The **hierarchical** content becomes enormous. The amount of content was far greater than ever imagined in the written proposal. In this case, the organization of the interface determines the content. An excellent example of this type of interactive guide has since been created called "The Adirondack Adventure Guide." You can examine the **design document** in detail.[2]

Many projects get out of control and cannot be finished because the design-versus-content relationship is not understood at the outset. In a professional world in which you are paying graphic artists, videographers, and sound engineers to create **assets** at great cost, you cannot afford to ask for content in a script phase without an **interactive design**. What you are selling or what the producer is selling is the interactive experience, not the content per se. It is rather a way of experiencing and using the content.

BREAKDOWN OF SCRIPT FORMATS

It is probably true to say that there is no industry-wide standard script layout for interactive programming. The layouts are still being invented to some extent. You will come across a patchwork of script formats. For example, if a game involves dialogue, then a miniscript, similar to a master scene script, might be useful for a dramatized section. An audio recording might be prepared like a single-column radio script. A description of a graphic can be a simple paragraph, but sooner or later, a graphic is going to have to be sketched in **storyboard** format. Finding ways to lay out the screens or sequences is probably manageable by common sense. You really need to group the different kinds of **assets** together. You need a shot list of all the audio and a folder with those scripts numbered or indexed to relate to a plan for the **navigation**. The same is true for video and graphics. The relationship between the scripting elements cannot be understood without this plan of **navigation** that explains the interactive sequencing and menu choices that must be built in with authoring software like Adobe Director. Although you need a written **design document** describing the objective, the interface, and how the **navigation** will work, you also need a new kind of document that is a diagram of the **navigation**. It is called a **flowchart**. In short, you cannot write much specific content without a **flowchart** because of the nature of the production process. The sequence is as follows:

1. Write a needs analysis defining the communications problem for the client.
2. Write a creative proposal demonstrating that interactivity is an answer.

---

[2] See Writer's Guild of America West's website at www.wga.org.

3. Write a **design document** describing the interface and how the **navigation** will work.
4. Map the interactive **navigation** by creating a **flowchart**.
5. Create **storyboards** for graphics/animation.
6. Write key miniscripts for video, audio, animation, and text.

The key is step 3: **navigation**. It is difficult to describe it thoroughly in prose. Should a writer be drawing? In the new media world, the role of writer is either breaking down or expanding, depending on how you define your role. Is the writer the designer of content and the designer of the audience interface with that content? The answer ought to be yes.[3] The Writers' Guild of Great Britain maintains "that writers, rather than designers, should be composing the scripts for games."[4] This suggests that designers are writing and that writers need to encompass design.

The capacity to think about the final experience and media result before production resources are committed to the project has always defined the role of the writer. The writer has to have a grasp of what interactive code and computer *scripting language* can do to describe interactive possibilities. The carriage builder has to become an autoworker. It is a symptom of change in the media landscape.

It seems awkward to introduce drawing, storyboarding, and charts into a work on writing for visual media. Writers do not necessarily have artistic skills. What if you cannot draw? If you do not conceptualize **navigation**, you take a backseat to some other member of the team. The question is whether the writer becomes a co-designer or just a wordsmith called in to write dialogue, commentary, or text. Perhaps collaboration is possible. Writers could also be designers and vice versa. There is a parallel between this and the writer/director relationship in **linear** media. Writers lose control to directors once production begins.

So what enables you to think about, conceive, and express **navigation**?

Branching

The easiest concept to grasp is **branching**. The metaphor is a tree that starts with a single trunk and then grows branches, which in turn grow smaller branches until there are thousands of twigs with leaves on them. The directory structure of a computer hard drive in most operating systems is presented to the user in this way. You navigate through directories and subdirectories until you find a specific file. This is known as a **hierarchical** structure. It is not an interactive structure because you can only go backward or forward in your click stream. You find this out if you construct too many folders and sub-folders. Computer directory structures can be unwieldy unless you have a tool like Windows Explorer to look down on the branching structure from above and navigate around it. Those who remember MS-DOS will remember the tedium of switching drives and changing directories to find a file.

You are probably familiar with organizational charts that show a chain of command or a chain of relationships. The limitation of this model as an interactive plan is apparent as soon as you go down

---

[3] A sample of opinions by writers who have worked on interactive projects can be found in *Interactive Writer's Handbook*, 2nd edition, by Darryl Wimberly and Jon Samsel (San Francisco: Carronade Group, 1996).
[4] See http://cgi.writersguild.force9.co.uk/News/index.php?ArtID=147.

or up a few levels. The number of branches increases geometrically. Getting from one branch to another is workable if you look at a page because your eye can jump from one part of the **hierarchy** to another. If the structure has embedded sequences that are hidden from view through menu choices, we are stuck with a tedious backtracking procedure that is like turning a book into a scroll. The depth of certain websites leads to real **navigational** problems. To return to the model of a tree, we need to be like a bird that hops or flies from branch to branch at will, not an ant that has to crawl down one branch to the trunk in order to go up another branch. Hence, we create **hyperlinks** between branches—active buttons or screen areas that switch us instantaneously to another page or another file. The cross-referencing can become very complex. You cannot link everything to everything else because the permutations and combinations would quickly become astronomical. This is the point at which you begin to design interactivity. You start to think about those links that will be either indispensable or useful. This thinking has to be set down. It is not just a crisscross of links; it must also be an interface that reveals the intention of your **interactive design**. You need to invent a **visual metaphor** that immediately communicates the organizing idea. This is the visual imagination at work. Once again, can you do it in prose? Partly!

Although it overlaps graphic design, inventing and organizing content and designing the look are two different tasks. The organizing idea could be that you see a bulletin board. Each of the notes posted on it is an active link. For another example, you have a room. In this room each object has a visual meaning and links to the other areas of content. Doors or windows can lead to subsets of information. Obviously, the **visual metaphor** should relate to the content, the objective, and the target audience. If you are designing learning materials for children, you might want cartoon animals in a zoo or a space fantasy. If you are creating an interactive brochure for a suite of software tools, you would look for a classy and clever interface (say a stack of CD-ROMs that slide out when you mouse over) that expresses something unique about the applications. Once again, can you do it in prose? Partly!

Computers now depend on **visual metaphors** codified as icons to communicate functions: a trash can for Macs, a recycle bin for Windows, the hand with the pointing finger, the hourglass, the hands turning on a clock face, or the animated bar graphing the amount of time left for a download. The visual writer has a talent that works with images projected on a screen and should be able to propose **visual metaphors** for **navigation** and organization. In fact, the best writers can manage content and communicate ideas precisely through **visual metaphor** and visual sequencing. So the visual writer has an imagination that can migrate from the **linear** to the **nonlinear** world. It is probably the key to your professional future and essential to a lot of media creation in the years to come.

We can represent the **linear** paradigm as a piece of string. We thread beads—events, scenes, chapters, sequences—on the string to create **linear** programming. Once we break with the **linear** world, we have no specific model as an alternative. We should consider other analogues or metaphors of organization that will lead us out of **linear** into **nonlinear**. For example, take the **wheel**. It is a **nonlinear** paradigm. It has a hub, spokes, and a circular rim. There is no beginning and no end. You can go from the center down a spoke (think link!) to any part of the circumference and vice versa. A variation would be a **hub with satellites**. You can combine branching with other structures after one or two levels, somewhat like a plan for an airport. Then there are pentangle patterns, which join up all **nodes** to all other **nodes**. A narrative journey can follow **parallel paths** with alternative routes, useful for interactive video games.

Again, witness certain websites, particularly university websites! You know the problem. You spend hours trying to find your way through the maze. You also have to grasp the organizational idea presented in the home page. Website design is a problem of visual organization but also of **navigation**. If you want to express an interactive idea, limiting yourself to writing only a word script would be like tying one hand behind your back when you can also draw a diagram with a purpose-built computer tool.

Flowcharts

A **flowchart** is a schematic drawing that represents the flow of choices or the click stream that a user can follow (Figure 11.1). If you don't plan it, it won't be there. Although you can compel the user to make a choice, you do not know which choice. Although users may think of choices that you haven't, they cannot insert new choices into the finished interactive program. If a link is not there, users cannot put it in. They cannot build their own bridges or impose their own **interactive design** on a program that is already authored.

Interactive multimedia designers have come to think of the **flowchart** as the first step in designing interactive choice. This map or diagram of the interactive click stream has become the ubiquitous planning document for **interactive design**. The problem of communicating the **flowchart** has resulted in a convention that reduces verbal explanations of choice to symbols. In fact, you can use the tables and boxes of a word processor to create flowcharts. More versatile tools exist, such as Inspiration, Smartdraw, Storyvision, and StoryBoard Artist. Each has a dictionary of shapes and symbols and drawing tools that enable anyone to create a **flowchart**. How else are you going to design **navigation**?[5] These software applications were invented to cope with the complexity of relating **navigation** diagrams or **flowcharts** with multiple storylines to the text that describes scenes. You are able to manipulate text files and graphics in a way that is beyond the scope of word processors. Movie Magic Screenwriter also has a template for an interactive script format that you can consult in the Appendix.

Storyboards

We saw that television commercials and public service announcements made use of **storyboard** techniques to lay out clear visual sequences for clients. **Storyboards** are very useful for graphics and animation sequences (see the First Union example on the website). Computer software exists that enables nonartists to visualize directly in the medium and design motion sequences for animation and live action. Storyboard Artist is a software program that allows you to create animated sequences out of a repertoire of characters and backgrounds that you can play as a movie.

AUTHORING TOOLS AND INTERACTIVE CONCEPTS

To understand interactivity, it is helpful to grasp how it is constructed. All of the **assets**—video, graphics, text, audio—have to be assembled as computer files and set into an interactive script that plays them when the user clicks on a button or link. So all the scripts or miniscripts of individual pieces of media do nothing until you orchestrate them into an interactive scenario by means of an **authoring tool**. This is a software application that writes a **scripting language** with commands in computer code

---

[5] See Smartdraw at www.smartdraw.com/exp/ste/home and Storyboard Artist at www.powerproduction.com.

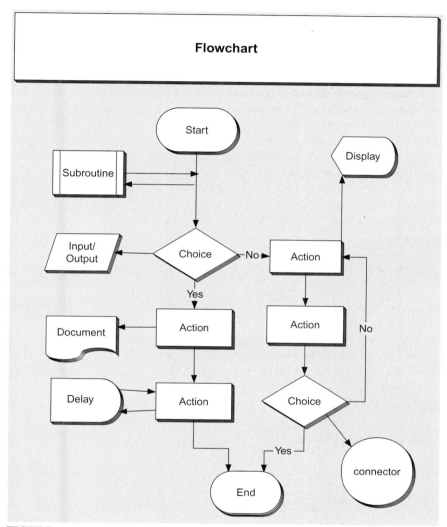

FIGURE 11.1
Flowchart symbols.

that make the various files display on screen in response to user input from the mouse. You cannot author this interactivity from a script easily unless it is expressed as a **flowchart**. The way an **authoring tool** works illustrates exactly why scripting content in segments does not express the interactivity.

The professional **authoring tool** of choice for fixed media is Adobe Director.[6] Video game **authoring tools** or programming software are often proprietary, such as Electronic Arts' RenderWare. The

[6] See Phil Gross, *Director 8 and Lingo Authorized* 3rd edition (Berkeley, CA: Macromedia Press, 2000).

function is the same, which is to encode the interactive choices available to the player or user. In Director, all the graphics, movie clips, audio clips, and text exist as separate cast members that are called onto the stage, that is the screen display, as "sprites." Each cast member, when it comes to the stage, becomes a sprite, which occupies a frame in a complex score (Figure 11.2). Each sprite and each cast member can be assigned behaviors that tell it to respond to a command such as "mouse enter" or "mouse down." The way the score plays, with its pauses for user input that jumps from one screen to another, is controlled by a computer **scripting language** called *Lingo*. This code makes the events happen in response to user input—clicking on a button—or a rollover or a link to a website outside the CD or DVD. The sophisticated coding of the score at the high end requires a programmer, somewhat like a movie or a video requires an editor, to create the final shape of the program by writing the Lingo code which tells the computer what to do.

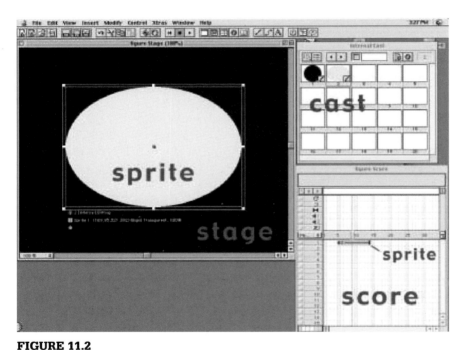

FIGURE 11.2
An example of Stage, Cast, Sprite, and Score in Adobe Director showing their relationship.

From Director, Macromedia (now Adobe) derived a web animation tool called Flash that copes with frames that move and layers of visual elements. The same software developer devised Dreamweaver for website design so that you do not have to master **hyper text markup language (HTML)**, which is the open source computer code with which web pages are constructed. It is the primary computer language of the World Wide Web. There are many other web page **authoring tools** that put the web page designer at one step removed from **HTML**; nevertheless, webmasters still need to know the actual code that makes the pages work, both for the execution of design and for maintenance.

To summarize production:

Step 1 is to assemble the media elements.

Step 2 is to position the media elements on stage or screen display.

Step 3 is to write the interactivity by means of a **scripting language**.

Step 4 is to render it as a stand-alone program that will play from a CD-ROM or DVD on any computer platform, or translate it into **HTML**.[7]

Director can also publish a Shockwave version of an interactive program, which can be embedded in an **HTML** document and played on the web.

It probably makes sense to divide the world of interactivity into two broad categories. The first is fixed interactive, including storage media such as CD-ROMs, DVD-ROMs, BDs, and proprietary disks or cartridges that companies like Sony and Nintendo use for video game consoles. When the program is completed, the producer publishes it, manufactures it, and distributes it in physical form. To change it means going back to the **authoring tool** and burning a new glass master from which to manufacture new disks. That is what we had to do to revise the DVD that went with this book for the second edition. We changed from a CD to a DVD and now to a website to gain real estate for all the new media content.

The second category is web-based nonfixed media, or interactive pages, uploaded to a server that is linked to a network. Most of the time, this network is the Internet. Then that site becomes part of the World Wide Web, which is a construction of unlimited connectivity between servers on that network. In practice, the network on which the nonfixed media work could also be a local area network (LAN) or a wide area network (WAN) not connected to the public Internet or part of the World Wide Web. Many corporations and organizations maintain their own networks that work on the same principle as the Internet, but you and I have no access to them. In fact, the Internet itself was originally the growth of a Pentagon WAN (called ARPANET) to decentralize command functions, which was then used by the defense establishment and the research establishment to send documents and messages. The Internet is simply a network that is not owned by anyone and to which anyone can have access so long as they can connect their computer to a **portal**, or an Internet service provider (ISP). Companies that maintain the servers and the infrastructure of the network (fiber-optic cable, satellites, microwave circuits) and provide access to this network charge a tariff and rent space on their servers for the web page files to reside and be accessible to browsers.

All this background is perhaps more than we need to know as writers. However, because of the relatively recent emergence of the Internet, it seems wise to ensure this understanding so that we can see how writing is different for different interactive media, just as writing for movies is different from writing for television or video. The difference comes about because of the nature of production and

---

[7] See Timothy Garrand, *Writing for Multimedia*, 2nd edition (Burlington: Focal Press, 2000) and also Darryl Wimberly and Jon Samsel, *Interactive Writer's Handbook*, 2nd edition (San Francisco: Carronade Group, 1996) Larry Elin, *Designing and Developing Multimedia: A Practical Guide for the Producer, Director, and Writer* (Boston: Allyn & Bacon, 2000).

distribution in each. Fixed and changing interactive media rest on different computer languages. One can be translated into the other, but there is a different **functionality** between a closed disk with a predetermined audience and use and a computer file open to anyone in the world with a computer and a connection to the Internet. This difference is dramatized by the problem of hackers, who can enter and modify those files, whether on a server or on your computer. This is not true for a manufactured disk.

Now we should consider what kind of communication problems find better solutions in interactive media. Always remember that the writer is paid to think as much as to write. So the question arises whether traditional **linear** video will do a job better, or whether it is better to create an interactive solution. To think clearly about the uses of interactive media and understand how to write for them, we need to observe to what uses they are put. The uses are not always confined to either fixed or fluid media. For example, video games can reside on a website or be distributed on a disk. Multiple users can access a web-based game, whereas only those with access to the player console have access to a game on fixed media. The same is true for, say, an interactive training or educational program. Broadly, the uses of interactive media are similar to **linear** media except that the new capabilities of interactive media allow some new applications. You can't use **linear** media for a kiosk in a mall, for example, where you want to provide shoppers with an interactive guide.

MULTIMEDIA COMPONENTS

Although the writer is not directly concerned with the production issues of making sure a program works **cross-platform** or is compatible with the average computer speed and RAM, it is wise to be aware of them. Any knowledge of how graphics, animation, and **authoring tools** work changes everything for a writer of interactive media. The more you know, the more intelligently you can write. If you make something interactive on tools like Dreamweaver or Director, you get a much clearer idea of what the process is and what you need on paper as a planning document before you create **assets** or start programming. Just as a screenwriter should understand the language of cinema and how the camera frames shots and how shots can be edited, so a writer of interactive media would learn from using an **authoring tool**.

The interactive world is made up of several components: text, graphics, animation (2-D and 3-D), still photos, video, and audio. Each of these **assets** is produced independently with a different production tool. Some, such as text, graphics, and animations, can be created within the computer environment. Still photos, video, and audio originate in other media and have to be produced externally and digitized as computer files so that they can be edited with sound editing software and video editing software.

FINDING A SCRIPT FORMAT

The jury still seems to be out on what script formats are acceptable to interactive media producers. No clearly defined format has come to the fore such as those that exist for the film and television worlds. Published books that cover the subject in most depth cite a number of variants that leads one to think that the format can be tailored to the writer, the production company's established format, and the interactive nature of the project. *The Interactive Writer's Handbook* cites 13 key elements in a **design document**. Some of them, such as a budget, schedule, marketing strategies, and sample graphics, require input other than the writer's. There is an area of overlap between layout, graphic design, and visual writing. Graphic design is the technique of visual communication, not necessarily the visual conceptualizing of content that precedes it. The graphic designer chooses fonts, colors, layout, and orchestrates the look and coordinates the aesthetic detail to make the idea work. Writing precedes graphic design, which is a facet of production and execution of the vision. Visual thinking, or **meta-writing**, is a way of construing the content with an organizing idea that precedes conceptual writing. The **design document** then embodies that **meta-writing** in a creative concept that becomes the solution to a communication problem.

To understand **meta-writing** or visual thinking in website communication, we can contrast several sites and see that the look and **navigational** design are wholly different and at the same time apt complements to the nature of the product or business that the website serves. The first example would be the website you use for online banking or a credit card to access your accounts and effect transactions. The financial sites are relatively clean, simple, and functional because they have a primary utilitarian function. However, a site like www.RedBull.com has no text, only images and Flash movies that respond to mouseovers. The **navigation** is intuitive and the visuals communicate lifestyle activities that sell a world, the world of Red Bull. You can see that the visual **meta-writing** behind these is different. Yet another would be www.Nabisco.com because its demographic and target audience is young and responds to bright primary colors and product pictures and games that the surfer can play. In other words, it is trying to be **sticky** and keep youthful surfers engaged and exposed to product marketing. Go to www.nike.com and you will find another approach which, like Red Bull, relies on streaming video clips of sports and hyperlinks embodied in images rather than text. It combines sidebar navigation via hyperlinked text menus to navigate to e-commerce, other countries and corporate information. The look and **functionality** of the website are related and are critical to the objective of the website. The objectives of large corporate websites are inevitably multiple. Banks tend to open with **functionality**; whereas Nike and Red Bull engage he user in a world of sports, achievement, and image that are not about the products so much as the aura of this world in which the products are to be perceived. Nevertheless, all corporate websites have to manage several publics such as investors, shareholders, financial analysts, public relations, and annual reports. They also serve human resources recruiting as well as communicating product information and sales. A great deal of conceptual thinking has to precede the huge developing and programming cost. Something has to be written down so as to coordinate multiple facets of production.

A game presents a different set of design problems and demands different writing. Visual writing would come into play for a concept, a story summary, character descriptions, and an interactive screenplay. Where characters and drama are involved, a modified master scene script works very well to describe setting, characters, and dialogue. When characters have different responses depending on choice, the format has to indicate a numbered sequence of choices. *Where in the World Is Carmen Sandiego?* has encounters with characters in different locations. Different interactive choices produce different responses from the characters, which give you information and clues. So in a given location, the character's replies are going to have to be numbered and related to where the player clicks on active parts of the screen. So the script format is going to vary with the type of project. Scripting has to provide instructions for production and programming. We can see how the medium demands another way of writing by consulting examples in the appendix and on our website.

CONCLUSION

Most writers of traditional media seem to be afraid of interactive media. It dethrones the writer to some extent. Linear media present the writer with a clear task, a clear role, and a definite authorship from which all production proceeds. Interactive media do not make the script the premise or predecessor of the product. Writing is necessary to flesh out a design. A number of different writing skills can be employed in the same production. One interactive producer explained to me that he uses three kinds of writers: one for text on screen, one for concept, and one for dialogue or voice-over. Sometimes he gets all three skills in one writer. This is why writers are not the authors of interactive media in the same way that they are for movies or television.[8] Collaboration is, has, and always will be indispensable to creative media program content. It seems even truer for interactive media because of the very nature of the medium. We now need to examine more closely the uses to which interactive media and interactive writing can be put.

Exercises

1. Write an organization chart to document the chain of responsibility for an organization such as a company where you work, a college or university, or a club or other organization to which you belong.
2. Write or draw a logical branching sequence for an interactive CD on (a) pasta, (b) automobile racing, (c) solar energy, or (d) cats.
3. Devise **visual metaphors** for the commands "Wait," "Think," "Danger," and "Important."
4. Describe the **navigation** in prose for an interactive CD on (a) cooking with pasta, (b) automobile racing, (c) solar energy, or (d) cats.
5. Write a **flowchart** for a simple game in which you have to click on a moving circle to score points, which are then displayed on screen.
6. Design an interactive multimedia résumé for yourself.
7. Describe an interactive game based on a world concept. Describe the main characters and what the objective of the game is.
8. Write a proposal for a training CD-ROM that teaches the highway code for your state with an interactive test at the end.

---

[8] Of course, the French new wave cinema has always asserted that the director is the auteur of the film. That is hard to see if the screenplay is an original.

CHAPTER 12

Writing for Interactive Communications

KEY TERMS

assets	fixed media	miniscript
B2B	flowchart	navigational design
banners	frames	parallel paths
branching	functionality	sidebars
circle	hub with satellites	third dimension
cloud computing	hyperlinks	vertical dimension
clusters	inverted pyramid	web 2.0
design document	meta-writing	wheel with spokes

In the previous chapter, we drew a distinction between fixed interactive media and web-based interactive media that consist of pages of HTML code residing on a server. At one stage, it seemed a good idea to write a chapter on each. In the end, it became clear that the media writing involved is independent of the computer code or the type of authoring tool employed in production. The same distinction applies here that related to our consideration of linear media when we found it useful to separate the writing in Part 2: Solving Communications Problems with Visual Media from the writing considered in Part 3: Entertaining with Visual Media. It is more helpful to group the types of interactive media according to their broad objectives. Some websites are predominantly informational and commercial, but others are dedicated to entertainment, whether it be zines, blogs, e-books, or online video games. Put another way, it is useful to separate, once more, writing that solves communication problems from writing that trawls the imagination to amuse, divert, and tell stories. Some web portals certainly combine both functions. A third category would be online journalism. Not only are most daily newspapers in America also published online, but television news organizations also edit the same stories for their websites and web portals linked to the journalistic side of their empires.

Doi: 10.1016/B978-0-240-81235-9.00012-2

Newspapers are in crisis because so many readers, including the author, read newspapers online. It is not just that most of them are free and paperless, which allows readers to avoid the smell of newsprint and the problem of recycling; they are metamorphosing into something different than the print version. New dimensions are added so that we interact with them in a different way. *The Boston Globe* is one of the best online newspapers. Some features that illustrate what makes an online interactive newspaper different are unique to the web edition:

1. Articles and reports have hyperlinks to related articles and to sources so that a reader can drill down into the background if need be.

2. Articles can be accompanied with a gallery of pictures, not just one picture that is chosen for the print edition. Slide shows can be attached.

3. Articles are often multimedia; they incorporate not only stills but video clips and graphics.

4. Graphics can be interactive so that they present complex information easily whether it is the location of crime across the city in different categories or economic data evolving over time. A mouse-over or click can bring up ancillary data or trigger animation.

5. No print edition runs the same article or feature in multiple editions. In online editions, important articles can stay on the website for extended periods. There isn't a problem of space and cost. Major stories that might run over weeks can be assimilated and reread in one place and be available to a wider readership.

6. Readers can email journalists and contributors and can post reader comments to the story. Although many comments are banal, even ignorant, it democratizes the letter to the editor that is so restrictive in print editions.

7. Articles and images can be saved and downloaded and forwarded to friends and acquaintances.

8. Readership of most newspapers, even a so-called national newspaper like the *New York Times*, is local, whereas access to the online edition is not limited by geography.

All this means online writing has to change. Although we cannot deal extensively with journalism in this book, it is easy to see how convergence of media imposes visual thinking on print journalists whose future now seems intimately involved with interactive media.

The Internet is really a huge network of connected computers. It has a parallel in the voice network of the telephone linked through exchanges. In fact, the Internet began by the invention of modems that enabled computers to connect to one another using the telephone voice network. Then dedicated infrastructure grew to meet the needs of this new network of servers. Now email and other data communications can be established between computers via various Internet service providers utilizing cable, twisted copper wires, or wireless links between the computer and that worldwide network.

The World Wide Web, however, adds another dimension to that Internet by virtue of a connectivity built out of a new computer language, hyper text markup language, known as HTML.[1] It is a universal

---

[1] This breakthrough idea came from Tim Berners-Lee, who is still involved in the transnational committees that establish protocol for the continued functioning of the web.

computer language with open-source code. That means it doesn't belong to its developer like operating systems (excluding Linux) and other proprietary software programs do. Anyone can use it free of charge and also modify it. This language describes what a web page looks like as to colors, fonts, type, and layout. In order to find web pages, you not only need a connection to a server that is the portal to the Internet, you need a browser, a piece of software that will display the HTML code as a page on your desktop, and the universal resource locator (URL)—the web address of the location of any page. Because thousands of web pages are added to the web every day to the millions that already exist, the World Wide Web is pretty much inaccessible without a search engine. This software will scan all web pages that fit limiting descriptions you provide. You can enter a word. Or you can enter phrases in quotation marks, or use Boolean statements that limit the list to "Presidents" NOT "Republican" or "Presidents" AND "Vice Presidents." Websites are tagged by key words, which the creator puts in a header (called a meta-tag) and are also indexed for content by the search engines. Different search engines use different criteria and search differently to bring up a list of sites that potentially relate to your search.

The World Wide Web now looms over our world and is the transforming phenomenon of the age. It changes business, lifestyles, leisure, commerce, journalism, education, research, and information so that there is almost universal connectivity. Interactivity links web pages through *hyperlinks*, embedded in pictures, graphics, or animation. The link can be to a page on the same website or anywhere on the World Wide Web.

DIFFERENT WRITING FOR WEBSITES

Websites are now well established as a fundamental form of communication that can solve a number of communication problems. We should go back to basics. We can get further value from the seven-step method set out in Chapter 2. The potential answers to the six analytic questions will lead to solutions that include websites, which then require a certain kind of writing. The sixth step, which asks what media can deliver the solution, becomes the key to this present chapter. Understanding why we should choose an interactive solution is critical before selecting that option. Then choosing which interactive solution, fixed or web-based, becomes a further refinement of that selection. Let's remind ourselves of the questions and consider how they might be answered when interactive solutions are probably appropriate.

1. First we define the communication problem. What communication need does it fill?

2. Then we define the target audience. Who are the intended visitors to the site? What are their demographic and psychographic characteristics?

3. Now we want to define the communication objective. What is the purpose of the site? Sales, marketing, information, instruction, presentation, public relations, or personal?

We always need to ask ourselves about the strategy for achieving the objective. Think about all the websites you have visited. Some of them, like Nike's and Red Bull's, are intensely visual with Flash animation, stunning graphics, and color experiences that require a visual response.[2] Some sites are

---

[2] See www.nike.com and www.redbull.com.

dominated by text and links. Other sites, such as Apple's, combine visuals and text. E-commerce sites have pragmatic features such as catalogues, shopping carts, and secure payment links. Corporate websites serve multiple needs that can include public relations, financial information for investors and shareholders, production information, recruitment of personnel, customer services, billing and payment capability, and finally sales.

Most Internet portals, such as Netscape, Yahoo!, and MSN, are somewhat like electronic newspapers. They present news, and some columns are rewritten daily or hourly. They are different from newspapers in that the home page is not the equivalent of the front page. A newspaper puts leading stories on the front page to complete them on inner pages. An Internet portal is also a table of contents as well as a provider of leading stories. Most of the site has to be apparent on the home page. Sometimes this leads to too much business, distraction, and confusion. The front page of a portal links you to many other types of information and activities, such as stock market and finance news, popular culture forums, chat, email, commerce, and specialized interests. Sidebars list all the headings under which you can explore the site. There is no dominant theme in the home page experience that many corporate sites try to achieve. Their home pages make a statement of corporate identity, mission, and purpose; or the best do and the rest should.

We can apply our classifications from an earlier chapter on corporate communications that divide objectives into broad types: informational, motivational, and behavioral. Without being exhaustive, we could categorize website functions in the following ways:

- Informational: Internet portals, government sites, library sites, colleges, corporations, newspapers, databases

- Motivational: entertainment, marketing, advertising, selling, pornography, movie trailers, games

- Behavioral: e-commerce, shopping carts, payments, instruction, surveys, video games, email feedback

Many sites combine one or more of these objectives.

Linear writing, or prose exposition, which is the centuries-old model for print writing, requires a sequential development of ideas moving from a beginning through a body of argument or narration to some kind of conclusion. The whole experience of reading is contained in the pages of the article or book. In contrast, web writing, which at its simplest could be a box containing the equivalent of a print article, is not limited to linear delivery in a frame of text. The information or idea can be developed with hyperlinks that highlight themes in the article that explore, sideways as it were, tangents that supply a lot of detail about something that would otherwise interrupt the flow of the main text. It is the same idea as the footnote in print media. Many writers, especially those presenting factual arguments, want to back up their points with sources or comments or asides, which are then put at the foot of the page or at the end of the chapter. In a sense, the web expands the footnote by making it interactive, by linking and branching to the actual source or another line of argument.

Another way of thinking about the difference of web writing is to see it as multilayered writing. By means of **hyperlinks**, panels, sidebars, fonts, and colors, you can reach more than one audience at a time. In fact, one problem of web writing lies in the unpredictable demographics of the surfer in your domain. On some sites, there is something for everyone. It is like the sections of a newspaper. You go for the sports pages; I go for international news; someone else goes for the classifieds. Websites are also the broadsides of the information age. In Shakespeare's time, a printer would put together a news sheet and run out on the street to sell it to curious passers-by until the innovation of the weekly and daily newspaper in a later century. Websites look for passing trade among the surfers as well as formal communication generated by emails and published links. The bloggers, who might be private individuals with a passion or interest in some subject, providing some alternative views or sources of information, resemble the seventeenth century broadsheet publishers.

In Shakespeare's theater, every class of person from educated gentlemen to illiterate groundlings sat in the audience. The plays contained comedy, tragedy, vulgarity, sublime poetry, suspense, gripping plots, history, and profound psychology. Portals and browsers are a kind of Internet theatre. They have something for everyone. So what we encounter is an omnibus of writing drawn from multiple sources. Websites make generous use of text. Some, like the portals of the major browsers, are cluttered with text leads and banners. So short, effective prose that headlines ideas and topics does the job. To communicate effectively, you need to conceptualize interactivity and introduce effective, functional graphics so that the options and functions are clear. At the moment, the home pages of AOL, MSN, Yahoo!, and other major portals and Internet service providers have a format that is akin to a newspaper front page, except that the headlines and tag lines are **hyperlinks**. Therefore, the writers and editors of these websites need a strong background in journalism and in the editing of breaking stories and weaving together of a combination of news and entertainment. However, the home pages also use still pictures, video, color, and graphic design to present opportunities to users.[3]

Multilayered Writing

Most of us are so familiar with web pages that we do not stop to think how they get conceived, designed, or written. Most web pages contain text of some sort, whether titles, headings, or labels. We might call that design text, the same use of text that we find on posters, billboards, and print ads. It has a graphic function as well as verbal exposition. Then there is the text that works like text in a book, newspaper, or magazine. It is prose exposition. It is meant to be read for content. It reads like print media, even though it may incorporate hypertext links to other pages. Gutenberg technology survives inside the web site although the prose style may change in ways that reflect a busy screen full of **banners** and **sidebars**. Website articles have to be written at multiple levels. The first level is broad outline. The succeeding levels amplify and link the story to an ever-widening circle of archival and related materials.

In the early days of journalism, when the early telegraph could break down or the correspondent could run out of money, wire stories were written with the most important, leading elements first. Detail and elaboration came later. This is called the **inverted pyramid**. A parallel problem exists today. Surfers come on to your site from all directions and may be bounced back off other links. A website needs to follow the same **inverted pyramid** practice developed in wire service journalism so that leading

---

[3] Interestingly, the OECD argues in its published standard for web communication that there should be "a text equivalent for every nontext element." See www.w3.org/TR/WAI-WEBCONTENT/full-checklist.html 1.1.

ideas come first and the impatient surfer does not click away. A new dimension is the multimedia content that tempts surfers to click on pictures, listen to audio, or find out answers to leading questions like *Is She Cheating On You? How to Tell* or *The Ten Hottest Jobs for Graduates*. There are tax tips, real estate advice, and celebrity news to distract the surfer and compete for attention. This changes the game from print newspapers and magazines. The web is a visual medium that is also a text medium. Although this primarily applies to web portals, there is a similar phenomenon on commercial sites such as Amazon.com. Who has not had the experience of searching for information on the web and then losing sight of the original intent of that search because of spontaneous response to **hyperlinks** that take you away from your main search? It is even possible to forget what you were trying to find in the first place and, what is worse, be unable to back up to where you started. The web is not just nonlinear, it is organic.

Conceptual Writing Versus Content Writing

Writing for a website means thinking clearly and analytically about its function. We have raised the question of whether the writer's and the designer's work overlap. Similarly, the writer and the webmaster's work overlap. Because a website is a kind of living organism that changes, evolves, and adapts over time, maintenance, pruning, and updating become critical to web success. Clearly, the webmaster is going to make decision about how to lay out and incorporate disparate and diverse elements on the website. So let us consider this to be an editing function, not a writing function. However, interactive writing also includes editing and hyperlinking pictures. The interactive journalist can say more with pictures, video clips, and audio clips. This new media writer has to conceptualize interactively and think more about the relation of text to other elements. Although interactive media are laid out visually, their content does not necessarily involve visual writing in the sense that we have defined it. The distinction lies in the difference between something that is written and read to be made into media as opposed to writing of text that is incorporated into this interactive medium. After all, a journalist or a feature writer for magazines could be published on a website. *Time* magazine and CNN stories and articles were linked to AOL. They all belonged to the same corporate entity. The rationale behind the merger of AOL and Time-Warner was to match content to the medium.[4] Can this be considered writing for the web? Isn't it writing that is cannibalized for web content? The writing that has to be unique to the web is the writing that the surfer never reads because, just as the moviegoer doesn't read the script of the movie, it lies behind the interactive planning and construction of the site.

The most important writing, consistent with the writing philosophy of this book, has to be conceptual. Such writing is not apparent to the eye. The writing that analyzes the communication problem, articulates the solution in the form of a concept, and then describes the **functionality** of the website is design. The fruit of such thinking and writing is **navigational design**. The strongest kind of **navigational design** communicates to the user by intuitive visual metaphors. We know that kind of thinking from the graphical user interface that is now fundamental to operating systems. The trash can on the Mac, the recycling bin in Windows, the turning circle or spinning color wheel for a process, a progress bar for a download—all these are elements of **navigational design**. Tabs for folders use an intuitive

---

[4] This merger has now broken up at the end of 2009, and AOL is once again an independent company.

metaphor. It is everywhere. Whatever engages the intuitive visual response of the user elevates the communication and invites the participation of the use. A writer/designer must think of that. Conceptual writing leads to production of various kinds such as graphic design and audio and video recording. Thinking through the function of the website, being able to translate that function into visual ideas, and organizing its content by visual metaphors would be the most critical work to precede the costly phase of production. The internal content of a web page keeps changing, sometimes daily. The question of how the website will serve a corporate communication needs writing of a different order—**meta-writing**—that relates **functionality**, look, and mission. It is the writing behind the writing. It is the writing that the audience does not read, as opposed to the written text on the website that the user gets to read. Writing for the web and interactive media involves structural writing—that is, writing out the idea of what the content is going to be and how it will work. A well-designed website has to have a concept behind it that addresses its organization in terms of the structure, the links, and the layout. A thoughtful, creative proposal is essential. Call a writer—but a writer who understands interactive media!

On the web, we have broken with the linear through line of content. Other paradigms for organizing content than beads on a string or an arrow become relevant:

- **Branching** (tree metaphor: trunk, branch, twig, leaf). This is hierarchical; navigation is arduous.

- **Circle**. Anything on the circumference is connected; there is no beginning and no end, and all points on the circle can connect with all other points across the circumference.

- **Wheel with spokes**. This is really a variation of the circle, but with a center so that points on the outside connect to a single central point.

- **Hub with satellites**. This is really a circle with smaller attached circles or systems and subsystems.

- **Clusters**. These allow random relationships between groups of objects.

- **Parallel paths**. These allow direction but with exchanges between the paths.

In interactive design, these relational forms can be combined. Different structures lend themselves to different material so that ideas and media can be accommodated. Content can consist of clusters of cognate or related material, sometimes raw material. In fixed interactive media, such as a training module, the **parallel path** might be ideal to get to a goal. A website allows unlimited links to source material that would sink a linear exposition. **Branching** in websites is a natural tendency, but it can quickly lead to exponential increase at every level and to surfers losing their way, like ants crawling up a tree trunk to get to one particular leaf.

WEBSITE CONCEPTS

If you wear the hat of a conceptual writer, you have to think through the function of the site. What is the objective, the purpose of the site? Again, we confront the writer/designer issue. It seems clear that this kind of writing implies design and therefore must express design concepts that in production become design features. A website makes a statement. Many websites make wrong or inadvertent statements. They are not only ugly but also confusing. A website must almost always be functional. It must be clear to users how they can interact with the site and get what they want or get what you want them to get. A site makes a visual statement and demonstrate **functionality**. The two should coincide and reinforce one another. A site has style and personality. In some cases, it is that of the creator, of that one person, but normally corporate communication is not personal expression. The site has to reflect the identity and mission of the corporation or the portal. More often than not, there is a conscious design, which a writer can articulate and a graphic designer and webmaster can execute. Why is web writing visual writing? A site makes a statement visually, verbally and functionally. Deciding how the home page should be organized is conceptual writing for design. Should it be bold and brash to attract attention, like Red Bull's site? Should it be sober and functional so that a bank or financial services company can inspire confidence, like the sites for T. Rowe Price or Bank of America? Should it be minimalist and intuitive to draw in the surfer, like the Nike site? How much Flash animation will succeed in visual seduction or, conversely, confuse the user. Nowadays, certain functions such as email in a "Contact Us" link, or "About Us" are almost universal. The questions we need to ask are: What is unique about this site? What will engage the surfer or user at an intuitive level visually that relates to the overall objective of the site? What keeps users on the site and gets them to go deeper. Writing out the idea for the website is a thinking-writing function, crucial in all scriptwriting and crucial to interactive media, both web-based and fixed.

Although a designer might make decisions about layout and build the look, it has to flow from a concept that unites function and look, articulated by a writer thinking through the organization of content. But maintenance then falls to the webmaster. A great many sites are put together in an impromptu way, where the creators make it up as they go along. We have to separate sites and writing intended to solve a communication problem from sites that are, if you like, pure expression.

WRITING TO BE READ ON THE WEB

You see words on the printed page just as you see text on the web page. In fact, text dominates web communications. The Gutenberg concept of a page has migrated across to the web. However, web pages are not laid out the same way and do not restrict themselves to text. They make use of boxes, panels, **sidebars**, color, different fonts and typefaces, and, of course, animation such as animated GIFs and Flash animation, so that the eye is engaged visually by the design rather than the text. On the other hand, web pages have fallen back into pre-Gutenberg ways of arranging text—scrolls and folding palm leaves. We have the expression "scrolling" up and down to describe our navigation through a web page document. At the same time, there are navigation arrows or "next" buttons or numbers to jump to the next page. Page turning does not make for true interactivity. It is really more like a slide show or a PowerPoint presentation. Arabic and Hebrew read right to left and Japanese and Chinese ideograms read vertically. The web page seems to accommodate all possible ways of arranging and sequencing text. The writing of text for web pages has to be different from ordinary print media because text has to be organized in layers of hypertext with links that draw together concentric circles of information. So although paragraphs of text may read just like print media, the editing and thinking must take into account another dimension that does not exist in print media. Print media, or straight text, has backward and forward relationships, whereas web text has a third dimension, a **vertical dimension**, which links and positions it in a matrix of information or of associations.

If you monitor your own experience of surfing, common sense tells you that when you read an online article you do not always read it as a stand-alone piece. More often than not, you find the article through links embedded in a previous text or in a list compiled by a search engine. So the web complicates life for the writer and the reader to some extent. Both can lose track of where they intend to go or where they came from.

So we come to the writing of the text we read in the columns and boxes that we find on a website. The conceptual writer might also write this content, but there are legions of freelance writers who modify traditional print content to fit into the interactive environment. They have to think of reading as seeing. Although you read a web page, you also see it. It is a visual experience. Editors who work on web content have to incorporate those visual values. It might be a simple issue of managing the fonts, the size of the block of text, or the relationship of text to pictures or video or audio links. However, in the best sites, the visual experience arises from the conceptual design, which is visual writing.

NAVIGATION: THE THIRD DIMENSION

Reading web pages involves navigation. So navigation is involved in writing web pages. This is the problem of the **third dimension**. Whatever you read, whatever you write, exists in a vertical context as well as a linear one like reading a book or an article. This has to modify the style of writing. So it makes sense to think carefully about links to offsite pages. Because **hypertext** is the same whether it jumps to a page on or off the site, users do not necessarily know where they are. There need to be signposts. You can't look down every rabbit hole.

It must make sense to think about how you want to define the cyber-boundaries and how you allow or direct your user to leave the site. Some websites are fairly self-contained and present opportunities for navigation around the site. Other websites fan out with ever denser links. Most e-commerce sites will want to be self-contained. However, with Amazon.com, the links across the web through a title or a product become so heavily layered that it is easy to lose your way because of links. But think about the concept. Amazon is not organized to be self-contained because its original main products—books and videos—by their nature take you down a road of exploration. Now Amazon is a virtual department store. Many sites compete within themselves for your attention. This is true of web portals. You are called to follow so many different directions and links, which are not necessarily related, that you become pole axed with indecision. This arrangement would not be good for a corporate website. Clear navigation and accessibility govern successful interactivity inside websites.

Consider Yahoo.com, which is a relatively clean web portal. Nevertheless, there is a bewildering range of directions to take from obvious news headlines to "9 Simple Things Women Want." These can be a distraction. It works for entertainment but not for business or corporate sites. Linking within a site helps organization. Linking to the web, or diverse sites, can fragment the user experience. You forget what you were looking for in the first place because you followed incidental links and ended up wandering in a maze of links.

WRITING ISSUES

Once again, we have to contemplate that fascinating transition from something conceptual written on paper to something visual and fully produced in the medium itself. We know that in the professional world, you cannot just keep this in one individual's head. Ideas have to be pitched to a client, costed out in a budget, and communicated to a team of specialists who will translate them into concrete visuals. Translating from the page to the screen—the computer screen, in this case—is the essence of the media business.

Concept

Production methods and the role of scripting are not standardized and predictable in the way that they are in the world of linear media. Nevertheless, we can outline a best practice that will ensure a satisfactory result. If more than one person is working on a project, a written concept and more is essential. It is probably indispensable even for a single creator to define a concept before committing resources.

Design Document

A **design document** is unique to interactive media. It addresses the need to know two important characteristics of a website: what it will look like and how it will be organized. **Navigational design** sets apart the pros from the amateurs. All interactivity is based on links. Anybody can create links. The question is whether the links serve a coherent purpose and whether the navigational idea is well communicated to the user. If this stage has any equivalence to the linear world, it would be to the treatment.

Flowchart

No question about it! A **flowchart** is a diagram. The thinking behind a **flowchart** could be the responsibility of a writer or a designer. It does not require writing skills per se. It requires skills to order spatially and sequentially. Making this diagram is enabled by software such as Inspiration, Smartdraw, and Storyvision. Whether a writer, developer, designer, or programmer does it, it has to be done so that the production team knows what it is trying to create. For each click and link, there is another page on screen. So it has to be designed and laid out and the assets necessary to that page assembled. The purpose of the flowchart is to chart the intended navigation to be presented to the user. It becomes a way of verifying **functionality** and a basis for a programmer to write the code that will make the links work.

Breakdown for Production

Any given web page is comprised of multiple media. Each of these media elements is an **asset**. If your idea calls for a still picture, you have to create that picture or buy it from some copyright owner. If you need a video clip, once again you have to shoot it or buy it ready made from some source. A list of **assets** for each page of the website must be compiled and broken down into production-specific categories: video, audio, graphics, still photography, and text. A production manager or project manager can assign to graphic designers, video producers, or animators the list of needed **assets** in each category that have to be assembled for construction of the site. We could probably find that in practice, the writer hands over to the project manager, developer, or designer.

Text

Text, of course, is a job for a writer reappearing as writing to be read. This writer may not be the writer/designer who conceptualized the site. Text content is itself an **asset**. It may be writing that is technical or that is based on specialized knowledge that has to be commissioned. Web writing differs from print writing because interactivity is part of the way it is put together and contributes to the experience of the web user. The use of colors in text and backgrounds changes the web reading experience. Key words or sources offer potential links in the form of tangents, statements, and questions. Writing for web content is visual writing in that it involves media other than text.

Video, Stills, and Audio

Images, video, and audio clips can enhance the user experience and bolster the content. The web writer has to write with multimedia content in mind and consider where additional content such as still photographs, video, and audio might be appropriate. If a video clip or other media is anticipated for a given page, you may need a short script (we will call it a **miniscript**) to tell a video production crew what to shoot, or an audio technician what to record, or a photo researcher what picture to search for in the libraries or archives. Once again, this writer may not be the writer/designer who conceptualized the site.

Applying the Seven-Step Method

To construct a site, without a doubt, we will want to go through the first six steps of the method outlined in Chapter 2 to come up with a concept. Many students getting involved in website construction or interactive media want to compose their interactivity directly with the authoring tool and are impatient about the writing that precedes it. It is important to keep in mind that what you do in higher education is free of commercial pressure, such as competition and cost. In the professional world, however, you need conceptualizing skills. Not the least of these problems involves cost. If you promise to build a website or an interactive CD for x dollars and then find that it costs more than your estimate, you will be working for nothing or actually making a charitable gift to your client. I don't believe in corporate welfare. Back in the first chapter, we explored how the need for scripts arose in the early film industry for the simple reason that in an expensive production medium you need a plan. This same principle applies to interactive media. The more you can get down on paper, the more secure your project!

We cannot illustrate all the issues of concept writing. Suppose we are going to create a writing website. Let the domain name be MediaWriting.com.[5] Although we have argued the importance of thinking through the six steps, in the professional world, this may not be presented to a client in writing. Personally, I always write a response to a client briefing setting out my understanding of the communication problem and my rationale for my creative solution. The six steps are embedded in that

---

[5] See www.MediaWriting.com.

preamble to the creative concept or treatment. We will begin with our six-point analysis of MediaWriting.com's needs:

1. The communication problem arises from the fact that many corporations do not know how to solve communication problems in written and visual media. We want to market a consultancy service to corporations and a coaching service to other writers who have ambitions to write for various media, mainly the visual media, and don't exactly know how to go about it. They need a guide, a writing clinic, a list of resources and information concerning the professional writing world.

2. The target audience is businesses and media writers who have an ambition to write for corporate or entertainment media. They might be beginners or experienced writers who need a second opinion. We need to accommodate these levels. The interactive characteristic of the medium will facilitate self-selection.

3. The objective is to provide a reassuring environment that is also commercial and useful to professionals. A forum for writing issues and chat rooms should be directed at creating a virtual community. Training and script-reading and critiquing is fee based. Click-through signage is desirable to generate supplementary income. An email function is important for communication.

4. The main strategy has to be a unique proposition of some kind that will invite the browser to click. Some video clips and stills might help break up text, but the main visual impact has to be in the look and design. It has to be clear and to the point in delivering services and information. The look and design should be professional and attractive.

5. The content comprises tutorials for purchase, advice columns, a forum, a chat room for writers, a virtual bookstore with click through links to Amazon.com, a resources guide that includes lists of agents, links to other writing websites and competitions, script reading and doctoring, corporate scriptwriting service for clients, email, a hit counter, script samples, the author's writing, and a personal profile.

6. There is dynamic interaction between users over the Internet. Because this function involves interactive exchange, the web is the unique medium that can deliver all this. Everything is updateable.

Step 7, as you will remember from Chapter 2, is to state the creative concept. Because the chosen medium is an interactive website, the concept must address things such as look and navigational design that will be developed later. This concept could be a memo for a meeting to pitch to a client for team clarification.

Concept

The first impression of the surfer has to be a combination of intrigue and efficiency. Something has to catch the eye, but then immediately engage the brain. The layout of the home page has to present clear options. There should be a discrete Flash movie that keeps interest without being distracting. The visual metaphor could be a quill pen morphing into a fountain pen, a typewriter, a computer, or a handheld PDA. A clean sidebar should list the major navigational links: Bookstore, Tutoring, Personal Profile, Script Samples, Writing Links, Email, and Login/ Logout. There should be a hit counter.

Sidebars with headings are a way of organizing text topics that are related. Mouse-overs cue submenus, and subtopics can be set in a different color and become hypertext. Body text should be in sans serif type, which generally reads better on the web.

The objective of the site is to generate inquiries and sell consulting services and writing instruction.

We want to see a clean, sober, easy-to-read site that presents an uncluttered spectrum of writing services both to the client needing a writer or consultation and to the writer needing information, advice, or writers' goods. If there is Flash animation, it has to be clean and simple. It has to be functional. It has to be fresh in content. The website www.mediawriting.com is up and running, a work in progress that is harder to create than to imagine. Budget and resources are significant in writing design concepts for clients.

INSTRUCTIONAL AND UTILITARIAN PROGRAMS

Interactive media apart from websites serve most of the main needs of corporations. These include public relations/marketing, catalogues, brochures, product manuals, and training. What used to be print media can now be interactive catalogues on websites. What used to be print brochures can now be interactive CDs or DVDs. What used to be a linear video solution to corporate communication is often now an interactive CD that may include video clips and much more besides. So much linear program content for corporate use involves a transfer of information to the audience. Audiences have difficulty following, absorbing, and retaining a lot of factual detail. Traditional linear video works best as a way to motivate by dramatizing or documenting corporate stories and presenting corporate personalities. Video works well in management groups and large motivational meetings at which an audience has a viewing experience as a group. In contrast, interactive media rarely involve a group experience, even across a network, because interactive responses are, by definition, individual. Whenever the corporate communication problem involves information transfer, complex data, or training, the intelligent solution must be interactive. The limitation on **fixed media** is the degree to which the information is volatile and needs frequent updates. Websites on intranets work better for this because the cost of site maintenance is lower than it is for manufacturing CDs or DVDs. Understanding these issues enables a writer to think critically and creatively in interactive media and do the **meta-writing** into which the writing of **frames** and blocks will fit.

INTERACTIVE CATALOGUES AND BROCHURES

One of the best uses of interactive media in business involves a fundamental need to list large amounts of information about products, which were formerly exclusively delivered in print. Now a catalogue can be a searchable database with pictures and web links either on a website or on fixed media. Typically, websites of business that have a large inventory are well served by an online catalogue which is enhanced by being interactive, even if it is not directly linked to e-commerce and a shopping cart checkout, which it often is. Then there is business-to-business (**B2B**) inventory with added functions of online ordering and invoicing.

Print brochures had, and still have, the function of presenting essential information about a company, a service, or a product. Although you can print expensive glossy brochures, you cannot know whether they are read. An interactive brochure allows user selection and allows readers to select the informational depth that matches their interest. Consequently, corporations can create denser brochures without the risk of overloading the audience, which might happen with a print brochure expounding information in a linear fashion. Customers or clients can choose how much technical detail they need to know. Thus, a web brochure for Sony video cameras can satisfy both the engineer and the videographer as well as the casual shopper.

EDUCATION AND TRAINING

In a previous chapter, we noted how enormous the need for training is in the corporate world, in government, and in the military—how to fire an antitank missile, how to service a jet engine to Federal Aviation Administration standards, how to invest in stocks and shares, how to bake bread, or how to speak French. Interactive media lend themselves very effectively to the learning process. There are several advantages. The learner sees pictures, hears audio, and reads text. Multiple sensory inputs reinforce ideas. Many studies show that learning and retention improve with visual intake. In addition, the learner has to interact with the program by thinking, choosing, and applying incremental blocks of knowledge. The learner can pace the process to suit an individual rate of assimilation, repeating where necessary. Most interactive learning programs test and track performance on the host computer or on a server. Training problems also cry out for interactive solutions, although there is still some life in the old-fashioned training video. **Interactive design** for training tends to lean on the use of **branching** and **hierarchies**, although testing and learning games can be effective components. Testing enhances interactivity by giving the user a role beyond a page-turner. Basic interactivity is just a menu and links, which can be created with Adobe Acrobat or PowerPoint.

Interactive learning programs can be set up on websites as well. In the educational environment, there are systems such as Blackboard, which allows asynchronous delivery of course content and online drop boxes, white boards and chat rooms, and testing. Macromedia (now Adobe) Breeze extends the spectrum of functions to include real-time video conferencing and desktop sharing as well as presentations and tests that can be downloaded. The possibility of web-based learning and web-based testing facilitate corporate training needs, continuing education, and traditional academic learning. Blackboard allows the delivery of asynchronous learning. Students are able to take the test in their own time by a certain date by logging on, or they can engage in class discussion on a bulletin board. Likewise, corporate training, which is a huge problem for companies that constantly need to train new hires and upgrade the knowledge of existing personnel, can run interactive training from a centralized website and serve an international, or nationally dispersed, population of workers. In many businesses, licensing or laws governing an industry entail compliance that is a legal responsibility. To create these learning programs, writers are going to be increasingly in demand. Someone who can combine media writing skills with instructional design and training will have a strong combination for future employment.

KIOSKS

Most people have had the experience of needing to search a small database of information at a location such as a shopping mall. You might want to know what stores are in the mall or find out where a store is in a large mall. I was on a university campus, which had addressed a fundamental communication problem of direction on campus by using an interactive touch-screen kiosk to guide students and visitors to faculty offices, classroom locations, and campus buildings. The kiosk application works well for cruise ships, theme parks, museums, malls, and department stores. Most kiosks rely on touch-screen interactivity.

CONCLUSION

The video production economic model, which charges for time and creative services, doesn't apply well when the product is really software or code or something you do with a product. The software developer spends a large amount up front in development and debugging and then shrink-wraps boxed copies that sell in increasing numbers and are upgraded and provide a revenue stream. The other model is the advertising agency that has an account and can develop campaigns and brand awareness and can charge a retainer plus commission on media buys. None of these models exactly fits nonlinear production businesses which, in effect, combine all three. However, some companies like Planet Interactive in Boston see no problem in charging for the time of highly skilled creative people, including writers, marking it up and billing a client, just like traditional video production companies.

The most important idea to carry forward to the next chapter makes the distinction between a certain kind of writing for content and what we now call **meta-writing**, which addresses site functional objectives, visual design, and navigation. This writing requires thinking through all the communication problems and thinking across parts to grasp the whole. This is true for all interactive media, but the website has evolved in a short time span to serve critical communication needs in the twenty-first century. Websites will extend their own **functionality** and importance because of accessibility via portable wireless devices such as personal digital assistants (PDAs) and cell phones. These new input and output devices will be leveraged to provide more services and enable buyer response to advertising—for example, websites that allow you to book a table at a restaurant from your cell phone. Voice recognition and smaller phones will change the traffic and function of the device, which was originally engineered just to enable wireless access to the voice network.[6] Voice recognition means that functions that now depend on keyboards and text input will operate by voice commands like on

---

[6] The growth of mobile platforms and their evolving content are discussed in Chapter 14.

Star Trek and in other science fiction worlds. Voice recognition is already being used in customer service voice menus.

We have laid down some foundations for interactive writing for the web. Apart from the need to consult more specialized works, if you want to develop your writing in this area, you will need to stay in touch with developing trends and techniques as the Internet continues to evolve as **Web 2.0** and **cloud computing** assumes greater importance. It seems clear that writing for interactive media, particularly for websites, is going to evolve rapidly, perhaps more rapidly in the next 10 years than over its first 10.

Exercises

1. Compare three web portals, such as Yahoo!, AOL, and MSN, and analyze the **functionality** of the sites.
2. Compare some major corporate websites, such as Nike, IBM, or Hewlett-Packard, with the website at your college or university.
3. Invent an interactive kiosk for a ski resort, or a national park, or a tourist guide for your area.
4. Write an interactive training proposal for how to apply to college, how to make salads, or how to use your campus library.
5. Pick a familiar product and write an interactive manual of instruction for it.
6. Write a high-level design document for a website or a CD-ROM on mountain biking, in-line skating, or any other sport or leisure activity of your choice.
7. Write and **flowchart** an interactive kiosk guide to your local museum or shopping mall.

Writing for Interactive Entertainment

AI
avatar
cloud computing
cut-scenes
design document
dialogue engine
dialogue scripting
engine
first person

flight simulator
game bible
HUD
isometric view
massively multiplayer
   online role-playing games
   (MMORPGs)
multiuser domains (MUDs)
narrative design

platform
RPG
shooter
simulation games
storymapping
third person
webisodes
world building

The previous chapter explored writing for interactive media that basically serve a utilitarian, commercial, or informational objective. This chapter looks at writing for interactive media that are primarily designed to divert, amuse, or entertain an audience. The media discussed in the previous chapter usually have some corporate or organizational function. The kind of interactive media we want to consider here generally offers an experience for which the audience is prepared to pay, and which satisfies a need for knowledge or entertainment, or both.

INTERACTIVE REFERENCE WORKS

Although we have had dictionaries ever since the eighteenth century when Dr. Johnson put together a dictionary of the English language, and later encyclopedias and other reference works in book form, the emergence of interactive media on CD-ROM offered an increase in the versatility of interactive

Doi: 10.1016/B978-0-240-81235-9.00013-4

referencing. Although cross-referencing was always part of the concept in print, the multiplicity of the links and the speed of linking in CD-ROMs enhance the user's experience. In addition, the old concept of the illustrated encyclopedia could be expanded to include not only more still pictures in color but video clips, audio clips, and graphic animations. Reference works such as encyclopedias were quick to see how they could enrich the content by introducing stills (already part of the print editions), video, and audio with links to make searching and cross-referencing more dynamic. Grolier's Encyclopedia and Microsoft Encarta are now given away as part of the software packages in new computers. They are maps to giant websites that can be updated continually. The primary interactive structure would seem to be more or less dictated by the traditional alphabetical listing. Hypertext and other links thread new instant interactivity through the content by topic or theme. Seeing video of President Kennedy's inaugural speech, hearing the voice of Martin Luther King's "I Have a Dream" speech, seeing a 3-D graphic of a part of the human anatomy—all transform hypertext cross-referencing into multimedia interactivity. Medical, legal, and other technical references works on CD make knowledge more accessible. Databases and search engines online make information available that would otherwise be inaccessible, but more to the point, they enable the processing of statistical data from commerce and government in ways that would defy research in the days before the invention of computers. With the invention of the personal computer, all those capabilities are within the reach of the individual.

Since the previous edition of this book, Wikipedia has emerged as a collective web encyclopedia to which anyone can contribute. It is the knowledge-based equivalent of open architecture in software that can be modified and improved by anyone. Although you hear complaints that some entries are not authoritative, there is review, and ultimately inaccuracies or incompleteness will be challenged and corrected by experts or interested readers and contributors. It is a manifestation of the new movement for **cloud computing** in which applications and data exist on servers in cyberspace off the desktop and are always accessible.

E-COMMERCE AND INTERACTIVE BOOKS

Although the first interactive media were reference works, there were also early attempts to make interactive entertainment. The best-selling CD-ROM for many years was *Virtual Valerie*, an interactive strip tease, which allowed the user to tell Valerie, the stripper character, what to do. Porn always seems to drive new media, whether it was the belly dancer in George Eastman's demonstration of moving picture at the Chicago Exhibition in 1895 or the pornography that drove the consumer VHS format to triumph over Sony's superior Betamax format, not to mention the early dominance of porn websites. Online pornography has pioneered the techniques of e-commerce because it fits, accidentally, the ideal business model for e-commerce. In that model, you can shop, choose, sample, pay for, and have delivered directly to your desktop the data, goods, or service that you seek. Amazon.com, on the other hand, is still warehousing books and videos and physically shipping them to the customer, as are most other web-based extensions of mail-order businesses. The true e-businesses actually deliver goods and services and take payment over the Internet. Banking and online stock trading fit the criteria. Another business that leads the way is software. You can buy and download software directly to your hard drive, or you can use it on a remote server. Why should you buy highly marked-up, shrink-wrapped packages of CDs or software that have to be manufactured, warehoused, shipped, and displayed on shelves in expensive retail floor space that you have to travel to, park near, and spend time getting to when you can get the software directly from a website?

Just as the music and film industries have been thrown into confusion by the rapid evolution of media compression technology (including MP3s and DivX movies), combined with high-speed Internet access, so the publishing business is also bound to change. Books and music cannot only be sold over the Internet, they can also be distributed over the Internet. The major media companies have been slow on the uptake. Authors can now self-publish on the web. Stephen King experimented with publishing a serial novel on the web.[1] Books on websites could become more interactive and could be sold as incremental chapters or selections, much like music tracks can be sold individually rather than as albums. This book could be fully interactive on the website that comes with it. It could be made more interactive, integrating the text and the online media, and be consulted on an hourly basis, or sold chapter by chapter, or by subscription. No doubt traditional writers will have to rethink how they write when the market for their product is an interactive marketplace. Fiction has enormous interactive possibilities. Perhaps games and storytelling will converge in a way that we cannot now predict. Lastly, video games can be played on the web, joining the circle of e-commerce innovation. **Multiuser domains (MUDs)** and **massively multiplayer online role-playing games (MMORPGs)** enable global game-playing between players logged on to a website from anywhere in the world.

GAMES, NARRATIVE, AND ENTERTAINMENT

Video Games

In the early 1990s, a number of educational games combining play and learning came out. I bought *Maths Blaster* and *Where in the World Is Carmen Sandiego?* for my son to make learning more fun. Play is a profound need of human nature. Children's play is a form of learning, and computers enable us to engage the natural propensity for play in the cause of learning to add or subtract fractions or learn geography. Interactive entertainment is a natural outcome of the marriage of computers, graphics, and video, and it is consistent with the interactive structure of the web. Computer graphics can now create any world, any fantasy, and any morphology that you can imagine. The interactive game market, whether distributed on proprietary cartridges for platforms, DVD, or posted to a website, reaches a huge market. Although the demographic is primarily under 30 (the average age is 29 and rising), that demographic is probably changing as the gamers mature (17 percent are over 50). Video gaming is international or transnational. Gaming competitions, supported by corporate promotional money, have produced gaming professionals who make a living playing video games. We are looking at a growth industry. Cell phones now link to the web and are able to download games and video and act as portable game consoles. Universal portable handheld devices on which all networked communications are accessible are the trend of the future, which we examine in greater detail in Chapter 14.

Video games are now big business. The Writer's Guild of America website says that this is "an enormous and continually evolving area of entertainment that now rivals feature films in terms of profits and

---

[1] *The Plant* (2000) is now offline; www.stephenking.com/index_flash.php.

popularity. Video games have become one of the three major forms of screen-based entertainment, alongside motion pictures and TV."[2] Statistics quoted in an article in *The Boston Globe Magazine* put the figure at $9.9 billion for video games, software, and hardware and another $1 billion for PC games.[3] However, the Writers Guild of America website mentions $15 billion as an estimate of the size of the industry. Video game developers bid millions for video game rights to movie properties, and it can cost millions to develop a video game. Development budgets are starting to rival feature film dollars. Games can easily cost $500,000 to produce at the low end and a record $40 million at the high end. Although most of that money is spent on programming and sometimes elaborate 3-D animation, some money has to be spent on writing. As with feature film, the higher the budget, the more important the writing!

In the beginning, video games were an arcade novelty like Pong, which came out in 1972, or Pac-Man, which soon followed. They were software or programming creations that did not need a script or a story. We can draw a parallel to the early days of movies, which also began as coin-operated arcade entertainment. Soon the moving picture novelty embraced more ambitious storytelling. At that point, you couldn't run out into the woods with a camera and a bunch of actors and make up a story as you went along. In the first place, it would not produce a good result. Second, it would be an expensive way of producing film. So as video game development budgets climb into the millions, the need for preproduction, creative **storymapping**, and planning becomes indispensable. Just as the scriptwriter became the key creator in movie preproduction, writing promises to become a key instrument to construct, imagine, and design a complex game. A video game has to have all the things that writers are good at creating—characters, plot, and dialogue. A game that has characters and dialogue needs a writer to invent the characters, write their dialogue, and create a storyline.

Exactly how writers are employed and what kind of writing they do vary a great deal depending on the producers and developers of games. The Writers' Guild of Great Britain website indicates that "some writers are being asked to write dialogue for characters and animation that have already been put together. Writing the script for a game can be the very last part of the process."[4] A similar observation can be found on the website of the International Game Developers Association (IGDA), which has a special interest group for writers. The association published a white paper, "IGDA's Guide to Writing for Games," in November 2003. In it, the association discussed the cross-over between writer and designer that we addressed in Chapter 11. One person can do both, but increasingly, higher budgets and more complex game design will create opportunities for writers. Today, few writers make a living writing only for games, but that time is likely to come. Meanwhile, the white paper identifies two main writing skills that are particular to video games: **narrative design** (creating a story) and **interactive dialogue scripting**. The role of writers is not standardized as it is in the film and television industry. Indeed, "the role of the game writer remains ill-defined and poorly understood." At the same time, the authors of this document, who are all professional game developers, believe that the medium has to "mature and broaden its potential audience." They see the need for "new material and new ideas" and they think the "game writer will have an important role to play in facilitating this evolution."[5]

---

[2] The WGA has established a *pro forma* contract for this kind of writing and formed a New Media Writers Caucus in 2004. See www.wga.org.

[3] Tracy Mayor, "What Are Video Games Turning Us Into?" *The Boston Globe Magazine*, February 20, 2005.

[4] See www.writersguild.org.uk/News/index.php?ArtID=14.

[5] See www.igda.org/writing.

The locus of the writer in the process also varies from one developer to another. Sometimes writers are called in relatively late to create or polish dialogue, especially when the game has originated in another country and another language and needs what is essentially a foreign version for the local market. A significant writing task involves writing the **game bible**, with descriptions of characters, for a large development team to work on. Also every game comes in a box with significant text describing settings, worlds, and game objectives and with a more detailed instruction booklet that the player will read. As with films and television, there are two basic ways to originate a game. Either you create it from scratch, or you buy a license to create a game out of source material such as a movie, a comic, or a book. This adaptation process depends on a unique writer's skills. Behind every game is some kind of written proposal and some kind of script. So where there are video games, there must be writers.

Writers work on project pitches, intellectual property development, **narrative design**, **world building**, **dialogue scripting**, and **dialogue engine design**. A project pitch is not going to differ a lot from concepts in the traditional linear media, except that it has to be thought out in terms of interactive values and appeal. It will necessitate composing something like a log line or a premise—a brief and provocative statement that tells us what the game is about. Let us remind ourselves of the concept of meta-writing. The writing is not in the words so much as the thinking and conceptualizing behind the words. That is where the specialized knowledge and understanding of interactivity and gaming will enable someone to write for this industry. According to the IGDA's white paper, "Game writers need to be game-literate, which is to say, they must understand how games function." Clearly there is a vocabulary and a jargon that the industry uses and understands that sets it apart.

Games are defined in terms of the point of view and the type of game. The point of view also has implications for the structure and design of the interactivity. The **first-person game** presents a subjective reality type of experience, with the real-life player seeing and hearing what the player character sees and hears. An example would be HalfLife, produced by Valve Software and distributed by Sierra. Flight simulators also tend to follow that model for obvious reasons. Then there is a **third-person** or objective narrative, somewhat like the omniscient narrator of the novelist. An example would be Tomb Raider. You see Lara Croft as a character, but she only makes the moves you decide and input via a player console. The third kind is the **platform game**. In this, a camera sees the character. The camera can pan and track, showing the player all points of view including maps of position. The player can switch between angles and viewpoints and can do inventory of weapons or energy. An example would be the PlayStation game Metal Gear Solid.

Then there are **simulation games** such as SimCity and Civilization that have apparently limitless combinations that occur following your choices of different scenarios. If you build roads or public transport in SimCity, you could run out of funds and have to raise taxes or deal with an economic crisis. Every choice has huge numbers of permutations and combinations with unpredictable results. So it seems that every game you play is unique compared to challenge games like Tomb Raider in which you have to progress by scoring and by problem-solving strategies that you can learn and repeat. There is even a game that allows you to simulate running a university. Simulation games seem to be very reliant on strong navigation and design work.

Games have developed a terminology or jargon that describes the type of game and the point of view:

- **Platform game**: Involves jumping on platforms of various sizes and jumping on enemies to destroy them. Examples include Super Mario Bros. (NES), Sonic the Hedgehog (Genesis), and Jak and Daxter (PS2).

- **RPG**: (role-playing game). A game genre for both PCs and consoles in which the player develops intelligence and skills by collecting points and solving puzzles.

- **Platform**: The type of system a game is played on such as PlayStation 2, Xbox, Game Boy, and GameCube.

- **Flight simulator**: Simulates the action of flying an aircraft. Realistic controls make the flying itself the point of the game. Driving simulators do the same thing for car racing.

- **Shooter**: A game in which the object is to kill an enemy with a weapon that fires bullets or rays while avoiding being shot by the adversaries. Such games are usually constructed in a 3-D environment, assume a first-person perspective, and are referred to as FPS, or "first-person shooters."

Then there is a defining question of the point of view that the player enjoys:

- **First person**: You see the action through the eyes of your characters. You don't see your own body.

- **Third person**: An omniscient point of view that lets you see the character you are controlling in contrast to first person.

- **Isometric view**: A view of a game and its action from an angle instead of directly from above or directly from the side.

Some other terms that help define video games are as follows:

- **Cut-scenes**: Live or computer-generated videos clips, usually not interactive, interludes between stages that furnish additional information, such as story elements, tips, tricks, or secrets.

- **Avatar**: The character that you control in the game or that you create in a multiplayer game.

- **AI** (artificial intelligence): The programmed characteristics of behavior and response of a nonhuman character. All characters not controlled by the player have some form of AI.

- **HUD** (heads up display): Used most in first-person games, the heads-up display, like a flight deck or a dashboard, presents information on the screen, such as the life meter, level, weapons, ammunition, map, and so on.

- **Engine**: The application that powers a game. One primary engine (the graphics engine) and several smaller engines power AI and sound. People refer to the whole product as the engine, meaning "the computer code that is programmable and usually proprietary to a platform or publisher."[6]

---

[6] See http://jobs.ea.com/how_ea_makes_games.html; Mark S. Meadows, *Pause & Effect: The Art of Interactive Narrative*, New Riders Press, Indianapolis, Indiana, 2002.

Characters in interactive media have to be developed differently. They may have back stories as characters in linear media do, but they behave differently and are unique to an environment. Lara Croft in the early Tomb Raider games can only walk, jump, climb, shoot, and react in terms of the script for the environment and her given weapons and responses. In Rockstar's game Grand Theft Auto: San Andreas, the third-person character that the player controls, has to be fed to maintain his energy. If you over feed him, he gets fat and can't run fast. So you can have him work out and build strength. There is also the relationship to the player. Is there interaction with the player or just with other characters, or with environment, or with robots or other nonhuman characters? How will communication take place? What actions are scripted for the character? What dialogue supports the game? How will change of strength, health, and energy level affect the character and be impacted by scenarios that are imagined for encounters with other characters or environments?

We have already established that writing for interactive media is different. Writing interactive entertainment can be exceedingly challenging. It is difficult to represent multiple-choice and alternate scenarios that result from user choice. What changes from linear media plots is that the writer has to create player choice. In a sense, the player becomes a character.

Dialogue is an important component of linear narrative and game narrative. However, the way dialogue functions in games is different. First, it might appear as text. It might be a narrow range of responses to specific questions or situations. The character may not develop and can be affected by the environment rather than the plot or interaction with another character. Although dialogue has to fit character, it has an altered functionality in games. It may present choice to the player with critical consequences for the outcome of the game. Dialogue may be voice-over or text as opposed to lip-sync delivery by an actor with body language to go with it. You lose actors and acting.

Writers are called on to develop game ideas from intellectual property of a nongame source such as a movie or a book. Although this is a form of adaptation, it bears little relationship to writing a movie script based on a book or a play. The game writer has to translate a story into interactive choice and play that keeps the spirit and style of the source but creates a wholly new experience and even extends the story and perhaps develops fuller minor characters in the game. *The Matrix* movies furnish a good example because the success of the movies generated games that extend the world of the matrix. In the **MMORPG**, you can create a character and teach it skills to navigate the world of the matrix after the third and last episode of the movie.

This brings us to the most complex and demanding form of writing for games, which is **narrative design**. Design implies some understanding of programming, or at least what it is capable of doing. It requires imagining the style and scope of the game, often within the framework of narrative set by the game developer. Its nearest relative in the linear entertainment world is the treatment. Whereas the treatment in film or television comes early on in story development, **narrative design** may occur in tandem with, or parallel to, the game design of the developer. If writers assume a stronger role, by grace or by choice, in the process of game development, perhaps the writing of **narrative design** will become stronger. It goes back to the question we have raised elsewhere—whether the writer designs or the designer writes.

World building involves writing that imagines and describes the world or environment that the player experiences in the world of the game: what it looks like graphically, what kind of laws govern its physical and psychic space, and what kind of creatures or behaviors are part of that world. These determine colors, the sounds, and the style or look of the game. It seems that, once again, this can happen after the basic game design is already in place. It fleshes out the game environment.

Second Life is a new game-like phenomenon. It is a virtual world you enter as a person whose identity you create—an **avatar**. You can be anything you want to be. You can create the virtual environment in which that person (**avatar**) moves. Now you can buy and sell clothes, weapons, and décor through virtual Second Life commerce, which involves real dollar transactions. Corporations use Second Life for meetings, training, and product launches. Real products are advertised on Second life. Social networking meets gaming.

In contrast to the linear entertainment world, writing for games might involve a stable of writers, who might have differentiated, specialized writing skills. Scriptwriting breaks down into three types. There is scriptwriting for text that appears on screen; there is scriptwriting for video segments or modules that run as QuickTime movies or 3-D animation; there is scriptwriting for voice narrative. Sometimes this can involve three different writers. Sometimes, a writer has the skills for all three. A fourth type would be the conceptual writing, the meta-writing of the **narrative design**. One writer might be able to do all the types of writing, but there will likely be specialization.

Another area of concern would be researching the background so that dialogue is consistent with the world that prevails in the game. Just as TV series have a series bible, so the video game needs a **game bible**, which details all the back story of the game and its characters and defines the objectives and the outcomes for the player. Its first function is to provide the production team with a common body of knowledge so that consistency of style and story is maintained. This would give rise to the booklet that is normally delivered with a game to prime the player/purchaser in order to get started. There is a clear writing job to be done here.

Some idea of the writing can be gleaned from the pro forma contracts for game writing and interactive writing that are obtainable on the website of the Writer's Guild of America.[7] Although the writers who would seem to be closest in background and talent would be the movie and TV scriptwriter, there would have to be a radical shift in mind set to deal with the nonlinear nature of composition. It is analogous to the early days of screenwriting when the writers were either novelists or playwrights, often with little understanding of the new medium. Gradually, a new kind of writer would emerge (a scriptwriter) that could see the particular writing problem of the medium and would do the meta-writing that would lead to strong program content.

GRAPHICS VERSUS LIVE ACTION

A game could be created with computer graphics or live-action video. Take, for example, the PlayStation game, Metal Gear Solid. This game world is created purely out of computer graphics. It is a challenge

---

[7] See www.wga.org/subpage_writersresources.aspx?id=90.

adventure that requires the player to infiltrate a military base for disarming nuclear war heads in Alaska that has been overrun by terrorists, find out if they have the capacity to launch a nuclear strike, prevent a nuclear launch at all costs, and rescue two high-level hostages, one military and one the president of Arms Tech. This game, like many others, has evolved over more than a decade. There is a complete **game bible**. The game introduces you to the characters, who are played by voice actors. The player has an inventory of weapons and rations. There is a bank of clues to call on when the player gets stuck.

The majority of games are created on a computer with 2-D or 3-D graphics tools. Not many are produced with photographic backgrounds and live-action sequences. There are practical reasons for this. Actors and video production are expensive, but you don't have to pay computer graphic characters for their performance. You merely have to record their voices. Audio production is less expensive. Video requires a huge amount of bandwidth, or it has to be severely compressed. Most of the worlds of computer games are extravagant fantasy worlds in space with aliens or in mythical kingdoms with monsters. It is easier and probably cheaper to create those environments and their characters with computer graphics tools than with live-action video. The animation occupies less drive space than full-motion video. With graphics and animation, you can create whatever you can imagine.

THE ORDER OF WRITING

Broadly speaking, video games face similar production problems to video, film, and television. You have to start with an idea. That seed idea has to be a written concept of the content and style of the game and how it will look and play. It then has to be elaborated in a treatment or **design document** that articulates the vision for a larger production team. As with film and video, content has to be created except that production involves huge amounts of graphic design and programming as well as audio recording of dialogue sound effects, and music. Video editing roughly corresponds to programming and debugging. However, the relation of writing to linear production inevitably differs from interactive production.

Electronic Arts, the world's leading independent developer and publisher of interactive entertainment software, outlines the video game production process on its website. The writing phase is somewhat concealed in the description of their **design document** "that specifies game play, fiction, characters, and levels."[8] In preproduction, artists and software developers work up a prototype 2-D and 3-D design, animation, and programming from the design document. Production assistants then break down and prioritize the tasks to create the finished product. Teams of artists and animators are coordinated as they create the assets that are the visual experience of the game. Likewise, teams of software engineers write the code with game authoring tools that create the interactivity. As with all interactive media production, there is a chicken and egg situation near the beginning in which developers have to toggle between creating interactive play choices and then translating that into visual assets that are needed,

---

[8] See www.igda.org/writing/WritersGlossary.htm for another useful glossary of gaming jargon.

whether video, audio, or graphics, to fulfill the vision. The miniscript for some dialogue or a story-board for an animation sequence could be written in response to the evolving game. The chicken and egg situation in which you are working from a written concept that becomes modified in production, then leads to renewed writing and or design. This is not true of film and video. Production proceeds from a finished script and its breakdown into a shooting schedule.

To summarize, the logical sequence of game development follows these steps:

- Concept /Proposal (writing)
- Preproduction (design, writing story, characters, levels, game play)
- Prototyping (continued writing as design evolves)
- Full production (continues writing as design evolves + scripting for software engineering)
- Postproduction (alpha, beta, and final testing + marketing and promotion)

Writing and rewriting for video games is not confined to one stage.[9] Conceptual writing that imagines the game play and design is meta-writing, whereas dialogue and character description is content writing. The conceptual writing at the early stage should contain a short premise, describe the type of game play, and outline a map of the game story, challenge, or goal. It should describe the look and style of the world of the game.[10] As production begins, the sequence of writing and its relationship to production is harder to pin down and seems to vary with the developer and the way the production team is structured. Dialogue writing for characters and the **cut-scenes** can arise after considerable game design but necessarily before production of the assets (picture and sound). You cannot write dialogue for stages of the play until you know the game design and the kind of choices that the player has, which trigger alternate responses.

FORMATS

We have not tackled the thorny question of a format for this writing. Unlike with other media we have discussed, we cannot be final and definitive: "Game writing has no real corollary in mainstream entertainment. Books, movies, television, theater—they all involve the creation of specific documents with established formats, which the interactive industry does not have."[11] There are some emerging patterns, dictated by logic and need. The appendix shows one example from the Movie Magic Screenwriter templates.

An example of dialogue writing for a kung-fu style game called Seven Shades illustrates one approach:[12]

---

[9] See www.erasmatazz.com/library/Le_Morte_DArthur/Index.html for a rich documentation of written development of ideas for a game.

[10] See http://www.ihobo.com/archive/index2.shtml for an archive containing well-thought-out concepts, elaborated game designs, and scripts. See also http://jhorneman.typepad.com.photos/ico_gdc_2004/dscn5686.html for a presentation of the Game design Methods of ICO.

[11] See the article, "How Do You Become a Game Writer?" at www.igda.org/writing/HowDoYouBecomeAGameWriter.htm.

[12] See www.ihobo.com/archive/scr_7shades.shtml.

Fox. Known is set TRUE if Xia Tu has learnt that Zhapian Hu is a fox spirit and not a human being.

Bandits. Wuhan is set TRUE if the bandits led by Shao Lung are currently hiding in the Wuhan marshes. If not, they have no fixed base of operations at this time in the script.

AREA: Kongmoon

SCENE: Mansion

//The upper floor of FOX's mansion; plushly furnished. HARE enters through the window, looking around furtively. She moves forward, looking for any sign of habitation. FOX opens the shutters to a lantern, illuminating the room, and casting HARE's shadow against the wall. FOX: It seems impatient to steal from a Nobleman's estate without waiting for the master of the house to be absent.

HARE: Forgive me; I meant no disrespect. I bring a message of vital importance to the safety of Kongmoon.

FOX: Messengers come by doors. Thieves come by windows.

HARE: And thieves who bring messages?

FOX (amused): So you admit that you are a thief?

CONDITION: if Fox. Known

{

HARE (pointedly): An honourable thief would do so, I would hope.

FOX: Can there be honour among those who steal?

HARE: Those who steal treasures? Assuredly. We shall see about those who steal cities.

FOX (amused): You are remarkably well informed for a common thief.

HARE: There is nothing common about anyone in this room, fox spirit.

}

ELSE

{

HARE: It would be dishonourable to do otherwise.

FOX: That must make it difficult to avoid justice.

HARE: Have you not heard? There is no justice in Honan.

}

FOX (somewhat surprised; then moving the conversation forward): Indeed? You said you brought a message.

HARE: Huang Leng plans to march upon Kongmoon and bend it to his will. He is ruthless, and intent on procuring not only the throne, but dominion over the entire middle kingdom. Already his agents are within the walls of the city, seeking a way to subdue your defences.

Reproduced by permission of ihobo international.

As you can see, the dialogue has to relate to another kind of document, which is a **design document**, in order to make sense because of player choice that is the essence of any game. As you look through the examples of **design documents**, you find diversity. However, something has to be written down at the beginning. Something very elaborate mapping out of the production is indispensable to production but may be modified as graphic artists develop scenes and programmers code play. Dialogue for the sound track and for **cut-scenes** must be written to keep pace with the evolving game and precede the creation of those assets.

INTERACTIVE TELEVISION

You might have noticed that a number of programs on television run a subtitle with a web page address that extends or continues the content of the program. The Public Broadcasting System channels pioneered this and seem to be the most evolved. WGBH in Boston produces *Frontline*, a current affairs documentary program, which has a very complete website with transcripts and background material. During many documentary and current affairs programs, a website universal resource locator (URL) is periodically superimposed as a subtitle. If you are online, during or after the program you can explore in-depth interviews and outtakes that are not in the edited broadcast footage. There are associated chat rooms and forums for audience participation in discussion about the content. Most network news programs post website links on screen so that viewers can consult other levels of information and background online while viewing the program. Television sets can also be linked via broadband cable to the web and serve as monitors for browsing. The program URLs can then become active links. A few television series, such as *CSI* and *The Practice*, have created websites that extend the story and create enhanced experiences for the audience.

I have seen a Saturday night movie program, which holds audience attention by running a quiz and interactive exchange on a website posted on the program and announced by an anchor before commercials so that audiences will stay with the program by going to the website and playing to win prizes. There are also websites that sell products in the program. This is only going to increase because as cable and Internet converge, the same monitor can display both. Product placement, which has become an important part of film and television financing, enables interactivity to grow audience responses beyond mere recognition and selling to actually buying what they see. The ideal marketing technology will enable the viewer to click on the object in the picture and be linked to a website to buy the article. One wonders how this will change writing and conceiving program content.

As the phenomenon of convergence continues with broadband access to cable and the Internet, we are likely to find more widespread adoption of devices that have polyvalent uses for both media. Some manufacturers are selling television sets that can be connected to the Internet by means of a modem. Computers can display television broadcasts and tune into podcast programs of cable and radio. HDTV monitors that will display high definition programming are readily available, which means that digital television and Internet can be delivered through the same fiber to the household. This potential has hardly been exploited to date in terms of cross-collateralizing cable, TV and Internet. The question for writers, producers, and directors is how this will impact the concept of programming. Viewer response or even viewer choice of program outcomes could become a feature of next-generation entertainment.

At the moment, most television programs and most movies have web pages that enrich the audience interaction with the program content. Remember that the moving picture medium began as a silent medium. Writers and producers did not think in terms of sound. When sound was introduced, whole new ways of imagining and writing scripts must have opened up opportunities for those who could exploit the new dimension. The potential of interactive movies is technically feasible with Blu-Ray technology and DVD authoring software. The same will be true for cable television. Nevertheless, the kind of story that can be made interactive is limited to a certain type. There is a potential convergence between video games and television.

Personally, I don't like the idea of interactive television because I am comfortable with the existing format. However, narrative innovation in the series *Once and Again*, which was mentioned in Chapter 10, is fascinating. The cutaway technique to the black-and-white asides that allow characters to communicate inner thoughts to the audience suggests an interactive potential with different writing and production so that an audience could choose to hear an inner thought or back story at any given moment. Interactivity could develop in this way so that audiences could select deeper levels of back story or character information rather than audiences choosing story outcomes.

The possibilities with documentary programming, reality TV, and game shows are not hard to imagine. Documentary could easily escape the restrictions of linear editing by presenting outtakes, background interviews, text, and interactive chat rooms not much different from the current PBS practice. Game and quiz shows could easily add an interactive dimension from the viewer audience. In 2000 a new series, *Survivor*, captured the ratings, pushing out the popular *Who Wants to Be a Millionaire?* The format of the show requires the "survivors" to vote one of their number "off the island" each week and become thereby ineligible to win the million-dollar prize. It is easy to imagine the audience being asked to vote online and interact with the program in real time as the survivors present themselves to the mass audience voters. Reality TV has mushroomed both because it is cheaper to produce than scripted series and because audiences become involved with the outcomes of fierce competitions and eliminations of contestants. All this spills over into the social networks and blogs.

WEBISODES AND TELEVISION WEB CONTENT

Television series have developed a significant web presence with blogs, chat rooms, bios, and added value content for fans and followers of the series. In particular, a web-based extension of series storylines has spawned what is popularly known as **webisodes**. These are short supplementary story extensions and offshoots of the main series, using the same characters. Viewers can expand their sense of that imaginary world and find story dimensions that might otherwise be restricted by primetime episodes. These **webisodes** are by definition separate scripted extensions of the story. So it is a new form of writing. There are also web-based series that are only distributed as webcasts or podcasts. These are discussed at greater length in the next chapter on mobile media.

INTERACTIVE MOVIES

A few producers are already experimenting with interactive drama in which the viewer response affects the outcome. At the National Association of Broadcasters annual convention several years ago, I attended a panel on interactive entertainment that featured some of these pioneers. A movie theater in New Jersey was built to allow the audience to interact with the storyline and select different story outcomes, which depended on majority vote by means of some control buttons at every seat. The panelist reported that the experience was addictive and that people kept buying new tickets to the movie to explore the alternative plot outcomes. I have never found this kind of entertainment in any neighborhood near me. This may change. However, I think there are inherent limitations quite apart from the capital cost of equipping cinemas with wiring and individual seat controls to input into the program. It also requires a digital cinema.

The likely method of distribution for feature film entertainment in the future will probably be digital, across a network or by satellite to the exhibition theater to avoid the cost of heavy film prints that have to be shipped and stored and which wear out. Although digital projection does not yet equal film projection in quality for size of image, the changeover seems inevitable. If the movie is therefore in electronic form, it will be much easier to embed interactive choices in the program. Nevertheless, theaters would have to be modified to furnish interactive controls to the audience. That system of controls would have to enjoy universality for producers to create product for it. Looked at another way, a successful story usually compels viewer attention because it seems inevitable and true. The audience believes in the story and the characters such that alternatives do not even occur to us. That is the nature of great writing. Maybe there is an alternative *Hamlet* in which he doesn't kill Polonius and, with the help of his only friend Horatio, organizes a palace coup, takes back the throne, and marries Ophelia. Great stories and great characters are so because they reflect some kind of emotional truth about human experience. Conventional movies have a long life ahead of them even while interactive novelty may begin to appear. Stories with multiple outcome choice will have to be restricted in scope and choice. The model is akin to a video game. That kind of experience is satisfied in video games. Television appears to be the more likely candidate for interactive story telling. It is going to become digital and can be married to a computer in the home. In the near future, interactivity could be coupled with on-demand digital television.

CONCLUSION

Writing for interactive media is no doubt the fastest growing opportunity for new writers. It is also the most elusive because of the newness of the field. Clearly, video games are overtaking movies and television in dollar terms. The situation of writers is somewhat like that of writers at the beginning of the twentieth century in the early days of the movies. Nobody knew exactly what a scriptwriter was, but the need for preproduction writing quickly emerged. As we noted in Chapter 1, novelists, dramatists, and even journalists turned to the new kind of writing required by the first visual medium. The difference now is that we have had a century of films, television, and video scriptwriting that, although linear in content, is not so far removed from nonlinear interactive content. The formats have yet to be firmly established, but the need for them clearly exists. Those who want to develop their writing for interactive media further can turn to a growing list of specialized titles dedicated to this kind of writing listed in the bibliography.

Exercises

1. Write a concept for an interactive quiz show.
2. Write a concept, then a **design document**, and a flowchart for a simple video game based on animation.
3. Look at your favorite video game and write a **design document** for it so that a game developer from another planet could re-create the game.
4. Using Inspiration or Storyvision, construct a flowchart for the game in Exercise 3.

CHAPTER 14

Writing for Mobile Media

KEY TERMS

Advanced Television Systems Committee (ATSC)	mobile media broadband	product integration
apps	mobile TV	product placement
bandwidth	mobisode™	"snackable" media
branded content	nielson	video strips
minisode	open mobile video coalition	webisode
	pre-roll ads	wiMax

The mobile device originated as a cellular phone made to connect to a new cellular wireless network and through it to the existing copper wire voice network. As all the world knows, this portable device has evolved into a multimedia, multifunction digital platform now converging with the portable computer and television. Companies are innovating and jockeying to find the business model to exploit the preferences of the public that uses cell phones and mobile media. By the time a fourth edition of this book might go to press, many uncertainties of the present moment will have become clear. But we can't wait, because the rate of change in Internet and **mobile media broadband** is accelerating as we write.

The metamorphosis of the cell phone into a multimedia mobile platform raises interesting questions about the video content that is delivered to subscribers. Are traditional linear media simply being redistributed over a new channel? Redistributing existing TV series on a mobile platform does not change the narrative style or the scriptwriting because clearly the product was already preconceived for broadcast television. Or does the design of this new mobile platform and the sociology of its users point to new formats unique to the medium? If the latter, then writers need to think about how they are going to tell stories that exploit mobile formats. We can extrapolate from early and current experiments in content for mobile media to plot the curve into the near term future. So we need to turn to examples of unique content and investigate how they modify visual narrative for mobile platforms. Are mobile platforms just another channel for delivery of existing content or a new medium with unique content that demands a new kind of writing? The nascent signs of content unique to mobile platforms suggest there is a new kind of content and therefore a new kind of writing and producing specific to mobile platforms. If the use of mobile media platforms is going to drive the demand for new and original content, content providers will turn to writers for their proven narrative skills. However, writers will have to think differently.

ANTECEDENTS

With the birth of television and its flowering post World War II, the need for content was ferocious. The lineup had to be filled. Content providers, who were the networks, basically taped the content of radio shows that were familiar—soaps, quiz shows, comedians, and variety shows. Then as the potential of the television medium became better understood, producers invented content unique to television from series to miniseries, talk shows, and most recently reality television. Going from an audio medium to a video medium is a radical shift, whereas going from one visual medium to another form of visual medium with a change in screen size and mode of access is less so. We can draw a parallel to the difference between movies and television. The size of the television screen, the viewing context in the living room, and the multiplicity of channels offered a different form of visual entertainment than movies. Initially, they were deadly rivals. Film studios forbade their contract stars to appear on television and would not allow movies to be shown on television. Movies set themselves apart by turning to color cinematography and new widescreen formats that prevail to this day and even 3-D formats (now reemerging), while television was stuck with a black-and-white image, a small screen, and the academy ratio of the 4:3 screen format. Even though television screens grew in size, and the quality of the video and audio improved and eventually became digital high definition, there was, and still is, a difference between television and movies.

Movies narrate more by means of action and setting, whereas television series resort to more dialogue often in series sets that become familiar spaces to the audience—the bar in *Cheers*, the living room in *Married with Children*, Gerry's apartment in *Seinfeld*, the couch in *Friends*, the office set in *The Office*, or the emergency room in *ER*. There is a different kind of writing and thinking that lies behind each medium. Even though films can be shown on television, seeing them on the small screen interrupted by commercials is not the same experience. By the same token, you could argue that seeing episodes of television series through mobile broadband or on a cell phone by subscription to a service provided by the carrier is not the equivalent of viewing content written and produced expressly for mobile platforms. The length, the pace, the screen size, the viewing context—all of these elements, once again, impact on the meta-writing and the kind of storytelling that engages a new sensibility in the audience. The fact is that it has already begun. A new word has been added to the lexicon. The Internet viewing experience spawned the word **webisode** to mean a segment tailor made for streaming on the web. Now we have the new term—**mobisode**™.[1] It is a short serial form of narrative uniquely adapted to the cell phone or mobile platform. So there is no question that new media formats have begun to emerge. The question is, what makes them different and how might they develop?

---

[1] The word has been registered as a trademark by Fox after the term came into use in connection with new media produced for Verizon.

Another interesting parallel that comes to mind is the change in content and readership styles that emerged with the flourishing of newspapers when compared to books. Books involve long sessions of reading that must be repeated over days and sometimes weeks to absorb the content. Newspapers, evolving from broadsheets and newsletters, accommodate short sessions of reading and are made up of multiple parallel segments of unconnected content. Newspapers are portable and fill in time while riding on a bus, train, or a plane. Likewise, cell phones are portable and serve both functional and spontaneous entertainment needs in unpredictable intervals between activities. The advent of the comic strip in the late nineteenth century as a new form of quick self-contained or serial narrative made sense in the context of the daily, expendable nature of newspaper content and the conditions under which newspapers were read. Comic strips are still going strong well more than 100 years later. Another change has occurred with the evolution of interactive editions of newspapers that are published on websites. Context and use alter the way content works. Prose narrative has become multimedia and in many ways reconceived to exploit the hyperlinks across the World Wide Web and the interactive potential of the computer through which it is delivered.

Mobile phone content could be seen as **video strips**, a video form of comic strip that is short, entertaining, and apt for the viewing device. For newspapers, successful comic strips built audiences, readership, and cult followings. The **video strip**, or **mobisode**™, or other kinds of content for mobile devices such as games keep the user on the channel and paying for data or time, and this type of content also sells other features. It might be like an electronic version of newspapers, attracting readers with the "funnies" who then go on to read other parts of the newspaper and see the ads.

Traditional prose storytelling has consisted of the short story and the novel. In the nineteenth century, authors like Dickens in Britain and Melville in America serialized novels in magazines. In recent years, something called flash fiction has emerged. It tells a story in 500 words or less. Younger generations have less time and less inclination to read. These short narratives for magazines and websites alter the dynamics of storytelling. Many have heard of the *haiku*, a Japanese 17-syllable poem that captures a fleeting but essential sentiment or perception. We see 15- and 20-second television advertising spots that are highly compressed forms of visual statement. This has evolved as a narrative form that has taught audiences to read visual messages in condensed, rapid, staccato narratives that depend on stripping editing down to the absolute bare minimum for visual comprehension. This often involves shots cut to fractions of a second, a matter of frames, accelerating the pace of visual narrative. Audiences, habituated since childhood from thousands of hours of watching television, have altered their response time, sense of visual literacy, and expectations. Watch a few older movies from the black-and-white era, and you will see the change in pace!

TECHNICAL ANTECEDENTS

My first cell phone was a monster with a separate battery pack you had to carry around that weighed a ton. It was simply a portable phone that connected to the wireless network of one of the carriers. What began as a portable, wireless apparatus designed initially to connect to a voice network has evolved over a dozen years into a multifunction device that uses the available networks in multiple ways. The cellular phone has metamorphosed into the iPhone, the Palm Pre, the Blackberry, and other phones with operating systems that enable burgeoning numbers of downloadable **apps**. The speed and complexity of this evolution flabbergasts even those business professionals who expect technological development at a rapid pace. The iPhone has probably driven this evolution because it has changed expectations of the design and functionality of a pocket-size mobile platform. This has made it the leader in sales volume and compelled other manufacturers to innovate in their design and functionality. The question now is whether the Apple propriety operating system, exclusive to its own device, will prevail over that of other cell phones whose functionality is enabled by transferable operating systems like Android and Palm Pre that will open up the **apps** that developers can write. It will be difficult to catch up with the iPhone **apps** lead. Perhaps it will be a rerun of the Apple versus PC marketing contest in which Apple led with its innovation of the graphical user interface but lost market share because the IBM PC was licensed to other enterprises to manufacture clones, which in turn brought the price down and increased the population of PC owners. When Microsoft Windows incorporated the graphical user interface in the operating system for cheaper PCs, that move eventually attracted developers to invest more time, energy, and money in more applications for PCs, which then became cheaper due to increased sales volume.

Although voice communications are still fundamental, text messaging or **texting** as it is now called, has taken on a huge importance as has the transmission of visual media, whether stills or video. Some portable digital phones already come with an FM radio chipset, which may well become standard now that the new Google phone Nexus One announced for 2010 will incorporate an FM chipset.[2] Increasing numbers of models can connect to the Internet to read and send email and browse websites. Keyboards, physical or virtual, have become more important features of cell phones. Yawn! I know all this, you say. What is fairly new at this writing is the prospect of **mobile TV**.

Let's begin with standards. There are basically five ways to access video on a mobile platform. The carrier provides a service like Verizon's VCast, to which you subscribe for its content, somewhat like you might subscribe to a premium cable channel. Several independent content producers are positioned to service the carriers. Only subscribers to the carrier's network can access this content where the carrier's signal is available. Each carrier has its own video entertainment stream.

Any device that can access the web through any carrier's network and has a browser can open the video stream of a broadcaster's website or YouTube or Hulu. However, a lot of video requires a Flash player and for this and other technical reasons will not play on every cell phone. The strength of the signal and traffic on carriers' circuits will also affect this viewing experience. There is also a question of cost to the user paying for the data stream over significant stretches of time. We'll call this the second way.

The third way is not yet fully operational. It is digital television broadcast from an antenna to any device that has the receiver for the broadcast signal built into its chipset and is within range of the transmitter. This method exists and works in a number of mobile devices for FM radio. Because all

---

[2] David Ayala, "Google's Nexus One Specs Leaked," *PC World*, December 16, 2009 (www.pcworld.com/article/184778/googles_nexus_one_specs_leaked. html). Radio executives approached the FCC in November 2009 to advocate incorporating HD FM in all cell phones for public safety (RBR-TVBR Newsletters 2009-11-11)

broadcast stations are local, mobile TV will be determined by your physical location. When you buy a television set, you don't buy a TV set that will work in Seattle as opposed to one that will work in New York; you expect it to work anywhere in the country. If you move from Seattle to New York or vice versa, you know the television set you take with you will work in the new location. Likewise, the mobile platform that has the digital TV receiver built in will work wherever you are in range of a transmitter. It will be like carrying a television set around with you except that this one fits into your pocket or perhaps on your wrist. Who has not wondered when the wristwatch video featured in the Dick Tracy comic strips of our youth will become a reality?

Open Mobile Video Coalition[3] (OMVC) is a group of some 800 stations that have been trying to establish a mobile digital television (DTV) standard enabling the "DTV Triple Play"—a multiplex of high-definition, standard-definition, and mobile DTV program streams. Until the standard was fixed, manufacturers of mobile devices could not know what chip set to put in the phone to receive the signal. The challenges are technical, legal, and content driven. Meanwhile, 11 companies have also filed patent disclosure statements with the **Advanced Television Systems Committee (ATSC)**. It raises a question about the cost for open access.[4] The ATSC, the U.S. digital TV standards body, ratified the ATSC-Mobile/Handheld (ATSC-M/H)[5] while this manuscript was in copyedit stage. This will pave the way for consumer mobile platforms such as cell phones, netbooks, and DVD players incorporating the receiver chip set to show up on retail shelves in 2010. Some 70 stations have already committed to begin mobile DTV broadcasts in 2009.[6] The DTV signal comprises not only the television content but parallel packets of information that allow device executable functions that can map location and possibly open up a wholly new form of advertising similar to Internet contextual banners and messages.

There is really a fourth way hidden in the first. Qualcomm's MediaFLO division is building its own nationwide network using the old bandwidth of UHF channel 55, which it bought at auction, to broadcast its own DTV signal. This means that phones must have the Qualcomm receiver chip built in to the device to receive its network signal, and that requires a relationship with a carrier and its locked phones. Both AT&T and Verizon have a relationship with this company to bring video content to their subscribers.[7] Qualcomm is making a huge bet that this network based on its chip set will be superior to broadcast and superior to streaming websites through a phone's Internet connection. The carrier benefits by not having the video stream occupy huge chunks of its bandwidth. However, MediaFLO doesn't have the local content. There is a loose parallel between this and satellite radio, which is a uniform national signal but does not have any of the local content that terrestrial radio stations have and that television stations do in each market. This changes the way advertising can work and changes the business model. Producers like GoTV Networks provide original content and

---

[3] See http://open-mobile.org.

[4] I am indebted to John Hane of the law firm Pillsbury Winthrop Shaw Pittman LLP, Washington, D.C., for making this point in his presentation on the panel at NAB 2009 on April 22: *Finding the Distribution Model for Mobile Television: The Decidedly Unsexy Legal Issues We Would All Prefer to Ignore.*

[5] Glen Dickson, *Broadcasting & Cable,* July 6, 2009.

[6] *Broadcasting & Cable* (July 22, 2009): "DTV enables us to reach millions of more people with higher picture quality and more programming choices," said Brandon Burgess, ION media networks chairman and CEO, in a statement. "Also, mobile television will allow viewers to access broadcaster's content anytime, anywhere. The entertainment, educational, and business benefits of the nation's switch to digital television are vast."

[7] See MocoNewsNet, Jan 8, 2009.

programming to carriers that want to add value to the range of content accessible on their network. Their servers are accessed through the carrier network and programming is managed at their end. They can manage and program the content in real-time response to user demand.

The fifth way involves the manufacturers of mobile devices like Ericcson, Nokia, and Motorola building into their product a capability to receive a dedicated video stream. Even though the device must use a carrier's network to do so, the access to the content now becomes device specific. Motorola has contracted with Blockbuster to stream movies to new feature-rich cell phones. The difference between this and the fourth way described earlier rests on exclusivity tied to the hardware. The fourth way is more like a cable channel that may or may not be in the bundle your cable provider offers, or at least be part of a premium package that increases your subscription cost. Christy Wyatt, vice president of software platforms at Motorola, said, "Mobile video entertainment is exploding, as consumers are demanding the widest selection of content: the movies they love in their living room and on their PC, now also available on their mobile phone, while on the go."[8] Ericsson has a contract with Sprint to manage its network. Its new CEO Hans Vestberg sees mobile broadband becoming predominant in the future as the number of mobile broadband subscribers grows (an 84 percent increase in 2008) with unpredictable implications for the shape of mobile media and what business model will work.[9]

This initiative by mobile device manufacturers to make money from content, not just from making the mobile platforms, begs a question. Which service, which channel, or which form of access to entertainment content will the public prefer? The business model for radio and television, and cable for that matter, is well understood. Not so for mobile media! Revenue can accrue to the provider either by subscription, somewhat like cable, or by selling ads around content or in preroll while providing the content free. The business model is in interactive relationship to the behavior of its users and subscribers. What do they want? What are they willing to pay for? And how do they use their mobile devices? Is the revenue in the network provider's data stream or in the content provider, and what is their relationship?

VIDEO AND CELL PHONE USE

The question of what will shape cell phone content and hence the question of how content and the writing for that content may differ from traditional media rests on understanding some technological issues and sociological issues of user behavior. To plot the curve into the future, we need to understand the demographic of users and more particularly how this demographic uses these ever-more-versatile mobile platforms. *The Boston Globe* reported that landline phones are being replaced by cell phones: "18 percent in cell-only households compares with 16 percent in the second half of 2007,

---

[8] See article by Marin Perez, *Information Week*, accessed Aug. 18, 2009, www.informationweek.com/story/showArticle.jhtml?articleID=219400486.

[9] The incoming CEO of Ericsson, Hans Vestberg was quoted in a *New York Times* report as seeing hope for growth in the rise of the mobile Internet: "I definitely see mobile broadband overtaking fixed broadband in a few years." *New York Times*, July 25 2009.

and just 7 percent in the first half of 2005. Leading the way are households made up of unrelated adults, such as roommates or unmarried couples. Sixty-three percent of such households only have cellphones. About one-third of renters and about the same number of people under age 30 live in homes with only cells. About a quarter of low-income people also have [sic] only wireless phones, nearly double the proportion of higher-earning people."[10]

Clearly, a change in viewing habits and behavior derives from new options furnished by the mobile platform. Data gathered by media tracking organizations suggests certain changes. The *Wall Street Journal*[11] reported some key facts gathered by Nielson that even though traditional linear television is still the most popular means for viewing video content, habits are in transition.

The number of users and the time spent watching each of the media screens rose. The number of viewers watching video on mobile devices increased the most. In the fourth quarter of 2008, some 11 million people viewed content on mobile media. Larger numbers viewed DVR programming and Internet video viewing increased.

The *Nielson* data show that the average length of viewing on a mobile phone is longer than for watching on the Internet. In the first three months of 2009, according to Nielson, about 13 million people watched video on their cell phones, about 6 percent of all mobile subscribers—a 50 percent increase over the year before.[12] This is confirmed by Transpera, the largest mobile video ad-network in the

Monthly users and time spent on selected media platforms

	User, in millions		Average minutes	
	4Q'08	4Q'07	4Q'08	4Q'07
Watching TV in the home	285.3	281.4	151:03	145:49
Watching Timeshifted TV	73.9	53.9	7:11	5:24
Using the Internet	161.5	156.3	27:04	26:08
Watching Video on Internet	123.2	n/a	2:53	n/a
Using a Mobile Phone	228.9	n/a		
Mobile Subscribers Watching Video on a Mobile Phone	11.2	n/a	3:42	n/a

Note: For people 2 and over except mobile users which are for ages 13 and over
Source: The Nielsen Company

FIGURE 14.1

---

[10] December 18, 2008.

[11] February 23, 2009.

[12] *LA Times*, June 9, 2009, www.latimes.com/business/la-fi-mobiletv9-2009jun09,0,6821495.story. These figures will date quickly.

United States, which anticipates increased ad revenue with increasing audience numbers.[13] Forbes.com reports that the U.S. mobile TV broadcasting market, subscription based and advertising funded, was estimated at $200 million in 2008. It is expected to jump 50 percent in 2009. Advertising across all mobile platforms, including mobile display and short messaging, grew 35 percent to $648 million in 2008.[14] All these data are telling us that there is a growing audience of mobile phone users and a growing revenue stream even if the exact business model is yet to be defined. A parallel trend in the period 2008/2009 has been the decline in television viewing and advertising revenue and the gain in web-based audiences and revenue.

At the National Association of Broadcasters convention on April 22, 2009, at the Mobile Entertainment Summit on a panel organized to discuss "Mobile, TV and Online: Successful Cross-Platform Strategies," Glenn Reitmeier, vice president of technology standards policy and strategy at NBC Universal and chair of the **Advanced Television Systems Committee** overseeing the mobile DTV standard, said that broadcasters have every reason to work with mobile operators because wireless is critical to the industry's future. The industry is trying to figure out what the mobile TV business really is. The video entertainment market has become fractured and thus affected advertising revenues. Most commentators in the industry seem to agree the future is going to be determined by an audience that will want to watch anything they choose on a platform of their choice and at a time of their choosing. The ability to deliver on-demand content to mobile viewers has to be incorporated into broadcasting.[15] Panelists posed the question we want to ask, namely, what is going to be the "nature of that content (long form versus short form)" and how is it going to be "delivered (streaming versus downloading)." Carriers and broadcasters are trying to figure out how to get as much content to users on screens of varying sizes. Payment models could include free over-the-air, subscription-based, and pay-as-you-go services. Reitmeier thought it unwise to project a business model onto a device and to expect several business models to evolve.[16]

The business model will succeed or fail with the assent of the mobile user public. QuickPlay Media, a Toronto-based provider of mobile TV and video services, surveyed 1000 mobile users between the ages of 18 and 25 and found that the primary reason the respondents have shunned mobile TV is the perceived cost; 51 percent said they would be willing to accept advertising if they got to watch for free.

---

[13] "If the numbers keep rising, so will the ad dollars—or at least that's the hope of television networks, which have been mourning their own loss: $1.5 billion in ad revenue in the first quarter of 2009, a drop of nearly 11% from $12 billion at the same time last year, says the Television Bureau of Advertising." (Forbes.com, accessed on July 14, 2009). "Advertisers, including Ford and Microsoft, are buying spots within mobile network content because it helps them reach younger audiences, says Frank Barbieri, chairman and CEO of San Francisco–based Transpera. Other brands prefer it because the phone is captivating and free of clutter. Screens are too small to have multiple ads on one page and mobile viewers can only activate one Internet page or iPhone application at a time." (Forbes.com, accessed July 14, 2009).

[14] Source: Strategy Analytics, quoted on Forbes.com.

[15] Mobile Entertainment Summit, Session S219/220 General Session: Mobile TV, TV and Online: Successful Cross-Platform Strategies. Participants: Glenn Reitmeier, VP, Technology, Chairman, Advanced Television Systems Committee, NBC-Universal; Arnaud Robert, VP Emerging Technology Strategy, Walt Disney Co.; Nandhu Nandhakumar, Sr. VP LG Electronics; John Zehr, Sr. VP Digital Media Productions, ESPN Digital Media; Nash Parker, Director, Emerging Technology & Media, Alcatel-Lucent; Moderator, Michael Stroud CEO, iHollywoodforum. See http://link.brightcove.com/services/player/bcpid1138353221?bclid=1149463430&bctid=1184468252. Glenn Reimeier kindly agreed to a telephone interview to discuss these issues on August 26, 2009.

[16] See the article by Glenn Dickson covering the NAB panel in *Broadcasting & Cable* (4/15/2009).

The survey also revealed that "a quarter of mobile TV users say they watch between daily activities, 16 percent while in transit (on a bus, for instance) and 11 percent while waiting in line."[17]

The mobile phone is portable, personal, and aggregates numerous functions such as voice communications, text messaging, calendars, alarms, still and video image capture, music, and (for cell phones with an operating system) hundreds of potential killer **apps** that facilitate life in a multitasking world such as conference calling and geopositioning. It could be that the immediate accessibility of the mobile phone will make it the viewing platform of choice. iPhones lead the way for devices that can download and store content, which means that the cell phone, if we should still call it that, can increasingly function as an offline viewer and as portable storage for media that can then be played back through laptops, desktops, and even television with USB inputs. So cellular phones now become satellites of our mothership platforms that duplicate functionality and furnish greater speed, power, and more **apps**. Will the cell phone be a storage device to carry content to plug into a larger screen for viewing, or will it be the viewing device itself? Although I crave the cinematic experience of the projected image, a whole new generation that cannot live without mobile phones doesn't really care that much. Convenience, accessibility, and personalized viewing drive the next generation. We hear the term **"snackable" media** as denoting dispensable, instantly gratifying media content that is not just scaled down but maybe different in style and flavor. Technical quality and the size of the image may be less important than the program content and the fact that it is controllable and on demand. Most mobile phone users whip out the phone when they have downtime or nothing special to do, or even while they are otherwise occupied (for instance, in my classes). If the average viewing time is about 3½ minutes (see Nielson data above), it might be a clue as to the kind of content that will succeed on mobile platforms.

Historically, the idea of unique content for mobile platforms is relatively old. In fact, it predates the previous edition of this book, which gives pause for thought. Media technology often develops under the radar, and innovation is of necessity not mainstream but the province of early adopters. Fox Mobile Entertainment, a new division of News Corp., was commissioned to produce a new media serial for cell phone distribution by Verizon, which shared it subsequently with European Vodaphone, the world's largest cellular phone carrier, to develop content for the 3G launch of Vodaphone's services.[18] The producer working for Twentieth Television and running the Foxlab at the time, Daniel Tibbets, was instrumental in putting together the first **"mobisode™,"** a term that Fox then registered as a trademark.[19] Several such series were made before the Fox unit was closed down. The idea was probably ahead of its time and the technology in 2004/2005. Since then, **bandwidth** has increased, phone screens have become larger and switchable between portrait and landscape format according

---

[17] TVNEWSDAY, Mar 13, 2009.

[18] See http://en.wikipedia.org/wiki/Mobisode: "Lucy Hood, then head of FME, conceived the idea of a short video series produced by Daniel Tibbets which then FME SVP Mitch Feinman coined a Mobisode™ Series and trademarked for News Corp." The word came into popularity as Vodafone, its US partner Verizon and FME launched several Mobisode™ Series.... around the world in nearly 30 countries and 7 languages. Over the next few years several other Mobisode™ series launched including some original ones produced by Daniel Tibbets of FoxLab Inc., a division of 20th Television's syndication arm, which shut down shortly thereafter." The Wikipedia entry is inaccurate. By email exchange with Daniel Tibbetts and Paul Palmieri, I have established that Verizon was indeed the first carrier/company to commission an original mobile series.

[19] See http://en.wikipedia.org/wiki/Daniel_Tibbets.

to the function desired with touch screen controls. Above all, battery life and efficiency have improved so that watching TV or video on a mobile phone is manageable. Fourth-generation(4G) networks already launched by Verizon, with other carriers close behind, offer speeds 5 to 10 times faster than 3G.[20] A competing network technology called **WiMax** promises similar speeds that, whatever the technology, could challenge DSL and cable broadband, while alternate parallel networks like Qualcomm's Media Flo provide a mobile TV service of licensed, *content* from broadcast and cable channels. On March 1, 2007, Verizon launched VCAST TV incorporating the MediaFLO-specific technology, which, as noted earlier, is a separate signal that does not take up **bandwidth** on the voice and data networks. AT&T Mobility launched its MediaFLO service on May 4, 2008. Video and TV content on cell phones is here to stay and will grow its audience and hence its advertising and revenue.

Since this is a book about writing rather than technology or marketing, our interest must be in the content and in the writing behind that content. More particularly, our interest must be in innovative writing specific to mobile platforms. Redistributing existing TV series on a mobile platform does not change the narrative style and scriptwriting, because clearly the product was already preconceived for broadcast television. So we need to turn to the unique content and investigate how it modifies visual narrative for mobile platforms. If the use of mobile media platforms is going to drive the demand for new and original content, content providers will turn to writers for their proven narrative skills. However, writers will have to think differently.

WEBISODES

Before **mobisodes**™, there were **webisodes**. Whereas "**mobisode**™" is trade marked, "**webisode**" is in the public domain and has been included as a new word in the latest edition of *Merriam-Webster's Collegiate Dictionary*. As the name implies, webisodes were a new form of video content consisting of short serial episodes found on websites of successful television shows such as *Battlestar Galactica*. They are often preceded by **pre-roll ads**. In some ways, they could be seen as satellites to the network series or trailers to promote the full-length series on cable or network television. The website for *The Office* offers webisodes and full-length episodes. However, certain webisodes exist in their own right, not as offshoots of conventional series. They take existing characters and add story not found in the broadcast version but scaled down in length and free of the three-act structure of the main series. Webisodes are not like outtakes that adorn DVDs where you get to see what the director and editor painstakingly removed from the final version. They are more like footnotes or excursions into tangential story matter that would interrupt the flow of a conventional television episode. There is another form of **webisode** to complicate matters, which is freestanding serial narrative that exists only on a website.

The Spot or thespot.com pioneered serialized fiction on a website, which ran from 1995 to 1997, and also pioneered a business model that included paid advertising banners and product placement in the interactive journals that characters wrote to engage the audience and get them to participate in the story by posting advice to characters on bulletin boards and emailing ideas. The "Spot" was a beach house in Santa Monica, California, that rented out rooms to cool 20-somethings. It flourished,

---

[20] Hiawatha Bray, *The Boston Globe*, August 13, 2009.

attracted investment and then failed as a commercial venture. It was briefly revived by two of its producers in 2004 with an exclusive wireless connection to Sprint, but it has not survived.[21] Thus, we find the first instance of a **webisode** migrating to mobile media.

Something to Be Desired, about a group of young people working as deejays in a Pittsburgh radio station, originated in 2003 as a dedicated entertainment website rather than a satellite of a network series. It is still going and represents a form of pure web-based serial narrative with episodes of 5 to 6 minutes duration. It shoots in real locations and has an ensemble cast. Its audience demographic must be roughly equivalent to the demographic of its characters. The website has interactive features that allow voting and rating of episodes and audience comments as well as a forum (www.somethingtobedesired.com).

The Strand (www.strandvenice.com/), set in Venice, California, is another web original brought to life in 2005 by one of the creators of *The Blair Witch Project* (1999), whose success was very much due to the brilliant and pioneering viral marketing through its website. This **webisode** mingles actors and real characters and exploits an improvisational style. The audience cannot interact directly with the storyline but can explore background blogs and anecdotal details of production.[22]

Bigger players are getting involved in the format with bigger budgets. Michael Eisner has produced *Prom Queen* with 90-second minisodes and a production cost of $3000 per segment.[23] It achieved an audience of 15 million, which led to a sequel, *Prom Queen: Summer Heat*. Let us note that the production costs are fractions of the cost of broadcast television. This is going to have implications for the kind of writing you can do. In chapter 1, we pointed out the production consequences that can arise from a few words on the script page. The concept has to be clean and simple and must allow some kind of narrative shorthand. **Webisodes** are often launched on social networks like MySpace and YouTube. Mainstream Hollywood producers Marshall Herskovitz and Ed Zwick's *Quarterlife* premiered on MySpace. It was then picked up by NBC.[24] The consensus seems to be that this is a new media frontier, and nobody is certain how to monetize the **webisode**. The audience demographic is adolescents to young adults who have adopted social networks, send video over cell phones, and snack on media tidbits grabbed on the fly. It is viral and unpredictable. The **webisode** offers an alternative experience to traditional television. It innovates on-demand viewing, interactivity, and personal viewing—on a laptop or computer monitor rather than a living room TV. It is not interrupted by ads like traditional television. It is free of constraints imposed on broadcasters licensed by the Federal Communications Commission to use public airwaves. The innovative style, format, and content are noticeably different than network TV driven by ratings and hunger for advertising dollars tied to the size of audiences, which ultimately limits the kind of writing and subject matter that the viewer will see. The **webisode** invites unconventional writing and storylines that push the envelope of the medium. It is still going and will now be accessible to mobile platforms that can access the web. It is also migrating to mobile media and becoming part of the media mix available through cell phone carriers and mobile broadband.

---

[21] See http://en.wikipedia.org/wiki/The_Spot.

[22] Carolyn Handler Miller, *Digital Storytelling,* 2nd Edition (Focal Press, 2008), pp. 261–2.

[23] Marisa Guthrie, *Broadcasting & Cable,* 11/24/2007.

[24] Ibid.

THE MOBISODE™

What's different? The abbreviated length and style of the **webisode** is transposed to a new network. The name **"webisode"** has embedded in it the association with the web, whereas the **"mobisode™"** suggests the new network and is a trademarked piece of terminology. In both, the writer is faced with extreme compression of storytelling techniques. However, the **modisode™** compresses narrative into a shorter and more elliptical style. Dialogue takes screen time. Visual narration becomes key. Think back to the dialogue balloons of comic strips and their relation to picture. There is a movement toward downsizing and compression. As life speeds up, there is less time to watch and to read. The comic strip really invented the EXTREME CLOSE UP and established key frame narration as a way to tell a story. In mobile media minisodes (to coin another phrase), it is almost as if the key frame of a storyboard becomes the program. The storyboard is, after all, a kind of comic strip of a full-motion linear narrative. Whereas the writing formats for games and interactive media are almost impossible to tie down, the script format for mobile media follows the linear media script for film and television. Do they differ in the meta-writing or conception that responds to the new qualities of this new medium? That is the question. To answer it, let us turn to a pioneering **mobisode™**.

Daniel Tibbets produced *Love and Hate* and *Sunset Hotel*, which were the original **mobisodes™** for Fox Mobile entertainment. *Love and Hate* and, later, the existing series 24 were re-edited for mobile streaming, but *Sunset Hotel* was scripted specifically as mobile content by Jana Veverka. Daniel Tibbets was quite clear at the time that cell phones invited a new kind of narrative content. Since then he has continued to develop unique mobile content as Executive Vice President and Studio Chief of GoTVNetworks.[25] Likewise, Jana Veverka was keenly aware that they were engaged in a new form of short narrative episode that had to tell a serial story in short episodes of 1 to 2 minutes for cell phone viewers.[26]

Sunset Hotel consists of a storyline centered in a Los Angeles hotel. This recalls the California settings of *The Strand* and *Something to Be Desired*. The characters are straight out of film noir and crime/suspense genres with good guys and bad guys and an alienated demi-monde femme fatale. Genre provides an immediate frame of reference and a way for audiences to recognize characters and situations. It is probably fair to say that this mobile series does not resonate with any profound philosophy or solve any existential problems. The bad guy is Peter, the womanizing, manipulative manager/owner and pimp. We discover this world through Jack, the new bartender. Bianca is a sexy call girl who has a working relationship with Peter and a suite at the hotel. There is a maid, Robin, who makes up the rooms and her friend, Charlie, whose picture-taking cell phone is a key prop and plot device that exposes the culprit of the murder of a client staying in the hotel. Jack is attracted to Bianca, who falls in love with him. Jack's sister, Emily, comes to visit him, and Peter uses her as a courier. The dialogue is mostly stylish and smart with comeback repartees and put-downs. While Peter is a classic domineering villain, Bianca is an unconventional free spirit who challenges Jack. Jack cannot deal with Bianca's chosen profession as call girl until his baby sister gives him a lesson on love. In the end, Charlie saves Bianca from being set up by Peter. Emily's relative purity and innocence are preserved, and Jack nearly misses out on Bianca because of his conventional scruples about returning love from a call girl. This is

---

[25] Based on a telephone interview and email communication in July 2009.
[26] Based on telephone interviews July/August 2009.

probably the most interesting part. What is characteristic of the writing and the storyline is its curt style and unresolved story issues. The premise is the story in the sense that we do not need complete third act resolution. Jack gets a one-way telephone message in the last episode of Bianca's address. The use of cell phone ring tones makes the content use the medium it's on to good effect. The **mobisodes**™ are like snapshots of a fictional world that seems familiar because of film noir and other suspense films.

Let's take the episode in which Emily comments on Jack's relationship with Bianca before she goes home:

"REALITY"

EXT. GARDENS BY BRIDGE - DAY

JACK says goodbye to EMILY.

>   EMILY
>
> You're staying because of Bianca.
>
> Aren't you.
>
>   JACK
>
> I'm not sure.
>
>   EMILY
>
> What's your problem?
>
>   JACK
>
>   (incredulous)
>
> My problem? I don't have a problem,
> she does.
>
>   EMILY
>
> You're such a guy. So damn
> territorial. How many girls you
> slept with, Jack?
>
>   JACK
>
> That's none of your business.
>
>   EMILY
>
> Exactly! Bet she never asked you.
>
> Because it doesn't matter to her.
>
>   JACK
>
> I never paid for sex.

EMILY

Everybody pays, Jack. One way or the
other. The point is, why can't you
accept her for who she is. Not what
she is.

JACK

How am I supposed to get over that?

EMILY

I don't know what she sees in you
anyway.

JACK

Thanks. I needed that.

In effect, a scene becomes an episode. So the scene is like the key frame of a comic strip or a story-board. If it is going to work in 1-minute **mobisodes**™, playing of genre helps, but conventional television writing has to be stripped down to essentials. Now the plot question has to resolve.

EMILY

Oh, stop. You love her. She loves you.
What else matters, Jack. How many
times have you told me that?

JACK

Never!

EMILY

Yeah, but you will someday!

EXT. TERRACE/BIANCA'S SUITE - DAY 2

BIANCA stands at the edge looking down.

BIANCA'S POV

Jack and Emily in the gardens.

RESUME SCENE

PETER (O.S.)

Back to business as usual.

Peter stands next to her looking down. Her phone RINGS. Her special "Client Ring." She doesn't move.

                    PETER

          Aren't you going to get that?

                    BIANCA

          In time.

                    PETER

          The police found your scarf in
          Tommy's room.

               (off her look)

          I've forgotten who it belongs to.

Her phone rings again.

                    PETER

          Our regulars are back.

He walks to the door.

                    PETER

          So are you. Time's up.

               FADE TO BLACK.

At this point we have to resolve whether Jack will have the courage of his love and whether Bianca will break her business arrangement with Peter.

Each episode is set up with a tag line, a boiled-down quintessence of the **mobisode™**, which is itself almost like a trailer for a bigger story. The storyline is like a series of pods or seeds that grow in the audience's imagination. In *Sunset Hotel*, each episode is stitched together with a voice-over narrative somewhat like the nondialogue narrative of comic strips. The voice-over, which is not in the original script, provides a string to thread through the beads of the episodes. In the final cut, the voice-over of Jack reveals some interior dialogue. *Sunset Hotel* as shot and edited is perhaps shorter than the script. The shooting style evolves from television shooting, which relies on close ups and two-shots, but with an even tighter, more elliptical style.[27] The scenes are shot like key frames of a storyboard and tell the story through staccato scenes with minimal dialogue and a voice-over link. Body language in close-up becomes more critical in **mobisodes™**. Cutting style changes—jump cuts compress action. We have learned to read short cuts from the narrative compression of so many TV ads, which also influences the narrative style, shooting, and editing techniques.

---

[27] In a phone interview with the director, Joe Rassulo explained he shot 26 1-minute episodes in four days. He confirmed the idea of a compressed staccato style of narrative derived from film noir and the comic strip.

One way to understand this new format is to realize that even though television episodes and even movies can be downloaded to cell phones or viewed on cell phones, the kind of content developed specifically for the cell phone format would never really work on television because our viewing expectations differ in the living room. GoTV Networks has developed other content, which you can sample on its website.[28] Segments are 2.5 to 4 minutes in length. Some of the content involves **branded entertainment** centered around strong **product integration** for corporate sponsors such as Tide for the hilarious mobile sitcom *Crescent Heights*. It is really the old soap opera model from radio.

It is interesting that this idea has been expanded in recent TV spots created from *Desperate Housewives* for Sprint, in which the carrier's Palm Pre figures in the interaction of the characters and then becomes incorporated in the on air script later so that there is seamless connection between the advertisement and the content.[29] **Product integration** is the new commercialism of the mobile media age. It began in feature film production as a way of selling opportunities for companies to expose their products when necessary props had to be in shot. The art director or Property master could arbitrarily or accidentally choose one brand over another of a car, a soft drink, or other commonly used product. Or producers could mine the script for props that could be sold as **product placement** opportunities and defray the cost of production.

The next step that has emerged in the context of the unstructured, undefined, and shifting business models of the mobile media worlds is **branded entertainment**. This involves more than **product placement**. **Branded entertainment** allows advertisers to have products written into the storyline and even fabricate story moments that walk a fine line between a detour to feature a product and a product that happens to be a logical part of the story. This blending requires skillful writing and is going to be part of the **webisode** writer's almanac. The advertiser then underwrites the production cost, somewhat similar to the old soap opera model and sponsored TV show. A defining characteristic of **minisodes** is their length and hence their production cost. A 1-minute **minisode** is not that much longer than a TV commercial spot. Moreover, the spots are an intrusion that the audience can reject or screen out either by means of technology or by simply leaving the screen to get a snack or go to the bathroom. **Branded content** makes the message unavoidable for any audience that is absorbed in the story.

Comedy is comedy in any format because it is funny. The quick comic sketches of *Crescent Heights* use well-understood comic devices but with a refreshing structural efficiency. The setting is an apartment complex with a typical laundry room that becomes the venue for several episodes and numerous encounters. Because Tide is the series sponsor, laundry themes are frequent. Here is an episode that exploits the comic hero as victim. Our hero has a temp job that terminates in disaster on the first day—in fact, morning, to be more accurate. While in the laundry room, Will tells it as a flashback to his roommate Eddie, from whom he borrowed a white shirt that he has ruined. A dragon office lady tells him that he must have coffee on his boss's desk by 8:45 or face a ballistic rage and termination.

---

[28] See www.gotvnetworks.com.
[29] Brian Steinberg,"Sprint Teams with Producers to Integrate Campaign with Hit Show" *Advertising Age*, September 28, 2009.

In minisodes, we skip dialogue and once the comic problem is set up we go straight to the sequence of physical comedy that ends with our hero knocking himself out in the kitchenette while trying to make the coffee. We see him on a stretcher, and then we understand why he is talking to his roommate with a bandage round his head. In mobile serials, we have to strip the action to its essence and allow the audience to fill in. It is not that this doesn't happen in regular television or even movies; in mobile media, it drives the **mobisode™**. In a feature film, we see someone hail a taxi in the street. Maybe we let the character get in the cab. We cut to the character at his destination. We don't want to watch a cab ride. It is a form of elision that shortens the action and relies on the audience's powers of deduction to fill in what happened that is not shown on screen. Audiences like contributing their imaginations to interpret the story. In **minisodes**, the action is constantly stripped down to its bare minimum, in this case a slapstick disaster. The character Will goes to the coffee machine. He sees no filters. So he looks at the empty paper towel dispenser in frustration then seizes on toilet paper to make a coffee filter. He searches the cabinets for coffee. He finds a packet of coffee. In tearing it open, he spills the contents on the floor. Cut to Will scooping coffee off the floor and sticking it in the machine. Enter the dragon to drop the line: "I hope you didn't add water. It's connected." She exits.

INT. OFFICE CUBICLE - MORNING

Will sits at his desk and unloads a box of his personal items. He places a framed photo on the desk along with a miniature hula girl figurine.

CAROL, 40's, annoyingly cheerful, suddenly pops into Will's cubicle. Surprised, Will jumps back.

> CAROL
> Good morning, I'm Carol. You must be
> Mr. Eubanks's new temp.

> WILL
> Yeah, I'm Will.

Carol looks at the desk and sees all of Will's personal items.

> CAROL
> I see you brought a few knickknacks
> with you. Personalizing your area on
> the first day. Quite a bold move, temp.

> WILL
> Well, I was kind of hoping that maybe
> this will turn into a full time
> position.

> CAROL
> I wouldn't count on it cubicle
> squatter, because while you were
> "unpacking", precious time was
> slipping away.

                    WILL
          What do you mean?

Carol gets in Will's face - she's uncomfortably close. She looks around making sure that her next words will be private.

                    CAROL
               (intense)
          If Mr. Eubanks's coffee is not on
          his desk when he walks in at 8:45,
          he'll go B - A - double L - istic!

                    WILL
          B-A- double L - istic?

                    CAROL
          Ballistic! Tick-tock, you've only
          got five minutes until Mr. Eubanks
          gets here. And if he blows, you goes.

Carol suddenly makes an EXPLOSION sound which startles Will. She quickly composes herself and breezes away. Will is a bit shaken.

                    WILL
          What's the big deal, it's just coffee?

Carol pops up again, surprising Will - he jumps out of his seat.

                    CAROL
          Remember...

Carol makes another EXPLOSION sound.

                    CAROL (CONT'D)
               (cheerful)

               Have a nice day!

Carol disappears. Will looks up at the clock - it reads 8:41 a.m.. He bolts from his desk.

We then get the physical comedy, which is much more compressed and faster than the script might suggest (see the website).

Will looks at the empty coffee filter basket. He shrugs.

                    WILL (CONT"D)
          It is paper.

Will pulls off a few sheets of toilet paper and lines the coffee filter basket.

> WILL (CONT'D)
> Now for the coffee grounds.

He grabs the last bag of coffee grounds. Will struggles to open it but cannot.

He looks up, it's 8:44. More sweat builds on his brow.

Will wrestles frantically with the bag of coffee grounds. Then with huge GROAN, will pulls on the bag with all of his might.

The bag explodes - covering Will and the rest of the kitchen in a thick layer of coffee grounds.

Will looks up and sees a large photo on the wall of Carol with the words, "Employee of the Month". It looks like she is leering down at him.

> WILL (CONT'D)
> Oh no.

Will quickly sweeps the grounds off the floor with his hands and dumps them into the basket. He shakes the remainder of the coffee grounds off of his shirt and into the basket as well. Then he slides the basket back into the machine.

Will grabs the coffee pot and fills it with water. He pours the water into the machine and hits BREW. Proud, will steps back and watches the coffee fill the pot.

Suddenly, Carol enters the kitchen, opens the fridge and grabs a yogurt.

> CAROL
> I hope you didn't add water because it's already connected to the tap.

Carol takes a bite of her yogurt.

> CAROL (CONT'D)
> Mmmm, peaches and cream. Yummy!

Carol breezes out of the kitchen.

Will turns to the machine, slips on the coffee grounds on the floor, then bangs his head and knocks himself out. Cut to exiting the building on a rolling gurney with all his office knick-knacks around him. A single scene implies the outcome of the previous scene and implies the missing scene of the emergency room. Time is also a character. Will is racing against the clock—a classic comic device. (See the website.)

Being Bailey is a teen drama for a key demographic distributed on AT&T, Sprint, and alltel that works like a kind of video diary of Bailey and her two best friends who are starting high school.[30] Information net-casting or mobile information content and even documentary are part of the mix. *Imaginings,* sponsored by Lexus through Saatchi and Saatchi, exploits the high-definition *slo-mo* action shot at 1000 frames per second. It is a gallery of the poetry of motion to be found in the movement of athletes and animals. It reminds one of the early silent movie days of the mutoscope and the kinetoscope, which offered short clips without storylines to be viewed for sensation. You watch the clips of *Imaginings* for pure visual sensation and, in this age, for its hi-tech multicam montage of extreme observation. This kind of content and the rest of the documentary coverage of music, news, and other events do not need narrative scripting.

The **Writers Guild of America** has recognized these new formats and that creative script writing is involved: "New Media includes all writing for the Internet and mobile devices as well as any new devices using these technologies as they evolve, or any other platform thought of as 'new media' by the industry as of the start of the 2008 MBA, which was February 13, 2008."[31] A scale of minimum fees has been negotiated that binds the Alliance of Motion Picture and Television Producers, which refers to programs up to 2 minutes in length as sort of standard units, clearly recognizing the kind of **minisode** for mobile platforms that we have discussed in this chapter. [32]

WRITING DOS AND DON'TS

How must writing change for the new market of mobile media scripts? Clearly, characters have to become easily recognizable. Genre will probably help, but that can mean capturing comic strip conventions of compressed narrative that leave intervening frames and action to the imagination. Shorter length means shorter dialogue because speech takes screen time. In this respect, movie dialogue might be the model. When dialogue plays, it must be hip, short, and to the point. Action trumps dialogue. Stories built around a product are going to sell to sponsors. The style must be contemporary and reach a primarily younger demographic below the age of 30. Single location settings will match the limited production budgets.

CONCLUSION

Enough evidence exists to warrant the prediction that new streams of video content can be delivered to mobile devices in a number of ways. Although a dominant technology of transmission and reception

---

[30] See gotvnetworks.com.

[31] See www.wga.org/content/default.aspx?id=1116.

[32] See www.wga.org/contract_07/NewMediaSideletter.pdf. "A *New Media Program* is deemed original and covered by the WGA Minimum Basic Agreement ("MBA") if it is produced by a signatory company ("Company") for the Internet, a mobile device, or any other platform thought of as "new media" by the industry, and meets either of the following tests: First, the program is covered if the Company employs or purchases literary material from a "professional writer" as that term is defined in the MBA.1 Second, the program is covered if the actual cost of production exceeds any one of the following limits, even if the writer is not a professional writer: • *$15,000 per minute of program material as* between the writer and the Company.*exhibited; or* • *$300,000 per single production as exhibited; or* • *$500,000 per series of programs produced for a single order.* When a New Media Program meets one of the above criteria, the WGA has jurisdiction over it. Under WGA jurisdiction, certain terms of the MBA automatically apply, while other terms remain freely negotiable."

has not emerged, the arrow points to growth and development of smart phones and mobile operating systems that allow more sophisticated entertainment options. As more eyeballs turn to mobile devices, carriers, broadcasters, and content providers search for the business model that will monetize the potential. Many consider this to be a new media marketplace, even a new media industry even though it is in part an offshoot of existing media. You could argue that the portable wireless platform and its adoption as a personal mobile entertainment device is a kind of genetic mutation of media into a new species. There are signs that although recognizable brand entertainment of movies and TV shows are the bait to attract early adopters, a mass audience will follow.

We can identify a number of innovative forms of program content that are specific to the medium and beg the question of how you invent narrative and write scripts specifically for mobile media production. Although a limited amount of original work is produced for mobile and Internet formats, talent agencies and producers are waking up to the potential of this content and the discovery of new voices.[33] Once again, where there is demand for content, there has to be demand for writers who know how to create content and tell stories. We may well find new formats and new narrative styles evolving to meet the unique viewing habits of a generation brought up on a new kind web and mobile media. Historical parallels and antecedents support the likelihood of content evolving to exploit and fulfill the new potential of a mobile viewing experience with miniformats.

Exercises

1. Look on your cell phone for content that is original video, not retransmitted content from another medium.
2. Write a 2- to 4-minute story.
3. Based on your review of Chapter 8, write a premise for a cell phone series that will break down into 2- to 3-minute episodes and write a scene outline.
4. Write a 1-minute video strip.
5. Storyboard an extreme moment in sports or wildlife for a cell phone video interval.

---

[33] iHollyfoodforum.com at a Mobile Entertainment Summit in March 2009 has interviews with two major agency department heads who are specifically targeting mobile and web-based authors and content.

Anticipating Professional Issues

Writers hope that there will be an audience for what they write and that they can get paid for their writing. To come full circle, we should remember the opening chapter of the book in which we made the point that scripts are blueprints, instructions to a production team, and that audiences don't generally read scripts. Although writing may begin as a purely creative act, at some point the question arises: What is the value of this writing? If writing is a professional skill, then how much is it worth? What is someone paying you for? What are your obligations? Can you support yourself by writing for one or other of the visual media?

The answers to these questions can vary according to the market sector in which you choose to practice your craft. Broadly, the writing market divides between the entertainment world, the nonprofit world, and the corporate world. The first is perhaps more glamorous, more competitive, and more highly paid but is also a great deal riskier than the second and third, which is less familiar to most would-be writers. In any of these worlds, the overwhelming majority of writers is freelance.

The essential transaction between a writer and any media enterprise involves a transfer of ownership or an assignment of copyright. This is governed by the law of the country in which the contract is made and by the Berne Convention for the Protection of Literary and Artistic Works of 1886 to which 196 countries are signatory.

You Can Get Paid to Do This

WRITING FOR THE ENTERTAINMENT WORLD

The writer is indispensable, yet not always valued—at least in the entertainment world. Sam Goldwyn, in one of his classic aphorisms, is reported to have called scriptwriters "schmucks with Underwoods." An Underwood, for those who have no cultural memory about this, was a make of manual typewriter. So you're a schmuck with a laptop. Robert Altman's brilliant film *The Player* (1992) gives you an idea of what life as a writer in Hollywood might be like, even though it is edged with satire and more in-jokes about the industry than most of the audience would understand. In the movie, a studio executive makes an interesting statement that goes something like, "My studio accepts a thousand submissions a year and puts twelve of them into production." There are probably no formal statistics to support this, but it sounds reasonably accurate. Multiply that by several studios, and you can estimate the number of screenplay submissions in any given year. Let's say 10,000 as a round number. That's a lot of competition. Of those, many are bought or optioned, but few are ever actually produced. So income from writing, as I know from personal experience, does not necessarily lead to screen credits. There is no way of knowing how effective or systematic the selection process is. Most studios and independent producers have readers who read all submissions and write a report that often determines the fate of the particular script. This hidden process causes much heartache and frustration and maybe prevents quite a few brilliant but idiosyncratic scripts from being produced. Every time you see a bad movie, you wonder how it got into production. Although people make mistakes in judgment, we like to assume that overall, the best scripts eventually rise to the top. No one intends to make a bad film although many producers make low-budget product for the video market that never gets a theatrical release.

Script readers and editors need a writing background. Producers who commission writers benefit enormously from having tried to write themselves, as do directors. A director has to work very closely with a scriptwriter especially if the director cannot write. Writing and directing can go hand in hand. Financial backers make decisions about large investments based, in part, on scripts. Other opportunities exist in the corporate world where the stakes are not as high. You still get to write professionally while you work on that screenplay.

In its own right, the corporate world is a highly creative and stimulating place to work. Every job is different. Although some assignments are less exciting than others, my personal experience writing for corporate media has been rewarding. You can perfect your craft and be paid, which might enable you to write your screenplay nights and weekends. As we learned in the chapter on corporate writing, dramatization is one of the devices that work well for certain corporate communication problems. This means writing dialogue, casting talent, and directing. Corporate work also is a good training for documentary because it relies on clear visual exposition.

To get ready to earn a living by writing for media, you should read the work of professionals and read books by professionals about the craft and about the business of writing. There is a selected bibliography at the end of this book. There are also a number of websites dedicated to writing to be found on the website and also listed in the bibliography. Above all, you have to have conviction about your writing. It can be a lonely business. Nobody will recognize you until you have produced work that you can show. So persistence is indispensable. It is difficult to give advice on this matter. What would you say to a basketball player or any athlete who has ambitions to play professionally? You'll never know if you don't try. At some point, you realize that even though you have talent, you are not succeeding. So you go to plan B. Or economic necessity drives you to take up some other activity, perhaps related.[1] These choices are intensely personal in nature.

WRITING CONTRACTS

If you are hired to write for compensation, make sure you have a contract. A contract can take many forms. The first is a verbal agreement. Surprisingly, many people work on terms negotiated verbally. It is good practice, however, to follow up any verbal agreement with a letter stating the terms under

---

[1] Lorian Tamara Elbert (Editor), *Why We Write: Personal Statements and Photographic Portraits of 25 Top Screenwriters* (Los Angeles: Silman-James Press, 1999), p. xiv: "only five percent of the approximately 8,500 Writers Guild members actually make a living from their writing."

which you are going to proceed with the project. A verbal contract can be legally binding. It's just hard to enforce it. Hence, writing out the terms in a letter of confirmation saves misunderstanding. I have never used a lawyer or an agent for a corporate job. Agents do very little business in the corporate world because the fees are low. Agents prefer to spend time and energy in the entertainment world where they are indispensable and make more money.

If you have an agent, the agent will negotiate the remuneration and the details of the contract that affect your delivery schedule and responsibilities. Of course, getting an agent to represent you is half the battle. Most studios and producers will not read any submission that does not come from a recognized agent. In the entertainment world, a number of trade union agreements are in force. The **Writers Guild of America(East and West)** and the **Writers' Guild of Great Britain**, which have reciprocal agreements, have contract models and minimum payment scales for film, television, and radio. The **Writers Guild of America** recently worked out a contract for the newest field of writing— the Internet. Even if you are not a member of these guilds, their standards are industry models that are mandatory. A signatory studio or producer may not pay less than the minimums set by the unions. You and they are governed by these agreements even if you are not a guild member because the industry producers are signatories to these agreements. Many readers will remember the writers' strike of 2008, which stopped all production for many months. The writers' guilds in different countries are strongest in the film and television industry. They have virtually no presence or influence in the corporate field. In my experience, however, the market in corporate video seems to reward competent writers adequately without the need for union representation.

As of 2009, the **Writers Guild of America** minimum for an original screenplay was $113,626 for films with budgets over $5 million and $60,523 for films budgeted between $1.2 and $5 million, and slightly less for adapted screenplays.[2] Successful writers with a track record of box office successes earn 10 to 20 times the minimum. A sought-after writer can sell a screenplay for $1 million and up. Some writers are able to negotiate a profit participation position in the producer's net. Major actors and other talent can negotiate a **percentage of the gross**, that is, the total revenue collected by the distributor. This is the most desirable position because it is the most transparent and hardest to disguise by creative accounting. The most likely profit participation that a writer can expect is a percentage of the net, the money that the distributor pays to the producer after its commission and expenses are deducted off the top. Whatever revenue comes in after that goes first to the cash investors until their production investment is paid off with interest. If the movie makes a profit, the money is split **pari passu** (a legal term meaning proportionately to each at each step) according to the original deal with a percentage split between investors and the producer. The producer's share is known as the **producer's net**. If actors, writers, or other creative people have given up money payment up front for a percentage, they get a percentage of this net revenue coming to the producer. Many movies make money but never make a profit, in which case there is no **producer's net**. Five percent of zero is zero.

Writing for money means someone is paying you to think creatively and represent that thinking in coherent form on the page. In the entertainment world, this process is well understood in its three

---

[2] www.wga.org/uploadedFiles/writers_resources/contracts/min2008.pdf. These rates have built-in increases over time. Writers employed for a term are paid around $4.926 per week, increasing in 2010.

stages that we have explained in the preceding chapters. It begins with a concept that expresses the **premise** and outlines the theme or story idea. This may be what starts the project after **pitching**. A lot of discussion with producers, directors, and possibly actors who are part of the project precedes the **treatment**.

The **treatment** is described in the contract and involves a partial payment of the total fee. A producer is usually entitled to pay for the treatment and then withdraw, depending on how the contract was negotiated. After the **treatment** has been read, a great deal of discussion ensues that allows the producer to react to the storyline and the vision expressed and, indeed, to ask for changes. Apart from the fact that money is changing hands, there is a strong need to look at story and character issues before committing further time and money to create the screenplay or script.

The **first-draft screenplay** is the next stage of the contract that involves a delivery date and a payment schedule. This stage involves the most substantial investment of time and money. Most contracts provide for one revision after reading and discussion. After this, the contract is complete. When payment is made in full, the writer no longer owns the work. The producer might pay another writer to rewrite, or an actor or director might want his or her chosen writer to rework and revise the script. The producer then has to raise finance for the production, complete a production deal, and make the script into film or television programming that can be sold. More than one writer often works on a script. I have rewritten scripts and, in turn, my scripts have been rewritten by someone else. This is less common in the corporate world. However, I had to rewrite a corporate video made by for Shell that had been rejected by the client within the Shell group. Television scripts go through many rewrites by teams of writers. The writer is by turns a craftsman, a hack, a professional wordsmith, and an image maker. There are triumphs and disappointments. Live to write another day!

PITCHING

In the entertainment world, the process of script development is a serious activity on which all production depends. The name of the game is to get money behind a project at the earliest stage possible, namely, the writing stage. The most desirable situation to be in is to have a multiple-picture development deal. Only successful producers and directors get this kind of speculative backing. Writers and other producers and directors often have to develop scripts to the **treatment** stage or even **first-draft screenplays** before seeking financial backing. For the studios, commissioning scripts is like sowing seeds. Some will germinate. Others will not. As mentioned earlier, even those that become fully developed scripts might be bought and paid for and never get into production. Script development is the cheapest part of the process of movie production. Distributors need product. Studios need scripts and story ideas to stay in business. A movie idea begins as something relatively simple—a story premise—which is often presented in meetings to agents, producers, and other principals in a process known as **pitching**.

We have discussed **pitching** in other contexts, but we should revisit the issue now. In the entertainment business, a writer must be able to talk about movie concepts as well as write them. A lot of ideas and projects are bought and sold on the basis of meetings at which creative people such as writers, producers, and directors talk their ideas to a production executive. This process is called **pitching**. It is a skill. A writer should be able to pitch, but it is a skill that does not always accompany writing talent.

To some extent, there is an element of salesmanship. You have to carry conviction in your manner, in your voice, and in your language. The pitch has to go beyond the reason why you want to write or do the project. It has to give reasons why someone else should want to get involved. It has to indicate how you see the project. It has to do this in language that makes sense to the executive making the decision to commit funds to your project over all of the other projects vying for the same resources. As we have noted, there is no shortage of scripts and projects, only good scripts and good projects.

Many executives who make decisions about development don't read. They don't have time, ability, or inclination. They have readers who cover the standard submissions as we have mentioned earlier. Most writers and their **agents** want to bypass the readers and get straight to the main decision maker. They do listen to pitches. **Pitching** must be an efficient way to process proposals. Otherwise, why would major studios and distributors keep doing it. I learned about **pitching** the hard way failing to do it successfully. I was commissioned to write a movie script for American International Pictures. I was working in London at the time with an executive in the London office. The day came when Samuel Arkoff, president of the company, came to town to decide what to do about this sequel, which the company had commissioned from me, to their remake of *Wuthering Heights* (1970). He checked into a suite at the Savoy. A meeting was scheduled at the hotel with me and the London executive producer. Sam Arkoff was in his bathrobe and slippers. He ordered a sumptuous lunch of oysters, smoked salmon, and chateau bottled French wine, which was brought to the room. Then the moment came. He asked me what the movie was about. I was stunned. I assumed that if the company had paid me to write the script (it had been sent to the Hollywood office), he would have read it. He hadn't read it.[3]

He wanted the premise expressed; he wanted a **log line**. A **log line** should not tell the whole story but provide a compelling and concise statement of who the lead character is, what his problem is and how he is going to solve it. This must be expressed in a sentence or two. As we discussed in Chapter 8, it contains the premise of the plot or story. What was the approach? What was the driving idea that would hold audiences and give him the conviction to put money into producing the movie? I made a mess of it. I got bogged down in too much detail. In retrospect, I realize I was being paid to pitch. To get my movie into production and to direct it, I had to pitch to save the project and the London executive. I earned the scriptwriting fee, but the movie was never made and the London executive was let go and the office shut down as the industry hit a crisis of rising debt and falling box office.

The Player (1992), mentioned earlier, was an original screenplay written and produced by Michael Tolkin. This movie provides excellent insight into the art of **pitching**. **Pitching** is a brief oral delivery of a summary or key concept of a movie. If the idea is strong, it is somehow seen as a firm anchor for the ensuing work. Sometimes development deals are made on this basis.

In the end, this is a commercial business. Hollywood is in business to make money. Of course, nobody knows for sure what makes money. There are tried-and-true formulas that keep resurfacing. You put money into a movie just like another one that made money or that is going to make money. The me-too syndrome is evident in every season's releases. Another way to try and minimize risk is to build a project around proven box office elements, usually an "A list" of actors and actresses whose movies have nearly always made money. Of course, their agents know this and push for the highest

---

[3] Correspondence included on the website shows that he had read the treatment.

fee and participation they can. So movies get more expensive. If a project starts to become a package with the elements of stars, director, and so on, it usually affects the script both before and after it is written. William Goldman's book is the best document from a writer's point of view of how and why this happens.[4]

Big-time **pitching** is not a real possibility at the beginning of a writer's career. There is an amazingly vigorous independent movie sector of low-budget, interesting movies. These movies are made outside the mainstream studio system. There are money finders who work on putting finance deals together for low budget independent productions like *The Blair Witch Project* (1999) that might make it into release. There are a lot of hungry, ambitious people. You have to become one of them. You have to learn the business. **Pitching** at this level means finding like-minded people and persuading them that your idea or your script is worth spending time and effort on to move forward. In every generation, new talent arises and old talent retires. Each generation produces a new audience that craves to see its realities reflected in movie and television stories and images. Life is a pitch, as someone once said.

IDEOLOGY, MORALITY, AND CONTENT

Broadly speaking, the entertainment industry is an uneasy alliance between expressive storytelling, the box office, and the bottom line. It is a simple fact that no one will back a movie or television project without the belief that there is a large audience for the finished program. And why should they? Hollywood producers and distributors speak of movies as product. "Produce" is the key verb of the industry. Product is the result of production. Product is what generates revenue that allows a company to survive, grow, and pay dividends. More particularly, it allows a producer to stay in business and produce again. To a considerable extent, the same rationale governs the work of writers and directors. If your movies don't make money—that is, don't attract an audience large enough to generate a return of at least the cost of production and distribution—your talent will be viewed with suspicion.

The uneasy alliance between art and commerce makes for a permanent tension and a continuing debate. Remember—it is called "the film industry!" The extreme of the Hollywood industrial view is epitomized by the classic *bon mot* of Samuel Goldwyn, "If you've got a message, take it to Western Union." MGM's movies were about entertainment, pleasing the public, and supplying it with whatever sensations would make the most money. Movie distributors are often contemptuous of art house movies because they are hard to sell and have smaller audiences and, therefore, less return for the same effort. The predominant mentality seems to be the hunt for the biggest box office rather than the smaller budget films that bring a proportionate return from smaller audiences. In the words of Sam Goldwyn about one of his films, "I don't care if it doesn't make a nickel. I just want every man, woman, and child in America to see it."

The dilemma here lies in the question of what appeals to audiences. If you survey the movies you know and those that are celebrated successes, you could very well argue that large audiences thrive on messages. Some of these messages can be paraphrased:

- Good ultimately triumphs over evil (westerns, police thrillers).
- Life is basically good and worth living (*It's a Wonderful Life*).

---

[4] William Goldman, *Adventures in the Screen Trade* (New York: Warner Books, 1983).

- Sacrifice for a cause such as your country is noble—the old Roman dictum *dulce et decorum est pro patria mori*, meaning "It is sweet and proper to die for your country" (most war films).
- Love conquers all (most romantic comedies).
- True love is happiness, or happiness is true love (most love stories).
- Action trumps intellect (most action films celebrate the man of action, not the man of rational thought).
- Revenge is sweet (killing your enemy who has done you wrong is your right).
- The underdog can win (*Rocky*, 1976 and whole host of films about reversal of fortune).

In *Ecclesiastes*, "The race is not to the swift nor the battle to the strong," but if you are a betting man, as Damon Runyon said, or a movie producer, that's who you put your money on. To put it simply, most popular movies are stuffed with messages about heroism and myths about love conquering all. The biggest message of all is the happy ending. It is difficult to sell stories without a happy ending, whether it is the triumph of the hero or the proposal of marriage that concludes a romance. There usually has to be a strong message of hope, of overcoming adversity, or at least benefiting the nation or the human race. This is not a bad thing. However, tragedy, loss, and pain have another truth that audiences also recognize.

A number of ideological themes are woven into a lot of movies and television. World War II movies are nearly always patriotic propaganda. Although characters might die, they do not die in vain, and they die heroically. It was noticeable how few movies about Vietnam were filmed because that undeclared war brought humiliation to the United States and discord at home. The movies that were made, like *The Deer Hunter* (1978), *Apocalypse Now* (1979), and *Full Metal Jacket* (1987), had to deal with the dark side of America—the My Lai massacre of civilians, the defoliation of jungles with Agent Orange, the high-altitude bombing of Hanoi with B-52s, and the draft dodging and political protest. Coppola made *Apocalypse Now* into a parable about moral degeneration based on Joseph Conrad's *Heart of Darkness*. It was difficult to find redemption in these three movies unless it was the refusal to shoot the noble stag at the end of *The Deer Hunter*, thereby celebrating life.

We see a constant ambivalence concerning crime and law and order. The movies have always glamorized gangsters even though they may have to die in a hail of bullets in the end. Until then, the audience gets a kind of fantasy outing in which power and invincibility rule. The writer has to make the central characters interesting. The movie and television series literature about the Mafia reveals the greatest ambivalence. The Mafia began as neighborhood protection of poor immigrants but ended up as a cancer corrupting everything it touched. Only the *Godfather* trilogy made by Francis Ford Coppola really shows the destruction of family, self, and relationships that are the inevitable consequence of the Mafia code of silence, violence, and revenge. Sometimes it seems as if the movies are a propaganda machine for the Mafia itself, showing its power, creating larger-than-life characters, and solidifying its mythic status in American society. *The Sopranos* became a major television hit. A mass audience could cozy up to a mafia family as if it were a next-door neighbor and just another way to make good in America. Tony Soprano even goes into therapy. Crime is just a psychological adjustment.

Crime makes for more interesting dramatic material than the humdrum life of law-abiding citizens. In films, the police are often the butt of ridicule. Their cruisers are involved in spectacular pileups.

The cliché chase sequence makes you root for the fleeing criminal rather than the police. Television, in contrast, seems to favor the police and the heroic public service of the keepers of law and order. In either medium and in every script, the depiction of violence is an overwhelming fact of screen entertainment. It began in the modern era with the slow-motion shootout in *The Wild Bunch* (1969). It becomes a kind of stylized entertainment in kung-fu movies, and it is delivered with clever, almost blasé ruthlessness in *Pulp Fiction* (1994). The trick seems to be to provide a legitimate excuse for the audience to indulge in a spectacle of violence by setting up a character with a plausible motive for revenge. For a century, the movies have evolved certain cliché set pieces—the fistfight, the shootout, and the car chase—that each generation seems to reinvent. Although this is not a forum in which these issues can be resolved, it is difficult not to suspect a relationship between the violent themes and images of big and small screen entertainment and the sickening violence that pervades American society. Adolescent kids, the most vulnerable audience, resort to guns and mass killing to express their anger and frustration. Are they acting out what they see on the screen? Movies glamorize violence and sensationalize life on the one hand, while sentimentalizing it on the other with fantasy relationships. Who is responsible? Producers, directors, or writers?

Like an addict who needs larger doses of a drug to get high, modern audiences seem to need more and more graphic violence to get their fix. How do you deal with these issues as a writer? There is a definite pressure to do likewise, or even to up the ante, to go further, and think up a novel way to present violence to the audience so as to sell your work. Whatever you write, you will have to think about whether you are writing imitative scripts or writing something that is authentic. There is no doubt that commercial pressure places the media writer in a moral dilemma.

EMOTIONAL HONESTY AND SENTIMENTALITY

Movies and television are about human emotions. People in conflict and under stress react emotionally. Their principles and morals are tested. The spectacle of a character confronting destiny and undergoing evolution through challenges fascinates audiences. Just as the Greeks explored the tragic dilemmas and comic absurdities of their society in their theatre, movies and TV mirror all our cultural dilemmas and moral conflicts. We have a long list of social issues such as drugs, HIV-AIDS, racial discrimination, disabilities, crime, abortion, and so on. It is interesting to speculate whether the program content reflects or leads the cultural consciousness of the day. Many movies and television programs have a distinct cultural bias and a subtle and even not so subtle a political agenda. The story plays to an ideological message as surely as Communist countries used to make films that celebrated the working class hero.

GI Jane (1997) seems to me an example of an agenda-driven storyline. A woman wants to become a Navy SEAL. At a political level, she is the pawn of a woman senator who wants to push the issue of gender equality in the armed services. The heroine is shown going through the training, including being physically beaten up by the master chief—total equality. Her head is shaven. She has to meet the same standards of physical endurance as the male recruits. It ends with a secret raid inside Libya in which she proves her operational skills and gains acceptance as one of the guys. It is easy to fabricate the endurance and the performance in the movies, which in real life would not be likely. It is in a sense exploitation and sensationalism. A star like Demi Moore is always a star. So her character has to be written to succeed.[5]

The feminist agenda is quite prevalent in movies and television today. Although many issues of gender equality are topical and meaningful, men in turn become stereotyped and masculinity pilloried. Sometimes there is a bias that distorts the truth. John Updike's novel *The Witches of Eastwick* (1987) was made into a movie that turned it upside down. The three leading ladies, Cher, Susan Sarandon, and Michelle Pfeiffer, played the witches who became the victims instead of the persecutors of a new man in the neighborhood who in the movie becomes the Devil incarnate, played by Jack Nicholson. Instead of three women trying to undo the man, who is the victim in the novel, with spells and esoteric practices, it is politically more attractive to play it the other way around. The basic message is female power is good, male power is bad. There used to be a grade-school chant, "What are little boys made of? Slugs and snails and puppy dogs tails—that's what little boys are made of. What are little girls made of? Sugar and spice and all that's nice. That's what little girls are made of." It is interesting to note how easily men's bodies are used as cannon fodder, men's lives are expendable, and men's pain allowable. Think how often you see men getting kicked or hit in the genitals. This is often made into a joke. Men kick men. Women kick men. You never see a woman kicked in the genitals or punched in the breast, and it wouldn't ever be particularly funny. Alert yourself to the amount and the extent of ideological agendas that are built into many scripts.

The most important form of emotional dishonesty is sentimentality. It is the substitution of a lesser emotion for a greater one while trying to achieve the same result. It appeals to the lowest common denominator of emotion. It oversimplifies life, death, and love to perpetuate a comfortable illusion. It is escape versus realism, glossing over the complexities of experience to provide an easy formula for getting a tear, a laugh, or a patriotic swelling of the chest. It turns complexity and subtlety into cartoons. Indeed, the Disney product, whether in movies or in theme parks, has always been larded with great dollops of sentimentality. Disney presents images of innocence and purity with all the nasty bits cleansed away. The projection of human emotions onto animal characters, cuteness as virtue, love without sexuality—it all gets served up as an easy substitute for experience, like processed food with sugar and coloring added to make it more attractive.[6]

Sentimentality drives *Pretty Woman* (1990)—the fantasy that a hooker is really a lady and gets to marry a millionaire and be treated like a princess. This is betrayed by the tag line "She walked off the street, into his life and stole his heart." Once Julia Roberts is cast in the role, we know there has to be a romantic triumph of these proportions. None of the sordid reality of this profession is ever revealed. Nor is the psychology of prostitution ever dealt with. It is a fantasy world. Julia Roberts is just playing at being a streetwalker. She is really never anything but an actress and a nice girl in hooker's clothing, who knows that by the end of the movie she is going to change her costume. The contrast is with her hooker friend, Kit, played by Laura San Giacomo. The movies have glossed over American historical realities such as slavery, genocide, discrimination, lynching, social inequalities,

---

[5] See the review at the Internet Movie Data Base website, http://us.imdb.com/CommentsShow?119173.
[6] See *Rethinking Disney: Private Control, Public Dimensions*, ed. Mike Budd and Max H. Kirsch, Middletown, Connecticut: Wesleyan University Press, 2005. See also my review in *Scope* (an online journal of film and TV studies), Institute of Film & TV Studies, University of Nottingham (www.scope.nottingham.ac.uk/bookreview.php?issue=11&id=1031&section=book_rev&q=friedmann)

and political corruption. They have even advocated racism. D. W. Griffith, one of the greatest and most inventive pioneers in the medium, made the first feature-length epic, *Birth of a Nation* (1915), which celebrated the Ku Klux Klan. Then movies have also become a way to change public perception. *In the Heat of the Night* (1967), with Sidney Poitier, showed how a black detective in the South dealt with prejudice and a Southern sheriff. Sidney Poitier also pioneered in portraying a mixed-race relationship in *Guess Who's Coming to Dinner* (1967). Kevin Costner made a 4-hour movie (director's cut), *Dances with Wolves* (1990) that reexamined the racist and genocidal assumptions that lie behind the American folklore of the frontier.

European films have less of the sentimental tradition. However, few of them receive wide distribution. If they do, they often are remade into a softened version for American consumption. *Trois Hommes et un Couffin* (1985), about three men who get stuck with a baby and have to learn to look after it—a great comic premise—was turned into an American version, *Three Men and a Baby* (1987), that takes gritty social observation and turns it into sentimentality. The British TV sitcom *Until Death Do Us Part* was bought, tamed, and turned into *All in the Family*. Although there are cultural reasons why one country's humor won't play in another's, there is also a Puritanism in American culture that has always restricted the way movies treat many themes.

Reflect about those movies that command attention and hold audiences long after their initial release and the video sales have dwindled! Their success is difficult to predict beforehand. Big box office is sometimes ephemeral, resulting from a fad or a public mood. Some big grossing movies fade into oblivion. *Citizen Kane* (1941) was not a box office hit, but it is a great movie that is technically brilliant and compelling viewing every time you watch it. Of course, its release was sabotaged by William Randolph Hearst, whose life it paraphrased in an unflattering way. *Casablanca* (1942) is a great love story that is compelling because it is not sentimental. Rick does not get Ilsa. Although he is bitter about losing her, he deals with the reality. He salvages something from it. They love one another, but they are not going to be together. Rick helps his rival instead of beating him up, as is the custom in American movies of the day.

It is very difficult to write without conviction. Ultimately, you have to write what your gut tells you is true for you and true for the audience. Nevertheless, there are many commercial pressures to create or include elements that are imitative—the car chase, the fight, the love scene with the movie kiss. It is hard to be original. It is hard to be truthful. Many of the best American movies come from the independent sector—interesting, gritty movies that explore out-of-the-way themes. They go to the Sundance Film Festival and get picked up for distribution, and the makers move on to bigger budgets and greater temptations. Complex, subtle movies are difficult to create, such as *Sling Blade* (1996), which was rewarded with an Oscar. *Election* (1999) looks at ambition and sexuality in a high school election that hints at the realities of the larger political world in which the heroine ends up. *Chasing Amy* (1997) deals with youth, gender, and sexuality in a way that is refreshing and funny. *Body Shots* (1999) is a tightly observed comment on the complexity of the social and sexual behavior of men and women and their different expectations in post feminist Los Angeles at the end of the 1990s. The script uses the theatrical aside in an interesting way so that characters break off and speak to the audience through the camera lens, making comments about the way a man or a woman sees the opposite sex. It recalls the innovation in the 1999 television series *Once and Again*.

Think about it! Most people experience a lot of pain from the experience of falling in love. Half the time it is with the wrong person, or the love is not requited, or the relationship stagnates into a routine, low-temperature marriage full of compromises and the extinction of passion. Fifty percent of marriages end in divorce. Everyday relationships are not often the stuff of movies and television. Passion, lust, and jealousy are. So movies and soaps are seldom about the routine married life unless they satirize it. A television show like *Married with Children* mocks the state of marriage as daily warfare and endless insults. The Academy Award–winning original screenplay and movie of 2000 was *American Beauty* (1999), which is a searing exposure of the social and emotional failure of the American family at the turn of the century. So truthfulness without a happy ending can result in commercial success.

There is no easy answer. There is no future in writing scripts that are never produced. You can train yourself to be a journeyman hack and make a living. Despite craft and technique, the animus for your writing has to come from your center, from what you know and believe. That voice of authenticity is what carries the day in the end. It is probably true to say that there is room for so many kinds of writing that you would be foolish to fabricate writing that you cannot sustain and that you do not genuinely want to do.

WRITING FOR THE CORPORATE WORLD

At first, most beginners are ambitious to work in the entertainment side of the industry. Although it is the most lucrative, it is also the hardest to get into. The largest employer, both in terms of salaried jobs and freelance work, is the business world. The need for writers who can design content for corporate communications needs is immense. In every major town across America, wherever businesses are to be found, you will also find production companies and advertising agencies that are in business to solve their communications problems. They need writers. It is not just that this pays the rent while you are waiting for your screenplay to be read and optioned; it is a fascinating and creative field in itself. It is innovative and requires you to be able to think about new media and keep up with what is happening in the industry. Every job exposes you to a new product or service and introduces you to whole new worlds of business activity. Sometimes these are highly technical and about business-to-business products and services that you don't normally come across. These jobs require a curious and adaptive spirit and someone who is able to assimilate new material quickly and get to the heart of a problem. You have to be able to communicate your ideas to clients and producers that employ you.

How do you start? One way is to write for no pay for a charity or public service organization that usually gets *pro bono* creative help from the industry. In the corporate chapter, we discussed a public service announcement about addictive gambling. This was produced by Pontes/Buckley Advertising, Inc. and by writers, technicians, and talent from the Boston chapter of the Media Communications Association.

There is a chicken-and-egg problem. You need experience before someone will entrust you with a high-value corporate job. To get experience you need to get a job. Another way would be to write for cable access channels, which exist in every community. You can even produce the program yourself. If the program is successful, it can be played on other cable access channels or even taken up by a commercial cable channel. More important is that you have a "reel" that shows program content for which you have a writing credit. It can become a calling card.

CLIENT RELATIONSHIPS

When you work for a client, you have entered into a business relationship. You are being paid to do a job to your client's satisfaction. A client pays you for your creative writing talent to solve a communication problem that they cannot solve on their own. A creative service is somewhat of a mystery. I once worked for a management consultant writing training videos. I had to go to Belgium and visit their client's site—the national steel company. I was given a desk to write at. The manager would come in now and then and wonder what I had produced in the last couple of hours because he was paying for my services by the day. His idea of writing was constant output. My approach was to visit the factory for visual input, read background, and stare out of the window with my feet on the desk until I had thought the problem through and found a solution, somewhat like the seven steps outlined in Chapter 2. Once I knew the answers to the questions and I had the creative concept, I could write quickly. Needless to say, the manager of this consultancy job was getting more and more agitated with me. He just did not understand the writing process. However, he was pleased with the script that resulted.

The point is that clients do not always understand what they are paying a writer for. It is problematic for them to put a value on the work. Are they paying by the hour? The hour that you chew pencils also counts but seems a waste of money to the client. On the whole, writers are paid for **piecework**. You quote a fee for the whole job, broken down into stages with a schedule of payments. Some people pay by the minute, say, $200 **per minute of finished program**. These last two methods of payment hide the pencil chewing and the thinking time and deal with a measurable result. The most common mode of payment for corporate work is a **flat fee** for the finished script. You estimate what time is involved in terms of research, travel, and writing. You multiply that by your notional or daily fee. You come up with a price for the whole job. Your producer or your client either agrees or negotiates. Sometimes you need to be working on more than one job at a time because there is waiting time while your producer/client reads the script or circulates it to others for reading. You need to be productive during this downtime.

CORPORATE CONTRACTS

The transfer of **intellectual property** is implicit in all corporate writing. Either you are employed as a writer by a corporation that by virtue of paying you a salary for your work owns your writing output, or you are a freelance writer who is contracted by the corporation or a producer in a production company to create a script. That contract may often be, and usually is, verbal and implicit, governed by custom and practice in the industry. You will not often have a written contract because to provide a written contract usually incurs legal costs. The nature of the contract and its salient features are so well understood that most work is done on trust.

Nevertheless, it is a wise practice to follow up all verbal agreements with a letter confirming the understanding. For instance, when a client signs off on a treatment or a script, I always write a letter saying that following our meeting and discussion on such and such a date, I am now proceeding with the treatment/script/revision based on agreement of the following points. Mentioning delivery dates is also a good idea. The letters have legal value in the event of a dispute or in the event that the client changes his mind. You need to have an agreement about a payment schedule and state what it is in a confirming letter. It is vitally important to get some form of partial payment up front as a sign of good faith. You do not expect to get final payment until the client has signed off on the final draft. Once again, your **copyright** in your work is assigned to the person who pays you, but only after you've been paid. The problem is that if you are not paid, the custom-crafted script is of little value to you as the writer.

Several types of payment agreement are used for corporate writing. You can divide the project into **concept**/outline, **treatment**, and **shooting script**. Each stage is valued at a third of the total and paid for in increments. This method of payment allows producers to pay as they go and protects you, the writer, from not getting paid at the end. In fact, it is a good idea to get one-third up front. Production companies use other formulas also. One way of valuing writing is by the minute of final program. Another is as a percentage of the production budget. A script for a video that costs $100,000 to make might have a script element that is worth a percentage of the production budget, say, $5000. All of these ways of calculating a writing fee are based on experience and history. You can generally work out what it takes to write a minute of script based on research time, outline and treatment work, and final scriptwriting. You express that time and effort as a figure defined by the end result.

Writing involves two elements that both cost money. The first is time. It takes time to think and write. Based on your experience, how long will it take you to write a 10-minute video? You calculate the hours and put a price on your time. You round out the figure. You also have to think about what other writers are charging. If you are experienced and respected in the industry, you have your price and can afford to be choosy. If you are a beginner, you have to be as flexible as you can. There are producers who try to exploit writers by asking for a script at a knockdown price on the promise of other work to come. I have learned that this other work never comes. I usually refuse these kinds of deals or offer to discount the second script. That usually flushes out the dishonest operators.

The second aspect of writing is creativity. Creative work and imagination have a value. It is hard to measure and impossible to cost. When it works, it is priceless. Advertising agencies charge for creative services. Graphic designers charge for creative flair. The writer is in the same business: selling creative ideas. A great creative idea cannot be costed in terms of time. Sometimes I have made it through my seven steps in a flash. I know before I leave the meeting how I will solve the problem. Creative talent has a value. To the extent that the market will bear, you can charge for creative flair and originality. You hope to build a reputation that people will be glad to pay a premium for. Your demonstrated track record and finished work back it up. It takes a lot of work to build this kind of reputation. It also gets you prestige projects to work on rather than run-of-the-mill training videos. So different jobs can be costed and charged differently based on the nature of the product and the client.

WORK FOR HIRE

Marketing yourself and your work

In the business world, you hope for repeat business. You must also build business by introducing yourself to new producers and new corporate clients, usually by showing them some of your work and a résumé. Whenever you are not writing, you should be on the phone trying to make new contacts. You have to sell your talent and your creative services. There are not many agents who represent corporate media writers. There is not enough money in it for the agent, and it is too specialized. This is an advantage because you are not shut out of the game by an agent barrier, which can indeed inhibit your entry into the entertainment world. In addition, you get to keep all the money earned without having to pay a commission.

Copyright

Copyright is an agreement, either in **common law** or **statute**, that the original work of a creator of words, images, music, or other media is an **intellectual property** as opposed to a physical property. The creator has a right in what is created and owns that work until that ownership is assigned to another for payment. The purpose of the contract is to transfer title in the property parallel to the transfer of title in real estate. If you do not **copyright** your work in the United States, it falls into the **public domain**. This means anyone can use it. Eventually, all **intellectual property** falls into the **public domain** 70 years after the author dies. **Copyright** law is different in different countries. In Europe, for instance, you do not have to create **copyright** as you do in the United States. It is deemed to exist *de facto* because of the act of creation. **Copyright** therefore inheres in what you write or create. The Berne Convention dating back to 1886 assures the protection of creative work beyond the national borders of its country of origin.

You need to understand that you cannot **copyright** an idea. You have to create something that has recognizable shape and form and individuality in order to **copyright** it. This is very important when dealing with scripts and ideas for entertainment program content. An idea or **concept** for a movie is hard to **copyright**. A **treatment** is an expressed idea that has particular characterisitcs and acquires the quality of **intellectual property**. A screenplay, book manuscript, or play manuscript has clear identity as the output of a particular creator. Because you cannot **copyright** an idea, it is important not to discuss it before making it into **intellectual property**. The Writers Guilds provide a service that enables you to register a script. This becomes a strong, dated proof of ownership, although it does not create **copyright** under U.S. law. You should register your script if you submit your work to any potential buyer.

Copyright and **clear title** to **intellectual property** are crucial to the entertainment industry. Whether the source is an original screenplay, a book in the public domain, or existing **intellectual property** in a book, play, or manuscript of the same, it is essential that at each stage of production and distribution, every element of writing, performance, and sound track has clear title. Any flaw in title puts a huge investment at risk and leaves the producer open to claims for payment from any party who holds title to a part of that **intellectual property**. All contracts involving the assignment of **intellectual property** require the grantor of the right to indemnify the grantee against any flaw in title and to assume all liability for any flaw. Investors, studios, and end distributors, right down to the end exhibitor, demand this **indemnity**.

The integrity of the title is of paramount importance. Lawyers involved in drafting contracts will always demand proof of title or an **indemnity** against all liability and any future claims resulting from any flaw in that title. Again, there is a parallel to real estate transactions. You cannot acquire title in something the seller does not have title to. This is why you buy title insurance in a real estate transaction. However, it is easier to verify title in the registry office of a town that probably keeps very good records of ownership for reasons of taxation levied on the property. Title in works of imagination expressed in words that anyone can copy, or ideas that anyone can copy, are more difficult to protect.

Students sometimes take plagiarism lightly and are careless about identifying their sources. As a professional writer, you must have a vigorous respect for these issues because you are proposing to sell a piece of **intellectual property**. You must be able to assert your title to what you have created and what you propose to the buyer. For example, you cannot sell a script or screenplay based on a work that you do not own. You can write it, but it will have no value. Although you have created **copyright** in writing your screenplay, you will have created a piece of work that has a split **copyright**. I once optioned a novel through an agent. I wrote a screenplay to set it up as a movie. The option expired before I could get any preproduction going. Of course, I could go back and re-option the book. In the end, it didn't work out. My screenplay is a work with split **copyright**. Any producer can buy the underlying work and decouple it from my screenplay and get someone else to write another screenplay based on the same source work. I have no rights. When novels or plays are popular, their media rights have value.

Only major players in the entertainment business can ante up the option money or bid for these rights. For this reason, it is better to adapt work in the **public domain**. However, there is still a split **copyright** because anyone else can go to the same source in the **public domain** and create a new derivative work equal to yours and independent of yours. This happened to me. I wrote an adaptation of Henry James's *Daisy Miller*. I approached Peter Bogdanovich, the director, with the idea that it would be a great idea for a movie and a perfect role for Cybill Shepherd, his girlfriend at the time. It just so happened that he had had the same idea and was developing *Daisy Miller* as his next project. I had no claim, and he had no obligation. For legal protection and to stop a rival production, he bought the screenplay.

Work-made-for-hire and freelance

Writers who are employees of a company, such as a production company or, indeed, journalists working for a publication, are deemed to be offering a **service for hire** so that the employer who pays the writer's salary automatically owns what the writer produces. The analogy is to the worker on a shop floor. Ford does not have to pay a worker for creating a car but only for the time on the job. By analogy, a freelance writer who is paid by the hour or by the minute of finished script or for a completed script is governed by a **work-made-for-hire** principle. If a company pays a writer in this way, it owns the **copyright** in the work produced completely.

There is another way to govern the contractual relationship. A freelance writer is paid for a piece of work, created by the writer as an independent, imaginative enterprise. It remains the property of the creator until a bargain is struck and terms are set by which the ownership in the creation is transferred. Freelance writers enter into agreements to transfer ownership in their **intellectual properties** for payment. Broadly speaking, there are two ways to do this. It is sometimes part of the agreement that the writer retains some rights for some media or some territories, especially in journalism, where content can be resold or sold in another medium like a website. So a writer might be paid by the word for a specific publication. In media writing, scripts are usually dedicated to one production and can have no afterlife. Nevertheless, in the entertainment world, new media are springing up all the time. There is some dispute now about whether content that is delivered to cell phones is covered by agreements that did not include those rights. Writers' guilds try to defend writers' **copyright**. Publishers, producers, and employers of writing talent try to word contracts to include all media and those not yet invented because they have been burned so many times by having to renegotiate rights for sales for new media. We take videotape, DVDs, MP3s, and the Internet for granted, but writers want participation in the revenue for sales of content based on their work in new forms of distribution. These issues constituted one of the principal reasons for writers striking in 2008.

AGENTS AND SUBMISSIONS

Agents have become indispensable in the entertainment business for selling ideas and scripts. To get a start in the entertainment side of the business, you need an **agent** who can represent you and in turn sell your work to producers and studios. You understand now why producers and studios are extremely prudent about where their material originates. Unsolicited manuscripts and scripts are usually rejected because of negative past experiences of lawsuits and claims by people who submitted work, had it rejected, and then saw a movie that contained what they saw as their idea. By dealing with **agents, intellectual property** lawyers, and professional intermediaries, studios are protected from frivolous lawsuits and are ensured they are acquiring bona fide **intellectual property** rights.

Agents work speculatively, of course. They earn no commission until they sell your work. Obviously, they have to be convinced that their work of representing your work and your talent will bear fruit. A relationship with an **agent** can be good and bad. It can be deceptive. You have to work in good faith. Sometimes you can make assumptions about how well you are being represented that are unfounded. This is a business relationship that is very important and a difficult one to make work well.

A good place to start is the Writers Guild website, which lists **agents** by state, classified according to their business orientation.[7] Those **agents** who will read unsolicited manuscripts are identified, as are those who won't. A number of **agents** or script advisors will read and critique your work for a fee. Some of them may be legitimate and give value for money. Some advertise merely to make money from the endless stream of "wannabes" who dream of success. The best advice would be to get a reference or a recommendation from someone you know. Even better, make use of your writing classes. Your writing instructor is a sounding board and is duty-bound to read your work and give you feedback. Any course you take, therefore, provides a structured way to test your writing talent. You will get a clue as to whether it is worth the struggle to go forward and commit the time, energy, and ambition necessary to succeed professionally.

NETWORKING, CONVENTIONS, AND SEMINARS

Writers are rather solitary creatures on the whole. For the most part, they work alone. Getting to know other writers is not that easy. That is why going to seminars and attending conventions are good ideas. In a way, it doesn't matter whether you meet other writers. You want to meet the people who will commission your work—producers, directors, and corporate advertising, and public relations executives. Networking is key. There are social networking tools such as LinkedIn through which you can build a network of trustworthiness. Today, having a website is a strong way to market yourself and display your work.

---

[7] See www.writersguild.org.

A number of traveling writing seminars are given by scriptwriters and script doctors.[8] One of them is sure to be coming to a venue near you during the year. That is a good way of getting a fast track to real professional issues. These events are not cheap. They are usually 2- to 3-day affairs and cost about $500. If travel and hotel accommodations are added, attendance can be a costly exercise, but it is worth doing at least once to get professional advice and meet other like-minded people.

Writing seminars and panels are also given at a number of professional conventions. The Media Communications Association International has an annual convention at which there are always some panels devoted to scripting issues and marketing of writing skills in the corporate media market-place. The National Association of Broadcasters brings most of the people on all sides of the industry together. Again, panels are conducted and papers presented that are of interest to writers, particularly new media and interactive writers. These conventions are quite expensive when you add the costs of registration, travel, and the hotel. If you are making an income as a writer, these expenses become tax deductible, as do independent writing seminars.

SURFING THE WEB

With the spread of the World Wide Web, writing and scriptwriting have benefited from dedicated web-sites full of valuable information, such as the one for the Writers Guild and other professional bodies. Sites provide valuable databases of scripts, movies, and television production, as cited throughout this book. You can download or buy copies of scripts from most films and television series. There are chat rooms, script competitions, and websites for current television series and movies in production. There are online writing courses and script services. You have huge resources at your fingertips for research and for professional contacts. There are sites that provide shop windows for scripts looking for a pro-ducer, which provide a way for writers to circumvent the problem of finding an agent. In the accom-panying website, you will find a long list of active links that will take you directly to the sites. Because you have to use a computer and its browser to explore them, there seems no point in listing URLs in print to be typed into a browser's search window when you can click on an active link on the website.

HYBRID CAREERS

Some writers also have knowledge of production. They have, or can develop, skills as a producer or director or both. We have alluded to multitalented figures throughout the book, from Orson Welles to James Cameron. Both in the entertainment world and in the corporate world, a combination of talents can be useful. You have to do whatever it takes. The path of development for each person always involves an element of character and an element of destiny.

CONCLUSION

Writing is a risky business. It is a bet on your own talent like most artistic pursuits. You can train and develop your talent. There is, however, no guarantee of success. If you are going to try to make a living

---

[8] See links on the website.

as a writer of scripts, you have to be professional and disciplined. You have to want to reach audiences. You have to want to move audiences. That is your motivation, not just the money. You have to be the audience as well as the writer. You have to be obsessed with understanding what makes people choke with emotion, laugh, feel outrage, and cheer for a character they identify with. This feeling for the audience must underlie any writing. Even writing a training video for a corporate client requires careful consideration of the people in the audience. You need to think about what they need to know, how they will understand, and whether you have communicated successfully. An audience is an audience, whether for a big-screen movie, a how-to training video, or a website that presents a corporate face to the world.

As you become more adept at creating for one or another media, you will want to explore the works of other professionals who have written more specialized works, as listed in the bibliography at the end of this book. Remember, many write; few are chosen. Whatever you do, whatever you become, this writer wishes you the best possible breaks and the courage to fulfill your creative potential. In this spirit, I hope this book has been a worthwhile learning experience and will provide you with a foundation for your chosen craft.

Exercises

1. Call up a few **agents** and try to find out whether they will accept new writers or read unsolicited manuscripts.
2. Visit the **Writers Guild** websites (UK and USA East and West) and find out what you have to do to register a script.
3. Contact a television series editor and find out whether you can submit a spec script for that series.
4. Make a plan for your professional development as a writer.
5. Call up three corporate production companies in your area and find out whether they will look at some of your work.
6. Contact a nonprofit organization or a charity and ask the organizers if they have any media projects planned and whether you can do some writing for them at no cost.

Script Formats

DUAL COLUMN: PSA, DOCUMENTARY, CORPORATE

The visual look is cold, monochromatic blue.	
FADE UP ON…	(*MUSIC—increasing tension.*)
EXT. ALLEY – DAY	(*SFX—The pulse of a racing heart.*)
(4 seconds)	
An urban alley in a poor part of town.	(*Over this sound, we hear a series of DESPERATE VOICES.*)
Garbage and debris litter the ground.	
From a low angle, we look up at a tough, angry thirteen-year-old BOY. A CIGARETTE is jammed into the corner of his mouth. He walks through the alley with anger and attitude, kicking at the trash and smashing his book bag against the wall.	VO: WOMAN'S VOICE (angry, frustrated, desperate, rising in pitch, losing control) The school called again. What am I going to do with you?!
The image in the alley is interrupted by a FLASH CUT (1 second)	(*SFX—Glass cracking.*)
(Full color.)	(*1 second*)

© 2010, Elsevier Inc. All rights reserved
Doi: 10.1016/B978-0-240-81235-9.00022-5

A happy family PORTRAIT. A single mother and the thirteen-year-old boy.	
He's dressed neatly in a tie.	
A jagged CRACK slices across the glass.	*(SFX—Woman crying. Struggling. Bottle breaking.)*
CUT TO…	
INT. ROOM – NIGHT	VO: FATHER'S VOICE (angry, drunk, slurred speech)
(4 seconds)	
A young BOY, six or seven huddles against a wall, terror and pain in his eyes.	
Behind him, we see the SILHOUETTES of a man hitting a woman.	(SFX—SLAP.) Don't you ever turn away (SLAP) for me when I'm talking! (SLAP)

DUAL COLUMN ANCHOR NEWS SCRIPT

ON CAMERA: SHERRY	DRIVERS BETTER KEEP THEIR EYES PEELED. NEW 55-MILE-AN-HOUR SPEED- LIMIT SIGNS ARE GOING UP… TO KEEP OUR POLLUTION DOWN. W-B 39'S KATIE McCALL TELLS US ABOUT THE CHANGES.
TAKE VTR	SOT 1:38
17 SUPER: JANELLE GBUR DEPT. OF TRANSPORTATION	
32 SUPER: KATIE MC CALL REPORTING	
40 SUPER: MIKE STAFFORD HARRIS COUNTY ATTORNEY	
1:38 TAPE OUT	1:38 STD OUT CUE

DUAL COLUMN MULTI CAMERA SCRIPT

FADE IN:	
CG title	FADE UP MUSIC INTRO
SEMINAR SET	SEGUE TO
WIDE SHOT of instructor and learners	INSTRUCTOR:(smiling) The industry has a standard layout for dual column scripts using for corporate, documentary and public service announcements.
Instructor to camera	
	EAGER LEARNER: Why is the action in caps?
WIDE ANGLE of seminar table	INSTRUCTOR VO: It doesn't have to be. I have seen the reverse where spoken dialogue is in caps and action is in lower case.
STILL STORE script page	
CU Eager Learner taking notes.	SECOND EAGER LEARNER: Can we choose?
WIDE ANGLE of the group	INSTRUCTOR: I advise putting speech into upper and lower case because it is easier to read. Action description can also be in lower case.
MS of Instructor	
	EAGER LEARNER: What font do we use?
CU Eager Learner	INSTRUCTOR: I use Courier New 12 point, but outside the entertainment industry, the rules are less rigid. The most important point about the dual column format is that the columns should be equal in width and action and speech should be related by horizontal position opposite one another.
LS Instructor	

PACKAGE SCRIPT FOR NEWS

VIDEO	AUDIO
NAT SOUND: "SPEED LIMIT 60" SIGN FALLS FORWARD & HITS GRASS, NATS WORKER TIGHTENING SCREWS	NAT SOUND :03
COVER BEGINNING OF BITE WITH FREEWAY SIGN THAT READS "SPEED LIMITS REDUCED THIS WEEK"	SOT :03 ALMA NICKELBERRY: "I DON'T LIKE IT. I THINK, WELL, I CAN'T REALLY SAY WHAT I THINK"
ALMA AT GAS PUMP NEW SPEED LIMIT SIGN CARS ON FREEWAY	ALMA NICKELBERRY AND OTHER HARRIS COUNTY DRIVERS GET THEIR FIRST GLIMPSE OF THE NEW 55-MILE-PER-HOUR SIGNS ON AREA FREEWAYS.
NAT SOUND: TRAFFIC ON FREEWAY	QUICK NAT SOUND TRAFFIC OF FREEWAY :01
SOT JANELLE GBUR COVER END OF BITE WITH TIRES ON FREEWAY	SOT JANELLE GBUR "IT BASICALLY MEANS IF THEY'RE GOING 55, IT'S TAKING THEM 14 SECONDS LONGER TO DRIVE THAT MILE." :06
WORKERS PUTTING UP SIGNS	THE PLAN IS TO GET ALL SIGNS UP BY MAY FIRST… TO HELP BRING HOUSTON INTO COMPLIANCE WITH THE CLEAN AIR ACT.
TRAFFIC	CARS ARE SUPPOSED TO EMIT LESS NOX… NITROGEN OXIDES… AT THESE SLOWER SPEEDS.
STANDUP (ZOOM OUT FROM 55-SPEED LIMIT SIGN TO KATIE MC CALL IN FREEWAY MEDIAN)	STANDUP: "BUT AS QUICKLY AS YOU'RE SEEING THESE SIGNS GO UP, THEY COULD COME RIGHT BACK DOWN. SOME SAY THERE'S NEW EVIDENCE THAT SHOWS SLOWING TRAFFIC DOWN WILL NOT CUT DOWN ON POLLUTION." :11

SOT MIKE STAFFORD	SOT MIKE STAFFORD "THE EPA MODEL INDICATES THAT WE ARE NOT GOING TO GET REDUCED NOX EMISSIONS BY LOWERING THE SPEED LIMIT." :06
STAFFORD AND REPORTER WALKING ALONG ROAD, IN FRONT OF SPEED LIMIT SIGN	COUNTY ATTORNEY MIKE STAFFORD HAS PETITIONED THE TEXAS NATURAL RESOURCES CONSERVATION COMMISSION TO STOP THE SIGN CHANGING… BECAUSE A
WORKER REMOVING SIGN	RECENT E-P-A STUDY SHOWS, CONTRARY TO PREVIOUS STUDIES, THIS –
SOT WORKER IN CHERRY-PICKER POSTING NEW SIGN	QUICK NAT SOUND SIGN GOING UP WILL NOT CLEAN UP THIS –
DOWNTOWN SKYLINE & SMOG SOT TRAFFIC	QUICK NAT SOUND SMOG & TRAFFIC
MIKE STAFFORD SOT	SOT MIKE STAFFORD "AT THE SAME TIME, THE TEXAS NATURAL RESOURCE CONSERVATION COMMISSION'S OWN STUDY INDICATES THAT EVEN IF YOU WERE TO REDUCE NOX EMISSIONS, THAT MAY NOT REDUCE THE GROUND OZONE THAT APPEARS AS SMOG ON OUR SKYLINE." :13
FREEWAY TRAFFIC & SMOG	STAFFORD, ALONG WITH COUNTY JUDGE ROBERT ECKELS AND GOVERNOR RICK PERRY, IS ASKING THE T-N-R-C-C TO LOOK AT OTHER WAYS TO REDUCE OZONE.
SKYLINE ON CLEAR DAY	IF IT CAN FIND THEM – AND PROVE THAT TO THE E-P-A—YOU COULD SEE AN OLD

SPEED LIMIT 60 SIGN	FAMILIAR FRIEND BACK ON THE FREEWAY.
FREEWAY OVERPASS	BUT UNTIL THEN, CHANGE IS IN THE AIR.
SPEED LIMIT 55 SIGN	KATIE MCCALL, W-B 39 NEWS, HOUSTON.

RADIO SCRIPT FORMAT

1. SOUND FX: INTERIOR CAR SOUND OF MOTOR AND EXTERIOR TRAFFIC

2. MUSIC BED CAR RADIO—HEAVY METAL FADE UNDER.

3. COLLEGE STUDENT 1 What a great party!

4. COLLEGE STUDENT 2 I'm wasted.

5. COLLEGE STUDENT 1 Are you all right to drive?

6. COLLEGE STUDENT 2 Hell yes.

7. COLLEGE STUDENT 1 (PANICKED) Look out!

8. MUSIC BED SEGUE TO

9. SOUND FX: SCREECH OF BRAKES THEN CAR CRASH

10. SOUND FX: AMBULANCE SIREN

11. ANNCR: If you drink and drive, death could be the chaser.

12. MUSIC STING ORGAN CHORD

MASTER SCENE SCRIPT: FEATURE FILM FOR CINEMA AND TELEVISION

EXT. LAKE FRONT - DAY

There is a lot of commotion as passengers board a steamer Moored along side. DAISY and WINTERBOURNE in LONG SHOT. She is quite sudden in her movements as she moves up the Gangway. The steamer blows its whistle and prepares to cast off. There is a summer breeze rippling the lake.

EXT. LAKE STEAMER DECK - DAY

WINTERBOURNE feels they are on an adventure as they stroll the deck.
DAISY is animated and charming. She is not flustered when she is aware
than people are staring at her. People look at her because she is pretty
and because of her unconventional manners and apparent liberty with
her escort. They find a seat on the deck and WINTERBOURNE looks at her
enchanted while she chatters on.

> DAISY
>
> I wish we had steamers like this in
> America.

> WINTERBOURNE
>
> Well what about on the Mississippi?

> DAISY
>
> I don't live near the Mississippi.

> WINTERBOURNE
>
> Well, we've got the trip back to look
> forward to.

> DAISY
>
> What's your first name, again?

> WINTERBOURNE
>
> Frederick!

SCENE SCRIPT, VERSION 1: TELEVISION SITCOMS AND SERIES

EXT. LAKE FRONT - DAY

THERE IS A LOT OF COMMOTION AS PASSENGERS BOARD A STEAMER MOORED ALONG
SIDE. DAISY AND WINTER BOURNE IN LONG SHOT. SHE IS QUITE SUDDEN IN HER
MOVE MENTS AS SHE MOVES UP THE GANGWAY. THE STEAMER BLOWS ITS WHISTLE AND
PREPARES TO CAST OFF. THERE IS A SUMMER BREEZE RIPPLING THE LAKE.

EXT. LAKE STEAMER DECK - DAY

WINTERBOURNE FEELS THEY ARE ON AN ADVENTURE AS THEY STROLL THE DECK.
DAISY IS ANIMATED AND CHARMING. SHE IS NOT FLUSTERED WHEN SHE IS AWARE
THAN PEOLE ARE STARING AT HER. PEOPLE LOOK AT HER BECAUSE SHE IS PRETTY
AND BECAUSE OF HER UNCONVENTIONAL MANNERS AND APPARENT LIBERTY WITH
HER ESCORT. THEY FIND A SEAT ON THE DECK AND WINTERBOURNE LOOKS AT HER
ENCHANTED WHILE SHE CHATTERS ON.

                         DAISY

            I wish we had steamers like this in
            America.

                         WINTERBOURNE

            Well, what about on the Mississippi?

SCENE SCRIPT, VERSION 2: TELEVISION
SITCOMS AND SERIES

EXT. LAKE FRONT DAY

(THERE IS A LOT OF COMMOTION AS PASSENGERS BOARD A STEAMER MOORED ALONG
SIDE. DAISY AND WINTERBOURNE INLONG SHOT. SHE IS QUITE SUDDEN IN HER
MOVEMENTS AS SHE MOVES UP THE GANGWAY. THE STEAMER BLOWS ITS WHISTLE AND
PREPARES TO CAST OFF. THERE IS A SUMMER BREEZE RIPPLING THE LAKE.)

EXT. LAKE STEAMER DECK - DAY

(WINTERBOURNE FEELS THEY ARE ON AN ADVENTURE AS THEY STROLL THE DECK. DAISY
IS ANIMATED AND CHARMING. SHE IS NOT FLUSTERED WHEN SHE IS AWARE THAT
PEOPLE ARE STARING AT HER. PEOPLE LOOK AT HER BECAUSE SHE IS PRETTY AND
BECAUSE OF HER UNCONVENTIONAL MANNERS AND APPARENT LIBERTY WITH HER ESCORT.
THEY FIND A SEAT ON THE DECK AND WINTERBOUNRE LOOKS AT HER ENCHANTED WHILE
SHE CHATTERS ON.)

                         DAISY

            I wish we had steamers like this In
            America.

                         WINTERBOURNE

            Well what about on the Mississippi?

> DAISY
>
> I don't live near the Mississippi

INTERACTIVE GAME SCRIPT

(This Is One Type Of Interactive Script)

(Reproduced with permission of Screenplay Systems Movie Magic Scriptwriter.)

ROCKY COURTYARD

It is a rock-hewn courtyard, old and decaying, but clearly having once been elegant.

To the north is the imposing edifice of a temple, to the west is a gaping chasm, completely impassible.

South of us is a gate, an apple orchard just beyond it.

> **GO TO GATE (2)**
>
> **GO TO TEMPLE (3)**
>
> **GO TO CHASM (4)**

ORCHARD GATE

IF YOU TRY TO OPEN THE GATE THEN

IF YOU HAVE THE <KEY TO THE ORCHARD GATE> THEN The gate creaks open.

> **GO TO ORCHARD (5)**

> OTHERWISE

The gates rattle but you can't get through.

> ENDIF

> ENDIF

> **GO TO ROCKY COURTYARD (1)**

TEMPLE

The temple is elegant, bas-relief images of strange animals covering the walls.

You can go around the temple to the left or right.

> **GO TO RIGHT AROUND TEMPLE (7)**
>
> **GO TO LEFT AROUND TEMPLE (6)**

CHASM

An uncrossable chasm at your feet.

IF YOU JUMP THEN

GO TO YOU'RE DEAD (16)

END IF

GO TO ROCKY COURTYARD (1)

ORCHARD

Congratulations! You're in. Eat an apple while you're here.

GO TO ORCHARD GATE (2)

LEFT AROUND TEMPLE

Broken columns litter your path as you walk around the temple, finally opening up and leaving you at the inner buildings.

GO TO INNER BUILDINGS (8)

RIGHT AROUND TEMPLE

Broken columns litter your path as you walk around the Temple.

Midway around, you'll find an open door.

IF YOU ENTER THE DOOR THEN

GO TO TEMPLE ROOM (13)

ENDIF

The Walkway continues around finally opening up and leaving you at the inner building

GO TO INNER BUILDINGS (8)

INNER BUILDINGS

IF <CLOCK IS SET> THEN

GO TO BACK OF TEMPLE (10)

ENDIF

A large ornate door blocks your way, a lion headed knocker on the front door.

IF YOU USE THE KNOCKER THEN

It hits the door with a loud booming sound, but no one
opens it.

END IF

IF YOU LOOK UP THEN

You will see more carvings and a sign over the door,
held up by two clocks.

IF YOU EXAMINE THE SIGN THEN YOU'VE < EXAMINED SIGN> AND

It says:

When time and place are correct, then the doors to
opportunity will open.

END IF

IF YOU HAVE <EXAMINED SIGN> AND YOU CLIMB UP

THEN

You can reach the two clocks.

IF YOU SET THE TWO CLICK HANDS TO BOTH POINT

AT THE DOOR THEN THE <CLOCK IS SET> AND

The door opens silently.

GO TO HALLWAY OF INNER BUILDINGS (9)

GO TO BACK OF TEMPLE (10)

ENDIF

ENDIF

ENDIF

GO TO BACK OF TEMPLE (10)

HALLWAY OF INNER BUILDING

It's a long hallway, water on the floor.

There is a door to the right of you.

IF YOU TRY AND OPEN DOOR THEN

it creaks open.

```
      GO TO LIBRARY (14)

            ENDIF
the hallway extends to an inner courtyard

      GO TO INNER COURTYARD (15)

      GO TO INNER BUILDINGS (8)
```

BACK OF TEMPLE

More bas-relief, these even weirder. From here you can go either left or right around the temple.

```
      GO TO INNER BUILDINGS (8)

      GO TO RIGHT AROUND TEMPLE II (11)

      GO TO LEFT AROUND TEMPLE II (12)
```

RIGHT AROUND TEMPLE II

Broken columns litter your path as you walk around the Temple, finally opening up and leaving you at the rocky Courtyard.

```
      GO TO ROCKY COURTYARD (1)
```

LEFT AROUND TEMPLE II

Broken columns litter your path as you walk around the temple.

Midway around, you'll find an open door.

IF YOU ENTER THE DOOR THEN

```
      GO TO TEMPLE ROOM (13)

            ENDIF
```

The walkway continues around finally opening up and leaving you at the rocky courtyard.

```
      GO TO ROCKY COURTYARD (1)
```

TEMPLE ROOM

A small temple, long pews on either side.

An OLD PRIEST stands with his back to you at the alter, mumbling something in what sounds like Latin.

IF YOU SPEAK TO HIM THEN

                        PRIEST
                  (without turning)
              Go away!

IF YOU CONTINUE TRYING TO TALK TO HIM THEN

                     PRIEST (CONT'D)
                  (still without turning)

If you value your soul, then turn back before it's too late . . . go,
leave me!

          ENDIF

          ENDIF

IF YOU WALK UP TO THE PRIEST THEN

He turns, and you see that he's quite dead, maggots crawling in what's
left of his face . . . he lunges for you and you quickly join his
condition . . .

   GO TO YOU'RE DEAD (16)

          ENDIF

   GO TO RETURN (0)

                         LIBRARY

Lots of books and a large key on the table.

          IF YOU TAKE KEY THEN YOU HAVE <KEY TO THE ORCHARD GATE>.

   GO TO RETURN (0)

                      INNER COURTYARD

Lots of cool statues.

   GO TO HALLWAY OF INNER BUILDING (9)

                      YOU'RE DEAD

That's it!

Gods & Monsters

Video Game Concept for *Gods & Monsters* (copyright 2003 International Hobo Ltd.) reproduced with permission.

Premise

The story of two brothers, Telamon and Peleus, who were friends of Heracles, voyagers on the Argo and enemies of the goddess Athena. Quest-based gameplay in which the player controls Telamon to fight, but Peleus fights alongside using unique combat mechanics. Together they combine talents to defeat armies and mythic creatures. After playing Telamon and Peleus' story, more quests become unlocked telling tales of different pairs of heroes (e.g. Heracles, Jason etc.). All heroes can be powered up by an RPG-style mechanic.

MECHANICS

Controls

PS2	XBox	Meaning	Notes
X	A	Attack	Can press up to four times for a sequence of attacks
O	B	Power	Used with direction push to dive, flip etc Used with Attack to access special attacks
□	X	Shoot Arrow	If locked on, fires at target
△	Y	–	*Currently unused*
L1 or L2	L	Lock On	When held, locks player onto target enemy If no other button pressed, automatically blocks
R1 or R2	R	Call to Partner	Changes between Open, Co-op and Guard

Attacks & Special Attacks

The player's first three attacks (on the Attack button) come in quick succession; the fourth is more powerful, but much slower. The most efficient way to attack is therefore to get the rhythm of the first three attacks and never trigger the fourth (a standard fighting game mechanic).

Special attacks can be pressed by using the Power button after a different number of Attacks (A = attack button, P = power button, + = 'then press...'):

- **P:** if Power is used without a direction (or when pressing forwards), causes a jumping weapon attack carrying the player forward a short distance.

- **A + P:** power blow, that knocks back opponent a short distance

- **A + P + P:** as above, but followed by the jumping attack to close distance

- **A + A + P:** wide arc attack clears surrounding opponents (low damage)

■ **A + A + A + P**: crushing blow, which can stagger opponent and lower their shield

These different combinations are simple to enter, and hence 'button mashing' still produces useful actions.

Locking On

Holding the Left trigger locks on to an opponent in the front arc. In this mode, the player can use all of the attacks they can use when unlocked, plus they can press Shoot to fire an arrow at their opponent.

Partner Trigger

When the Right trigger is pressed, the player's hero calls out to their partner for help. The partner switches between three contexts:

■ **Open**: partner chooses own targets, staying within about 20 m radius of player.
■ **Guard**: partner stands back-to-back with player to protect their rear
■ **Co-op**: partner attacks the same target as the player, using co-operative attack.

Which context the partners goes into depends upon the circumstances, using a highly intuitive system which can easily be learned experientially:

	Final Context	
Current Context	**If no enemy locked**	**If enemy locked on (L-trigger held)**
Open	→ Guard	If enemies in rear arc, → Guard Else, → Co-op
Guard	→ Open	→ Co-op
Co-op	If enemies in rear arc, → Guard Else, → Open	If enemies in rear arc, → Guard Else, → Open

Informally, when unlocked, pressing Partner trigger switches between Open and Guard. When locked on, pressing Partner trigger switches between Open and Co-op.

If the player is being attacked from behind, pressing Partner trigger instead switches to Guard.

Armour

To help build atmosphere, the player's state of health is shown visually, by their armour. As they take damage, they lose items of armour. First, they lose their shoulder plate (75% Armour), then their breastplate (50% Armour), then finally their helmet (25% Armour). From 24 to 1% armour they are down to just a loincloth. At 0%, they are dead.

Their partner also has armour, *but cannot be killed*. Instead, when their armour runs out they automatically go into Guard position (the safest position).

THE LEGENDS

Initially, only Telamon & Peleus can be played, but the other legends unlock progressively:

1. **Telamon & Peleus:** the two brothers travel on the Argo, until Heracles leaves the voyage, and ultimately face off against the daughters of Medusa.

2. **Atalanta & Jason:** the first half of the story of the Argonauts, told from the perspective of Greece's legendary female warrior, Atalanta, who is partnered here with Jason.

3. **Jason & Medea:** the second half of the story of the Argonauts, as Jason returns to Greece with the Golden Fleece, partnered with his new wife, the sorceress Medea.

4. **Peleus & Heracles:** the tale of five of the twelve labours of Hercules (Heracles), told from the perspective of his friend Peleus, who helped him on several labours.

5. **Theseus & Telamon:** the legendary story of Theseus and the Minotaur, with Telamon partnering Theseus.

6. **Medea & Atalanta:** as Jason betrays Medea, she seeks revenge upon him, and partners with Atalanta for her own legend.

7. **Heracles & Theseus:** the story of mighty Heracles is concluded, with him partnered with his cousin and admirer, Theseus. Ultimately, Hercales ascends to Olympus as a god.

THE QUESTS

As well as the seven story-driven Legends above, the player can also complete seven quests – one for every hero. This is carried out in Quest Mode, in which the player can take any pair of heroes into any of the game levels. Each hero can acquire a mythic item (the Silver Bow of Artemis, Zeus' Thunderbolt, the Helm of Hades, the Winged Sandels of Hermes etc.) by completing a series of challenges which are 'hidden' in the levels, but marked with the seal of the hero's patron god. The hero then uses the item to complete a final challenge.

For example, Medea's quest begins when her patron deity, Hecate, orders her to acquire the head of one of the daughters of Medusa. To do this, she must find where the Adamantium Sickle is held (the only weapon strong enough to cut off the head), and also acquire the Kibisis Pouch (which can hold the head safely). Only when she has found, and defeated the guardians of, these items, can she go to the daughters of the Medusa and get a Gorgon's head. Then, Hecate sends her into the Underworld to 'rescue' Persephone from Hades, using the Gorgon's head to turn her enemies to stone.

These quests provide a reuse of resources at very little cost, and provide an extended play window, extending the value of word-of-mouth and other consumer-lead market effects.

Additionally, the player receives a letter grade (Epsilon, Delta, Gamma, Beta, Alpha or Omega) for each level in Quest Mode, allowing hardcore players to strive to get Omega on every level.

GAMEPLAY EXAMPLE

This is set in the first Legend, Telamon & Peleus, during the part of the voyage of the Argo when these two heroes were aboard. The player is Telamon; Peleus is their partner.

The Argo has set ashore on the Arcton penisula, en route to the Black Sea and Colchis (where the Golden Fleece is held). Desperately short of food, all the Argonauts are told to go out seeking supplies. Telamon briefly talks to Heracles, whom both he and Peleus have befriended. He tells them that the Arcton peninsula is notoriously home to certain Earth-born giants with a bad reputation. Heracles asks the two heroes to take care, and heads off on his own.

Telamon and Peleus talk amongst themselves as they head out into the peninsula – their conversation is ended by unintelligible talking from a ridge nearby. A short engine cut shows the group of six-armed nine-feet tall giants on the other side of the ridge.

The heroes engage. At first, Telamon wades into open combat (Peleus picks his own targets), but the enemy is strong. Soon, Telamon is surrounded. He tries a wide-arc attack to throw them off, then hits his trigger to call to Peleus ("I need some help here!"). Because there are enemies in Telamon's rear arc, Peleus rushes to fight back to back, guarding Telamon's back.

They cut the group down to just two opponents, but another giant arrives. This one is twelve feet tall, and is dressed in black armour – the leader of this group. Telamon hits his trigger to free up Peleus ("Go get them…"), and then locks onto the leader of the group. He starts hitting, but the giant's defence is too strong, and it keeps using a shield to block.

Telamon decides to take out the grunts first, then deal with the leader. Still locked, he hits his trigger to assign Peleus to that target ("Keep the leader busy for me!"), putting Peleus in Co-op mode, then releases the lock trigger (Peleus continues attacking the leader).

Locking onto a distant foe that Peleus has already reduced to just a helm, Telamon hits his arrow button repeatedly and the giant falls down dead – but as he does the other giant hits him and sends him flying. He loses his breastplate – he's down to 50% Armour. He's scored a 3-hit combo at the moment from the arrows, and Peleus hits the giant leader 4 times, extending this combo to 7 while the player while gets their bearings.

Quickly locking onto the last grunt before the combo fades, he starts hitting it just in time to continue the combo. Because a second opponent has been added to the combo, a x2 appears by the combo count, and after 8 hits (15 hits total) the giant falls.

The player locks back onto the leader (combo x3), but as he does, Peleus' last piece of armour is removed – Peleus falls into Guard ("I can't hold him any longer"). Telamon will have to defeat the giant on his own. After another 4 hits, the player is knocked back and with Peleus in Guard mode, the combo is broken at $19 \times 3 = 57$. The player's helm is knocked off – they only have 25% Armour left.

Falling back a safe distance, the player locks on and lets loose with arrows. Although Peleus is in Guard, Telamon hits trigger to toggle Peleus into Co-op... since Peleus cannot leave the Guard position without getting some armour, this causes Peleus to shoot arrows to defend Telamon – so the two unleash a rain of arrows together. The giant leader falls, and the highest combo score of the battle (57) is used to upgrade the loot – which includes full armour and a big plus to Attack.

The two carry on, and come to a flock of sheep. Perfect food for the voyage! Telamon tries to grab one, but they run away too fast. Flipping into Co-op ("Help me corner one of these damn sheep!"), the two co-operate to bring down the sheep. They round up the last few with arrows, leaving a dead flock and mutton for all.

The camera pans back to a nearby ridge. From behind it can be see a smooth mound, which rises upwards... then higher... and higher... until a huge thirty foot tall Cyclops shepherd can be seen towering angrily above it's now slaughtered flock!

Telamon locks on, and triggers Peleus into Co-op ("Try and hit its skullcap!"). Peleus begins hitting the Cyclops' skullcap (a context-specified behaviour in this case), which partly covers the single eye. When he does, the shepherd stops briefly to readjust its position. Telamon times his shot perfectly and an arrow pierces the Cyclops' eye, blinding it! The giant comes falls to its hands and knees and begins groping after the two heroes in a blind panic. The adventure continues...

NOTES

How does the game emotionally involve the player?

- "Buddy movie" stories following the adventures of various pairings of heroes
- Vivid, believable recreation of mythic Greece (rather than over-the-top fantasy)
- RPG structure immerses player as they work to 'power up' their heroes
- Strong non-linear interconnections between the stories ("Mythological *Pulp Fiction*")
- Later quests relate to the relationships between the heroes

How does the game function as wish-fulfillment?

- Player engages in larger-than-life heroics
- Epic quest format
- Player is immersed in famous mythology

How does the game appeal to the hardcore gamer?

- Multi-level controls allows hardcore players to perfect 'advanced' combat techniques (earning greater rewards in terms of character advancement by using combos to 'upgrade' power ups)
- RPG-style format popular with hardcore

- "Fantasy" settings popular with hardcore
- Constant unlocking of materials (new heroes, then mythic items) forms addictive motivating factor

How does the game appeal to the casual gamer?

- Easy controls, allows the player to "button-mash" and still progress
- RPG format allows less-expert players to "level up" to tackle tougher quests
- Immersive mechanics (very little displayed as HUD overlays) builds atmosphere
- Quasi-historical setting provides easy identification with game world

Market notes

- Greek monsters are the most recognizable mythic creatures in the West and are perennially popular (especially amongst young males)

- *Shin Sangoku Musou* (*Dynasty Warriors* in the West) series succeeded incredibly in the Japanese market (top five sales positions) by drawing on an identifiable mythology – the Three Kingdoms. (This Three Kingdoms setting is extremely famous and popular in Japan and China). *Gods & Monsters* presents a Westernized version of this approach, using a recognizable Western mythology as the basis for the game.

- Multi-character progression (through reuse of materials in new story contexts) creates longer play window for hardcore players, resulting in longer shelf life and greater capacity to cross over into the casual audience.

Bibliography

GENERAL BIBLIOGRAPHY

Atkinson, C. (2009). Verizon chief: Hulu will be over in two years. *Broadcasting & Cable*, November 20.

Burkitt, L. (2009). Commercials on the Go. *Forbes.com*, 14th July.

Carr, N. (2009). The price of free. *New York Times*, November 15.

Cellphone-only homes are increasing. *Boston Globe*, December 18, 2008

Dickson, G. (2009). FLO TV makes retail push. *Broadcasting & Cable*, November 14.

Dickson, G. (2009). Mobile DTV standard approved. *Broadcasting & Cable*, October 16.

Gates, B. (1999). *Business @ the speed of thought*. New York: Penguin Books.

Guthrie, M. (2007). What's webisode worth. *Broadcasting & Cable*, November 24.

Holmes, E. (2009). Mobile, DVR video log fastest growth. *Wall Street Journal*, February 23.

Jessell, H. A. (2009). Mobile TV's new free market economy. *TVNEWSDAY, 5*, Mar 13.

O'Brien, K. J. (2009). Ericsson reports 61% decline in profit. *New York Times*, July 25.

Reitmeier, G., "A Bigger-Picture Perspective on the Small Screen and ATSC Mobile Broadcasting," A White Paper from NBC Universal, unpublished.

Toffler, A. (1991). *Future shock*. New York: Bantam Books.

Top level radio posse pushes cellular FM. *Radio Business Report*, 11th November 2009.

GENERAL TEXTBOOKS ON WRITING

Hilliard, R. L. (2007). *Writing for television, radio and new media* (9th ed). Belmont, CA: Cengage Learning.

Kauffman, T. (1997). *The script as blueprint: Content and form working together, writing for radio, TV, film and video*. New York: McGraw-Hill.

Mayeux, P. E. (1994). *Writing for the electronic media* (2nd ed). Madison, WI: Brown & Benchmark.

Ryan, M., & Tankard, J. W., Jr. (2005). *Writing for print and digital media*. New York: McGraw-Hill.

Rubenstein, P., & Maloney, M. (1988). *Writing for the media: film, television, video, and radio* (2nd ed). Englewood Cliffs, NJ: Prentice-Hall.

Yopp, J. J. (2009). *Reaching audiences: A guide to media writing*. Boston: Allyn & Bacon.

REFERENCE, HISTORY, AND CRITICISM

Bluestone, G. (1966). Bartleby: The tale, the film. In H. P. Vincent (Ed.), *Bartleby, the scrivener: The Melville annual*. Kent, OH: The Kent State University Press.

Bowser, E. (1990). The transformation of cinema 1907–1915. In C. Harpole (Ed.). *History of the American cinema: Vol. 2*. New York: Charles Scribner's Sons.

Brownlow, K. (1969). *The Parade's Gone By*. New York: Alfred A. Knopf.

Budd, M., & Kirsch, M. H. (Eds.), (2005). *Rethinking disney: Private control, public dimensions*. Middletown, Connecticut: Wesleyan University Press.

Campbell, J. (1949). *The hero with a thousand faces*. New York: Pantheon Books.

Campbell, J., & Bill, M. (1988). *The Power of myth*. New York: Doubleday.

Chomsky, N., Herman, E.S., (1988). Manufacturing Consent: The Political Economy of the Mass Media

Connelly, R. B. (1986). *The motion picture guide, silent film 1910–1936*. Chicago: Cinebooks.

Elsaesser, T., & Barker, A. (Eds.), (1990). *Early cinema: Space, frame, narrative*. London: BFI Publishing.

Fox, B. (2009). *Documentary media: History, theory, practice*. Boston: Allyn & Bacon.

Harpole, C. (Ed.), (1990). *Cinema: Vol. 1*. New York: Charles Scribner's Sons.

King Hanson, P. (Ed.), (1988). *The American film institute catalog of motion pictures produced in the United States 1911–1920*. Berkeley: University of California Press.

Masser, C. (1990). The emergence of cinema: The American screen to 1907. In C. Harpole (Ed.). *History of the American cinema: Vol. 2* . New York: Charles Scribner's Sons.

Packard, V. (1960). *The hidden persuaders*. New York: David McKay Company Inc.

Perrault, C., (1967). *Histoires et contes du temps passé , avec des moralités. Contes de ma mè re l'Oye*

Schrader, P., & Jackson, K. (Eds.), (1992). *Schrader on schrader & other writings*, Directors on Directors Series. London: Faber & Faber.

Vogler, C. (1992). *The writer's journey: Mythic structure for writers*. Studio City, CA: M. Wiese Productions.

EARLY SCRIPT WRITING MANUALS

Ball, E. H. (1917). *Photoplay scenarios: How to write and sell them*. New York: Hearst's International Library Company.

Beck, L. J. (1915). *The scenario writers guide*. Brooklyn: Henry Harris.

Bertsch, M. (1917). *How to write for moving pictures: A manual of instruction and information*. New York: Duran.

Bradley, W. K. (1926). *Inside secrets of photoplay writing*. New York: Funk & Wagnalls.

Esenwein, J. B., & Leeds, A. (1913). *Writing the photoplay*. Springfield, MA: The Home Correspondence School.

Farquarson, J. (1916). *Picture plays and how to write them*. London: Hodder & Stoughton.

Fine, R. (1985). *Hollywood and the profession of authorship, 1929–1940*. Ann Arbor, MI: UMI Research Press.

Gaudreault, A. (1990). Detours in film narrative, The development of cross-cutting. In T. Elsaesser & A. Barker (Eds.), *Early cinema: space, frame, narrative*. London: BFI Publishing.

Palmer, F., & Howard, E. (1920). *Photoplay plot encyclopedia: An analysis of the use in photoplays of the thirty-six dramatic situations and their subdivisions*. Los Angeles, CA: Palmer Photoplay Corporation.

Parsons, L. O. (1915). *How to write for the "Movies"*. Chicago: A. C. McClurg & Company.

Patterson, F. T. (1921). *Cinema craftsmanship: A book for photo playwrights* (2nd ed). New York: Harcourt, Brace & Company.

FILM AND TELEVISION

Armer, A. A. (1993). *Writing the screenplay: TV and film* (2nd ed). Belmont, CA: Wadsworth.

Bluestone, G. (1961). *Novels into film.* Los Angeles: University of California Press.

Blum, R. A. (1995). *Television and screen writing: From concept to contract* (3rd ed). Boston: Focal Press.

Dancyger, K., & Rush, J. (2006). *Alternative scriptwriting; Successfully breaking the rules* (5th ed). Burlington: Focal Press.

Elbert, L. T. (Ed.), (1999). *Why we write: Personal statements and photographic portraits of 25 top screen-writers.* Los Angeles: Silman-James Press.

Goldman, W. (1983). *Adventures in the screen trade.* New York: Warner Books.

Gotham Writers' Workshop. (1981). *Writing movies: The practical guide to creating stellar screenplays the way to write for television.* London: Hamish Hamilton.

Hamp, B. (1997). *Making documentary films and reality videos.* New York: Henry Holt & Company.

Koch, J., Kosberg, R., & Meureur, T., *Pitching Hollywood: How to Sell Your TV and Movie Ideas*

Portnoy, K. (1998). *Screen adaptation: A scriptwriting handbook* (2nd ed). Burlington: Focal Press.

Rouveral, J. (1984). *Writing for the soaps.* Cincinnati, OH: Writer's Digest Books.

Schwartz, M. E., *How to write a screenplay* (2nd Ed).

Swain, D. V. (1982). *Film scriptwriting: A practical manual.* Burlington: Focal Press.

Taylor, T. (1999). *The big deal: Hollywood's million dollar spec script market.* New York: William Morrow.

Thompson, K. (1999). *Story telling in the new Hollywood: Understanding classical narrative technique.* Cambridge, MA: Harvard University Press.

Trottier, D., *The Screenwriter's Bible: A Complete Guide to Writing, Formatting, and Selling Your Script.*

Vale, E. (1998). *Vale's technique of screen and television writing.* Burlington: Focal Press.

Whiteside, R. (1998). *The screen writing life: The dream, the job, and the reality.* New York: Berkeley Boulevard Books.

SCREENPLAYS, STORIES AND NOVELS

Arndt, M., *Little Miss Sunshine: The Shooting Script*, (New Market Shooting Scripts Series)

Barnett, M., & Alison, J., *Casablanca*, The Script Shop (www.scriptshop.com).

Campion, J., *The Piano Player*, The Script Shop (www.scriptshop.com).

Ephron, N., *When Harry Met Sally* . . .

Friedmann, A., *Bartleby*, unpublished script, New York: Museum of Modern Art.

Goldman, W. (1983). *Butch cassidy and the sundance kid in adventures in the screen trade.* New York: Warner Books.

Hecht, B., *A Farewell to Arms*, The Script Shop (www.scriptshop.com).

Hemingway, E. (1962). *A farewell to arms in three novels of Ernest Hemingway.* New York: Charles Scribner's Sons.

Melville, H. (1853). Bartleby, the scrivener (a story of Wall Street). *Putnam's Magazine, Nov-Dec.*

Melville, H. (1952). Bartleby: The scrivener. In *Selected writings of Herman Melville*, The modern library. New York: Random House.

Schrader, P. (1990). *Taxi Driver.* London: Faber and Faber.

Sorkin, A. (2002). *The west wing script book.* New York: New Market Press.

Stern, P. (1996). *Van Dorn, It's a Wonderful Life, Penguin Studio Edition.* New York.

Vincent, H. P. (Ed.), (1966). *Bartleby, the scrivener: The melville annual.* The Kent State University Press.

Welland, C., *Chariots of Fire*, The Script Shop (www.scriptshop.com).

Welles, O., & Manckiewicz, H. J. (1946). *Citizen Kane.*

Niccol, A., & Peter W., *The Truman Show: The Shooting Script*

Payne, A., & Jim, T., *Sideways: The Shooting Script*

BROADCAST WRITING

Carroll, V. M. (1997). *Writing news for television: style and format.* Iowa City, IA: Iowa State University Press.

Orlik, P. B. (1998). *Broadcast cable copywriting.* Boston: Allyn & Bacon.

Wulfemeyer, K. T. (1993). *Beginning broadcast newswriting: A self-instructional learning experience* (3rd ed). Iowa City, IA: Iowa State University Press.

Wulfemeyer, K. T. (1995). *Radio-TV newswriting: A workbook.* Iowa City, IA: Iowa State University Press.

CORPORATE AND TRAINING

DiZazzo, R. (2000). *Corporate media production.* Boston: Focal Press.

DiZazzo, R. (1992). *Corporate scriptwriting: A professional's guide.* Boston: Focal Press.

Matrazzo, D. (1980). *The corporate scriptwriting book.* Philadelphia: Media Concepts Press.

Van Nostran, W. J. (1996). *The scriptwriter's workbook: A media writer's companion.* Boston: Focal Press.

Van Nostran, W. J. (1996). *The Scriptwriter's handbook: Corporate and educational media writing.* Boston: Focal Press.

Van Nostran, W. J. (1999). *The Media writer's guide, writing for business and education.* Boston: Focal Press.

INTERACTIVE MULTIMEDIA

Elin, L. (2001). *Designing and developing multimedia.* Boston: Allyn & Bacon.

Garrand, T. (2001). *Writing for multimedia and the web* (2nd ed). Burlington: Focal Press.

Gross, P. (1999). *Director 7 and lingo authorized.* Berkeley, CA: Macromedia Press.

IGDA's Guide to Writing for Games, Game Writers' Special Interest Group, 2003 (http://www.igda.org/writing/index.html

Iuppa, N. V. (1998). *Designing interactive digital media.* Burlington, MA: Focal Press.

Maciuba-Koppel, D. (2002). *The web writer's guide: Tips and tools.* Burlington: Focal Press.

Miller, C. H. (2004). *Digital storytelling, a creator's guide to interactive entertainment.* Burlington: Focal Press.

Siegel, D. (1996). *Creating killer web sites*. Indianapolis, IN: Hayden Books.
Thurlow, C., Laura, L., & Alice, T. (2004). *Computer mediated communication: Social interaction and the internet*. London: Sage Publications Ltd.
Varchal, D. J. (1996). *The multimedia scriptwriting workshop*. Subex Inc.
Wimberly, D., & Samsel, J. (1996). *Interactive writer's handbook* (2nd ed). San Francisco: Carronade Group.

RADIO-TV NEWSWRITING

McCullough, V. C. (1997). *Writing news for television, style and format*. Iowa City, IA: Iowa State University Press.
Wulfemeyer, K. T. (1993). *Radio-TV newswriting, A workbook*. Iowa City, IA: Iowa State University Press.

ARTICLES, JOURNALS, PAPERS & NEWSPAPERS

Ayala, D. (2009). Google's Nexus one specs leaked. *PC World*, December 16 (www.pcworld.com/article/184778/googles_nexus_one_specs_leaked.html).
Bray, H. (2009). *The Boston Globe*, August 13.
Dickson, G. (2009). *Broadcasting & Cable*, July 6, *Broadcasting & Cable*, July 22.
Perez, M. (2009). *Information Week*, accessed Aug. 18, 2009, www.informationweek.com/story/showArticle.jhtml?articleID219400486.
Meyer, N. (2000, April). *The situation comedy script format: Its evolution from radio comedy and the traditional screenplay* unpublished paper. Broadcast Education Association Panel.
MocoNewsNet (2009, Jan 8).
Substance Abuse: The Nation's Number One Health Problem, prepared by the Institute for Health Policy, Brandeis University for the Robert Wood Johnson Foundation, Princeton, NJ, October 1993.

SCRIPTWRITING SOFTWARE

Final Draft, Final Draft Inc., 1600 Ventura Boulevard, Suite 800, Encino, CA 91436 (http://www.finaldraft.com).
Inspiration, Inspiration Software, Inc., 7412 SW Beaverton Hillsdale Highway, Suite 102, Portland, OR 97225-2167 (http://www.inspiration.com).
Movie Magic Screenwriter, Movie Magic Dramatica, Screenplay Systems Inc., 150 E. Olive Avenue, Suite 203, Burbank, CA 91502 (http://www.screenplay.com).
Movie Master, Movie Master Hollywood Cinema Software, 12A Chestnut Street, Ridgewood, NJ 07450, e-mail: MMsupport@aol.com. Scriptware, Cinovation Inc. 1750 30tj Street, Suite 360, Boulder CO 80301-1005 (http://www.scriptware.com).
Scriptwerx, Parnassus Software, 1923 Lyans Drive, La Canada, CA 91011 (http://www.originalvision.com).
StoryLinePro, Truby's Writers Studio, 1737 Midvale Avenue, Los Angeles, CA 90024.
StoryVision, 171 Pier Avenue, Suite 204, Santa Monica, CA 90405, e-mail: storyvisn@aol.com.

Glossary

(Note: Glossary entries which are also Key Terms are in *italics*)

4:3 academy or television ratio   The standard format and screen ratio for movies at the time television was invented.

A sequence of images   The basic narrative concept of storytelling in motion picture.

A "spec" script   A script for an established series that is not commissioned by written by a new writer who hopes to get a commission from a series editor or head writer.

Academy of Motion Picture Arts and Sciences   This renowned industry organization, recognizing the need for some kind of format for screenplays when sound came into motion picture, began to standardize the screenplay format, which has led to the modern-day master scene script.

Act   A term borrowed from the theater to signify a key story point in motion picture narrative.

Action   The events and choices whose consequences impact characters and constitute the storyline; the fundamental component of visual narration in visual media.

Adaptation   Using a source that is a fully developed story in fiction or drama and reconceiving it for a motion picture medium.

Advertising on the Internet   Changes the game from linear to interactive responses and uses contextual targeting a click mapping.

Agents   Individuals or companies that represent talent of all kinds including writers. They negotiate fees and, if good, become a clearinghouse for a lot of jobs and put packages together.

AI   Artificial intelligence is the programmed characteristics of behavior and response of a nonhuman character.

Analytic steps   The critical thinking about a communication problem that can be summarized as six steps in the form of a question and answer that lead to the creative concept.

Angle of acceptance   A term that describes how wide or narrow a given lens frames the scene in front of it.

Antagonist   Derived from the Greek word *agon*, meaning action, and refers to the character who is the adversary or opponent of the PROTAGONIST.

Apps   An abbreviation for applications or software written to run on a given operating system.

Aristotle   Aristotle was the fourth-century BC author of *The Poetics* defining literary modes of communication.

Aristotle's Rhetoric   A work of literary and communication dating from analysis that explains how persuasion works on the recipient of written and oral argument.

Artificial intelligence   A behavior programmed in to an avatar, object, robot, or character that enables it to make choices.

Assets   Media elements that are created independently and imported into a multimedia environment.

Audience   The receiver of a one-way communication whose response determines the success of dramatic and media writing.

Audio writing   Writing to designate a series of sounds, whether speech, music, or sound effects, that tell or help to tell a story.

Authoring tool   Software that enables the writing of code that can program interactivity and create an interface for the user.

Avatar   The character that you control in the game or that you create in a multiplayer game.

Axiom   A given that is a logical foundation to an argument, in this case, that no communication is necessary unless there is a problem of knowledge or understanding on the part of a potential audience.

B2B   Business-to-business.

Background   The farthest part of a camera frame along the optical axis of the lens.

Background research and investigation   The process that sometimes precedes the concept and certainly the treatment of both corporate and entertainment scripts.

Backstory   Refers to the life and background of a character that does not appear in the film or TV episode but that explains who the person is and why he or she is that way. Backstory is usually written up for a series or video game BIBLE.

Bandwidth   Describes the size of the data stream in bits or the measure of the speed of a network connection.

BCU (Big Close-Up) or ECU (Extreme Close-Up)   A big close-up or extreme close-up frames the head so that the top of the frame clips the forehead or hairline and the bottom of the frame clips the neck.

Beat   A scriptwriting term written in caps to indicate a wait or a pause in the delivery of dialogue. It implies a reaction or when some business intervenes between lines of dialogue.

Beat sheet   A scriptwriting term associated with television writing for series, which often substitutes for a TREATMENT and outlines the numbered scenes or sequences for an episode.

Behavioral objective   One of three types of objective that engenders actual change in action or behavior as a result of media communication.

Bible   Combined with the word "series" or "video game," refers to a substantial compilation of BACKSTORIES and includes explanation of the setting, world, characters, and story background for the benefit of all writers and creative talent involved.

Billboards   A form of visual medium that often incorporates on visual metaphor and meta-writing.

Blogs   A contraction of web logs or websites maintained by one person who writes and collects links to other sites concerning a given topic.

Brainstorming   A well-recognized process of free associative thinking that takes place at the beginning of the creative process.

Branching   A basic schematic for organizing hierarchical relationships.

Branded content   A relatively new idea of entertainment conceived around a product or a brand so that advertising is integrated into storylines and content, separate from product placement, which is the incorporation of specific brands as props.

Business theatre   A live presentation of product, corporate policy, or annual results with prescribed speech and multimedia modules to motivate personnel, usually in a special sometimes exotic location.

Camera angles   Always in uppercase.

Camera directions   A repertoire of camera angles that refer to the size of the frame around the human figure.

Camera lens   The image forming optical device that makes film and video.

Camera movements   A repertoire of displacements of the camera platform in all the different possible axes of movement.

Camera plot   A diagram of camera positions and moves for a given scene in relation to the action.

Capture audience attention   Involves an essential strategic device to hold the audience.

Case history   A story of someone's experience that illustrates the issue or idea that is the subject of a video.

CG (Character Generator)   The electronic text-composing device that is the most downstream device in a television switcher before program. In video postproduction, a character generator is now integrated with desktop editors. See TITLES.

Character   The fundamental element of drama and story that an audience relates to.

Character as victim   A comic device that makes a spectacle out of a character's mishap or misfortune.

Character names   Always in uppercase.

Children, babies, and animals   One of the principal persuasive strategies.

Cinematography and videography record in the present   Motion picture media transpire in the present and therefore narrate in the present.

Circle   A paradigm for representing graphically which interactive elements can relate so that all elements are equal, as any part of the circumference of a circle is equivalent to any other part.

Clear title   As with a physical property title that has no lien or encumberment.

Cloud computing   A web 2.0 idea of storing data and operating software from server-based applications accessible from anywhere rather than limited to a single desktop or laptop.

Clusters   Another paradigm for linked islands of information.

Comedy   The outcome of conflict that is hilarious or, as Aristotle says, a situation in which people appear to be worse than they are in real life.

Common denominator of a production   The script becomes the unifying reference point for all production decisions.

Common law   A British tradition of law made by precedent and tradition.

Communication objective   An identified outcome to any media communication that can be stated and expressed before commencing the scripting process.

Communication problem   The essential need or lack of knowledge or understanding that must be identified before any meaningful analytic or creative thinking can occur.

Communication strategy   A choice of persuasive device, story, or image that addresses the psychographic of the audience and disarms resistance or lack of receptivity to a given message or objective.

Computer graphic imaging (CGI)   Images created and rendered as pixels that are not produced by light forming an image through a lens onto focal plane.

Concept   The first formal document you create in the scriptwriting process is called a concept. It is also sometimes called an outline. Whatever you call it, its function is the same, namely, to set down in writing the key ideas and vision of the program. This document is written in conventional prose. There is no special format for it. It does not cover all the plot or content; nor does it include dialogue or voice narration. It is primarily an idea in a nutshell from which the script in all its detail will grow.

Content   The articulated matter that carries the story or the message that the audience sees and hears.

Copy platform   An advertising term that is an agency formula that approximates the seven-step process of developing a script concept.

Copyright   A right of ownership established by registering a work with the Library of Congress.

Copywriting and scriptwriting   These functions overlap but are not identical in that scriptwriters are not necessarily copywriters and copywriters in ad agencies are not necessarily scriptwriters.

Copywriting for the web   A new form of writing, thinking, and visualizing.

Cost benefit   An analytic concept that relates cost for any communication exercise to the theoretical money-saving benefit accruing from it with the idea that the demonstrable value of the benefit should exceed the cost.

Cover   A director must shoot the same SCENE from several different camera setups so that action and dialogue are repeated, or covered, in different camera angles in order for the editor to cut between them and create continuity from shot to shot within a scene. Without such cover, a scene cannot be edited.

Crane   A crane shot is made by raising or lowering a camera platform, usually with a crane or boom. It could also be achieved with a helicopter-mounted camera at great expense. In a low-budget production, a smaller-scale crane effect can be done by bending and straightening the knees while handholding the camera.

Creative concept   The key idea or seed from which a script grows; also a form of meta-writing.

Creative visual idea   The basis of a script is usually some visual idea or story idea that plays out in some action that can be visualized.

Cross-platform   Usually means something that can work in Windows or Mac OS but can also mean applications that are operational across other kinds of platforms or operational software.

CU (Close-Up)   A close-up frames the head and shoulders, leaving headroom above the head. A close-up is a way to frame the face or to highlight detail of inanimate objects.

Cut-scenes   Live or computer-generated video clips, usually not interactive; interludes between stages that furnish additional information, such as story elements, tips, tricks, or secrets.

D. W. Griffith An early pioneer of moving picture art for the Biograph Company who extended the vocabulary of visual narrative.

DAY or NIGHT   The third piece of production information in a scene heading that has implications for lighting.

Decorum   A term derived from class rhetorical theory that the style of speech, diction, and vocabulary should match the person or setting.

Demographics   The definition of an audience with respect to age, income, education, gender, race, and other key characteristics.

Denouement   A French word meaning, literally, unknotting, which refers to the resolution of the basic conflict that drives a story.

Depth of Field   The nearest point of focus to the farthest point of focus in any given shot. This is a function of the focal length of the lens, the f-stop setting, and the shutter speed, usually fixed in film at a 1/48th of a second and in video at 1/30th of a second. Shutter angles can be varied on professional cameras to a small degree that changes exposure.

Design document   A commonplace term that refers to the meta-writing or conceptual writing behind interactive media.

Deus ex machina   A Latin phrase that means the god outside the mechanism, found in Aristotle's *Poetics* to explain a weak dramatic device; undermines true tragic drama because it is arbitrary and not connected to human action or choice.

Dialogue   Lines written for characters that are acted by talent.

Dialogue cards   Written dialogue seen on screen as text to be read by the audience and a beginning to the need for a script to put words in the mouths of characters.

Disguise   Deception of one character by another through physical disguise or false identity.

Dissolve/Mix   In film production, anything other than a cut has to be created in the optical printer from A- and B-roll offsets. The editor marks up the film so that the lab technician can move the printer from the outgoing shot on the A roll to the incoming shot on the B roll. In video, the mix is made with a fader bar that diminishes input from one video source as a second is added. In the middle of a dissolve, when 50 percent of the printer light or video source comes from each picture, a temporary effect called a SUPERIMPOSITION occurs. This effect is now created digitally within nonlinear editors.

Dolly   A dolly shot is similar to a tracking shot in that the camera platform moves, but it moves toward or away from the subject so that the frame size gets larger or smaller.

Double-take   Like many comic devices, the double-take is a compact with the audience. The character takes an extra long time to react to a put down or before delivering a reply. Although it can be an acting technique, it is also very much a comic effect that can be written into a script. It needs the right line or situation with an indication in the script. You do this by writing PAUSE, BEAT, or DOUBLE-TAKE.

Dramatic irony   A dramatic device in which the audience knows more than one of the characters in the drama such as Little Red Riding Hood not knowing that the Wolf has eaten Grandma and is waiting for her disguised in Grandma's clothes.

Dramatization   A technique that explains concepts, policy, or actions in a corporate context by means of dramatic scenarios with character and dialogue.

Dual-column format   This refers to a script layout in which all action is described in the left-hand column and all audio is described in the right-hand column.

Dub   Used as both a noun and a verb, the term refers to the copying of an electronic signal, both audio and video or either by itself, from one source to a new tape, disk, or new location on a tape or disk.

DVE (Digital Video Effect)   Transitions between shots have become so numerous because of the advent of DVEs in computer-based editors and mixers that it would be impossible to list the dozens of patterns and effects. Once again, this is the province of postproduction unless you have a strong reason to incorporate a specific visual effect into your script.

Edison   Thomas Edison is credited with improving the movie camera and inventing 35-mm film, although simultaneous development of the movie camera and projector by the Lumière brothers in Paris moderates that claim.

Educational documentary   A form of linear moving picture narrative that is dedicated to imparting knowledge or understanding of a specific subject matter or specific ideas usually of an academic nature.

Emotion (pathos)   One of the modes of persuasion in Aristotle's *Poetics*.

Engine   The application that powers a game. One primary engine (the graphics engine) and several smaller engines power AI and sound. People refer to the whole product as the engine.

Establishing Shot   This SHOT establishes the setting and the dramatic components of the SCENE.

Ethical values (ethos)   One of the modes of persuasion in Aristotle's *Poetics*.

Ethos or an appeal to ethical values   Part of Aristotle's classic analysis of the way persuasion works.

EXT. (Exterior)   This is the standard abbreviation for an exterior (or outside) setting used in the SLUG LINE of a script.

Fade In   Almost all audio events are faded in and faded out to avoid the snap cut to music or effects at full level. This also permits us to use music cues that do not necessarily correspond to the beginning and end of a piece.

Fade In From Black   All programs begin with this effect, which is simply a mix from black to picture. Sometimes you might write in this effect to mark a break in time or sections of a program.

Fade Out   This is the audio cue that most people forget to use. They fade in music or effects and then forget to indicate where the audio event ends. The fade out eases out the sound so that an abrupt cut off or stop does not shock the ear or draw attention to itself. Many commercial recordings of popular music are faded out at the end.

Fade Out To Black   All programs end with this effect that is a mix from picture to black, the opposite of the fade in from black. Logically, these two fade effects go in pairs.

Fade Under   Fading an audio event such as music under is necessary when you want the event to continue but not compete with a new event that will mix from another track—typically dialogue or commentary. These decisions are largely made by audio mixers and editors. Nevertheless, you should know these terms for the rare occasion when you need to lock in a specific audio idea in your script.

FCC language codes   The Federal Communications Commission, the federal agency that regulates broadcasting over public airwaves, bleep-censures a list of seven unacceptable four-letter words and also can fine stations that broadcast them.

Final Draft Script   This is the final document that incorporates all the revisions and input of the client or producer and all the improvements and finishing touches that a writer gives to the writing job even when not explicitly asked for. A scriptwriter, like all writers, looks at his work with a critical eye and seeks constant improvement. This document should mark the end of the writer's task and the completion of any contractual arrangement.

First-Draft Script   This is the initial attempt to transpose the content of the treatment into a screenplay or script format appropriate to the medium. This is the cross-over from prose writing to script writing in which all the special conventions of camera and scene description are used. The layout of the page serves the special job of communicating action, camera angles, and audio to a production team. It is the idea of the program formulated as a blueprint for production. The producer, the client, and the director get their first chance to read a total account for every scene from beginning to end.

First Person   In video games, means you see the action through the eyes of your characters. You don't see your own body.

First-person plural   The preferred pronoun "we" is inclusive and puts the client and the writer on the same team, as it were, working together to solve a problem.

First-person singular   A fatal error of media writing because it interposes a personal self between the idea and the client who is paying for it and makes criticism awkward and harder for the client to bring forward.

Fixed media   Interactive media that is burned onto a disk and then manufactured.

Flashback/Flash Forward   These terms refer to a narrative device that both writers and editors use to manage the relationship of different moments of time in a dramatic story.

Flat fee   Compensation by a fixed amount irrespective of time or effort spent.

Flight simulator   Simulates the action of flying an aircraft. Realistic controls make the flying itself the point of the game.

Flowchart   A diagrammatic representation of interactivity by lines and symbols.

Focus group   A selected group representative of the demographic of the target audience.

Foreground   The near part of a camera frame along the optical axis of the lens.

Format   The special layout of the page and conventions of upper and lowercase that govern a script page.

Formative evaluation   An investigative test of potential audience response before production or other communication exercises.

Frame   The borders of the images or picture, which corresponds to the area seen in a viewfinder.

Frames   A border placed around an element of a web page such as a text block.

Friedmann's first law of media communication   The effectiveness of a message varies in inverse proportion to the size and breadth of its audience.

Friedmann's second law of media communication   The simplicity of the message must be in inverse proportion to the size of the audience. The larger the audience, the greater the need to simplify the content to reach the lowest common denominator of any given audience.

Functionality   A concept of web design that emphasizes function and purpose in design.

Funnel technique   An arrangement of questions that starts with broad general questions and progresses to specific, sometimes closed questions.

Gambling PSA   Sponsored by the Massachusetts Council on Compulsive Gambling, this PSA illustrates visual metaphor (see the website).

Game bible   The written story background that includes a description of characters and their powers and weapons.

GIF or JPEG   Two of many still picture codecs that computers and web pages still recognize.

Graphics   Media content created by artwork or computer-generated images that are not photographically recorded and illuminated images of the real world.

High Angle   A high angle means pointing the camera lens down to an object or a person.

High-Level Design   Refers to a comprehensive description of the content, style, and look of interactive media such as a video game, a website, or a CD-ROM.

Hook   A situation or action that captures the immediate interest of an audience.

Hopefully   A fatal adverb to use to qualify any written or oral pitch of an idea because it indicates the lack of conviction on the part of the author or presenter of any given idea.

How-to-do-it videos   A common use of video to explain a process, job, or task, usually by demonstration so that the viewer can imitate and achieve the same result.

HTML   Hyper text markup language that is the universal open architecture code on which all websites are based.

Hub with satellites   Another paradigm for the graphic representation of interactive elements.

Hubris   A Greek word meaning pride or self-delusion or the overconfidence that precedes misfortune.

HUD (Heads-Up Display)   A heads-up display is used most in first-person games. The heads-up display, like a flight deck or a dashboard, presents information on the screen, such as the life meter, level, weapons, ammunition, map, and so on.

Humor   A key ingredient or device of many corporate, training, and other media communications; one of the principal persuasive strategies.

Hyperlinks   An object, text, or area of a web page that has embedded links to other pages.

Hypertext   Text in an interactive medium in which a link to another part of the text or another website URL is embedded and activated by mouse click.

Indemnity   A warranty by the seller that the provenance of any piece of property is good in title and clear of liens.

Index cards   A common technique of outlining the scenes of a program or script either with cards or virtual cards in scriptwriting programs that can be shuffled and rearranged.

Infomercial   An extended form of advertising presented in the guise of programming.

Informational objective   One of three types of objective that delivers knowledge, fact, or understanding to an audience that did not know.

INT. (Interior)   This is the standard abbreviation for an interior (or inside) setting used in the SLUG LINE of a script.

Intellectual property   The legal notion that an idea or created work enjoys a status parallel to that of physical property. Interactive television allows real-time interaction with screen content on equipped TV sets that are also connected to the Internet.

Interviewing   Recording the responses of people to questions prepared or impromptu that are then edited either as sync shots or voice only for inclusion in a video.

Inverted funnel   An arrangement of questions that starts with closed questions and fans out to broader lines of questioning.

Inverted pyramid   The classic formula for writing news stories filed by wire services in which the lead goes first and the least important details are presented at the end.

Isometric View   A view of a video game and its action from an angle instead of directly from above or directly from the side.

Job   In training terms, refers to the overall job of work that has to be accomplished.

Key moment   The essential part of a story reality that makes up a scene.

Library Music   Library music is sold by needle time for specific synchronization rights for designated territories and is generally recorded without fades so that the audio mixer of a program can make the decisions about the length of fades. This music is recorded in convenient lengths of 30 and 60 seconds, as well as longer pieces with variations on the same basic theme so that the piece can be reprised at different moments on the sound track. Also, small music bridges and riffs and teasers are available off the shelf for editors and audio mixers to use.

Linear   A program that is structured as a straight-line progression from beginning to end, like music, movies, and television.

Lingo   The scripting language that Adobe Director uses to program interactivity.

Location research   A specialized business of finding places and settings in which to shoot that correspond to the designated setting in the scene headings of a script.

Log Line   A log line is a short sentence or even a phrase that rests on the premise of a film and captures its essential idea.

Logos, an appeal to reason and argument   Part of Aristotle's classic analysis of the way persuasion works.

Louis Lumiere   Louis Lumiere invented a motion picture camera, which also served as a projector, in 1895.

Low Angle   A low angle means pointing the camera lens up to a subject whether an object or a person.

LS (Long Shot) A long shot should include the whole human figure from head to foot so that this figure or figures are featured rather than the background.

Master Scene Script The standard form of the SCREENPLAY for feature film is sometimes referred to by this name because each SCENE is usually the description of an action from which a MASTER SHOT will come.

Master Shot This is a camera SHOT that captures the whole scene and its dialogue in one single shot or TAKE. The standard practice of directors is to shoot a master and then COVER it with other angles of the same action and dialogue.

Meta-writing The author's term used throughout the book to mean visual and conceptual thinking that underlies visual writing and that may not be explicit expressed in the program.

Minidrama One of the principal persuasive strategies.

Miniscript The author's term for small scripts that define various assets such as video clips, voice-over, and graphics.

Mistaken identity Confusion of identity, usually comic, that produces plot complications and mis-understandings for other characters.

Mobile media broadband Types of wireless high-speed Internet access via a portable modem.

Mobile TV Broadcast television that can be picked up by a chipset in a mobile platform.

Mobisode™ A term trade marked by Fox to denote a very short unit of a new serial narrative for mobile media.

MMORPG (Massively Multiplayer Online Role-Playing Game), MMP, or MMO (Massively Multiplayer Online) An online game that allows players to interact with a large number of other players in a real-time virtual environment.

Montage A montage is an assembly of shots that have no intrinsic continuity and no necessary relation to one another other than their function in the montage created by the editor. The term comes from the French *monter*, meaning to edit.

Morphing This refers to a computer-generated effect that makes one shape or object metamorphose into, or transform into, another object unlike the first. For example, a human face changes into an animal face.

Motivational objective One of three types of objective that induces an emotional response in the audience and so changes attitude and receptivity.

MS (Medium Shot) A medium shot allows headroom at the top of frame and puts the bottom of frame either above or below the waist. Keeping the hands in is one way to visualize the shot. It is definitely well above the knees.

MUD (Multiuser Domain) A website that hosts multiple players logged on to play one another. An example is a chat room for text-based games.

Multimedia time continuum   The essential problem of scriptwriting, which is to describe visual and audio that happen as an integral continuous experience for an audience but can only be described by alternating representation of one after the other in words.

Multipoint to multipoint communication   A form of communication that allows all parties connected to the network to communicate to all other points.

Music   A music track is created independently of production. Music videos begin with a defined sound track. Other programs have music added in postproduction to fit dialogue, sound effects, and mood. The writer does not usually pick music nor decide where music is necessary. The exception is where the music is integral to the idea, or in a short script such as a PSA in which detailed conception might include ideas for music. If you do write in music cues, there is a correct way to do it.

Music bed   A continuous piece of music that is mixed under other sound or is audio coloration of a visual sequence.

Music bridge   A short piece of music that indicates a dramatic transition.

Music cues   A vocabulary of descriptive terms that indicate how and when a musical event on a sound track occurs.

Music sting   A very short and emphatic musical sound that underlines a dramatic moment.

Narrative argument   A form of presenting content by means of a logical progression or exposition, usually without resorting to techniques or devices that entertain.

Narrative tense   The present tense is the convention of screenwriting in contrast to narrative fiction, which can adopt a past or present tense.

Navigation   Refers to the way in which a user can travel around a website or choose interactive hyperlinks to discover the in-depth layers of a site, CD-ROM, or DVD.

Navigational design   Refers to the way interactivity is communicated to the user by intuitive visual ideas.

New England Home for Little Wanderers   A PSA discussed for its strong visual metaphor (see the website).

Nielson   A company that collects audience data and sells it to broadcasters.

Nodes   A point on an interactive path that requires choice to proceed.

Nonlinear   Program content that has a beginning at some entry point or home page but no necessary end or order or play because it is determined by the user.

Omniscient narrator   A novelistic device that is virtually impossible to replicate in a motion picture.

Omniscient or third-person narrator   A narrative device or convention that is unique to prose fiction, although there is a kind of equivalent in an objective camera but never the exact equivalent of an author who can reveal the thoughts of multiple characters.

On-camera anchor   A presenter who speaks to the camera and looks at the audience through the lens to narrate program content, familiar from the television idiom of news and other factual programming.

Open Mobile Video Coalition Advanced Television Systems Committee (ATSC)   The official body of the broadcast industry that has determined the signal standard for all broadcasters to use known as Mobile DTV.

Outline   A common technique of laying out the spine of a story or the sequence of scenes for a program or script.

Over-The-Shoulder   This shot, as the name implies, frames two figures so that one is partially in frame quarter-back view at one side while the other is featured three-quarter front view. This shot is usually matched to a reverse angle of the same figures so that the values are reversed.

Pace   The rate at which a story and scenes unfold based on the length of scenes.

Pan (Panorama)   The most common movement of the camera. A pan can move from left to right, or vice versa, hence, sweeping across a scene to give a panoramic view. The most common use of this camera movement is to follow action while the camera platform remains stationary.

Parallel paths   Another paradigm for graphic representation of interactive elements that charts movement that can hop from one path to the other.

Pari passu   A Latin legal term meaning each one gets paid equally at each step.

Pathos, an appeal to emotion   Part of Aristotle's classic analysis of the way persuasion works.

Per minute of finished program   A practice of charging a sum per finished minute of program.

Percentage of the gross   Gross revenue is all the money received by the distributor of a film.

Picture libraries   Commercial collections of images that are sold for use in programs and print media by license for specific rights.

Picture researchers   Specialized researchers that know the different specialized collections and how to find pictures and video/film clips.

Piecework   Work paid for by the unit or piece.

Pitch/Pitching   Pitching is talking, not writing. It is the verbal communicating and selling of ideas in the media industries. You have to talk your ideas as well as write them down. To make a living as a writer, you often have to sell your ideas in meetings. The good pitch should capture the essential idea in a nutshell and tease listeners so that they are motivated to read what you have written.

Platform   The type of system a game is played on, such as PlayStation 3, Xbox 360, Nintendo DS, Nintendo Wii, etc.

Platform game   Involves jumping on platforms of various sizes and jumping on enemies to destroy them.

Plot   The sequence of events that simulate the dynamics of circumstance, destiny, and choice involving one or more characters.

Point of view   A narrative voice that can be injected into the narration of a story so that one character is the lens through which the audience sees a world, which in a moving picture medium can influence the visual point of view established by the camera.

Portal   A gateway to enter the World Wide Web.

Postproduction   Refers to all the activities that follow shooting such as editing, postsyncing, music recording, titling, and mastering that lead to a completed program or SHOW PRINT.

Premise   This term refers to a compact statement of the essential idea of a movie or program. It embodies the essential conflict or dilemma that will drive the plot and the characters.

Preproduction   This refers to all the activities before shooting that turn a script into a production. During this stage, scripts are broken down, scheduled, budgeted, crewed-up, and cast.

Present tense   A universal convention of media writing which is more convincing because it implies we are seeing it now as if it already existed. Writing in the future tense, a common error of beginners, implies doubt because what is in the future does not exist.

Primary target audience   The most important segment of any audience demographic, which corresponds metaphorically to the bull's-eye of a target.

Process   An understanding that scriptwriting evolves through stages and changes from prose to a unique format.

Producer's net   The money paid by the distributor to the producer minus a lot of distribution costs as well as a fat commission.

Protagonist   A protagonist is the main character, whose actions and choices determine the story (e.g., Hamlet, the character in the Shakespearen play).

PSA   The acronym stands for public service announcement, which is like a TV commercial that communicates a message on behalf of a nonprofit organization or government agency with a message intended for the public good; broadcasters play PSAs to fulfill service obligations under their FCC licences.

Psychographics   The definition of the mental, emotional, and psychological frame of mind of an audience that helps identify its receptivity or hostility or neutrality toward a given media message.

Public domain   A legal term referring to intellectual property rights that have expired or have no known authorship such as folk tales and fairy tales.

Public policy problem   The large-scale issue that uses media as one technique, usually a PSA, to reach and influence various publics.

Pull Focus/Rack Focus   Pulling or racking focus refers to a deliberate change of focus executed by twisting the focus ring on the barrel of a lens. This technique is typically used to shift attention from one character to another when they are speaking and the depth-of-field is insufficient to hold both in focus at the same time. It is commonly used in television drama and movies.

Random access   Data that are immediately accessible in any part at any time because of their digital nature.

Realism   A literal representation of reality.

Realistic   Representing the world we know in a way that makes it convincing, sometimes by artifice.

Reason (logos)   One of the modes of persuasion in Aristotle's *Poetics*.

Reverse Angle   A reverse angle is one of a typical pairing of two matched shots with converging eye-lines. They can be MEDIUM SHOTS, CLOSE-UPs, or OVER-THE-SHOULDER shots and are shot from two separate camera setups.

Revision   An inevitable part of all writing but especially scriptwriting for which contracts usually specify a certain amount of revision.

RPG (Role-Playing Game)   A role-playing game is a genre of game for both PCs and consoles in which the player develops intelligence and skills by collecting points and solving puzzles.

Running Gag   A running gag depends on repetition. It keeps running. The audience knows the premise of the gag, so that each new exploitation of the gag gets a rise from the previous one. You keep going back to the same premise to work it from another angle. This device enriches a lot of comedy.

Scenario   An early term of the silent movie industry to designate an outline dramatic idea, what might now be called a treatment.

Scene   The scene is the basic unit of visual narrative for the SCREENPLAY. It has unity of time and place. A new scene begins when either time or place changes.

Scene heading   Another name for a slug line.

Scene Outline   This term refers to a way a writer might compose a visual narrative by listing SCENES rather than writing a TREATMENT.

Screenplay   A screenplay or script is the translation of the TREATMENT into a visual blueprint for production laying end to end the particular scenes employing the specific descriptive language of the medium to describe what is to be seen on the screen and heard on the sound track. This means the action and its background and each new character in the SCENE must be delineated. Every word of dialogue intended to be spoken must be written down. Every SCENE must be described.

Script   A script is the final document that details the scenes that make up the narrative of a film or program. It describes action and provides the dialogue to be spoken and is laid out in a format according to the convention of the medium. MASTER SCENE SCRIPT or SCREENPLAY is appropriate to film, and a DUAL COLUMN FORMAT is appropriate to documentary or corporate programs.

Script Breakdown   This is an analysis of the elements of a script by reference to location, cast, props, costumes, and so on that enables the producer to find the most efficient order for shooting the script in a shooting schedule.

Script format   A specific way of arranging the description of an image or shot and its corresponding sound on the page together with scene information.

Scripting language   A computer language that is a meta-language or coding language that creates a sublanguage or set of commands for other users who do not have access to the scripting language (e.g., Windows, Visual Basic, or Lingo).

Scripting software   Computer programs, such as Movie Magic Screenwriter and Final Draft, that are specialized word processors that format the script page according to industry standards by keystrokes.

Scriptlets   The author's term for short miniscripts for PSAs and TV commercials.

Scriptwriting   The term that embodies all the visual thinking and writing down in specific format of the narrative.

Scriptwriting software   Computer software that formats the word processing to fit precise industry script formats.

Search engines   Web crawlers that read tags and metatags in the html of web pages to list search results.

Secondary target audience   A desirable audience that may or may not be affected by the communication and would be a bonus but for whom the message cannot be altered.

Segue To   This term means to cross-fade two audio events. It is the audio equivalent of the video mix. You do not need to write this into the audio side of a script every time you use a MIX TO transition. It is understood by all involved that one goes with the other.

Sequence   This term refers to a coherent section of visual narrative that might be composed of several SCENES or several shots in the case of a long SCENE.

Serials   Multiepisode narratives in which each episode is a continuation of the previous episode.

Series bible   The book of characters, backstories, and locations on which a series is based, built up by writers over time.

Series editor   The head writer of a series, either the original writer or someone who takes over from the original writer.

Setup   This refers to the placement of a camera in a specific place and with a specific focal length lens to shoot a SHOT.

Seven-step method   The method of asking and answering six questions analytically before writing a creative concept.

Sexual innuendo   One of the principal persuasive strategies.

SFX (Sound Effects)   Instead of describing a thunderstorm and the sound of thunder at length, it is sufficient to write, "SFX thunder." In postproduction, whoever assumes responsibility for the audio tracks will pull a stock effect from a bank of effects on a CD-ROM or audiotape. A sound effect is anything other than speech or music.

Shock   One of the principal persuasive strategies.

Shooter   A game in which the object is to kill an enemy with a weapon that fires bullets or rays while avoiding being shot by the adversaries. Such games are usually constructed in a 3-D environment, assume a first-person perspective, and are referred to as FPS or "first-person shooters."

Shooting Script   A writer builds a SCREENPLAY out of scenes, which is its fundamental building block. The director has to compose a SCENE out of shots. This means a director has to create a SHOOTING SCRIPT out of a SCREENPLAY. The director has both the right and the responsibility to break down the SCENE into camera setups or shots that will COVER the action of the SCENE.

Shot   A shot describes the way a lens produces an image. It frames the subject in the viewfinder and is usually defined in two dimensions by how much or little of the human figure is included in the frame. It also has a third dimension that is defined by the foreground and background in the frame. How much of this third dimension is in focus depends on the DEPTH OF FIELD. See also PULL FOCUS/RACK FOCUS. The shot is the basic unit of narrative for the camera and for the director who shoots the movie. A shot can also be defined as the smallest unit of uninterrupted live action in the finished program.

Shot List   This list consists of the SHOTS that are revealed by a SCRIPT BREAKDOWN. It can be a list of shots that a director visualizes to shoot a SCENE, or it can be a way for a writer to compose a SEQUENCE or outline a SCENE.

Show-and-tell   A traditional and literal approach to training or video exposition that avoids visual metaphor.

Show Print   A print or dub from an edit master that embodies the finished program as it will be distributed.

Sitcom   A standard abbreviation of situation comedy that is now virtually a word in its own right.

Slapstick   Physical comedy routines that were developed in vaudeville, evolved in early silent films, and continue to this day.

Slug line   A standardized scene heading in a script consisting of three specific pieces of information crucial to production personnel who need to know whether the scene is interior or exterior, what the location is, and whether the action happens at night or in the daytime.

"Snackable" media   A current term that likens media consumption on mobile platforms to food snacks.

Sound cues   A series of indicators of how audio events will be recorded, played, or edited on a sound track and how they will begin and end.

Sound effect   An effect recorded wild for laying up on a mutlitrack mix, whether during production or taken from a sound archive or prior recordings.

Special effects   One of the principal persuasive strategies.

Specialized kind of writing   Scriptwriting in the history of writing is a new and specialized kind of writing.

Stage directions   Taken from drama scripts and referring to directions for emotion or performance put in parentheses after a character's name.

Statute   Law created by a legislative body and signed into law.

Sticky   Web terminology that describes the quality of a website that keeps you on it by virtue of its navigational design and content.

Storyboard   An artist's rendition of key frames of action in a script, somewhat like a comic strip.

Storyline   A through line or story arc that threads through the events of the narrative.

Strategies   Ways of overcoming audience resistance to a message or its content.

Subject matter experts, or SMEs   People with specialized knowledge inside or outside corporate client organizations that scriptwriters consult for essential background.

Summative evaluation   A verification of results obtained by measuring audience response to a finished piece of media communication.

Superimposition   A superimposition (or SUPER as an instruction) is simply the mix or dissolve mixed into the midprinter light or midfader position and then out. Beginners often go to unnecessary lengths to describe the way titles superimpose on picture or a background. A sentence can be reduced to *SUPER TITLES over black, SUPER TITLES over LS of street,* or *SUPER name under CU of face.*

Survey of strategies   These are humor, suspense, shock, minidramas, use of children, babies and animals, testimonials, sexual innuendo, and involving the audience as a character.

Suspense   One of the principal persuasive strategies.

Sync   Action and sound that produced at the same moment in time and recorded as such, particularly dialogue that requires lip sync.

Tag Line   A phrase or sentence that invites you into the world of the movie and is usually part of the publicity for launching and selling the film (e.g., "In space, nobody can hear you scream").

Take   This refers to the discrete recording or filming of a shot from a given SETUP. More than one take may be shot from the same SETUP in order to correct technical or performance errors.

Target audience   The identified group of people who are on the receiving end of any media communication.

Task   A subset of a given job that involves specific actions or routines or skills.

Teaser   An introduction to an episode that contains a dramatic premise, sometimes functioning as a hook.

Testimonials   Real and fake; one of the principal persuasive strategies.

The audience as a character   One of the principal persuasive strategies.

The role of writer   Can be combined with producer or director but is usually an independent role preceding production.

The story of a day   A chronological narrative of the events in a 24-hour period of a person or an enterprise that explains the relation of parts to the whole or detail in the context of complex stories.

The third dimension   Any interactive text has a relational dimension to other text or web pages through hyperlinks.

The Writers Guild of America (East and West)   The trade union that represents screenwriters and negotiates with the Motion Picture and Television Producers Association.

Third Person   An omniscient point of view in a video game that lets you see the character you are controlling in contrast to FIRST PERSON.

Through Line   A scriptwriting term that refers to the comprehensible story thread discernible in the events or actions of the character or plot.

Tilt   Tilt is a movement of the camera platform to angle up or angle down in a continuous movement along a vertical axis. It is useful for following movement. Panning and tilting are often combined in one movement to follow motion in three dimensions.

Titles   A title is created either in a CHARACTER GENERATOR or as part of computer graphic imaging. It is part of postproduction and needs to be identified by another SLUG LINE separate from a SHOT or a SCENE. You can indicate this by a simple slug: TITLE or CG.

Title cards   The technique of representing the speech of characters in silent movies by interspersing text in full frame between cinematographic action shots.

Track   A track refers to a continuous movement of the camera platform in one direction, usually alongside an action or moving figure. This is accomplished by putting the camera on a dolly that runs on tracks or by handholding the camera while walking alongside the action. This enables the camera to make a shot that maintains a constant frame around a moving object or person. The camera platform can also be mounted on a vehicle or any other moving object.

Tragedy   Conflict or choice that results in self-destruction or an outcome that induces pity and awe in the audience.

Trailers   Quick summaries with key moments edited together to suggest the promise of an episode to come.

Transitions   A repertoire of changes from shot to shot, namely CUT, FADE TO, DISSOLVE, or WIPE.

Treatment   After the CONCEPT comes the treatment. Both these terms are universally used and understood. A writer must know what they are and how to write them. Writing the treatment involves expanding the concept to reveal the complete structure of the program with the basic content or storyline arranged in the order that will prevail in the final script. All characters and principal scenes should be introduced. Although this document is still written in normal prose, it frequently introduces key moments of voice narration or dramatic dialogue.

TV spot for First Union   The chapter example for sophisticated CGI and special effects (see the website).

Two-Shot   Although this is not an abbreviation, it is a common term that describes two people in CLOSE-UP or MEDIUM SHOT. The widescreen format of the movie screen and the new HDTV television format make good use of this frame.

Verbal comedy   Comedy reliant on dialogue repartee, wit or verbal humor.

Video news release   A form of public relations presenting a story in the guise of news.

Video strips   The author's terms for short bursts of serial narrative for mobile platforms.

Virtual space   A cyberspace that does not exist in physical reality but is accessible as a graphic world by one or more users.

Visual gags   A comedy routine that involves physical action, not dialogue.

Visual metaphor   Like literary metaphor, an image that allows an intensification of meaning by transference of qualities of one object to another.

Visual seduction   The use of the visual properties of a camera shot or sequence that by means of color, form, and composition enchant or captivate the viewer.

Visual writing   An essential characteristic of writing for visual media that means narrating through action and what the camera sees rather than by what people say.

VLS (Very Long Shot)   There is no precise definition about what is very long other than that it should include the whole human figure, the whole action, and a good view of the background.

Voice commentary   An important component of the PSA or ad that requires special attention.

Voice narration   A recorded commentary that is usually a voice confined to the sound track but can sometimes be the sync narrative of someone who appears on camera as presenter or interviewee.

Voice-over commentary   See voice narration.

Voice-overs   A recorded commentary that is dubbed over the picture without the speaker appearing in the shot or in the program.

Vox pops   From the Latin *vox populi*, a shorthand phrase that refers to random interviews of the man-on-the-street to find out the views and opinions of a cross section of the population.

Web 2.0   The next evolutionary phase of the World Wide Web—version 2.0.

Webisodes   Extensions of broadcast TV series podcast on the series website, and a series podcast from a website that has no broadcast presence.

What the camera sees   The basis for all screenwriting because there is nothing else.

Wheel   A paradigm for representing graphically how interactive elements relate.

Wheel with spokes   A variant of the circle with segments.

Where the action is taking place   The second piece of production information in a scene heading that the writer must determine.

Which medium?   A key question to ask about any concept to verify whether it will truly work in its chosen medium by exploiting the unique characteristics of that medium.

Wide Angle   This term is somewhat loose. It generally means a LONG SHOT or an establishing shot that shows the whole scene.

Widescreen 2:85 to 1   The standard widescreen ratio.

WiMax   *Worldwide Interoperability for Microwave Access* is a telecommunications technology that provides wireless transmission of data using a variety of transmission modes, from point-to-multipoint links to portable and fully mobile Internet access.

Wipe   A wipe is the effect of an incoming image pushing off the outgoing image. A wipe is more commonly a video effect. Every mixer has a number of standard wipe patterns. The most obvious are a horizontal and a vertical wipe in which the two images are separated by a line. The other basic patterns are circle wipes and rectangle wipes in which the incoming image grows from a point in the middle of the outgoing picture as an expanding shape. A scriptwriter should think carefully before writing in such detailed transitions. Leave it to the director and editor in postproduction.

Work-made-for-hire   Work commissioned and paid for by the acquirer.

World building   Conceptual writing of the nature of the game environment, real or imagined.

Write for the voice   Writing spoken dialogue or commentary that must work when read aloud by a voice artist or commentator.

Writers Guild of America   The trade union of film and television writers, which bargains with the movie and television producers.

Writers Guild of Great Britain   The British equivalent of the American guilds.

Writing in one medium for another   Represents the fundamental paradox of scriptwriting because the writing is a blueprint for something that is not words.

Zoom   A zoom is an optical effect created by changing the focal length during a SHOT in a specially designed lens that has a variable focal length. The effect makes the frame larger or smaller like a DOLLY SHOT. The important difference is that a dolly shot maintains the focal length and depth of field throughout, and the camera moves nearer or farther away. The zoom uses an optical effect without moving the camera to change from a wide angle lens to a telephoto lens so that it appears to the viewer that the subject is closer or farther away.

Index

A

Academy Award, 4, 12, 148, 333
Academy of Motion Picture Arts
    and Sciences, 8, 139
act, 69
action, 8, 10–13, 61–62, 189, 190,
    191, 192, 207–209
    vs. dialogue, 207–209
acts, 160, 165
actuality, 140
Adams, Amy, 195
adaptations, 10, 202–204
    problems of, 202–203
    writing for, 202
The Adirondack Adventure Guide,
    257
admissions video, 19–20
Adobe Director, 257, 261, 262
Advanced Television Systems
    Committee (ATSC), 303
Adventures in the Screen Trade, 201
adversary, 160, 161
advertisements (ad), 79, 80
    audience attention and, 83–88
    billboards, 97–100
    client needs, 81
    computer imaging techniques
        and, 90
    First Union, 89
    formats, 102
    graphics and, 90
    infomercials, 96–97
    on Internet, 100–102

miniscripts, 81–82, 83, 102, 260,
    292
sexuality, 95
special effects and, 94
strategies for, 90–94
in television, 226
transportation, 97–100
video news releases, 97
visual writing and, 82–83
A&E, 139
Age. *see* demographics
agents, 338
agreement. *see* contracts
algorithm, 102
Allen, Woody, 165, 169, 175
Altman, Robert, 50, 192, 323
America, 152
American Beauty, 333
American Experience, 139, 145
American Express, 20, 38, 127–128
American Gigolo, 177
American Psycho, 174
American Travel in Europe, 129
analytic steps, 20
anchors, 125–126
angle of acceptance, 60
animation. *see* graphics
Anna Karenina, 200
antagonist, 161, 164, 181
antismoking PSA, 39–40
    communication problem, 40
    concepts, 40
    contents, 40

medium, 40
objectives, 40
strategy, 40
target audience, 40
AOL, 82
apps, 302, 307
archetype, 160, 164, 169, 188
archives, 143
Aristotle *Rhetoric*, 33, 90
ARPANET. *see* Pentagon WAN
artificial intelligence, 253, 288
assets, 254–255, 257, 260, 264,
    276
ATSC. *see* Advanced Television
    Systems Committee (ATSC)
AT&T, 92, 93, 120
Attenborough, David, 91
attention span, 32–33
attitude, 29–30
audience(s), 4–5, 18–19, 23–25,
    188, 234
    as a character, 95–96
    demographics, 25–27, 149, 175
    devices to capture attention of,
        83–88
    psychographics, 27–30
    target, 23–25, 40
audio, 5, 10. *see also* Sound
    writing, 67
authoring tools, 260–264
    defined, 260–261
avatar, video games, 288
axiom, 18

B

babies, 92–93
The Bachelor, 168, 178
background, 10, 61
    research and investigation,
        44–49, 141, 143
The Bank Job, 198
Barrymore, Drew, 196
Bartleby, 14–15, 177, 205, 206,
    215–220
Bartleby, The Scrivener, 13, 215
B2B. *see* business-to-business (B2B)
    inventory
BCU/ ECU. *see* big close up/
    extreme close up (BCU/ ECU)
beat sheet, 231–232
Beauty and the Beast, 174
behavioral objective, 31
Being Bailey, 318
Beowulf, 94, 173
big close up/extreme close up
    (BCU/ ECU), 63
billboards, 97–100
biographies, 146, 174
biopics. *see* biographies
Birth of a Nation, 332
Blade Runner, 94
The Blair Witch Project, 155, 166,
    309, 328
bloggers, 271
Body Heat, 171, 201
Body of Evidence, 201
Bogart, Humphrey, 171
Bogdanovich, Peter, 220, 337
The Bold and the Beautiful, 225
books *vs.* newspapers, 301
The Boston Globe Magazine, 286
Boston Law, 224
Bowling for Columbine, 139
brainstorming, 49
branching, 258–260, 273
branded content, 308, 314
Breast Implants on Trial, 145
brochures, 279–280
browsers, 269, 271
Budd, Billy, 219

budgets
    documentary, 143
    limitations, working with, 134
    location research and, 48–49
    scriptwriting and, 4, 80
Burn After Reading, 196, 197
Burns, Ken, 44
business theater, 119
business-to-business (B2B)
    inventory, 280
Butch Cassidy and the Sundance Kid,
    44, 165, 171, 201

C

camera
    angles, 62
    directions, 63
    frames, 62–63, 209
    lens, 60
    movement. *see* camera
        movement
    plot, 56
    shots. *see* camera shots
camera movement, 64
    CRANE, 64
    DOLLY, 64
    PAN, 64
    TILT, 64
    TRACK, 64
    ZOOM, 64
camera shots, 62–63, 183
    BCU/ECU. *see* big close up/
        extreme close up (BCU/ ECU)
    CU, 63
    ECU. *see* big close up/extreme
        close up (BCU/ECU)
    HIGH ANGLE, 63
    LOW ANGLE, 63
    LS, 63
    MS, 63
    OTS, 63
    RACK FOCUS, 63
    REVERSE ANGLE, 63
    TWO SHOT, 63
    VLS, 63
    WIDE ANGLE, 63

Cameron, James, 4
Campion, Jane, 201
Capitalism: A Love Story,
    139
capture audience attention
    devices to, 83–88
    strategies, 83
Careers, hybrid, 339
Casablanca, 332
case histories, 130
catalogues, 279–280
CD-ROMs, 6, 19, 45, 95, 111
cell phone, 301–302
    mobisode. *see* mobisode™
    text messaging, 302
    video on, 304–308
    video strips, 301
CGI. *see* computer graphic imaging
    (CGI)
Chamberlain, Richard, 226
Chaplin, Charlie, 193
character, 188–189
    generator, 65
    names, 62
    as victim, 194
Chariots of Fire, 12
Charley Wheeler's Big Week, 121,
    130, 132
Chasing Amy, 332
Check It Out, 126
children. *see* kids
cinematography, 60
circle, 273
Citizen Kane, 167, 201, 332
Civilization, 152
Civil War, 44–45
clear title, 336. *see also* copyright
Cleese, John, 28, 121
client relationship, 334
clients
    communication problem,
        18–19
    developing script with inputs of,
        133
    needs and priorities, 81
Clooney, George, 197

closed questions, 47
Close Encounters of the Third Kind, 170
close up (CU), 63
cloud computing, 282, 284
clusters, 273
Columbo, 191
comedy, 157, 159, 168, 169, 170, 175, 179, 180, 193–197. *see also* humor
    romantic, 168–169
    television and, 235–243
Comedy of Errors, 196
comic device, 193–194
commentary
    anchors, 150
    clichés, 151
    counterpoint, 150
    fitting to film/video, 152
    recording, 152
    scratch, 151
    voice, 96, 133
    wall-to-wall, 150
    writing, 149–152
commentators, dual, 150–151
commercials. *see* advertisements
commissioned writing, 19, 81
common denominator of production, 7
communication
    in corporate world. *see* corporate writing
    objective, 30–31
    problem, 18–23, 40, 110–113
    strategy, 32–33, 40–41
computer graphic imaging (CGI), 65, 94
concepts, 35–39, 41, 49–52, 178–180
    high, 178–179
    low, 178–179
conceptual writing, 272–273
conflict, 158–160
Connections, 120
contents, 33, 41
content writing, 272–273

contracts, in corporate world. *see* corporate contracts
contracts, in entertainment industry, 324–326
    agent and, 325–326
    first-draft screenplay in, 326
    remuneration, 325
    treatment in, 326
Coppola, Francis Ford, 172, 329
copy platform, 36, 83
copyright, 336–337
copywriting, 80–81
    for web, 102
corporate communication. *see* corporate writing
corporate contracts, 334–335
    payment agreement, 335
    verbal, 334–335
    written, 334
corporate television, 107–108
corporate writing
    client relationships, 334
    contracts. *see* corporate contracts
    copyright, 336–337
    freelance writer, 337–338
    marketing, 335–336
    overview, 333
    work-made-for-hire, 337–338
cross-dressing, 195
cost benefit, 110
Costner, Kevin, 152
Cotillard, Marion, 174
cover-up, 195–196, 197
CRANE, 64
Creating a Loyal Client, 126
creative concept, 17. *see also* concepts
creative ideas, 133–134. *see also* concepts
creative visual idea, 43
creativity, 335
crime movies, 171
cross-cutting, 190
cross genre, 174–175
cross-platform, 264
The Crying Game, 196

C-SPAN, 140
CU. *see* close up (CU)
current affairs features, 149
Curtis, Tony, 195, 196
CUT, 65
cutaway, 9, 65, 184
Cutler, Peter, 123
cut-scenes, video games, 288

D
Daisy Miller, 220, 337
Dances with Wolves, 332
Dave, 196
The Day After Tomorrow, 172
A Day at the Races, 195
DAY or NIGHT, 61
The Day the Earth Stood Still, 170
Deadwood, 234
decorum, 54–55
Defiance, 171
The Defiant Ones, 171
de Mille, William, 8
demographics
    age, 25
    education, 26
    gender, 25
    income, 26–27
    race and ethnic origin, 26
dénouement, 162, 164, 176
depth of field, 63
design document, 276
deus ex machina, 158, 159, 189
devices
    for corporate messages, 119–131
    for entertainment, 119
    for training, 119
    for video exposition, 114
The Devil Wears Prada, 194–195
dialogue in television, 228–231
    breaking up, 231
    realistic, 228–229
dialogue(s), 12–14, 54–55, 189–192, 207–209
    cards, 8
    in television *see* dialogues, in television

dialogue(s) (*Continued*)
  vs. action, 207–209
  writing, 191, 192
Diamond, I. A. L., 195
Dick, Moby, 219
digital television (DTV), 303
digital video effects (DVE), 66
directors, 4, 7, 12
disaster movies, 172
Discovery Channel, 139
disguise, 196
DISSOLVE/MIX TO, 65, 66
Dix, Beulah Marie, 8
documentaries
  about making of feature films,
    149
  Cro-Magnon man and, 137
  current affairs, 149
  dramatized, 143, 146–147
  educational, 116
  expedition, 148
  expository, 147
  historical and biographical, 142
  investigative, 145–146
  Muybridge, Eadweard and, 138
  narrative, 128–129, 146
  objective, 141–142
  point of view, 141–142
  propaganda, 147–148
  research and formulating theme,
    143
  role of writer in, 143–144
  science, 147
  scripted/unscripted approaches
    in, 142
  techniques, types of, 144–148
  television, 116, 127
  travel, 148–149
  truth or fiction, 140–142
  wildlife, 149
  writing of commentary in,
    149–152
Dogma, 211
DOLLY, 64
double-barreled questions, 47
double takes, 242

Doubt, 198, 200
drafts
  final, 56
  first, 52–54
drama
  for corporate messages, 120–121
  origins of, 157–158
  for TV commercials, 92
drama and comedy, 197
dramatic irony, 196–197, 198
dramatic structures, 157, 160, 165
dramatized documentary, 143,
    146–147
Dreamweaver, 262
DTV. *see* digital television (DTV)
dual-column format, 71–73, 102
dual commentators, 150–151
The Duchess, 200
DVDs, 6, 45
DVE, digital video effect (DVE)

E
Eastwood, Clint, 168
Easy Rider, 169–170
Ecclesiastes, 329
e-commerce, 284–285
ECU. *see* big close up/extreme close
    up (BCU/ ECU)
Edison, Thomas, 5, 138
education, 26
educational documentary, 116
educational videos, 108–110, 116
effects, 65
Egoyan, Atom, 4
Eisner, Michael, 309
Election, 332
Electronic Arts, 291
Elegy, 201
Elvira Madigan, 28
email, 268
EMC Corporation, 11
emotions, 28–29
*The Endurance: Shackleton's
    Legendary Antarctic Expedition*,
    139
engine, video games, 288

Enterprise, 229
entertainment industry
  agents, 338
  content, 328–330
  ideology, 328–330
  morality, 328–330
  overview, 323–324
  pitching, 326–328
  sentimentality, 330–333
  writing contracts, 324–326
epics, 173
ER, 44, 224, 225, 229, 231, 232
ethical values (ethos), 33, 90
expedition documentary, 148
expository documentary, 147

F
FADE IN (audio), 68
FADE IN FROM BLACK, 66
FADE OUT (audio), 68
FADE OUT TO BLACK, 66
FADE UNDER, 69
FADE UP, 69
Fahrenheit 9/11, 139
Fairfax, Marion, 8
Family Man, 212
A Farewell to Arms, 9
Fargo, 4
FCC. *see* Federal Communications
    Commission (FCC)
fear, 158, 159
Federal Communications
    Commission (FCC), 80, 234,
    309
fiction, 140–142
film noir, 171–172
final draft, 56
first draft scripts, 52–54
first-person game, 287, 288
first-person plural, 39
first-person singular, 39
First Union, 89
500 Nations, 150, 152
fixed media, 118
  limitation on, 279
Flaherty, Robert, 139

flashback, 167
flat fee, 334
flowcharts, 260, 261, 276
focus group, 110
follow-up questions, 48
foreground, 10, 61
format, 43, 69
formative evaluation, 109
4:3 academy or television ratio, 228
Franju, Georges, 141
Frasier, 242
freelance writers, 337–338
Friedmann's first law of media communication, 29
Friedmann's second law of media communication, 30
Frontline, 139
Frost/Nixon, 199
funnel approach, 48, 145

G
gambling, 84–88
games
    computer, 291
    formats, 292–294
    graphics, 290–291
    live-action video, 290–291
    order of writing, 291–292
    video. *see* video games
gang movies, 172
gender, 25
genres, 167–175
    action, 173
    adventure, 173
    biographies, 174
    buddy movies, 171
    disaster movies, 172
    epics, 173
    gang movies, 172
    horror, 169
    martial arts, 172–173
    monster movies, 173–174
    murder mysteries, 171–172
    private eyes, 171
    road movies, 169–170

    romantic comedies, 168–169
    satire, 174
    science fiction, 170
    undercover cops, 172
    war, 170–171
    westerns, 167–168
Gentlemen Prefer Blondes, 8
GIF, 45
GI Jane, 330–331
Gladiator, 199
The Godfather, 172, 190, 329
Golden Globe Awards, 118
Goldman, William, 44, 201
The Gold Rush, 193
Goldwyn, Sam, 193, 323, 328
Got Milk? campaign, 35
graphic design, 259, 265
graphics, 64–65, 90, 94, 129, 290–291
Great Dictator, 194
The Greatest Gift, 214
The Great Train Robbery, 168
Grierson, John, 139
Griffith, D. W., 8
Groundhog Day, 211
Guess Who's Coming to Dinner, 332

H
haiku, 301
HDTV. *see* high-definition television (HDTV)
heads up display (HUD), 288
Hecht, Ben, 11
Hemingway, Ernest, 9–11
Herbal Essence, 95
hero. *see* main character
Herskovitz, Marshall, 309
HIGH ANGLE, 63
high-concept film, 178–180
high-definition television (HDTV), 63
High Noon, 9
historical and biographical documentary, 142
History Channel, 139

hook, 233
horror movies, 169
how-to-do-it videos, 108, 115, 116
HTML. *see* hyper text markup language (HTML)
hubris, 199
hub with satellites, 259, 273
HUD. *see* heads up display (HUD)
Hudson, Hugh, 82
humor
    for corporate messages, 122
    for TV commercials, 90–91
Hybrid careers, 339
hyperlinks, 269
hypertext, 252
hyper text markup language (HTML), 262, 263, 268–269
hypothetical questions, 47

I
idea, 9, 11, 34, 82–83
images, 44–45
IMAX theater, 139, 148
implied action, 209–210
In Bruges, 198
income, 26–27
In Dances with Wolves, 199
index cards, 44, 49
Industrial Light and Magic, 94, 129
infomercials, 96
informational objective, 31
information overload, 24–25
innovative techniques, television writing in, 243–244
The Insider, 147
Inside the Tobacco Deal, 147
instructional videos, 108–110, 116
intellectual property. *see* copyright
interactive applications, 119
interactive brochures, 279–280
interactive catalogue, 279–280
interactive design, 254–257, 260
interactive learning programs, 280–281

interactive media. *see also* Internet;
     print media; video games;
     World Wide Web
   authoring tools and, 260–264
   defined, 251–253
   reference work, 283–284
   script formats for, 264–266
   television, 294–296
   writing for, 254–257
interactive movies, 296–297
interactive television, 102
The Interactive Writer's Handbook,
     265
International Game Developers
     Association (IGDA), 286
Internet. *see also* World Wide Web
   email, 268
   modems, 268
Internet service provider (ISP), 263
interviews
   for corporate messages, 130
   for documentary, 145
   for scriptwriting, 46–48
Interview with the Vampire, 169
In the Heat of the Night, 332
In the Realm of the Senses, 201
INT.(interior) or EXT.(exterior), 60
inverted funnel approach, 48, 145
inverted pyramid, 271–272
investigative documentary,
     145–146
Irons, Jeremy, 201
isometric view, video games, 288
ISP. *see* Internet service provider
     (ISP)
It's a Wonderful Life, 177, 189, 210,
     212–213
Ivy college, 19–20, 24

J
James, Henry, 220, 337
Jaws, 174, 188
jobs, 115
jokes. *see* Humor
journalism, 46, 144
   in early days, 271

inverted pyramid practice, 271
JPEG, 45
The Jungle, 105
Jurassic Park, 94, 129, 199
Just Marcy, 236–239

K
Kasdan, Lawrence, 171, 201
Kaspar, David, 148
Kaufman, George S., 196
Keillor, Garrison, 67
key moment, 189
kids, 92–93
kiosks, 281
Kubrick, Stanley, 28, 170

L
L.A. Law, 224
LAN. *see* local area network (LAN)
language codes, 234
The Last Samurai, 173
laugh lines, 242–243
La Vie en Rose, 174, 199
leading questions, 47
Legends of the West, 146
Lemmon, Jack, 195, 196
length, 205
   of corporate video, 132–133
Le Sang des Bêtes, 140
Liar, Liar, 168
Library of Congress, 45
linear media, 252–254, 258, 259,
     264
linear writing, 270
lingo, 262
Little Big Man, 146
Little Red Riding Hood, 160–164,
     198
live-action video, 290–291
local area network (LAN), 263
location research
   for documentaries, 143
   for film/videos, 48–49
logical argument, 128–129
log lines, 50, 176–177
   characteristics of, 176

Lolita, 201, 219
Lonesome Dove, 226
long shot (LS), 63
Loos, Anita, 8
Lost in Translation, 194
Love and Hate, 310
The Lover, 200
The Lovers, 219
LOW ANGLE, 63
low-concept film, 178–180
LS. *see* long shot (LS)
Lucas, George, 94
Lumière, Louis, 5, 138

M
Madame Bovary, 200
main character, 160–164
The Maltese Falcon, 171
Mankiewicz, Herman J., 201
marketing oneself, for corporate
     writing, 335–336
Married with Children, 333
martial arts movies, 172–173
M*A*S*H, 192
Mason, James, 201
The Master of Disguise, 196
master scene script, 70–71,
     184–185, 234
The Matrix, 289
media
   corporate uses of, 117–118
   fixed, 118
   interactive, 106
   print, 106
   visual, 3–6. *see also*
     advertisements; PSAs
   written, 3
Media Communications
     Association International,
     339
medium, 34–35, 41
medium shot (MS), 63
meetings, 118–119
Melville, Herman, 14, 174, 188,
     215
Men in Black, 170

metaphor, 50, 101, 120, 129. *see also* visual metaphor
meta-writing, 11, 36, 82–83, 265–266, 273
Michael, 211
minidramas, 92
miniscripts, 82, 277
miniseries, television, 226
Mishima, 201
Miss Congeniality, 196
Miss Pettigrew Lives for a Day, 195
mistaken identity, 196, 197
    cover-up and, 197
    disguise and, 196
MIX TO. *see* DISSOLVE/MIX TO
mobile media
    antecedents, 300–301
    cell phone. *see* cell phone
    OMVC, 303
    overview, 299–300
    video content on, 302–304
mobisode™, 300, 307, 310–318
Moby Dick, 174, 188
modems, 268
Modern Times, 194
Monroe, Marilyn, 195
Moore, Michael, 139
motivational objective, 31
Movie Magic Screenwriter, 44, 68
movies, 6–7, 8, 139. *see also* Genres
    vs. television, 300
Mrs. Doubtfire, 195
MS. *see* medium shot (MS)
multilayered writing, 271–272
multimedia time continuum, 70
multipoint-to-multipoint communication, 253
The Mummy, 174
murder mysteries, 171
Murphy Brown, 239–241
Murray, Bill, 194
MUSIC, 68
music, 66
    bed, 67
    bridge, 68

cues, 68
    sting, 68
Muybridge, Eadweard, 138
My Big Fat Greek Wedding, 168–169
My Darling Clementine, 168

N

The Nanny, 242, 243
Nanook of the North, 145
narration, 10, 54–55
narrative argument, 128–129
narrative documentary, 128–129, 146
narrative paradigms, 253
narratives, 165–166
narrative tense, 206
narrators
    on camera, 125–126
    omniscient, 10
Nash Bridges, 234
Natural Gas: The Liquid Alternative, 126, 130
navigation, 256, 257, 258, 260, 265, 275
navigational design, 276
Never Been Kissed, 196
news anchor script format, 74
newspapers
    online, 268
    vs. books, 301
A Night at the Opera, 196
9 ½ Weeks, 201
No Country for Old Men, 4
nodes, 259
nonbroadcast industry, 105–106
non-linear media, 252–254, 259
Nova, 139
Now and Again, 211
Nuit et Brouillard, 141, 150
NYPD Blue, 225

O

objective documentary, 141–142
objectives, 30–32, 40
    behavioral, 31
    communication, 30–31

informational, 31
    motivational, 31
    observation, in documentary, 144–145
The Office, 308
The Old Man and the Sea, 188
omniscient narrator, 205
on-camera anchor, 125–126
Once and Again, 243–244, 296
one-liners, 242–243
online journalism, 267–268
online newspapers, 268
Open Mobile Video Coalition (OMVC), 303
open questions, 47
OTS. *see* over-the-shoulder (OTS)
The Outlaw Josey Wales, 168
outlines. *see* concepts
over-the-shoulder (OTS), 63

P

pacing, 231
    of corporate video, 132–133
PAN, 64
The Panama Deception, 148
parallel paths, 259, 273
Parker, Alan, 82
Patent Law, 225
payment, for writers, 325
Penn, Arthur, 146
Pentagon WAN, 263
percentage of the gross, 325
period, 206–207
Pfeiffer, Michelle, 331
The Phantom Menace, 94
The Philadelphia Story, 168
photo-dramas, 8
photography, 137–138
photoplays, 8, 158
The Piano, 201
picture libraries, 45
picture research, 143
picture researchers, 45
piecework, 334
pitching, 50–51, 176, 326–328
Pitt, Brad, 197

pity, 158–159
place, 60–61
platform game, 287, 288
The Player, 50, 323, 327
plays, 12
play-within-a-play, 166
playwriting, 12
plot, 9, 11, 192–193
point of view, 205
point of view documentary, 141–142
Poitier, Sidney, 332
Polidori, John, 169
portal, 263. *see also* Internet service
    provider (ISP)
portals, 269, 270, 271
postproduction, 65, 149–150
PowerProduction Software, 72
PR. *see* public relations (PR)
The Practice, 224
Prairie Home Companion, 67
premise, 177–178
present tense, 39
Pretty Woman, 331
primary target audiences, 21, 24
print media, 106
problem, 160, 161, 162, 164
process, scriptwriting, 43
producers, 4, 6–7
production crew, instructions to, 7
product knowledge, 113–114
Professional Writer's Teleplay/
    Screenplay Format Guide, 235
Prom Queen, 309
Prom Queen: Summer Heat, 309
propaganda, 147–148
proposal, 144
prose exposition. *see* linear writing
PSA. *see* public service
    announcement (PSA)
Psycho, 169
psychographics, 27–30
    attitude, 29–30
    emotion, 28–29
public domain, 203
Public Enemies, 171
public policy problem, 22

public relations (PR), 29–30
public service announcements
    (PSA). *see also* advertisements
antismoking, concept for, 39–41
for battered women, 20–21
concept for, smoked to death
    and, 50
first draft script for, smoked to
    death and, 52–54
gambling, 84–88
for New England Home for Little
    Wanderers, 87–88
for radio, 67
treatment for, smoked to death
    and, 51–52
Pudd'nhead Wilson, 197
Pulp Fiction, 330
Puttnam, David, 12

Q
Qualcomm, 303
Quantum Leap, 210
Quarterlife, 309
questionnaires, 110

R
race and ethnic origin, target
    audience and, 26
RACK FOCUS, 63
radio, format for, 67–68
random access, 253
Rashomon, 211
The Reader, 201
realism, 189–190, 191
    in television, 228–229
realistic dialogue, 228–229, 234
reality, 140
reality TV, 296
reason (logos), 33, 90
Reefer Madness, 147
reference works, 283–284
reportage, 144
research *see* background research;
    location research; pircture
    research
Resnais, Alain, 141

resolution, 162, 164, 176
revenge, 163
reversals, 160
REVERSE ANGLE, 63
revision, 56
Riefenstahl, Leni, 141, 147
The Right Direction, 120, 122, 123
role-playing game (RPG), 288
romantic comedy, 168–169
Romeo and Juliet, 200
Roots, 226
RPG. *see* role-playing game (RPG)
Run Lola Run, 211
running gags, 195, 236–241
Runyon, Damon, 329

S
satire, 174
A Scanner Darkly, 94
scenarios, 8
scene heading. *see* slug line
scene outline, 51, 184. *see also* beat
    sheet
Schrader, Paul, 177, 201
science documentary, 147
Scott, Ridley, 82
scratch commentary, 151
screenplays. *see* scripts
screen time, 206
screenwriting. *see* scriptwriting
screwball comedy, 195
Scripps Howard National Spelling
    Bee competition, 139
script development, 175–181
    seven-step method of,
        175–176
script formats, 70, 264–266
    for corporate videos, 132
    television, 234–235
scripting language, 255, 258, 260,
    262, 263
scripts, 4, 7, 8, 182–184
    with client input, 133
scriptwriters. *see* writers
scriptwriting, 3, 6–7, 12–14, 80–81
    software, 44, 69, 185

Sea Change, 123, 128
search engines, 101, 269
SEC. *see* Securities and Exchange
      Commission (SEC)
secondary target audiences, 24
Second Life, 290
Securities and Exchange
      Commission (SEC), 121
SEGUE TO, 69
Seinfeld, 228, 240
self-assessment questions, 47
seminars, 338–339
sequences, 69
   of images, 11
serials, 224
series bible, 233
series editor, 233
setbacks, 161, 163, 164
setting, 206–207
seven questions, 37
seven-step method, 18–39,
      175–176
   for web writing, 277–278
sexuality, 95
SFX. *see* sound effects (SFX)
Shell Gas International, 21–23
shock, 91–92
Shogun, 226
shoot, 182, 184
shooter, 288
shooting script, 56–57, 182, 184,
      185
shot(s), 69, 182. *see also* camera
      shots
show-and-tell videos, 114–115
Sicko, 139
Silence of the Lambs, 188
SimCity, 287
The Simpsons, 241
simulation games, 287
Sin City, 94
sitcoms, 223, 224–226
slapstick, 193
Sleepless in Seattle, 168
Sling Blade, 332
slug line, 64, 70, 184, 234

Slumdog Millionaire, 199
SME. *see* subject matter expert
      (SME)
soaps, 224, 225, 226, 228, 243
social networking, 338
Soft Image, 129
software, 44, 69
Some Like it Hot, 195, 196
Something's Gotta Give, 194
Something to Be Desired, 309
The Sopranos, 329
sound, 8, 67–69
sound cues, 68–69
      FADE IN, 68
      FADE OUT, 68
      FADE UNDER, 69
      FADE UP, 69
      MUSIC, 68
      SEGUE TO, 69
      SFX, 68
sound effects (SFX), 68
South Park, 242
spec, 55
special effects, 94
specialized kind of writing, 71
spec script, 233, 244–245
Spellbound, 139
Spielberg, Steven, 170
The Spot, 308–309
sprites, 262
stage directions, 235
Star Trek, 229
Star Wars, 94, 129
sticky, 265
story, 10, 141
StoryBoard Artist, 73
storyboards, 73–75, 102, 260
story engines, 180–181
storyforming, 181
storyline. *see* plot
the story of a day, 131
storytelling, 181
storyweaving, 181
The Strand, 309
strategies, 83
Strauss, Ricard, 28

subject matter experts (SME), 45,
      111, 114
summative evaluation, 109–110
Sunset Hotel, 310
SUPER, 65
survey of strategies, 90
Survivor, 295
suspense, 92
The Sweet Hereafter, 4
Switched at Birth, 197
sync, 66
synopsis. *see* concept

T
tag lines, 178
target audiences. *see* audience(s)
task, 115
Taxi Driver, 201
team writing, 233
teaser, 233
television series, 224, 225, 233,
      236, 244
television (TV), 79
   comedy in, 235–242
   commercial breaks in. *see*
      television (TV) commercials
   corporate, 107–108
   dialogue in, 228–231
   documentaries, 116, 126–127
   formats, 126
   interactive, 294–295
   premise for, 224
   realism in, 228–229
   script formats for, 234–235
   scripts, 73–75
   time slot in, 226–227
   vs. movies, 300
   web content. *see* webisodes
television (TV) commercials, 227.
      see also advertisements
   drama and, 92
   humor and, 90–91
   kids and, 92–93
   shock and, 91–92
   suspense and, 92
   testimonial, 93–94

television writing, 223, 225, 227, 228, 231, 244
    innovative techniques in, 243–244
tension, 158, 159, 161
testimonials: real and fake, 93–94
text messaging, 302
There Will Be Blood, 199, 200
third person game, 288
third-person narrator. *see* omniscient narrator
three-act structures, 160–164
    television, 226–227
3-D
    graphic animation, 129
    movie experiments, 139
300, 94
Three Men and a Baby, 332
three-stage process, 177
The Three Stooges, 241
Thus Spake Zarathustra, 28
Tibbets, Daniel, 310
TILT, 64
time, 60–61
time slots, television, 226–227
Titanic, 4, 11, 129
title cards, 191
Tomb Raider, 287
Tootsie, 195
Touched by an Angel, 211
Touching the Void, 139
TRACK, 64
tragedy, 157, 158, 159, 193, 194, 198
trailers, 233
training videos, 108–110
    how-to-do-it videos, 108, 115, 116
    show-and-tell, 114–115
transitions, 65–66
    CUT, 65
    CUTAWAY, 65
    DISSOLVE/MIX TO, 65
    DVE, 66
    FADE IN FROM BLACK, 66
    FADE OUT TO BLACK, 66

MIX TO. *see* DISSOLVE/MIX TO
SUPER, 65
WIPE, 66
transportation ads, 97–100
travel documentary, 148–149
Treasure of the Sierra Madre, 199
treatments, 181–182
    corporate, 131–132
    for documentary, 144
    script, 51–52
Trent, Barbara, 148
The Triumph of Evil, 147
The Triumph of the Will, 147
Trois Hommes et un Couffin, 332
TR: The Story of Theodore Roosevelt, 146
truth and fiction, 140–142
tunnel approach, 48
Turnbull, Margaret, 8
TV studio multi-camera script, 73–75
Twain, Mark, 197
Twelfth Night, 159, 196, 241
Two Lovers, 201
TWO SHOT, 63
2001: A Space Odyssey, 28, 170

U

undercover cops, 172
Unforgiven, 168
universal resource locator (URL), 269
URL. *see* universal resource locator (URL)

V

The Vampyre, 169
Vantage Point, 211
verbal comedy, 194–195
very long shot (VLS), 63
Vestberg, Hans, 304
Veverka, Jana, 310
Vicky Christina Barcelona, 169
video, 5. *see also* educational videos; instructional videos; training videos

corporate communication problems, 110–113
    as corporate communications tool, 106–107
    cost benefit, 112
    exposition, devices for, 114
    vs. interactive media, 106
    vs. print media, 106
Video Arts, 28
video games, 285–290
    business, 285–286
    defined terminologies, 287, 288
    dialogue, 289
    in early days, 286
    formats, 292–294
    graphics, 290–291
    IGDA on, 286
    order of writing, 291–292
    scriptwriting, 290
    simulation games, 287
    terminologies, 288
    Writer's Guild of America on, 285–286
    Writers' Guild of Great Britain on, 286
    writing, 286–287
videography, 60
video news releases, 97
video strips, 301
virtual space, 253
Virtual Valerie, 95, 284
virtual world, 290. *see also* video games
visual gags, 241
visual idea. *see* Idea
visual media, 3–6. *see also* advertisements; public service announcement (PSA)
visual metaphors, 11, 27, 82, 123–125, 259
visual narrative, 182, 184, 190
visual seduction, 129–130
visual thinking. *see* meta-writing
visual writing, 8, 9–12, 82–83
VLS. *see* very long shot (VLS)
voice commentary, 96, 133

voice narration. *see* Narration
voice-over commentary, 55, 125
   in documentary, 149–150
Von Karajan, Herbert, 28
vox pops, 127–128

W

Wall Street, 200
wall-to-wall commentary, 150
Wal-Mart, 26
WAN. *see* wide area network
   (WAN)
Warhol, Andy, 32
War of the Worlds, 170
Watchmen, 94
Web 2.0, 282
webisodes, 296, 304, 308–310
websites, 273–274. *see also* World
   Wide Web
web writing, 270–271
   breakdown for production,
      276–277
   concepts, 276, 278–279
   design document, 276
   flowchart, 276
   issues, 276–279
   multimedia content, 277
   seven-step method, 277–278
   text, 277
Welland, Colin, 12
Welles, Orson, 170, 201
We're No Angels, 196
westerns, 167–168
The West Wing, 228, 229
wheel, 259
wheel with spokes, 273

When Harry Met Sally, 95
*Where in the World Is Carmen
   Sandiego?* 265
Who Wants to Be a Millionaire?
   295
WIDE ANGLE, 63
wide area network (WAN), 263
wide screen, 228
Wikipedia, 284
The Wild Bunch, 330
Wilder, Billy, 195
wildlife documentary, 149
Winged Migration, 139
WIPE, 66
The Wire, 234
The Witches of Eastwick, 331
work-made-for-hire, 337–338
World building, 290
World Wide Web, 6, 19, 339
   advertising on, 100–102
   conceptual *vs.* content writing,
      272–273
   functions, categorization, 270
   HTML, 268–269
   hyperlinks, 269
   for images, 45
   inverted pyramid practice,
      271–272
   multilayered writing, 271–272
   navigation, 275
   search engines and, 269
   URL, 269
   websites, 273–274
   writing, 270–273
The Wrestler, 199
Writers Guild agreement, 6

Writers Guild of America, 159, 181,
   235, 247, 285, 286, 290, 318,
   325
   on video games, 286–287
Writers' Guild of Great Britain,
   258, 286, 325
writers, role, 4–5, 7–8
   in documenatry, 143–144
writing
   for audio, 66, 96
   commentaries, 149–152
   commissioned, 19, 81
   conceptual, 272–273
   content, 272–275
   copywriting, 80–81
   for corporate world.
      see corporate writing
   for entertainment industry.
      see entertainment industry
   issues, 276–279
   meta-writing, 11, 36, 82–83
   in one medium for another, 6
   for radio, 96
   visual, 8, 9–12, 82–83
   for voice, 67
   voice commentary, 133
writing schools, 8
Wuthering Heights, 327

Y

The Young and the Restless, 225

Z

ZOOM, 64
Zwick, Ed, 309

Rec
Aug 2010

DATE DUE

APR 0 3 2018			